Lecture Notes in Computer Science 2031

Edited by G. Goos, J. Hartmanis and J. van Leeuwen

T0205278

Springer
Berlin
Heidelberg
New York
Barcelona
Hong Kong
London
Milan
Paris
Singapore
Tokyo

Tiziana Margaria   Wang Yi (Eds.)

Tools and Algorithms for the Construction and Analysis of Systems

7th International Conference, TACAS 2001
Held as Part of the Joint European Conferences
on Theory and Practice of Software, ETAPS 2001
Genova, Italy, April 2-6, 2001
Proceedings

 Springer

Series Editors

Gerhard Goos, Karlsruhe University, Germany
Juris Hartmanis, Cornell University, NY, USA
Jan van Leeuwen, Utrecht University, The Netherlands

Volume Editors

Tiziana Margaria
Universit t Dortmund, Lehrstuhl f r Programmiersysteme
Baroper Str. 301, 44221 Dortmund, Germany
E-mail: tiziana@ls5.cs.uni-dortmund.de

Wang Yi
Uppsala University, Department of Information Technology
Box 337, 751 05 Uppsala, Sweden
E-mail: yi@docs.uu.se

Cataloging-in-Publication Data applied for

Die Deutsche Bibliothek - CIP-Einheitsaufnahme

Tools and algorithms for the construction and analysis of systems :
7th international conference ; proceedings / TACAS 2001, held as part
of the Joint European Conferences on Theory and Practice of Software,
ETAPS 2001, Genova, Italy, April 2 - 6, 2001. Tiziana Margaria ; Wang
Yi (ed.). - Berlin ; Heidelberg ; New York ; Barcelona ; Hong Kong ;
London ; Milan ; Paris ; Singapore ; Tokyo : Springer, 2001
    (Lecture notes in computer science ; Vol. 2031)
    ISBN 3-540-41865-2

CR Subject Classification (1998): F.3, D.2.4, D.2.2, C.2.4, F.2.2

ISSN 0302-9743
ISBN 3-540-41865-2 Springer-Verlag Berlin Heidelberg New York

Springer-Verlag Berlin Heidelberg New York
a member of BertelsmannSpringer Science+Business Media GmbH

http://www.springer.de

'   Springer-Verlag Berlin Heidelberg 2001
Printed in Germany

Typesetting: Camera-ready by author, data conversion by Claudia Herbers, Dortmund
Printed on acid-free paper   SPIN: 10782361   06/3142   5 4 3 2 1 0

Foreword

ETAPS 2001 was the fourth instance of the European Joint Conferences on Theory and Practice of Software. ETAPS is an annual federated conference that was established in 1998 by combining a number of existing and new conferences. This year it comprised five conferences (FOSSACS, FASE, ESOP, CC, TACAS), ten satellite workshops (CMCS, ETI Day, JOSES, LDTA, MMAABS, PFM, RelMiS, UNIGRA, W ADT, WTUML), seven invited lectures, a debate, and ten tutorials.

The events that comprise ETAPS address various aspects of the system development process, including specification, design, implementation, analysis, and improvement. The languages, methodologies, and tools which support these activities are all well within its scope. Different blends of theory and practice are represented, with an inclination towards theory with a practical motivation on one hand and soundly-based practice on the other. Many of the issues involved in software design apply to systems in general, including hardware systems, and the emphasis on software is not intended to be exclusive.

ETAPS is a loose confederation in which each event retains its own identity, with a separate program committee and independent proceedings. Its format is open-ended, allowing it to grow and evolve as time goes by. Contributed talks and system demonstrations are in synchronized parallel sessions, with invited lectures in plenary sessions. Two of the invited lectures are reserved for "unifying" talks on topics of interest to the whole range of ETAPS attendees. The aim of cramming all this activity into a single one-week meeting is to create a strong magnet for academic and industrial researchers working on topics within its scope, giving them the opportunity to learn about research in related areas, and thereby to foster new and existing links between work in areas that were formerly addressed in separate meetings.

ETAPS 2001 was hosted by the Dipartimento di Informatica e Scienze dell'Informazione (DISI) of the Università di Genova and was organized by the following team:

Egidio Astesiano (General Chair)
Eugenio Moggi (Organization Chair)
Maura Cerioli (Satellite Events Chair)
Gianna Reggio (Publicity Chair)
Davide Ancona
Giorgio Delzanno
Maurizio Martelli

with the assistance of Convention Bureau Genova. Tutorials were organized by Bernhard Rumpe (TU München). Overall planning for ETAPS conferences is the responsibility of the ETAPS Steering Committee, whose current membership is:

Egidio Astesiano (Genova), Ed Brinksma (Enschede), Pierpaolo Degano (Pisa), Hartmut Ehrig (Berlin), José Fiadeiro (Lisbon), Marie-Claude Gaudel (Paris), Susanne Graf (Grenoble), Furio Honsell (Udine), Nigel Horspool (Victoria), Heinrich Hußmann (Dresden), Paul Klint (Amsterdam), Daniel Le Métayer (Rennes), Tom Maibaum (London), Tiziana Margaria (Dortmund), Ugo Montanari (Pisa), Mogens Nielsen (Aarhus), Hanne Riis Nielson (Aarhus), Fernando Orejas (Barcelona), Andreas Podelski (Saarbrücken), David Sands (Göteborg), Don Sannella (Edinburgh), Perdita Stevens (Edinburgh), Jerzy Tiuryn (Warsaw), David Watt (Glasgow), Herbert Weber (Berlin), Reinhard Wilhelm (Saarbrücken)

ETAPS 2001 was organized in cooperation with

the Association for Computing Machinery
the European Association for Programming Languages and Systems
the European Association of Software Science and Technology
the European Association for Theoretical Computer Science

and received generous sponsorship from:

ELSAG
Fondazione Cassa di Risparmio di Genova e Imperia
INDAM - Gruppo Nazionale per l'Informatica Matematica (GNIM)
Marconi
Microsoft Research
Telecom Italia
TXT e-solutions
Università di Genova

I would like to express my sincere gratitude to all of these people and organizations, the program committee chairs and PC members of the ETAPS conferences, the organizers of the satellite events, the speakers themselves, and finally Springer-Verlag for agreeing to publish the ETAPS proceedings.

January 2001   Donald Sannella
                                      ETAPS Steering Committee chairman

Preface

This volume contains the proceedings of the 7th TACAS, International Conference on *Tools and Algorithms for the Construction and Analysis of Systems.*
TACAS 2001 took place in Genova, Italy, April 2nd to 6th, 2001, as part of the 4th European Joint Conference on Theory and Practice of Software (ETAPS), whose aims, organization, and history are detailed in the separate foreword by Donald Sannella.

It is the goal of TACAS to bring together researchers and practitioners interested in the development and application of tools and algorithms for specification, verification, analysis, and construction of software and hardware systems. In particular, it aims at creating an atmosphere that promotes a cross-fertilization of ideas between the different communities of theoreticians, tool builders, tool users, and system designers, in various specialized areas of computer science. In this respect, TACAS reflects the overall goal of ETAPS on a tool-oriented footing. In fact, the scope of TACAS intersects with all the other ETAPS events, which address more traditional areas of interest.

As a consequence, in addition to the standard criteria for acceptance, contributions have also been selected on the basis of their conceptual significance in the context of neighboring areas. This comprises the profile-driven comparison of various concepts and methods, their degree of support via interactive or fully automatic tools, and in particular case studies revealing the application profiles of the considered methods and tools.

In order to emphasize the practical importance of tools, TACAS allows tool presentations to be submitted (and reviewed) on equal footing with traditional scientific papers, treating them as 'first class citizens'. In practice, this entails their presentation in plenary conference sessions, and the integral inclusion of a tool report in the proceedings. The conference, of course, also included informal tool demonstrations, not announced in the official program.

TACAS 2001 comprised

- **Invited Lectures** by Moshe Vardi on **Branching vs. Linear Time: Final Showdown** and by Michael Fourman, **Propositional Reasoning**, as well as
- **Regular Sessions** featuring 36 papers selected out of 125 submissions, ranging from foundational contributions to tool presentations including online demos, and
- **ETAPS Tool Demonstration s** featuring 3 short contributions selected out of 9 submissions.

Grown itself out of a satellite meeting of TAPSOFT in 1995, TACAS 2001 featured the *ETI DAY*, a satellite event of ETAPS concerning the future development of the Electronic Tool Integration platform.

TACAS 2001 was hosted by the University of Genova, and, being part of ETAPS, it shared the sponsoring and support described in Don Sannella's foreword. Like ETAPS, TACAS will take place in Grenoble next year.

Warm thanks are due to the program committee and to all the referees for their assistance in selecting the papers, to the TACAS Steering Committee, to Don Sannella for mastering the coordination of the whole ETAPS, to Egidio Astesiano, Gianna Reggio, and the whole team in Genova for their brilliant organization.

Recognition is due to the technical support team: Matthias Weiß at the University of Dortmund together with Ben Lindner and Martin Karusseit of METAFrame Technologies provided invaluable assistance to all the involved people concerning the online service during the past three months.

Finally, we are deeply indebted to Claudia Herbers for her first class support in the preparation of this volume.

January 2001   Tiziana Margaria
                                                               and Wang Yi

Steering Committee

Ed Brinksma (NL)
Rance Cleaveland (USA)
Kim G. Larsen (DK)
Bernhard Steffen (D)

Program Committee

Chair: Tiziana Margaria (Dortmund University)
        Wang Yi (Uppsala University)

Rajeev Alur (University of Pennsylvania, USA)
Ed Brinksma (University of Twente, NL)
Rance Cleaveland (SUNY at Stony Brook, USA)
Hubert Garavel (INRIA Rhône-Alpes, France)
Susanne Graf (VERIMAG Grenoble, France)
Orna Grumberg (Technion Haifa, Israel)
John Hatcliff (Kansas State University, USA)
Hardi Hungar (METAFrame Research, Germany)
Claude Jard (IRISA Rennes, France)
Stuart Kent (University of Kent, UK)
Kim Larsen (University of Aalborg, Denmark)
Doron Peled (Bell Laboratories Murray Hill, USA)
Andreas Podelski (MPI Saarbrücken, Germany)
Mary Sheeran (Chalmers University, Sweden)
Bernhard Steffen (University of Dortmund, Germany)
Perdita Stevens (University of Edinburgh, UK)

Reviewers

Table of Contents

Hardware: Design and Verification

Software Verification

Symbolic Verification

Testing: Techniques and Tools

Implementation Techniques

Semantics and Compositional Verification

Logics and Model-Checking

ETAPS Tool Demonstration

Branching vs. Linear Time: Final Showdown

Moshe Y. Vardi*

Rice University, Department of Computer Science, Houston, TX 77005-1892, USA

Abstract. The discussion of the relative merits of linear- versus branching-time frameworks goes back to early 1980s. One of the beliefs dominating this discussion has been that "while specifying is easier in LTL (linear-temporal logic), verification is easier for CTL (branching-temporal logic)". Indeed, the restricted syntax of CTL limits its expressive power and many important behaviors (e.g., strong fairness) can not be specified in CTL. On the other hand, while model checking for CTL can be done in time that is linear in the size of the specification, it takes time that is exponential in the specification for LTL. Because of these arguments, and for historical reasons, the dominant temporal specification language in industrial use is CTL.

In this paper we argue that in spite of the phenomenal success of CTL-based model checking, CTL suffers from several fundamental limitations as a specification language, all stemming from the fact that CTL is a branching-time formalism: the language is unintuitive and hard to use, it does not lend itself to compositional reasoning, and it is fundamentally incompatible with semi-formal verification. These inherent limitations severely impede the functionality of CTL-based model checkers. In contrast, the linear-time framework is expressive and intuitive, supports compositional reasoning and semi-formal verification, and is amenable to combining enumerative and symbolic search methods. While we argue in favor of the linear-time framework, we also we argue that LTL is not expressive enough, and discuss what would be the "ultimate" temporal specification language.

1 Introduction

As indicated in the National Technology Roadmap for Semiconductors[1], the semiconductor industry faces a serious challenge: chip designers are finding it increasingly difficult to keep up with the advances in semiconductor manufacturing. As a result, they are unable to exploit the enormous capacity that this technology provides. The Roadmap suggests that the semiconductor industry will require productivity gains greater than the historical 30% per-year cost reduction. This is referred to as the "design productivity crisis".

Integrated circuits are currently designed through a series of steps that refine a more abstract specification into a more concrete implementation. The process starts at a "behavioral model", such as a program that implements the instruction set architecture of

---

* Supported in part by NSF grants CCR-9700061 and CCR-9988322, and by a grant from the Intel Corporation. URL: http://www.cs.rice.edu/~vardi.

[1] http://public.itrs.net/files/1999_SIA_Roadmap/Home.htm

T. Margaria and W. Yi (Eds.): TACAS 2001, LNCS 2031, pp. 1–22, 2001.

a processor. It ends in a description of the actual geometries of the transistors and wires on the chip. Each refinement step used to synthesize the processor must preserve the germane behavior of the abstract model. As designs grow more complex, it becomes easier to introduce flaws into the design during refinement. Thus, designers use various validation techniques to prove the correctness of the design after each refinement. Unfortunately, these techniques themselves grow more expensive and difficult with design complexity. Indeed, for many designs, the size of the validation team now exceeds that of the design team. As the validation process has begun to exceed half the design project resources, the semiconductor industry has begun to refer to this problem as the "validation crisis".

Formal verification provides a new approach to validating the correct behavior of logic designs. In simulation, the traditional mode of design validation, "confidence" is the result of running a large number of test cases through the design. Formal verification, in contrast, uses mathematical techniques to check the entire state space of the design for conformance to some specified behavior. Thus, while simulation is open-ended and fraught with uncertainty, formal verification is definitive and eliminates uncertainty [23].

One of the most significant recent developments in the area of formal design verification is the discovery of algorithmic methods for verifying temporal-logic properties of *finite-state* systems [19,68,86,103]. In temporal-logic *model checking*, we verify the correctness of a finite-state system with respect to a desired property by checking whether a labeled state-transition graph that models the system satisfies a temporal logic formula that specifies this property (see [22]). *Symbolic model checking* [14] has been used to successfully verify a large number of complex designs. This approach uses symbolic data structures, such as *binary decision diagrams* (BDDs), to efficiently represent and manipulate state spaces. Using symbolic model checking, designs containing on the order of 100 to 200 binary latches can be routinely verified automatically.

Model-checking tools have enjoyed a substantial and growing use over the last few years, showing ability to discover subtle flaws that result from extremely improbable events. While until recently these tools were viewed as of academic interest only, they are now routinely used in industrial applications [6,42]. Companies such as AT&T, Cadence, Fujitsu, HP, IBM, Intel, Motorola, NEC, SGI, Siemens, and Sun are using model checkers increasingly on their own designs to ensure outstanding product quality. Three model-checking tools are widely used in the semiconductor industry: SMV, a tool from Carnegie Mellon University [74], with many industrial incarnations (e.g., IBM's RuleBase [7]); VIS, a tool developed at the University of California, Berkeley [11]; and FormalCheck, a tool developed at Bell Labs [44] and marketed by Cadence.

A key issue in the design of a model-checking tool is the choice of the temporal language used to specify properties, as this language, which we refer to as the *temporal property-specification language*, is one of the primary interfaces to the tool. (The other primary interface is the modeling language, which is typically the hardware description language used by the designers). One of the major aspects of all temporal languages is their underlying model of time. Two possible views regarding the nature of time induce two types of temporal logics [65]. In *linear* temporal logics, time is treated as if each moment in time has a unique possible future. Thus, linear temporal logic formulas are interpreted over linear sequences and we regard them as describing a behavior of a single computation of a program. In *branching* temporal logics, each moment in time may split into various possible futures. Accordingly, the structures over which branching temporal logic formulas are interpreted can be viewed as infinite computation trees, each describing the behavior of the possible computations of a nondeterministic program.

In the linear temporal logic LTL, formulas are composed from the set of atomic propositions using the usual Boolean connectives as well as the temporal connective G ("always"), F ("eventually"), X ("next"), and U ("until"). The branching temporal logic CTL* augments LTL by the path quantifiers E ("there exists a computation") and A ("for all computations"). The branching temporal logic CTL is a fragment of CTL* in which every temporal connective is preceded by a path quantifier. Finally, the branching temporal logic ∀CTL is a fragment of CTL in which only universal path quantification is allowed. (Note that LTL has implicit universal path quantifiers in front of its formulas.)

The discussion of the relative merits of linear versus branching temporal logics goes back to 1980 [80,65,31,8,82,35,33,18,100,101]. As analyzed in [82], linear and branching time logics correspond to two distinct views of time. It is not surprising therefore that LTL and CTL are expressively incomparable [65,33,18]. The LTL formula FGp is not expressible in CTL, while the CTL formula $AFAGp$ is not expressible in LTL. On the other hand, CTL seems to be superior to LTL when it comes to algorithmic verification, as we now explain.

Given a transition system M and a linear temporal logic formula φ, the model-checking problem for M and φ is to decide whether φ holds in all the computations of M. When φ is a branching temporal logic formula, the problem is to decide whether φ holds in the computation tree of M. The complexity of model checking for both linear and branching temporal logics is well understood: suppose we are given a transition system of size n and a temporal logic formula of size m. For the branching temporal logic CTL, model-checking algorithms run in time $O(nm)$ [19], while, for the linear temporal logic LTL, model-checking algorithms run in time $n2^{O(m)}$ [68]. Since LTL model checking is PSPACE-complete [91], the latter bound probably cannot be improved.

The difference in the complexity of linear and branching model checking has been viewed as an argument in favor of the branching paradigm. In particular, the computational advantage of CTL model checking over LTL model checking makes CTL a popular choice, leading to efficient model-checking tools for this logic [20]. Today, the dominant temporal specification language in industrial use is CTL. This dominance stems from the phenomenal success of SMV, the first symbolic model checker, which is CTL-based, and its follower VIS, also CTL-based, which serve as the basis for many industrial model checkers. (Verification systems that use linear-time formalisms are the above mentioned FormalCheck, Bell Labs's SPIN [48], Intel's Prover, and Cadence SMV.)

In spite of the phenomenal success of CTL-based model checking, CTL suffers from several fundamental limitations as a temporal property-specification language, all stemming from the fact that CTL is a branching-time formalism: the language is unintuitive and hard to use, it does not lend itself to compositional reasoning, and it is fundamentally incompatible with semi-formal verification. In contrast, the linear-time framework is expressive and intuitive, supports compositional reasoning and semi-formal verification, and is amenable to combining enumerative and symbolic search methods. While we argue in favor of the linear-time framework, we also we argue that LTL is not expressive enough, and discuss what would be the ultimate temporal specification language.

We assume familiarity with the syntax and semantics of temporal logic [30,53,94].

2   CTL

2.1   Expressiveness

It is important to understand that expressiveness is not merely a theoretical issue; expressiveness is also a usability issue. Verification engineers find CTL unintuitive. The linear framework is simply more natural for verification engineers, who tend to think linearly, e.g., timing diagrams [37] and message-sequence charts [64], rather than "branchingly". IBM's experience with the RuleBase system has been that "nontrivial CTL equations are hard to understand and prone to error" [90] and "CTL is difficult to use for most users and requires a new way of thinking about hardware" [7]. Indeed, IBM has been trying to "linearize" CTL in their RuleBase system [7]. It is simply much harder to reason about computation trees than about linear computations.

As an example, consider the LTL formulas XFp and FXp. Both formulas say the same thing: "p holds sometimes in the strict future". In contrast, consider the CTL formulas $AFAXp$ and $AXAFp$. Are these formulas logically equivalent? Do they assert that "p holds sometimes in the strict future"? It takes a few minutes of serious pondering to realize that while $AXAFp$ does assert that "p holds sometimes in the strict future", this is not the case for $AFAXp$ (we challenge the reader to figure out the meaning of $AFAXp$). The unintuitiveness of CTL significantly reduces the usability of CTL-based formal-verification tools. A perusal of the literature reveals that the vast majority of CTL formulas used in formal verification are actually equivalent to LTL formulas. Thus, the branching nature of CTL is very rarely used in practice. As a consequence, even though LTL and CTL are expressively incomparable from a theoretical point of view, from a practical point of view LTL is more expressive than CTL.

One often hears the claim that expressiveness "is not an issue", since "all users want to verify are simple invariance property of the form AGp". Of course, the reason for that could be the difficulty of expressing in CTL more complicated properties. Industrial experience with linear-time formalism shows that verification engineers often use much more complicated temporal properties, when provided with a language that facilitates the expression of such properties. Further more, even when attempting to verify an invariance property, users often need to express relevant properties, which can be rather complex, of the environment of the unit under verification. We come back to this point later.

Reader who is steeped in the concurrency-theory literature may be somewhat surprised at the assertion that that CTL lacks expressive power. After all, it is known that CTL characterizes *bisimulation*, in the sense that two states in a transition system are bisimilar iff they satisfy exactly the same CTL formulas [12] (see also [46]), and bisimulation is considered to be the finest reasonable notion of equivalence between processes

[79,76]. This result, however, says little about the usefulness of CTL as a property-specification language. Bisimulation is a structural relation, while in the context of model checking what is needed is a way to specify behavioral properties rather than structural properties. Assertions about behavior are best stated in terms of traces rather than in terms of computation trees (recall, for example, the subtle distinction between $AFAXp$ and $AXAFp$).[2]

2.2 Complexity

As we saw earlier, the complexity bounds for CTL model checking are better than those for LTL model checking. We first show that this superiority disappears in the context of open systems.

In computer system design, we distinguish between *closed* and *open* systems. A closed system is a system whose behavior is completely determined by the state of the system. An open system is a system that interacts with its environment and whose behavior depends on this interaction. Such systems are called also *reactive systems* [45]. In closed systems, nondeterminism reflect an *internal* choice, while in open systems it can also reflect an *external* choice [47]. Formally, in a closed system, the environment can not modify any of the system variables. In contrast, in an open system, the environment can modify some of the system variables. In reality, the vast majority of interesting systems are open, since they have to interact with an external environment.

We can model finite-state open systems by *open modules*. An open module is simply a module with a partition of the states into two sets. One set contains *system states* and corresponds to locations where the system makes a transition. The second set contains *environment states* and corresponds to locations where the environment makes a transition.

As discussed in [72], when the specification is given in linear temporal logic, there is indeed no need to worry about uncertainty with respect to the environment. Since all the possible interactions of the system with its environment have to satisfy a linear temporal logic specification in order for a program to satisfy the specification, the distinction between internal and external nondeterminism is irrelevant. In contrast, when the specification is given in a branching temporal logic, this distinction is relevant. There is a need to define a different model-checking problem for open systems, and there is a need to adjust current model-checking tools to handle open systems correctly.

We now specify formally the problem of *model checking of open modules* (*module checking*, for short). As with usual model checking, the problem has two inputs: an open module M and a temporal logic formula φ. For an open module M, let V_M denote the unwinding of M into an infinite tree. We say that M satisfies φ iff φ holds in all the trees obtained by pruning from V_M subtrees whose root is a successor of an environment state. The intuition is that each such tree corresponds to a different (and possible) environment. We want φ to hold in every such tree, since, of course, we want the open system to satisfy its specification no matter how the environment behaves.

---

[2] It is also worth noting that when modeling systems in terms of transition systems, deadlocks have to be modeled explicitly. Once deadlocks are modeled explicitly, the two process $a(b+c)$ and $ab + ac$, which are typically considered to be trace equivalent but not bisimilar [76], become trace inequivalent.

A *module* $M = \langle W, W_0, R, V \rangle$ consists of a set W of states, a set W_0 of initial states, a total transition relation $R \subseteq W \times W$, and a labeling function $V : W \to 2^{Prop}$ that maps each state to a set of atomic propositions that hold in this state. We model an open system by an *open module* $M = \langle W_s, W_e, W_0, R, V \rangle$, where $\langle W_s \cup W_e, W_0, R, V \rangle$ is a module, W_s is a set of *system states*, and W_e is a set of *environment states*. We use W to denote $W_s \cup W_e$. For each state $w \in W$, let $succ(w)$ be the set of w's R-successors; i.e., $succ(w) = \{w' : R(w, w')\}$. Consider a system state w_s and an environment state w_e. When the current state is w_s, all the states in $succ(w_s)$ are possible next states. In contrast, when the current state is w_e, there is no certainty with respect to the environment transitions and not all the states in $succ(w_e)$ are necessarily possible next states. The only thing guaranteed is that not all the environment transitions are impossible, since the environment can never be blocked. For a state $w \in W$, let $step(w)$ denote the set of the possible sets of w's next successors during an execution. By the above, $step(w_s) = \{succ(w_s)\}$ and $step(w_e)$ contains all the nonempty subsets of $succ(w_e)$.

An *infinite tree* is a set $T \subseteq X^*$ such that if $x \cdot c \in T$ where $x \in X^*$ and $c \in X$, then also $x \in T$, and for all $0 \leq c' < c$, we have that $x \cdot c' \in T$. In addition, if $x \in T$, then $x \cdot 0 \in T$. The elements of T are called *nodes*, and the empty word ϵ is the *root* of T. Given an alphabet Σ, a *Σ-labeled tree* is a pair $\langle T, V \rangle$ where T is a tree and $V : T \to \Sigma$ maps each node of T to a letter in Σ. An open module M can be unwound into an infinite tree $\langle T_M, V_M \rangle$ in a straightforward way. When we examine a specification with respect to M, it should hold not only in $\langle T_M, V_M \rangle$ (which corresponds to a very specific environment that does never restrict the set of its next states), but in all the trees obtained by pruning from $\langle T_M, V_M \rangle$ subtrees whose root is a successor of a node corresponding to an environment state. Let $exec(M)$ denote the set of all these trees. Formally, $\langle T, V \rangle \in exec(M)$ iff the following holds:

- $\epsilon \in T$ and $V(\epsilon) = w_0$.
- For all $x \in T$ with $V(x) = w$, there exists $\{w_0, \ldots, w_n\} \in step(w)$ such that $T \cap X^{|x|+1} = \{x \cdot 0, x \cdot 1, \ldots, x \cdot n\}$ and for all $0 \leq c \leq n$ we have $V(x \cdot c) = w_c$.

Intuitively, each tree in $exec(M)$ corresponds to a different behavior of the environment. Note that a single environment state with more than one successor suffices to make $exec(M)$ infinite.

Given an open module M and a CTL* formula φ, we say that M satisfies φ, denoted $M \models_o \varphi$, if all the trees in $exec(M)$ satisfy φ. The problem of deciding whether M satisfies φ is called *module checking*. We use $M \models \varphi$ to indicate that when we regard M as a closed module (thus refer to all its states as system states), then M satisfies φ. The problem of deciding whether $M \models \varphi$ is the usual model-checking problem. Note that while $M \models_o \varphi$ entails $M \models \varphi$, all that $M \models \varphi$ entails is that $M \not\models_o \neg\varphi$. Indeed, $M \models_o \varphi$ requires all the trees in $exec(M)$ to satisfy φ. On the other hand, $M \models \varphi$ means that the tree $\langle T_M, V_M \rangle$ satisfies φ. Finally, $M \not\models_o \neg\varphi$ only tells us that there exists some tree in $exec(M)$ that satisfies φ. We can define module checking also with respect to linear-time specifications. We say that an open module M satisfies an LTL formula φ iff $M \models_o A\varphi$.

Theorem 1. [54,61]

(1) *The module-checking problem for LTL is PSPACE-complete.*
(2) *The module-checking problem for CTL is EXPTIME-complete.*
(3) *The module-checking problem for CTL* is 2EXPTIME-complete.*

Thus, module checking for LTL is easier than for CTL (assuming that EXPTIME is different than PSPACE), which is, in turn, easier than for CTL*. In particular, this results shows that branching is not "free", as has been claimed in [35].[3] See [100] for further discussion on the complexity-theoretic comparison between linear time and branching time.

Even in the context of closed systems, the alleged superiority of CTL from the complexity perspective is questionable. The traditional comparison is in terms of worst-case complexity. Since, however, CTL and LTL are expressively incomparable, a comparison in terms of worst-case complexity is not very meaningful. A more meaningful comparison would be with respect to properties that can be expressed in both CTL and LTL. We claim that under such a comparison the superiority of CTL disappears.

For simplicity, we consider systems M with no fairness conditions; i.e., systems in which all the computations are fair. As the "representative" CTL model checker we take the bottom-up labeling procedure of [19]. There, in order to check whether M satisfies φ, we label the states of M by subformulas of φ, starting from the innermost formulas and proceeding such that, when labeling a formula, all its subformulas are already labeled. Labeling subformulas that are atomic propositions, Boolean combinations of other subformulas, or of the form $AX\theta$ or $EX\theta$ is straightforward. Labeling subformulas of the form $A\theta_1 U\theta_2$, $E\theta_1 U\theta_2$, $A\theta_1 \tilde{U}\theta_2$, or $E\theta_1 \tilde{U}\theta_2$ involves a backward reachability test. As the "representative" LTL model checker, we take the automata-based algorithm of [103]. There, in order to check whether M satisfies φ, we construct a Büchi word automaton $\mathcal{A}_{\neg\varphi}$ for $\neg\varphi$ and check whether the intersection of the language of M with that of $\mathcal{A}_{\neg\varphi}$ is nonempty. In practice, the latter check proceeds by checking whether there exists an initial state in the intersection that satisfies CTL formula $EG\mathbf{true}$. For the construction of $\mathcal{A}_{\neg\varphi}$, we follow the algorithms in [41] or [29], which improve [103] by being demand-driven; that is, the state space of $\mathcal{A}_{\neg\varphi}$ is restricted to states that are reachable from the initial state.

The exponential term in the running time of LTL model checking comes from a potential exponential blow-up in the translation of φ into an automaton $\mathcal{A}_{\neg\varphi}$. It is shown, however, in [70] that for LTL formulas that can also be expressed in ∀CTL (the universal fragment of CTL) there is Büchi automaton $\mathcal{A}_{\neg\varphi}$ whose size is *linear* in $|\varphi|$. Furthermore, this automaton has a special structure (it is "weak"), which enables the model checker to apply improved algorithms for checking the emptiness of the intersection of M with $\mathcal{A}_{\neg\varphi}$ [10]. (See also [56,57] for a through analysis of the relationship between LTL and CTL model checkers.)

2.3 Compositionality

Model checking is known to suffer from the so-called *state-explosion* problem. In a concurrent setting, the system under consideration is typically the parallel composition

---

[3] Note also that while the satisfiability problem for LTL is PSPACE-complete [91], the problem is EXPTIME-complete for CTL [36,32] and 2EXPTIME-complete for CTL* [102,34].

of many modules. As a result, the size of the state space of the system is the product of the sizes of the state spaces of the participating modules. This gives rise to state spaces of exceedingly large sizes, which makes model-checking algorithms impractical. This issue is one of the most important ones in the area of computer-aided verification and is the subject of active research (cf. [15]).

Compositional, or *modular*, verification is one possible way to address the state-explosion problem, cf. [24]. In modular verification, one uses proof rules of the following form:

$$\left.\begin{array}{l} M_1 \models \psi_1 \\ M_2 \models \psi_2 \\ C(\psi_1, \psi_2, \psi) \end{array}\right\} M_1 \| M_2 \models \psi$$

Here $M \models \theta$ means that the module M satisfies the formula θ, the symbol "$\|$" denotes parallel composition, and $C(\psi_1, \psi_2, \psi)$ is some logical condition relating ψ_1, ψ_2, and ψ. The advantage of using modular proof rules is that it enables one to apply model checking only to the underlying modules, which have much smaller state spaces.

A key observation, see [77,66,50,93,81], is that in modular verification the specification should include two parts. One part describes the desired behavior of the module. The other part describes the assumed behavior of the system within which the module is interacting. This is called the *assume-guarantee* paradigm, as the specification describes what behavior the module is *guaranteed* to exhibit, *assuming* that the system behaves in the promised way.

For the linear temporal paradigm, an assume-guarantee specification is a pair $\langle \varphi, \psi \rangle$, where both φ and ψ are linear temporal logic formulas. The meaning of such a pair is that all the computations of the module are guaranteed to satisfy ψ, assuming that all the computations of the environment satisfy φ. As observed in [81], in this case the assume-guarantee pair $\langle \varphi, \psi \rangle$ can be combined to a single linear temporal logic formula $\varphi \rightarrow \psi$. Thus, model checking a module with respect to assume-guarantee specifications in which both the assumed and the guaranteed behaviors are linear temporal logic formulas is essentially the same as model checking the module with respect to linear temporal logic formulas.

The situation is different for the branching temporal paradigm, where assumptions are taken to apply to the computation tree of the system within which the module is interacting [43]. In this framework, a module M satisfies an assume-guarantee pair $\langle \varphi, \psi \rangle$ iff whenever M is part of a system satisfying φ, the system also satisfies ψ. (As is shown in [43], this is not equivalent to M satisfying $\varphi \rightarrow \psi$.) We call this *branching modular model checking*. Furthermore, it is argued in [43], as well as in [26,51,43,27], that in the context of modular verification it is advantageous to use only *universal* branching temporal logic, i.e., branching temporal logic without existential path quantifiers. In a universal branching temporal logic one can state properties of all computations of a program, but one cannot state that certain computations exist. Consequently, universal branching temporal logic formulas have the helpful property that once they are satisfied in a module, they are satisfied also in every system that contains this module. The focus in [43] is on using ∀CTL, the universal fragment of CTL, for both the assumption and the guarantee. We now focus on the branching modular model-checking problem, where assumptions and guarantees are in both $\forall$CTL and in the more expressive $\forall$CTL*, the universal fragment of CTL*.

Let $M = (W, W_0, R, V)$ and $M' = (W', W_0', R', V')$ be two modules with sets AP and AP' of atomic propositions. The *composition* of M and M', denoted $M\|M'$, is a module that has exactly these behaviors which are joint to M and M'. We define $M\|M'$ to be the module $\langle W'', W_{0''}, R, V'' \rangle$ over the set $AP'' = AP \cup AP'$ of atomic propositions, where $W'' = (W \times W') \cap \{\langle w, w' \rangle : V(w) \cap AP' = V'(w') \cap AP\}$, $W_{0''} = (W_0 \times W_{0'}) \cap W''$, $R'' = \{\langle \langle w, w' \rangle, \langle s, s' \rangle \rangle : \langle w, s \rangle \in R$ and $\langle w', s' \rangle \in R'\}$, and $V''(\langle w, w' \rangle) = V(w) \cup V'(w')$ for $\langle w, w' \rangle \in W''$.

In modular verification, one uses assertions of the form $\langle \varphi \rangle M \langle \psi \rangle$ to specify that whenever M is part of a system satisfying the universal branching temporal logic formula φ, the system satisfies the universal branching temporal logic formula ψ too. Formally, $\langle \varphi \rangle M \langle \psi \rangle$ holds if $M\|M' \models \psi$ for all M' such that $M\|M' \models \varphi$. Here φ is an assumption on the behavior of the system and ψ is the guarantee on the behavior of the module. Assume-guarantee assertions are used in modular proof rules of the following form:

$$
\left.
\begin{array}{l}
\langle \varphi_1 \rangle M_1 \langle \psi_1 \rangle \\
\langle \mathbf{true} \rangle M_1 \langle \varphi_1 \rangle \\
\langle \varphi_2 \rangle M_2 \langle \psi_2 \rangle \\
\langle \mathbf{true} \rangle M_2 \langle \varphi_2 \rangle
\end{array}
\right\}
\langle \mathbf{true} \rangle M_1 \| M_2 \langle \psi_1 \wedge \psi_2 \rangle
$$

Thus, a key step in modular verification is checking that assume-guarantee assertions of the form $\langle \varphi \rangle M \langle \psi \rangle$ hold, which we called the *branching modular model-checking problem*.

Theorem 2. [60]
(1) *The branching modular model-checking problem for $\forall$CTL is PSPACE-complete.*
(2) *The branching modular model-checking problem for $\forall$CTL* is EXPSPACE-complete.*

Thus, in the context of modular model checking, $\forall$CTL has the same computational complexity as LTL, while $\forall$CTL* is exponentially harder. The fact that the complexity for $\forall$CTL is the same as the complexity for LTL is, however, somewhat misleading. $\forall$CTL is simply not expressive enough to express assumptions that are strong enough to prove the desired guarantee. This motivated Josko to consider modular verification with guarantees in CTL and assumptions in LTL. Unfortunately, it is shown in [60] that the EXPSPACE lower bound above applies even for that setting.

Another approach to modular verification for $\forall$CTL is proposed in [43], where the following inference rule is proposed:

$$
\left.
\begin{array}{l}
M_1 \preceq A_1 \\
A_1 \| M_2 \preceq A_2 \\
M_1 \| A_2 \models \varphi
\end{array}
\right\}
M_1 \| M_2 \models \varphi
$$

Here A_1 and A_2 are modules that serve as assumptions, and $\preceq$ is the *simulation* refinement relation [75]. In other words, if M_1 guarantees the assumption A_1, M_2 under the assumption A_1 guarantees the assumption A_2, and M_1 under the assumption A_2

guarantees φ, then we know that $M_1 \| M_2$, under no assumption, guarantees φ. The advantage of this rule is that both the $\preceq$ and $\models$ relation can be evaluated in polynomial time. Unfortunately, the simulation relation is much finer than the trace-containment relation (which is the refinement relation in the linear-time framework). This makes it exceedingly difficult to come up with the assumptions A_1 and A_2 above.

What do CTL users do in practice? In practice, they use the following rule:

$$\left. \begin{array}{c} M_2 \preceq A_2 \\ M_1 \| A_2 \models \varphi \end{array} \right\} M_1 \| M_2 \models \varphi$$

That is, instead of checking that $M_1 \| M_2 \models \varphi$, one checks that $M_1 \| A_2 \models \varphi$, where A_2 is an abstraction of M_2. As CTL model checkers usually do not support the test $M_2 \preceq A_2$, users often rely on their "intuition", which is typically a "linear intuition" rather than "branching intuition".[4] In other words, a typical way users overcome the limited expressive power of CTL is by "escaping" outside the tool; they build the "stub" A_2 in a hardware description language. Unfortunately, since stubs themselves could be incorrect, this practice is unsafe. (Users often check that the abstraction A_2 satisfies some CTL properties, such as $AGEFp$, but this is not sufficient to establish that $M_2 \preceq A_2$.)

In summary, CTL is not adequate for modular verification, which explains why recent attempts to augment SMV with assume-guarantee reasoning are based on linear time reasoning [73].

2.4 Semi-formal Verification

Because of the state-explosion problem, it is unrealistic to expect formal-verification tools to handle full systems or even large components. At the same time, simulation-based dynamic validation, while being able to handle large designs, covers only a small fraction of the design space, due to resource constraints. Thus, it has become clear that future verification tools need to combine formal and informal verification [106]. The combined approach is called *semi-formal verification* (cf. [39]). Such a combination, however, is rather problematic for CTL-based tools. CTL specifications and model-checking algorithms are in terms of computation trees; in fact, it is known that there are CTL formulas, e.g., $AFAXp$, whose failure cannot be witnessed by a linear counterexample [18].[5] In contrast, dynamic validation is fundamentally linear, as simulation generates individual computations. Thus, there is an inherent "impedance mismatch"

---

[4] Note that linear-time refinement is defined in terms of trace containment, which is a behavioral relation, while branching-time refinement is defined in terms of simulation, which is a state-based relation. Thus, constructing an abstraction A_2 such that $M_2 \preceq A_2$ requires a very deep understanding of the environment M_2.

[5] One of the advertised advantages of model checking is that when the model checker returns a negative answer, that answer is accompanied by a counterexample [21]. Note, however, that validation engineers are usually interested in linear counterexamples, but there are CTL formulas whose failure cannot be witnessed by a linear counterexample. In general, CTL-based model checkers do always accompany a negative answer by a counterexample. A similar comment applies to positive witnesses [59].

between the two approaches. This explains why current approaches to semi-formal verification are limited to invariances, i.e., properties of the form AGp. While many design errors can be discovered by model checking invariances, modular verification of even simple invariances often requires rather complicated assumptions on the environment in which the component under verification operates. Current semi-formal approaches, however, cannot handle general assumptions. Thus, the restriction of semi-formal verification to invariances is quite severe, limiting the possibility of integrating CTL-based model checking in traditional validation environments.

3   Linear Time

Our conclusion from the previous section is that CTL-based model checking, while phenomenally successful over the last 20 years, suffers from some inherent limitations that severely impede its functionality. As we show now, the linear-time approach does not suffer from these limitations.

3.1   The Linear-Time Framework

LTL is interpreted over *computations*, which can be viewed as infinite sequences of truth assignments to the atomic propositions: i.e., a computation is a function $\pi : N \to 2^{Prop}$ that assigns truth values to the elements of a set $Prop$ of atomic propositions at each time instant (natural number). For a computation π and a point $i \in N$, the notation $\pi, i \models \varphi$ indicates that a formula φ holds at the point i of the computation π. For example, $\pi, i \models X\varphi$ iff $\pi, i + 1 \models \varphi$. We say that π *satisfies* a formula φ, denoted $\pi \models \varphi$, iff $\pi, 0 \models \varphi$.

Designs can be described in a variety of formal description formalisms. Regardless of the formalism used, a *finite-state design* can be abstractly viewed as a *labeled transition system*, i.e., as a module $M = (W, W_0, R, V)$, where W is the finite sets of states that the system can be in, $W_0 \subseteq W$ is the set of initial states of the system, $R \subseteq W^2$ is a total transition relation that indicates the allowable state transitions of the system, and $V : W \to 2^{Prop}$ assigns truth values to the atomic propositions in each state of the system. A *path* in M that *starts at* u is a possible infinite behavior of the system starting at u, i.e., it is an infinite sequence $u_0, u_1 \ldots$ of states in W such that $u_0 = u$, and $u_i\ R\ u_{i+1}$ for all $i \geq 0$.[6] The sequence $V(u_0), V(u_1) \ldots$ is a *computation* of M that *starts at* u. The *language* of M, denoted $L(M)$, consists of all computations of M that start at a state in W_0. We say that M *satisfies* an LTL formula φ if all computations of $L(M)$ satisfy φ.

The *verification problem* for LTL is to check whether a transition system P satisfies an LTL formula φ. The verification problem for LTL can be solved in time $O(|P| \cdot 2^{|\varphi|})$ [68]. In other words, there is a model-checking algorithm for LTL whose running time is *linear* in the size of the program and *exponential* in the size of the specification. This is acceptable since the size of the specification is typically significantly smaller than the size of the program.

---

[6] It is important to consider infinite paths, since we are interested in ongoing computations. Deadlock and termination can be modeled explicitly via sink state.

The dominant approach today to LTL model checking is the *automata-theoretic approach* [103] (see also [99]). The key idea underlying the automata-theoretic approach is that, given an LTL formula φ, it is possible to construct a finite-state automaton A_φ that accepts all computations that satisfy φ. The type of finite automata on infinite words we consider is the one defined by Büchi [13] (c.f. [96]). A *Büchi automaton* is a tuple $A = (\Sigma, S, S_0, \rho, F)$, where Σ is a finite alphabet, S is a finite set of states, $S_0 \subseteq S$ is a set of initial states, $\rho : S \times \Sigma \to 2^S$ is a nondeterministic transition function, and $F \subseteq S$ is a set of accepting states. A *run* of A over an infinite word $w = a_1 a_2 \cdots$, is a sequence $s_0 s_1 \cdots$, where $s_0 \in S_0$ and $s_i \in \rho(s_{i-1}, a_i)$ for all $i \geq 1$. A run $s_0, s_1, \ldots$ is *accepting* if there is some designated state that repeats infinitely often, i.e., for some $s \in F$ there are infinitely many i's such that $s_i = s$. The infinite word w is *accepted* by A if there is an accepting run of A over w. The *language* of infinite words accepted by A is denoted $L(A)$. The following fact establishes the correspondence between LTL and Büchi automata: Given an LTL formula φ, one can build a Büchi automaton $A_\varphi = (\Sigma, S, S_0, \rho, , F)$, where $\Sigma = 2^{Prop}$ and $|S| \leq 2^{O(|\varphi|)}$, such that $L(A_\varphi)$ is exactly the set of computations satisfying the formula φ [104].

This correspondence enables the reduction of the verification problem to an automata-theoretic problem as follows [103]. Suppose that we are given a system M and an LTL formula φ: (1) construct the automaton $A_{\neg\varphi}$ that corresponds to the *negation* of the formula φ, (2) take the product of the system M and the automaton $A_{\neg\varphi}$ to obtain an automaton $A_{M,\varphi}$, and (3) check that the automaton $A_{M,\varphi}$ is nonempty, i.e., that it accepts *some* input. If it does not, then the design is correct. If it does, then the design is incorrect and the accepted input is an incorrect computation. The incorrect computation is presented to the user as a finite trace, possibly followed by a cycle.

The linear-time framework is not limited to using LTL as a specification language. There are those who prefer to use automata on infinite words as a specification formalism [104]; in fact, this is the approach of FormalCheck [62]. In this approach, we are given a design represented as a finite transition system M and a property represented by a Büchi (or a related variant) automaton P. The design is correct if all computations in $L(M)$ are accepted by P, i.e., $L(M) \subseteq L(P)$. This approach is called the *language-containment* approach. To verify M with respect to P we: (1) construct the automaton P^c that *complements* P, (2) take the product of the system M and the automaton P^c to obtain an automaton $A_{M,P}$, and (3) check that the automaton $A_{M,P}$ is nonempty. As before, the design is correct iff $A_{M,P}$ is empty.

3.2 Advantages

The advantages of the linear-time framework are:

- Expressiveness: The linear framework is more natural for verification engineers. In the linear framework both designs and properties are represented as finite-state machines (we saw that even LTL formulas can be viewed as finite-state machines); thus verification engineers employ the same conceptual model when thinking about the implementation and the specification [67].
- Compositionality: The linear framework supports the assume-guarantee methodology. An assumption on the environment is simply expressed as a property E.

Thus, instead of checking that $L(M) \subseteq L(P)$, we check that $L(M) \cap L(E) \subseteq L(P)$ [81]. Furthermore, we can add assumptions incrementally. Given assumptions $E_1, \ldots, E_k$, one needs to check that $L(M) \cap L(E_1) \cap \ldots \cap L(E_k) \subseteq L(P)$. The linear formalism is strong enough to express very general assumptions, as it can describe arbitrary finite-state machines, nondeterminism, and fairness. In fact, it is known that to prove linear-time properties of the parallel composition $M \| E_1 \| \ldots \| E_k$, it suffices to consider the linear-time properties of the components $M, E_1, \ldots, E_k$ [71].

- **Semi-formal verification:** As we saw, in the linear framework language containment is reduced to language emptiness, i.e., a search for a single computation satisfying some conditions. But this is precisely the same principle underlying dynamic validation. Thus, the linear framework offers support for search procedures that can be varied continuously from dynamic validation to full formal verification. This means that techniques for semi-formal verification can be applied not only to invariances but to much more general properties and can also accommodate assumptions on the environment [58]. In particular, linear-time properties can be compiled into "checkers" of simulation traces, facilitating the integration of formal verification with a traditional validation environment [58]. Such checkers can also be run as run-time monitors, which can issue an error message during a run in which a safety property is violated [16].

- **Property-specific abstraction:** Abstraction is a powerful technique for combating state explosion. An abstraction suppresses information from a concrete state-space by mapping it into a smaller, abstract state-space. As we saw, language containment is reduced to checking emptiness of a system $A_{M,\varphi}$ (or $A_{M,P}$) that combines the design with the complement of the property. Thus, one can search for abstractions that are tailored to the specific property being checked, resulting in more dramatic state-space reductions [38].

- **Combined methods:** Nonemptiness of automata can be tested enumeratively [25] or symbolically [97]. Recent work has shown that for invariances enumerative and symbolic methods can be combined [89]. Since in the linear framework model checking of general safety properties can be reduced to invariance checking of the composite system $A_{M,\varphi}$ (or $A_{M,P}$) [58], the enumerative-symbolic approach can be applied to a large class of properties and can also handle assumptions.

- **Uniformity:** The linear framework offers a uniform treatment of model checking, abstraction, and refinement [1], as all are expressed as language containment. For example, to show that a design P_1 is a refinement a design P_2, we have to check that $L(P_1) \subseteq L(P_2)$. Similarly, one abstracts a design M by generating a design M' that has more behaviors than M, i.e., $L(M) \subseteq L(M')$. Thus, an implementor can focus on an efficient implementation of the language-containment test. This means that a linear-time model checker can also be used to check for *sequential equivalence* of finite-state machines [49]. Furthermore, the automata-theoretic approach can be easily adapted to perform quantitative timing analysis, which computes minimum and maximum delays over a selected subset of system executions [17].

- **Bounded Model Checking:** In linear-time model checking one searches for a counterexample trace, finite or infinite, which falsifies the desired temporal property. In bounded model checking, the search is restricted to a trace of a bounded length, in which the bound is selected before the search. The motivating idea is that many errors can be found in traces of relatively small length (say, less than 40 cycles). The restriction to bounded-length traces enables a reduction to propositional satisfiability (SAT). It was recently shown that SAT-based model checking can often significantly outperform BDD-based model checkers [9]. As bounded model checking is essentially a search for counterexample traces of bounded length, its fits naturally within the linear-time framework, but does not fit the branching rime framework.

3.3   Beyond LTL

Since the proposal by Pnueli [80] to apply LTL to the specification and verification of concurrent programs, the adequacy of LTL has been widely studied. One of the conclusions of this research is that LTL is not expressive enough for the task. The first to complain about the expressive power of LTL was Wolper [105] who observed that LTL cannot express certain ω-regular events (in fact, LTL expresses precisely the star-free ω-regular events [95]). As was shown later [69], this makes LTL inadequate for *compositional* verification, since LTL is not expressive enough to express assumptions about the environment in modular verification. It is now recognized that a linear temporal property logic has to be expressive enough to specify all ω-regular properties [104]. What then should be the "ultimate" temporal property-specification language?

Several extensions to LTL have been proposed with the goal of obtaining full ω-regularity:

- Vardi and Wolper proposed ETL, the extension of LTL with temporal connectives that correspond to ω-automata [105,104]), ETL essentially combines two perspective on hardware specification, the operational perspective (finite-state machines) with the behavioral perspective (temporal connectives). Experience has shown that both perspectives are useful in hardware specification.
- Banieqbal and Barringer proposed extending LTL with fixpoint operators [4] (see also [98]), yielding a linear μ-calculus (cf. [52]), and
- Sistla, Vardi, and Wolper proposed QPTL, the extension of LTL with quantification over propositional variables [92].

It is not clear, however, that any of these approaches provides an adequate solution from a pragmatic perspective: implementing full ETL requires a complementation construction for Büchi automata, which is still a topic under research [55]; fixpoint calculi are notoriously difficult for users, and are best thought as an intermediate language; and full QPTL has a nonelementary time complexity [92].

Another problem with these solutions is the lack of temporal connectives to describe past events. While such connectives are present in works on temporal logic by philosophers (e.g., [85,78]), they have been purged by many computer scientists, who were motivated by a strive for minimality, following the observation in [40] that in applications with infinite future but finite past, past connectives do not add expressive power. Somewhat later, however, arguments were made for the restoration of the past in temporal logic. The first argument is that while past temporal connectives do not add any expressive power the price for eliminating them can be high. Many natural statements in program specification are much easier to express using past connectives [87]. In fact, the best known procedure to eliminate past connectives in LTL may cause a significant blow-up of the considered formulas [69].

A more important motivation for the restoration of the past is again the use of temporal logic in modular verification. In global verification one uses temporal formulas that refer to locations in the program text [81]. This is absolutely *verboten* in modular verification, since in specifying a module one can refer only to its external behavior. Since we cannot refer to program location we have instead to refer to the history of the computation, and we can do that very easily with past connectives [5].

We can summarize the above arguments for the extension of LTL with a quote by Pnueli [81]: "In order to perform compositional specification and verification, it is *convenient* to use the past operators but *necessary* to have the full power of ETL."

3.4   A Pragmatic Proposal

The design of a temporal property-specification language in an industrial setting is not a mere theoretical exercise. Such an effort was recently undertaken by a formal-verification group at Intel. In designing such a language one has to balance competing needs:

- Expressiveness: The logic has to be expressive enough to cover most properties likely to be used by verification engineers. This should include not only properties of the unit under verification but also relevant properties of the unit's environment.
- Usability: The logic should be easy to understand and to use for verification engineers. At the same time, it is important that the logic has rigorous formal semantics to ensure correct compilation and optimization and enable formal reasoning.
- Closure: The logic should enable the expression of complex properties from simpler one. This enables maintaining libraries of properties and property templates. Thus, the logic should be closed under all of its logical connectives, both Boolean and temporal.
- History: An industrial tool is not developed in a vacuum. At Intel, there was already a community of model-checking users, who were used to a certain temporal property-specification language. While the new language was not expected to be fully backward compatible, the users demanded an easy migration path.
- Implementability: The design of the language went hand-in-hand with the design of the model-checking tool [2]. In considering various language features, their importance had to be balanced against the difficulty of ensuring that the implementation can handle these features.

The effort at Intel culminated with the design of FTL, a new temporal property specification language [3]. FTL is the temporal logic underlying *ForSpec*, which is Intel's new formal specification language. A model checker with FTL as its temporal logic is deployed at Intel [2]. The key features of FTL are as follows:

- FTL is a linear temporal logic, with a limited form of past connectives, and with the full expressive power of ω-regular languages,

- it is based on a rich set of logical and arithmetical operations on bit vectors to describe state properties,
- it enables the user to define temporal connectives over time windows,
- it enables the user to define regular events, which are regular sequences of Boolean events, and then relate such events via special connectives,
- it enables the user to quantify universally over propositional variables, and
- it contains constructs that enable the users to model multiple clock and reset signals, which is useful in the verification of hardware design.

Of particular interest is the way FTL achieves full ω-regularity. FTL borrows from both ETL (as well as PDL [36]), by extending LTL with regular events, and from QPTL, by extending LTL with universal quantification over propositional variables. Each of these extensions provides us with full ω-regularity. Why the redundancy? The rationale is that expressiveness is not just a theoretical issue, it is also a usability issue. It is not enough that the user is able to express certain properties; it is important that the user can express these properties without unnecessary contortions. Thus, one need not shy away from introducing redundant features, while at the same time attempting to keep the logic relatively simple.

There is no reason, however, to think that FTL is the final word on temporal property-specification languages. First, one would not expect to have an "ultimate" temporal property-specification language any more than one would expect to have an "ultimate" programming language. There are also, in effect, two competing languages. Formal-Check uses a built-in library of automata on infinite words as its property-specification language [63], while Cadence SMV[7] uses LTL with universal quantification over propositional variables. Our hope is that the publication of this paper and of [3], concomitant with the release of an FTL-based tool to Intel users, would result in a dialog on the subject of property-specification logic between the research community, tool developers, and tools users. It is time, we believe to close the debate on the linear-time vs. branching time issue, and open a debate on linear-time languages.

4   Discussion

Does the discussion above imply that 20 years of research into CTL-based model checking have led to a dead end? To the contrary! The key algorithms underlying symbolic model checking for CTL are efficient graph-theoretic reachability and fair-reachability procedures (cf. [88]). The essence of the language-containment approach is that verification of very general linear-time properties can be reduced to reachability or fair-reachability analysis, an analysis that is at the heart of CTL-based model-checking engines. Thus, a linear-time model checker can be built on top of a CTL model checker, as in Cadence SMV, leveraging two decades of science and technology in CTL-based model checking.

It should also be stated clearly that our criticism of CTL is in the specific context of property-specification languages for model checking. There are contexts in which the branching-time framework is the natural one. For example, when it comes to the

---

[7] http://www-cad.eecs.berkeley.edu/~kenmcmil/smv/

synthesis of reactive systems, one has to consider a branching-time framework, since all possible strategies by the environment need to be considered [83,84]. Even when the goal is a simple reachability goal, one is quickly driven towards using CTL as a specification language [28].

Even in the context of model checking, CTL has its place. In model checking one checks whether a transition system M satisfies a temporal formula φ. The transition system M is obtained either by compilation from an actual design, typically expressed using a *hardware description language* such as VHDL or Verilog, or is constructed manually by the user using a modeling language, such as SMV's SML [74]. In the latter case, the user often wishes to "play" with M, in order to ensure that M is a good model of the system under consideration. Using CTL, one can express properties such as $AGAFp$, which are structural rather than behavioral. A CTL-based model checker enables the user to "play" with M by checking its structural properties. Since the reachability and fair-reachability engine is at the heart of both CTL-based and linear-time-based model checkers, we believe that the "ultimate" model checker should have both a CTL front end and a linear-time front end, with a common reachability and fair-reachability engine.

Acknowledgment: I'd like to thank Orna Kupferman, my close collaborator over the last few years, for numerous discussions on linear vs. branching time. Also, my collaboration with members the formal-verification team in the Intel Design Center, Israel, during the 1997-2000 period, in particular, with Roy Armoni, Limor Fix, Ranan Fraer, Gila Kamhi, Yonit Kesten, Avner Landver, Sela Mador-Haim and Andreas Tiemeyer, gave me invaluables insights into formal verification in an industrial setting.

References

1. M. Abadi and L. Lamport. The existence of refinement mappings. *Theoretical Computer Science*, 82(2):253–284, 1991.
2. R. Armoni, L. Fix, A. Flaisher, R. Gerth, T. Kanza, A. Landver, S. Mador-Haim, A. Tiemeyer, M.Y. Vardi, and Y. Zbar. The ForSpec compiler. Submitted, 2001.
3. R. Armoni, L. Fix, R. Gerth, B. Ginsburg, T. Kanza, A. Landver, S. Mador-Haim, A. Tiemeyer, E. Singerman, and M.Y. Vardi. The ForSpec temporal language: A new temporal property-specification language. Submitted, 2001.
4. B. Banieqbal and H. Barringer. Temporal logic with fixed points. In B. Banieqbal, H. Barringer, and A. Pnueli, editors, *Temporal Logic in Specification*, volume 398 of *Lecture Notes in Computer Science*, pages 62–74. Springer-Verlag, 1987.
5. H. Barringer and R. Kuiper. Hierarchical development of concurrent systems in a framework. In S.D. Brookes et al., editor, *Seminar in Concurrency*, Lecture Notes in Computer Science, Vol. 197, pages 35–61. Springer-Verlag, Berlin/New York, 1985.
6. I. Beer, S. Ben-David, D. Geist, R. Gewirtzman, and M. Yoeli. Methodology and system for practical formal verification of reactive hardware. In *Proc. 6th Conference on Computer Aided Verification*, volume 818 of *Lecture Notes in Computer Science*, pages 182–193, Stanford, June 1994.
7. I. Beer, S. Ben-David, and A. Landver. On-the-fly model checking for RCTL formulas. In A.J. Hu and M.Y. Vardi, editors, *Computer Aided Verification, Proc. 10th Int'l Conf.*, volume 1427 of *Lecture Notes in Computer Science*, pages 184–194. Springer-Verlag, Berlin, 1998.

8. M. Ben-Ari, A. Pnueli, and Z. Manna. The temporal logic of branching time. *Acta Informatica*, 20:207–226, 1983.

9. A. Biere, A. Cimatti, E.M. Clarke, M. Fujita, and Y. Zhu. Symbolic model checking using SAT procedures instead of BDDs. In *Proc. 36th Design Automation Conference*, pages 317–320. IEEE Computer Society, 1999.

10. R. Bloem, K. Ravi, and F. Somenzi. Efficient decision prcedures for model checking of linear time logic properties. In *Computer Aided Verification, Proc. 11th Int. Conference*, volume 1633 of *Lecture Notes in Computer Science*, pages 222–235. Springer-Verlag, 1999.

11. R.K. Brayton, G.D. Hachtel, A. Sangiovanni-Vincentelli, F. Somenzi, A. Aziz, S.-T. Cheng, S. Edwards, S. Khatri, T. Kukimoto, A. Pardo, S. Qadeer, R.K. Ranjan, S. Sarwary, T.R. Shiple, G. Swamy, and T. Villa. VIS: a system for verification and synthesis. In *Computer Aided Verification, Proc. 8th Int. Conference*, volume 1102 of *Lecture Notes in Computer Science*, pages 428–432. Springer-Verlag, 1996.

12. M.C. Browne, E.M. Clarke, and O. Grumberg. Characterizing finite Kripke structures in propositional temporal logic. *Theoretical Computer Science*, 59:115–131, 1988.

13. J.R. Büchi. On a decision method in restricted second order arithmetic. In *Proc. Internat. Congr. Logic, Method. and Philos. Sci. 1960*, pages 1–12, Stanford, 1962. Stanford University Press.

14. J.R. Burch, E.M. Clarke, K.L. McMillan, D.L. Dill, and L.J. Hwang. Symbolic model checking: 10^{20} states and beyond. In *Proc. 5th Symp. on Logic in Computer Science*, pages 428–439, Philadelphia, June 1990.

15. J.R. Burch, E.M. Clarke, K.L. McMillan, D.L. Dill, and L.J. Hwang. Symbolic model checking: 10^{20} states and beyond. *Information and Computation*, 98(2):142–170, June 1992.

16. W. Cai and S.J. Turner. An approach to the run-time monitoring of parallel programs. *The Computer JournaL*, 37(4):333–345, 1994.

17. S. Campos, E.M. Clarke, and O. Grumberg. Selective quantitative analysis and interval model checking: Verifying different facets of a system. In *Computer-Aided Verification, Proc. 8th Int'l Conf.*, volume 1102 of *Lecture Notes in Computer Science*, pages 257–268. Springer-Verlag, Berlin, 1996.

18. E.M. Clarke and I.A. Draghicescu. Expressibility results for linear-time and branching-time logics. In J.W. de Bakker, W.P. de Roever, and G. Rozenberg, editors, *Proc. Workshop on Linear Time, Branching Time, and Partial Order in Logics and Models for Concurrency*, volume 354 of *Lecture Notes in Computer Science*, pages 428–437. Springer-Verlag, 1988.

19. E.M. Clarke, E.A. Emerson, and A.P. Sistla. Automatic verification of finite-state concurrent systems using temporal logic specifications. *ACM Transactions on Programming Languages and Systems*, 8(2):244–263, January 1986.

20. E.M. Clarke, O. Grumberg, and D. Long. Verification tools for finite-state concurrent systems. In J.W. de Bakker, W.-P. de Roever, and G. Rozenberg, editors, *Decade of Concurrency – Reflections and Perspectives (Proceedings of REX School)*, volume 803 of *Lecture Notes in Computer Science*, pages 124–175. Springer-Verlag, 1993.

21. E.M. Clarke, O. Grumberg, K.L. McMillan, and X. Zhao. Efficient generation of counterexamples and witnesses in symbolic model checking. In *Proc. 32nd Design Automation Conference*, pages 427–432. IEEE Computer Society, 1995.

22. E.M. Clarke, O. Grumberg, and D. Peled. *Model Checking*. MIT Press, 1999.

23. E.M. Clarke and R.P. Kurshan. Computer aided verification. *IEEE Spectrum*, 33:61–67, 1986.

24. E.M. Clarke, D.E. Long, and K.L. McMillan. Compositional model checking. In R. Parikh, editor, *Proc. 4th IEEE Symp. on Logic in Computer Science*, pages 353–362. IEEE Computer Society Press, 1989.

25. C. Courcoubetis, M.Y. Vardi, P. Wolper, and M. Yannakakis. Memory efficient algorithms for the verification of temporal properties. *Formal Methods in System Design*, 1:275–288, 1992.
26. W. Damm, G. Döhmen, V. Gerstner, and B. Josko. Modular verification of Petri nets: the temporal logic approach. In *Stepwise Refinement of Distributed Systems: Models, Formalisms, Correctness (Proceedings of REX Workshop)*, volume 430 of *Lecture Notes in Computer Science*, pages 180–207, Mook, The Netherlands, May/June 1989. Springer-Verlag.
27. D. Dams, O. Grumberg, and R. Gerth. Generation of reduced models for checking fragments of CTL. In *Proc. 5th Conf. on Computer Aided Verification*, volume 697 of *Lecture Notes in Computer Science*, pages 479–490. Springer-Verlag, June 1993.
28. M. Daniele, P. Traverso, and M.Y. Vardi. Strong cyclic planning revisited. In S. Biundo and M. Fox, editors, *5th European Conference on Planning*, pages 34–46, 1999.
29. N. Daniele, F.Guinchiglia, and M.Y. Vardi. Improved automata generation for linear temporal logic. In *Computer Aided Verification, Proc. 11th Int. Conference*, volume 1633 of *Lecture Notes in Computer Science*, pages 249–260. Springer-Verlag, 1999.
30. E.A. Emerson. Temporal and modal logic. *Handbook of Theoretical Computer Science*, pages 997–1072, 1990.
31. E.A. Emerson and E.M. Clarke. Characterizing correctness properties of parallel programs using fixpoints. In *Proc. 7th Int'l Colloq. on Automata, Languages and Programming*, pages 169–181, 1980.
32. E.A. Emerson and J.Y. Halpern. Decision procedures and expressiveness in the temporal logic of branching time. *Journal of Computer and System Sciences*, 30:1–24, 1985.
33. E.A. Emerson and J.Y. Halpern. Sometimes and not never revisited: On branching versus linear time. *Journal of the ACM*, 33(1):151–178, 1986.
34. E.A. Emerson and C. Jutla. The complexity of tree automata and logics of programs. In *Proc. 29th IEEE Symp. on Foundations of Computer Science*, pages 328–337, White Plains, October 1988.
35. E.A. Emerson and C.-L. Lei. Modalities for model checking: Branching time logic strikes back. In *Proc. 20th ACM Symp. on Principles of Programming Languages*, pages 84–96, New Orleans, January 1985.
36. M.J. Fischer and R.E. Ladner. Propositional dynamic logic of regular programs. *Journal of Computer and Systems Sciences*, 18:194–211, 1979.
37. K. Fisler. Timing diagrams: Formalization and algorithmic verification. *Journal of Logic, Language, and Information*, 8:323–361, 1999.
38. K. Fisler and M.Y. Vardi. Bisimulation minimization in an automata-theoretic verification framework. In G. Gopalakrishnan and P. Windley, editors, *Proc. Intl. Conference on Formal Methods in Computer-Aided Design (FMCAD)*, number 1522 in Lecture Notes in Computer Science, pages 115–132. Springer-Verlag, 1998.
39. R. Fraer, G. Kamhi, L. Fix, and M.Y. Vardi. Evaluating semi-exhausting verification techniques for bug hunting. In *Proc. 1st Int'l Workshop on Symbolic Model Checking (SMC'99)*, Electronic Notes in Theoretical Computer Science, pages 11–22. Elsevier, 1999.
40. D. Gabbay, A. Pnueli, S. Shelah, and J. Stavi. On the temporal analysis of fairness. In *Proc. 7th ACM Symp. on Principles of Programming Languages*, pages 163–173, January 1980.
41. R. Gerth, D. Peled, M.Y. Vardi, and P. Wolper. Simple on-the-fly automatic verification of linear temporal logic. In P. Dembiski and M. Sredniawa, editors, *Protocol Specification, Testing, and Verification*, pages 3–18. Chapman & Hall, August 1995.
42. R. Goering. Model checking expands verification's scope. *Electronic Engineering Today*, February 1997.
43. O. Grumberg and D.E. Long. Model checking and modular verification. *ACM Trans. on Programming Languages and Systems*, 16(3):843–871, 1994.

44. R.H. Hardin, Z. Har'el, and R.P. Kurshan. COSPAN. In *Computer Aided Verification, Proc. 8th Int. Conference*, volume 1102 of *Lecture Notes in Computer Science*, pages 423–427. Springer-Verlag, 1996.

45. D. Harel and A. Pnueli. On the development of reactive systems. In K. Apt, editor, *Logics and Models of Concurrent Systems*, volume F-13 of *NATO Advanced Summer Institutes*, pages 477–498. Springer-Verlag, 1985.

46. M. Hennessy and R. Milner. Algebraic laws for nondeterminism and concurrency. *Journal of ACM*, 32:137–161, 1985.

47. C.A.R. Hoare. *Communicating Sequential Processes*. Prentice-Hall, 1985.

48. G.J. Holzmann. The model checker SPIN. *IEEE Trans. on Software Engineering*, 23(5):279–295, May 1997. Special issue on Formal Methods in Software Practice.

49. S.Y. Huang and K.T. Cheng. *Formal Equivalence Checking and Design Debugging*. Kluwer Academic publishers, 1998.

50. C.B. Jones. Specification and design of (parallel) programs. In R.E.A. Mason, editor, *Information Processing 83: Proc. IFIP 9th World Congress*, pages 321–332. IFIP, North-Holland, 1983.

51. B. Josko. Verifying the correctness of AADL modules using model chekcing. In *Stepwise Refinement of Distributed Systems: Models, Formalisms, Correctness (Proceedings of REX Workshop)*, volume 430 of *Lecture Notes in Computer Science*, pages 386–400, Mook, The Netherlands, May/June 1989. Springer-Verlag.

52. D. Kozen. Results on the propositional μ-calculus. *Theoretical Computer Science*, 27:333–354, 1983.

53. D. Kozen and L. Tiuryn. Logics of programs. *Handbook of Theoretical Computer Science*, pages 789–840, 1990.

54. O. Kupferman and M.Y. Vardi. Module checking. In *Computer Aided Verification, Proc. 8th Int. Conference*, volume 1102 of *Lecture Notes in Computer Science*, pages 75–86. Springer-Verlag, 1996.

55. O. Kupferman and M.Y. Vardi. Weak alternating automata are not that weak. In *Proc. 5th Israeli Symp. on Theory of Computing and Systems*, pages 147–158. IEEE Computer Society Press, 1997.

56. O. Kupferman and M.Y. Vardi. Freedom, weakness, and determinism: from linear-time to branching-time. In *Proc. 13th IEEE Symp. on Logic in Computer Science*, pages 81–92, June 1998.

57. O. Kupferman and M.Y. Vardi. Relating linear and branching model checking. In *IFIP Working Conference on Programming Concepts and Methods*, pages 304 – 326, New York, June 1998. Chapman & Hall.

58. O. Kupferman and M.Y. Vardi. Model checking of safety properties. In *Computer Aided Verification, Proc. 11th Int. Conference*, volume 1633 of *Lecture Notes in Computer Science*, pages 172–183. Springer-Verlag, 1999.

59. O. Kupferman and M.Y. Vardi. Vacuity detection in temporal model checking. In *10th Advanced Research Working Conference on Correct Hardware Design and Verification Methods*, volume 1703 of *Lecture Notes in Computer Science*, pages 82–96. Springer-Verlag, 1999.

60. O. Kupferman and M.Y. Vardi. An automata-theoretic approach to modular model checking. *ACM Transactions on Programming Languages and Systems*, 22:87–128, 2000.

61. O. Kupferman, M.Y. Vardi, and P. Wolper. Module checking. *To appear in Information and Computation*, 2001.

62. R.P. Kurshan. *Computer Aided Verification of Coordinating Processes*. Princeton Univ. Press, 1994.

63. R.P. Kurshan. *FormalCheck User's Manual*. Cadence Design, Inc., 1998.

64. P. Ladkin and S. Leue. What do message sequence charts means? In R.L. Tenney, P.D. Amer, and M.Ü. Uyar, editors, *Proc. 6th Int'l Conf. on Formal Description Techniques.* North Holland, 1994.

65. L. Lamport. Sometimes is sometimes "not never" - on the temporal logic of programs. In *Proc. 7th ACM Symp. on Principles of Programming Languages*, pages 174–185, January 1980.

66. L. Lamport. Specifying concurrent program modules. *ACM Trans. on Programming Languages and Systenms*, 5:190–222, 1983.

67. L. Lamport. The temporal logic of actions. *ACM Transactions on Programming Languages and Systems*, 16:872–923, 1994.

68. O. Lichtenstein and A. Pnueli. Checking that finite state concurrent programs satisfy their linear specification. In *Proc. 12th ACM Symp. on Principles of Programming Languages*, pages 97–107, New Orleans, January 1985.

69. O. Lichtenstein, A. Pnueli, and L. Zuck. The glory of the past. In *Logics of Programs*, volume 193 of *Lecture Notes in Computer Science*, pages 196–218, Brooklyn, June 1985. Springer-Verlag.

70. Monika Maidl. The common fragment of CTL and LTL. In *Proc. 41th Symp. on Foundations of Computer Science*, pages 643–652, 2000.

71. Z. Manna and A. Pnueli. The anchored version of the temporal framework. In *Linear time, branching time, and partial order in logics and models for concurrency*, volume 345 of *Lecture Notes in Computer Science*, pages 201–284. Springer-Verlag, 1989.

72. Z. Manna and A. Pnueli. Temporal specification and verification of reactive modules. 1992.

73. K. L. McMillan. Verification of an implementation of Tomasulo's algorithm by compositional model checking. In *Proc. 10th Conference on Computer Aided Verification*, volume 1427 of *Lecture Notes in Computer Science*, pages 110–121. Springer-Verlag, 1998.

74. K.L. McMillan. *Symbolic Model Checking*. Kluwer Academic Publishers, 1993.

75. R. Milner. An algebraic definition of simulation between programs. In *Proc. 2nd International Joint Conference on Artificial Intelligence*, pages 481–489. British Computer Society, September 1971.

76. R. Milner. *Communication and Concurrecny*. Prentice-Hall, Englewood Clifs, 1989.

77. B. Misra and K.M. Chandy. Proofs of networks of processes. *IEEE Trans. on Software Engineering*, 7:417–426, 1981.

78. A. Urquhart N. Rescher. *Temporal Logic*. Springer-Verlag, 1971.

79. D. Park. Concurrency and automata on infinite sequences. In P. Deussen, editor, *Proc. 5th GI Conf. on Theoretical Computer Science*, Lecture Notes in Computer Science, Vol. 104. Springer-Verlag, Berlin/New York, 1981.

80. A. Pnueli. The temporal logic of programs. In *Proc. 18th IEEE Symp. on Foundation of Computer Science*, pages 46–57, 1977.

81. A. Pnueli. In transition from global to modular temporal reasoning about programs. In K. Apt, editor, *Logics and Models of Concurrent Systems*, volume F-13 of *NATO Advanced Summer Institutes*, pages 123–144. Springer-Verlag, 1985.

82. A. Pnueli. Linear and branching structures in the semantics and logics of reactive systems. In *Proc. 12th Int. Colloquium on Automata, Languages and Programming*, pages 15–32. Lecture Notes in Computer Science, Springer-Verlag, 1985.

83. A. Pnueli and R. Rosner. On the synthesis of a reactive module. In *Proc. 16th ACM Symp. on Principles of Programming Languages*, pages 179–190, Austin, January 1989.

84. A. Pnueli and R. Rosner. On the synthesis of an asynchronous reactive module. In *Proc. 16th Int. Colloquium on Automata, Languages and Programming*, volume 372, pages 652–671. Lecture Notes in Computer Science, Springer-Verlag, July 1989.

85. A. Prior. *Past, Present, and Future*. Oxford Univ. Press, 1951.

86. J.P. Queille and J. Sifakis. Specification and verification of concurrent systems in Cesar. In *Proc. 5th International Symp. on Programming*, volume 137 of *Lecture Notes in Computer Science*, pages 337–351. Springer-Verlag, 1981.

87. W.P. DeRoever R. Koymans, J. Vytopil. Real-time programming and asynchronous message passing. In *Proc. 2nd ACM Symp. on Principles of Distributed Computing*, pages 187–197, 1983.

88. K. Ravi, R. Bloem, and F. Somenzi. A comparative study of symbolic algorithms for the computation of fair cycles. In W. A. Hunt, Jr. and S. D. Johnson, editors, *Formal Methods in Computer Aided Design*, Lecture Notes in Computer Science 1954, pages 143–160. Springer-Verlag, 2000.

89. K. Ravi and F. Somenzi. High-density reachability analysis. In *Proc. Int'l Conf. on Computer-Aided Design*, pages 154–158, San Jose, 1995.

90. T. Schlipf, T. Buechner, R. Fritz, M. Helms, and J. Koehl. Formal verification made easy. *IBM Journal of Research and Development*, 41(4:5), 1997.

91. A.P. Sistla and E.M. Clarke. The complexity of propositional linear temporal logic. *Journal ACM*, 32:733–749, 1985.

92. A.P. Sistla, M.Y. Vardi, and P. Wolper. The complementation problem for Büchi automata with applications to temporal logic. *Theoretical Computer Science*, 49:217–237, 1987.

93. E.W. Stark. *Foundations of theory of specifications for distributed systems*. PhD thesis, M.I.T., 1984.

94. C. Stirling. Modal and temporal logics. *Handbook of Logic in Computer Science*, 2:477–563, 1992.

95. W. Thomas. A combinatorial approach to the theory of ω-automata. *Information and Computation*, 48:261–283, 1981.

96. W. Thomas. Automata on infinite objects. *Handbook of Theoretical Computer Science*, pages 165–191, 1990.

97. H.J. Touati, R.K. Brayton, and R. Kurshan. Testing language containment for ω-automata using BDD's. *Information and Computation*, 118(1):101–109, April 1995.

98. M.Y. Vardi. A temporal fixpoint calculus. In *Proc. 15th ACM Symp. on Principles of Programming Languages*, pages 250–259, San Diego, January 1988.

99. M.Y. Vardi. An automata-theoretic approach to linear temporal logic. In F. Moller and G. Birtwistle, editors, *Logics for Concurrency: Structure versus Automata*, volume 1043 of *Lecture Notes in Computer Science*, pages 238–266. Springer-Verlag, Berlin, 1996.

100. M.Y. Vardi. Linear vs. branching time: A complexity-theoretic perspective. In *Proc. 13th IEEE Sym.. on Logic in Computer Science*, pages 394–405, 1998.

101. M.Y. Vardi. Sometimes and not never re-revisited: on branching vs. linear time. In D. Sangiorgi and R. de Simone, editors, *Proc. 9th Int'l Conf. on Concurrency Theory*, Lecture Notes in Computer Science 1466, pages 1–17, 1998.

102. M.Y. Vardi and L. Stockmeyer. Improved upper and lower bounds for modal logics of programs. In *Proc 17th ACM Symp. on Theory of Computing*, pages 240–251, 1985.

103. M.Y. Vardi and P. Wolper. An automata-theoretic approach to automatic program verification. In *Proc. 1st Symp. on Logic in Computer Science*, pages 332–344, Cambridge, June 1986.

104. M.Y. Vardi and P. Wolper. Reasoning about infinite computations. *Information and Computation*, 115(1):1–37, November 1994.

105. P. Wolper. Temporal logic can be more expressive. *Information and Control*, 56(1–2):72–99, 1983.

106. J. Yuan, J. Shen, J. Abraham, and A. Aziz. On combining formal and informal verification. In *Computer Aided Verification, Proc. 9th Int. Conference*, volume 1254 of *Lecture Notes in Computer Science*, pages 376–387. Springer-Verlag, 1997.

Propositional Reasoning

Michael P. Fourman

Institute for Representation and Reasoning
Division of Informatics
The University of Edinburgh
Scotland, UK
Michael.Fourman@ed.ac.uk

Abstract. Propositional (Boolean) logic is conceptually simple. It provides a rich basis for the representation of finite structures, but is computationally complex. Many current verification techniques are based on propositional encodings.

Propositional representations lead to problems that are, in general, computationally intractable. Nevertheless, datastructures for representing propositional formulae, and algorithms for reasoning about them, provide generic tools that can be applied to a wide variety of computational problems. Natural problem instances are often effectively solved by these generic approaches.

There is a growing literature of algorithms for propositional reasoning, and of techniques for propositional representation of tasks in areas ranging from cryptography, constraint satisfaction and planning, to system design, validation and verification.

We present a model-theoretic account of propositional encodings for questions of logical validity. Validity is characterised model-thoretically. For restricted logics, checking validity in a restricted class of models may suffice. Classes of structures on a finite domain can be encoded as propositional theories, and validity in such a class is encoded propositionally, by means of a syntactic translation to a propositional formula.

This provides a unified setting for generating efficient propositional encodings suitable for analysis using BDD or SAT packages.

T. Margaria and W. Yi (Eds.): TACAS 2001, LNCS 2031, p. 23, 2001.
© Springer-Verlag Berlin Heidelberg 2001

Language Containmen t Chec king with Nondeterministic BDDs *

Bernd Finkbeiner

Computer Science Department
Stanford University
Stanford, CA 94305-9045
finkbein@cs.stanford.edu

Abstract. Checking for language containment between nondeterministic ω-automata is a central task in automata-based hierarchical verification. We present a symbolic procedure for language containment checking between two Büchi automata. Our algorithm avoids determinization by intersecting the implementation automaton with the complement of the specification automaton as an alternating automaton. We present a fixpoint algorithm for the emptiness check of alternating automata. The main data structure is a nondeterministic extension of binary decision diagrams that canonically represents sets of Boolean functions.

1 Introduction

Binary decision diagrams (BDDs) have greatly extended the scope of systems that can be verified automatically: instead of searching the entire state space of a model, the verification algorithm works with a symbolic representation of relevant state sets. Symbolic methods have been developed for many verification problems, in particular for temporal logic model c hecking [CGP99].

For the language containment problem $\mathcal{L}(\mathcal{A}) \subseteq \mathcal{L}(\mathcal{B})$ between two ω-automata $\mathcal{A}$ and $\mathcal{B}$, symbolic algorithms have so far only been proposed in the case where $\mathcal{B}$ is deterministic [TBK95]. This is a serious restriction: in property-oriented verification it is advantageous to allow for nondeterminism, since it usually leads to simpler specifications (see [THB95] for examples). Having the same type of automaton for $\mathcal{A}$ and $\mathcal{B}$ also makes hierarchical verification possible, where an intermediate automaton appears as an implemen tation in one verification problem and as a specification in the next; the verification can follow a chain of increasingly more complex models and ensure that observ able properties are preserved.

The standard approach to the language containment check $\mathcal{L}(\mathcal{A}) \subseteq \mathcal{L}(\mathcal{B})$ is to first complemen t $\mathcal{B}$, and then check the intersection with $\mathcal{A}$ for emptiness.

---

* This research was supported in part by the National Science Foundation grant CCR-99-00984-001, by ARO grant DAAG55-98-1-0471, by ARO/MURI grant DAAH04-96-1-0341, by ARPA/Army contract DABT63-96-C-0096, and by ARPA/AirForce contracts F33615-00-C-1693 and F33615-99-C-3014.

T. Margaria and W. Yi (Eds.): TACAS 2001, LNCS 2031, pp. 24–38, 2001.
© Springer-Verlag Berlin Heidelberg 2001

The difficulty with this approach is that the classic constructions for the complementation of ω-automata are all based on determinization. Determinization algorithms for ω-automata, like Safra's construction [Saf88], use an intricate structure to describe deterministic states. Such states not only encode sets of nondeterministic states reachable by the same input prefix, but also keep track of the acceptance status of the nondeterministic computations. Safra-trees have been found to be too complex to be directly encoded in a BDD [THB95].

In our solution we sidestep the determinization construction by intersecting $\mathcal{L}(\mathcal{A})$ and $\overline{\mathcal{L}(\mathcal{B})}$ not in their representation as nondeterministic automata, but in the more general framework of alternating automata, where complementation can be achieved by dualizing the transition function and acceptance condition. This approach makes use of concepts from a new complementation construction by Kupferman and Vardi [KV97]. The use of alternation not only simplifies the algorithm, it also allows us to combine the two automata before any analysis takes place. Thus, no effort is wasted on parts of $\mathcal{B}$ that are not reachable in the combined automaton.

We describe a fixpoint algorithm that checks the resulting alternating automaton for emptiness. This construction involves reasoning about sets of sets of states, one level of aggregation above the sets of states that can be represented by a BDD. We therefore propose an extension to BDDs: by allowing the underlying automaton to be nondeterministic, sets of (deterministic) BDDs can be embedded in a single (nondeterministic) structure.

Overview. In the following Section 2 we briefly survey related work. Section 3 provides background on automata over infinite words. We review deterministic BDDs in Section 4 and present our nondeterministic extension in Section 5. In Section 6 we develop the fixpoint construction for the emptiness check on alternating automata.

2   Related Work

Language containment checking. There are two systems that provide completely automatic language containment checking. Omega [BMUV97] is a package of procedures related to ω-automata and infinite games over finite graphs. Omega implements Safra's construction and uses a completely explicit representation of the state space. HSIS [THB95] is a partially symbolic implementation, again based on Safra's construction. While the state space is still represented explicitly, HSIS makes auxiliary use of BDDs to represent relations on states.

Simulation checking. Simulation is a strictly stronger property than language containment. Tools capable of simulation checking, such as Mocha [AHM+98], can therefore be used to prove language containment (usually with some user interaction), but a failed simulation check does not contradict language containment.

Nondeterministic BDDs. There is a rich literature on extensions to BDDs. In particular the idea to add nondeterminism has been exploited before, but with a different objective: parallel-access diagrams [BD96] interpret

Fig. 1. Büchi automata $\mathcal{A}$ and $\mathcal{B}$. Accepting states are shown in gray.

nondeterminism as disjunction to achieve a more compact representation of certain Boolean functions. Takagi et al. [TNB$^+$97] show that certain methods for the satisfiability checking of combinatorial circuits and techniques that represent Boolean functions as sets of product terms can be regarded as nondeterministic BDDs.

Alternation. Muller and Schupp [MS87] observed that complementing an alternating automaton corresponds to dualizing the transition function and acceptance condition. The application of alternation in verification methods has been studied both for automata-based algorithms [Var95] and in deductive verification [MS00]. Alternating automata have been used in a new complementation constructions for Büchi automata [KV97].

3   Automata on Infinite Words

Automata on infinite words differ from automata on finite words in their acceptance mechanism: there are no final states; instead, acceptance is determined w.r.t. the set of states that are visited infinitely often. Different types of acceptance conditions are studied (see [Tho94] for an overview). In the following we will work with Büchi conditions.

Definition 1. *A (nondeterministic) Büchi-automaton $\mathcal{A} = \langle \Sigma, Q, \theta, \rho, \alpha \rangle$ consists of a finite input alphabet Σ, a finite set of states Q, a set of initial states θ, a transition function $\rho : Q \times \Sigma \to 2^Q$ and a set of accepting states $\alpha \subseteq Q$.*

A *run* of $\mathcal{A}$ on an input string $l_0, l_1, \ldots \in \Sigma^\omega$ is an infinite sequence of states $\sigma = v_0, v_1, \ldots$ s.t. $v_0 \in \theta$ and for every $i \geq 0$, $v_{i+1} \in \rho(v_i, l_i)$, i.e., the first state is an initial state and each successor state is included in the successor set given by the transition function.

A run is *accepting* if some accepting state is visited infinitely often. The *language* $\mathcal{L}(\mathcal{A})$ of a Büchi automaton consists of those input strings that have accepting runs.

Example 1. The automaton $\mathcal{A}$ in Figure 1 accepts all infinite words over the alphabet $\{0, 1\}$ that begin with 0 and contain infinitely many 0s. Since $\mathcal{B}$ does not accept the word 0^ω, $\mathcal{L}(\mathcal{A}) \not\subseteq \mathcal{L}(\mathcal{B})$.

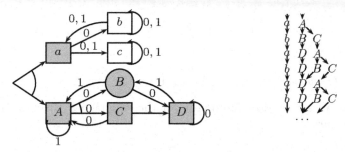

Fig. 2. Alternating automaton $\mathcal{C}$ and a computation for input word 0^ω. Accepting states $\alpha = \{a, A, B, C, D\}$ are shown in gray, stable states $\beta = \{a, b, c, A, C, D\}$ as boxes.

The branching mode in a nondeterministic automaton is existen tial; a word is accepted if its suffix is accepted in one of the successor states. Alternating automata com bine existential branching with universal branching. Again, man y different acceptance conditions are studied. W e will work with a com bined Büchi and co-Büchi condition.

Definition 2. *An* alternating automaton *is a tuple* $\mathcal{A} = \langle \Sigma, Q, \theta, \rho, \alpha, \beta \rangle$ *with* Σ, Q, α *as before; a set of stable states* β, *a set of initial state sets* $\theta \in 2^{2^Q}$; *and the transition function* $\rho : Q \times \Sigma \to 2^{2^Q}$, *a function from states and alphabet letters to sets of successor state sets.*

A *run* of an alternating automaton is a directed acyclic graph (dag) (N, E), where the nodes are labeled with states *state* : $N \to Q$. It is often useful to view the dag as a sequence of sets of nodes which we call *slices*: the i-th slice is the set of nodes that are reached after traversing i edges from root nodes. W e call the set of states that occur on the nodes of the i-th slice the i-th *configuration*. Let configuration 0 be the *root configuration*, and, for finite segments of a run, call the first configuration *source* and the last configuration *target*.

In a run for the input string $l_0, l_1, \ldots \in \Sigma^\omega$, the root configuration is one of the sets in θ, and, for each state v in the i-th configuration, the set of states on successor nodes is one of the successor sets in $\rho(v, l_i)$. A run is accepting if every path visits some α-state infinitely often, and eventually only visits states in β.

Finding a Büchi automaton that accepts the complemen t of a nondeterministic Büchi automaton is complicated and leads to an exponen tial blow-up [Saf88]. Alternating automata can be complemen ted without blow-up by dualizing the transition function and acceptance condition [MS87]. Thus, it is also very simple to construct an alternating automaton that accepts those words that are accepted by the first but not by the second automaton:

Theorem 1. *For two Büchi automata* $\mathcal{A}_1 = \langle \Sigma, Q_1, \theta_1, \rho_1, \alpha_1 \rangle$, $\mathcal{A}_2 = \langle \Sigma, Q_2, \theta_2, \rho_2, \alpha_2 \rangle$ *(where* $\rho_2(p, l) \neq \emptyset$ *for all* $p \in Q_2, l \in \Sigma$*), the alternating automaton* $\mathcal{A} = \langle \Sigma, Q, \theta, \rho, \alpha, \beta \rangle$ *with*

 – $Q = Q_1 \cup Q_2$,

- $\theta = \{\theta_2 \cup \{p\} \mid p \in \theta_1\}$,
- $\rho(s, a) = if \ (s \in Q_1) \ then \ \{\{p\} \mid p \in \rho_1(s,a)\} \ else \ \{\rho_2(s,a)\}$,
- $\alpha = \alpha_1 \cup Q_2$,
- $\beta = (Q_2 \backslash \alpha_2) \cup Q_1$

accepts the language $\mathcal{L}(\mathcal{A}) = \mathcal{L}(\mathcal{A}_1) \cap \overline{\mathcal{L}(\mathcal{A}_2)}$.

Example 2. An alternating automaton for the language $\mathcal{L}(\mathcal{C}) = \mathcal{L}(\mathcal{A}) \cap \overline{\mathcal{L}(\mathcal{B})}$ is shown in Figure 2.

4 Binary Decision Diagrams

A binary decision diagram (BDD) [Bry86] is a data structure for the representation of Boolean functions $f : \mathbb{B}^n \to \mathbb{B}$. In their reduced and ordered form, BDDs represent Boolean functions canonically for fixed variable orderings. For many examples BDDs significantly outperform other representations. BDDs can be used to store sets of states, represented by their characteristic function: Boolean "or" corresponds to set union, "and" to intersection. BDDs are also used to represent relations on states, such as the transition function of an automaton. This is done by adding a second "primed" copy for each variable.

Definition 3 (BDD). *A (deterministic) binary decision diagram (BDD) $(\mathcal{V}, Q, E_0, E_1, \phi)$ is a directed acyclic graph with internal nodes Q, edges $E_0 \cup E_1$, a single root ϕ and two terminal nodes $\mathbf{0}, \mathbf{1}$. Each internal node $n \in Q$ has exactly two departing edges $low(n) \in E_0, high(n) \in E_1$. Every internal node $n \in Q$ is labeled with a variable $var(n) \in \mathcal{V}$.*

The successor nodes along the $low(n)$ and $high(n)$ edges are referred to as the *low* and *high* successors of n. A BDD d with root node ϕ defines a Boolean function $f_d = f_\phi : \mathbb{B}^n \to \mathbb{B}$ as follows:

- the terminal node $\mathbf{1}$ defines the constant function *true*.
- the terminal node $\mathbf{0}$ defines the constant function *false*.
- an internal node $n \in Q$ represents the function

$$f \ : \ (\text{if } var(n) \text{ then } f_1 \text{ else } f_0)$$

where f_0, f_1 are the functions represented by the *low* and *high* successors, respectively.

Of special interest are BDDs in a canonical form called reduced and ordered.

Definition 4. *A BDD is ordered (OBDD), if on all paths through the graph the labeling respects a given linear order on the variables $v_1 > v_2 > \cdots > v_n$; i.e., on all paths through the graph, smaller variables are traversed first. An OBDD is reduced (ROBDD) if*

1. *no two different internal nodes have the same label and the same high and low successors,*
2. *no internal node has identical high and low successor.*

Theorem 2. *[Bry86] For any Boolean function $f : \mathbb{B}^n \to \mathbb{B}$ and a given variable ordering, there is (up to isomorphism) exactly one ROBDD d s.t. $f_d = f$.*

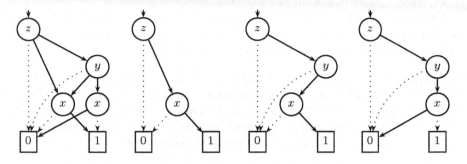

Fig. 3. Nondeterministic BDD (left) and three embedded deterministic BDDs. Solid edges are *high*-successors, dotted edges *low*-successors.

5 Nondetermini stic Binary Decision Diagrams

For the analysis of alternating automata we need a more expressive representation than BDDs. Sets of sets of states as they occur, for example, in the initial condition or as sets of configurations, cannot be represented as a conventional BDD. The extension we present in this section uses nondeterministic BDDs to represent sets of Boolean functions. We interpret the nondeterministic BDD to describe the set of all deterministic BDDs that can be embedded in it.

Example 3. Figure 3 shows a nondeterministic BDD and the three embedded deterministic BDDs.

Nondeterministic BDDs may have more than one root node, and the out-degree of internal nodes may be higher than two, so we consider the sets of *High* and *Low* departing edges.

Definition 5. *A nondeterministic binary decision diagram (NBDD) $(\mathcal{V}, Q, E_0, E_1, \Phi)$ is a directed acyclic graph with internal nodes Q, edges $E_0 \cup E_1$, a set of root nodes $\Phi \subseteq Q$, and two terminal nodes $\mathbf{0}, \mathbf{1}$. The set of departing edges from an internal node $n \in Q$ is partitioned into $Low(n) \subseteq E_0$ and $High(n) \subseteq E_1$. Every internal node $n \in Q$ is labeled with a variable $var(n) \in \mathcal{V}$.*

A NBDD D with root set Φ defines a set of Boolean functions $\mathcal{F}_D = \mathcal{F}_\Phi \subseteq 2^{\mathbb{B}^n \to \mathbb{B}}$ as follows:

- the terminal node $\mathbf{1}$ defines the set $\mathcal{F}_\mathbf{1} = \{true\}$.
- the terminal node $\mathbf{0}$ defines the set $\mathcal{F}_\mathbf{0} = \{false\}$.
- a set of nodes Ψ defines the union of the sets represented by the individual nodes: $\mathcal{F}_\Psi = \bigcup_{n \in \Psi} \mathcal{F}_n$.
- for an internal node $n \in Q$, let $\mathcal{H}, \mathcal{L}$ denote the sets defined by its *High* and *Low* successors, respectively. Then n defines the set:

$$\mathcal{F} = \left\{ \begin{array}{c} (\text{if } var(n) \text{ then } f_1 \text{ else } f_0) \\ \text{s.t. } f_0 \in \mathcal{L} \text{ and } f_1 \in \mathcal{H} \end{array} \right\}$$

BDDs are therefore a special (deterministic) case of NBDDs: for a given BDD $(\mathcal{V}, Q, E_0, E_1, \phi)$ the NBDD $(\mathcal{V}, Q, E_0, E_1, \{\phi\})$ characterizes the singleton set containing the Boolean function defined by the BDD.

Definition 6. *A BDD $d = (\mathcal{V}, Q^d, E_0{}^d, E_1^d, \phi^d)$ is embedded in an NBDD $D = (\mathcal{V}, Q^D, E_0{}^D, E_1^D, \Phi^D)$ iff there is a simulation function $\gamma : Q^d \to Q^D$ with $\gamma(\mathbf{0}) = \mathbf{0}, \gamma(\mathbf{1}) = \mathbf{1}$, $\gamma(\phi^d) \in \Phi^D$ and for all nodes $n \in Q^d$, $var(n) = var(\gamma(n))$, if n' is the low^d-successor of n then $\gamma(n')$ is a Low^D-successor of $\gamma(n)$, if n' is the $high^d$-successor of n then $\gamma(n')$ is a $High^D$-successor of $\gamma(n)$.*

We say that two node sets Φ_1, Φ_2 in an NBDD are *mutually exclusive* iff there is no BDD that is embedded in both the NBDD with root node set Φ_1 and the NBDD with root node set Φ_2. The notions of ordered and reduced diagrams can now be lifted to NBDDs:

Definition 7. *A NBDD is ordered (ONBDD), if on all paths through the graph the labeling respects a given linear order on the variables $v_1 > v_2 > \ldots > v_n$. An ONBDD is reduced (RONBDD) if*

1. *no two different internal nodes have the same label and the same High and Low successor sets,*
2. *the High and Low successor sets of an internal node are mutually exclusive.*

Theorem 3. *Let d be a OBDD and D a ONBDD with the same variable order. d is embedded in D iff $f_d \in \mathcal{F}_D$.*

Proof. By structural induction. $\qquad\qquad\qquad\qquad\qquad\qquad\qquad\qquad\qquad$ $\square$

RONBDDs are not a canonical representation of sets of Boolean functions. To achieve canonicity, more restrictions on the grouping of functions (if v then f^1 else f^0) that have a common negative cofactor f^0 or a common positive cofactor f^1 are necessary. One such restriction, which we will call the *negative-normal form*, is to require that the functions are grouped by their negative cofactors f_0.

Definition 8. *A RONBDD $D = (\mathcal{V}, Q, E_0, E_1, \Phi)$ is in negative-normal form iff the following holds for all nodes $n \in Q$:*

1. *there is only one low-successor: $Low(n) = \{low(n)\}$,*
2. *the low-successor is a BDD,*
3. *no two different High-successors or root nodes are labeled by the same variable and have the same low-successor.*

Theorem 4. *For any set of Boolean functions $\mathcal{F} \subseteq 2^{\mathbb{B}^n \to \mathbb{B}}$ and a given variable ordering, there is (up to isomorphism) exactly one RONBDD D in negative-normal form s.t. $\mathcal{F}_D = \mathcal{F}$.*

Proof. We show, by induction on m, that for any subset of the set of variables $\{v_1, \ldots, v_m\} \subseteq \{v_1, \ldots, v_n\}$ (with variable order $v_1 > v_2 > \cdots > v_n$), any set of functions $\mathcal{F}_m \subseteq (2^{\mathbb{B}^n \to \mathbb{B}})$ that only depend on variables in $\{v_1, \ldots, v_m\}$ can be canonically represented by a RONBDD in negative-normal form. In the following we will assume sharing of subgraphs, and identify NBDDs by their root node sets, BDDs by their root node.

$m = 0$: There are four different sets of functions not depending on any variable: $\emptyset, \{true\}, \{false\}, \{true, false\}$. These sets are uniquely represented by the RONBDDs with root node sets $\emptyset, \{0\}, \{1\}, \{0, 1\}$, respectively.

$m \to m+1$: We construct the set of root nodes F for a set $\mathcal{F}_{m+1}$, where v_{m+1} is the least variable some function in $\mathcal{F}_{m+1}$ depends on. For each function f in $\mathcal{F}_{m+1}$ we consider the positive and negative cofactor $f^b(x_1, \ldots, x_{m+1}, \ldots, x_n) = f(x_1, \ldots, b, \ldots, x_n), b \in \mathbb{B}$ [the $(m+1)$st argument is replaced by b]. This allows us to separate the subset of functions A that do not depend on v_{m+1}:

$$A = \{ f \mid f \in F_{m+1} \text{ and } f^0 = f^1 \}.$$

For all other functions we separate the positive and negative cofactor in the following set of pairs:

$$B = \{ (f^0, f^1) \mid f \in F_{m+1} \text{ and } f^0 \neq f^1 \}.$$

Next, we group the positive cofactors by the negative cofactors:

$$C = \{ (f, X) \mid \exists g \,.\, (f, g) \in B, \ X = \{g \mid (f, g) \in B\} \}.$$

The resulting sets of positive cofactors contain only functions that do not depend on v_{m+1}. The same holds for the set of functions in A. By the induction hypothesis, we can therefore find negative-normal RONBDDs as follows:

$$D = \{ (d_f, D_Y) \mid d_f \text{ is the canonical ROBDD for } f,$$
$$D_Y \text{ is the root node set of the canonical RONBDD}$$
$$\text{for } Y \text{ with } (f, Y) \in C \},$$

$E = $ the root node set of the canonical RONBDD for A.

Finally, we can construct the set of root nodes for $\mathcal{F}_{m+1}$:

$$F = \{\langle var = v_{m+1}, low = d_f, High = D_Y\rangle \mid (d_f, D_Y) \in D\} \cup E.$$

The constructed NBDD is ordered, reduced and in negative-normal form since the NBDDs in D and E are, and the newly constructed nodes maintain all conditions. It remains to show that the RONBDD is unique.

Assume there was a different negative-normal RONBDD with root node set F' defining $\mathcal{F}_{m+1}$. Consider the functions in $\mathcal{F}_{m+1}$ that do not depend on v_{m+1}: since the *High* and *Low* successors of any node must be mutually exclusive, they cannot be contained in the set represented by a node labeled by v_{m+1} (reducedness). By the induction hypothesis we know that the set of all nodes in F that are not labeled by v_{m+1} is canonical (the functions represented by the subset depend only on greater variables). Thus F and F' must differ in nodes that are both labeled by v_{m+1}.

Suppose there are two functions f_1, f_2 that are characterized by the same root node in one diagram but by two different root nodes in the other. All functions characterized by the same node in a ROBDD in negative-normal form have the same negative cofactor (conditions 1 and 2 and Theorem 2). Thus the diagram that represents them on two different nodes cannot be in negative-normal form (condition 3). □

```
UNION(N, M)
1  R ← (N ∪ M) ∩ {0, 1}
2  for all  n ∈ N
3     if ∃m ∈ M . var(n) = var(m), low(n) = low(m)
4        then R ← R ∪ { ⟨var(n), low(n), UNION(High(n), High(m))⟩ }
5     else R ← R ∪ {n}
6  for all  m ∈ M
7     if ∄n ∈ N . var(n) = var(m), low(n) = low(m)
8        then R ← R ∪ {m}
9  return R
```

Fig. 4. Operation UNION, computing the union of two sets represented by negative-normal NBDDs.

It is straightforward to implement traditional BDD operations (like the application of boolean operations, variable substitution, or quantification) and set operations on NBDDs. As an example, consider UNION, shown in Figure 4. We assume sharing of subgraphs and identify BDDs with their root nodes and NBDDs with their root node sets. The UNION operation computes the negative-normal RONBDD representing the union of two sets represented by two negative-normal RONBDDs. This is done by considering corresponding nodes in the two root node sets. Two nodes *correspond* if they are labeled with the same variable and have the same *low*-successor. The union is computed by recursing on pairs of corresponding nodes and simply adding nodes that do not have a corresponding node in the other set.

6   Emptiness of Alternating Automata

As discussed in Section 3, the language containment problem between non-deterministic Büchi automata is easily reduced to the emptiness problem of alternating automata. In this section we develop a fixpoint algorithm for the emptiness problem. The reachable configurations of an alternating automaton can be computed in a forward propagation from θ. To decide if the finite dag leading to such a configuration can be completed into an accepting run we identify gratifying segments, i.e., segments that would, if repeated infinitely often, form the suffix of an accepting run.

Gratifying segments. Consider an alternating automaton $\mathcal{A} = \langle \Sigma, Q, \theta, \rho, \alpha, \beta \rangle$. A run segment is a finite dag (N, E), where the nodes are labeled with states $state : N \to Q$, such that for each state v in a configuration, the set of states on successor nodes is one of the successor sets in $\rho(v, l)$ for some input letter $l \in \Sigma$. We characterize gratifying segments w.r.t. a complete preorder $\preceq$ on the states in the source configuration. It will be helpful to identify nodes that are on some path from a source node p to a target node p', s.t. $state(p) \approx state(p')$; we call such nodes *fixed*. A run segment S is *gratifying* if

1. the source and target configuration are the same,
2. all fixed nodes are labeled by β-states,
3. all paths in S visit a node with an α-state,
4. all paths originating from a source node labeled by a state p lead to nodes in the target slice that are labeled with states equivalent to, or smaller than p, and
5. all paths originating from a source node labeled by a state p that visit a non-fixed node lead to target nodes that are labeled with states strictly smaller than p.

Example 4. The segment from slice 2 to slice 4 (configurations $\{a, D, A\}$, $\{b, D, B, C\}$, $\{a, D, A\}$) of the computation in Figure 2 is gratifying w.r.t. the preorder $a \approx D \prec A$. In slices 2 and 4 all nodes are fixed; in slice 3 the nodes labeled by b, D and C are fixed.

Lemma 1. *Let L be a gratifying run segment of an alternating automaton, and P a finite run prefix leading to the source slice of L. Then the dag $G = P \cdot L^\omega$, constructed by appending an infinite number of copies of L to P, is a computation of $\mathcal{A}$.*

Proof. All paths in L visit an accepting state; the paths in L^ω therefore visit an accepting state infinitely often. A path that does not visit a fixed node in L leads to a target node that is labeled by a strictly smaller state than the state on the node it visited in the source slice. Thus, since there are only finitely many states in the source configuration of L, every path in L^ω eventually visits a fixed node. From there, a path can either (1) stay forever in fixed nodes (and therefore in stable states) or (2) visit a non-fixed node and, again, lead to a target node with a strictly smaller state. Hence, eventually (1) must occur.   □

Lemma 2. *Let G be a computation of the alternating automaton $\mathcal{A}$. There is a preorder $\preceq$ s.t. G can be partitioned into a finite prefix P and an infinite number of copies of a segment L that is gratifying w.r.t. $\preceq$.*

Proof. For the given computation G we apply a ranking construction by Kupferman and Vardi [KV97]. Consider the following sequence of subgraphs of G.

- $G_0 = G$.
- $G_{2i+1} = G_{2i}$ minus all nodes from which there are only finitely many nodes reachable. Assign rank $2i$ to all the subtracted nodes.
- $G_{2i+2} = G_{2i+1}$ minus all nodes from which only nodes with β-states are reachable. Assign rank $2i + 1$ to all the subtracted nodes.

$G_{2|Q|+1}$ is empty [KV97], i.e., the number of ranks is bounded. There must be infinitely many occurrences of some configuration x, s.t. the nodes with the same state label have the same rank in the two occurrences. We select two occurrences s.t. all paths on the run segment L between them visit an α-state and a node with odd rank. L is a gratifying segment with the order $\preceq$ induced by the ranking. The fixed states have odd rank, non-fixed states even rank. Along a path the rank never increases.   □

Annotated Configurations. To recognize gratifying segments we keep track of the gratification conditions in configurations. An *annotated configuration* is a tuple $\langle x, f, t, u, \preceq \rangle$ where x is a set of states, f, t, u are subsets of x, and $\preceq$ is a complete preorder on x. The goal is to capture the states on fixed nodes in f, "trapped" states (i.e., states on nodes s.t. all originating paths visit a fixed node) in t, and "fulfilling" states (i.e., states on nodes s.t. all paths that originate from this node visit an α-node) in u. We now introduce constraints that ensure that these sets are propagated consistently in a sequence of annotated configurations. Consider two consecutive configurations $\langle x, f, t, u, \preceq \rangle$ and $\langle x', f', t', u', \preceq' \rangle$. We require that there exists a letter l of the input alphabet s.t. for each state $v \in x$ there is a set $y_v \in \rho(v, l)$ so that the following constraints are satisfied:

1. for all $v \in x$, $y_v \subseteq x'$,
2. for all $v' \in f'$ there is a $v \in f$ s.t. $v' \in y_v$,
3. for all $v \in f$, $f' \cap y_v \neq \emptyset$,
4. for all $v \in t - f$, $y_v \subseteq t'$,
5. for all $v \in u - \alpha$, $y_v \subseteq u'$,
6. for all $v' \in f'$ and $v \in x$, s.t. $v' \in y_v$, there is a $w \in f$ s.t. $v' \in y_w$ and $w \prec v$,
7. for all $v' \in f'$ and all $w' \in x'$ with $w' \prec v'$, there exists a $v \in f$ s.t. $v' \in y_v$ and for all $w \in x$ with $w' \in y_w$, $v \prec w$, and
8. for all $v \in f$ s.t. there is a $w \in x$ with $w \prec v$, there exists a $v' \in f'$ with $v' \in y_v$ s.t. for all $w' \in y_w$, $w' \prec' v'$.

Let Y be a set of annotated configurations. We say that an annotated configuration a is *eventually accepting* w.r.t. Y iff there is a sequence of annotated configurations, where a is the first and some $b \in Y$ the last configuration, and where every two consecutive configurations satisfy the constraints above. Let EVENTUALACCEPT(Y) denote the set of annotated configurations that are eventually accepting w.r.t. Y.

Lemma 3. *Let S be a gratifying segment leading from a configuration x back to x; then there is an annotation for the source configuration $a = \langle x, f, t = x, u = x, \preceq \rangle$ and an annotation for the target configuration $a' = \langle x' = x, f' = f, t' = f, u' = x \cap \alpha, \preceq \rangle$ s.t. for every set Y of annotated configurations that includes a', $a \in$ EVENTUALACCEPT(Y).*

Proof. First, we construct a segment S' in which every path visits a fixed node (by appending as many copies of S as needed). For each slice s in S' we define the following annotated configuration $\langle x_s, f_s, t_s, u_s, \preceq_s \rangle$:

- x_s contains the states on nodes in s,
- f_s contains exactly the states on the fixed nodes in s,
- t_s contains exactly the states on those nodes for which all paths that originate from the node visit a fixed node,
- u_s contains exactly the states on those nodes for which all paths that originate from the node visit an α-node,

- $\preceq_s$ is the following preorder:

for two states v, w on nodes p, q that are both in f_s or both in $x_s - f_s$,
$v \prec_s w$ iff there is a target node q' reachable from q s.t. for all target nodes
p' reachable from p, $state(p') \prec state(q')$;
for two states $v \in f_s, w \in x_s - f_s$ or $v \in x_s - f_s, w \in f_s$ on nodes p, q,
$v \prec_s w$ iff there is a target node q' reachable from q s.t. for all target nodes
p' reachable from p, $state(p') \preceq state(q')$.

The resulting sequence of annotated configurations satisfies the constraints. Due
to space limitations we skip the detailed argument here.   □

Let UNMARK(X) denote the set of annotated configurations, s.t. $\langle x, f, f, x \cap$
$\alpha, \preceq \rangle \in$ UNMARK(X) for $\langle x, f, t, u, \preceq \rangle \in X$. Let FILTER($X$) be the subset of the
set of annotated configurations X s.t. $u = x, t = x$.

Lemma 4. *Let $a = \langle x, f, t, u, \preceq \rangle$ be an annotated configuration in a set Y s.t.
$a \in$ FILTER(EVENTUALACCEPT(UNMARK(Y))). Then there is a gratifying seg-
ment S that leads from configuration x to x.*

Proof. Because of constraint (1) there is a run segment S corresponding to the
sequence of configurations in the construction of EVENTUALACCEPT. We show
that S is gratifying. For a slice s, let $\langle x_s, f_s, t_s, u_s, \preceq_s \rangle$ denote the corresponding
annotated configuration.

Claim 1: For two nodes p, q in the same slice s, if $state(q) \prec_s state(p)$,
$state(p) \in f_s$ then there is a path from p to a node p' in the target slice labeled
by an f-state, s.t. for all nodes q' in the target slice that can be reached from q,
$state(q') \prec state(p')$.
Proof by induction on the length of S using constraint (8).

Claim 2: For two nodes p', q' in the same slice s, if $state(p') \prec_s state(q')$,
$state(p') \in f_s$ then there is a path from a source node p, with $state(p) \in f$, to
p', s.t. for all nodes q in the source slice that can reach q', $state(p) \prec state(q)$.
Proof by induction on the length of S using constraint (7).

Claim 3: For all nodes p' in the target slice that are reachable from a source
node p: $state(p') \preceq state(p)$.
Proof: Case (A): $state(p) \in f$. Assume there is a path from p to a node p'
in the target slice with $state(p) \prec state(p')$. Let q' be the node in the target
s.t. $state(q') = state(p)$. By Claim 2, there is a path from a node q in the
source slice with $state(q) \in f$ to q' with $state(q) \prec state(p')$, $state(q) \in f$.
Hence, $state(q) \prec state(p) = state(q')$. Let o' be the node in the target slice
s.t. $state(o') = state(q)$. Again, using Claim 2, we can find a node in the source
slice with an f-state that is smaller than $state(q)$. Since this argument can be
repeated infinitely often the source configuration must contain infinitely many
different states.
Case (B): $state(p) \notin f$. Let s' be the first slice with a $f_{s'}$-node p_1 on the path
from p to p', and s the slice with the non-f_s predecessor p_0 of p_1. By constraint
(6) there must be a f_s-predecessor p'_0 of p_1, s.t. $state(p'_0) \prec state(p_0)$. By Claim
2, there is a source node q with $state(q) \in f$ and $state(q) \prec state(p)$. By case

(A) all target nodes that are reachable from q are labeled by states smaller than or equivalent to $state(q)$. In particular, $state(p') \preceq state(q) \prec state(p)$.

Claim 4: For a node p' in some slice s with $state(p') \in f_s$ there is a path from a source node p to a target node p'' with $state(p) \approx state(p'')$ and $state(p) \in f$, $state(p'') \in f$ that visits p'.

Proof: An induction on the size of the segment of S up to s using constraint (2) and a second induction on the size of the segment beginning with s using constraint (3) shows that there is indeed a source node $p \in f$ and a target node $p'' \in f$ s.t. p' is on a path between them. By Claim 3, $state(p'') \preceq state(p)$. Now assume $state(p'') \prec state(p)$. By Claim 2, there is a source node $q \in f$ s.t. $state(q) \prec state(q)$. Let o be the node in the target slice labeled by $state(q)$. Again, using Claim 2, we can find a node in the source slice with an f-state smaller than $state(q)$. Since this argument can be repeated infinitely often the source configuration must contain infinitely many different states.

Claim 5: If there is a path from a source node p to a target node p'' with $state(p) \approx state(p'')$, then for all nodes p' on the path (where p' is a node in slice s), $state(p') \in f_s$.

Proof: Since all states in the source slice are contained in t, we know (because of constraint 4) that every path in S visits at least one $f_{s'}$-node in some slice s'. Consider the case that $state(p) \notin f$. Now let s' be the first slice with a $f_{s'}$-node p_1 that is visited on the path from p to p''. Let s be the previous slice containing p_0, the non-f_s predecessor of p_1. By constraint (6), there is a node q_0 in s, s.t. p_1 is a successor of q_0, $state(q_0) \in f_s$ and $state(q_0) \prec_s state(p_0)$. By Claim 2, there is a source node q s.t. $state(q) \prec state(p)$ and there is a path from q to q_0. Since p'' is reachable from q, by Claim 3, $state(p'') \preceq state(q)$. This is in contradiction to $state(p) \approx state(p'')$.

Now consider the case that $state(p) \in f$. Let s' be the first slice with a non-$f_{s'}$-node p_1 that is visited on the path from p to p''. Let s be the previous slice containing p_0, the f_s-predecessor of p_1. By constraint (8) there is a node q_1 in s', s.t. p_0 is a predecessor of p_1, $state(q_1) \in f_{s'}$, and $state(p_1) \prec_{s'} state(q_1)$. By Claim 1, there is a target node q'' s.t. $state(m'') \prec state(q'')$, and there is a path from q_1 to q''. Since q'' is reachable from p, by Claim 3 $state(q'') \preceq state(p)$. This again is in contradiction to $state(p) \approx state(p'')$.

Proof of the lemma: By Claims 4 and 5, the fixed nodes are exactly the nodes labeled by f_s-states. Because of $u = x$ and constraint 5 all paths in S visit an α-node. By Claim 3, all paths lead to smaller or equivalent states in the target. Paths that visit a non-fixed node lead to target nodes with strictly smaller states by Claim 5. □

With these results we can now formulate the algorithm for the emptiness check of alternating automata, shown in Figure 5. Let REACHABLE($\mathcal{A}$) denote the set of reachable configurations. ANNOTATE(X) computes for a set of configurations X a set of annotated configurations, s.t. for a configuration x all annotations $\langle x, f, f, x \cap \alpha, \preceq \rangle$ are added where $f \subseteq x \cap \beta$. We state the correctness of the algorithm as the following two theorems.

Theorem 5. *If $\mathcal{L}(\mathcal{A}) = \emptyset$ then* EMPTY($\mathcal{A}$).

```
EMPTY(A)
1  A ← ∅
2  B ← ANNOTATE(REACHABLE(A))
3  while (A ≠ B) do
4     A ← B
5     B ← B ∩ FILTER(EVENTUALACCEPT(UNMARK(B)))
6  return (B = ∅)
```

Fig. 5. Fixpoint algorithm for the emptiness check of alternating automata.

Proof. Suppose there is an annotated configuration $\langle x, f, t, u, \preceq \rangle \in B$. By Lemma 4 there exists a gratifying segment L leading from configuration x to x. Since $x \in$ REACHABLE(A) there is a run segment P leading from an initial configuration to x. Thus, by Lemma 1, A has a computation $P \cdot L^\omega$. □

Theorem 6. *If* EMPTY(A) *then* $\mathcal{L}(A) = \emptyset$.

Proof. Suppose there is a computation G of A. By Lemma 2, G can be partitioned into an initial segment P and an infinitely often repeated gratifying segment L. Let x be the source configuration of L. $x \in$ REACHABLE(A). By Lemma 3 there is an annotated configuration $a = \langle x, f, t = x, u = x, \preceq \rangle$ that is included in EVENTUALACCEPT(Y), if $a' = \langle x, f, t' = f, u' = x \cap \alpha, \preceq \rangle \in Y$. Since $a \in$ ANNOTATE(REACHABLE(A)), $a' \in$ UNMARK(Y) if $a \in Y$, and $a \in$ FILTER(Y) if $a \in Y$, a is included in every iteration of B. □

7 Conclusions

The data structures and algorithms presented in this paper are the basis of a symbolic verification system for language containment. In comparison to the classic construction, that starts with the determinization of the specification automaton, our algorithm is both simpler and, for certain problems, more efficient: because the two automata are combined early, no effort is wasted on the determinization of parts of the specification automaton that are not reachable in the intersection with the implementation automaton.

It should be noted, however, that our solution does not improve on the worst-case complexity of the standard algorithm. While first results with our prototype implementation are encouraging, advanced implementations and case studies are necessary to determine the characteristics of systems for which the symbolic approach is useful. The performance of NBDDs depends strongly on implementation issues like the constraints of the chosen normal form.

Efficient representations of sets of Boolean functions are of interest beyond the language containment problem. An example is the state minimization of incompletely specified finite state machines [KVBSV94]: the standard algorithm computes sets of sets of (compatible) states.

Acknowledgemen ts:I am grateful to the mem bers of the STeP research group at Stanford University for our discussions and their commen ts on drafts of this paper, as well as to the anonymous referees for their commen ts and suggestions.

References

AHM+98. R. Alur, T. Henzinger, F. Mang, S. Qadeer, S. Rajamani, and S. Tasiran. MOCHA: modularity in model checking. In A. Hu and M. Vardi, editors, *CAV 98: Computer-aided Verification*, Lecture Notes in Computer Science 1427, pages 521–525. Springer-Verlag, 1998.

BD96.   V. Bertacco and M. Damiani. Boolean function representation using parallel access diagrams. In *The Sixth Great Lakes Symposium on VLSI*. IEEE, 1996.

BMUV97. N. Buhrke, O. Matz, S. Ulbrand, and J. Vöge. The automata theory package omega. In *WIA '97*, vol. 1436 of *LNCS*. Springer-Verlag, 1997.

Bry86.   R.E. Bryant. Graph-based algorithms for Boolean function manipulation. *IEEE Transactions on Computers*, C-35(8):677–691, August 1986.

CGP99.   E. Clarke, O. Grumberg, and D. Peled. *Model Checking*. MIT Press, 1999.

KV97.   O. Kupferman and M. Vardi. Weak alternating automata are not that weak. In *5th Israeli Symposium on Theory of Computing and Systems*, pages 147–158. IEEE Computer Society Press, 1997.

KVBSV94. T. Kam, T. Villa, R. Brayton, and A. Sangiovanni-Vincentelli. A fully implicit algorithm for exact state minimization. In *31st ACM/IEEE Design Automation Conference*, pages 684–690. ACM, 1994.

MS87.   D.E. Muller and P.E. Schupp. Alternating automata on infinite trees. *Theoretical Computer Science*, 54(2–3):267–276, October 1987.

MS00.   Z. Manna and H.B. Sipma. Alternating the temporal picture for safety. In U. Montanari, J.D. Rolim, and E. Welzl, editors, *Proc. 27th Intl. Colloq. Aut. Lang. Prog.*, vol. 1853, pages 429–450, Geneva, Switzerland, July 2000. Springer-Verlag.

Saf88.   S. Safra. On the complexity of ω-automata. In *Proc. 29th IEEE Symp. Found. of Comp. Sci.*, pages 319–327, 1988.

TBK95.   H. Touati, R.K. Brayton, and R. Kurshan. Testing language containment for ω-automata using BDDs. *Inf. and Comp.*, 118(1):101–109, April 1995.

THB95.   S. Tasiran, R. Hojati, and R.K. Brayton. Language containment using non-deterministic omega-automata. In *Proc. of CHARME '95: Advanced Research Working Conference on Correct Hardware design and verification methods*, vol. 987 of *LNCS*. Springer-Verlag, 1995.

Tho94.   W. Thomas. Automata on infinite objects. In J. v an Leeuwen, editor, *Handbook of Theoretical Computer Science*. Elsevier Science Publishers (North-Holland), 1994.

TNB+97. K. Takagi, K. Nitta, H. Bouno, Y. Takenaga, and S. Yajima. Computational power of nondeterministic ordered binary decision diagrams and their subclasses. *IEICE Transactions on Fundamentals*, E80-A(4):663–669, April 1997.

Var95.   M.Y. Vardi. Alternating automata and program verification. In J. van Leeuwen, editor, *Computer Science Today. Recent Trends and Developments*, vol. 1000 of *LNCS*, pages 471–485. Springer-Verlag, 1995.

Satisfiabilit y Chec king
Using
Boolean Expression Diagrams

Poul Frederick William s, Henrik Reif Andersen, and Henrik Hulgaard

IT University of Copenhagen
Glentevej 67, DK-2400 Copenhagen NV, Denmark
{pfw,hra,henrik}@it-c.dk

Abstract. In this paper we present an algorithm for determining satisfiability of general Boolean formulas which are *not* necessarily on conjunctive normal form. The algorithm extends the well-known Davis-Putnam algorithm to work on Boolean formulas represented using Boolean Expression Diagrams (BEDs). The BED data structure allows the algorithm to take advantage of the built-in reduction rules and the sharing of sub-formulas. Furthermore, it is possible to combine the algorithm with traditional BDD construction (using Bryant's APPLY-procedure). By adjusting a single parameter to the BEDSAT algorithm it is possible to control to what extent the algorithm behaves like the APPLY-algorithm or like a SAT-solver. Thus the algorithm can be seen as bridging the gap between standard SAT-solvers and BDDs. We present promising experimental results for 566 non-clausal formulas obtained from the multi-level combinational circuits in the ISCAS'85 benchmark suite and from performing model checking of a shift-and-add multiplier.

1 Introduction

In this paper we address the problem of determining satisfiabilit y of non-clausal Boolean formulas, i.e., formulas which are *not* necessarily on conjunctive normal form. One area where such formulas arise is in formal verification. For example, in equivalence checking of combinational circuits we connect the outputs of the circuits with exclusive-or gates and construct a Boolean formulas for the combined circuits. The formulas is satisfiable if the two circuits are not functionally equivalent.

Another important area in which non-clausal formulas arise is in model checking [1,4,5,6,24]. In bounded model checking, the reachable state space is approximated by (syntactically) unfolding the transition relation and obtaining a propositional formula which is not in clausal form. In order to check whether the approximated state space R violates a given invariant I, one has to determine whether the formula $\neg I \wedge R$ is satisfiable.

Boolean Expression Diagrams (BEDs) [2,3] is an extension of Binary Decision Diagram (BDD) [9] which allows Boolean operator vertices in the DAG. BEDs

T. Margaria and W. Yi (Eds.): TACAS 2001, LNCS 2031, pp. 39–51, 2001.
© Springer-Verlag Berlin Heidelberg 2001

can represent any Boolean formulas in linear space at the price of being non-canonical. However, since converting a Boolean formula into a BDD via a BED can always be done at least as efficiently as constructing the BDD directly, many of the desirable properties of BDDs are maintained.

Given a BED for a formula, one way of proving satisfiability is to convert the BED to a BDD. The formula is satisfiable if and only if the resulting BDD is different from the terminal **0** (a contradiction). BDDs have become highly popular since they often are able to represent large formulas compactly. However, by converting the BED into a BDD, more information is obtained than just a "yes, the formula is satisfiable" or a "no, the formula is not satisfiable" answer. The resulting BDD encodes *all* possible variable assignments satisfying the formula. In some cases this extra information is not needed since we may only be interested in *some* satisfying assignment or simply in whether such an assignment exists. The canonicity of BDDs also means that some formulas (such as the formulas for the multiplication function) cannot be efficiently represented and thus the approach to convert the BED to a BDD will be inefficient.

Instead of converting the BED to a BDD, one can use a dedicated satisfiability solver such as SATO [25] or GRASP [17]. These tools are highly efficient in finding a satisfiable assignment if one exists. On the other hand, they are often much slower than the BDD construction when the formula is unsatisfiable. Another problem with these algorithms is that the Boolean formula must be given in conjunctive normal form (CNF), and converting a general formula (whether represented as a BED or as a Boolean circuit) to CNF is inefficient: either k new variables are introduced (where k is the number of non-terminal vertices in the BED) or the size of the CNF may grow exponentially in the size of the formula.

The BEDSAT algorithm presented in this paper attempts to exploit the advantages of the two above approaches. The algorithm extends the Davis-Putnam algorithm to work directly on the BED data structure (thus avoiding the conversion to CNF). By using the BED representation, the algorithm can take advantage of the built-in reduction rules and the sharing of isomorphic subformulas. For small sub-BEDs (i.e., for small sub-formulas), it turns out that it is faster than running Davis-Putnam to simply construct the BDD and checking whether the result is different from **0**. In the BEDSAT algorithm, this observation is used by having the user provide an input N to the algorithm. When a sub-formula contains less than N BED vertices, the algorithm simply builds the BDD for the sub-formula and checks whether the result is different from the terminal **0**. When using $N = 0$, the BEDSAT algorithm reduces to an implementation of Davis-Putnam on the BED data structure (which is interesting in itself) and when using $N = \infty$, the BEDSAT algorithm reduces to Bryant's APPLY-algorithm for constructing BDDs bottom-up. Experiments show that the BEDSAT algorithm is significantly faster than both pure BDD construction and the dedicated satisfiability-solvers GRASP and SATO, both on satisfiable and unsatisfiable formulas, when choosing a value of N of 400 vertices.

Related W ork

Determining whether a Boolean form ula is satisfiable is one of the classical NP-complete problems and algorithms for determining satisfiability have been studied for a long time. The Davis-Putnam [11,12] SAT-procedure has been known for about 40 years and it is still considered one of the best procedures for determining satisfiability. More recen tly, incomplete algorithms lik e Greedy SAT (GSAT) [20] have appeared. These algorithms are faster than the complete methods, but b y their very nature, they are not always able to complete with a definitive answer.

Most SA T-solvers expect the input formula to be in CNF. However, Giunchiglia and Sebastiani [13,19] have examined GSAT and Davis-Putnam for use on non-CNF form ulas. Although these algorithm avoid the explicit conversion of the form ula to CNF, they often implicitly add the same n umber of extra variable which would have been needed if one converted the form ula to CNF. Stålmarck's method [21] is another algorithm which does not need the conversion to CNF.

BDDs [9] and variations thereof [10] have until recently been the dominating data structures in the area of formal verification. However, recently researchers have started studying the use of SAT-solvers as an alternative. Biere *et al.* [4,5,6] introduce bounded model checking where SAT-solvers are used to find counterexamples of a given depth in the Kripke structures. Abdulla *et al.* [1] and William s *et al.* [24] study SAT-solvers in fixed-point iterations for model checking. Bjesse and Claessen [7] apply SAT-solvers to van Eijk's BDD-based method [22] for verification without state space traversal.

2 Boolean Expression Diagrams

A Boolean Expression Diagram [2,3] is a data structure for representing and manipulating Boolean form ulas. In this section we briefly review the data structure.

Definition 1 (Boolean Expression Diagram). *A Boolean Expression Diagram (BED) is a directed acyclic graph $G = (V, E)$ with vertex set V and edge set E. The vertex set V contains three types of vertices: terminal, variable, and operator vertices.*

- *A terminal vertex v has as attribute a value $val(v) \in \{0, 1\}$.*
- *A variable vertex v has as attributes a Boolean variable $var(v)$, and two children $low(v), high(v) \in V$.*
- *An operator vertex v has as attributes a binary Boolean operator $op(v)$, and two children $low(v), high(v) \in V$.*

The edge set E is defined by

$$E = \big\{ (v, low(v)), (v, high(v)) \mid v \in V \text{ and } v \text{ is a non-terminal vertex} \big\}.$$

The relation between a BED and the Boolean function it represents is straightforward. Terminal v ertices correspond to the constant functions 0 (false) and 1 (true). Variable vertices have the same semantics as vertices of BDDs and correspond to the *if-then-else* operator $x \rightarrow f_1, f_0$ defined as $(x \wedge f_1) \vee (\neg x \wedge f_0)$. Operator vertices correspond to their respective Boolean connectives. This leads to the following correspondence between BEDs and Boolean functions:

Definition 2. *A vertex v in a BED denotes a Boolean function f^v defined recursively as:*

- *If v is a terminal vertex, then $f^v = val(v)$.*
- *If v is a variable vertex, then $f^v = var(v) \rightarrow f^{high(v)}, f^{low(v)}$.*
- *If v is an operator vertex, then $f^v = f^{low(v)} \ op(v) \ f^{high(v)}$.*

A BDD is simply a BED without operators, thus a strategy for converting BEDs into BDDs is to gradually eliminate the operators, keeping all the intermediate BEDs functionally equivalent. There are two very different ways of eliminating operators, called UP_ALL and UP_ONE. The UP_ALL algorithm constructs the BDD in a bottom-up way similar to the APPLY algorithm by Bryant [9].

The UP_ONE algorithm is unique to BEDs and is based on repeated use of the following identity (called the *up-step*):

$$(x \rightarrow f_1, f_0) \ op \ (x \rightarrow f_1', f_0') = x \rightarrow (f_1 \ op \ f_1'), (f_0 \ op \ f_0'), \qquad (1)$$

where op is an arbitrary binary Boolean operator, x is a Boolean variable, and f_i and f_i' $(i = 0, 1)$ are arbitrary Boolean expressions. This identity is used to move the variable x above the operator op. In this way, it moves operators closer to the terminal vertices and if some of the expressions f_i are terminal vertices, the operators are evaluated and the BED simplified. By repeatedly moving variable vertices above operator vertices, all operator vertices are eliminated and the BED is turned into a BDD. (Equation (1) also holds if the operator vertex op is a variable vertex. In that case, the up-step is identical to the level exchange operation typically used in BDDs to dynamically change the variable ordering [18].)

The UP_ONE algorithm gradually converts a BED into a BDD by pulling up variables one by one. The main advantage of this algorithm is that it can exploit structural information in the expression. We refer the reader to [2,3,15,23] for a more detailed description of UP_ONE, UP_ALL and their applications.

3 Satisfiability of Formulas in CNF

A Boolean formula is in conjunctive normal form (on clausal form) if it is represented as a conjunction (AND) of clauses, each of which is the disjunction (OR) of one or more literals. A literal is either a variable or the negation of a variable. The Davis-Putnam algorithm [11,12] (see Algorithm 1) determines whether a Boolean formula ϕ in CNF is satisfiable. Line 1 is the base case where ϕ is the empty set of clauses which represents "true." Line 3 is the backtracking step where ϕ contains an empty clause which represents "false." Line 5 handles unit

Algorithm 1 The basic version of Davis-Putnam. The function $assign(l, \phi)$ applies the truth value of literal l to the CNF formula ϕ. The function *choose-literal*(ϕ) selects a literal for DP to split on.

Name: DP ϕ
1: **if** ϕ is the empty set of clauses **then**
2:     **return** true
3: **else if** ϕ contains the empty clause **then**
4:     **return** false
5: **else if** a unit clause l occurs in ϕ **then**
6:     **return** DP$(assign(l, \phi))$
7: **else**
8:     $l \leftarrow$ *choose-literal*(ϕ)
9:     **return** DP$(assign(l, \phi)) \vee$ DP$(assign(\neg l, \phi))$

clauses, i.e., clauses of the form x or $\neg x$. In this case, the value of the variable in the unit clause l is assigned in all remaining clauses of ϕ using the $assign(l, \phi)$ procedure. Line 8 and 9 handles the general case where a literal is chosen and the algorithm splits on whether the literal is true or false. There are a number of different heuristics for choosing a "good" literal in line 8 and the SAT-solvers based on Davis-Putnam differ by how they choose the literals to split on. A simple heuristic is to choose the literal in such a way that the assignments in line 9 produce the most unit clauses.

4   Satisfiability of Non-clausal Formulas

Using BEDs, the effect of splitting on a literal is obtained by pulling a variable to the root using UP_ONE. After pulling a variable x up using UP_ONE, there are two situations:

- The new root vertex contains the variable x. Both *low* and *high* children are BEDs. The formula is satisfiable if either the *low* child or the *high* child (or both) represents a satisfiable formula.
- The new BED does not contain the variable x anywhere. The formula does not depend on x and we can pick a new variable to pull up.

This suggests a recursive algorithm that pulls variables up one at a time. If the algorithm at any point reaches the terminal **1**, then a satisfying assignment has been found (the path from the root to the terminal **1** gives the assignment). The test for the empty set of clauses (line 1 in Algorithm 1) becomes a test for the terminal **1**. The test for whether ϕ contains the empty clause (line 3) becomes a test for the terminal **0**. It's not possible to test for unit clauses in the BED and thus lines 5 and 6 have no correspondence in the BED algorithm. The only use of the unit clause detection in the Davis-Putnam algorithm is to reduce the size of the CNF representation. However, the BED data structure has a large number of built-in reduction rules such as the distributive laws and the absorption laws [23].

Algorithm 2 The BEDSAT algorithm. The argument u is a BED. The function *choose-variable(u)* selects a variable to split on.

Name: BEDSAT u
1: **if** $u = 1$ **then**
2:     **return** true
3: **else if** $u = 0$ **then**
4:     **return** false
5: **else**
6:     $x \leftarrow$ *choose-variable(u)*
7:     $u' \leftarrow$ UP_ONE(x, u)
8:     **if** u' is a variable x vertex **then**
9:         **return** BEDSAT *low(u')* $\lor$ BEDSAT *high(u')*
10:    **else**
11:        **return** BEDSAT u'

These reduction rules are applied each time a new BED vertex is created and can potentially reduce the size of the representation considerably. Algorithm 2 shows the pseudo-code for the SAT-procedure BEDSAT.

The function *choose-variable* in line 6 of Algorithm 2 selects a variable to split on. With a clausal representation of the formula, it is natural to pick the variable in such a way as to obtain the most unit clauses after the split. This gives the most reductions due to unit propagation. Although we do not have a clausal representation of the formulas when using BEDs, it is still possible to choose good candidate variables. In [23], several different heuristics for picking good variable orderings for UP_ONE are discussed. The first variable in such an ordering is probably a good variable to split on. In the prototype implementation, a simple strategy has been implemented: the first variable encountered during a depth-first search is used in the spilt. Notice that we do not need to split on the variables in the same order along different branches, i.e., it is not necessary to choose a single global variable ordering. Thus, the variable ordering can be adjusted to each sub-BED as the algorithm executes.

In line 9 the algorithm branches out in two: one branch for the low child and one for the high child. If a satisfying assignment is found in one branch (and thus BEDSAT returns true), it is not necessary to consider the other branch. We have implemented a simple greedy strategy of first examining the branch with the smaller BED size (least number of vertices).

An interesting feature of the BEDSAT algorithm is that it is possible to compute the fraction of the state space that has been examined at any point in the execution. It is known that the algorithm will terminate when 100% of the state space has been examined (it may of course terminate earlier if a satisfying assignment is found.) Figure 1 shows graphically how to determine the fraction of the state space that has been examined by the BEDSAT algorithm. The circles correspond to splitting points and the triangles correspond to parts of the BED which have (gray triangles) or have not (white triangles) been examined. The numbers next to the triangles indicate the size of the state space represented by

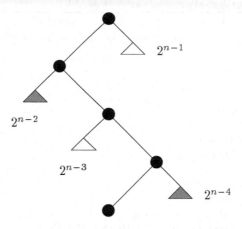

Fig. 1. Illustration of how to determine the percentage of the state space that has been examined. Each circle represents a split on a variable. The top circle is the starting point. The triangles represent sub-BEDs; the white ones are as yet unexamined while the gray ones have already been examined. Assume that there are n variables in total and that the current position in BedSat corresponds to the bottom circle. Then the fraction of the state space which has already been examined is $\frac{2^{n-2}+2^{n-4}}{2^n}$.

each triangle assuming that there are n variables in total. The fraction of the state space examined so far is determined by adding the numbers from the gray triangles and dividing by 2^n which is the size of the complete state space.

Of course, the percentage of the state space that has been examined does not say much about the time remaining in the computation. However, it does allow us to detect whether the algorithm is making progress. One could imagine a SAT-solver which jumps back a number of splits if the user felt that the current choice of split variables did not produce any progress. This could also be done automatically by tracking how the percentage changes over time. No or little growth could indicate that the choosen sequence of variables to split on is inefficient and the algorithm should backtrack and pick new split variables. Such backtracking is called *premature* and the technique is used in many implementations of Davis-Putnam. It works the best for satisfiable functions since it allows the search to give up on a particular part of the state space and concentrate on other, and hopefully easier, parts. If a satisfying assignment is found in the easy part of the state space, then the difficult part never needs to be revisited. For unsatisfiable functions, the entire state space needs to be examined, and giving up on one part just postpones the problems. The only hope is that by choosing a different sequence of variables to split on, the BED reduction rules collapse the difficult part of the state space.

The BedSat algorithm can be improved by combining it with traditional BDD construction. As more and more splits are performed, more and more

---

Algorithm 3 The BEDSAT algorithm with cutoff size N. $|u|$ is the number of vertices in the BED u. Line 6 returns whether the BED u represents a satisfiable function.

Name: BEDSAT u

1: **if** $u = 1$ **then**
2:   **return** true
3: **else if** $u = 0$ **then**
4:   **return** false
5: **else if** $|u| < N$ **then**
6:   **return** (UP_ALL(u) $\neq$ **0**)
7: **else**
8:   $x \leftarrow$ *choose-variable*(u)
9:   $u' \leftarrow$ UP_ONE(x, u)
10:   **if** u' is a variable x vertex **then**
11:     **return** BEDSAT *low*(u') $\lor$ BEDSAT *high*(u')
12:   **else**
13:     **return** BEDSAT u'

---

variables are assigned a value and the remaining BED shrinks. The BEDSAT algorithm, as described above, continues this process until either reaching a terminal **1**, or the entire BED is reduced to **0** (i.e., the BED is unsatisfiable). However, at some point it becomes more efficient to convert the BED into a BDD from which it can be decided immediately whether the original formula is satisfiable (the BDD is *not* **0**) or the algorithm has to backtrack and continue spliting (the BDD is **0**).

As discussed in the introduction, there is a trade-off between building the BDD and splitting on variables. The BDD construction computes too much information and is slow for large BEDs. On the other hand, splitting on variables tend to be slow when the depth is large. To be able to find the optimal point between the BDD construction and splitting on variables, we use a *cutoff size* N for the remaining BED; see Algorithm 3. If the size of the BED of a sub-problem less than the cutoff size, the BED is converted into a BDD, otherwise we continue splitting. For large values of N, the revised version of BEDSAT reduces to pure BDD construction. For N equal to 0, the revised algorithm is identical to Algorithm 2.

5   Experimental Results

To see how well BEDSAT works in practice, we compare it to other techniques for solving satisfiability problems. Unfortunately, the standard benchmarks used to evaluate SAT-solvers are all in CNF (see for example [14]). To compare the performance of BEDSAT with existing algorithm on non-clausal Boolean formulas, we obtain Boolean formulas from the circuits in the ISCAS'85 benchmark siute [8] and from model checking [24].

We compare BEDSAT to the BDD construction algorithms UP_ONE and UP_ALL, both using the FANIN variabel ordering heuristic. Furthermore, we compare BEDSAT with the state-of-the-art SAT-solvers SATO and GRASP. Since both SATO and GRASP require their input to be in CNF form, we convert the BEDs to CNF although this increases the number of variables and thus also the state space for SATO and GRASP.

The experiments are performed on a 450 MHz Pentium III PC running Linux. For the BDD construction in Algorithm 3 we use UP_ALL with the FANIN variable ordering heuristic [23]. All runs are limited to 32 MB of memory and 15 minutes of CPU time.

Table 1 shows the ISCAS'85 results. The ISCAS'85 benchmark consists of eleven multi-level combinational circuits, nine of which exist both in a redundant and a non-redundant version. Furthermore, the benchmark contains five circuits that originally were believed to be non-redundant versions but it turned out that they contained errors and weren't functionally equivalent to the original circuits [16]. The nine equivalent pairs of circuits corresponds to 475 unsatisfiable Boolean formulas (the circuits have several outputs) when the outputs of the circuits are pairwise exclusive-or'ed. The first nine rows of Table 1 show the runtimes to prove that the 475 fomulas are unsatisfiable using UP_ONE, UP_ALL, SATO, GRASP, and the BEDSAT algorithm with the cutoff size equal to 0, 100, 400 and 1000. UP_ONE and UP_ALL perform quite well on all nine circuits. The SAT-solvers SATO and GRASP perform well on the smaller circuits (the number in the circuit names indicate the size), but give up on several of the larger ones. With 0 as cutoff size, BEDSAT does not perform well at all. The runtimes are an order of magnitude larger than the runtimes for the other methods. The long runtimes are due to BEDSAT's poor performance on some (but not all) unsatisfiable formulas. Increasing the cutoff size to 100 or 400 improves BEDSAT's performance. In fact, with cutoff size 400, BEDSAT yields runtimes comparable to or better than all other methods except the case of c6288/nr with UP_ONE.

The last five rows of Table 1 show the results for the erroneous circuits. Here there are 340 Boolean formulas in total out of which 267 are unsatisfiable and 73 are satisfiable. We indicate this with "S/U" in the second column. The UP_ONE and UP_ALL methods take slightly longer on the erroneous circuits since not all BDDs collapse to a terminal. The SAT-solvers (SATO, GRASP and BEDSAT) perform considerably better on the erroneous circuits compared to the correct circuits; sometimes going from impossible to possible as for SATO and BEDSAT (with a cutoff size of 0 and 100) on c7552. BEDSAT is the only SAT-solver to handle c3540 and it outperforms SATO and GRASP on c5315. On c7552, BEDSAT is two orders of magnitude slower with a cutoff of 0, but yields comparable results when the cutoff size increases.

Consider the case of BEDSAT on c3540 with a cutoff size of 0. In the correct version of the circuits, BEDSAT uses 185 seconds. This number reduces to 35.9 seconds for the erroneous circuits. The c3540 circuit has 22 outputs where five are faulty in the erroneous version. BEDSAT has no problem detecting the errors in the five faulty outputs. In the correct version, about 149 seconds are spent on proving those five outputs to be unsatisfiable. Another example is c1908 where, in the correct case, BEDSAT spends all the time (242 seconds) on one

Table 1. Runtimes in seconds for determining satisfiability of problems arising in verification of the ISCAS'85 benchmarks using different approaches. In the "Result" column, "U" indicates unsatisfiable problems while "S/U" indicates both satisfiable and unsatisfiable problems. Both UP_ONE and UP_ALL use the FANIN variable ordering heuristic. The last three columns show the results for BEDSAT. The numbers 0, 100, 400 and 1000 indicate the cutoff sizes in number of vertices. A dash indicates that the computation could not be done within the resource limits.

Description	Result	UP_ONE	UP_ALL	SATO	GRASP	BEDSAT			
						0	100	400	1000
c432/nr	U	2.1	1.7	0.5	0.4	36.4	3.5	1.4	1.4
c499/nr	U	4.3	1.8	1.8	1.4	17.8	16.7	1.7	1.7
c1355/nr	U	4.3	1.8	1.8	1.5	18.1	16.5	1.7	1.7
c1908/nr	U	0.7	0.6	0.4	0.4	242	11.1	0.2	0.2
c2670/nr	U	1.2	0.6	1.0	0.9	38.6	1.9	0.3	0.3
c3540/nr	U	32.3	39.2	–	–	185	133	10.9	16.3
c5315/nr	U	16.2	1.9	–	15.0	1.1	1.0	0.9	1.3
c6288/nr	U	2.7	–	–	–	–	–	–	–
c7552/nr	U	3.6	1.1	–	4.4	–	–	0.7	0.7
c1908/nr−err	S/U	0.7	0.6	0.4	0.4	0.1	0.1	0.2	0.2
c2670/nr−err	S/U	2.9	0.7	0.9	0.8	0.4	0.3	0.3	0.3
c3540/nr−err	S/U	42.8	40.2	–	–	35.9	15.8	4.6	6.5
c5315/nr−err	S/U	32.7	2.4	31.7	10.3	0.7	1.6	1.5	1.8
c7552/nr−err	S/U	8.1	1.8	2.5	2.6	176	2.0	1.3	1.3

unsatisfiable output. In the erroneous version the difficult output has an error and the corresponding Boolean formula becomes satisfiable. BEDSAT finds a satisfying assignment instantaneously (0.1 seconds).

By varying the cutoff size, we can control whether BEDSAT works mostly as the standard BDD construction (when using a high cutoff size) or as a Davis-Putnam SAT-solver (a low cutoff size). From Table 1 it is observed that for the ISCAS circuits, a cutoff size of 400 seems to be the optimal value. Using this value for the cutoff size, the BEDSAT algorithm outperforms both pure BDD construction (UP_ALL and UP_ONE) and standard SAT-solvers (SATO, GRASP, and BEDSAT with 0 cutoff) for all the larger circuits except **c6288/nr** and for all the errorneous (and thus satisfiable) ISCAS circuits.

The Boolean formulas obtained from the ISCAS'85 circuits have many identical sub-formulas since they are obtained by comparing two similar circuits. To test the BEDSAT algorithm on a more reaslistic example (at least from the point of view of formal verification), we have extracted Boolean formulas that arise during the fixed-point iteration when performing model checking of a 16-bit shift-and-add multiplier [23]. Table 2 shows the results for the model checking problems. The numbers 10, 20 and 30 indicate the output bit we are considering. The word "final" indicates the satisfiability problem for the check for whether the

Table 2. Runtimes in seconds for determining satisfiabilit y of problems arising in model checking using different approaches. In the "Result" column, "U" indicates unsatisfiable problems while "S" indicates satisfiable problems. Both UP_ONE and UP_ALL use the FANIN variable ordering heuristic. The BEDSAT experimen ts have cutoff size 0 (i.e., no cutoff) except for the one marked with † which has cutoff size 400. A dash indicates that the computation could not be done within the resource limits.

Description	Result	UP_ONE	UP_ALL	SATO	GRASP	BEDSAT
mult_10_final	U	13.1	43.5	-	-	31.9†
mult_10_last_fp	U	10.3	-	0.1	0.1	0.2
mult_10_second_last_fp	S	-	-	0.1	0.1	0.1
mult_20_final	?	-	-	-	-	-
mult_20_last_fp	U	-	-	0.1	0.1	0.1
mult_20_second_last_fp	S	-	-	0.5	40.9	0.5
mult_30_final	S	-	-	0.3	0.6	0.2
mult_30_last_fp	U	-	-	0.1	0.2	0.2
mult_30_second_last_fp	S	-	-	0.6	1.4	0.5
mult_bug_10_final	S	13.0	-	6.7	0.1	0.1
mult_bug_10_last_fp	U	9.9	-	0.1	0.1	0.2
mult_bug_10_second_last_fp	S	-	-	0.1	0.1	0.1
mult_bug_20_final	S	-	-	113	-	0.3
mult_bug_20_last_fp	U	-	-	0.1	0.1	0.1
mult_bug_20_second_last_fp	S	-	-	0.5	499	0.5
mult_bug_30_final	S	-	-	0.3	0.6	0.2
mult_bug_30_last_fp	U	-	-	0.1	0.2	0.2
mult_bug_30_second_last_fp	S	-	-	0.6	1.5	0.5

implem entation satisfies the specification. The word "last_fp" indicates the sat-isfiability problem for the last iteration in the fixed-poin t computation (where it is detected that the fixed-point is reached). The word "second_last_fp" indicates the satisfiability problem for the previous iteration in the fixed-point iteration. The result column indicates whether the satisfiabilit y problem is satisfiable (S) or not (U).

For the model checking problems, UP_ONE and UP_ALL perform very poorly. UP_ONE is only able to handle four out of 18 problems and UP_ALL only handles a single one. However, both UP_ONE and UP_ALL handle the mult_10_final problem which is difficult for the SAT-solvers. The SAT-solvers perform quite well – both on the satisfiable and the unsatisfiable problems. Most of the prob-lems are solved in less than a second by all three SAT-solvers. While both SATO and GRASP take a long time on a few of the problems, BEDSAT is more consistent in its performance.

6   Conclusion

This paper has presented the BEDSAT algorithm for solving the satisfiabilit y problem on BEDs. The algorithm adopts the Da vis-Putnam algorithm to the

BED data structure. Traditional SAT-solvers require the Boolean formula to be given in CNF, but BEDSAT works directly on the BED and thus avoids the conversion of the formula to CNF which either adds extra variables or may result in an exponentially larger CNF formula. The BEDSAT algorithm is also able to take advantage of the BED data structure by using the reduction rules from [23] during the algorithm and by taking advantage of the sharing of sub-formulas.

We have described how the BEDSAT algorithm is combined with traditional BDD construction. By adjusting a single parameter to the BEDSAT algorithm it is possible to control to what extent the algorithm behaves like the APPLY-algorithm or like a SAT-solver. Thus the algorithm can be seen as bridging the gap between standard SAT-solvers and BDDs.

We present promising experimental results for 566 non-clausal formulas obtained from the multi-level combinational circuits in the ISCAS'85 benchmark suite and from performing bounded model checking of a shift-and-add multiplier. For these formulas, the BEDSAT algorithm is more efficient than both pure SAT-solvers (SATO and GRASP) and standard BDD construction. The combination works especially well on formulas which are unsatisfiable and thus difficult for pure SAT-solvers.

References

1. P. A. Abdulla, P. Bjesse, and N. Eén. Symbolic reachability analysis based on SAT solvers. In *Tools and Algorithms for the Construction and Analysis of Systems (TACAS)*, 2000.
2. H. R. Andersen and H. Hulgaard. Boolean expression diagrams. *Information and Computation*. (To appear).
3. H. R. Andersen and H. Hulgaard. Boolean expression diagrams. In *IEEE Symposium on Logic in Computer Science (LICS)*, July 1997.
4. A. Biere, A. Cimatti, E. M. Clarke, M. Fujita, and Y. Zhu. Symbolic model checking using SAT procedures instead of BDDs. In *Proc. ACM/IEEE Design Automation Conference (DAC)*, 1999.
5. A. Biere, A. Cimatti, E. M. Clarke, and Y. Zhu. Symbolic model checking without BDDs. In *Tools and Algorithms for the Construction and Analysis of Systems (TACAS)*, volume 1579 of *Lecture Notes in Computer Science*. Springer-Verlag, 1999.
6. A. Biere, E. Clarke, R. Raimi, and Y. Zhu. Verifying safety properties of a PowerPC microprocessor using symbolic model checking without BDDs. In *Computer Aided Verification (CAV)*, volume 1633 of *Lecture Notes in Computer Science*. Springer-Verlag, 1999.
7. P. Bjesse. SAT-based verification without state space traversal. In *Proc. Formal Methods in Computer-Aided Design, Third International Conference, FMCAD'00, Austin, Texas, USA*, Lecture Notes in Computer Science, November 2000.
8. F. Brglez and H. Fujiware. A neutral netlist of 10 combinational benchmarks circuits and a target translator in Fortran. In *Special Session International Symposium on Circuits and Systems (ISCAS)*, 1985.
9. R. E. Bryant. Graph-based algorithms for boolean function manipulation. *IEEE Transactions on Computers*, 35(8):677–691, August 1986.

10. R. E. Bryant. Binary decision diagrams and beyond: Enabling technologies for formal verification. In *Proc. International Conf. Computer-Aided Design (ICCAD)*, pages 236–243, November 1995.

11. M. Davis, G. Longemann, and D. Loveland. A machine program for theorem-proving. *Communications of the ACM*, 5(7):394–397, July 1962.

12. M. Davis and H. Putnam. A computing procedure for quantification theory. *Journal of the ACM*, 7:201–215, 1960.

13. E. Giunchiglia and R. Sebastiani. Applying the Davis-Putnam procedure to non-clausal formulas. In *Proc. Italian National Conference on Artificial Intelligence*, volume 1792 of *Lecture Notes in Computer Science*, Bologna, Italy, September 1999. Springer-Verlag.

14. Holger H. Hoos and Thomas Sttzle. SATLIB – the satisfiability library. http://aida.intellektik.informatik.tu-darmstadt.de/~hoos/SATLIB/.

15. H. Hulgaard, P. F. Williams, and H. R. Andersen. Equivalence checking of combinational circuits using boolean expression diagrams. *IEEE Transactions on Computer Aided Design*, July 1999.

16. W. Kunz and D. K. Pradhan. Recursive learning: A new implication technique for efficient solutions to CAD problems – test, verification, and optimization. *IEEE Transactions on Computer Aided Design*, 13(9):1143–1158, September 1994.

17. J. P. Marques-Silva and K. A. Sakallah. GRASP: A search algorithm for propositional satisfiability. *IEEE Transactions on Computers*, 48, 1999.

18. R. Rudell. Dynamic variable ordering for ordered binary decision diagrams. In *Proc. International Conf. Computer-Aided Design (ICCAD)*, pages 42–47, 1993.

19. R. Sebastiani. Applying GSAT to non-clausal formulas. *Journal of Artificial Intelligence Research (JAIR)*, 1:309–314, January 1994.

20. B. Selman, H. J. Levesque, and D. Mitchell. A new method for solving hard satisfiability problems. In P. Rosenbloom and P. Szolovits, editors, *Proc. Tenth National Conference on Artificial Intelligence*, pages 440–446, Menlo Park, California, 1992. American Association for Artificial Intelligence, AAAI Press.

21. M. Sheeran and G. Stålmarck. A tutorial on Stålmarck's proof procedure for propositional logic. In G. Gopalakrishnan and P. J. Windley, editors, *Proc. Formal Methods in Computer-Aided Design, Second International Conference, FM-CAD'98, Palo Alto/CA, USA*, volume 1522 of *Lecture Notes in Computer Science*, pages 82–99, November 1998.

22. C.A.J. van Eijk. Sequential equivalence checking without state space traversal. In *Proc. International Conf. on Design Automation and Test of Electronic-based Systems (DATE)*, 1998.

23. P. F. Williams. *Formal Verification Based on Boolean Expression Diagrams*. PhD thesis, Dept. of Information Technology, Technical University of Denmark, Lyngby, Denmark, August 2000. ISBN 87-89112-59-8.

24. P. F. Williams, A. Biere, E. M. Clarke, and A. Gupta. Combining decision diagrams and SAT procedures for efficient symbolic model checking. In *Computer Aided Verification (CAV)*, volume 1855 of *Lecture Notes in Computer Science*, pages 124–138, Chicago, U.S.A., July 2000. Springer-Verlag.

25. H. Zhang. SATO: An efficient propositional prover. In William McCune, editor, *Proceedings of the 14th International Conference on Automated deduction*, volume 1249 of *Lecture Notes in Artificial Intelligence*, pages 272–275, Berlin, July 1997. Springer-Verlag.

A Library for Composite Symbolic Represen tations

Tuba Yavuz-Kahveci, Murat Tuncer, and Tevfik Bultan

Department of Computer Science, University of California,
Santa Barbara, CA 93106, USA
{tuba, mtuncer, bultan}@cs.ucsb.edu

Abstract. In this paper, we present the design and the implementation of a composite model checking library. Our tool combines different symbolic representations, such as BDDs for representing boolean logic formulas and polyhedral representations for linear arithmetic formulas, with a single interface. Based on this common interface, these data structures are combined using what we call a *composite representation*. We used an object-oriented design to implement the composite symbolic library. We imported CUDD (a BDD library) and Omega Library (a linear arithmetic constraint manipulator that uses polyhedral representations) to our tool by writing wrappers around them which conform to our symbolic representation interface. Our tool supports polymorphic verification procedures which dynamically select symbolic representations based on the input specification. Our symbolic representation library forms an interface between different symbolic libraries, model checkers, and specification languages. We expect our tool to be useful in integrating different tools and techniques for symbolic model checking, and in comparing their performance.

1 Introduction

In symbolic model checking sets of states and transitions are represented symbolically (implicitly) to avoid the state-space explosion problem [BCM+90,McM93]. Success of symbolic model checking has been mainly due to efficiency of the data structures used to represent the state space. For example, binary decision diagrams (BDDs) [Bry86] have been successfully used in verification of finite-state systems which could not be verified explicitly due to size of the state space [BCM+90,McM93]. Linear arithmetic constraint representations have been used in verification of real-time systems, and infinite-state systems [ACH+95,AHH96,BGP99,HRP94] which are not possible to verify using explicit representations. Any data structure that supports operations such as intersection, union, complement, equivalence checking and existential quantifier elimination (used to implement relational image computations) can be used as a

---

This work is supported in part by NSF grant CCR-9970976 and NSF CAREER award CCR-9984822.

T. Margaria and W. Yi (Eds.): TACAS 2001, LNCS 2031, pp. 52–66, 2001.

symbolic representation in model checking. The motivation is to find symbolic representations which can represent the state space compactly to avoid state-space explosion problem. However, symbolic representations may have their own deficiencies. For example BDDs are incapable of representing infinite sets. On the other hand linear arithmetic constraint representations, which are capable of representing infinite sets, are expensive to manipulate due to increased expressivity.

Generally, model checking tools have been built using a single symbolic representation [McM93,AHH96]. The representation used depends on the target application domain for the model checker. Inefficiencies of the symbolic representation used in a model checker can be addressed using various abstraction techniques, some ad hoc, such as restricting variables to finite domains, some formal, such as predicate-abstraction [Sai00]. These abstraction techniques can be used independent of the symbolic representation. As model checkers become more widely used, it is not hard to imagine that a user would like to use a model checker built for real-time systems on a system with lots of boolean variables and only a couple of real variables. Similarly another user may want to use a BDD-based model checker to check a system with few boolean variables but lots of integer variables. Currently, such users may need to get a new model-checker for these instances, or use various abstraction techniques to solve a problem which may not be suitable for the symbolic representation their model checker is using. More importantly, as symbolic model-checkers are applied to larger problems, they are bound to encounter specifications with different variable types which may not be efficiently representable using a single symbolic representation.

In this paper we present a verification tool which combines several symbolic representations instead of using a single symbolic representation. Different symbolic representations are combined using the *composite model checking* approach presented in [BGL98,BGL00b]. Each variable type in the input specification is assigned to the most efficient representation for that variable type. The goal is to have a platform where strength of each symbolic representation is utilized as much as possible, and deficiencies of a representation are compensated by the existence of other representations.

We use an object oriented design for our tool. First we declare an interface for symbolic representations. This interface is specified as an abstract class. All symbolic representations are defined as classes derived from this interface. We integrated CUDD and Omega Library to our tool by writing wrappers around them which implements this interface. This makes it possible for our verifier to interact with these libraries using a single interface. The symbolic representations based on these tools form the basic representation types of our composite library. Our composite class is also derived from the abstract symbolic representation class. A composite representation consists of a disjunction of composite atoms where each composite atom is a conjunction of basic symbolic representations. Composite class manipulates this representation to compute operations such as union, intersection, complement, forward-image, backward-image, equivalence check, etc.

There have been other studies which use different symbolic representations together. In [CABN97], Chan *et al.* present a technique in which (both linear and non-linear) constraints are mapped to BDD variables (similar representations were also used in [AB96,AG93]) and a constraint solver is used during model checking computations (in conjunction with SMV) to prune infeasible combinations of these constraints. Although this technique is capable of handling non-linear constraints, it is restricted to systems where transitions are either *data-memoryless* (i.e., next state value of a data variable does not depend on its current state value), or *data-invariant* (i.e., data variables remain unchanged). Hence, even a transition which increments a variable (i.e., $x' = x + 1$) is ruled out. It is reported in [CABN97] that this restriction is partly motivated by the semantics of RSML, and it allows modeling of a significant portion of TCAS II system.

In [BS00], a tool for checking inductive invariants on SCR specifications is described. This tool combines automata based representations for linear arithmetic constraints with BDDs. This approach is similar to our approach but it is specialized for inductive invariant checking. Another difference is our tool uses polyhedral representations as opposed to automata based representations for linear arithmetic. However, because of the modular design of our tool it should be easy to extend it with automata-based linear constraint representations.

Symbolic Analysis Laboratory (SAL) is a recent attempt to develop a framework for combining different tools in verifying properties of concurrent systems [BGL+00a]. The heart of the tool is a language for specifying concurrent systems in a compositional manner. Our composite symbolic library is a low-level approach compared to SAL. We are combining different libraries at the symbolic representation level as opposed to developing a specification language to integrate different tools.

The rest of the paper is organized as follows. We explain the design of our composite symbolic library in Section 2. In Section 3, we describe the algorithms for manipulating composite representations. Section 4 presents the polymorphic verification procedure. In Section 5 we show the performance of the composite model checker on a simple example. Finally, in Section 6 we conclude and give some future directions.

2   Composite Symbolic Library

To combine different symbolic representations we use the composite model checking approach presented in [BGL98,BGL00b]. The basic idea in composite model checking is to map each variable in the input specification to a symbolic representation type. For example, boolean and enumerated variables can be mapped to BDD representation, and integers can be mapped to an arithmetic constraint representation. Then, each atomic event in the input specification is conjunctively partitioned where each conjunct specifies the effect of the event on the variables represented by a single symbolic representation. For example, one conjunct specifies the effect of the event on variables encoded using BDDs, whereas another conjunct specifies the effects of the event on variables encoded using linear arithmetic constraints. We encode the sets of system states as a disjunction of conjunctively partitioned type specific representations (e.g., a disjunct may consist of a boolean formula stored as a BDD representing the states of boolean and enumerated variables, and a linear arithmetic constraint representation representing the states of integer variables). The forward and backward image computations are computed independently for each symbolic representation by exploiting the conjunctive partitioning of the atomic events. We also implement algorithms for intersection, union, complement and equivalence checking computations for the disjunctive *composite* representation that use the corresponding methods for different symbolic representations. The key observation here is the fact that conjunctive partitioning of the atomic events allows forward and backward image computations to distribute over different symbolic representations.

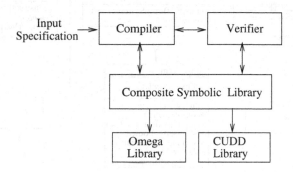

Fig. 1. Architecture of the composite model checker

Our current implementation of the composite symbolic library uses two symbolic representations: BDDs and polyhedral representation for Presburger arithmetic formulas. For the BDD representations we use the Colorado University Decision Diagram Package (CUDD) [CUD]. For the Presburger arithmetic formula manipulation we use the Omega Library [KMP+95,Ome]. Fig. 1 illustrates a general picture of our composite model checking system. We will focus on the symbolic library and verifier parts of the system in this paper.

We implemented our composite symbolic library in C++ and Fig. 2 shows its class hierarchy as a UML class diagram[1]. The abstract class **Symbolic** serves as an interface to all symbolic representations including the composite representation. Our current specification language supports enumerated, boolean, and integer variables. Our system maps enumerated variables to boolean variables. The classes **BoolSym** and **IntSym** are the symbolic representations for boolean and integer variable types, respectively. Class **BoolSym** serves as a wrapper for

---

[1] In UML class diagrams, triangle arcs denote *generalization*, diamond arcs denote *aggregation*, dashed arcs denote *dependency*, and solid lines denote *association* among classes.

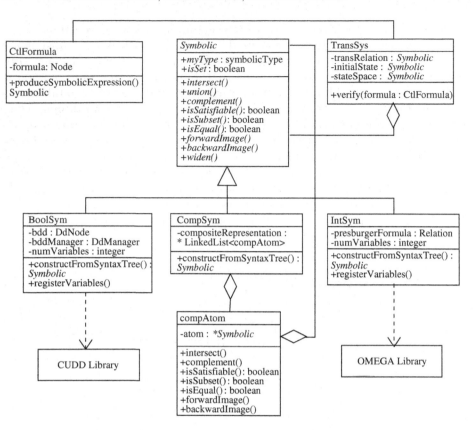

Fig. 2. Class diagram for the composite sym bolic library

the BDD library CUDD [CUD]. It is derived from the abstract class `Symbolic`. Similarly, `IntSym` is also derived from abstract class `Symbolic` and serves as a wrapper for the Omega Library [Ome].

The class `CompSym` is the class for composite representations. It is derived from `Symbolic` and uses `IntSym` and `BoolSym` (through the `Symbolic` interface) to manipulate composite represen tations. Note that this design is an instance of the composite design pattern given in [GHJV94].

To verify a system with our tool, one has to specify its initial condition, transition relation, and state space using a set of *composite formulas*. The syntax of a composite form ula is defined as follows:

$$CF ::= CF \land CF \mid CF \lor CF \mid \neg CF \mid BF \mid IF$$
$$BF ::= BF \land BF \mid BF \lor BF \mid \neg BF \mid Term_{bool}$$
$$IF ::= IF \land IF \mid IF \lor IF \mid \neg IF \mid Term_{int} \; Rop \; Term_{int}$$
$$Term_{bool} ::= id_{bool} \mid true \mid false$$
$$Term_{int} ::= Term_{int} \; Aop \; Term_{int} \mid -Term_{int} \mid id_{int} \mid constant$$

where CF, BF, IF, Rop, and Aop denote composite formula, boolean formula, integer formula, relational operator, and arithmetic operator, respectively. Since symbolic representations in our composite library currently support only boolean and linear arithmetic formulas, we restrict arithmetic operators to $+$ and $-$ (we actually allow multiplication with a constant). In the future, by adding new symbolic representations we can extend this grammar.

A transition relation can be specified using a composite formula by using unprimed variables to denote current state variables and primed variables to denote next state variables. A method called `registerVariables` in `BoolSym` and `IntSym` is used to register current and next state variable names during the initialization of the representation.

Given a composite formula, the method `constructFromSyntaxTree()` in `CompSym` traverses the syntax tree and calls `constructFromSyntaxTree()` method of `BoolSym` when a boolean formula is encountered and calls `constructFromSyntaxTree()` method of `IntSym` when an integer formula is encountered. In `CompSym`, a composite formula, A, is represented in Disjunctive Normal Form (DNF) as

$$A = \bigvee_{i=1}^{n} \bigwedge_{j=1}^{t} a_{ij}$$

where a_{ij} denotes the the formula of type j in the ith disjunct, and n and t denote the number of disjuncts and the number of types, respectively.

Each disjunct $\bigwedge_{j=1}^{t} a_{ij}$ is implemented as an instance of a class called `compAtom` (see Fig. 2). Each `compAtom` object represents a conjunction of formulas each of which is either a boolean or an integer formula.

A composite formula stored in a `CompSym` object is implemented as a list of `compAtom` objects, which corresponds to the disjunction in the DNF form above. Figure 3 shows internal representation of the composite formula

$$(a > 0 \ \wedge \ a' = a + 1 \ \wedge \ b') \ \vee \ (a \leq 0 \ \wedge \ a' = a \ \wedge \ b' = b)$$

in a `CompSym` object. The field *atom* is an array of pointer to class `Symbolic` and the size of the array is the number of basic symbolic representations.

`CompSym` and `compAtom` classes use a `TypeDescriptor` class which records the variable types used in the input specification. Our library can adapt itself to any subset of the supported variable types, i.e., if a variable type is not present in the input specification, the symbolic library for that type will not be called during the execution. For example, given an input specification with no integer variables our tool will behave as a BDD-based model checker without making any calls to Omega Library.

A `Simplifier` class implements a simplifier engine that reduces the number of disjuncts in the composite representations. Given a disjunctive formula A it searches for pairs of disjuncts $\bigwedge_{j=1}^{t} a_{ij}$ and $\bigwedge_{j=1}^{t} a_{kj}$ that can be expressed as a single disjunct $\bigwedge_{j=1}^{t} b_j$. Two disjuncts $\bigwedge_{j=1}^{t} a_{ij}$ and $\bigwedge_{j=1}^{t} a_{kj}$ can be simplified to a single disjunct $\bigwedge_{j=1}^{t} b_j$ if one of the following holds:

- $\bigwedge_{j=1}^{t} a_{ij}$ is subset of $\bigwedge_{j=1}^{t} a_{kj}$. Then $\bigwedge_{j=1}^{t} b_j = \bigwedge_{j=1}^{t} a_{kj}$.

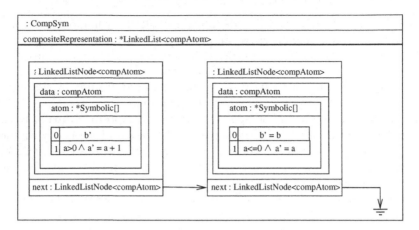

Fig. 3. An instance of `CompSym` class

- $\wedge_{j=1}^{t} a_{ij}$ is superset of $\wedge_{j=1}^{t} a_{kj}$. Then $\wedge_{j=1}^{t} b_j = \wedge_{j=1}^{t} a_{ij}$.
- There exists j such that a_{ij} is not equal to a_{kj} and for $1 \leq m \leq t$, $m \neq j$, a_{im} is equal to a_{km}. Then for $1 \leq m \leq t$, $m \neq j$, $b_m = a_{im}$ and $b_j = a_{ij} \vee a_{kj}$.

3 Algorithms for Manipulating Composite Representations

In this section, we present the algorithms used in `compAtom` and `CompSym` classes to implement the methods of `Symbolic` interface such as intersection, union, complement, image computations, subset, equality and satisfiability checks. Note that the algorithms given below are independent of the type and number of basic symbolic representations used.

Throughout this section, `CompSym` objects A and B are assumed to be in the following forms:

$$A = \bigvee_{i=1}^{n_A} \bigwedge_{j=1}^{t} a_{ij} \quad \text{and} \quad B = \bigvee_{i=1}^{n_B} \bigwedge_{j=1}^{t} b_{ij}$$

and $n_A(n_B)$, t, and T_{Op}^{i} denote the number of `compAtom` objects in `CompSym` object $A(B)$, the number of basic symbolic representations in the composite library, and time complexity of ith symbolic representation for operation Op.

Subset Relation Checking: Given two `compAtom` objects a and b, $a.\text{isSubset}(b)$ is evaluated by checking the corresponding symbolic representations in a and b for subset relation (step 2 of the algorithm given below). Checking subset relation for `CompSym` objects is more complicated. Given two `CompSym` objects, A and B, $A.\text{isSubset}(B)$ is evaluated as shown in the algorithm below. First, both A and B are simplified, which has a time complexity of $O((n_A^3 + n_B^3) \times \sum_{i=1}^{t}(T_{equal}^{i} + T_{isSubset}^{i}))$. Then for each `compAtom` object a in A we check if a is a subset of B.

An efficient way to check if a `compAtom` object a is subset of `CompSym` object B is to compare a with each `compAtom` object b in B till a.`isSubset`(b) evaluates to true. This is done in steps 7-11 below. However, if no such b can be found, this does not mean that a is not a subset of B. Next, we create a new `CompSym` object C, which consists of a single `compAtom` object a. We take the intersection of C and *not* B to obtain the `CompSym` object D. Then D is checked for satisfiability. If D is satisfiable then it means a is not a subset of B (steps 13-19). Time complexity of checking subset relation between two `CompSym` objects, A and B, is $O(n_A \times n_B \times t^{2n_B} \times \sum_{i=1}^{t} T_{isSatisfiable}^{i})$.

```
boolean compAtom::isSubset(compAtom other)
1  for i=1 to numBasicTypes do
2       if not atom[i].isSubset(other.getAtom(basicTypes[i])) then
3            return false;
4  return true;
```

```
boolean CompSym::isSubset(Symbolic other)
1   compAtom thisatom,otheratom; boolean found;
2   LinkedList<compAtom> otherlist = other.getCompAtomList();
3   this.simplify();
4   other.simplify();
5   for compRep.hasMore() do
6        thisatom = compRep.getNext();
         found = false;
7        for otherlist.hasMore() do
8             otheratom = otherlist.getNext();
9             if thisatom.isSubset(otheratom) then
10                 found = true;
11                 break;
12       if not found then
13            CompSym newsym1 = new CompSym(thisatom,isSet);
14            CompSym newsym2 = new CompSym(otherlist,isSet);
15            newsym2.complement();
16            newsym1.intersect(newsym2);
17            if newsym1.isSatisfiable() then
18                 return false;
19            else break;
20   return true;
```

Equivalence Checking: Checking equivalence of two `compAtom` objects is performed by calling `isEqual()` method of each symbolic representation similar to subset checking. Equivalence of two `CompSym` objects is checked by calling `isSubset()` method of `CompSym` class and time complexity of `isEqual()` method is the same as `CompSym::isSubset()` method.

Satisfiability Checking: Checking satisfiability of a `compAtom` object is performed by calling `isSatisfiable()` method of each symbolic representation. The condition for satisfiability of a `compAtom` object, a, is that each symbolic representation in a must be satisfiable. Satisfiability of a `CompSym` object A

is equivalent to existence of a `compAtom` object a in A such that a is satisfiable. Time complexity of checking satisfiability of `CompSym` object A is $O(n_A \times \sum_{i=1}^{t} T^i_{isSatisfiable})$.

Backward Image Computation: Backward image computation takes the transition relation as the input parameter. Backward image of a `compAtom` object is computed by calling `backwardImage()` method of each symbolic representation and passing the corresponding symbolic representation of the input `compAtom` object, as the parameter. While computing backward image for a `CompSym` object A, a new list of `compAtoms` is created and for each `compAtom` object in A as many copies as the number of `compAtom` objects in the input `CompSym` object are created. On each copy `backwardImage()` method is called with a `compAtom` object in the input `CompSym` object and the resulting `compAtom` object is inserted in the new list. At the end the `compAtom` list of A is replaced with this new list. Time complexity of computing backward image of `CompSym` object A over `CompSym` object B is $O(n_A \times n_B \times \sum_{i=1}^{t} T^i_{backwardImage})$.

```
compAtom::backwardImage(compAtom other)
1  for i=1 to numBasicTypes do
2      atom[i].backwardImage(other[i]);

CompSym::backwardImage(Symbolic other)
1  compAtom thisatom,newatom;
2  LinkedList<compAtom> newlist();
3  LinkedList<compAtom> otherlist = other.getCompAtomList();
4  for compRep.hasMore() do
5      thisatom = compRep.getNext();
6      for otherlist.hasMore() do
7          newatom = thisatom;
8          newatom.backwardImage(otherlist.getNext());
9          newlist.insert(newatom);
10 compRep = newlist;
```

Intersection : Given two composite formula, A and B, we define A intersection B as

$$A \wedge B = \bigvee_{i=1}^{n_A} \bigvee_{k=1}^{n_B} \bigwedge_{j=1}^{t} (a_{ij} \wedge b_{kj}) \tag{1}$$

Intersection of two `compAtom` objects is computed by calling `intersect()` method of each symbolic representation and passing the corresponding symbolic representation in the input `compAtom` object. To compute intersection of two `CompSym` objects, A and B, a new list of `compAtoms` is created and for each `compAtom` a in A and for each `compAtom` object b in B, intersection of a and b is computed and the resulting `compAtom` object is inserted into the new list. At the end `compAtom` list of A is replaced with the new list. The number of disjuncts in the resulting `CompSym` object after intersection of two `CompSym` objects, A and B, is $O(n_A \times n_B)$.

Complement : Given a composite formula A we define A's complement as

$$\neg A = \bigvee_{1 \le k \le t} \bigwedge_{i=1}^{n_A} \neg a_{ik} \tag{2}$$

Complement of a `compAtom` object is computed by creating a new `Compsym` object for negation of each symbolic representation in the `compAtom` object. Then the union of each newly created `CompSym` object is the result of the complement as seen in the algorithm below. To compute the complement of a `CompSym` object A, a new `CompSym` object B, which is initialized to *True*, is created. For each `compAtom` object a in A, complement of a is intersected with B (steps 4-6). The number of disjuncts in the resulting `CompSym` object after complementation of `CompSym` object A is $O(t^{n_A})$.

```
CompSym compAtom::complement()
1   CompSym result,temp;
2   Symbolic sym;
3   result = null;
4   for i=1 to numBasicTypes do
5       if result != null then
6           sym = atom[i];
7           sym.complement();
8           result.union(new CompSym(sym,isSet));
9       else
10          result = new CompSym(atom[i],isSet);
11 return result;
```

```
CompSym::complement()
1   CompSym result(true,isSet);
2   compAtom thisatom;
3   for compRep.hasMore() do
4       thisatom = compRep.getNext();
5       thisatom.complement();
6       result.intersect(thisatom);
7   this = result;
```

Union : Given two composite formula, A and B, we define A union B as

$$A \vee B = \bigvee_{i=1}^{n_A + n_B} \bigwedge_{j=1}^{t} c_{ij} \tag{3}$$

where for $1 \le i \le n_A$ $c_{ij} = a_{ij}$ and for $n_A + 1 \le i \le n_A + n_B$ $c_{ij} = b_{ij}$. Union of two `CompSym` objects, A and B, is computed by inserting the `compAtom` objects in B to the list of `compAtom` objects in A. The number of disjuncts in the union of two `CompSym` objects, A and B, is $O(n_A + n_B)$.

4   A Polymorphic V erifier

Module **TransSys** in Fig. 2 is responsible for verification. It contains two main functions **check** and **verify** . Check is a recursive function that traverses the syntax tree of CTL formula to compute a sym bolic representation for its truth set.

TransSys contains following mem bers : **transRelation** (transition relation), **stateSpace** (defined by the domains of the variables in the input specification) and **initialState** (defined by the initial condition of the input specification). These define the transition system for the input specification.

The **verify** function determines whether the given CTL formula is satisfied by the input specification by calling the **check** function. It prints the initial states that violate the formula if the CTL formula is not satisfied by the input specification.

Function **check** is the main part of the module. All computation is done within this function. There are two types of operations : evaluation of logical operators (and, or, not), and evaluation of CTL operators (EX, AX, EF, AF). It assumes that all occurrences of atomic form ulas (subformulas with no CTL operators in them) are already converted into **Symbolic** representation. Note that CTL operators that can be expressed in terms of these primitiv es are first converted into an equivalent representation (e.g. $AG(f) \equiv \neg EF(\neg f)$).

```
Symbolic TransSys::check(Node n) {
  if (n.ofType() == CTLFORMULA)
     switch n.getOperator()
       case AND: s = check(n.left).intersectWith(check(n.right)); break;
       case OR: s = check(n.left).unionWith(check(n.right)); break;
       case NOT: s = check(n.left).complement(); break;
       case NONE: s = check(n.left);
  else if (n.ofType() == CTLOPERATOR)
     s = check (n.left);
     switch n.getOperator()
       case EX:
         s.backwardImage(transRelation);
         break;
       case AX:
         s.complement();
         s.backwardImage(transRelation);
         s.complement();
         break;
       case EF:
         do
           snew = s;
           sold = s;
           snew.backwardImage(transRelation);
           s.unionWith(snew);
         while not sold.isEquals(s)
         break;
```

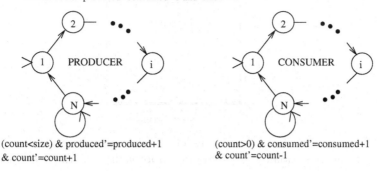

Initial: count=produced=consumed=0 and size >= 1

(count<size) & produced'=produced+1
& count'=count+1

(count>0) & consumed'=consumed+1
& count'=count-1

Fig. 4. A simple bounded-buffer producer-consumer example

```
      case AF:
        do
          snew = s;
          sold = s;
          snew.complement();
          snew.backwardImage(transRelation);
          snew.complement();
          s.backwardImage(transRelation);
          s.intersectWith(snew);
          s.unionWith(sold);
        while not sold.isEquals(s)
        break;
    else if (n.ofType() == ATOMIC)
        s = n;
    return s;
}
```

An important feature of function **check** is polymorphism. It is independent of underlying **Symbolic** type. Since each subclass of **Symbolic** implements basic functions (e.g. **intersectWith**, **backwardImage**, etc.) used, verifier does not need to know which type of representation it is working on. If we introduce a new symbolic type, we do not need to modify the verification procedure. Also, using this feature the verifier can decide which symbolic representation to use at run-time. For example given an input specification with just boolean and enumerated variables, our verifier becomes a BDD-based model checker. Hence, such specifications can be checked efficiently without introducing the cost of manipulating composite representations.

5   A Simple Example

In Fig. 4 we show a simple producer-consumer system. Both *producer* and *consumer* components have N control states. Producer produces an item only when

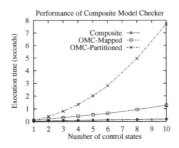

Fig. 5. Performance of composite model checker and Omega Library model checker (using partitioning or mapping approach) on the bounded-buffer producer-consumer example

it is in control state N and there is available space in the buffer (*count < size*). When it produces an item it increases *produced* and *count* by 1. Similarly, consumer consumes an item only when it is in control state N and there is an item in the buffer (*count > 0*). When it consumes an item it increases *consumed* by 1 and decreases *count* by 1. An invariant of this system is *count ≤ size ∧ produced − consumed = count*.

Initial condition for this system can be represented with the composite formula:

pstate = 1 ∧ cstate = 1 ∧ count = 0 ∧ produced = 0 ∧ consumed = 0 ∧ size >= 0

where *pstate* and *cstate* are variables introduced to model the control states of producer and consumer. Self-loop on state N for producer can be represented with the composite formula:

pstate = N ∧ pstate' = N ∧ count < size ∧ produced' = produced + 1 ∧ count' = count + 1

The overall transition relation is the disjunction of the formulas that correspond to each arc in Figure 4. (We are assuming that if a variable is not modified it preserves its value. These constraints have to be added to the composite formula before generating a `CompSym` object).

We used this example to compare the performance of our composite model checker with OMC (Omega Library Model Checker) presented in [BGP97,BGP99]. OMC uses polyhedral representations of arithmetic constraints as a symbolic representation. To represent the control states of the system given in Fig. 4 in such a tool, there are two options, 1) to partition the state space based on the control states, creating N partition classes, 2) to map the control states to an integer variable. Either option is not very efficient because of the high complexity of manipulating arithmetic constraint representations. In our composite library the control states in the above example are mapped to an enumerated variable which is encoded using BDDs. Integer variables are still encoded using the polyhedral representation, however the unnecessary mapping to integers is prevented. Fig. 5 shows the execution time of the composite model checker and the OMC (using both partitioning and integer-mapping) with the increasing number of control states for the system given in Fig. 4. Although this is a small example, it demonstrates the inefficiency of using a model checker which is solely based on polyhedral representations.

6 Conclusion and Future Work

The composite symbolic library presented in this paper can be used as a platform to integrate different symbolic representations. Using composite representations one can improve the efficiency of verification procedures by mapping each variable type in the input specification to a suitable symbolic representation.

The `Symbolic` interface provided by our tool can be useful in integrating different symbolic libraries. Once a wrapper for a symbolic library is written the internal representations of that library will be hidden. This can also help in comparing performances of different symbolic representations by isolating them from the verification procedures.

Using the composite symbolic library we were able to develop polymorphic verification procedures which are oblivious to the symbolic representation used. Hence, the decision of which symbolic representation to use can be made at run-time, based on the input specification. If the input specification has only boolean and enumerated variables, then our verifier becomes a BDD-based symbolic model checker. However, if both integer and boolean variables are present in the input specification, then it is able to use arithmetic constraints and BDDs together using the composite representation.

References

AB96.   J. M. Atlee and M. A. Buckley. A logic-model semantics for SCR software requirements. In *Proceedings of the 1996 ACM SIGSOFT International Symposium on Software Testing and Analysis*, pages 280–292, January 1996.

ACH+95.   R. Alur, C. Courcoubetis, N. Halbwachs, T. A. Henzinger, X. Nicollin P. H. Ho, A. Olivero, J. Sifakis, and S. Yovine. The algorithmic analysis of hybrid systems. *Theoretical Computer Science*, 138(1):3–34, 1995.

AG93.   J. M. Atlee and J. Gannon. State-based model checking of event-driven system requirements. *IEEE Transactions on Software Engineering*, 19(1):24–40, January 1993.

AHH96.   R. Alur, T. A. Henzinger, and P. Ho. Automatic symbolic verification of embedded systems. *IEEE Transactions on Software Engineering*, 22(3):181–201, March 1996.

BCM+90.   J. R. Burch, E. M. Clarke, K. L. McMillan, D. L. Dill, and L. H. Hwang. Symbolic model checking: 10^{20} states and beyond. In *Proceedings of the 5th Annual IEEE Symposium on Logic in Computer Science*, pages 428–439, January 1990.

BGL98.   T. Bultan, R. Gerber, and C. League. Verifying systems with integer constraints and boolean predicates: A composite approach. In *Proceedings of the 1998 ACM SIGSOFT International Symposium on Software Testing and Analysis*, pages 113–123, March 1998.

BGL⁺00a. S. Bensalem, V. Ganesh, Y. Lakhnech, C. Munoz, S. Owre, H. Rueb, J. Rushby, V. Rusu, H. Saidi, N. Shankar, E. Singerman, and A. Tiwari. An overview of SAL. In *Proceedings of the Fifth Langley Formal Methods Workshop*, June 2000.

BGL00b. T. Bultan, R. Gerber, and C. League. Composite model checking: Verification with type-specific symbolic representations. *ACM Transactions on Software Engineering and Methodology*, 9(1):3–50, January 2000.

BGP97. T. Bultan, R. Gerber, and W. Pugh. Symbolic model checking of infinite state systems using Presburger arithmetic. In O. Grumberg, editor, *Proceedings of the 9th International Conference on Computer Aided Verification*, volume 1254 of *Lecture Notes in Computer Science*, pages 400–411. Springer, June 1997.

BGP99. T. Bultan, R. Gerber, and W. Pugh. Model-checking concurrent systems with unbounded integer variables: Symbolic representations, approximations, and experimental results. *ACM Transactions on Programming Languages and Systems*, 21(4):747–789, July 1999.

Bry86. R. E. Bryant. Graph-based algorithms for boolean function manipulation. *IEEE Transactions on Computers*, 35(8):677–691, 1986.

BS00. R. Bharadwaj and S. Sims. Salsa: Combining constraint solvers with bdds for automatic invariant checking. In S. Graf and M. Schwartzbach, editors, *Proceedings of the 6th International Conference on Tools and Algorithms for the Construction and Analysis of Systems*, Lecture Notes in Computer Science, pages 378–394. Springer, April 2000.

CABN97. W. Chan, R. J. Anderson, P. Beame, and D. Notkin. Combining constraint solving and symbolic model checking for a class of systems with non-linear constraints. In O. Grumberg, editor, *Proceedings of the 9th International Conference on Computer Aided Verification*, volume 1254 of *Lecture Notes in Computer Science*, pages 316–327. Springer, June 1997.

CUD. CUDD: CU decision diagram package, http://vlsi.colorado.edu/ fabio/cudd/.

GHJV94. E. Gamma, R. Helm, R. Johnson, and J. Vlissides. *Design Patterns: Elements of Reusable Object-Oriented Software*. Addison-Wesley, Reading, Massachusetts, 1994.

HRP94. N. Halbwachs, P. Raymond, and Y. Proy. Verification of linear hybrid systems by means of convex approximations. In B. LeCharlier, editor, *Proceedings of International Symposium on Static Analysis*, volume 864 of *Lecture Notes in Computer Science*. Springer-Verlag, September 1994.

KMP⁺95. W. Kelly, V. Maslov, W. Pugh, E. Rosser, T. Shpeisman, and D. Wonnacott. The Omega library interface guide. Technical Report CS-TR-3445, Department of Computer Science, University of Maryland, College Park, March 1995.

McM93. K. L. McMillan. *Symbolic model checking*. Kluwer Academic Publishers, Massachusetts, 1993.

Ome. The Omega project, http://www.cs.umd.edu/projects/omega/.

Sai00. H. Saidi. Model checking guided abstraction and analysis. In *Proceedings of Statica Analysis Symposium*, Lecture Notes in Computer Science. Springer, 2000.

Synthesis of Linear Ranking Functions

Michael A. Colón and Henny B. Sipma*

Computer Science Department
Stanford University
Stanford, CA. 94305-9045
{colon,sipma}@cs.stanford.edu

Abstract. Deductive verification of progress properties relies on finding ranking functions to prove termination of program cycles. We present an algorithm to synthesize linear ranking functions that can establish such termination. Fundamental to our approach is the representation of systems of linear inequalities and sets of linear expressions as polyhedral cones. This representation allows us to reduce the search for linear ranking functions to the computation of polars, intersections and projections of polyhedral cones, problems which have well-known solutions.

1 Introduction

Deductive verification of reactive systems relies on finding invariants and ranking functions. While automatic generation of invariants has received much attention [GW75,KM76,BLS96,BBM97], automatic generation of ranking functions has only recently started to emerge [DGG00].

Proofs of progress properties of systems (that is, properties that the system will achieve a certain goal) involve showing that cycles on the path to the goal terminate. The classical method for establishing such termination is the use of well-founded domains together with so-called ranking functions that assign a value from these domains to each program state. Progress is then shown by demonstrating that each step in the cycle reduces the measure assigned by the ranking function. As there can be no infinite descending chain of elements of a well-founded domain, the cycle must eventually terminate. Clearly the existence of such a ranking function implies termination. Conversely, it has been proven that if a cycle terminates, a ranking function exists.

Recent years have seen great progress in automating deductive verification by improvements in decision procedures, invariant generation and automatic abstraction. However, the synthesis of ranking functions remains largely a manual task. Some heuristics have been proposed in [DGG00], but these are limited to functions that appear as expressions in the program text.

* This research was supported in part by the National Science Foundation grant CCR-99-00984-001, by ARO grant DAAG55-98-1-0471, by ARO/MURI grant DAAH04-96-1-0341, by ARPA/Army contract DABT63-96-C-0096, and by ARPA/AirForce contracts F33615-00-C-1693 and F33615-99-C-3014.

T. Margaria and W. Yi (Eds.): TACAS 2001, LNCS 2031, pp. 67–81, 2001.

In this paper we propose an algorithm that generates ranking functions for a program cycle that are linear in the program variables. The algorithm consists of three steps. First, it derives a set of linear expressions that are bounded inside the cycle from some cycle invariant. Second, it derives a set of linear expressions that decrease discretely around the cycle from the cycle's transition relation. The third step then computes the intersection of these two sets. Any expression in the intersection serves as a ranking function, and thus nonemptiness of the intersection proves termination of the cycle.

The remainder of the paper is organized as follows. Section 2 presents our computational model of transition systems, it gives some background on well-founded domains, and it introduces the running example. In Sec. 3 we introduce polyhedral cones and demonstrate that problems involving systems of linear inequalities can be reduced to problems over cones. Our algorithm is presented in Sec. 4, and its application is illustrated on the example program. In Sec. 5 we discuss a more complex application of the algorithm, and in Sec. 6 we conclude with some discussion and limitations of our approach.

2   Preliminarie s

The computational model used to describe programs is that of a *transition system* [MP95] (FTS), $\mathcal{S} = \langle V, \Theta, \mathcal{T} \rangle$, where V is a finite set of variables, Θ is an initial condition, and $\mathcal{T}$ is a finite set of transitions. A *state s* is an interpretation of V. Each transition $\tau \in \mathcal{T}$ is represented by a *transition relation* ρ_τ, an assertion that expresses the relation between the values of V in some state s and the values of V (referred to by V') in any state s' to which the system can transition by taking τ. A *run* of $\mathcal{S}$ is a sequence of states such that the first state satisfies Θ and any two consecutive states satisfy ρ_τ for some $\tau \in \mathcal{T}$. A state s is *accessible* if s appears in some run of $\mathcal{S}$. The set of all accessible states is Σ.

A *relational domain* (or just *domain*) $\langle \mathcal{D}, \succ \rangle$ is a set $\mathcal{D}$ paired with a binary relation $\succ$ on $\mathcal{D}$. A domain is said to be *well-founded* if there are no infinite sequences of elements of $\mathcal{D}$ which decrease under $\succ$. A function f is said to *map* $\langle \mathcal{D}_1, \succ_1 \rangle$ *into* $\langle \mathcal{D}_2, \succ_2 \rangle$ if f maps $\mathcal{D}_1$ into $\mathcal{D}_2$ and is monotone, that is, $f(d_1) \succ_2 f(d_2)$ for all $d_1, d_2 \in \mathcal{D}_1$ such that $d_1 \succ_1 d_2$. Notice that f maps infinite decreasing sequences in $\langle \mathcal{D}_1, \succ_1 \rangle$ to infinite decreasing sequences in $\langle \mathcal{D}_2, \succ_2 \rangle$. A *ranking function* for a domain is any function that maps it into some domain that is known to be well-founded, such as the non-negative integers with the greater-than relation. Notice that any domain for which a ranking function exists is well-founded.

Ranking functions can also be used to establish the termination of transition systems. Let $\mathcal{R} = \bigcup \{ \rho_\tau \mid \tau \in \mathcal{T} \}$ be the combined transition relation of $\mathcal{S}$. The decreasing sequences of $\langle \Sigma, \mathcal{R} \rangle$ are precisely the suffixes of runs of $\mathcal{S}$. Thus $\mathcal{S}$ has an infinite run iff the domain $\langle \Sigma, \mathcal{R} \rangle$ has an infinite decreasing sequence. Therefore the termination of $\mathcal{S}$ is equivalent to the well-foundedness of $\langle \Sigma, \mathcal{R} \rangle$, and a ranking function for $\langle \Sigma, \mathcal{R} \rangle$ certifies that $\mathcal{S}$ terminates.

Our algorithm generates ranking functions that map $\langle \Sigma, \mathcal{R} \rangle$ into the well-founded domain $\langle Rat_\Lambda, >_\Delta \rangle$ of rationals greater than some constant value Λ, with the *discretely-greater-than* relation $>_\Delta$, defined by

$$x >_\Delta y \quad \text{iff} \quad x \geq y + \Delta \ ,$$

where Δ is a positive constant.

Example

Consider the program TERMINATE, presented in Fig. 1. The expression $-i - j$ decreases by 1 with each iteration of the cycle $\{\ell_0, \ell_1, \ell_2\}$, and its value is bounded from below by $-100 - k_0$, where k_0 is the value of k upon entry into the loop. Therefore, $-i - j$ defines a ranking function for the cycle, and the program terminates.

$$
\begin{aligned}
&\textbf{local } i, j, k : \textbf{integer} \\
&\ell_0 : \textbf{while } i \leq 100 \wedge j \leq k \textbf{ do} \\
&\qquad \begin{bmatrix} \ell_1 : (i, j) := (j, i + 1) \\ \ell_2 : k := k - 1 \end{bmatrix} \\
&\ell_3 : \textbf{halt}
\end{aligned}
$$

Fig. 1. Program TERMINATE

Notice that this system is not finite-state, so termination cannot be established by model checking. In addition, the expression $-i - j$ does not appear anywhere in the program, so analytic heuristics of the form proposed in [DGG00] are unlikely to discover it. Furthermore, the expression k, which seems the most promising analytic ranking function, has no obvious lower bound. In fact, it is bounded from below by $\min(i_0, j_0)$, but it is not clear that discovering this bound is any easier than finding the expression $-i - j$.

In Sec. 4 we will demonstrate that the ranking function $-i - j$ can be generated automatically.

3   Linear Inequalities and Polyhedral Cones

Our method is inherently deductive. It reduces the synthesis of linear ranking functions to the search for linear inequalities implied by systems of inequalities extracted from the program. Essential to the method, then, is the approach used to derive such consequences.

Consider any system of linear inequalities $\alpha_{i1} x_1 + \cdots + \alpha_{id} x_d \leq 0$. Recall that the inequality $\alpha_1 x_1 + \cdots + \alpha_d x_d \leq 0$ is a *consequence* of the system iff it is satisfied by every solution of the system. Two well-known rules for deducing consequences of such systems are that any inequality can be scaled by a non-negative factor, and that any pair of inequalities can be added. These two inference rules can be combined to yield a single rule which derives any non-negative linear combination of inequalities. It is this sound and complete inference rule which motivates the treatment of linear inequalities developed here.

A vector w is a *conic combination* of vectors $v_1, \ldots, v_n$ iff $w = \Sigma_i \lambda_i v_i$ for scalars $\lambda_i \geq 0$. A *cone* is any set of vectors closed under conic combinations. Thus a cone is a (vector) space in which the linear combinations are restricted to non-negative factors. Every space is a cone since spaces are closed under negation. As the vector 0 is the conic combination of the empty set, the least cone is $\{0\}$, not $\emptyset$. The greatest cone is the set containing all vectors (of a given dimension).

It is easy to see that the intersection of two cones is again a cone. However, the union of two cones need not form a cone. This observation motivates the introduction of the following two concepts. The *conic hull* of a set of vectors V, written $Con(V)$, is the set of conic combinations of V. The *conic union* of two cones C_1, C_2, written $C_1 \uplus C_2$, is the cone $Con(C_1 \cup C_2)$. Thus the conic hull of a set is the least cone containing it, while the conic union of two cones is the least cone containing both.

A set of vectors R is called a *ray* (or *half-line*) if $R = Con(r)$ for some vector $r \neq 0$. A set of vectors L is called a *line* if $L = \mathcal{L}in(l)$ for some vector $l \neq 0$, where the *linear hull* $\mathcal{L}in(V)$ is the set of linear combinations of V. Thus a ray is a unit cone, while a line is a unit space. A pair $G = \langle L, R \rangle$ of lines L and rays R is called a *generator* of the cone C iff $C = \mathcal{L}in(L) \uplus Con(R)$. Lines are not essential components of generators. Since $\mathcal{L}in(l) = Con(l) \uplus Con(-l)$, every line can be replaced by a pair of rays in opposite directions without changing the generated cone. To simplify the theory, we assume all lines have been eliminated in this manner. In practice, however, maintaining an explicit representation of lines improves both the space and time complexity of algorithms on cones [Tel82,Wil93].

Notice that every cone has a generator, as C certainly generates itself. However, unlike spaces, some cones admit only infinite generators. Cones which do admit finite generators are said to be *polyhedral*.

Returning to linear inequalities, the inequality $\alpha_1 x_1 + \cdots + \alpha_d x_d \leq 0$ can be represented by the vector $(\alpha_1, \ldots, \alpha_d)$ of its coefficients, and the ray determined by this vector is the set of consequences of the inequality. A system of inequalities is represented by the set of its coefficient vectors, and the cone generated by these rays yields precisely the consequences of the system – a fact which we prove presently. Should the system also contain equalities, they can be represented either implicitly, as pairs of rays in opposite directions, or explicitly, as lines.

The *polar* C^* of a cone C is the set of vectors forming non-acute angles with every member of C, i.e., the set $\{u \mid u \cdot v \leq 0 \text{ for all } v \in C\}$, as illustrated in Fig. 2. The polar of a cone is itself a cone. In fact, the polar of any set of vectors is a cone, but our interest here lies in polars of cones. Polars of cones have the following properties

- $(C^*)^* \supseteq C$,
- $(C_1 \cap C_2)^* \supseteq C_1^* \uplus C_2^*$,
- $(C_1 \uplus C_2)^* = C_1^* \cap C_2^*$.

For arbitrary cones, the two inclusions cannot be strengthened to equalities. However, for polyhedral cones we have

- $(C^*)^* = C$,
- $(C_1 \cap C_2)^* = C_1^* \uplus C_2^*$.

These equalities are implied by a fundamental result, due to Weyl and Minkowski, that a cone is polyhedral iff its polar is polyhedral. Another fundamental theorem concerning polars of polyhedral cones is the following.

Theorem 1 (Alternative) *Let $G = \{r_1, \ldots, r_n\}$ be a set of vectors and r be a vector. Either i) $r \in Con(G)$ or ii) $v \cdot r > 0$ for some $v \in G^*$, but not both.*

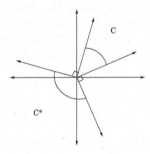

Fig. 2. A cone and its polar.

Our primary interest in polar cones is driven by the relationship they bear to solutions of systems of inequalities. A vector $(x_1, \ldots, x_d)$ is a solution of the inequality $\alpha_1 x_1 + \cdots + \alpha_d x_d \leq 0$ iff $(x_1, \ldots, x_d) \cdot (\alpha_1, \ldots, \alpha_d) \leq 0$. For a system of inequalities, the set of all solutions is precisely the polar of its set of coefficient vectors. With this observation, we are in a position to justify the soundness and completeness of the inference rule presented above.

Theorem 2 (Farkas' Lemma) *Let $\alpha_{i1} x_1 + \cdots + \alpha_{id} x_d \leq 0$ be a system of inequalities. Let $G = \{r_i\}$, where $r_i = (\alpha_{i1}, \ldots \alpha_{id})$. Then $\alpha_1 x_1 + \cdots + \alpha_d x_d \leq 0$ is a consequence of the system iff $(\alpha_1, \ldots, \alpha_d) \in Con(G)$.*

This result is easily proved using the theorem of the alternative. In the case of soundness, assume $(\alpha_1, \ldots, \alpha_d) \in Con(G)$. Then for all $(x_1, \ldots, x_d) \in G^*$, $(x_1, \ldots, x_d) \cdot (\alpha_1, \ldots, \alpha_d) \leq 0$. That is, every solution of the system satisfies the inequality. For completeness, assume $(\alpha_1, \ldots, \alpha_d) \notin Con(G)$. Then for some

$(x_1, \ldots, x_d) \in G^*$, $(x_1, \ldots, x_d) \cdot (\alpha_1, \ldots, \alpha_d) > 0$. That is, some solution of the system fails to satisfy the inequality.

Thus far, we have demonstrated that the polar of a system of linear inequalities represents its solutions. Another perspective on these polars is that they too represent systems of inequalities. In this case, the inequalities are constraints not on solutions, but on the coefficients of consequences of the original system. That is, any solution $(\alpha_1, \ldots, \alpha_d)$ of the polar is in fact the coefficient vector of an inequality implied by the original system, as $(C^*)^* = C$. This perspective on polars of systems of linear inequalities is also integral to the method for synthesizing ranking functions presented here. By computing the polar of a system, adding additional inequalities, and computing the polar of the augmented polar, the algorithm presented in Sec. 4 derives those consequences of systems which satisfy syntactic criteria sufficient to guarantee the existence of ranking functions.

To compute polars, our method uses an algorithm, known as the Double Description Method, which is based on Motzkin's constructive proof of Minkowski's theorem [MRTT53,FP96]. This algorithm constructs the generator of the polar incrementally by successively intersecting the generator of the entire space with the polar of each ray in the generator of the cone.

The algorithm also serves as the basis for implementing additional operators on cones. For two polyhedral cones C_1, C_2 such that $C_i = \mathcal{C}on(G_i) = Con(H_i)^*$,

- $C_1 \uplus C_2 = \mathcal{C}on(G_1 \cup G_2)$,
- $C_1 \cap C_2 = \mathcal{C}on(H_1 \cup H_2)^*$, and
- $C_1 \subseteq C_2$ iff $r \cdot s \leq 0$ for every $r \in G_1$ and $s \in H_2$.

Another useful operation on polyhedral cones is projection onto a space. It is performed by intersecting the cone with the space and eliminating positions that are zero in every ray of the resulting generator. When the space has a basis consisting of canonical unit vectors, we can simply eliminate those positions in the generator of the cone that are zero in every line of the basis of the space.

For a more thorough discussion of the theory of polyhedral cones, the reader is referred to [Gal60,Sch86]. Those interested in the implementation of algorithms on cones should consult [Wil93].

Inhomogeneous Inequalities

Having demonstrated the equivalence of systems of homogeneous inequalities and polyhedral cones, we turn now to inhomogeneous systems and argue that they too can be represented as polyhedral cones.

Consider an inhomogeneous system $\alpha_{i1}x_1 + \cdots + \alpha_{id}x_d + \beta_i \leq 0$. The set of solutions of such a system is no longer a polyhedral cone, but rather a polyhedral convex set. However, by the addition of a single variable χ, the solutions of an inhomogeneous system can be embedded in a polyhedral cone. To see this, consider that the inhomogeneous system is equivalent to the homogeneous system $\alpha_{i1}x_1 + \cdots + \alpha_{id}x_d + \beta_i\chi \leq 0$, along with the single inhomogeneous side condition $\chi = 1$. That is, $(x_1, \ldots, x_d)$ is a solution of the inhomogeneous system iff $(x_1, \ldots, x_d, 1)$ is a solution of its homogeneous embedding.

While the set of solutions of an inhomogeneous system is a polyhedron, not a cone, its set of consequences remains a cone. Taking conic combinations of inequalities continues to be a sound inference rule when applied to inhomogeneous systems. Furthermore, with two minor modifications, it is also complete. First, the tautology $-1 \leq 0$ must be added to the system. The need for this apparently redundant inequality can be attributed to the side condition of the homogeneous embedding. Although $\chi = 1$ cannot be represented explicitly in the embedding, it has as a consequence the homogeneous inequality $-\chi \leq 0$, which is representable, but not derivable. Therefore, this inequality must be added explicitly.

The second modification concerns unsatisfiable systems. Consider the system consisting of the single inequality $1 \leq 0$. The system is unsatisfiable, so every inequality is a consequence of it. For example, $x_i \leq 0$ is a consequence for any i. However, $x_i \leq 0$ is not a conic combination of $1 \leq 0$ and $-1 \leq 0$, where the second inequality is added for the reasons previously given. For unsatisfiable systems, the taking of conic combinations is sound, but incomplete. Care must be taken, then, to detect unsatisfiablility and to replace unsatisfiable systems with an equivalent system which generates all inequalities.

The next theorem, which we state without proof, provides a procedure for detecting unsatisfiability and shows that inferring conic combinations is sound and complete for satisfiable systems.

Theorem 3 *Let* $\alpha_{i1}x_1 + \cdots + \alpha_{id}x_d + \beta_i \leq 0$ *be a system of inequalities. Let* $r_0 = (0, \ldots, 0, -1)$, *and let* $r_i = (\alpha_{i1}, \ldots, \alpha_{id}, \beta_i)$. *Let* $G = \{r_i\}$. *The system is unsatisfiable iff* $(0, \ldots, 0, 1) \in Con(G)$. *When satisfiable,* $\alpha_1 x_1 + \cdots + \alpha_d x_d + \beta \leq 0$ *is a consequence iff* $(\alpha_1, \ldots, \alpha_d, \beta) \in Con(G)$.

Strict Inequalities

Consider now the mixed inhomogeneous system $\alpha_{i1}x_1 + \cdots + \alpha_{id}x_d + \beta_i \{<, \leq\} 0$, containing both strict and weak inequalities. The solutions of this system are embedded in the cone of solutions of the weak homogeneous system $\alpha_{i1}x_1 + \cdots + \alpha_{id}x_d + \beta_i \chi + \delta_i \epsilon \leq 0$, where δ_i is positive or zero depending on whether the ith inequality is strict or weak, along with the side conditions $\chi = 1$ and $\epsilon > 0$. That is, $(x_1, \ldots, x_d)$ is a solution of the original system iff $(x_1, \ldots x_d, 1, \epsilon)$ is a solution of its embedding for some $\epsilon > 0$.

The consequences of the mixed inhomogeneous system are the members of the cone generated by its weak homogeneous embedding, provided the embedding is augmented with two additional inequalities. First, it is necessary to add $-\chi + \epsilon \leq 0$, which is the representation of the tautology $-1 < 0$. Second, $-\epsilon \leq 0$ must also be added, as it is a representable, but not derivable consequence of the side condition $\epsilon > 0$. The presence of this second inequality guarantees that the coefficient of ϵ in any consequence of the weak system can be driven to zero.

Thus, it plays the role of the well-known inference rule for mixed systems which allows any strict inequality to be weakened.

The following theorem, a variant of which appears to have been first proved by Kuhn [Kuh56], demonstrates the soundness and completeness of this approach to mixed inhomogeneous systems.

Theorem 4 *Let* $\alpha_{i1}x_1 + \cdots + \alpha_{id}x_d + \beta_i \{<, \leq\}$ 0 *be a system of inequalities. Let* $r_{-1} = (0, \ldots, -1, 1)$, $r_0 = (0, \ldots, 0, -1)$ *and* $r_i = (\alpha_{i1}, \ldots, \alpha_{id}, \beta_i, \delta_i)$, *where* $\delta_i > 0$ *when strict and* $\delta_i = 0$ *when weak. Let* $G = \{r_i\}$. *The system is unsatisfiable iff* $(0, \ldots, 0, 1) \in Con(G)$. *When satisfiable,* $\alpha_1 x_1 + \cdots + \alpha_d x_d + \beta \{<, \leq\}$ 0 *is a consequence iff* $(\alpha_1, \ldots, \alpha_d, \beta, \delta) \in Con(G)$ *for some appropriate* δ.

Note that if our interest lies in just the weak consequences of a mixed system, we can simply treat each strict inequality as if it were weak. However, there is no generator of only the strict consequences. In fact, that set is not a cone as it is not closed under scaling by zero.

4   Generating Linear Ranking Functions

Our objective is to show that a transition system $\mathcal{S} = \langle V, \Theta, \mathcal{T} \rangle$ terminates. We do so by attempting to find a ranking function for each cycle in $\mathcal{S}$.

Let $\langle \Sigma, \mathcal{R} \rangle$ be the domain associated with $\mathcal{S}$, as described in Sec. 2, and let $\langle \Sigma^{\mathcal{A}}, \mathcal{R}^{\mathcal{A}} \rangle$ be a finite abstraction of $\langle \Sigma, \mathcal{R} \rangle$ with abstraction function $\alpha : \Sigma \mapsto \Sigma^{\mathcal{A}}$ for some finite set $\Sigma^{\mathcal{A}}$. That is, $(s_1^{\mathcal{A}}, s_2^{\mathcal{A}}) \in \mathcal{R}^{\mathcal{A}}$ iff there exists $s_1, s_2 \in \Sigma$ such that $s_1^{\mathcal{A}} = \alpha(s_1)$ and $s_2^{\mathcal{A}} = \alpha(s_2)$ and $(s_1, s_2) \in \mathcal{R}$. Thus $\Sigma^{\mathcal{A}}$ induces a finite partition on Σ. When $\Sigma^{\mathcal{A}}$ is the partition induced by the control variables of the system, $\langle \Sigma^{\mathcal{A}}, \mathcal{R}^{\mathcal{A}} \rangle$ is a called the *control flow graph* of $\langle \Sigma, \mathcal{R} \rangle$. Let $\gamma : \Sigma^{\mathcal{A}} \mapsto 2^{\Sigma}$ be the function that maps each abstract state $s^{\mathcal{A}}$ to the set of concrete states it represents, i.e., $\{s \in \Sigma \mid \alpha(s) = s^{\mathcal{A}}\}$. To show that $\langle \Sigma, \mathcal{R} \rangle$ is well-founded it suffices to show that for each cycle in $\langle \Sigma^{\mathcal{A}}, \mathcal{R}^{\mathcal{A}} \rangle$, no infinite decreasing sequence of $\langle \Sigma, \mathcal{R} \rangle$ is mapped to that cycle. This is so because any infinite decreasing sequence in $\langle \Sigma, \mathcal{R} \rangle$ is mapped to an infinite decreasing sequence in $\langle \Sigma^{\mathcal{A}}, \mathcal{R}^{\mathcal{A}} \rangle$, which must end in a cycle, as $\Sigma^{\mathcal{A}}$ is finite.

Consider an arbitrary cycle $\mathcal{C}^{\mathcal{A}} \subseteq \Sigma^{\mathcal{A}}$ of $\langle \Sigma^{\mathcal{A}}, \mathcal{R}^{\mathcal{A}} \rangle$ and let $c^{\mathcal{A}} \in \mathcal{C}^{\mathcal{A}}$ be any element of that cycle. Let $\mathcal{R}_{\mathcal{C}}^{\mathcal{A}}$ be the composition of the transition relations along the cycle from $c^{\mathcal{A}}$ back to $c^{\mathcal{A}}$. Any infinite decreasing sequence that ends in this cycle induces an infinite decreasing sequence in $\langle \{c^{\mathcal{A}}\}, \mathcal{R}_{\mathcal{C}}^{\mathcal{A}} \rangle$ and hence in $\langle \gamma(c^{\mathcal{A}}), \gamma(\mathcal{R}_{\mathcal{C}}^{\mathcal{A}}) \rangle$. Our approach to proving the well-foundedness of $\langle \Sigma, \mathcal{R} \rangle$ is to prove that for each cycle of $\langle \Sigma^{\mathcal{A}}, \mathcal{R}^{\mathcal{A}} \rangle$ there exists some element $c^{\mathcal{A}}$ such that $\langle \gamma(c^{\mathcal{A}}), \gamma(\mathcal{R}_{\mathcal{C}}^{\mathcal{A}}) \rangle$ is well-founded.

In the remainder of this section we will assume that the well-foundedness of $\langle \Sigma, \mathcal{R} \rangle$ is to be established, where Σ stands for $\gamma(c^{\mathcal{A}})$, the set of states accessible at the chosen element of the cycle, and $\mathcal{R}$ stands for $\gamma(\mathcal{R}^{\mathcal{A}})$, the transition relation around the cycle. To show that $\langle \Sigma, \mathcal{R} \rangle$ is well-founded, our algorithm attempts to generate all functions f of the form

$$f : \alpha_1 x_1 + \ldots + \alpha_d x_d,$$

that map $\langle \Sigma, \mathcal{R} \rangle$ into the well-founded domain $\langle Rat_\Lambda, >_\Delta \rangle$, for some constant Λ and positive constant Δ. The algorithm computes all functions definable as linear expressions over the rational program variables $x_1, \ldots, x_d$, which are bounded and discretely decreasing for $\langle \Sigma, \mathcal{R} \rangle$. It does so by computing approximations of the set of bounded expressions and the set of decreasing expressions and taking their intersection.

The principle behind the algorithm is the representation of these sets as polyhedral cones. Up to this point, we have demonstrated that polyhedral cones can conveniently represent systems of linear inequalities. But notice that the generator of all inequalities implied by the system is also the generator of all linear expressions that are non-positive in every solution of the system. Our algorithm exploits this observation to derive a generator of the bounded decreasing expressions for $\langle \Sigma, \mathcal{R} \rangle$ from two systems of linear inequalities – the first characterizing the set Σ and the second characterizing $\mathcal{R}$.

Computing the Cycle Invariant

The first step of the algorithm is to compute an invariant $\mathcal{I}$ characterizing Σ. For this step we assume the existence of an invariant generator that extracts an invariant for each control location from the description of the system. Furthermore we posit that the generated invariants are systems of linear inequalities, and that they are sufficiently strong. These assumptions are reasonable, given the success of the automatic invariant generation techniques proposed in [CH77].

In an effort to increase the utility of the generated invariant for computing the set of bounded expressions in the next step of the algorithm, we automatically augment the system with auxiliary variables. For each system variable, an auxiliary variable is added which assumes the value of the corresponding system variable upon entry into the cycle and which never changes in value while the computation remains within the cycle. Thus, these variables can be considered symbolic constants within the cycle.

To see the effect of such augmentation, consider again the program TERMINATE, shown in Fig. 1. An invariant for location ℓ_1 is

$$\mathcal{I}_- : \ i \leq 100 \ \wedge \ j - k \leq 0 \ .$$

This invariant bounds i from above by the constant 100, but neither j nor k is bounded. However, the augmented program, shown in Fig. 3, produces the invariant

$$\mathcal{I} : \ i \leq 100 \ \wedge \ j - k \leq 0 \ \wedge \ k - k_0 \leq 0 \ ,$$

in which i, j, and k are all bounded (since $j \leq k_0$ is a consequence of $j - k \leq 0$ and $k - k_0 \leq 0$).

Fig. 4 shows the generator of the consequences of $\mathcal{I}$, where, as explained in Sec. 3, the first ray represents the tautology $-1 < 0$, the second ray allows strict inequalities to be weakened, and the remaining rays represent the three conjuncts of the invariant.

$$i, j, k : \textbf{integer}$$
$$i_0, j_0, k_0 : \textbf{integer}$$

$$\ell_{-1} : (i_0, j_0, k_0) := (i, j, k)$$
$$\ell_0 : \textbf{while } i \le 100 \wedge j \le k \textbf{ do}$$
$$\left[\begin{array}{l} \ell_1 : (i, j) := (j, i + 1) \\ \ell_2 : k := k - 1 \end{array} \right]$$
$$\ell_3 : \textbf{halt}$$

Fig. 3. Augmented version of TERMINATE

$$G_1 : \left\{ \begin{array}{l} \quad\quad i, \quad j, \quad k, \; i_0, \; j_0, \; k_0, \quad\quad \chi, \quad \epsilon \\[4pt] r_{-1}^1 : (0, 0, \quad 0, \; 0, \; 0, \quad 0, \quad -1, \quad 1) \quad -1 < 0 \\[4pt] r_0^1 : (0, 0, \quad 0, \; 0, \; 0, \quad 0, \quad\;\; 0, -1) \quad < \to \le \\[4pt] r_1^1 : (1, 0, \quad 0, \; 0, \; 0, \quad 0, -100, \quad 0) \quad i - 100 \le 0 \\[4pt] r_2^1 : (0, 1, -1, \; 0, \; 0, \quad 0, \quad\;\; 0, \quad 0) \quad j - k \le 0 \\[4pt] r_3^1 : (0, 0, \quad 1, \; 0, \; 0, -1, \quad\;\; 0, \quad 0) \quad k - k_0 \le 0 \end{array} \right\}$$

Fig. 4. Generator of the consequences of $\mathcal{I}$

Computing the Bounded Expressions

The second step of the algorithm is to compute the generator of bounded expressions. Recall that a function $f : \Sigma \mapsto Rat$ is bounded if there exists a constant Λ such that $f(s) \ge \Lambda$ for every $s \in \Sigma$. That is, f is bounded if $-f + \Lambda \le 0$ is implied by $\mathcal{I}$, or equivalently, if $-f + \Lambda$ is in the cone generated by $\mathcal{I}$, for some constant expression Λ. The generator of negations of bounded expressions is computed by projecting $\mathcal{I}$ onto the system variables. In fact, we project $\mathcal{I}$ with the ray $(0, \ldots, 0, 1)$ added, since strictness is not relevant for establishing boundedness. We then negate this generator, using the following result.

Proposition 1 *Let $G = \{r_i\}$, where $r_i = (\alpha_{i1}, \ldots, \alpha_{id}, \delta_i)$, and $G' = \{r_i'\}$, with $r_i' = (-\alpha_{i1}, \ldots, -\alpha_{id}, \delta_i)$. Then $(\alpha_1, \ldots, \alpha_d, \delta) \in G$ iff $(-\alpha_1, \ldots, -\alpha_d, \delta) \in G'$.*

Fig. 5 presents the generator of bounded expressions for program TERMINATE.

Computing the Decreasing Expressions

The third step of the algorithm is to compute a generator of expressions that decrease discretely around the cycle. Recall that a function $f : \Sigma \mapsto Rat$ is discretely decreasing if there exists a positive constant Δ such that, for every $(s, s') \in \mathcal{R}$, $f(s) \ge f(s') + \Delta$. Thus, the discretely decreasing expressions are exactly those expressions f such that $f \ge f' + \Delta$ is implied by the transition

$$G_2 : \left\{ \begin{array}{ll} \quad\quad i, \quad j, \quad k, \epsilon & \\ l_1^2 : (0, \quad 0, \quad 0, 1) & \text{any strictness} \\ r_1^2 : (-1, \quad 0, \quad 0, 0) & -i \text{ is bounded} \\ r_2^2 : (0, -1, \quad 1, 0) & -j + k \text{ is bounded} \\ r_3^2 : (0, \quad 0, -1, 0) & -k \text{ is bounded} \end{array} \right\}$$

Fig. 5. Generator of bounded expressions

relation $\mathcal{R}$, for some positive constant Δ. Alternatively, they are those f for which $-f + f' + \Delta$ is in the cone generated by $\mathcal{R}$, with $\Delta > 0$ implied by $\mathcal{I}$.

The generator of the decreasing expressions is computed incrementally: First we transform $\mathcal{I}$ into a generator of the positive constant expressions Δ. Then we restrict $\mathcal{R}$ to generate only those expressions of the form $-f + f' + \Delta$, with Δ a constant expression. This restricted generator is then further constrained to ensure that Δ is in fact positive. This result, when projected onto the coefficients of primed system variables, yields the set of decreasing expressions.

The positive constant expressions Δ cannot be represented directly, as they do not form a cone. For example, they are not closed under scaling by zero. Therefore, we adopt the technique introduced in Sec. 3 for representing strict inequalities, and compute a generator of the non-negative constant expressions along with an indication of strictness. Now, Δ is a non-negative constant expression iff $-\Delta$ is non-positive and the coefficients of the system variables, both primed and unprimed, are zero in Δ. That is, for Δ to be a constant expression, only the auxiliary variables can have non-zero coefficients.

Recall that $\mathcal{I}$ generates the set of all non-positive expressions. So the polar of $\mathcal{I}$ is a system of constraints on the coefficients of these expressions, and every solution of the polar is the coefficient vector of some non-positive expression. Adding the equalities $\alpha_1 = 0$, ..., $\alpha_d = 0$ to the polar yields the subset of non-positive expressions in which the system variables all have zero coefficients, assuming d system variables. Thus, the polar of the augmented polar is precisely the set of non-positive constant expressions. By negating the generator of this set, we arrive at a generator of non-negative constant expressions.

Applying this transformation to the invariant $\mathcal{I}$ of TERMINATE and eliminating the system variables yields the generator shown in Fig. 6. The only positive constant expression is 1.

Next we compute the generator of that subset of the expressions generated by $\mathcal{R}$ which have the form $-f + f' + \Delta$, for some non-negative constant expression Δ. Again, this result is achieved by taking the polar of an augmented polar. First, the ray $(0, \ldots, 0, 1)$ is added to $\mathcal{R}$, and the polar of the augmented generator is computed. The strictness of the non-negativity of expressions in $\mathcal{R}$ is not relevant, and adding the ray eliminates any constraints which $\mathcal{R}$ places on δ. Next, the equalities $\alpha_1 = -\alpha_{d+1}, \ldots, \alpha_d = -\alpha_{2d}$ are added to the polar,

$$G_3 : \left\{ \begin{array}{l} \quad i_0\ j_0\ k_0\ \chi\ \epsilon \\[4pt] r_1^3 : (0,\ 0,\ 0,\ 1,\ 1) \quad 1 \text{ is positive} \\[4pt] r_2^3 : (0,\ 0,\ 0,\ 1,\ 0) \quad 1 \text{ is non-negative} \end{array} \right\}$$

Fig. 6. Generator of non-negative constant expressions.

thereby restricting its solutions to those expressions in which the coefficient of each unprimed system variable is the negation of the coefficient of the corresponding primed system variable. Finally, the system is augmented with all of the constraints on the coefficients of non-negative constant expressions. That is, we add all equalities and inequalities that result from taking the polar of the non-negative constant expressions computed earlier.

The resulting system is precisely the set of constraints satisfied by the coefficients of the expressions we seek. The vector $(\alpha_1, \ldots, \alpha_{3d}, \beta, \delta)$ is a solution of this system iff the corresponding expression has the form $-f + f' + \Delta$, where Δ is a non-negative constant expression. Furthermore, if $\delta > 0$, then Δ is positive. Taking the polar of this system and projecting the result onto the coefficients of the primed system variables and ϵ yields the generator of a set of expressions all of whose strict members are discretely decreasing.

Continuing with the program TERMINATE, the generator of the decreasing expressions is shown in Fig. 7.

$$G_4 : \left\{ \begin{array}{l} \quad i,\ j,\ k,\ \epsilon \\[4pt] l_1^4 : (1,\ 1,\ 1,\ 0) \quad i + j + k \text{ is invariant} \\[4pt] r_1^4 : (0,\ 0,\ 1,\ 1) \quad k \text{ decreases} \\[4pt] r_2^4 : (0,\ 0,\ 1,\ 0) \quad k \text{ does not increase} \end{array} \right\}$$

Fig. 7. Generator of decreasing expressions.

Computing the Ranking Functions

The final step of the algorithm intersects the bounded expressions with the decreasing expressions. Any strict member of the resulting cone is a ranking function.

The generator of the ranking functions for TERMINATE is shown in Fig. 8. Thus $-i - j + k$ is a ranking function. Notice that $-i - j$ is also a ranking function, since $\frac{1}{2}r_1^5 + \frac{1}{2}r_2^5 = (-1, -1, 0, 1)$ is a strict member of the generated cone.

$$G_5 : \left\{ \begin{array}{lll} & i, \quad j, \quad k, \epsilon & \\ r_1^5 : (-1, -1, -1, 0) & -i - j - k \text{ weakly} \\ r_2^5 : (-1, -1, \quad 1, 2) & -i - j + k \text{ strictly} \\ r_3^5 : (-1, -1, \quad 1, 0) & -i - j + k \text{ weakly} \end{array} \right\}$$

Fig. 8. Generator of ranking functions.

5   Application

W e applied our algorithm to a system modeling the biological mec hanism of lateral inhibition in cells, brought to our attention by Ronojoy and Tomlin [RT00]. Lateral inhibition, a mechanism extensively studied in biology [CMML96], causes a group of initially equivalent cells to differentiate. It is based on an intra- and intercellular feedback mechanism, whereby a cell developing into one type inhibits its neighbors from developing into the same type. The result is a more or less regular pattern of cells of different types.

In collaboration with David Dill, we abstracted the (continuous) model of differentiation of skin cells described in [CMML96] and [RT00] into a discrete transition system. The system consists of a planar hexagonal configuration of cells. Cells can be black, white or gray, where black and white cells, if stable, lead to specialization into ciliated and unciliated cells, respectively. Cells transition based on their own color and the colors of their six imm ediate neighbors. Therefore we define the state of a cell by the two variables $color \in \{w, g, b\}$ and $ncolor \in \{W, G, B\}$, where the value of $ncolor$ is determined as follows:

$$\begin{array}{ll} W : & \forall i.(n_i = white \lor n_i = gray) \land \exists i.(n_i = white) \\ G : & \forall i.(n_i = gray) \\ B : & \exists i.(n_i = black) \end{array}$$

with n_i the neighbor cells. The transitions of a cell can then be described by

$$\begin{array}{lll} \tau_1 : w \land W \land g' & \tau_2 : g \land W \land b' & \tau_3 : g \land G \land (b' \lor w') \\ \tau_4 : b \land B \land g' & \tau_5 : g \land B \land w' \end{array}$$

The objective is to prove that this system, like its biological counterpart, stabilizes for an arbitrary num ber of cells. To do so we attempt to find a ranking function F for the entire plane of cells $\mathcal{C}$. We assume F has the form

$$F = \Sigma_{c \in \mathcal{C}} f(c) \ ,$$

where $f(c)$ is the measure of a single cell. To show that F is a ranking function, it is sufficient to show that its value decreases whenever any cell c transitions. Let c be an arbitrary cell. W e can write F as $F = G_c + H_c$ with

$$G_c = f(c) + \Sigma_{i=1}^6 f(n_i(c)) \quad \text{and} \quad H_c = \Sigma_{d \in \mathcal{C} \setminus \{c, n_1(c) \ldots n_6(c)\}} f(d) \ .$$

To show that F is decreased by every transition of c, it is sufficient to show that G_c is decreased by every transition of c, as transitions of c can affect only the state of c and the state of c's neighbors, so H_c is unaffected. Thus it suffices to consider a group of seven cells (c and its six neighbors) and determine whether a function f exists such that G_c is a ranking function.

Capitalizing on the symmetry in the description, we take as variables the nine states in which a cell and its neighbors can be: $\mathcal{N}_{wW}$, $\mathcal{N}_{wG}$, $\mathcal{N}_{wB}$, $\mathcal{N}_{gW}$, $\mathcal{N}_{gG}$, $\mathcal{N}_{gB}$, $\mathcal{N}_{bW}$, $\mathcal{N}_{bG}$, $\mathcal{N}_{bB}$, with each variable denoting the number of cells among the seven with that configuration, also taking into consideration the colors of the neighbors of the neighbors. For example, if the set consists of a black center cell with six white neighbors, then $\mathcal{N}_{bW} = 1$, $\mathcal{N}_{wB} = 6$ and all other variables are zero[1].

Applying the algorithm to the transition system leads to the following ranking function:

$$24\mathcal{N}_{bB} + 6\mathcal{N}_{wW} + 4\mathcal{N}_{wG} + 5\left(\mathcal{N}_{gW} + \mathcal{N}_{gG} + \mathcal{N}_{gB}\right)$$

This ranking function was found earlier by Dill [Dil00] using an ILP solver. From this ranking function we can conclude that with

$$f(c) = \begin{cases} 24 & \text{if } color = b \text{ and } ncolor = B \\ 6 & \text{if } color = w \text{ and } ncolor = W \\ 4 & \text{if } color = w \text{ and } ncolor = G \\ 5 & \text{if } color = g \\ 0 & \text{otherwise} \end{cases}$$

the function F is a ranking function for the entire plane of cells.

6   Conclusions

We have implemented our algorithm using the polyhedral cone library in the invariant generator of the Stanford Temporal Prover [BBC+95]. Our experience thus far is that simple systems are easily handled, but systems with complex transition relations often exhaust the available memory before a ranking function can be found. This is to be expected, as the library, based on the Double Description Method, represents each cone dually, i.e., by its generator and the generator of its polar. The generator of the polar, however, can be exponentially larger than the generator of the cone [McM70]. We are currently investigating an implementation of our method that avoids this explosion in space by maintaining parametric representations of cones, rather than computing polars explicitly.

Assuming a space-efficient implementation is possible, the method, as presented thus far, might still fail to find a ranking function when one exists. This incompleteness is due to the fact that the required bounds may not be linear expressions in the (auxiliary) variables. Future work includes finding a characterization of the class of systems for which our method is complete.

---

[1]   In this configuration the values of the variables are independent of the colors of the neighbors of the neighbors. In general however, the variables are dependent on them.

References

BBC+95.   Nikolaj S. Bjørner, Anca Browne, Eddie S. Chang, Michael Colón, Arjun Kapur, Zohar Manna, Henny B. Sipma, and Tomás E. Uribe. STeP: The Stanford Temporal Prover, User's Manual. Technical Report STAN-CS-TR-95-1562, Computer Science Department, Stanford University, 1995.

BBM97.   Nikolaj S. Bjørner, Anca Browne, and Zohar Manna. Automatic generation of invariants and intermediate assertions. *Theoretical Computer Science*, 173(1):49–87, 1997.

BLS96.   Saddek Bensalem, Yassine Lakhnech, and Hassen Saidi. Powerful techniques for the automatic generation of invariants. In Rajeev Alur and Thomas A. Henzinger, editors, *CAV'96*, volume 1102 of *LNCS*, pages 323–335. Springer-Verlag, 1996.

CH77.   Patrick Cousot and Nicolas Halbwachs. Automatic discovery of linear restraints among variables of a program. In *4th A.C.M. Symposium on Principles of Programming Languages*, 1977.

CMML96.   Joanne R. Collier, Nicholas A.M. Monk, Philip K. Maini, and Julian H. Lewis. Pattern formation by lateral inhibition with feedback: a mathematical model of delta-notch intercellular signalling. *J. Theoretical. Biology*, 183:429–446, 1996.

DGG00.   Dennis Dams, Rob Gerth, and Orna Grumberg. A heuristic for the automatic generation of ranking functions. In *Workshop on Advances in Verification (WAVe'00)*, pages 1–8, 2000.

Dil00.   David Dill. personal communication. August 2000.

FP96.   Komei Fukuda and Alain Prodon. Double description method revisited. In *Combinatorics and Computer Science*. 1996.

Gal60.   David Gale. *The Theory of Linear Economic Models*. McGraw Hill, 1960.

GW75.   Steven M. German and B. Wegbreit. A Synthesizer of Inductive Assertions. *IEEE transactions on Software Engineering*, 1(1):68–75, March 1975.

KM76.   Shmuel Katz and Zohar Manna. Logical analysis of programs. *Communications of the ACM*, 19(4):188–206, April 1976.

Kuh56.   H. W. Kuhn. Solvability and consistency for linear equations and inequalities. *American Mathematics Monthly*, 63, 1956.

McM70.   P. McMullen. The maximum numbers of faces of a convex polytope. *Mathematika*, 17(4):179–184, 1970.

MP95.   Zohar Manna and Amir Pnueli. *Temporal Verification of Reactive Systems: Safety*. Springer-Verlag, New York, 1995.

MRTT53.   T.S. Motzkin, H. Raiffa, G. L. Thompson, and R. M. Thrall. The double description method. In H. W. Kuhn and A. W. Tucker, editors, *Contributions to the Theory of Games II*. Princeton University Press, 1953.

RT00.   Gosh Ronojoy and Claire Tomlin. Lateral inhibition through delta-notch signaling. a piecewise affine hybrid model. Technical report, Stanford University, 2000.

Sch86.   Alexander Schrijver. *Theory of Linear and Integer Programming*. Wiley, 1986.

Tel82.   J. Telgen. Minimal representation of convex polyhedral sets. *Journal of Optimization Theory and Application*, 38:1–24, 1982.

Wil93.   Doran K. Wilde. A library for doing polyhedral operations. Technical report, IRISA, 1993.

Automatic Deductive Verification with Invisible Invariants*

Amir Pnueli[1], Sitvanit Ruah[1], and Lenore Zuck[2]

[1] Dept. of Computer Science, Weizmann Institute of Science, Rehovot, Israel,
{amir,sitvanit}@wisdom.weizmann.ac.il
[2] Dept. of Computer Science, New York University, New York,
zuck@cs.nyu.edu

Abstract. The paper presents a method for the automatic verification of a certain class of parameterized systems. These are *bounded-data* systems consisting of N processes (N being the parameter), where each process is finite-state. First, we show that if we use the standard deductive INV rule for proving invariance properties, then all the generated verification conditions can be automatically resolved by finite-state (BDD-based) methods with no need for interactive theorem proving.

Next, we show how to use model-checking techniques over finite (and small) instances of the parameterized system in order to derive candidates for invariant assertions. Combining this automatic computation of invariants with the previously mentioned resolution of the VCs (verification conditions) yields a (necessarily) incomplete but fully automatic sound method for verifying bounded-data parameterized systems. The generated invariants can be transferred to the VC-validation phase without ever been examined by the user, which explains why we refer to them as "invisible".

We illustrate the method on a non-trivial example of a cache protocol, provided by Steve German.

1 Introduction

Automatic verification of infinite state systems in general, and parameterized systems in particular, have been the focus of much research recently (see, e.g., [ES96,ES97,CFJ96,GS97,ID96,LS97,RKR+00].) Most of this research concentrates on *model checking* techniques for verification of such systems, using symmetry reduction and similar methods to make model checking more tractable.

In this paper we present a method for the automatic verification of a certain class of parameterized systems using a deductive approach. The parameterized systems we study are *bounded-data* systems consisting of N processes (N being the parameter), where each process is finite-state and the number of its states is independent of N. We first show that for a large and interesting set of assertions, called *R-assertions*, there is a number, N_0, such that the verification condition

---

* This research was supported in part by the Minerva Center for Verification of Reactive Systems, a gift from Intel, a grant from the German - Israel Foundation for Scientific Research and Development, and ONR grant N00014-99-1-0131.

T. Margaria and W. Yi (Eds.): TACAS 2001, LNCS 2031, pp. 82–97, 2001.

claiming that an R-assertion φ is preserved by any step of the system is valid for every $N > 1$ iff it is valid for every $N \leq N_0$. Thus, to check for validity of such verification conditions, it suffices to consider only parameterized systems with up to N_0 processes. The number N_0 is small. In fact, it is linear in the number of the local state variables of an individual process (i.e. logarithmic in the number of local states of a single process).

Using the standard deductive INV rule for proving invariance properties, all the generated verification conditions for the systems we are considering are R-assertions. Thus, for these systems, verification of invariance properties using INV can be automatically resolved by finite-state (BDD-based) methods, with no need for interactive theorem proving.

We also show how to use model-checking techniques over finite (N_0-process) instances of the parameterized system in order to derive candidates for invariant assertions. The combination of this automatic computation of invariants with the previously mentioned resolution of the verification conditions (VCs) yields a (necessarily) incomplete but fully automatic sound method for verifying bounded-data parameterized systems. The generated invariants can be transferred to the VC-validation phase without ever been examined by the user, which explains why we refer to them as "invisible".

We illustrate the method on a non-trivial example of a cache protocol, provided by Steve German. In this example, N client processes may request shared or exclusive access to a shared cache line. A *Home* process coordinates the cache access. Using our approach, we managed to automatically verify the property of *coherence* by which, if one process has an exclusive access to the cache line, then no other process may have any access right to the same line, even a shared one. We verified this property for any $N > 1$ using only the instance of $N = 4$.

Related Work

The problem of uniform verification of parameterized systems is, in general, undecidable [AK86]. There are two possible remedies to this situation: either we should look for restricted families of parameterized systems for which the problem becomes decidable, or devise methods which are sound but, necessarily incomplete, and hope that the system of interest will yield to one of these methods.

Among the representatives of the first approach we can count the work of German and Sistla [SG92] which assumes a parameterized system where processes communicate synchronously, and shows how to verify single-index properties. Similarly, Emerson and Namjoshi [EN96] proved a PSPACE complete algorithm for verification of synchronously communicating processes. Many of these methods fail when we move to asynchronous systems where processes communicate by shared variables.

Perhaps the most advanced of this approach is the paper [EK00] which considers a general parameterized system allowing several different classes of processes. However, this work provides separate algorithms for the cases that the guards are either all disjunctive or all conjunctive. A protocol such as the cache example we consider in Section 6 which contains some disjunctive and some conjunctive guards, cannot be handled by the methods of [EK00].

The sound but incomplete methods include methods based on explicit induction ([EN95]) network invariants, which can be viewed as implicit induction ([KM95], [WL89], [HLR92], [LHR97]), methods that can be viewed as abstraction and approximation of network invariants ([BCG86], [SG89], [CGJ95], [KP00]), and other methods that can be viewed as based on abstraction ([ID96]). The papers in [CR99a,CR99b,CR00] use structural induction based on the notion of a network invariant but significantly enhance its range of applicability by using a generalization of the data-independence approach which provides a powerful abstraction capability, allowing it to handle network with parameterized topologies. Most of these methods require the user to provide auxiliary constructs, such as a network invariant or an abstraction mapping. Other attempts to verify parameterized protocols such as Burn's protocol [JL98] and Szymanski's algorithm [GZ98,MAB+94,MP90] relied on abstraction functions or lemmas provided by the user. The work in [LS97] deals with the verification of safety properties of parameterized networks by abstracting the behavior of the system. PVS ([SOR93]) is used to discharge the generated VCs.

Among the automatic incomplete approaches, we should mention the methods relying on "regular model-checking" [KMM+97,ABJN99,JN00,PS00], where a class of systems which include our bounded-data systems as a special case is analyzed representing linear configurations of processes as a word in a regular language. Unfortunately, many of the systems analyzed by this method cause the analysis procedure to diverge and special *acceleration* procedures have to be applied which, again, requires user ingenuity and intervention.

The works in [ES96,ES97,CFJ96,GS97] study symmetry reduction in order to deal with state explosion. The work in [ID96] detects symmetries by inspection of the system description. Perhaps the closest in spirit to our work is the work of McMillan on compositional model-checking (e.g. [McM98]), which combines automatic abstraction with finite-instantiation due to symmetry. What started our research was the observation that, compared to fully deductive verification, McMillan's method requires significantly fewer auxiliary invariants, usually down to 2 auxiliary lemmas. Our explanation for this phenomenon was that, by performing model-checking instead of the usual one-step induction, his model-checker computes many of the necessary auxiliary invariants automatically. This led us to the conjecture that we can compute the full invariant characterizing the reachable states automatically by considering just a few processes, and then abstract and generalize it automatically to any number of processes, which is the basis for our method.

2   Bounded-Data Parameterized Systems

We consider systems whose variables can be declared as follows:

$$V = \begin{cases} N & : \textbf{natural where } N > 1 \\ x_1, \ldots, x_a & : \textbf{boolean} \\ y_1, \ldots, y_b & : [1..N] \\ z_1, \ldots, z_c & : \textbf{array } [1..N] \textbf{ of boolean} \end{cases}$$

Variable N is the system's parameter which, with no loss of generality, we assume to be bigger than 1. Note that we do not allow parameterized arrays whose elements range over $[1..N]$. Such data types will take us beyond the scope of bounded-data parameterized systems. We can easily extend the data-type restrictions to allow arbitrary finite types instead of just booleans. Thus, we could allow an z_r to be a parameterized array of any finite type, and let a x_r range over such a type.

We refer to the set of variables $\{y_1, \ldots, y_b\}$ as Y. In addition to the system variables, we also use a set of auxiliary variables $Aux = \{i, j, h, t, u \ldots : [1..N]\}$. We refer to the variables in $Y \cup Aux$, that range over the parametric domain $[1..N]$, as *Par-variables*. We define a class of assertions, to which we refer as R-assertions, as follows:

- x_s, $z_r[h]$, and $h = t$ are R-assertions, for $s = 1, \ldots, a$, every *Par*-variables h and t, and $r = 1, \ldots, c$. For the extended case that z_r is an array over the finite domain D_r, we also allow the atomic assertion $z_r[h] = d$ for every constant $d \in D_r$.

- If p and q are R-assertions, then so are $\neg p$, $p \vee q$, and $\exists h : p$, for every $h \in Aux$.

The other boolean operations and universal quantification can be defined using the existing operators and negation. We write $p(h)$, $q(h, t)$, to denote that the only auxiliary variables to which p (respectively q) may refer are h (respectively h, t). An R-assertion p is said to be *closed* if it contains no free occurrence of an auxiliary variable.

A *bounded-data discrete system* (BDS) $S = \langle V, \Theta, \rho \rangle$ consists of

- V – A set of *system variables*, as described above. A *state* of the system S provides a type-consistent interpretation of the system variables V. For a state s and a system variable $v \in V$, we denote by $s[v]$ the value assigned to v by the state s. Let Σ denote the set of states over V.

- $\Theta(V)$ – The *initial condition*. An R-assertion characterizing the initial states.

- $\rho(V, V')$ – The *transition relation*. An R-assertion, relating the values V of the variables in state $s \in \Sigma$ to the values V' in an S-successor state $s' \in \Sigma$.

We require that ρ has the special form

$$\rho = \exists h : \bigvee_{\ell = 1, \ldots, M} p_\ell(h) \wedge \forall t : q_\ell(h, t),$$

where $h, t \in Aux$, and $p_\ell(h)$, $q_\ell(h, t)$ are quantifier-free R-assertions which may refer to both V and V'.

Typically, a bounded-data parameterized system is a parallel composition $H \parallel P[1] \parallel \cdots \parallel P[N]$. The R-assertion $p_\ell(h)$ often describes the local effect of taking a transition τ_ℓ within process $P[h]$, while $q_\ell(h, t)$ describes the effect of this transition on all other processes. Usually, $q_\ell(h, t)$ will say that the local variables of all processes $P[t]$, for $t \neq h$, are preserved under a step of process $P[h]$. Note that a state s of a bounded-data system should also interpret the parameter N. We refer to $s[N]$ as the *size* of the global state s.

Since in this paper we only consider the verification of invariance properties, we omitted from the definition of a BDS the components that relate to fairness.

When w e will work on the extension of these methods to liveness, we will add
the relevant fairness components.

To illustrate the representation of a parameterized system as a BDS, consider
program MUX-SEM, presented in Fig. 1. The semaphore instructions "**request** x"
and "**release** x" appearing in the program stand, respectively, for

$\langle$**when** $x = 1$ **do** $x := 0 \rangle$ and $x := 1$

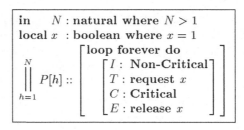

Fig. 1. Program MUX-SEM

In Fig. 2, we present the BDS which corresponds to program MUX-SEM. Note
that the BDS standardly contains the additional system array variable $\pi[1..N]$,
which represents the program counter in each of the processes.

$$
\begin{aligned}
&V : \begin{cases} N : \textbf{natural where } N > 1 \\ x : \textbf{ boolean where } x = 1 \\ \pi : \textbf{ array } [1..N] \textbf{ of } \{I, T, C, E\} \end{cases} \\[2mm]
&\Theta : x \ \wedge \ \forall h : [1..N] : \pi[h] = I \\[2mm]
&\rho : \ \exists h : [1..N] \left(\begin{array}{l} \pi'[h] = \pi[h] \ \wedge \ x' = x \\ \vee \ \pi[h] = I \ \wedge \ \pi'[h] = T \ \wedge \ x' = x \\ \vee \ \pi[h] = T \ \wedge \ x = 1 \ \wedge \ \pi'[h] = C \ \wedge \ x' = 0 \\ \vee \ \pi[h] = C \ \wedge \ \pi'[h] = E \ \wedge \ x' = x \\ \vee \ \pi[h] = E \ \wedge \ \pi'[h] = I \ \wedge \ x' = 1 \end{array} \right) \ \wedge \ \forall t \neq h : \pi'[t] = \pi[t]
\end{aligned}
$$

Fig. 2. The BDS corresponding to program MUX-SEM.

A computation of the BDS $S = \langle V, \Theta, \rho \rangle$ is an infinite sequence of states
$\sigma : s_0, s_1, s_2, ...$, satisfying the requirements:

- *Initiality* — s_0 is initial, i.e., $s_0 \models \Theta$.
- *Consecution* — For each $\ell = 0, 1, ...$, the state $s_{\ell+1}$ is a S-successor of s_ℓ.
  That is, $\langle s_\ell, s_{\ell+1} \rangle \models \rho(V, V')$ where, for each $v \in V$, we interpret v as $s_\ell[v]$
  and v' as $s_{\ell+1}[v]$.

The definitions of R-assertions and BDS are such that the only tests applied
to *Par*-variables are equalities (and disequalities). Consequently, states, computations, and satisfaction of R-assertions are all *symmetric* with respect to an
arbitrary permutation of indices. Consider the system instance $S(N_0)$, i.e., an
instance of the system in which N has the value N_0. Let $\Pi : [1..N_0] \to [1..N_0]$
be a permutation on the indices $[1..N_0]$. We say that the state $\widetilde{s}$ is a Π-variant
of s, denoted $\widetilde{s} = s[\Pi]$ if the following holds:

- $\widetilde{x}_r = x_r$, for every $r \in [1..a]$.
- $\widetilde{y}_r = \Pi^{-1}(y_r)$, for every $r \in [1..b]$.
- $\widetilde{z}_r[h] = z_r[\Pi(h)]$, for every $r \in [1..c]$, $h \in [1..N_0]$.

where, we write $\widetilde{v}$ to denote the value of $v \in V$ in $\widetilde{s}$, while writing simply v denotes the value of this variable in state s.

For example, applying the permutation

$$\Pi : 1 \to 2, \ 2 \to 3, \ 3 \to 1$$

to the state

$$s : \langle z[1] : 10, \ z[2] : 20, \ z[3] : 30; \ y_1 : 1; \ y_2 : 2 \rangle$$

yields the state

$$\widetilde{s} : \langle z[1] : 20, \ z[2] : 30, \ z[3] : 10; \ y_1 : 3; \ y_2 : 1 \rangle$$

Given an infinite state sequence, $\sigma : s_0, s_1, \ldots$ and a permutation Π, we define the Π-variant of σ, denoted $\sigma[\Pi]$ to be the state sequence $\sigma[\Pi] = s_0[\Pi], s_1[\Pi], \ldots$. The following claim makes the statement of symmetry precise.

Claim (Statement of Symmetry). Let $S = \langle V, \Theta, \rho \rangle$ be a BDS, and Π be a permutation with finite domain. Then

- For a closed R-assertion p and a state s, $s \models p$ iff $s[\Pi] \models p$. This leads to the following consequences:
- State $s \models \Theta$ is iff $s[\Pi] \models \Theta$.
- State s_2 is a ρ-successor of s_1 iff $s_2[\Pi]$ is a ρ-successor of $s_1[\Pi]$.
- $\sigma : s_0, s_1, \ldots$ is a computation of S iff $\sigma[\Pi]$ is a computation of S.

From now on, we will refer to R-assertions simply as assertions.

3 Verification Methods

In this section we will briefly survey the two main approaches to verification: Enumeration and Deduction. Both establish a property of the type $S \models \Box p$ for an assertion p.

3.1 The Method of Enumeration: Model Checking

For an assertion $p = p(V)$ and transition relation $\rho = \rho(V, V')$, we define the ρ-*postcondition* of p, denoted by $p \diamond \rho$, by the formula

$$p \diamond \rho = unprime(\exists V : p(V) \ \wedge \ \rho(V, V'))$$

The operation *unprime* is the syntactic replacement of each primed occurrence v' by its unprimed version v.

We can also define the iterated computation of postconditions:

$$p \diamond \rho^* = p \ \vee \ p \diamond \rho \ \vee \ (p \diamond \rho) \diamond \rho \ \vee \ ((p \diamond \rho) \diamond \rho) \diamond \rho \ \vee \ \cdots,$$

which, for finite-state systems, is guaranteed to terminate. Using this concise notation, verification by model checking can be summarized by the following claim:

Claim (Model Checking). Let $S = \langle V, \Theta, \rho \rangle$ be a finite-state system and p an assertion. Then, $S \models \Box p$ iff the implication

$$\Theta \diamond \rho^* \ \to \ p$$

is valid.

3.2   Deductive Verification: The Invariance Rule

Assume that we wish to prove that assertion p is an invariant of system S. The method of deductive verification suggests that the user comes up with an auxiliary assertion φ, intended to be an over-approximation of the set of reachable states, and then show that φ implies p. This can be summarized by rule INV, presented in Fig. 3.

$$
\begin{array}{ll}
\text{I1.} & \Theta \;\rightarrow\; \varphi \\
\text{I2.} & \varphi \wedge \rho \;\rightarrow\; \varphi' \\
\text{I3.} & \varphi \;\rightarrow\; p \\
\hline
& \Box\, p
\end{array}
$$

Fig. 3. The invariance Rule INV.

An assertion φ satisfying premises I1 and I2 is called *inductive*. An inductive assertion is always an over-approximation of the set of reachable states. Premise I3 ensures that assertion φ is a *strengthening* (under-approximation) of the property p. In rare cases, the original assertion p is already inductive. In all other cases, the deductive verifier has to perform the following tasks:

T1. Divine (invent) the auxiliary assertion φ.
T2. Establish the validity of premises I1–I3.

For the case that the system S is finite-state all the assertions can be represented by BDD's. Validity of these premises can then be checked by computing the BDD of their negations, and checking that it equals 0 (false). For the case that S is not a finite-state system, for example, if it is a BDS, one traditionally uses interactive theorem provers such as PVS [SOR93] and STeP [MAB+94].

Performing interactive first-order verification of implications such as the premises of rule INV for any non-trivial system is never an easy task. Neither is it a one-time task, since the process of developing the auxiliary invariants requires iterative verification trials, where failed efforts lead to correction of the previous candidate assertion into a new candidate. Therefore, our first efforts were directed towards the development of methods which will enable establishing the validity of the premises of Rule INV for bounded-data parameterized systems in a fully automated manner.

4   Deciding the Verification Conditions

In this section, we outline a decision procedure for establishing the validity of the verification conditions generated by rule INV for bounded-data parameterized systems. Consider first the case that the auxiliary assertion φ has the form $\varphi = \forall i : \psi(i)$, where $\psi(i)$ is a quantifier-free (R-)assertion. The most complex verification condition is premise I2 which can be written as:

$$
(\forall j : \psi(j)) \;\wedge\; (\exists h : \bigvee_{\ell = 1, \ldots, M} p_\ell(h) \;\wedge\; \forall t : q_\ell(h, t)) \;\rightarrow\; \forall i : \psi'(i) \tag{1}
$$

The following claim states that, for a bounded-data parameterized system $S(N)$, condition (1) can be decided by establishing it over finitely (and not too) many instances of $S(N)$.

Claim. Let $S(N)$ be a bounded-data parameterized system. Then, the implication (1) is valid over $S(N)$ for all $N > 1$ iff it is valid over $S(N)$ for all N, $1 < N \leq 2b + 2$, where b is the size of Y.

For example, the claim states that it is sufficient to check the premises of rule INV over MUX-SEM(2) in order to establish their validity over all instances of MUX-SEM(N).

Proof: (Sketch)   Let $N_0 = 2 + 2b$. To prove the claim, it is sufficient to show that the negation of condition (1), given by

$$(\forall j : \psi(j)) \wedge (\exists h : \bigvee_{\ell=1,\ldots,M} p_\ell(h) \wedge \forall t : q_\ell(h,t)) \wedge \exists i : \neg\psi'(i) \tag{2}$$

is satisfiable for some $N > 1$ iff it is satisfiable for some $1 < N \leq N_0$. Clearly, formula (2) is satisfiable iff the formula

$$(\forall j : \psi(j)) \wedge \bigvee_{\ell=1,\ldots,M} (p_\ell(h) \wedge \forall t : q_\ell(h,t)) \wedge \neg\psi'(i) \tag{3}$$

is satisfiable. It suffices to show that if formula (3) is satisfiable over a state (pair) of size $N > N_0$, it is also satisfiable over a state (pair) of size N_0.

Let s be a state of size $N_1 > N_0$ which satisfies assertion (3). The states s assigns to the variables $V_{aug} = \{h, i, y_1, y_1', \ldots, y_b, y_b'\}$ values in the domain $[1..N_1]$. Let $\alpha \leq N_0$ be the number of the *different* values assigned to those variables, and assume these values are $v_1 < v_2 < \cdots < v_\alpha$. There obviously exists a permutation Π on $[1..N_1]$ such that $\Pi^{-1}[v_k] = k$ for every $k = 1, \ldots, \alpha$. Let $\tilde{s}$ be the Π-variant of s, applying the permutation-induced transformation described in Section 2 to the augmented set of state variables $V_{aug} = V \cup \{h, i\}$. The size of $\tilde{s}$ is N_1, and, according to Claim 2, it satisfies assertion (3), which is a closed assertion relative to the augmented variable set $V \cup \{h, i\}$.

We proceed to show how to derive a new state $\hat{s}$ of size $\alpha \leq N_0$ which also satisfies assertion (3). The state $\hat{s}$ is defined by letting $\tilde{s}[N] = \alpha$ and letting $\hat{s}$ and $\tilde{s}$ agree on the interpretation of the variables in $h, i, y_1, y_1', \ldots, y_b, y_b', x_1, x_1', \ldots, x_a, x_a'$. For the remaining variables (the z_r's), we let $\hat{s}$ and $\tilde{s}$ agree on the interpretation of every variable $z_r[k]$ and $z_r'[k]$ where $r \in [1..c]$ and $k \leq \alpha$.

It remains to show that if $\tilde{s}$ satisfies the N_1-version of assertion (3) then $\hat{s}$ satisfies the α-version of assertion (3), where the assertions are

$$(\bigwedge_{j=1}^{N_1} \psi(j)) \wedge \bigvee_{\ell=1,\ldots,M} (p_\ell(h) \wedge \bigwedge_{t=1}^{N_1} q_\ell(h,t)) \wedge \neg\psi'(i), \tag{4}$$

and

$$(\bigwedge_{j=1}^{\alpha} \psi(j)) \wedge \bigvee_{\ell=1,\ldots,M} (p_\ell(h) \wedge \bigwedge_{t=1}^{\alpha} q_\ell(h,t)) \wedge \neg\psi'(i) \tag{5}$$

respectively.

Since the difference between the two assertions is that the conjunctions in assertion (5) extend only over the $[1..\alpha]$ subrange of the conjunctions in assertion

(4), and since $\hat{s}$ and $\tilde{s}$ agree on the interpretation of variables in this subrange, we conclude that $\hat{s}$ satisfies assertion (5). ◢

Claim 4 can be extended in several different ways. For example, we can trivially modify it to establish that premises I1 and I3 of Rule INV can also be checked only for systems of size not exceeding $2b+2$. Another useful modification applies to the case of *Par*-deterministic systems. A bounded-data system is said to be *Par-deterministic* if, for every *Par*-variable y_r and every disjunct $p_\ell(h)$ of the transition relation, $p_\ell(h)$ contains a conjunct of the form $y'_r = u$ for some unprimed *Par*-variable u. Recall that the bound of $2b + 2$ was derived in order to cover the possibility that $h, i, y_1, y'_1, \ldots, y_b, y'_b$ may all assume disjoint values. Under a *Par*-deterministic transition relation, all the primed variables must assume values that are equal to the values of some unprimed variables. Therefore, the set of variables $h, i, y_1, y'_1, \ldots, y_b, y'_b$ can assume at most $b + 2$ distinct values. This leads to the following corollary:

Corollary 1. *Let $S(N)$ be a Par-deterministic BDS. Then, the premises of rule INV are valid over $S(N)$ for all $N > 1$ iff they are valid over $S(N)$ for all N, $1 < N \leq b+2$.*

The last extension considers the case that both the property p to be proven and the auxiliary invariant φ have the form $\forall h, t : \psi(h, t)$ for some quantifier-free (R-)assertion ψ.

Corollary 2. *Let $S(N)$ be a bounded-data parameterized system, and let p and φ both have the form $\forall h, t : \psi(h, t)$. Then, the premises of rule INV are valid over $S(N)$ for all $N > 1$ iff they are valid over $S(N)$ for all N, $1 < N \leq 2b+3$. In the case that $S(N)$ is Par-deterministic, it is sufficient to check the premises for $N \leq b + 3$.*

5   Automatic Calculation of the Auxiliary Invariants

Providing a decision procedure for the premises of rule INV greatly simplifies the process of deductive verification. Yet, it still leaves open the task of inventing the strengthening assertion φ. As illustrated in the next section, this strengthening assertion may become quite complex for all but the simplest systems.

Here we propose a heuristic for an algorithmic construction of an inductive assertion for a given bounded-data parameterized system. Let us consider first the case that we are looking for an inductive assertion of the form $\varphi = \forall h : \psi(h)$. The construction algorithm can be described as follows:

Algorithm 1. *Compute Auxiliary Assertion of the form $\forall h : \psi(h)$*
1. Let *reach* be the assertion characterizing all the reachable states of system $S(N_0)$, where $N_0 = 2b + 2$ (or $b + 2$ if S is *Par*-deterministic). Since $S(N_0)$ is finite-state, *reach* can be computed by letting $reach := \Theta \diamond \rho^*$.
2. Let ψ_1 be the assertion obtained from *reach* by projecting away all the references to variables subscripted by indices other than 1. Technically, this is done by using BDD operations for computing
$$\psi_1 = \exists z_1[2], \ldots, z_1[N_0], \ldots, z_c[2], \ldots, z_c[N_0] : reach$$

3. Let $\psi(h)$ be the assertion obtained from ψ_1 by *abstraction*, which involves the following transformations:

   - Replace any reference to $z_r[1]$ by a reference to $z_r[h]$.
   - Replace any sub-formula of the form $y_r = 1$ by the formula $y_r = h$, and any sub-formula of the form $y_r = v$ for $v \neq 1$ by the formula $y_r \neq h$.

Let us illustrate the application of this algorithm to program MUX-SEM (as presented in Fig. 1). Since, for this program, $b = 0$, we take $N_0 = 2$ and obtain

$$reach : \left(\begin{array}{l} (x = 1) \wedge \pi[1] \in \{I, T\} \wedge \pi[2] \in \{I, T\} \\ \vee (x = 0) \wedge (\pi[1] \in \{I, T\} \leftrightarrow \pi[2] \notin \{I, T\}) \end{array} \right)$$

$$\psi_1 : \quad (x = 1) \rightarrow \pi[1] \in \{I, T\}$$
$$\psi(h) \quad (x = 1) \rightarrow \pi[h] \in \{I, T\}$$

Unfortunately, when we take the proposed assertion $\varphi : \forall h : (x = 1) \rightarrow \pi[h] \in \{I, T\}$ we find out that it is not inductive over $S(2)$. This illustrates the fact that the above algorithm is not guaranteed to produce inductive assertions in all cases.

Another version of the algorithm can be used to compute candidates for inductive assertions of the form $\varphi : \forall h \neq t : \psi(h, t)$.

Algorithm 2. *Compute Auxiliary Assertion of the form $\forall h \neq t : \psi(h, t)$*

1. Let *reach* be the assertion characterizing all the reachable states of system $S(N_0)$, where $N_0 = 2b + 3$ (or $b + 3$ if S is *Par*-deterministic).
2. Let $\psi_{1,2}$ be the assertion obtained from *reach* by projecting away all the references to variables subscripted by indices other than 1 or 2.
3. Let $\psi(h, t)$ be the assertion obtained from $\psi_{1,2}$ by *abstraction*, which involves the following transformations:

   - Replace any reference to $z_r[1]$ by a reference to $z_r[h]$ and any reference to $z_r[2]$ by a reference to $z_r[t]$.
   - Replace any sub-formula of the form $y_r = 1$ by the formula $y_r = h$, any sub-formula of the form $y_r = 2$ by the formula $y_r = t$, and any sub-formula of the form $y_r = v$ for $v \notin \{1, 2\}$ by the formula $y_r \neq h \wedge y_r \neq t$.

Let us apply this algorithm again to system MUX-SEM. This time, we take $N_0 = 3$ and compute:

$$reach : \quad (\pi[1] \in \{C, E\}) + (\pi[2] \in \{C, E\}) + (\pi[3] \in \{C, E\}) + y = 1$$

$$\psi_{1,2} : \left(\begin{array}{l} \pi[1] \in \{C, E\} \rightarrow (x = 0) \wedge \pi[2] \in \{I, T\} \\ \wedge \pi[2] \in \{C, E\} \rightarrow (x = 0) \wedge \pi[1] \in \{I, T\} \end{array} \right)$$

$$\psi(h, t) : \left(\begin{array}{l} \pi[h] \in \{C, E\} \rightarrow (x = 0) \wedge \pi[t] \in \{I, T\} \\ \wedge \pi[t] \in \{C, E\} \rightarrow (x = 0) \wedge \pi[h] \in \{I, T\} \end{array} \right)$$

Taking $\varphi = \forall h \neq t : \psi(h, t)$ yields an assertion which is inductive over $S(3)$. By Corollary (2), it follows that φ is inductive for all $S(N)$. It is straightforward to check that φ implies the property of mutual exclusion $\forall h \neq t : \neg(\pi[h] = C \wedge \pi[t] = C)$ which we wished to establish for program MUX-SEM.

5.1   The Integrated Processes

The description of the two algorithms for computing auxiliary assertions may have given some of the readers the false impression that there is a manual step involved. For example, that after computing ψ_1 in Algorithm (1), we print it out and ask the user to perform the abstraction herself. This is certainly not the case. The whole process of deriving the candidate for inductive auxiliary assertion and utilizing it for an attempt to verify the desired property is performed in a fully automated manner. In fact, without an explicit request, the user never sees the generated candidate assertion, which is the reason we refer to this method as "verification by invisible invariants".

To explain how the entire process is performed, we observe that steps (2) and (3) of Algorithm (1) obtain a symbolic representation of $\psi(h)$. However, to check that it is inductive over $S(N_0)$, we immediately instantiate h in $\psi(h)$ to form $\bigwedge_{j=1}^{N_0} \psi(j)$. In the integrated process, we perform these three steps together. This is done by defining an *abstraction relation* α_j for each $j \in [1..N_0]$. The abstraction relation is given by

$$\alpha_j : \quad \overset{a}{\underset{r=1}{\bigwedge}} (x'_r = x_r) \ \wedge \ \overset{b}{\underset{r=1}{\bigwedge}} \Big((y'_r = j) \leftrightarrow (y_r = 1) \Big) \ \wedge \ \overset{c}{\underset{r=1}{\bigwedge}} (z'_r[j] = z_r[1])$$

This relation defines an abstract state consisting of the interpretation of a primed copy V' which only cares about the interpretation of $z'_r[j]$, whether y'_r equals or is unequal to j, and the precise values of x_r. These values correspond to the interpretation of these variables for $j = 1$ in the unprimed state. Given the assertion *reach* which characterizes all the reachable states of $S(N_0)$, we can form the assertion $\psi_j = reach \diamond \alpha_j$. Then we claim that

The state $\tilde{s}$ is in $\|\psi_j\|$ iff there exists a state $s \in \|reach\|$, such that
$$\tilde{x}_r = x_r \qquad \text{for every } r \in [1..a]$$
$$\tilde{y}_r = j \text{ iff } y_r = 1 \text{ for every } r \in [1..b]$$
$$\tilde{z}_r[j] = z_r[1] \quad \text{for every } r \in [1..c]$$

Thus, we reuse the operator $\diamond$ for performing abstraction+instantiation instead of computation of a successor, which is its customary use.

With this notation, we can describe the full verification process as follows:

Verification Process 3. Verify property p, using a singly indexed auxiliary assertion.

1. Let *reach* := $\Theta \diamond \rho^*$, computed over $S(N_0)$ for an appropriately chosen N_0.
2. Let ψ_j := $reach \diamond \alpha_j$, for each $j \in [1..N_0]$.
3. Let φ := $\bigwedge_{j=1}^{N_0} \psi_j$.
4. Check that φ is inductive over $S(N_0)$.
5. Check that $\varphi \rightarrow p$ is valid.

If tests (4) and (5) both yield positive results, then property p has been verified.

To illustrate the application of Verification Process (3), consider the augmented version of program MUX-SEM, presented in Fig. 4. In this program, we added an auxiliary variable *last_entered* which is set to h whenever process $P[h]$ enters its critical section. Applying Verification Process (3) to this program, we obtained the calculated invariant

$$\begin{array}{|l|}
\hline
\textbf{in}\quad N \qquad\qquad\quad : \textbf{natural where } N > 1 \\
\textbf{local } x \qquad\qquad\quad : \textbf{boolean where } x = 1 \\
\textbf{local } \textit{last\_entered} : [1..N] \\
\displaystyle\prod_{h=1}^{N} P[h] :: \left[\begin{array}{l}
\textbf{loop forever do} \\
\left[\begin{array}{l}
I : \textbf{Non-Critical} \\
T : \langle\textbf{request } x;\ \textit{last\_entered} := h\rangle \\
C : \textbf{Critical} \\
E : \textbf{release } x
\end{array}\right]
\end{array}\right] \\
\hline
\end{array}$$

Fig. 4. Augmented Program MUX-SEM

$$\varphi : \quad \forall h : \pi[h] \in \{C, E\} \ \leftrightarrow \ (x = 0 \ \wedge \ \textit{last\_entered} = h)$$

The candidate assertion φ is inductive and also implies the property of mutual exclusion, specifiable as

$$p : \quad \forall h \neq t : \neg(\pi[h] = C \ \wedge \ \pi[t] = C)$$

To handle the case of an auxiliary assertion which depends on two different indices, we define the abstraction relations

$$\alpha_{ht} : \quad \left[\begin{array}{l}
\bigwedge_{r=1}^{a}(x'_r = x_r) \\
\wedge \bigwedge_{r=1}^{b}\Big((y'_r = h) \leftrightarrow (y_r = 1)\Big) \ \wedge \ \Big((y'_r = t) \leftrightarrow (y_r = 2)\Big) \\
\wedge \bigwedge_{r=1}^{c}(z'_r[h] = z_r[1]) \ \wedge \ (z'_r[t] = z_r[2])
\end{array}\right]$$

We then formulate the verification process for doubly indexed assertions:

Verification Process 4. Verify property p, using a doubly indexed auxiliary assertion.

1. Let $reach := \Theta \diamond \rho^*$, computed over $S(N_0)$ for an appropriately chosen N_0.
2. Let $\psi_{ht} := reach \diamond \alpha_{ht}$, for each $h < t \in [1..N_0]$.
3. Let $\varphi := \displaystyle\bigwedge_{h<t\in[1..N_0]} \psi_{ht}$.
4. Check that φ is inductive over $S(N_0)$.
5. Check that $\varphi \to p$ is valid.

6   German's Cac he Case Study

In this section we illustrate the application of the invisible-invariants verification method to a case study which is a simple cache algorithm provided to us by Steve German [Ger00]. The algorithm consists of a central controller called *Home* and N client processes $P[1], \ldots, P[N]$. Each of the clients communicates with *Home* via the following channels:

- *channel1* – Client $P[c]$ uses this channel to send *Home* requests for either *shared* or *exclusive* access to the cache line.
- *channel2* –*Home* uses this channel to send $P[c]$ permissions (grants) for the requested access rights. It also sends on this channel requests to $P[c]$ to invalidate its cache status.

---

in N : **natural where** $N > 1$
type $message = \{empty, req\_shared, req\_exclusive, invalidate, invalidate\_ack,$
$\qquad\qquad\qquad\qquad\qquad\qquad\qquad\qquad grant\_shared, grant\_exclusive\}$
type $cache\_state$ = $\{invalid, shared, exclusive\}$
local $channel1, channel2, channel3$: **array**$[1..N]$ **of message where**
$\qquad\qquad\qquad \forall i : [1..N].(channel1[i] = channel2[i] = channel3[i] = empty)$
local $sharer\_list, invalidate\_list$: **array**$[1..N]$ **of bool where**
$\qquad\qquad\qquad \forall i : [1..N].(sharer\_list[i] = invalidate\_list[i] = 0)$
local $exclusive\_granted$: **bool where** $exclusive\_granted = 0$
local $curr\_command$: **message where** $curr\_command = empty$
local $curr\_client$: $[1..N]$ **where** $curr\_client = 1$
local $cache$: **array**$[1..N]$ **of cache_state where** $\forall i : [1..N].(cache[i] = empty)$

Fig. 5. Variables for German's cache algorithm

– $channel3$ – Client $P[c]$ uses this channel to send $Home$ acknowledgments of invalidation of the client's cache status.

Fig. 5 presents the variables used in the algorithm.

The algorithm can be presented as

$$Home \quad \| \quad \overset{N}{\underset{c=1}{\|}} P[c]$$

An SPL program for $Home$ is presented in Figure Fig. 6, and an SPL program for $P[c]$ is presented in Fig. 7.

The main property we wish to verify for this system is that of *coherence* by which there cannot be two clients, c and d, such that $P[c]$ holds an exclusive access to the cache line while $P[d]$ holds a shared access to the same cache line at the same time. This can be specified by the invariance of the assertion

$$\forall c \neq d : \neg(cache[c] = exclusive \ \wedge \ cache[d] = shared) \tag{6}$$

Following are the results of our verification experiments applied to the cache algorithm:

1. We applied Verification Process (3) to the cache program. The computed candidate assertion failed to be inductive.
2. We augmented the cache program with an auxiliary variable $last\_granted$ which is assigned the value of $curr\_client$ in transitions m_0 and m_1. We then applied Verification Process (3) to the augmented program. This time, the candidate assertion proved to be inductive and implied the property of coherence. It took 1.97 seconds to compute the candidate assertion, and 31.43 seconds to check that it is inductive (over an instance of the program with $N = 4$).
3. We applied Verification Process (4) to the original cache program. It produced an inductive assertion which implied the property of coherence. It took 15.42 seconds to compute the candidate assertion, and 186.82 seconds to check that it is inductive.

```
loop forever do
  m₀: ⟨when (    curr_command = req_shared  ∧  ¬exclusive_granted    )
              ∧  channel2[curr_client] = empty
            do [ sharer_list[curr_client] := true; curr_command := empty; ]⟩
               [ channel2[curr_client] := grant_shared                   ]
  or
  m₁: ⟨when (   curr_command = req_exclusive ∧ channel2[curr_client] = empty   )
              ∧ ∀i : [1..N].sharer_list[i] = false
            do [ sharer_list[curr_client] := true;  curr_command := empty;      ]
               [ exclusive_granted := true;       x_granted := curr_client; ]⟩
               [ channel2[curr_client] := grant_exclusive                       ]
  or
  m₂: ⟨when curr_command = empty  ∧  channel1[c] ≠ empty do
            [ curr_command := channel1[c]; channel1[c] := empty; ]⟩
            [ invalidate_list := sharer_list;   curr_client := c  ]
  or
  m₃: ⟨when ( (curr_command = req_shared  ∧  exclusive_granted )
             (         ∨ curr_command = req_exclusive)
             ( ∧ invalidate_list[c]  ∧  channel2[c] = empty      )
            do [channel2[c] := invalidate; invalidate_list[c] := false]⟩
  or
  m₄: ⟨when curr_command ≠ empty  ∧  channel3[c] = invalidate_ack do
            [sharer_list[c] := false; exclusive_granted := false; channel3[c] := empty]⟩
```

Fig. 6. Program for *Home*

We repeated these experiments over two erroneous versions of the cache program, also provided to us by Steve German. In both cases, Verification Process (4) produced inductive assertions but they failed to imply the property of coherence.

References

ABJN99. P.A. Abdulla, A. Bouajjani, B. Jonsson, and M. Nilsson. Handling global conditions in parametrized system verification. In *CAV'99*, LNCS 1633, pages 134–145, 1999.

AK86. K. R. Apt and D. Kozen. Limits for automatic program verification of finite-state concurrent systems. *Information Processing Letters*, 22(6), 1986.

BCG86. M.C. Browne, E.M. Clarke, and O. Grumberg. Reasoning about networks with many finite state processes. In *Proc. 5th ACM Symp. Princ. of Dist. Comp.*, pages 240–248, 1986.

CFJ96. E.M. Clarke, , R. Enders T. Filkron, and S. Jha. Exploiting symmetry in temporal logic model checking. *Formal Methods in System Design*, 9(1/2), 8 1996. Preliminary version appeared in 5th CAV, 1993.

CGJ95. E.M. Clarke, O. Grumberg, and S. Jha. Verifying parametrized networks using abstraction and regular languages. In *6th International Conference on Concurrency Theory (CONCUR'95)*, pages 395–407, Philadelphia, PA, August 1995.

$$
\begin{bmatrix}
\ell_0 \colon \textbf{skip} \\
\quad \textbf{or} \\
\ell_1 \colon \langle \textbf{when } cache[c] = invalid \ \wedge \ channel1[c] = empty \ \textbf{do} \\
\qquad\qquad\qquad\qquad\qquad\qquad [channel1[c] := req\_shared] \rangle \\
\quad \textbf{or} \\
\ell_2 \colon \langle \textbf{when } (cache[c] = invalid \ \vee \ cache[c] = shared) \wedge channel1[c] = empty \ \textbf{do} \\
\qquad\qquad\qquad\qquad\qquad\qquad [channel1[c] := req\_exclusive] \rangle \\
\quad \textbf{or} \\
\ell_3 \colon \langle \textbf{when } channel2[c] = invalidate \ \wedge \ channel3[c] = empty \ \textbf{do} \\
\qquad\quad [channel2[c] := empty; channel3[c] := invalidate\_ack; cache[c] := invalid] \rangle \\
\quad \textbf{or} \\
\ell_4 \colon \langle \textbf{when } channel2[c] = grant\_shared \ \textbf{do} \\
\qquad\qquad\qquad\qquad\qquad [cache[c] := shared; channel2[c] := empty] \rangle \\
\quad \textbf{or} \\
\ell_5 \colon \langle \textbf{when } channel2[c] = grant\_exclusive \ \textbf{do} \\
\qquad\qquad\qquad\qquad\qquad [cache[c] := exclusive; channel2[c] := empty] \rangle
\end{bmatrix}
$$

Fig. 7. Program for Process $P[c]$

CR99a.   S.J. Creese and A.W. Roscoe. Formal verification of arbitrary network topologies. In *Proc. of the Int. Conf. on Parallel and Distributed Processing Techniques and Applications (PDPTA '99)*, Las Vegas, 1999. CSREA Press.

CR99b.   S.J. Creese and A.W. Roscoe. Verifying an infinite family of inductions simultaneously using data independence and fdr. In *Formal Description Techniques for Distributed Systems and Communication Protocols and Protocol Specification, Testing and Verification (FORTE/PSTV'99)*, Beijing, 1999. Kluwer Academic Publishers.

CR00.   S.J. Creese and A.W. Roscoe. Data independent induction over structured networks. In *Proc. of the Int. Conf. on Parallel and Distributed Processing Techniques and Applications (PDPTA '00)*, Las Vegas, June 2000. CSREA Press.

EK00.   E.A. Emerson and V. Kahlon. Reducing model checking of the many to the few. In *17th International Conference on Automated Deduction (CADE-17)*, pages 236–255, 2000.

EN95.   E. A. Emerson and K. S. Namjoshi. Reasoning about rings. In POPL'95, 1995.

EN96.   E.A. Emerson and K.S. Namjoshi. Automatic verification of parameterized synchronous systems. In CAV'96, LNCS 1102, 1996.

ES96.   E. A. Emerson and A. P. Sistla. Symmetry and model checking. *Formal Methods in System Design*, 9(1/2), 8 1996. Preliminary version appeared in 5th CAV, 1993.

ES97.   E. A. Emerson and A. P. Sistla. Utilizing symmetry when model checking under fairness assumptions. *ACM Trans. Prog. Lang. Sys.*, 19(4), 1997. Preliminary version appeared in 7th CAV, 1995.

Ger00.   S. German. Personal Communication, 2000.

GS97.   V. Gyuris and A. P. Sistla. On-the-fly model checking under fairness that exploits symmetry. In CAV'97, LNCS 1254, 1997.

GZ98.   E.P. Gribomont and G. Zenner. Automated verification of szymanski's algorithm. In TACAS'98, LNCS 1384, pages 424–438, 1998.

HLR92.   N. Halbwachs, F. Lagnier, and C. Ratel. An experience in proving regular networks of processes by modular model checking. *Acta Informatica*, 29(6/7):523–543, 1992.

ID96.   C.N. Ip and D. Dill. Verifying systems with replicated components in Murφ. In CAV'96, LNCS 1102, 1996.

JL98.   E. Jensen and N.A. Lynch. A proof of burn's n-process mutual exclusion algorithm using abstraction. In TACAS'98, LNCS 1384, pages 409–423, 1998.

JN00.   B. Jonsson and M. Nilsson. Transitive closures of regular relations for verifying infinite-state systems. In TACAS'00, LNCS 1785, 2000.

KM95.   R.P. Kurshan and K.L. McMillan. A structural induction theorem for processes. *Information and Computation*, 117:1–11, 1995.

KMM$^+$97. Y. Kesten, O. Maler, M. Marcus, A. Pnueli, and E. Shahar. Symbolic model checking with rich assertional languages. In CAV'97, LNCS 1254, pages 424–435, 1997.

KP00.   Y. Kesten and A. Pnueli. Control and data abstractions: The cornerstones of practical formal verification. *Software Tools for Technology Transfer*, 4(2):328–342, 2000.

LHR97.   D. Lesens, N. Halbwachs, and P. Raymond. Automatic verification of parameterized linear networks of processes. In POPL'97, 1997.

LS97.   D. Lesens and H. Saidi. Automatic verification of parameterized networks of processes by abstraction. In *2nd International Workshop on the Verification of Infinite State Systems (INFINITY'97)*, 1997.

MAB$^+$94. Z. Manna, A. Anuchitanukul, N. Bjørner, A. Browne, E. Chang, M. Colón, L. De Alfaro, H. Devarajan, H. Sipma, and T.E. Uribe. STeP: The Stanford Temporal Prover. Technical Report STAN-CS-TR-94-1518, Dept. of Comp. Sci., Stanford University, Stanford, California, 1994.

McM98.   K.L. McMillan. Verification of an implementation of Tomasulo's algorithm by compositional model checking. In CAV'98, LNCS 1427, pages 110–121, 1998.

MP90.   Z. Manna and A. Pnueli. An exercise in the verification of multi – process programs. In W.H.J. Feijen, A.J.M van Gasteren, D. Gries, and J. Misra, editors, *Beauty is Our Business*, pages 289–301. Springer-Verlag, 1990.

PS00.   A. Pnueli and E. Shahar. Livenss and acceleraiton in parameterized verification. In CAV'00, LNCS 1855, 2000.

RKR$^+$00. A. Roychoudhury, K. Narayan Kumar, C. R. Ramakrishnan, I.V. Ramakrishnan, and S.A. Smolka. Verification of parameterized systems using logic program transformations. In TACAS'00, LNCS 1785, 2000.

SG89.   Z. Shtadler and O. Grumberg. Network grammars, communication behaviors and automatic verification. In CAV'89, LNCS 407, pages 151–165, 1989.

SG92.   A.P. Sistla and S.M. German. Reasoning about systems with many processes. *J. ACM*, 39:675–735, 1992.

SOR93.   N. Shankar, S. Owre, and J.M. Rushby. The PVS proof checker: A reference manual (draft). Technical report, Comp. Sci.,Laboratory, SRI International, Menlo Park, CA, 1993.

WL89.   P. Wolper and V. Lovinfosse. Verifying properties of large sets of processes with network invariants. In CAV'89, LNCS 407, pages 68–80, 1989.

Incremental Verification by Abstraction

Y. Lakhnech[1][**], S. Bensalem[1], S.Berezin[2], and S. Owre[3]

[1] VERIMAG, Centre Equation 2 Av. de Vignate, 38610 Gières, France.
{bensalem, lakhnech}@imag.fr
[2] Carnegie Mellon University, Department of Computer Science,5000 Forbes Ave.
Pittsburgh, PA 15213. Email: berez+@cs.cmu.edu
[3] Computer Science Laboratory, SRI International, Menlo Park, CA 94025, USA.
Email : owre@csl.sri.com

Abstract. We present a methodology for constructing abstractions and refining them by analyzing counter-examples. We also present a uniform verification method that combines abstraction, model-checking and deductive verification in a novel way. In particular, it allows and shows how to use the set of reachable states of the abstract system in a deductive proof even when the abstract model does not satisfy the specification and when it simulates the concrete system with respect to a weaker simulation notion than Milner's.

1 Introduction

Verification by abstraction (e.g. [15,16,12,25,13]) is a major technique for verifying infinite-state and very large systems. This technique consists in finding an abstraction relation and an abstract system that simulates the concrete one and that is amenable to algorithmic verification. One then checks that the abstract system satisfies an abstract version of the property of interest. Well established preservation results allow then to deduce for a large class of properties that the concrete system satisfies the concrete property, if the abstract system satisfies the abstract one.

In order for this technique to be used more widely, automatic techniques are needed for 1) finding an accurate abstraction relation and 2) automatically generating an abstract property and an abstract system that simulates the concrete one. Several papers have discussed the automatic construction of the abstract system, e.g. [17,6,14] for infinite-state systems. A less studied issue is that of finding/constructing the abstract domain and the abstraction relation. The situation is somewhat different in the case of program analysis where one is interested in rather generic properties mainly concerning run-time errors. In this case, depending on the programming paradigm (imperative, functional, or logic) and depending on the properties to be checked, several adequate abstract domains

---

[*] This work has been partly performed while the first two authors were visiting the Computer Science Laboratory, SRI International. Their visits were funded by NSF Grants No. CCR-9712383 and CCR-9509931.
[**] Contact Author.

T. Margaria and W. Yi (Eds.): TACAS 2001, LNCS 2031, pp. 98–112, 2001.

together with abstraction functions have been designed and extensively studied [28]. In model-checking, however, as one is interested in verifying properties specific to a given system, one usually needs to generate for every system and property a new abstract domain and abstraction relation. Therefore, it is mandatory to have automatic techniques assisting the user in finding the abstraction.

In this paper, we describe an automatic abstraction technique for invariance properties which is based on the set of atomic formulas appearing in successive applications of the weakest (liberal) predicate transformer on the invariant to be proved. This technique allows us to derive an abstraction function which is then used to construct an abstract system and an abstract property. When the property is true in the abstract system, we can conclude that the concrete system satisfies the invariant. The question arises, however, how to proceed in case the property is not satisfied in the abstract system. There are three possible reasons why the abstract system may not satisfy the abstract property: 1) the abstraction function is not fine enough to prove the property, that is, it identifies concrete states that should be distinguished, 2) the abstract system contains superfluous transitions that can be safely removed, that is, without altering the fact that it is an upper approximation and 3) the concrete system does not satisfy the specification [1]. The main contributions of this paper are on one hand algorithms for analyzing counter-examples that allow either to construct concrete counter-examples when this is possible or to refine the abstraction function. On the other hand, we present a uniform verification method that combines abstraction, model-checking and deductive verification in a novel way. In particular, it allows and shows how to use the set of reachable states of the abstract system in a deductive proof even when it simulates the concrete system in a weaker sense than Milner's notion of simulation.

For analyzing counter-examples, we present an algorithm that allows in many cases to analyze an infinite number of counter-examples at once. That is, the algorithm can deal with counter-examples that contain unfoldings of loops and where each time we unfold the loop we obtain a new counter-example.

Using counter-examples to refine abstract systems has been investigated by a number of other researchers, e.g. [23,1,11]. Closest to our work is Clarke et al's techniques [11]. The main differences are, however, that we focus on infinite-state systems and that our algorithms for analyzing counter-examples work backwards while their algorithms are forward. This difference can lead to completely different abstractions. Moreover, our technique allows in many cases to do in one step a refinement that cannot be done in finitely many ones using their method. The key issue here is that our technique incorporates accelerating the analysis of counter-examples that involve the unfolding of loops. On the other hand, we do not consider liveness properties. Also close to our work is Namjoshi and Kur-

---

[1] In the case of finite-state systems only reason 1) and 3) are relevant as a least non-deterministic abstract system exists and can always be computed, if we consider abstraction functions which is the case here. Computing this abstract system is, in general, not possible for infinite-state system as incomplete decision procedures have to be used for constructing the abstract system.

shan's work [29] on computing finite bisimulations/simulations of infinite-state systems. The main idea there is to start from a finite set of atomic formulae and to successively split the abstract state space induced by these formulae until stabilization. However, in contrast to [8,24,21], the splitting in [29] is done on atomic formulae instead of equivalence classes which correspond to boolean combinations of these. A similar idea is applied in [30].

2   Preliminarie s

2.1   Invariants

Given a set X of typed variables, a *state over* X is a type-consistent mapping that associates with each variable $x \in X$ a value.

A *transition system* is given by a triple (Σ, I, R), where Σ is a set of states over a set X of variables, $I \subseteq \Sigma$ is a set of initial states, and $R \subseteq \Sigma^2$ is the transition relation. A *syntactic* transition system is given by a triple $(X, \theta(X), \rho(X, X'))$, where X is a set of typed variables, $\theta(X)$ is a predicate describing the set of initial states and $\rho(X, X')$ is a predicate describing the transition relation. We associate in the usual way a transition system with every syntactic transition system.

A *computation* of a transition system $S = (\Sigma, I, R)$ is a sequence $s_0, \cdots, s_n$ such that $s_0 \in I$ and $(s_i, s_{i+1}) \in R$, for $i \leq n - 1$. A state $s \in \Sigma$ is called *reachable* in S, if there is a computation $s_0, \cdots, s_n$ of S with $s_n = s$. We denote by $\mathcal{R}(S)$ the set of states reachable in S.

A set $P \subseteq \Sigma$ is called an *invariant* of S, denoted by $S \models \Box P$, if every state that is reachable in S is in P. Given a set $P \subseteq \Sigma$ of states and a relation $R \subseteq \Sigma^2$ the *weakest liberal precondition* of R with respect to P, denoted by $wp(R, P)$ or $wp_R(P)$, is the set consisting of states s such that for every state s', if $(s, s') \in R$ then $s' \in P$. The *precondition* of R with respect to P, denoted by $pre_R(P)$, is the pre-image of P by R. We also sometimes write $pre(R)(P)$ instead of $pre_R(P)$.

All the semantic notions introduced so far have their syntactic counterparts which we assume as known. Moreover, we will tacitly interchange syntax and semantics, e.g. predicates and sets of states etc., unless there is a necessity to make a distinction.

2.2   Abstractions

Abstraction techniques [15,10] can be used to compute an over-approximation of $\mathcal{R}(S)$. Basically, the idea consists in abstracting the considered system S to a finite system S^a such the concretization of $\mathcal{R}(S^a)$ is a super-set of $\mathcal{R}(S)$. The use of abstractions techniques in the context of model-checking is well-studied [12,25]. The theory is based on the notion of simulation (also called L-simulation, forward-simulation,...) and on preservation results which tell us which properties that are satisfied by S^a are also satisfied by S.

A drawback of this method is that the simulation notion used does not take into account the invariance property we want to prove. To overcome this, we proposed in [7], the following invariant-dependent simulation notion.

Definition 1. *We say that S^a is an abstraction of S with respect to $\alpha \subseteq \Sigma \times \Sigma^a$ and $P \subseteq \Sigma$, denoted by $S \sqsubseteq_\alpha^P S^a$, if the following conditions are satisfied:*

1. *α is a total relation,*
2. *for every state $s_0, s_1 \in \Sigma$ and $s_0^a \in \Sigma^a$ with $s_0 \in P$ and $(s_0, s_0^a) \in \alpha$, if $(s_0, s_1) \in R$ then there exists a state $s_1^a \in \Sigma^a$ such that $(s_0^a, s_1^a) \in R^a$ and $(s_1, s_1^a) \in \alpha$,*
3. *$I \subseteq P$, and*
4. *for every state s in I there exists a state s^a in I^a such that $(s, s^a) \in \alpha$.* □

Now, it can be proved by induction on n that for every computation $s_0, \cdots, s_n$ of S such that $s_i \in P$, for every $i = 0, \cdots, n-1$, there exists a computation $s_0^a, \cdots, s_n^a$ of S^a such that $(s_i, s_i^a) \in \alpha$, for every $i \leq n$. Therefore, we can state the following preservation result:

Theorem 1. *Let S and S^a be transition systems such that $S \sqsubseteq_\alpha^P S^a$. Let $P^a \subseteq \Sigma^a$ and $P' \subseteq \Sigma$. If $\alpha^{-1}(P^a) \subseteq P \cap P'$, and $S^a \models \Box P^a$, then $S \models \Box(P \cap P')$.* □

3 A General V erification Rule

In this section, we present a general rule for verifying invariance properties which combines the two main approachs to the verification of invariance properties of infinite-state systems:

1. the *deductive approach* which consists in applying a rule that allows to reduce the verification to proving a set of 1st-order formulas, and
2. the *verification by abstraction approach* which consists in abstracting the system in hand to a finite system which is then analyzed algorithmically using model-checking techniques.

To do so, we fix throughout this section a transition system $S = (\Sigma, I, R)$ and a set $P \subseteq \Sigma$ of states. W e then consider the problem of showing that S satisfies the invariant P.

A uniform rule While Theorem 1 allo ws us to deduce $S \models \Box P$ in case $S^a \models \Box P^a$, they do not tell us whether it is possible to take advantage from S^a in case $S^a \not\models \Box P^a$. Rule (Inv-Uni) (see Fig. 1), which can be seen as a uniform presentation of the deductive and the verification by abstraction approaches, addresses this question. Indeed, the proof rule shows how concretizations of invariants of the abstract system can be used to prove that the predicate P is preserved by the transition relation of S. In fact, these concretizations are used to weaken the third premise of the rule (Inv-Uni).

Theorem 2. *The proof Rule (Inv-Uni) (see Figure 1) is sound and complete.*

Proof. Let us first show soundness. Let S and S^a be transition systems such that (P1) $S \sqsubseteq_\alpha^P S^a$, (P2): $\alpha^{-1}(\mathcal{R}(S^a)) \subseteq Q$, (P3): $Q \cap P \cap P' \subseteq wp(R, P \cap P')$, and (P4): $I \subseteq P'$.

$$\frac{\begin{array}{l} \text{There exists } \alpha \subseteq \Sigma \times \Sigma^a \\ S \sqsubseteq_\alpha^P S^a \\ \alpha^{-1}(\mathcal{R}(S^a)) \subseteq Q \\ Q \cap P \cap P' \subseteq wp(R, P \cap P') \\ I \subseteq P' \end{array}}{S \models \Box(P \cap P')}$$

Fig. 1. Proof rule (Inv-Uni).

Let $s_0, \cdots, s_n$ be a computation of S. We prove by induction on n that $s_n \in P \cap P'$. Now, since (P1) implies that all initial states of S satisfy P, and since $I \subseteq P'$, we have $s_0 \in P \cap P'$. Moreover, from (P1) and (P2), we have $s_{n-1} \in Q$, and hence by induction hypothesis, $s_{n-1} \in Q \cap P \cap P'$. Therefore, from (P3), $s_n \in P \cap P'$.

Completeness of Rule (Inv-Uni) is easily proved along the same lines as for the completeness of the standard rule for proving invariants, e.g. [26].   □

3.1   Concretizing OBDD's

To be able to apply Rule (Inv-Uni) we need:

1. a finite representation of the set R^a of abstract reachable states and
2. to transform this representation into a finite representation of its concretisation, that is, $\alpha^{-1}(R^a)$.

Symbolic model checkers like SMV use ordered binary decision diagrams (OB-DDs) to represent sets of states. To do so, all abstract variables are encoded by boolean variables. An OBDD is very easily transformed into a proposional formula in disjunctive normal form. Such representation can, however, be unnecessarily cumbersome.

In this section, we describe an algorithm for converting an OBDD into a propositional formula over the original state variables (not necessarily boolean), which is often almost as compact as the original OBDD.

Consider first a simple case when the top variable x of an OBDD b is boolean. Then, by the Shannon-Boole expansion law, $b = x \cdot b|_{x=\text{true}} + \bar{x} \cdot b|_{x=\text{false}}$. Equivalently, this can be written as a formula

$$(x = \text{false} \to \text{formula}(b|_{x=\text{false}})) \land (x = \text{true} \to \text{formula}(b|_{x=\text{true}})),$$

where formula(b) is a formula corresponding to the BDD b. Generalizing this to program variables with arbitrary number of possible values represented as a vector of boolean variables $x = (x_1, \ldots, x_n)$, and assuming that x_i's are the n top variables in b, we can recursively construct a formula

$$\bigwedge_{v \in \text{type}(x)} (x = v \to \text{formula}(b|_{x=v})).$$

```
bdd2f(b: BDD, var_list: list of variables): formula =
if b ∈ H then return H(b);
if b = true_bdd then res := TRUE;
else if b = false_bdd then res := FALSE;
else
x := car(var_list);
res := TRUE;
for every v ∈ type(x) do
tmp := bdd2f(b|ₓ₌ᵥ, cdr(var_list));
res := res ∧ (x = v → tmp);
end;
H → (b, res);
end if
return res;
end bdd2f
```

Fig. 2. Basic algorithm converting BDD to a formula.

The basic algorithm is shown on Figure 2. It takes a BDD b and the list of program state variables (not necessarily boolean), and returns a formula equivalent to b. It uses a hash table H that hashes pairs of the form (b, f), where f is a formula previously constructed for a BDD b. At the very beginning the algorithm checks whether b is already in the table, and if it is, it simply returns the associated formula. If the formula has not been constructed yet, it checks for the trivial base cases (TRUE or FALSE). If we are not at the base case, then it constructs a formula recursively on the BDD structure. For every value in the type of the first variable[2] we restrict b to that value, remove the variable from the list, construct the formula recursively for that restricted BDD, and add the result into the final formula. Finally, the result is included into the hash table before it is returned.

If the internal representation of the formula being constructed is done using pointers, then multiple occurences of the same subformula in the final formula does not cause the formula to grow exponentially in the size of b. In fact, its size is only linear. However, the formula cannot be easily printed without losing this structure sharing. A simple solution to that would be to print the subformulas collected in the hash table with names assigned to them, and then print the final formula that has the names instead of these subformulas. However, the formula will be ugly and hardly manageable both for a human and for a mechanical tool reading it. We designed a set of simplifications that make the formula look a lot more understandable and even more compact. These transformations are applied for each program variable before the function returns from the recursive call.

Example 1. Let us consider the abstract system of the Bakery example (see e.g. [7]). If we apply the basic algorithm (see Figure 2) to the obdd that char-

---

[2] We assume that the types are always finite.

acterizes the reachable states of this abstract system, we obtain the following formula:

$$(a1 \Rightarrow (a2 \Rightarrow a3 \land pc1 = l11 \land pc2 = l21) \land$$
$$(\neg a2 \Rightarrow a3 \land pc1 = l11 \land pc2 \neq l21)) \land$$
$$(\neg a1 \Rightarrow (a2 \Rightarrow \neg a3 \land pc1 \neq l11 \land pc2 = l21) \land$$
$$(\neg a2 \Rightarrow (a3 \Rightarrow pc1 \neq l11 \land pc2 = l22) \land$$
$$(\neg a3 \Rightarrow pc1 = l12 \land pc2 \neq l21)))$$

The concretization of the above formula yields the conjunction of following formulae:

$$(y1 = 0 \land y2 = 0) \Rightarrow pc1 = l11 \land pc1 = l21 \tag{1}$$

$$(y1 = 0 \land y2 > 0) \Rightarrow pc1 = l11 \land pc1 \neq l21 \tag{2}$$

$$(y1 \neq 0 \land y2 = 0) \Rightarrow pc1 \neq l11 \land pc1 = l21 \tag{3}$$

$$y1 \neq 0 \land y2 \neq 0 \land y1 \leq y2 \Rightarrow pc1 \neq l11 \land pc1 = l22 \tag{4}$$

$$y1 \neq 0 \land y2 \neq 0 \land y1 > y2 \Rightarrow pc1 = l12 \land pc1 \neq l21 \tag{5}$$

In this example, the concrete invariant obtained by this approach is stronger than the invariant generated by the method presented in [9,5]. The invariants (4) and (5) cannot be immediately obtained by these methods. Indeed, these methods cannot easily generate invariants relating the variables of different processes.

4   Analyzing Counter-examples and Refining Abstraction Relations

A key issue in applying the verification method described by Theorem 1, respectively Rule (Inv-Uni), is finding a suitable abstraction relation α. In this section, we discuss a heuristic for finding an initial abstraction relation and present a method for refining it by analyzing abstract counter-examples, that is, counter-examples of the abstract system.

4.1   Initial Abstraction Relation

Assume that we are given a syntactic transition system $S = (X, \theta, \rho)$ and a quantifier-free formula P with free variables in X. Henceforth, we assume that ρ is given as a finite disjunction of transitions $\tau_1, \cdots, \tau_n$, where each τ_i is given by a guard g_i that is quantifier-free formula and a multiple-assignment $x_1, \cdots, x_n :=$ $e_1, \cdots, e_n$.

We want to prove that P is an invariant of S. To do so, we choose a constant $N \in \omega$ and compute $\bigwedge_{i < N} wp_\rho^i(P)$. Then, $\bigwedge_{i \leq N} wp_\rho^i(P)$ is also a quantifier-free formula. Let $F = \{f_1, \cdots, f_m\}$ be the set of atomic formulas that appear in $\bigwedge_{i < N} wp_\rho^i(P)$ in the predicate describing the initial states or in the property. (Notice that one can choose N sufficiently large to include the atomic formulae in the guards.) Then, we introduce for every formula f_i an abstract variable a_i and define the abstraction function α defined by $a_i \equiv f_i$. In [6], we show how given a transition system S, a predicate P and an abstraction function α, we compute a system S^a such that $S \sqsubseteq_\alpha^P S^a$ and a predicate P^a such that $\alpha^{-1}(P^a) \subseteq P$. Rule (Inv-Uni) addresses the question of how to benefit from computing the set of reachable states of S^a even when S^a does not satisfy $\Box P^a$. In this, section we address the following questions:

1. given a counter-example for $S^a \models \Box P^a$ does it correspond to some behavior in the concrete system and
2. in case the answer to the first question is no, how can we use the given counter-example to refine the abstraction function.

Identifying false negatives As in this paper, we focus on invariance properties, counter-examples are finite computations. Let $\sigma^a = s_0^a \tau_1^a s_1^a \cdots \tau_n^a s_n^a$ be a counter-example for $S^a \models \Box P^a$. The concretization $\alpha^{-1}(\sigma^a)$ of σ^a is the sequence $\alpha^{-1}(s_0^a)\tau_0\alpha^{-1}(s_1^a) \cdots \tau_{n-1}\alpha^{-1}(s_n^a)$. We call $\alpha^{-1}(\sigma^a)$ a symbolic computation of S, if there exists a computation $s_0\tau_1 s_1 \cdots \tau_n s_n$ of S such that $s_i \in \alpha^{-1}(s_i^a)$, for $i = 0, \cdots, n$. Clearly, this definition can be generalized to arbitrary sequences $Q_0\tau_1 Q_1 \cdots \tau_n Q_n$, with $Q_i \subseteq \Sigma$. Then, we have the following:

Lemma 1. *A sequence $Q_0\tau_1 Q_1 \cdots \tau_n Q_n$, with $Q_i \subseteq \Sigma$ is a symbolic computation iff $\theta \cap X_0 \neq \emptyset$, where $X_n = Q_n$ and $X_{n-i-1} = Q_{n-i-1} \cap \mathrm{pre}_{\tau_{n-i}}(X_{n-i})$.*
$\Box$

Lemma 1 suggests the procedure CouAnal given in Figure 3 for checking whether an abstract counter-example is a false negative or whether it corresponds to a behavior of the concrete system.

Input: An abstract counter-example $\sigma^a = s_0^a \tau_1^a s_1^a \cdots \tau_n^a s_n^a$
$X := \alpha^{-1}(s_n^a)$;
$i := n$;
while ($X \neq \emptyset$ and $i > 0$) do
    $Y := X$;
    $X := \mathrm{pre}_{\tau_i}(X) \cap \alpha^{-1}(s_{i-1}^a)$;
    $i := i - 1$
od
if $i = 0$ and $\theta \cap X \neq \emptyset$ then return "the following is a counter-example:"
    Take any $s \in \theta \cap X \neq \emptyset$
    Let $s_0 := s, s_1 := \tau_1(s_0) \cdots, s_n := \tau_n(s_{n-1})$
    write $s_0 \cdots s_n$
else return i, Y
fi

Fig. 3. Counter-example Analyzer: CouAnal

Refining the abstraction function First, we consider a simple refinement strategy of the abstraction function. Thus, let $\sigma^a = s_0^a \tau_1^a s_1^a \cdots \tau_n^a s_n^a$ be a counter-example for $S^a \models \square P^a$ that is not a symbolic computation of S. By Lemma 1, procedure CouAnal returns some $i \leq n$ and a set $Y = X_i \subseteq \Sigma$ such that $X_{i-1} = \emptyset^3$. Now, since $X_{i-1} = \emptyset$, $Q_{i-1} \subseteq wp_{\tau_i}(\neg X_i)$ and abstract transitions from abstractions of states in Q_{i-1} to abstractions of states in X_i are superfluous and should be omitted. To achieve this, we add for every atomic formula f in $\neg X_i$ which is not already in α, a corresponding new abstract variable a_f with $a_f \equiv f$. Let α_e denote the so-obtained new abstraction function. Moreover, let S_e^a be the abstract system with $(s_1^a, s_2^a) \in \rho_e$ iff there exist concrete states s_1, s_2 such that $(s_i, s_i^a) \in \alpha_e$, for $i = 1, 2$, and $(s_1, s_2) \in \rho$. Then, σ^a is not a computation of S_e^a.

Speeding-up refinement of abstraction functions The simple illustrative example given in Figure 4 shows that in general applying finitely many times the procedure CouAnal is not sufficient. In this example, we want to show that location l_2 is not reachable and we initially take the abstraction function defined $a \equiv x = y$. After the n-th application of CouAnal we will have the abstraction function defined by $a_1 \equiv x = y, \cdots, a_i \equiv x + i = y, \cdots, a_n \equiv x + n = y$. However, the abstraction function we need is $a \equiv x = y, a_1 \equiv x > y$. The problem here is clearly that the abstract counter-examples contain abstract transitions that correspond to the unfolding of a loop in the concrete system. In the following, we generalize procedure CouAnal to cope with this situation. Let us first explain the main idea.

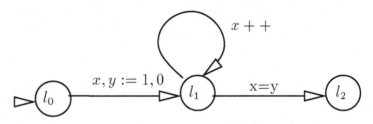

Fig. 4. Example for showing that speeding-up is needed

Henceforth, we assume that the description of the concrete system makes a clear distinction between control and data variables. That is, we assume that the concrete system is given by an extended transition system as in Figure 4, where l_0, l_1, l_2 are the control locations and x and y are the data variables. Let $\sigma^a = s_0^a \tau_1^a s_1^a \cdots \tau_n^a s_n^a$ be a counter-example for $S^a \models \square P^a$. Assume that $\tau_{i_0}, \cdots, \tau_{i_1}$ is a loop in the control graph of the concrete system. In the procedure CouAnal we apply one time pre_{τ_i} on each X_i. However, since $\tau_{i_0}, \cdots, \tau_{i_1}$ is a loop, it is more interesting to apply an arbitrary number of times $pre(\tau_{i_0}, \cdots, \tau_{i_1})$ on X_{i_1}, that is, to consider $\bigvee_{i \in \omega} pre^i(\tau_{i_0}, \cdots, \tau_{i_1})$ on X_{i_1}.

---

[3] We assume that $i > 0$ as the case of $i = 0$ is easily handled

For instance, in the example of Figure 4, applying $\bigvee_{i \in \omega} pre^i(x++)$ on $x = y$ gives after quantifier elimination the predicate $x \leq y$. Now, since $pre(x, y :=$ $1, 0)(x \leq y)$ is empty our strategy consists in adding an abstract variable b such that b is true in the abstraction of a state s iff s satisfies $\neg(x \leq y)$ which is $x > y$; what we indeed expect.

This idea of speeding-up counter-example analyzes leads to the procedure AccCouAnal given in Figure 5. There are several remarks to say about pro-

---

Input: An abstract counter-example $\sigma^a = s_0^a \tau_1^a s_1^a \cdots \tau_n^a s_n^a$;
Let $L_1, \cdots, L_m$ be loops in the concrete system such that
$L_j = \tau_{i_j}, \cdots, \tau_{i_j + k_j}$ and
$\tau_1, \cdots, \tau_n = \tau_1, \cdots, \tau_{i_1-1} L_1, \tau_{i_1+k_1+1}, \cdots, L_m, \tau_{i_m+k_m+1}, \cdots, \tau_n$;
$X := \alpha^{-1}(s_n^a)$;
$i := n$;
$k := m$;
while $(X \neq \emptyset$ and $i > 0)$ do
    $Y := X$;
    if $i = i_k$ then
        $X := \bigvee_{j \in \omega} pre_{L_k}^j(X) \cap \alpha^{-1}(s_{i-1}^a)$;
        $i := i - \text{length}(L_k)$
    else $X := pre_{\tau_i}(X) \cap \alpha^{-1}(s_{i-1}^a)$
    fi
    $i := i - 1$
od
if $i = 0$ and $\theta \cap X \neq \emptyset$ then return "S does not satisfy the property"
else return i, Y
fi

Fig. 5. Accelerated Counter-example Analyzer: AccCouAnal

---

cedure AccCouAnal. The first one is that for a sequence $\tau_1, \cdots, \tau_n$ of transitions there are in general several but finitely many ways to partition it in $\tau_1, \cdots, \tau_{i_1-1} L_1, \tau_{i_1+k_1+1}, \cdots, L_m$. The accuracy of the obtained abstraction function depends on this choice. In principle, one could, however, consider all possible choices and combine the obtained abstraction functions into a single one (take their conjunction). An other point is that in order to have reasonably simple abstraction functions one needs to simplify the predicates $\bigvee_{j \in \omega} pre_{L_k}^j(X) \cap$ $\alpha^{-1}(Q_{i-1})$, in particular, when possible, one should eliminate the existential quantification on i.

5   Example

To illustrate how we can use the procedure CouAnal, we consider the verification
of the Bounded Retransmission protocol [27,18,20,19], BRP for short.

The BRP accepts requirements from a producer to transmit a file of data to
a consumer. The protocol consists of a sender at the producer side and a receiver
at the consumer side (see Figure 6). Sender transmits data frames to the receiver

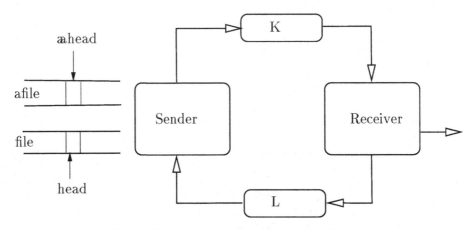

Fig. 6. The Bounded Retransmission Protocol.

via channel K and waits for acknowledgment via channel L. Since these channels
may lose messages timeouts are used to identify a loss of messages. After sending
a message, the sender waits for an acknowledgment. When the acknowledgment
arrives, the sender either proceeds with the next message in the file, if there
is one, or sends a confirmation message to the producer. However, if a timeout
occurs before reception of an acknowledgment, the sender retransmits the same
message. This procedure is repeated as often as specified by a parameter max. On
its side, the receiver after acknowledging a message that is not the last one waits
for further messages. If no new message arrives before a timeout, it concludes
that there is a loss of contact to the sender and reports this to the consumer.
Since the same message may be sent several times by the sender, a data frame
includes a bit to indicate whether the same datum is resent or not. In fact, the
BRP protocol can be seen as an extension of the alternating bit protocol [2].
The protocol is responsible for informing the producer whether the file has been
transmitted correctly. On the consumer side, the protocol passes data frames
indicating whether the datum is the first one in a file, the last one, or whether it
is an intermediate one. Thus, a data frame contains also the information whether
the data is the first, the last, or an intermediate. A third timeout is used in case
a transmission has been interrupted to ensure that the sender waits enough to
be sure that the receiver is prepared to receive new frames.

Correctness Criterion In the original formulation the requirements on the protocol are given by an abstract BRP-spec, and the task is to prove that BRP implements BRP-spec. To reduce the problem of proving that BRP implements BRP-spec to an invariance problem, we consider a superposition of BRP and BRP-spec and prove that the superposed protocol, BRP^+, satisfies the invariance property $\Box Safe$, where *Safe* is a variable that is set to *false* as soon as BRP makes a transition that is not allowed by BRP-spec. It should be realized that BRP^+ contains for many variables of the protocol two different copies corresponding to the variable in BRP and BRP-spec, respectively. So, for instance there are two variables *file* and *afile* which correspond to the file to be sent and two variables *head* and *ahead* which correspond to the position of the data being processed in *file* and *afile*, respectively. It is also worth mentioning that the variables *head* and *ahead* are never compared in BRP^+. Any relation between them these variables can not be deduced from the specification of BRP^+. The property that says the data transmitted is the same as the data received is important for the verification of this protocol.

5.1 Verification of the Protocol

The BRP protocol represents a family of parameterized protocols. The parameters are the number of allowed retransmissions *max*, the length of a file *last*, and finally, the data type *Data*. Let us describe now the main steps we followed in the verification of BRP using InVeSt [7].

An initial abstraction function is generated automatically and used to compute an abstract system of the BRP^+. This initial abstraction function is obtained from the predicates describing the initial states, the specification and $\bigwedge_{i \leq N} wp_\rho^i(P)$ with $i = 1$. The abstraction is the identity on variables ranging over finite domains . The concrete variables that range over an infinite, resp. parameterized domain, and their abstract versions are (partially) given in the following table:

head<last ≡ file = MANY	(afile[ahead]=data(msg)) ≡ msgafile
(head=last) ≡ (file=ONE)	(afile[ahead]=data(k)) ≡ kafile
(head=last+1) ≡ (file=NONE)	rn=0 ≡ ¬Rn
⋮	⋮

It turns out the abstract system obtained by the initial abstraction does not satisfy the specification. The provided trace by the model-checker SMV has 6 states, each state contains 39 variables (not all of them booleans). This trace is concretized and checked using CouAnal. The result of this analysis is that this counter-example is spurious. Moreover, the result of this analyzes is that we have to add a boolean abstract variable $h_a h$ that is true iff *head = ahead*. Then, analyzing the abstract system obtained by this new abstraction shows a new counter-example. In this new counter-example, first *head* is incremented which on the abstract level assigns false to $h_a h$ as initially *head = ahead*. Then, after a few steps, *ahead* is incremented. Thus, though, at the concrete level

$head = ahead$, this cannot be inferred at the abstract level. Indeed, applying CouAnal shows us that we have to add a new abstract variable corresponding to $head = ahead + 1$. Again, the abstract system obtained by this new abstraction shows a new counter-example. This time the incrementation of $ahead$ precedes $head$ and we have to add a new abstract variable corresponding to $head + 1 = ahead$. And now we are done. The new abstraction is fine enough for proving the property; the constructed finite abstract system satisfies the specification.

As a second experimentation we used the proof rule (Inv-Uni) to verify the BRP protocol. We started with the initial abstract system. But rather than going through the refinement process of the abstraction function, we concretized, using the procedure described in section 3, the OBDD that characterizes the abstract reachable states of the first abstract system. One iteration of strengthening was needed to prove the desired property of BRP protocol.

6   Conclusion

We have presented a novel verification methodology that combines abstraction, model-checking and deductive methods. To support this methodology, and in particular, the verification by abstraction method we developed techniques for refining abstraction functions. These are based on the analysis of counter-examples and allow in many cases the simultaneous analysis of infinitely many examples by applying acceleration techniques. These techniques have been implemented in the tool InVeSt, which is a tool for verifying invariance properties of infinite-state systems. InVeSt is based on PVS and connected to SMV. Since then we applied these techniques to several interesting examples and the results are promising.

In contrast to [11] we did not consider liveness properties. For infinite-state systems, the key issue is techniques for automatically generating ranking functions and fairness conditions (cf. [3,4,22]).

References

1. F. Balarin and A.L. Sangiovanni-Vincentelli. Am iterative approach to language containment. In Costas Courcoubetis, editor, *Computer Aided Verification: 5th International Conference*, volume 697 of *Lecture Notes in Computer Science*, pages 29–40. Springer-Verlag, 1993.
2. K.A. Barlett, R.A. Scantlebury, and P.T. Wilkinson. A note on reliable full-duplex transmission over half-duplex links. *Communications of the ACM*, 12(5), 1969.
3. K. Baukus, S. Bensalem, Y. Lakhnech, and K. Stahl. Abstracting WS1S Systems to Verify Parameterized Networks. In S. Graf and M. Schwartzbach, editors, *TACAS'00*, volume 1785 of *Lecture Notes in Computer Science*. Springer-Verlag, 2000.
4. K. Baukus, Y. Lakhnech, and K. Stahl. Verifying universal properties of parameterized networks. In M. Joseph, editor, *Formal Techniques in Real-Time and Fault-Tolerant Systems*, volume 1926 of *Lecture Notes in Computer Science*, pages 291–304. Springer-Verlag, 2000.

5. S. Bensalem and Y. Lakhnech. Automatic generation of invariants. *Formal Methods in System Design*, 1999. To appear.
6. S. Bensalem, Y. Lakhnech, and S. Owre. Computing abstractions of infinite state systems automatically and compositionally. In Alan J. Hu and Moshe Y. vardi, editors, *Computer Aided Verification*, volume 1427 of *Lecture Notes in Computer Science*, pages 319–331. Springer-Verlag, 1998.
7. S. Bensalem, Y. Lakhnech, and S. Owre. Invest: A tool for the verification of invariants. In Alan J. Hu and Moshe Y. vardi, editors, *Computer Aided Verification*, volume 1427 of *Lecture Notes in Computer Science*, pages 505–510. Springer-Verlag, 1998.
8. A. Bouajjani, J. Cl. Fernandez, and N. Halbwachs. Minimal model generation. In *Workshop on Computer-aided Verification*. Rutgers – American Mathematical Society, Association for Computing Machinery, June 1990.
9. Ahmed Bouajjani, Yassine Lakhnech, and Sergio Yovine. Model checking for extended timed temporal logics. In B. Jonsson and J. Parrow, editors, *4th International Symposium on Formal Techniques in Real-Time and Fault-Tolerant Systems FTRTFT'96*, volume 1135 of *Lecture Notes in Computer Science*, pages 306–326. Springer-Verlag, 1996.
10. Bettina Buth, Karl-Heinz Buth, Martin Fränzle, Burghard v. Karger, Yassine Lakhnech, Hans Langmaack, and Markus Müller-Olm. Provably correct compiler development and implementation. Compiler Construction, 1992.
11. E. Clarke, O. Grumberg, S. Jha, Y. Lu, and H. Veith. Counterexample-guided abstraction refinement. In *Computer Aided Verification*, Lecture Notes in Computer Science, pages 154–169. Springer-Verlag, 2000.
12. E.M. Clarke, O. Grumberg, and D.E. Long. Model checking and abstraction. *ACM Transactions on Programming Languages and Systems*, 16(5), 1994.
13. R. Cleaveland, P. Iyer, and D. Yankelevitch. Optimality in abstractions of model checking. In A Mycroft, editor, *Static Analysis*, volume 983 of *Lecture Notes in Computer Science*, pages 51–63, 1995.
14. M. A. Colon and T. E. Uribe. Generating finite-state abstractions of reactive systems using decision procedures. *Lecture Notes in Computer Science*, 1427:293–304, 1998.
15. P. Cousot and R. Cousot. Abstract interpretation: A unified lattice model for static analysis of programs by construction or approximation of fixpoints. In *4th ACM symp. of Prog. Lang.*, pages 238–252. ACM Press, 1977.
16. P. Cousot and R. Cousot. Systematic design of program analysis frameworks. In *6th ACM POPL*, pages 269–282, 1979.
17. S. Graf and H. Saidi. Construction of abstract state graphs with PVS. In *Computer Aided Verification*, volume 1254 of *Lecture Notes in Computer Science*, 1997.
18. F.F. Groote and J.C. van de Pol. A bounded retransmission protocol for large packets. In *A case study in computer checked verification*, Logic Group Preprint Series 100. Utrecht University, 1993.
19. K. Havelund and N. Shankar. Experiments in theorem proving and model checking for protocol verification. In *Formal Methods Europe, FME'96 Symposium*, volume 1051 of *Lecture Notes in Computer Science*. Springer-Verlag, 1996.
20. L. Helmink, M.P.A. Sellink, and F.W. Vaandrager. Proof-checking a data link protocol. Technical Report CS-R9420, Centrum voor Wiskunde en Informatica (CWI), March 1994.
21. M. R. Henzinger, T. A. Henzinger, and P. W. Kopke. Computing simulations on finite and infinite graphs. In *36th Annual Symposium on Foundations of Computer*

Science (FOCS'95), pages 453–462, Los Alamitos, October 1995. IEEE Computer Society Press.

22. Y. Kesten and A. Pnueli. Verification by augmented finitary abstraction. *Information and Computation*, To appear, 2000.

23. R.P. Kurshan. *Computer-Aided Verification of Coordinating Processes, the automata theoretic approach*. Princeton Series in Computer Science. Princeton University Press, 1994.

24. David Lee and Mihalis Yannakakis. Online minimization of transition systems (extended abstract). In *Proceedings of the Twenty-Fourth Annual ACM Symposium on the Theory of Computing*, pages 264–274, Victoria, British Columbia, Canada, 4–6 May 1992.

25. C. Loiseaux, S. Graf, J. Sifakis, A. Bouajjani, and S. Bensalem. Property preserving abstractions for the verification of concurrent systems. *Formal Methods in System Design*, 6(1), 1995.

26. Z. Manna and A. Pnueli. *Temporal Verification of Reactive Systems: Safety*. Springer-Verlag, 1995.

27. S. Mauw and G.J. Veltink editors. *Algebraic Specification of Communication Protocols*. Number 36 in Cambridge Tracts in Theoretical Computer Science. 1993.

28. S.S. Muchnick and N. D. Jones, editors. *Program Flow Analysis*. Prentice-Hall, 1981.

29. K. S. Namjoshi and R .P. Kurshan. Syntactic program transformations for automatic abstraction. In *Computer Aided Verification*, Lecture Notes in Computer Science, pages 435–449. Springer-Verlag, 2000.

30. H. Sipma, T.E. Uribe, and Z. Manna. Deductive model checking. In R. Alur and T.A. Henzinger, editors, *8th International Conference on Computer Aided Verification*, volume 1102 of *Lecture Notes in Computer Science*, pages 208–219. Springer-Verlag, 1996.

A Technique for Invariant Generation

A. Tiwari, H. Rueß, H. Saïdi, and N. Shankar

SRI International,
333 Ravenswood Ave,
Menlo Park, CA, U.S.A
{tiwari,ruess,saidi,shankar}@csl.sri.com

Abstract. Most of the properties established during verification are either invariants or depend crucially on invariants. The effectiveness of automated formal verification is therefore sensitive to the ease with which invariants, even trivial ones, can be automatically deduced. While the strongest invariant can be defined as the least fixed point of the strongest post-condition of a transition system starting with the set of initial states, this symbolic computation rarely converges. We present a method for invariant generation and strengthening that relies on the simultaneous construction of least and greatest fixed points, restricted widening and narrowing, and quantifier elimination. The effectiveness of the method is demonstrated on a number of examples.

1 Introduction

The majority of properties established during the verification of programs are either invariants or depend crucially on invariants. Indeed, safety properties can be reduced to invariant properties, and to prove progress one usually needs to establish auxiliary invariance properties too. Consequently, the discovery and strengthening of invariants is a central technique in the analysis and verification of both sequential programs and reactive systems, especially for infinite state systems.

Consider, for example, a program with state variables pc and x. The program counter pc is interpreted over the control locations inc and dec, and x is interpreted over the integers. Initially, the program counter pc is set to inc and x to 0. The dynamics of the system is described in terms of the guarded commands:

$$pc = inc \;\longmapsto\; x := x + 2; \; pc := dec$$
$$pc = dec \wedge x > 0 \;\longmapsto\; x := x - 2; \; pc \in \{inc, dec\}$$

Suppose we are interested in establishing the invariant $pc = inc \to x = 0$. A naïve proof attempt fails, and consequently, the invariant needs to be strengthened to an inductive invariant $(pc = inc \to x = 0) \wedge (pc = dec \to x = 2)$. Such strengthenings are typically needed in induction proofs. In general, the main

---

* The research described in this paper was supported in part by NSF contract CCR-9712383 and DARPA/AFRL contract F33615-00-C-3043.

T. Margaria and W. Yi (Eds.): TACAS 2001, LNCS 2031, pp. 113–127, 2001.
© Springer-Verlag Berlin Heidelberg 2001

principle for proving that a predicate ϕ is an invariant of some program or system S, consists in finding an *auxiliary* predicate ψ such that ψ is stronger than ϕ and ψ is inductive; i.e., every initial state of S satisfies ψ, and ψ is preserved under all transitions. This rule is sound and (relatively) complete. On the other hand, finding a strengthening ψ is not always obvious, and usually requires a microscopic examination of failed verification attempts.

Most approaches for generating and strengthening invariants are based on symbolic computation of the system at hand [10, 15, 4]. The *bottom-up* method performs an abstract forward propagation to compute the set of all reachable configurations, while the *top-down* method starts from an invariant candidate ϕ and performs an abstract backward propagation to compute a strengthened invariant ψ. There is, however, no guarantee for success in exact forward or backward propagation. This may be due either to infinite or unmanageably large configuration spaces or to the failure to detect convergence of the propagation methods altogether. Consequently, approximation techniques such as widening or narrowing [8] are needed to enforce termination of symbolic computation. The basic idea is to accelerate the convergence of symbolic computations in infinite abstract domains.

The framework of abstract interpretation with widening and narrowing as outlined in [8], however, is not immediately applicable to the discovery and strengthening of inductive invariants, since not every over-approximation of an inductive invariant is necessarily an inductive invariant. Our main contributions are: first, we provide an abstract description of the process of *inductive* invariant generation and strengthening based on computing under- and over-approximations of the reachable state set; second, this framework is instantiated with a novel technique based on combining concrete widening and narrowing operators. Our techniques can uniformly be used on a wide class of examples including transition systems where both forward and backward propagation do not converge. We demonstrate the effectiveness of our approach through a variety of examples.

Our algorithm is based on the symbolic computation of a sequence of under- and over-approximations of the reachable state set. These computations rely heavily on the elimination of quantifiers in the underlying theory. Quantifier elimination, however, is not required to return equivalent formulas, since our algorithm tolerates weakened quantifier-eliminated formulas. Whenever the computation of the sequence of under-approximations terminates, we get an inductive invariant. Moreover, since every element in the sequence of decreasing over-approximations is an inductive invariant, our algorithm can be stopped at *any time* and it outputs the best (strongest) inductive invariant computed up to this point. In the example above, our procedure yields the invariant $(pc = inc \rightarrow x = 0) \wedge (pc = dec \rightarrow x = 2)$.[1]

The approach faces two problems. First, the computation of the sequence of under-approximations usually does not terminate. Second, the computation of

---

[1]   This example can also be handled by some other invariant generation techniques based on forward reachability or abstraction [3, 17].

the sequence of over-approximations terminates with very weak invariants, in practice. For instance, forward reachability does not converge in case the initial value for x is unspecified in the example above. In order to overcome these problems we add specialized widening and narrowing operators to our algorithm. One of the distinguishing features of our algorithm is the use of unreachable configurations for detecting unreachable strongly connected components and computing corresponding narrowing operators. In this way, our algorithm terminates with the invariant $x > -2$ in case the initial value for x is unspecified in our running example.

The paper is structured as follows. In Section 2 we introduce notation and definitions, Section 3 presents the theoretical framework that is used in Section 4 to obtain a procedure for generating invariants using affirmation and propagation rules along with widening and narrowing. Finally, we conclude in Section 5 with a short investigation of the relationship between invariant generation and abstract interpretation, and comparisons with related work.

2   Preliminarie s

Let Σ be a first-order language containing interpreted symbols for standard concrete domains like booleans, integers and reals. Let $\Re$ denote the (first-order) theory of interest over the language Σ. We fix the set $\mathcal{V} = \{x_1, \ldots, x_n\}$ of (typed) variables and denote by $\mathcal{F}$ the set of first-order formulas over Σ with free variables contained in the set $\mathcal{V}$. A *transition system* S is a tuple $(\mathcal{V}, \Theta, \Phi)$, where $\Theta \in \mathcal{F}$ and Φ is a first-order formula over Σ with free variables contained in the set $\mathcal{V} \cup \mathcal{V}'$, where $\mathcal{V}' = \{x'_1, \ldots, x'_n\}$. The formula Θ is called the *initial predicate* and the formula Φ a *transition predicate* of the system S. We shall denote the sequence $x_1, \ldots, x_n$ by $\boldsymbol{x}$ and the sequence $x'_1, \ldots, x'_n$ by $\boldsymbol{x}'$.

A *state* σ of a transition system S $= (\mathcal{V}, \Theta, \Phi)$ is a mapping from $\mathcal{V}$ to values from the corresponding domains. If ρ is a state, we denote by ρ' the mapping obtained by renaming variables x_i to x'_i in ρ. A formula $\phi(\boldsymbol{x})$ is interpreted as the set $[\![\phi(\boldsymbol{x})]\!]$ of all states σ such that $\Re, \sigma \models \phi(\boldsymbol{x})$. We define the set $Reach(\Phi)(\Theta)$ of states *reachable* from the states represented by Θ via the transition predicate Φ as the smallest set such that (i) $[\![\Theta]\!] \subset Reach(\Phi)(\Theta)$ and (ii) the state $\sigma \in Reach(\Phi)(\Theta)$ whenever $\Re, \rho, \sigma' \models \Phi(\boldsymbol{x}, \boldsymbol{x}')$ for some $\rho \in Reach(\Phi)(\Theta)$. Since the theory $\Re$ is fixed, we shall not mention it explicitly when we talk about satisfiability and validity in $\Re$. Thus, validity in $\Re$ is denoted by $\models$.

A *formula transformer* Γ is a function mapping formulas to formulas. The *strongest postcondition* transformer, denoted by $\mathtt{SP}(\Phi)$, is defined as $\mathtt{SP}(\Phi)(\phi(\boldsymbol{x})) = \exists \boldsymbol{y}.(\Phi(\boldsymbol{y}, \boldsymbol{x}) \wedge \phi(\boldsymbol{y}))$. The formula $\mathtt{SP}(\Phi)(\phi(\boldsymbol{x}))$ denotes the set of states reachable in one step from the set of states represented by ϕ. Similarly, the *weakest precondition* transformer, $\mathtt{WP}(\Phi)$, is defined as $\mathtt{WP}(\Phi)(\phi(\boldsymbol{x})) = \forall \boldsymbol{y}.(\Phi(\boldsymbol{x}, \boldsymbol{y}) \rightarrow \phi(\boldsymbol{y}))$.

A *fixed point* of a formula transformer Γ is a formula ϕ such that $\models \Gamma(\phi) \leftrightarrow \phi$. A formula transformer Γ is *monotonic* if $\models \Gamma(\phi) \rightarrow \Gamma(\psi)$ whenever $\models \phi \rightarrow \psi$. A *least* fixed point of Γ, denoted by $\mu\psi.\Gamma(\psi)$, is a fixed point ϕ such that for any other fixed point ψ of Γ, it is the case that $\models (\phi \rightarrow \psi)$. A *greatest* fixed point of Γ, denoted by $\nu\psi.\Gamma(\psi)$, is a fixed point ϕ such that for any other fixed point ψ of Γ, it is the case that $\models (\psi \rightarrow \phi)$. Whenever the transition system $\langle \mathcal{V}, \Theta, \Phi \rangle$ is clear from the context, we define the transformer $\mathcal{I}$ by $\mathcal{I}(\phi) = \mathsf{SP}(\Phi)(\phi) \vee \Theta$. Note that the transformer $\mathcal{I}$ is monotonic. The least fixed point of this operator, $\mu\psi.\mathcal{I}(\psi)$, whenever it exists in the first-order language, represents the set $Reach(\Phi)(\Theta)$ of reachable states.

2.1   Invariants

A formula ϕ is an *S-invariant* if $Reach(\Phi)(\Theta) \subset [\![\phi]\!]$. Thus, an invariant describes an over-approximation of the set of reachable states. An *S-inductive invariant* is a formula ϕ such that (i) ϕ is an S-invariant, and (ii) ϕ is inductive, i.e., $\models \mathsf{SP}(\Phi)(\phi) \rightarrow \phi$. Condition (ii) can be equivalently stated as $\models \phi \rightarrow \mathsf{WP}(\Phi)(\phi)$. In other words, ϕ is an S-inductive invariant if $\models \mathcal{I}(\phi) \rightarrow \phi$. Note that the definition does not require an equivalence, but only an implication.

It is easy to establish that the set of reachable states $Reach(\Phi)(\Theta)$ of a system S represents the strongest (inductive) invariant. By this we mean that if ψ is any other (inductive) invariant, then, $Reach(\mathrm{S})(\Theta) \subset [\![\psi]\!]$. However, note that if ϕ is an inductive invariant, and $\models (\phi \rightarrow \psi)$, then ψ need not be an inductive invariant because ψ might violate condition (ii). For purposes of this paper, we will only be interested in inductive invariants. Thus, we are *not* interested in just obtaining *any* over-approximation of the set of reachable states, but only those that also satisfy condition (ii). This is because the inductive property provides a sufficient local characterization of invariance property, which makes the task of proving easier.

Given a transition system $\mathrm{S} = (\mathcal{V}, \Theta, \Phi)$, the *converse* transition system $\mathrm{S}^{-1} = (\mathcal{V}, \Theta, \Phi^{-1})$ is defined by $\Phi^{-1}(\boldsymbol{x}, \boldsymbol{y}) = \Phi(\boldsymbol{y}, \boldsymbol{x})$. The following well-known theorem says that if none of the initial states is backward reachable from the states represented by ϕ, then $\neg\phi$ is an invariant.

Theorem 1. *Let $S = \langle \mathcal{V}, \Theta, \Phi \rangle$ be a transition system and ϕ an arbitrary formula. If ψ is such that $\models (\mathsf{SP}(\Phi^{-1})(\psi) \vee \phi) \rightarrow \psi$ and the formula $\Theta \wedge \psi$ is unsatisfiable, then $\neg\psi$ is an S-inductive invariant.*

Corollary 1. *If $Reach(\Phi^{-1})(\phi) \cap [\![\Theta]\!] = \emptyset$, then the formula corresponding to the complement of the set $Reach(\Phi^{-1})(\phi)$ is an S-inductive invariant.*

We remark here that although application of the $\mathsf{SP}(\Phi)$ transformer is called "forward propagation", the term "backward propagation" is typically used for the transformer $\mathsf{WP}(\Phi)$. But there is no anomaly here as the transformers $\mathsf{SP}(\Phi^{-1})$ and $\mathsf{WP}(\Phi)$ are duals in the sense that $\mathsf{SP}(\Phi^{-1})(\phi)$ is logically equivalent to $\neg\mathsf{WP}(\Phi)(\neg\phi)$. Hence, Theorem 1 can be stated in terms of $\mathsf{WP}(\Phi)$. It also follows that if formula ϕ is an invariant, then the formula $\nu\psi.\phi \wedge \mathsf{WP}(\Phi)(\psi)$ is an inductive invariant that is a strengthening of ϕ[2]. Similarly, it is easy to see that there is a corresponding connection between the $\mathsf{SP}(\Phi)$ and $\mathsf{WP}(\Phi^{-1})$ transformers.

---

[2] It follows from this duality that the the least (greatest) fixed point iterations of $\mathsf{SP}(\Phi^{-1}) \vee \phi$ are logically equivalent to the negations of the greatest (least) fixed point iterations of $\mathsf{WP}(\Phi) \wedge \neg\phi$.

3   Inductive Invariant Generation

In this section, we discuss the problem of automatically generating some useful inductive invariants for a given transition system. It is a simple observation that the greatest fixed point $\nu\phi.\mathcal{I}(\phi)$, whenever it exists, is an S-inductive invariant.

Lemma 1. *Let $S = \langle \mathcal{V}, \Theta, \Phi \rangle$ be a transition system. Recursively define the sequence of formulas $\phi_0, \phi_1, \ldots$, as follows.*

$$\phi_0 = \texttt{true} \qquad \phi_{i+1} = \texttt{SP}(\Phi)(\phi_i) \vee \Theta$$

Then, every formula ϕ_i is an S-inductive invariant. Furthermore, every formula ϕ_i in the above sequence can be decomposed as $\psi_i \vee \chi_i$, where

$$\psi_0 = \texttt{false} \qquad \psi_{i+1} = \texttt{SP}(\Phi)(\psi_i) \vee \Theta$$
$$\chi_0 = \texttt{true} \qquad \chi_{i+1} = \texttt{SP}(\Phi)(\chi_i).$$

The sequence $\psi_0, \psi_1, \ldots$, represents iterations in a least fixed point computation of the $\mathcal{I}$ transformer. The sequence $\chi_0, \chi_1, \ldots$, represents the greatest fixed point component. The formulas ψ_i provide successive under-approximations of the set $Reach(\Phi)(\Theta)$ of reachable states. The formulas ϕ_i are inductive over-approximations. The sequence $\psi_0, \psi_1, \ldots$, usually does not terminate, whereas the sequence $\phi_0, \phi_1, \ldots$, often terminates with very weak invariants.

It should be observed here that the greatest fixed point of the $\texttt{SP}(\Phi)(\_) \vee \Theta$ transformer characterizes states σ such that there exists a backward path starting from σ which is either infinite, or contains some initial state. In case of finite state transition systems, this is exactly the set of states that either belong to a strongly connected component, or, that are reachable from either some initial state or some strongly connected component. Hence, the greatest fixed point may not be the strongest S-inductive invariant even in the case of finite systems. Despite its shortcomings, this simple method is attractive since (i) we do not need to detect that the iterations have converged[3], and (ii) every formula ϕ_i is an S-inductive invariant. Detecting convergence is difficult as it involves deciding if $\models \phi_i \leftrightarrow \phi_{i+1}$.

Example 1. Consider the transition system over ten states presented in Figure 1.

3.1   Widening and Narrowing

In the case when the state space is either infinite, or finite but too large, the symbolic computation of (greatest or least) fixed points of various transformers is restricted by the finite space and time resources available. A well-known solution to this problem is the use of *widening* and *narrowing* to respectively enhance the

---

[3]   If ϕ is an S-invariant, then every iteration in the greatest fixed point computation of $\texttt{WP}(\Phi)(\_) \wedge \phi$ is also an S-invariant. But, if ϕ is inductive, then this method yields ϕ.

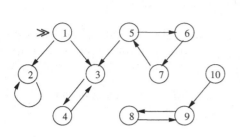

States are represented by nodes with integer labels and transitions are represented by edges. State 1 is the initial state. Clearly, the set of reachable states is the set

$$\{1, 2, 3, 4\}.$$

The greatest fixed point of the SP(Φ) $\vee$ Θ is the set consisting of states

$$\{1, 2, 3, 4, 5, 6, 7, 8, 9\}.$$

Fig. 1. A finite state transition system.

least and greatest fixed point computation (with gains obtained both in terms of space and time).

A *widening* operator $\triangledown : \mathcal{F} \times \mathcal{F} \mapsto \mathcal{F}$ is a function such that for all formulas $\phi, \phi' \in \mathcal{F}$, $\models (\phi \vee \phi') \rightarrow \triangledown(\phi, \phi')$. Similarly, a *narrowing* operator $\triangle : \mathcal{F} \times \mathcal{F} \mapsto \mathcal{F}$ is a function such that for all formulas $\phi, \phi' \in \mathcal{F}$, $\models \triangle(\phi, \phi') \rightarrow (\phi \wedge \phi')$. Thus, logical disjunction $\vee$ is a trivial widening operator, and logical conjunction $\wedge$ is a trivial narrowing operator.

The definitions of widening and narrowing are slightly different from the standard ones [8, 9]. First, we do not include any conditions to guarantee that increasing (decreasing) sequences are transformed to finite, hence converging, increasing (decreasing) sequences by widening (narrowing). Secondly, in the case of narrowing, the standard definition requires that whenever $\phi' \rightarrow \phi$, the formula $\triangle(\phi, \phi')$ is such that $\phi' \rightarrow \triangle(\phi, \phi')$ and $\triangle(\phi, \phi') \rightarrow \phi$. In our definition, $\triangle(\phi, \phi')$ is stronger than both ϕ and ϕ' as our interest is in the use of narrowing to obtain *under*-approximations of the greatest fixed point. But we have to be careful so as to not eliminate any reachable states by overly aggressive under-approximation, see Lemma 3.

A particularly simple narrowing operator, denoted by $\triangle(\psi)$, is defined by $\triangle(\psi)(\phi, \phi') = \phi \wedge \phi' \wedge \psi$, where ψ is an arbitrary formula. Similarly, we can define $\triangledown(\psi)(\phi, \phi') = \phi \vee \phi' \vee \psi$. Since we are interested in generating inductive invariants, it turns out that in order to guarantee correctness, we can use any arbitrary widening operator, but not any narrowing operator.

Lemma 2. *[Upward iteration sequence with widening] Let $\psi_0, \psi_1, \ldots$, be a sequence of formulas such that ψ_0 is Θ, and for every $i > 0$, either*
   (i) ψ_i is SP(Φ)(ψ_{i-1}) $\vee \psi_{i-1}$, or
   (ii) ψ_i is $\triangledown(\alpha_i)(\psi_{i-2}, \psi_{i-1})$, where α_i is any arbitrary formula.
Then, if for some $n > 0$, $\models$ SP(Φ)(ψ_n) $\rightarrow \psi_n$, then the formula ψ_n is an S-inductive invariant.

Lemma 3. *[Downward iteration sequence with narrowing] Let $\phi_0, \phi_1, \ldots$, be a sequence of formulas such that ϕ_0 is* **true***, and for every $i > 0$, either* *(i)* ϕ_i is $\mathsf{SP}(\Phi)(\phi_{i-1}) \vee \Theta$, *or*

(ii) ϕ_i is $\triangle(\beta_i)(\phi_{i-2}, \phi_{i-1})$, *where β_i is some S-inductive invariant.*
Then, for every i, ϕ_i is an S-inductive invariant[4] such that $\models \phi_i \to \beta_i$.

Lemma 3 extends the greatest fixed point iterations in Lemma 1 by a narrowing operator. Similarly, Lemma 2 extends the least fixed point computation that is hidden inside the iterations in Lemma 1 by a widening operator.

We obtain the formula β_i used in Lemma 3 by identifying strongly connected components consisting of unreachable states. This is achieved using backward propagation from an unreachable state, as outlined in Theorem 1. These unreachable states are not automatically eliminated by the greatest fixed point computation outlined in Lemma 1. Furthermore, an S-inductive invariant obtained using Lemma 2 can be used in Step (ii) of Lemma 3. Thus, Lemma 3 gives a method for systematically strengthening known invariants.

Example 2. Following up on Example 1, let $N = \{1, 2, \ldots, 10\}$ denote the set of all states. In order to strengthen the over-approximation, viz. $N - \{10\}$, of the set of reachable states obtained via the greatest fixed point computation, we can try removing certain states. But if we remove a subset of states that is not strongly connected, the subsequent fixed point computation may no longer be monotonic, and could fail to converge.

For instance, removing state 5 from the above set gives a new set $N_1 = N - \{5, 10\}$. Now, $\mathsf{SP}(\Phi)(\phi_{N_1}) \vee \Theta$, where ϕ_{N_1} is the characteristic predicate of N_1, represents the set $N_2 = N - \{6, 10\}$. Clearly, $N_2 \not\subseteq N_1$, and hence the sequence of formulas obtained in the greatest fixed point computation is no longer monotonic. Note that all formulas in the sequence are invariants, but they are not inductive.

In order to identify unreachable states, we note that if we start with the set $N_3 = \{7, 8\}$, and we assign ϕ in Theorem 1 to the characteristic predicate ϕ_{N_3} of N_3. The least fixed point of $\mathsf{SP}(\Phi^{-1}) \vee \phi_{N_3}$ represents the set $N_4 = \{5, 6, 7, 8, 9, 10\}$. Now, since the formula $\Theta \wedge \phi_{N_4}$ is unsatisfiable (i.e. the set $\{1\} \cap N_4 = \emptyset$), it follows from Theorem 1 that the set $N_5 = \{1, 2, 3, 4\}$ represented by $\neg\phi_{N_4}$ is an S-inductive invariant.

4   An Any-Time Algorithm for Generating Inductive Invariants

The transition predicate Φ of a transition system $\mathsf{S} = (\mathcal{V} = \{x_1, \ldots, x_n\}, \Theta, \Phi)$ is typically specified using a finite set of *guarded transitions*, where a guarded transition consists of a guard $\gamma \in \mathcal{F}$, and a finite set of assignments $\{x_1 := e_1(\boldsymbol{x}), \ldots, x_n := e_n(\boldsymbol{x})\}$. A guarded transition τ is written as

$$\gamma \longmapsto x_1 := e_1(\boldsymbol{x}); \ldots; x_n := e_n(\boldsymbol{x})$$

---

[4] Note that the lemma also holds if we drop the word "inductive" from the statement.

where e_i is some expression with free variables in the set x. We shall also use the compact notation $x := e(x)$ to represent the above assignments.

A typical specification of a guarded transition system contains at least one control variable, usually the program counter $pc \in \{x_1, \ldots, x_n\}$, which takes values from a finite set, say $\{1, \ldots, p\}$. Control states are defined by formulas of the form $pc = i$, $i \in \{1, \ldots, p\}$. This transition system then has p different control states. Additionally, we assume that the source states of each guarded transition belong to some *fixed* source control state, $pc = i$, (and similarly for the target states) so that each transition τ can be written as

$$pc = i \wedge \gamma \longmapsto x := e(x); pc := j$$

where x denotes variables in $\mathcal{V} - \{pc\}$. In this case, we define $src(\tau) = i$ and $tgt(\tau) = j$. By $\Phi_\tau(x, x')$, we denote the formula $\gamma(x) \wedge x' = e(x)$. If $\mathcal{T}$ is a set of such transitions, then the transition predicate Φ is itself defined by $\bigvee_{\tau \in \mathcal{T}} pc = src(\tau) \wedge pc' = tgt(\tau) \wedge \Phi_\tau$. Similarly, we assume that $\models \Theta \to pc = 1$.

Whenever such a decomposition of the state space into finitely many control states is available such that every transition has a unique source and target control state, the S-invariant can be maintained as a conjunction of local invariants indexed by the control locations. We assume that every formula is represented as an array of formulas indexed by integers $\{1, \ldots, p\}$. Given an S-inductive invariant φ (as an array of formulas), and a transition predicate Φ, the function `propagation`$(\Theta, \Phi, \varphi, k)$ returns the strengthened S-inductive invariant $\mathcal{I}^k(\varphi)$.

```
function propagation(Θ, Φ, φ, k) {
    let Θ be pc = 1 ∧ Θ';
    for k iterations do: for every i in parallel do {
        T_i := {τ ∈ T : tgt(τ) = i};
        φ[i] := { ⋁_{τ∈T_i} SP(Φ_τ)(φ[src(τ)]) ∨ Θ'   if i = 1 };
                { ⋁_{τ∈T_i} SP(Φ_τ)(φ[src(τ)])         if i ≠ 1 }
        φ[i] := ℜ-simplify(φ[i]);
    }
    return(φ);
}
```

The function $\mathfrak{R}$-`simplify` performs quantifier-elimination and simplification in the theory $\mathfrak{R}$ and is described in Section 4.2.

Lemma 4. *Let $S = (\mathcal{V}, \Theta, \Phi)$ be a transition system and let φ_0 be an array of formulas initialized to* **true**. *Let φ_k denotes the array* `propagation`$(\Theta, \Phi, \varphi_0, k)$ *of formulas (assuming $\mathfrak{R}$-`simplify` always returns equivalent formulas), and ϕ_k be as defined in Lemma 1. Then, for all $k \geq 0$, $\models \phi_k \leftrightarrow \bigwedge_{i=1}^p (pc = i \to \varphi_k[i])$. Consequently, the formula $\bigwedge_{i=1}^p (pc = i \to \varphi_k[i])$ is an S-inductive invariant, for every k.*

Notice that the formula $\bigwedge_{i=1}^p (pc = i \to \varphi[i])$ is equivalent to the formula $\bigvee_{i=1}^p (pc = i \wedge \varphi[i])$ under the assumption that $\bigvee_{i=1}^p (pc = i)$. The computations outlined in other lemmas and theorems can be suitably cast in terms of local invariants at control locations.

4.1   Combining $\mathtt{SP}(\varPhi)$ and $\mathtt{SP}(\varPhi^{-1})$ Iterations

The basic algorithm for the automatic generation of inductive invariants consists of affirmation and propagation steps—the essence of whic h is captured in Lemma 1 and function **propagation**. In order to get stronger invariants, we propose the use of narrowing and widening.

The function $\mathtt{widening}(\vartheta, \varphi, k)$ starts with a given under-approximation ϑ of the set of reachable states, and widens it using a subformula α of the over-approximation φ. If this widening yields an S-inductive invariant (see Lemma 2) in k propagation steps, then the function returns this invariant, otherwise it just returns **true**[5].

```
function widening(ϑ, φ, k) {
    χ := ϑ;
    choose j ∈ {1, . . . , p} and a formula α s.t.
        φ[j] is of the form φ' ∨ α, and ϑ[j] ∧ α is satisfiable;
    χ[j] := χ[j] ∨ α;                          /* widening */
    χ := propagation(Θ, Φ, χ, k);
    if (⊨ propagation(Θ, Φ, χ, 1)[i] → χ[i] for all i)
        return(χ);                             /* new invariant */
    return(true);
}
```

Lemma 5. *For any value of the constant k, if χ denotes the array of formulas returned by* $\mathtt{widening}(\vartheta, \varphi, k)$, *then the formula* $\bigwedge_{i=1}^{p} pc = i \rightarrow \chi[i]$ *is an S-inductive invariant.*

Strongly connected components of unreachable states are detected using backward propagation, and if successful, this information is used for strengthening the current invariant. The subroutine $\mathtt{narrowing}(\vartheta, \varphi, k)$ chooses a subformula β of the over-approximation φ which could possibly represent unreachable states. Thereafter, it computes the set of states that are backward reachable from the conjectured unreachable states β and if we successfully terminate without intersecting Θ (see Theorem 1), then we again have an S-inductive invariant.

```
function narrowing(ϑ, φ, k) {
    choose j ∈ {1, . . . , p} and a formula β s.t.
        φ[j] is of the form φ' ∨ β, and ϑ[j] ∧ β is unsatisfiable;
    χ := propagation(pc = j ∧ β, Φ⁻¹, false, k);
    if (⊨propagation(pc = j ∧ β, Φ⁻¹, χ, 1)[i] → χ[i] for all i)
        if (⊨ ¬(χ ∧ Θ))
            return(Invariant(¬χ));
        else if (χ ∧ Θ is satisfiable)        /* β is reachable */
            return(Reachable(pc = j ∧ β));
```

---

[5]   We shall overload **true** (**false**) to also denote arrays in which every element is **true** (**false**), and use assignments between arrays to mean element-wise copying.

```
    return(Invariant(true));
}
```

The return value Reachable(ψ) of the function narrowing(ϑ, φ, k) says that the states represented by ψ are reachable, and the return value Invariant(ψ) denotes that the formula represented by ψ is an inductive invariant.

Lemma 6. *For any value of the constant k, if the function* narrowing(ϑ, φ, k) *returns* Reachable(ψ), *then* $[\![\psi]\!] \subset Reach(\Phi)(\Theta)$. *Similarly, for any value of the constant k, if* narrowing(ϑ, φ, k) *returns* Invariant(ψ), *then the formula* $\bigwedge_{i=1}^{p}(pc = i \rightarrow \psi[i])$ *is an S-inductive invariant.*

Finally, we outline a procedure that uses the various functions described above by combining the least fixed point and greatest fixed point computations with narrowing and widening. In the procedure, the formula ψ always stores an under-approximation of the set of reachable states, and the formula ϕ always stores an S-inductive invariant. The procedure essentially consists of doing one of four different steps—(i) Augmen ting ψ using propagation(Θ, Φ, ψ, k), where k is some constant; (ii) Strengthening the current invariant ϕ using the function propagation(Θ, Φ, ϕ, k); (iii) Use of widening on the under-approximation for generating an invariant; and, (iv) Use of narrowing to detect and eliminate unreachable states from the over-approximation.

```
/* Given: S = (V, Θ, Φ), a transition system with p control states.
   The transition predicate Φ is indexed by guarded transitions.
   k is an upper bound on the number of iterations. */
Procedure InvGen:
   φ, ψ: Array [1...p] of formula
   Initialization:
       φ := true;
       ψ := false;
   repeatedly do the following {{
       ψ := propagation(Θ, Φ, ψ, k);
       if (⊨ propagation(Θ, Φ, ψ, 1)[i] → ψ[i] for all i)
           φ := ψ; terminate the program;
   } OR {
       φ := propagation(Θ, Φ, φ, k);
   } OR {
       φ := φ ∧ widening(ψ, φ, k);
   } OR {
       if (narrowing(ψ, φ, k) returns Reachable(β))
           ψ[j] := ψ[j] ∨ χ where β is pc = j ∧ χ;
       else (assuming narrowing returns Invariant(β))
           φ[i] := φ[i] ∧ β[i] for all i;
   }}
```

Theorem 2. *Let ϕ be the array of formulas in the procedure* InvGen. *Then, at any stage of the procedure, the formula $\bigwedge_i (pc = i \rightarrow \phi[i])$ is an S-inductive invariant.*

Our procedure does not consider the control structure of the transition graph to generate invariants. Though specific control structures, like loops, are not relevant for correctness of the basic procedure, they can be important in choosing specific points for widening or narrowing [6]. We wish to point out that the procedure is tolerant to theorem proving failures and only assumes a refutationally complete prover. In particular, note that the satisfiability test in widening can be eliminated.

4.2 Quantifier Elimination and Simplification

We remark here that implementation of propagation requires elimination of existential quantifiers. The existential quantifier in $\text{SP}(\Phi^{-1})(\phi)$ and the universal quantifier in $\text{WP}(\Phi)(\phi)$ can both be easily eliminated using substitutions. The quantifiers in $\text{SP}(\Phi)(\phi)$ and $\text{WP}(\Phi^{-1})(\phi)$ cannot be eliminated so easily in general. But in special cases, for instance when the transition is "reversible" (for example, the effect of assignment $x := x + y$ can be reversed by the assignment $x := x - y$), quantifier elimination reduces to substitution again. In cases where exact quantifier elimination is not possible, we can still get a correct procedure using a quantifier elimination procedure that returns a "weaker" formula, i.e., we do *not* need an equivalence preserving quantifier elimination procedure.

Let $\Re$-simplify be a function such that $\models \phi \rightarrow \Re\text{-simplify}(\phi)$. We shall denote the formula $\Re$-simplify(ϕ) by $\overline{\phi}$ in the next theorem.

Theorem 3. *Let $\psi_0, \psi_1, \ldots, \psi_i$ be an upward iteration sequence with widening and $\phi_0, \phi_1, \ldots, \phi_i$ be a downward iteration sequence with narrowing (see Lemmas 2 and 3). Then the sequence $\psi_0, \psi_1, \ldots, \psi_i, \overline{\psi_i}$ is also an upward iteration sequence with widening. Similarly, the sequence $\phi_0, \phi_1, \ldots, \phi_{i-1}, \phi'_i$, where ϕ'_i is $\phi_{i-1} \wedge \overline{\phi_i}$, is also a downward iteration sequence with narrowing.*

Note that the formula ϕ'_i in Theorem 3 can be seen as results of "narrowing" in the sense of [9]. Theorem 3 makes it possible for simple (and possibly incomplete) quantifier elimination procedures to suffice for our purposes. For instance, when it is not possible to eliminate the existential quantifier from $\exists x. p(x) \wedge q(x)$, we could weaken this to $\exists x. p(x) \wedge \exists x. q(x)$ and perform quantifier elimination on atomic formulas. With suitable modifications as outlined in Theorem 3, our procedure continues to be correct. In fact, such simplifications help in the convergence of the iterations as well.

Finally, as pointed out in Lemma 1, implementation of the above procedure can be optimized by combining the arrays ψ and ϕ into a single array, say φ. If individual formulas $\varphi[i]$ are always stored in disjunctive normal form, then we can distinguish the disjuncts that would appear in $\psi[i]$ by marking them. In this way, a single propagation step can be used to update both ψ and ϕ. The implementation of the above procedure is being done in the framework of SAL [1], which is a collection of different tools for analyzing concurrent systems.

4.3   Illustrative Examples

W e shall provide certain simple examples to illustrate the procedure. The theory of interest is the theory of linear arithmetic, and we assume that we have an exact quantifier elimination procedure.

Example 3. Consider the example outlined in Section 1. In this case, the least fixed point sequence converges in two steps. In particular, we obtain the invariant $pc = inc \rightarrow x = 0 \wedge pc = dec \rightarrow x = 2$.

Example 4. A simplified version of the Bakery mutual exclusion protocol $S = (\mathcal{V}, \Theta, \Phi)$ for two processes $p1$ and $p2$ accessing a critical section cs is given by $\mathcal{V} = \{y1 : int, y2 : int, pc1 : \{1, 2, 3\}, pc2 : \{1, 2, 3\}\}$, Θ is $pc1 = 1 \wedge pc2 = 1 \wedge y1 = 0 \wedge y2 = 0$, and Φ is defined by the following set of guarded transitions:

$$
\begin{array}{rcll}
pc1 = 1 & \longmapsto & y1 := y2 + 1; pc1 := 2; & // \text{ p1: try} \\
pc1 = 2 \wedge (y2 = 0 \vee y1 \le y2) & \longmapsto & pc1 := 3; & // \text{ p1: enter cs} \\
pc1 = 3 & \longmapsto & y1 := 0; pc1 := 1; & // \text{ p1: exit cs} \\
pc2 = 1 & \longmapsto & y2 := y1 + 1; pc2 := 2; & // \text{ p2: try} \\
pc2 = 2 \wedge (y1 = 0 \vee y2 < y1) & \longmapsto & pc2 := 3; & // \text{ p2: enter cs} \\
pc2 = 3 & \longmapsto & y2 := 0; pc2 := 1; & // \text{ p2: exit cs}
\end{array}
$$

Since this system has an infinite number of reachable states, the least fixed point computation sequence does not converge. We choose to define 9 control locations based on the values of $pc1$ and $pc2$ variables, and we shall use the notation $\phi[i, j]$ to denote the current invariant at control location $pc1 = i \wedge pc2 = j$. After a few iterations, the greatest fixed point iterations yield a formula ϕ, with the following three local invariants (due to space restrictions, we are not writing down the complete formula here):

$$
\begin{array}{l}
\phi[3, 1] : y2 = 0 \\
\phi[3, 2] : (y2 = y1 + 1) \vee (y1 = 1 \wedge y2 = 0) \\
\phi[3, 3] : (y1 = 0 \wedge y2 = 1) \vee (y1 = 1 \wedge y2 = 0)
\end{array}
$$

The disjunct β, defined as $y1 = 0 \wedge y2 = 1$, in control location $pc1 = 3 \wedge pc2 = 3$ can be conjectured to be unreachable (as the formula $\psi[3, 3]$ in the least fixed point iterations is always **false**) and for a suitable choice of k, the formula $\chi := \texttt{propagation}(pc1 = 3 \wedge pc2 = 3 \wedge \beta, \Phi^{-1}, \texttt{false}, k)$ contains the following strongly connected set of unreachable states,

$$
\begin{array}{lll}
\chi[3, 3] : y1 = 0 & \chi[3, 2] : y1 = 0 & \chi[2, 3] : y1 = 0 \\
\chi[3, 1] : y1 = 0 & \chi[2, 2] : y1 = 0 & \chi[2, 1] : y1 = 0
\end{array}
$$

Similarly, we can eliminate the other possibility ($y1 = 1 \wedge y2 = 0$) at control location $pc1 = 3 \wedge pc2 = 3$. This proves mutual exclusion. W e can also use a single widening step to obtain an inductive invariant strong enough to prove mutual exclusion. Note that it was pointed out in [5] that the computation of $\nu\phi.(\texttt{WP}(\Phi)(\phi) \wedge (pc1 = 3 \wedge pc2 = 3 \rightarrow \texttt{false}))$ terminates in a finite number of steps and yields an invariant that proves mutual exclusion.

Example 5. Consider the following transitions:

$$pc = 1 \longmapsto x := x + 2; y := y + 2; pc := 2;$$
$$pc = 2 \longmapsto x := x - 2; y := y + 2; pc := 1;$$

with initial state predicate $pc = 1 \wedge x = 0 \wedge y = 0$. Assuming that the variables x and y are declared to be integers, neither the least fixed point sequence, nor the greatest fixed point sequence converges. After a few iterations for computing the greatest fixed point, the formula ϕ we obtain is:

$$pc = 1 \rightarrow (x = 0 \wedge y = 0) \vee (x = 0 \wedge y = 4) \vee (x \geq 0 \wedge y \geq 8)$$
$$pc = 2 \rightarrow (x = 2 \wedge y = 2) \vee (x = 2 \wedge y = 6) \vee (x \geq 2 \wedge y \geq 10)$$

The predicate $\geq$ can be replaced by the predicates $=$ and $>$. Now, the disjunct β can be chosen as $x > 0 \wedge y \geq 8$ and it can be conjectured to be unreachable. The formula $\texttt{propagation}(pc = 1 \wedge \beta, \Phi^{-1}, \texttt{false}, 2)$ contains the following strongly connected set of unreachable states,

$$pc = 1 \rightarrow x > 0 \wedge y \geq 8 \qquad pc = 2 \rightarrow x > 2 \wedge y \geq 6$$

Conjunction of the negation of this formula with the original invariant ϕ gives the following new invariant,

$$pc = 1 \rightarrow (x = 0 \wedge y = 0) \vee (x = 0 \wedge y = 4) \vee (x = 0 \wedge y \geq 8)$$
$$pc = 2 \rightarrow (x = 2 \wedge y = 2) \vee (x = 2 \wedge y = 6) \vee (x = 2 \wedge y \geq 10)$$

As before, in this case again widening can also be used to obtain a similar invariant.

5   Related Work and Concluding Remarks

Early work [12, 10] on generating invariant for sequential programs has been extended to the case of reactive systems in [16, 13, 5, 11, 2]. These methods are usually based on the propagation of invariants through the control structure of the different components and by combining local invariants of each component to construct global invariants of the system.

Forward and backward propagation using operators $\texttt{SP}(\Phi)$ and $\texttt{WP}(\Phi)$ is also used in [5] as the basic technique for generating invariants. In addition, over-approximations such as the convex hull of the union of polyhedra, are used for widening fixed point computations. Our approach differs in that we consider simultaneous forward and backward propagation for computing both lower and upper bounds of the reachable state sets. These bounds are also used for computing suitable narrowing and widening operators. The combination of these techniques usually yields much stronger invariants. Moreover, our algorithm is an any-time algorithm, in the sense that it can be interrupted at any time to yield the most refined inductive invariant computed up to the point of interruption.

The method of generalized reaffirmed in variance and propagation was introduced in [2] and is based on *affirming* local invariants of the form $\mathrm{SP}(\varPhi(\tau))(\texttt{true})$ and *propagating* these local invariants along all transitions. This process of affirmation and propagation, however, is performed only in the special case when all the existential quantifiers arising in the process are trivial, i.e., when the quantified variables do not occur in the rest of the formula; the *twos* example in the introduction does not possess this property. The technique presented in [2] also uses information about the control transition graph, especially knowledge about cycles and how variables are manipulated in the cycle transitions, to generate stronger invariants. In some cases, these stronger local invariants can be generated by repeated propagation (in the stronger sense defined in this paper). In general, however, the detection of unreachable cycles is crucial, as outlined in Theorem 1.

Techniques based on abstraction have also been proposed for generating invariants [14,3]. It appears attractive to first create (finite) abstractions for large programs and then to use standard propagation techniques to obtain the set of states reachable in the abstract system. This set can then be concretized to obtain invariants of the concrete system. Abstraction can be cast as a special widening strategy in our procedure. More specifically, let (α, γ) be an abstraction and concretization pair (Galois connection) for a transition system $S = (\mathcal{V}, \Theta, \varPhi)$. Let $S_a = (\mathcal{V}_a, \Theta_a, \varPhi_a)$ denote the abstract transition system. If

$$\psi_a^{(0)}, \psi_a^{(1)}, \psi_a^{(2)}, \ldots$$

is a least fixed point computation on the abstract transition system S_a, then one obtains a corresponding fixed point computation with widening on the concrete system

$$\psi^{(0)}, \psi^{(1)}, \psi^{(1')}, \psi^{(2)}, \psi^{(2')}, \ldots$$

as follows: the formula $\psi^{(i)}$ is $\mathrm{SP}(\varPhi)(\psi^{(i-1')}) \vee \psi^{(i-1')}$ (Step (i) of Lemma 2), and $\psi^{(i')}$ is $\psi^{(i)} \vee \gamma(\alpha(\psi^{(i)}))$ (Step (ii) of Lemma 2). Now, if $\models \gamma(\psi_a^{(i)}) \leftrightarrow \psi^{(i')}$, then it is also the case that $\models \gamma(\psi_a^{(i+1)}) \leftrightarrow \psi^{(i+1')}$. Thus, the fixed point computation on the abstract transition system can be suitably captured in the concrete system. We shall not prove this claim here, but refer to [9] for a similar result.

Note that the set of generated invariants is restricted to the ones expressible in the language of the theory $\Re$. A program that performs multiplication by repeated addition, for example, never uses the multiplication operator, but any expression that describes the set of reachable states typically would use the multiplication operator.

In summary, we present a technique for generation of inductive invariants using a combination of least and greatest fixed point computations of the forward and backward propagation operators. With obvious modifications, the results can be used to strengthen invariants. Thus, any technique for generation of invariants, inductive or not, can be incorporated with the techniques in this paper.

Acknowledgements We would like to thank S. Bensalem, S. Owre, Y. Lakhnech, J. Rushby, J. Sifakis, and the referees for their helpful comments.

References

[1] S. Bensalem, V. Ganesh, Y. Lakhnech, C. Muñoz, S. Owre, H. Rueß, J. Rushby, V. Rusu, H. Saïdi, N. Shankar, E. Singerman, and A. Tiwari. An overview of SAL. In C. M. Holloway, editor, *LFM 2000: Fifth NASA Langley Formal Methods Workshop*, pages 187–196, 2000. Available at http://shemesh.larc.nasa.gov/fm/Lfm2000/Proc/.

[2] S. Bensalem and Y. Lakhnech. Automatic generation of invariants. *Formal Methods in System Design*, 15:75–92, 1999.

[3] S. Bensalem, Y. Lakhnech, and S. Owre. Computing abstractions of infinite state systems compositionally and automatically. In *Proc. of the 9th Conference on Computer-Aided Verification, CAV'98*, LNCS. Springer Verlag, June 1998.

[4] S. Bensalem, Y. Lakhnech, and H. Saïdi. Powerful techniques for the automatic generation of invariants. In R. Alur and T. A. Henzinger, editors, *Computer-Aided Verification, CAV '96*, number 1102 in LNCS, pages 323–335. Springer-Verlag, 1996.

[5] N. Bjørner, A. Browne, and Z. Manna. Automatic Generation of Invariants and Intermediate Assertions. *Theoretical Computer Science*, 1997.

[6] F. Bourdoncle. Efficient chaotic iteration strategies with widenings. In *Proceedings of the Intl Conf on Formal Methods in Programming and their Applications*, volume 735 of *LNCS*, pages 128–141. Springer Verlag, 1993.

[7] E. M. Clarke, O. Grumberg, and D. E. Long. Model checking and abstraction. *ACM Transactions on Programming Languages and Systems*, 16(5):1512–1542, September 1994.

[8] P. Cousot and R. Cousot. Abstract interpretation: a unified lattice model for static analysis of programs by construction or approximation of fixpoints. In *4th POPL*, January 1977.

[9] P. Cousot and R. Cousot. Comparing the Galois connection and widening/narrowing approaches to abstract interpretation. In M. Bruynooghe and M. Wirsing, editors, *Proc. of the 4th Intl. Symposium on Programming Language Implementation and Logic Programming (PLILP '92)*, volume 631 of *LNCS*, pages 269–295, Berlin, 1992. Springer-Verlag.

[10] S. M. German and B. Wegbreit. A synthesizer of inductive assertions. *IEEE Transactions on Software Engineering*, 1(1):68–75, March 1975.

[11] S. Graf and H. Saïdi. Verifying invariants using theorem proving. In *Conference on Computer Aided Verification CAV'96*, LNCS 1102, Springer Verlag, 1996.

[12] S. Katz and Z. Manna. Logical analysis of programs. *Communications of the ACM*, 19(4):188–206, April 1976.

[13] L. Lamport. The 'Hoare logic' of concurrent programs. In *Acta Informatica 14*, pages 21–37, 1980.

[14] C. Loiseaux, S. Graf, J. Sifakis, A. Bouajjani, and S. Bensalem. Property preserving abstractions for the verification of concurrent systems. *Formal Methods in System Design*, 6(1), January 1995.

[15] Z. Manna and A. Pnueli. *The Temporal Verification of Reactive Systems: Safety*. Springer-Verlag, 1995.

[16] S. Owicki and D. Gries. An axiomatic proof technique for parallel programs. *Acta Informatica*, 6:319–340, 1976.

[17] H. Saïdi and N. Shankar. Abstract and model check while you prove. In *Computer-Aided Verification, CAV '99*, Trento, Italy, July 1999.

Model Checking Syllabi and Student Careers [*]

Roberto Sebastiani[1], Alessandro Tomasi[1], and Fausto Giunchiglia[1,2]

[1] University of Trento, I-38050 Povo, Trento, Italy,
[2] ITC-IRST, I-38050 Povo, Trento, Italy
{rseba,atomasi,fausto}@cs.unitn.it

Abstract. Model checking has been conceived as a powerful tool for hardware, software and protocol verification, which has its main application fields in the development of hi-tech and safety-critical systems. We present here a completely novel application in the field of university administration processes, in which model checking is applied to the verification of the coherence of syllabi and to the automated synthesis/simulation of correct student careers under given requirements.

1 Motivations and Goals

Recently the Italian Ministry of University and Scientific & Technological Research, MURST —*the Ministry* from now on— has approved the reform of the Italian university, which will come into force in the year 2001-2002 [MURST2000a]. The result is a complex hybrid between the Anglo-Saxon and the traditional Italian university organizations. In order to forestall the many problems arising from the reform, the University of Trento and CINECA [1] have started a joint project, named SS2, whose goal is to build a model of the post-reform structure and administration processes of a university, and to develop a new information system for the university admission & examination offices.

One major problem with the reform evidenced by the project model is the much increased difficulty of reasoning on regulations, syllabi and student careers. For instance, the new autonomy given to the universities in organizing their degrees allows them to drastically enlarge the number of degrees of freedom for the student's career choices. Moreover, the introduction of new distinct didactic activity types, and of the different weights in credits, has further complicated both the planning and the verification of the student careers.

To partially cope with this problem, the project model allows for encoding the ordinance regulations for student careers as a set of *formal rules*, so that they can be read and understood by an automated device. This allows for an automatic verification of the correctness of a career wrt. the rules.

---

[*] The first and the third author are part of the SS2 project team. The other team members provided feedback on the formalization. Alessandro Cimatti, Marco Roveri and Paolo Traverso from ITC-IRST provided help on Symbolic Model Checking.
[1] Italian university consortium for automated computing.

T. Margaria and W. Yi (Eds.): TACAS 2001, LNCS 2031, pp. 128–142, 2001.

In this paper we go much further, and we describe how to apply model checking to solve the much harder problems of automatically planning/synthesizing correct student careers under given requirements, and of automatically verifying the coherence of syllabi wrt. the rules. The ultimate goal is to develop an automated support tool, to be integrated with the project's information system.

The paper is organized as follows. In Section 2, we describe in detail the domain and the problems of both career synthesis and syllabus coherence verification; in Section 3, we show how we encode the latter two problems as CTL model checking problems; in Section 4, we describe a prototype tool we have implemented; in Section 5, we present and discuss some preliminary empirical results; in Section 6, we discuss the ongoing and future work.

As a notational remark, many of the Italian terms we use do not have a straightforward translation into English. This is due to the fact that there is not a direct correspondence between the structure and administration processes of Italian and Anglo-Saxon universities. (E.g., the meaning of *ordinance* here may not be the same as it is in Oxford or Harvard.) Thus we will define the meaning of all non-obvious terms explicitly, reporting the corresponding Italian terms.

2   The Problem

2.1   A Model for the Domain

Didactic activities and syllabi By *didactic activity* ("attività didattica") we mean any activity a student can perform to enhance his/her career. Examples of didactic activities are, courses, seminars, theses, stages, projects. Most didactic activities are courses. Subjects are grouped into *subject areas* ("settore scientifico-disciplinare"), whose complete list is published by the Ministry [MURST2000b]. The estimated workload related to each activity is measured in *credits*. At the beginning of the year, the student has to register to a new *matriculation year* ("anno di corso"), which is either the successor of the old one —if the student is reasonably on schedule— or the old one itself —if the student is behind schedule and decides, or is forced, to repeat the year.

A didactic activity is modeled as a record; the fields which are relevant for our discussion are the following:

- the activity *code*;
- one activity *type*. Possible values are *course, seminars, stage, thesis*, etc.;
- one *subject area*;
- one *weight in credits*;
- the list of the codes of the *prerequisite didactic activities*; [2]
- the minimum *matriculation year* at which one can perform the activity.

Some examples of courses are given in Figure 1.

---

[2] Prerequisites obtained by transitivity are omitted.

	Code	Type	Subject area	Credit weight	Prerequisite courses	Matriculation year
1.	CSI	*course*	$INF01$	5	$\{\}$	1
2.	$CSII$	*course*	$INF01$	5	$\{CSI\}$	2
3.	OOP	*course*	$INF01$	5	$\{CSII\}$	2
4.	GEO	*course*	$MAT03$	5	$\{\}$	1
5.	AI	*course*	$INF01$	5	$\{CSI\}$	3
	...	...	...	...	...	...

Fig. 1. Examples of Courses.

Every year, for every degree course ordinance, the proper entity (faculty, department, ...) presents a *syllabus* ("offerta didattica"), i.e., the list of courses which are active that year. The other didactic activities (theses, stages, etc.) are proposed either by the teachers or by the students themselves. (For simplicity, from now on we will consider all didactic activities as part of the syllabus.)

Student careers We see a student's career C as an ordered list of didactic activities performed, each tagged with the matriculation year of the student when he/she performed it, —whic h has to be greater or equal than the minim um matriculation year of the didactic activity. We say that C is *on* a set of didactic activities A if all the didactic activities in C are in A. When matriculating, a student is given an empty career and is registered to the first matriculation year. Each time a student performs a didactic activity (passes an exam, presents successfully a seminar, defends a thesis, etc.), this activity is appended to the student career, together with the student's current matriculation year. If a didactic activity is a prerequisite of another, the former m ust occur before the latter. For instance,

$$C = \{\langle GEO, 1\rangle, \langle CSI, 2\rangle, \langle CSII, 2\rangle, \langle OOP, 2\rangle\} \tag{1}$$

is a career on the set of courses in Figure 1.

Ordinances and Rules When matriculating, a studen t is associated to an *ordinance* ("ordinamento didattico"), which states the regulations for the student's career, that is, the goals to achieve and the constraints to satisfy for graduation. In the project model this is represented by a set of formal rules for the student career. Some examples of rules are giv en in Figure 2. From a syntactic viewpoint, each rule is built on the following components:

- a *quantity*, in the form *at least|at most N*. N is an integer, called the *bound*;
- a *unit of measure*, in the form *credits|units*;
- an *activity type*. The values correspond to those of the didactic activities, plus the value *any*, which matches all values;
- a *scope*, given by a *scope type*, in the form *subject areas|courses|all*, and a *scope list*, which is a list of elements of scope type. If the latter is *all* ("any scope"), then no scope list is provided.

	Quantity	Unit of Measure	Activity Type	Scope Type	Scope List
r_1 :	at least 180	credits	any	all	
r_2 :	at least 90	credits	course	subject areas	{MAT01,...,MAT08}
r_3 :	at least 38	credits	course	subject areas	{FIS01,...,FIS08, INF01,ING-INF05}
r_4 :	at least 10	credits	course	subject areas	{INF01,ING-INF05}
r_5 :	at least 5	credits	thesis	all	
r_6 :	at least 9	credits	stage	all	
r_7 :	at least 2	units	course	courses	$\{CSI, CSII\}$
r_8 :	at most 15	credits	course	subject areas	{INF01,ING-INF05}
r_9 :	...	...	...	...	...

Fig. 2. Examples of Rules.

We call a rule *explicit* if its scope type is *courses*, *implicit* otherwise. Explicit rules —e.g., r_7 in Figure 2— make explicit reference to course codes, which have to be defined a priori wrt. the rules themselves. Implicit rules —e.g., r_2, r_3, r_4 and r_8 in Figure 2— make no explicit reference to courses.

From a semantic viewpoint, each rule tells a student the amount of didactic activities of given kind and scope he/she has to cash into his/her career to achieve graduation. For instance, the intuitive meaning of the rule set in Figure 2 is that, a student has to cash into his/her career, respectively:

R_1: at least 180 credits on the whole (in any activities of any scope), of which:
R_2: at least 90 credits in courses in the subject area(s) $\{MAT01, ..., MAT08\}$,
R_3: at least 38 credits in courses in subject area(s) $\{FIS01, ..., ING\text{-}INF05\}$, ...

Notice the usage of the expression "of which". This applies when the scope and activity type of a rule r_i are subsets of the scope and activity type of another rule r_j, and the bound of r_i is smaller than the bound of r_j. (Remarkably, explicit scopes are treated as subsets of the scopes given by the corresponding subject areas; e.g., "courses $\{CSI, CSII\}$" is treated as a subset of "*subject areas* $\{INF01\}$".) Some rules with explicit scopes —like, e.g.,r_7— can be used to force the student to perform some courses. We call such courses*mandatory*.

We divide the rules into*goal rules* and *constraint rules*. We call a goal rule any rule in the form "at least N ...". (Typically most rules in ordinances — often all— are goals.) A career *satisfies* a goal rule when the sum of units of the activities of the desired type and scope performed is greater or equal than the bound of the rule. For instance, the career (1) satisfies rule r_4 in Figure 2, as the 2nd, 3rd and 4th courses provide $5 + 5 + 5 \geq 10$ credits in the subject area *INF01*. The goal rules are not satisfied at the beginning of a career and must be satisfied when the student graduates. When a career satisfies a goal, all extensions of that career satisfy it.

We call a constraint rule any rule in the form "at most N ...". (Typically very few rules in ordinances —often none— are constraints.) A career*violates* a constraint rule when the sum of units of the activities of the desired type and scope performed is greater than the bound of the rule. For instance, in the career (1), the student cannot pass the exam of the sixth course of Figure 1, because doing so it would violate rule r_8 in Figure 2, as the courses 2, 3, 4 and 5 would provide $5 + 5 + 5 + 5 > 15$ credits in the subject area *INF01*. The constraint rules are not violated at the beginning of a career and none should be violated until the student graduates. If a career violated a constraint, all extensions of that career would violate it.

Given a career C and a rule set R, we say that:

(i) C *violates* R if it violates one constraint rule $c_j \in R$;

(ii) C *satisfies* R if it satisfies every goal rule $g_k \in R$ and violates no constraint rule $c_j \in R$.

C neither satisfies nor violates R if none of the two conditions above holds. Notice that a rule set is interpreted as a conjunction of rules.

2.2   A Model for the Problems

Career planning/synthesis A student has to plan his/her career when matriculating, and possibly to re-plan it every new year's registration, according to the rules he/she is given, the activities available, plus his/her own *desiderata*. (In many universities, such a plan must be presented and renewed explicitly.) Desiderata are mainly represented in terms of career elements $\langle a_i, y_i \rangle$ —e.g., $\langle OOP, 2 \rangle$ means "I want to pass OOP at the second matriculation year"— which we call *self-imposed didactic activities*. It is also possible to add to the rules of the ordinance self-imposed rules like, e.g., "At most 180 credits any all".

Because of the overlapping rule scopes, the different didactic activity types and credit weights, and the high number of degrees of freedom, the planning task may be rather complicate, and can cause mistakes. Thus, it is highly desirable to provide for the students a sort of *electronic advisor of studies* (EAS), an interactive support tool interfaced with the information system which, at each step,

(*a*) displays the student's current career and status wrt. the rule set and self-imposed didactic activities, and the complete list of activities available;

(*b*) allows the student to input and edit his/her own set of desiderata, and simulate interactively the evolution of his/her career

(*c*) can *synthesize automatically* careers which satisfy both the rule set and the desiderata.

The EAS can be used also by a secretary to verify the correctness of a complete student's career wrt. the ordinance rules.

While the steps (*a*) and (*b*) can be implemented with the standard technology of information systems, the step (*c*) can not, and it requires an external tool. The kernel of such a tool is an exhaustive search engine which, given the syllabus A, the rule set R, the current career C, plus the student's set of self-imposed didactic activities $\mathcal{A}'$, searches for a career $\mathcal{C}'$, extending $\mathcal{C}$ and including all elements of $\mathcal{A}'$, which satisfies $\mathcal{R}$. This can be a very hard task, as it may require exploring all possible career combinations before finding one, or that there is none.

Remark 1. A syllabus lists only the courses which are taught the current year, and makes no statement about the future. Thus, any plan for a student's future career is necessarily based on the implicit assumption that the syllabus will not be modified in the future years. Luckily, the course list of the syllabus typically does not change much from year to year and, if it does, changes concern only with minor optional courses. (Mandatory courses are set by ordinance rules.) In general, in this paper we assume that syllabi are static. We are currently experimenting an implementation with dynamic syllabi. □

Verifying the coherence of a syllabus wrt. a rule set Defining the rule set of an ordinance, and defining new syllabi, are hard tasks. In fact, the rule set of an ordinance constrains not only the student careers, but also the syllabi. For instance, if the rule set defines some mandatory courses, the syllabi are forced to provide such courses; e.g., the goal r_7 of Figure 2 forces all syllabi to provide a couple of courses with code CSI and CSII, and corresponding subject area INF01. More generally, syllabi must always be *coherent* with the rule set, that is, they must always provide enough courses to give to every students who have never violated a constraint a chance to complete his/her degree course and graduate. We formulate the latter fact as follows.

Definition 1. Given a rule set $\mathcal{R}$ and set of didactic activities $\mathcal{A}$, we say that $\mathcal{A}$ is *coherent* wrt. $\mathcal{R}$ if it is always the case that, for every student's partial career $\mathcal{C}$ on $\mathcal{A}$ which does not violate $\mathcal{R}$, there exists at least one career $\mathcal{C}'$ on $\mathcal{A}$ extending $\mathcal{C}$ which satisfies $\mathcal{R}$.

Verifying exhaustively the coherence of the syllabi is in many cases out of the reach of a human mind. Thus, it would be highly desirable to provide a support tool able to verify it automatically.

In general, verifying the coherence of syllabi with the rule sets is by far out of the reach of standard technology of information systems, for it requires a (double) exhaustive search engine. In fact, the basic step is similar to that of the EAS, that is, to search for a new career $\mathcal{C}'$ extending $\mathcal{C}$ which satisfies $\mathcal{R}$. As before, this means exploring up to all possible career combinations before finding one. Much worse, this must be done *for every student's partial career $\mathcal{C}$*, which requires exploring up to all possible combinations.

Remark 2. One may wonder whether Definition 1 is too restrictive. Consider, for instance, the case in which the courses *OOP* and *AI* in Figure 1 had no prerequisite. Then the partial career $\mathcal{C} = \{OOP, AI\}$ would not violate r_8, but there would be no career $\mathcal{C}'$ extending $\mathcal{C}$ satisfying r_7 without violating r_8. Thus, according to Definition 1, the syllabus would not be considered coherent with the rule set. On the other hand, one can reply that, given a constraint c_j, if we provide a set of didactic activities $\{a_1, ..., a_k\}$ containing mandatory courses which is big enough to violate c_j, we should also introduce prerequisites to force the student to perform all the mandatory courses before violating the constraint. We will further discuss the topic in Section 4.   □

3 Formalization in to Model Chec king

The main idea of this paper is to encode and solve the problems of the synthesis of student careers and of the verification the coherence of the syllabi wrt. rule sets, as CTL model checking problems. For lack of space, we omit any description of CTL and OBDD-based CTL model checking, which can be found in, e.g., [Clarke et al.1986; McMillan1993].

3.1 Career Evolutions as a Finite State Mac hine

We represent all the possible evolutions of a student's career within a given set of didactic activities as a finite state machine (FSM from no w on). Consider Figure 3. Broadly speaking, a state is characterized by the set of the activities performed so far. In the initial state no activity has been performed; each transition represents the performance of a new activity, and adds it to the career.

More in detail, let $\mathcal{A}$ be the set of didactic activities a_i's of a given syllabus; let $\mathcal{R}$ be the rule set of a given ordinance; let g_j and c_k denote the goal rules and the constraint rules in $\mathcal{R}$ respectively. We represent all the possible evolutions of a student's career within $\mathcal{A}$ as a FSM $\mathcal{M}$.

The state variables of $\mathcal{M}$ are given by:

- an array $\mathbf{v}$ of booleans, one for each didactic activity a_i in $\mathcal{A}$, such that $\mathbf{v}[i]$ is **true** if and only if the didactic activity a_i has been performed.
- a bounded integer $y \in \{1, ..., y_{max}\}$, representing the student's current matriculation year;
- an array $\mathbf{b}$ of bounded integers, one for each rule r_j in $\mathcal{R}$, s.t. $\mathbf{b}[j]$ is the sum of the credit/unit weights of the activities in the current career which match the type and scope of r_j.
- an array of booleans $\mathbf{p}$, one for each a_i in $\mathcal{A}$, s.t $\mathbf{p}[i]$ is **true** if and only if a_i satisfies its matriculation year and prerequisite constraints.

Notice that $\mathbf{b}$ and $\mathbf{p}$ are not state variables in the strict sense, as their values derive deterministically from the v alues of $\mathbf{v}$ and y. A state is univocally denoted by the values of $\mathbf{v}$ and y, so that the size of the state space is upper-bounded by $y_{max} \cdot 2^{||\mathcal{A}||}$, $||\mathcal{A}||$ being the number of didactic activities in $\mathcal{A}$.

In the initial state of the FSM $\mathcal{M}$, the matriculation year y is 1; every boolean $\mathbf{v}[i]$s is set to **false** (no activity performed); every bounded integer $\mathbf{b}[j]$ is set to 0; for each a_i, $\mathbf{p}[i]$ is set to **true** if a_i's minimum matriculation y ear is 1 and a_i has no prerequisite courses, to **false** otherwise.

The transition relation of $\mathcal{M}$ is defined in such a way that

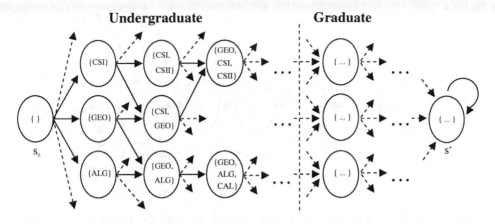

Fig. 3. The FSM representing all the possible evolutions of a student's career within a given syllabus. Within each state, "{}" is the set of didactic activities performed. (For simplicity, information regarding matriculation years and prerequisites is ignored.)

- one boolean $\mathbf{v}[i]$, corresponding to the performed activity a_i, passes from **false** to **true**, the others keep their values. If all $\mathbf{v}[i]$'s are **true**, then they all keep their values;
- y may either keep its value or be incremented by 1. If y equals its bound y_{max}, then it is not changed. If all $\mathbf{v}[i]$'s are **true** and y is smaller than the bound, it is incremented by 1;

The other variables are automatically updated from the new values of $\mathbf{v}$ and y in the following way:

- for each rule r_j in $\mathcal{R}$, if the performed activity a_i matches the type and scope of r_j, then $\mathbf{b}[j]$ is incremented by the weight of a_i, otherwise $\mathbf{b}[j]$ keeps its value.
- for each a_k, $\mathbf{p}[k]$ is set to **true** if a_k's minimum matriculation year is smaller or equal y, and a_k has no prerequisite courses a_l s.t. $\mathbf{v}[l]$ is **false**, it is set to **false** otherwise.

The goal and constraint rules in $\mathcal{R}$ are the atomic propositions of the CTL formulas representing the specifications. Thus, for every state s of $\mathcal{M}$ and for every goal rule g_k and constraint rule c_j in $\mathcal{R}$, we say that

$$\mathcal{M}, s \models g_k \iff \mathbf{b}[k](s) \geq bound(g_k),$$
$$\mathcal{M}, s \models c_j \iff \mathbf{b}[j](s) \leq bound(c_j), \tag{2}$$

where $\mathbf{b}[i](s)$ denotes the value of $\mathbf{b}[i]$ in s. Intuitively, this means that the goal rule g_k "at least N credits ...." is true in the state s of the FSM $\mathcal{M}$ if and only if, in the state s, the amount of credits $\mathbf{b}[k]$ matching the scope and type of g_k is greater or equal than N, and that the constraint rule c_j "at most N credits ...."

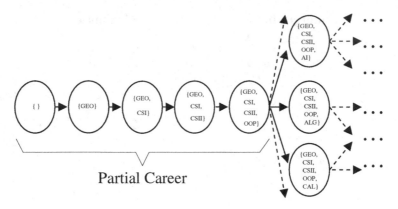

Fig. 4. The FSM representing all the possible evolutions of a student's career starting from a given partial career. (For simplicity, information regarding matriculation years and prerequisites is ignored.)

is true in the state s of the FSM $\mathcal{M}$ if and only if, in the state s, the amount of credits $\mathbf{b}[j]$ matching the scope and type of c_j is smaller or equal than N.

To handle the case when the evolutions starts from a given partial career $\mathcal{C}'$, we modify $\mathcal{M}$ by forcing an initial deterministic behavior until the given career $\mathcal{C}$ is emulated. This is represented in Figure 4. Let $\mathcal{C}$ be the career $\{\langle a_{i_1}, y_{i_1} \rangle, ..., \langle a_{i_N}, y_{i_N} \rangle\}$. At the k-th step, $k \leq N$, $\mathcal{M}$ "chooses" deterministically the didactic activity a_{i_k}, sets $\mathbf{v}[i_k]$ to **true** and y to y_{i_k}, and updates $\mathbf{b}$ and $\mathbf{p}$ accordingly. After the Nth step, $\mathcal{M}$ starts behaving in the usual nondeterministic way. To handle the presence of self-imposed didactic activities $\langle a_i, y_i \rangle$'s, we modify $\mathcal{M}$ by forcing the deterministic choice of a_i as soon as possible when $y \geq y_i$. [3]

Property 1 (Monotonicity). Assume **true** > **false**. Let s and s' denote two generic states of the FSM $\mathcal{M}$ described above such that s' is a successor of s. Let x and x' denote the values of the generic variable x in s and s' respectively. Then we always have that, for every i and j, $y' \geq y$, $\mathbf{v}[i]' \geq \mathbf{v}[i]$, $\mathbf{b}[j]' \geq \mathbf{b}[j]$, $\mathbf{p}[i]' \geq \mathbf{p}[i]$. We say that $\mathcal{M}$ is *monotonic*.   □

A consequence of the definition of $\mathcal{M}$ is that, except for the very last state s^* where all $\mathbf{v}[i]$s are **true** and y equals its bound, it is always the case that $y' > y$ or $\mathbf{v}[i]' > \mathbf{v}[i]$ for one i, that is, the monotonicity of $\mathcal{M}$ is "strict". Thus we have no loops except than in s^*, which is the successor of itself (see Figure 3).

From (2) and Property 1 we have that, for every goal rule g_k and constraint rule c_j in $\mathcal{R}$,

$$\mathcal{M}, s \models g_k \implies \mathcal{M}, s' \models g_k,$$
$$\mathcal{M}, s \not\models c_j \implies \mathcal{M}, s' \not\models c_j. \tag{3}$$

---

[3] This means interpreting $\langle a_i, y_i \rangle$ as "I want to perform a_i *as soon as possible* in the y_i-th matriculation year". Anyway, as self-imposed didactic activities can be used only in career synthesis, this is not a significant restriction.

This matches the intuitive statements of Section 2.1: when a career satisfies a goal, all extensions of that career satisfy it, and when a career violates a constraint, all extensions of that career violate it.

3.2   Encodings of the Different Problems

Let $C =_{def} \bigwedge_j c_j$ and $G =_{def} \bigwedge_k g_k$, where c_j and g_k denote the constraint and goals in $\mathcal{R}$. Let s_0 denote the initial state in $\mathcal{M}$. We represent the different kinds of problems described in Section 2.2 as CTL model checking problems by means of different specification formulas.

Career's synthesis The problem of synthesizing a career matching the rules and desiderata is a typical *reachability* problem: given a set of initial states Δ, a set of goal states Γ (the states which verify all goals and constraints) and a transition relation T, find a path $s_0, ..., s_n$ such that $s_o \in \Delta$, $s_n \in \Gamma$ and $T(s_{i-1}, s_i)$ holds for every $i \in \{1, ..., n\}$. Following the approach of [Cimatti *et al.*1998], we model the problem as:

$$\mathcal{M}, s_0 \models \mathbf{A}\mathbf{G}\neg(C \wedge G). \tag{4}$$

The CTL specification formula means "invariantly, at least one rule is false". The model checker tries to verify exhaustively this property, and, when it finds a counter-example (a state s_n where all rules are true) it returns a path π leading to it. The property (3) guarantees that, if a constraint is not violated in s_n, then it is not violated in all the states of the path. Thus a path π returned represents the progression of a career which satisfies all goals and violates no constraint. If a breadth-first search strategy is used (as in standard OBDD-based CTL model checking), then the length of the career returned is minimal. If the synthesis starts from a partial career C', or it contains self-imposed didactic activities, $\mathcal{M}$ is modified as described in the previous section.

Verifying the coherence of a syllabus Following Definition 1, we model the problem of verifying the coherence of a syllabus as follows:

$$\mathcal{M}, s_0 \models \mathbf{A}\mathbf{G}(C \rightarrow \mathbf{E}(C\mathbf{U}(C \wedge G))). \tag{5}$$

The CTL specification formula means "invariantly, if in a state s all constraints are true, then there exist a path π starting from s in which all constraints are always true and eventually all goals become true." The intermediate state s represents that of the partial career C in Definition 1, and the path π represents the career prosecution C'/C. Because of the monotonicity property (3), (5) can be simplified into:

$$\mathcal{M}, s_0 \models \mathbf{A}\mathbf{G}(C \rightarrow \mathbf{E}\mathbf{F}(C \wedge G)). \tag{6}$$

Moreover, as the goals are monotonic (3) and the FSM has no loop except for the one in the final state s^*, if there is no constraint rule, then (6) can be further be simplified into:

$$\mathcal{M}, s_0 \models \mathbf{A}\mathbf{F}\, G, \tag{7}$$

which means "for all paths, eventually all goals become true".

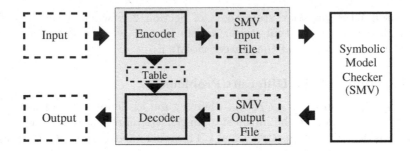

Fig. 5. Schema of the prototype tool.

4   A Protot ype Impleme ntation

The project information system will be ready no earlier than the second half of 2001. In the meantime, to verify the feasibility of the approach, we have implem ented a simple prototype tool interfaced with a new version of the SMV symbolic model checker [McMillan1993]. The tool provides a set of commands and options to perform the tasks described in Section 3. It takes as input a set of didactic activities $\mathcal{A}$, a rule set $\mathcal{R}$, and, in case of career synthesis, an optional partial career $\mathcal{C}$ and an optional set of self-imposed didactic activities $\mathcal{A}'$. The output depends of the kind of problem addressed: in case of career synthesis, either it returns a career $\mathcal{C}'$ extending $\mathcal{C}$ and including all elements of $\mathcal{A}'$ which satisfies $\mathcal{R}$, or it fails; in case of syllabus coherence verification, it returns **true** if $\mathcal{A}$ is coherent wrt. $\mathcal{R}$, **false** otherwise.

The schema of the tool is reported in Figure 5. An ENCODER generates from the input a SMV input file describing the FSM $\mathcal{M}$ and the CTL specification formula, as in Section 3, plus a TABLE, keeping track of the symbol encodings. A DECODER converts the SMV output file in a readable output format using the TABLE; in particular, it converts an output path of states into a career. The search engine of the tool is the symbolic model checker, which is used as a blackbox. The choice for an OBDD-based CTL model checker was forced by the particular formalization of the problems, as in Section 3, and by the very regular structure and high symmetry of the FSM $\mathcal{M}$.

The tool provides some options to impro ve its performances. First, we notice that a significant source of resources consumption is the presence of lots of counters $\mathbf{b}[j]$: OBDD-based model checkers handle with difficulty (bounded) integers, as they have to be encoded into their bitwise representations. Thus, if an apposite option is set, the tool applies the following reduction: if the greatest common divisor (GCD) n of the credit weights of all the didactic activities in $\mathcal{A}$ is strictly greater than 1, then all the credit values are divided by n by the ENCODER and the results are re-multiplied by n by the DECODER. This allows the model checker to handle smaller integer values. For the goal and constraint rule bounds b's, it is considered respectively the ceiling $\lceil b/n \rceil$ and the floor $\lfloor b/n \rfloor$. In fact, e.g., if the weights of all didactic activities are multiple of 5, "at least 9" is equivalent to "at least 10", and "at most 7" is equivalent to "at most 5". We call this option, *GCD*.

Moreover, the number of possible paths may be huge, and most are groupwise identical modulo order permutations. We notice that non-mandatory didactic activities cannot be prerequisites for mandatory courses (this fact is checked by the ENCODER). Thus, one may want to restrict the search to careers in which mandatory courses are performed as soon as possible —that is, at the beginning of their corresponding minimum matriculation year. Moreover, from the students' viewpoint, non-mandatory didactic activities are the only matter of choice in a career, so that, once the mandatory courses are clustered at the beginning of their matriculation years, their relative order within each cluster can be considered insignificant. Thus, one may want to impose a fixed order among the clustered mandatory courses, which is compatible with the prerequisites. We call this option, *Restrict*. Notice that the Restrict option allows the model checker to avoid situations like the one highlighted in Remark 2.

Finally, if an apposite option is set, all rules stating mandatory courses — like, e.g., r_7 in Figure 2— can be merged into one rule, requiring thus only one counter. We call this option, *Merge*.

5   Preliminary Empirical Results

The reform will come into force in the year 2001-2002, so that so far the universities have not yet presented their post-reform ordinances and syllabi. Thus, to verify the feasibility of the approach, we have modeled as a test-case the proposal of post-reform ordinance and syllabus of the Mathematics and Physics degree of the University of Trento. [4] Both degree course ordinances require 180 credits on the whole, of which at least 5 credits are for a thesis and 9 are for a stage, with no scope restriction. Both rule sets contain no constraint rule. The Math syllabus offers 55 5-credit courses, among which 22 are mandatory; the Physics syllabus offers 39 5-credit courses, among which 25 are mandatory.

As stages and theses are not explicitly inserted in the syllabi, we have added them in two distinct ways: in the first ($Math_1$ and $Phys_1$) the syllabi are added one 5-credit didactic activity of type **thesis** and a 10-credit one of type **stage**; in the second ($Math_2$ and $Phys_2$) the syllabi are added one 5-credit and one 6-credit didactic activity of type **thesis** and one 9-credit and one 10-credit didactic activity of type **stage**; a constraint rule "at most 1 unit [of type] thesis" is added in order to cope with the uniqueness of the thesis.

The results of the empirical tests are summarized in Table 1. (All tests have been obtained by running the model checker on a bi-processor PC **PentiumIII 667MHz 1GB RAM** with **Debian Linux**; the RAM consumption and CPU time required by the ENCODER and the DECODER are negligible wrt. those of the model checker.) We have considered both the problems of career synthesis and syllabus coherence verification. For all problems, we have analyzed all possible

---

[4]   Available at http://www-math.science.unitn.it/CCLM/ (in Italian). As they are just proposals, they may eventually change wrt. the current version (October 2000).

GCD	off	off	off	off	on	on	on	on	ordinance/	
Restrict	off	off	on	on	off	off	on	on	syllabus	Problem
Merge	off	on	off	on	off	on	off	on		
BDD Nodes	???	25M	288K	244K	???	27M	219K	198K	$Math_1$	
CPU Time		26'	11"	6"		22'	6"	4,5"	[GCD=5]	
BDD Nodes	???	???	314K	254K	???	???	314K	254K	$Math_2$	Career
CPU Time			11"	7"			11"	7"	[GCD=1]	synthesis
BDD Nodes	???	825K	97K	65K	???	801K	107K	61K	$Phys_1$	
CPU Time		27"	5"	2,5"		26"	2,5"	1,5"	[GCD=5]	
BDD Nodes	???	1,5M	122K	103K	???	1,5M	122K	103K	$Phys_2$	
CPU Time		51"	5"	3"		51"	5"	3"	[GCD=1]	
BDD Nodes	???	???	10M	4,3M	???	???	2,9M	1,0M	$Math_1$	
CPU Time			488"	300"			75"	40"	[GCD=5]	
BDD Nodes	???	???	7,2M	9,2M	???	???	7,2M	9,2M	$Math_2$	Syllabus
CPU Time			24'	24'			24'	24'	[GCD=1]	verification
BDD Nodes	???	3,4M	258K	111K	???	3,7M	253K	96K	$Phys_1$	
CPU Time		149"	19"	15"		127"	3,5"	2"	[GCD=5]	
BDD Nodes	???	15M	499K	353K	???	15M	499K	353K	$Phys_2$	
CPU Time		28'	36"	31"		28'	36"	31"	[GCD=1]	

Table 1. The results of the tests. "???" means "Exceeding 600MB RAM consumption". (Here "K" and "M" denote 10^3 and 10^6 rather than 2^{10} and 2^{20}.)

combinations of the *GCD*, *Restrict* and *Merge* options. (For $Math_2$ and $Phys_2$, the GCD option is ineffective, so that the values in the left half of the table are pairwise identical to those of the right half.)

On one hand, we notice that the problems are intrinsically very hard: with all the options disabled, no problem can be solved within 600MB RAM consumption, as the size of the state space, and thus of the BDD's, tend to explode. The same happens when both Restrict and Merge options are off. On the other hand, with all the options set, all problems are well at the reach of the model checker, mostly solved in a bunch of seconds. In between, we notice that:

- with the GCD option on, when applicable ($Math_1$ and $Phys_1$), there are mostly sensible, but not dramatic, performance impro vements. In fact, it reduces the number of boolean variables necessary to encode bounded integers, but the reduction is only logarithmic with the value of the GCD;
- with the Restrict option on, the improvements are very relevant. In fact, it reduces the number of non-deterministic choices and restricts the search only to non-mandatory didactic activities, causing a very relevant reduction of the size of the state space.
- with the Merge option on, there are mostly relev ant performance impro vements. In fact, it allows for a reduction of the number of the counters —i.e., of the boolean variables encoding it— and reduces the size of the corresponding BDD.

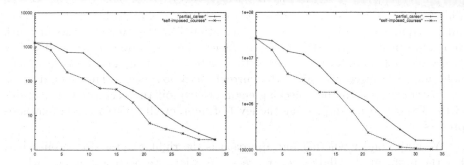

Fig. 6. Results obtained with $Math_1$, GCD=on, Merge=on and Restrict=off, adding either a partial career or a set of self-imposed didactic activities of increasing size. Y axis: (Left) CPU time in seconds; (Right) number of BDD nodes. X axis: number of didactic activities inserted.

We notice that $Math_2$ and $Phys_2$ are always harder or much harder than $Math_1$ and $Phys_1$ respectively. The motivations for this fact are manifold: first, we have two more non-mandatory didactic activities; second, the new 6-credits and 9-credits didactic activities hinder the applicability of the GCD option ($gcd(5,6,9) = 1$); finally, for the syllabus verification problem, with $Math_1$ and $Phys_1$ we use the simplified encoding (7), while with $Math_2$ and $Phys_2$ the constraint rule added forces the usage of the much harder encoding (6).

As a side observation, we also notice that the problem of career synthesis is always easier or much easier than the corresponding problem of syllabus verification. In fact, when both problems have solution, the latter requires an exhaustive exploration of the whole search space, while the former can stop when it finds one path.

For the problem of career synthesis, we wonder how the efficiency changes when we add partial careers and self-imposed didactic activities. To provide an intuition, in Figure 6 we have taken the problem $Math_1$ with GCD=on, Merge=on and Restrict=off, and we have added either a partial career or a set of self-imposed didactic activities of increasing size. Both the CPU times and number of OBDD nodes decrease significantly with the size of both the partial career and the set of self-imposed didactic activities. In fact, as with Restrict=on, the pre-compiled presence of the input didactic activities in the career reduces the number of non-deterministic choices and restricts thus the search, causing a relevant reduction of the size of the state space.

6   Ongoing and Future Work

The currently implemented prototype is actually more complex than we have described. First, it can handle multiple choices for the credit weight of one didactic activity. E.g., for theses, this prevents introducing extra constraints like the one in Section 5, which is the main source of the performance gaps between $Math_1$, $Phis_1$ and $Math_2$, $Phis_2$. Second, it can also handle dynamic syllabi.

This feature, which is still at experimental level and has to be further investigated, requires handling some extra information, like the range of years in which an exam can be passed and the equivalence relations among courses. The key future research step, however, will be to pass to a direct integration with a symbolic model checker instead of the current blackbox usage. This should allow for customizing the model checking engine to exploit the very peculiar features of the FSM, and for improving the level of interactivity of the career synthesis process.

We may wonder whether our approach is the right one for this application. For the problem of syllabus coherence verification, we need a language which, like CTL, is expressive enough to represent boolean and temporal information as well as constraints on bounded integers, and we need a search technique which, like OBDD-based Model Checking, is able to exploit the very regular structure of the FSM to cope with the combinatorial explosion of the state space. Therefore, although we cannot exclude a priori the existence and effectiveness of other approaches, we believe that symbolic model checking is a natural and very effective way to encode this problem.

For career synthesis, the problem is significantly simpler, and we are considering also other approaches like planning combined with linear programming [Wolfman & Weld1999] and SAT-based model checking [Biere et al.1999], with some tricks from [Giunchiglia et al.1998] to exploit the dependencies among the state variables of the FSM.

References

Biere et al.1999. A. Biere, A. Cimatti, E. M. Clarke, and Y. Zhu. Symbolic Model Checking without BDDs. In Proc. TACAS'99, pages 193–207, 1999.

Cimatti et al.1998. A. Cimatti, M. Roveri, and P. Traverso. Strong Planning in Non-Deterministic Domains via Model Checking. In Proc. Fourth International Conference on Artificial Intelligence Planning Systems (AIPS-98), 1998.

Clarke et al.1986. E. Clarke, E. Emerson, and A. Sistla. Automatic verification of finite-state concurrent systems using temporal logic specifications. ACM Transactions on Programming Languages and Systems, 8(2):244–263, 1986.

Giunchiglia et al.1998. E. Giunchiglia, A. Massarotto, and R. Sebastiani. Act, and the Rest Will Follow: Exploiting Determinism in Planning as Satisfiability. In Proc. AAAI'98, pages 948–953, 1998.

McMillan1993. K. McMillan. Symbolic Model Checking. Kluwer Acad. Publ., 1993.

MURST2000a. MURST. Regolamento in materia di autonomia didattica degli atenei (Regulations on the didactic autonomy of universities). Gazzetta Ufficiale, 2, January 2000. In Italian. Available at http://www.murst.it/regolame/1999/adq.htm.

MURST2000b. MURST. Rideterminazione dei settori scientifico-disciplinari (Redefinition of subject areas). Gazzetta Ufficiale, 3, January 2000. In Italian. Available at http://www.murst.it/atti/2000/dSettori.htm.

Wolfman & Weld1999. S. Wolfman and D. Weld. The LPSAT Engine & its Application to Resource Planning. In Proc. IJCAI, 1999.

Verification of Vortex Workflows

Xiang Fu[1], Tevfik Bultan[1], Richard Hull[2], and Jianwen Su[1]

[1] Department of Computer Science, University of California,
Santa Barbara, CA 93106, USA. {fuxiang, bultan, su}@cs.ucsb.edu.
[2] Bell Laboratories, Lucent Technologies, 600 Mountain Ave.,
Murray Hill, NJ 07974. hull@research.bell-labs.com.

Abstract. Vortex is a workflow language to support decision making activities. It centers around gathering and computing attributes of input objects. The semantics of Vortex is declarative, and the dependency graphs of Vortex programs are acyclic. This paper discusses the application of symbolic model checking techniques to verification of Vortex programs. As a case study we used a Vortex program MIHU for online customer support. The control structure and the declarative semantics of Vortex programs enabled us to develop various optimization techniques for the purpose of verification. These techniques include constructing a disjunctive transition BDD, variable pruning, projection of initial constraints, and predicate abstraction.

1 Introduction

A workflow management system provides a mechanism for organizing the execution of multiple tasks, typically in support of a business or scientific process. A variety of workflow models and implementation strategies have been proposed [8,19]. Workflows concentrate on the control and coordination of tasks performed by software systems or humans. Workflows are typically represented using some form of directed graphs [8,6], often based on variations of Petri nets. A workflow specification describes both data and control flows between tasks as well as the application programs that implement the tasks. In contrast, recent work in the area of scientific workflows emphasize the need to promote a dataflow view of the workflow at the specification level. [1] presented an "object view" where the focal point is the data used and generated during workflow execution. There, workflows are considered as graphs of objects with the processes that created them being expressed through the links between them. A mixed view is proposed in [14], wherein both data and control flow are expressible and the user can navigate from an activity to its input data structure.

Many workflow applications require highly differentiated treatments for different kinds of inputs. A substantial class of examples arises in customer care (e.g., e-commerce, insurance claims processing) where enterprises attempt to provide goods and services to a mass market. Such individualized treatments can cater to the individual preferences of customers, and can support targeted marketing initiatives and promotions by the host enterprises. This is especially important in connection with establishing and maintaining a loyal customer base, a cornerstone to success in business in general and e-commerce in particular.

T. Margaria and W. Yi (Eds.): TACAS 2001, LNCS 2031, pp. 143–157, 2001.
© Springer-Verlag Berlin Heidelberg 2001

To support this need, Vortex [10] is developed recently and focuses on determining attribute values, and the means by which these values are obtained are modeled essentially as side-effects of this. However, attributes in Vortex can either model the execution status of some task or the output data of a task. This approach offers a lot of flexibility, which enables to alternatively focus on tasks or data as needed by the decision process incarnated by the workflow. Vortex enables a declarative specification of workflows, which matches the need for high-level specification languages for designing and prototyping workflows usable by non computer trained users (e.g., a natural scientist) emphasized by existing work on scientific workflows.

Increasingly more people are getting information and services online, many of which are supported by workflow systems. Failure of these systems will have potentially a huge impact (e.g., the server attacks on CNN and other Internet sites some time ago). Moreover, workflow specifications (programs) are becoming more and more complex. For example, a Vortex workflow program [10] in practical use may consist of hundreds of variables and thousands lines of code. It is unlikely that one can develop large workflow systems free of errors with no tools. An interesting issue here is to develop appropriate tools to aid the design of workflow specifications. Good design tools can not only improve the quality of workflow specifications and but also improve the design and maintenance process. Verification techniques can allow the designer to "debug" the specifications of workflow processing logic. Among important properties of workflow specification are logical properties such as each insurance claim is eventually approved or disapproved, existence of nondeterministic behaviors, and properties related to tasks with side effects (such as issuing a check).

Research on model-checking produced tools such as SMV [13] has been successfully applied to verification of control-intensive systems [12]. Symbolic model checking has been used in verification of systems with up to 10^{100} states. However, large number of variables, complex program logic, or arithmetic operations can easily exceed the capabilities of verification tools such as SMV. The control structure and the declarative semantics of Vortex programs provide opportunities for various optimizations which can result in scalable verification techniques.

In [15], modeling checking was applied to verification of Mentor workflow specifications. More specifically, the focus is on properties over graph structures (rather than execution results). A similar approach was taken using Petri-net based structures in [18]. A technique for translating business processes in the process interchange format (PIF) to CCS was developed in [17] which can then be verified by appropriate tools. Clearly, a direct verification that considers not only the structures but also the executions is more accurate and desirable. This is the focus of the present paper.

In this paper we present techniques such as constructing a disjunctive transition BDD, variable pruning, projection of initial constraints, and predicate abstraction for verification of Vortex programs. As a case study we use a Vortex program "May-I-Help-You" (MIHU), a system to improve the effectiveness of web-based storefronts. MIHU has over 40 integer attributes and consists of more than 800 lines of Vortex code. A straightforward mapping of the MIHU program to SMV results in a BDD of size too large to be computed. By introducing execution order on Vortex programs we were able to construct a much smaller disjunctive transition BDD in 10 seconds. However, even using the disjunctive transition BDD we were not able to check all the properties of the MIHU program. Based on the dependencies among attributes we were able to develop a variable pruning technique which only preserves the variables that are *active* during the computation. This technique is motivated by the acyclic nature of dependencies in Vortex programs and can be applied to other such systems. Variable pruning requires the projection of the initial image to different stages of the computation. This also reduces the size of the initial image, since complicated predicates on various attributes, such as sorted arrays, are decomposed. Using these techniques we were able to check all the properties of the MIHU program using SMV.

The remainder of the paper is organized as follows. § 2 reviews necessary concepts of Vortex. § 3 describes a Vortex application system "May I Help yoU" (MIHU), which we use as a case study. § 4 gives the mapping from Vortex to SMV and compares two different approaches to construct an efficient transition BDD. § 5 presents two optimization methods: variable pruning and decomposition of initial constraints. § 6 is an experimental exploration on predicates abstraction, which sheds a light on solving the exponential problem size over integer width.

2   Vortex Decision Flows

Vortex [10] is a programming paradigm for online decision making, an important component in workflow systems. A Vortex program focuses on information gathering, decision making, and launching and monitoring of external tasks. The Vortex language is declarative and it allows programmers to specify the conditions under which decisions and tasks should be performed, but the flow of control is not specified explicitly. As a result, Vortex programs are more succinct and easier to analyze formally than equivalent procedural programs, and are easier for humans to understand and modify. Because the core semantics of Vortex is declarative, analysis is simpler than with procedural workflow languages.

A Vortex decision flow consists of a family of attributes that may be evaluated during execution. One attribute will be "target" and embody the output of a decision flow, e.g., what priority of service to give this customer, or what promotional image to display on the next web page. Other attributes correspond to intermediate results of the decision flow. For example, a "promo hit list" attribute might hold a listing of potential promo messages to display, along with scores combining the likelihood that a customer will buy the promo and the potential profit that might be derived. Some intermediate attributes might gather data from external sources, such as databases. Since attribute evaluation can have a real cost, enabling conditions are used to decide which attributes should be evaluated. The set of data flow and control flow dependencies in a decision flow must be acyclic. This and the enabling conditions restrict Vortex decision flows to be "monotonic": once an attribute obtains a value the value will not be changed before the end of execution. This "attribute-centric" perspective of decision flows permits a systematic approach for specifying what factors to be incorporated as a decision is being made.

Individual Vortex programs are centered around the decision making and processing needed to react to a single event, e.g., a new claim input to an insurance claims workflow, or a customer contact through a web-based storefront. Programmers specify what tasks might potentially be performed for an incoming event, and specify logical conditions under which these tasks should be performed. A typical Vortex application will involve several Vortex programs, each for dealing with a different class of events.

Programs in Vortex focus on how values should be assigned to the attributes of an input object. In particular, each Vortex execution begins with values only for the *source* attributes. As execution continues values for additional attributes are obtained, perhaps by computation or synthesis based on previously obtained attribute values, by information retrieval, or by interaction with humans or other software systems. Not all attributes need take values. External actions (e.g., issue checks) may be launched as a side-effect of attribute evaluation.

A Vortex program includes *enabling conditions* to determine whether an attribute will be evaluated for a particular execution. These are similar to the enabling rules in Meteor [11] with a crucial difference: the enabling rules of Meteor explicitly mention events, and can be fired only if the mentioned event(s) occur and the remainder of the condition is true at that time. Thus, an analysis of tasks and enabling rules in Meteor requires an understanding of the relative timing of tasks executions. In contrast, the assignment of attribute values in Vortex is monotonic (i.e., once assigned an attribute value cannot change), and the enabling conditions refer only to attribute values and states (i.e., whether an attribute has been enabled or disabled). This makes it possible for Vortex to have a simple declarative semantics that ignores issues around order of execution except for those implied by data flow constraints between tasks.

Thus the computation of an attribute value in a Vortex program may depend on values of other attributes (*data dependencies*) and the execution of the computation depends on attributes occurring in the enabling condition (*control dependencies*).

The attribute-centric paradigm and assumption of monotonicity make possible a natural mechanism for querying the status and history of workflow processing. This is based on the notion of *snapshot* of a Vortex execution. Suppose a Vortex program is being executed. At a given point in time the snapshot associated with this execution is a mapping from attributes to the current state of the attribute (not-yet-considered, enabled or disabled), and if the attribute is enabled either a value for the attribute or the "value" **uninitialized**. Once an execution completes then its snapshot can be archived.

Although attribute computation in Vortex can be specified in several different ways including by external systems (black boxes), an interesting class of computation is specified by *decision modules*. These provide an eclectic mix of mechanisms for aggregating and synthesizing previously obtained attribute values. As a very simple illustration, suppose that multiple vendors are being considered in connection with a given purchase. Different factors might need to be weighed, e.g., the price quoted by different vendors, the availability date, previous history with the vendor, and etc. A Vortex decision module (or family of decision modules) might be used to associate a weight to each vendor and then pick the vendor with highest weight. As a simplified illustration, a rule such as "If vendor V gave lowest price quote, then contribute $[V, 10]$" can be used to contribute a weight of 10 in favor of V; and the total weight for V would be obtained by adding this with the other weights contributed for V. Vortex supports a broad family of simple and intricate semantics for combining the contributions of the rules in a decision module. Decision modules provide a simple mechanism for using a broad variety of heuristics when combining information. This is useful in contexts that involve business considerations, e.g., customer care, automated resolution of exceptions, and reconciling dirty data.

3   A Vortex System "May I Help yoU" (MIHU)

Need for online decision making arises frequently in electronic commerce applications. For example, many web storefronts have human agents for online customer support, in case when customers feel lost while shopping at the website. However in such an application the web storefront has to automatically decide who needs the service and when it is appropriate to prompt a customer to launch the service. A decision process behind the web server can track each shopping session, collect data, analyze the status of a customer, and make decisions to provide online support. MIHU is such a Vortex workflow that runs behind web server to improve customer satisfaction.

The purpose of MIHU is to make the decision whether to provide a customer service called AWD (Automated Web Dialog). The target attribute is a boolean attribute **offer_AWD**, as shown in Fig. 1. Each time a web page is accessed, MIHU will be called by the web server before the page is delivered to the customer. In each run of MIHU, it will monitor several key attributes of a customer (e.g. the business value, the frustration score, and the opportunity score of the current session, and the current agent load of the web store). The goal is to respond as soon as possible whenever the customer's frustration level becomes high or the customer has potential to buy more. As shown in Fig. 1, MIHU will also compute some intermediate attributes such as **AWD_score** and **AWD_override_score** during its execution. The target attribute **offer_AWD** is computed using **AWD_score**, **AWD_override_score** and **agent_load**. Note that there are many source attributes in the program, such as **card_color**, **log**, and **shopping_count** etc. The source attributes are passed by the web server or fetched from databases. The control and data dependencies between all attributes are also shown in Fig. 1, where the graph is acyclic as explained in Section 2.

One characteristic of Vortex programs is that they are heavily "control intensive." A great proportion of a Vortex program consists of case-statements which are specified as conditions on attributes. Let us take a look at a module in MIHU which computes the attribute **frustration_aggregate**.

```
MODULE compute_frustration_aggregate{
enabling condition: true;
computation: frustration_aggregate=
  eval_rules(
    //if no rule is true, the default value is 0
    policy: max_of_true_rules(0),
    rules:{
      if (sorted_vector[1] >= 100) then contribute
        2*(sorted_vector[0]+sorted_vector[1]+sorted_vector[2]);

      if (sorted_vector[0] >= 100) then contribute
```

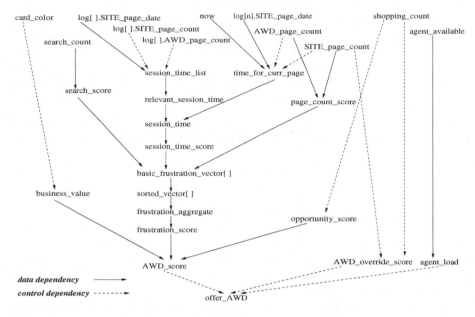

Fig. 1. Dependency Graph for MIHU

```
        (sorted_vector[0]+sorted_vector[1]+sorted_vector[2]);
    if (sorted_vector[0] < 100) then contribute
        (sorted_vector[0]+sorted_vector[1]/2+sorted_vector[2]/4);
    }
  )
}
```

There are three case statements in the module, referred as *rules* in Vortex. The three cases are all evaluated, and the maximum result value is assigned to the attribute **frustration_aggregate**. If none of the cases are satisfied, the attribute is assigned a default value. Note that each Vortex module has an enabling condition (e.g. the above module has an enabling condition which is **true**).

A collection of properties were proposed on MIHU, so that commercial policy and integrity can be ensured. Some of them are listed in the following.

1. AWD should not be provided when there are no human agents for support.
2. MIHU should not provide AWD when one AWD has already been launched.
3. Do not show AWD to any user who has been idle for two hours or more.
4. No AWD should be displayed within the first three pages in any session.

We define P as: there are no human agents for support, or at least one AWD has already been launched, or the user has been idle for more than two hours, or no more than three pages has been displayed. If P is **false**, then the following properties should hold.

5. MIHU should guarantee that the frustration score of any customer is below 90, or an AWD should be launched.
6. When a customer has more than 5 items in his shopping cart, an AWD frame should be launched (to encourage shopping).

7. When a customer has searc hed the same item for o ver 5 times, an AWD frame should be launched to help him.

These properties can be expressed as invariants using the Vortex attributes. For example, property (1) can be expressed as `AG( IsEndOfExecution -> ( agent_available==0 -> !offer_AWD) )`, using the CTL operator AG.

4   From V ortex to SMV

It is not unusual for a Vortex workflow system to have many integer variables (e.g., more than 50). Assuming 50 in teger variables with 16-bit integer width, the state space would exceed 10^{200}. Explicit exploration on such a huge state space would be computationally very expensive. On the other hand, BDD-based symbolic model checking can cope with large state spaces, given that they can be represented compactly using BDDs. It is true that in the presence of nonlinear constraints BDD representation is not efficient. However a large class of workflow and decision flow used on applications is linear. MIHU is such an example. Therefore we chose the BDD-based symbolic model checker SMV to investigate the feasibility of automated verification of Vortex programs.

4.1   Straightforward Mapping

Specification constructs provided in SMV input language enables a straight-forward translation of the Vortex programs. Since SMV does not have global variables, a module named `Attributes` is set up to hold attributes, and passed as an argument to each computation module. Any attribute in Vortex program is mapped into one or a set of boolean variables, depending on whether it is a boolean or an integer attribute. Also for each attribute $attr_i$, a boolean variable $attr_i\_enabled$ is set up to represent the status of $attr_i$. Notice that since integer attributes are translated into a set of boolean variables in SMV, the arithmetic computation over them should be translated to a series of logical relations over those boolean variables. Since SMV's mapping of in teger variables is inefficient, we used a macro developed by Chan for this purpose [4].

As shown in Fig. 2, for each module in Vortex, the mapped SMV module contains two assignments, one for the attribute, and the other is for the status variable. The two assignments are both case-statements, and each rule in Vor-tex modules corresponds to a case of the case-statement. The construction of the condition for each case varies according to different rule policies provided in Vortex language such as `first_rule_win` and `max_rule_win`. The methodology to build the condition is the same. For example, if the policy is `first_rule_win`, the condition for each case in the SMV case statemen t is constructed by conjoin-ing the enabling condition of the module with the rule condition and another condition called `anc_enabled`. The boolean condition `anc_enabled` is defined as the conjunction of all status variables of attributes that are direct predecessors of the attribute that is being computed in the dependency graph. Another ex-ample on policy `max_rule_win` is shown in Fig. 2. Notice that the first case states that when the attribute has already been assigned its value, it should keep that value. This helps reduce the size of transition BDD.

```
// anc_enabled: all direct predecessors of attr have been computed
// IsMax(res): among all available results, res is the largest.
// It is defined as follows:
//   (cond1 ->(res>=r1)) & (cond2 ->(res>=r2)) &...& (condn ->(res>=rn))
```

Vortex Module	SMV Module

```
MODULE compute_attr            MODULE compute_attr
enabling condition: e_cond;
                               ASSIGN
attr=eval_rules{               next(attr):= case
  policy: max_rule_wins,         //if already assigned, keep the value
                                 attr_enabled:attr;
  rules:{
  //rule1                        //rule 1
  if cond1 then contribute r1;   e_cond & anc_enabled & cond1 &
                                 IsMax(r1):r1;

  //rule2                        //rule 2
  if cond2 then contribute r2;   e_cond & anc_enabled & cond2 &
                                 IsMax(r2):r2;

  //rule n                       //rule n
  if condn then contribute rn;   e_cond & anc_enabled & condn &
                                 IsMax(rn):rn;
  }                              esac;
}
                               //now for status variable
                               next(attr_enabled):= case

                                 e_cond & anc_enabled: 1;
                                 1:                     0;//default

                               esac;
```

Fig. 2. SMV Translation of a Vortex Module

4.2 Sequential Execution

Unfortunately experimental results have shown that the straightforward mapping is inefficient. It took more than 24 hours of CPU time to build the transition BDD of 10-bit integer width for MIHU even without verifying any properties. The reason is that, given a BDD variable order in which all integer bits are interleaved, building a monolithic transition BDD for multiple computations can be exponentially expensive. For example, if there are two computation $c := a + b$ and $f := d + e$ that can be executed in parallel, then there are two options to build the transition BDD. One is to build the monolithic transition BDD that incorporates both computations. The other is to introduce a sequence number, and split the computation in two steps. If the integer width is 16, given an interleaved integer variable order, a single addition BDD is 131 nodes, the transition BDD by first approach is 506 nodes, and the BDD by second method is 266 nodes. Obviously, the second approach, to split the computation in sequential steps, is better.

It might be argued that if we rearrange a, b, c and d, e, f in two groups, and interleave them separately, a much smaller transition BDD can be generated for the first approach. It is true for this little example. However it is not applicable to Vortex programs. Since in a Vortex program, all attributes contribute to the target attribute, any two attributes are logically related. This prevents a grouping of variables based on the dependency. Therefore, a natural BDD variable order for Vortex programs is to interleave all integer variables together.

For such a BDD variable order, the straightforward translation fails because it incorporates too many computations in one step.

In our straightforward mapping, the set of status variables for attributes dictates the execution order. Each snapshot (the values of status variables) will decide which module can be executed. However, multiple modules can be executed in one step, which finally leads to an unreasonably large transition BDD. Our improved approach is quite simple. Just replace those status variables with a sequence variable explicitly, and make sure that at each step, only a small number of computations can be executed. Generally, we assign one sequence number for each Vortex module. If a module contains too much computation, then several sequence numbers can be assigned to a single module.

Fig. 3 shows the structure of the transition relation BDD using sequence numbers. The SMV translation in Fig. 3 is similar to the one in Fig. 2 except that the conditions on status variables are replaced by conditions on sequence numbers.

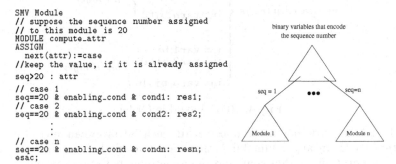

```
SMV Module
// suppose the sequence number assigned
// to this module is 20
MODULE compute_attr
ASSIGN
  next(attr):=case
//keep the value, if it is already assigned
seq>20 : attr

// case 1
seq==20 & enabling_cond & cond1: res1;
// case 2
seq==20 & enabling_cond & cond2: res2;
      :
// case n
seq==20 & enabling_cond & condn: resn;
esac;
```

Fig. 3. Disjunctive Structured Transition BDD

As shown in Fig. 3, the transition BDD has a disjunctive structure. So the overall transition BDD size is at worst the sum of all these submodules. Notice that these submodules can share components, which would further reduce the overall transition BDD size. Given a fixed integer width, if all the computations are linear, the total transition BDD size is linear on the program size. It can also be proved that the size is linear on the integer width.

Because of the declarative semantics of Vortex programs, if an execution sequence satisfies the partial order defined in the dependency graph, the final snapshot of all attributes of SMV translation will be the same as the original SMV program. Note that all properties are expressed over the final values of attributes. It is clear that restricting to a particular execution sequence does not affect the verification.

4.3   BDD Variable Order

The BDD variable order we use in mapping Vortex programs to SMV modules is shown in Fig. 4. The first part is all the bits of the sequence variable **seq** which holds the current sequence number. This part leads to the disjunctive transition BDD structure. As shown in Fig. 4, in the second part we list all the boolean variables that correspond to boolean attributes in Vortex. Finally, the third part corresponds to the boolean variables that encode the bits of integer attributes. Note that if the ranges of integers are not the same, then we can interleave starting from the least significant bit.

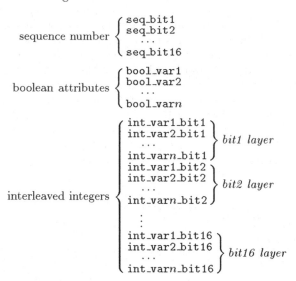

Fig. 4. BDD Variable Order

In Fig. 4, the ordering of variables within each bit layer can affect the size of transition BDD. In any submodules, there are two kinds of computations: the "main computation" of that step, and the assignments to preserve old values for some attributes. If there are too many such attributes, preserving assignment can also result in quite a large BDD, especially when these attributes were mixed with the attributes for main computation. It is better to move these unrelated attributes outside the group of attributes used in main computation, as illustrated in Fig. 5. (In Fig. 5 the edges toward BDD node 0 are all omitted. Attributes u1, u2 are unrelated attributes for the main computation; and r1, r2, r3 are attributes used in computation. The attributes with quotation (e.g. r3′) are next values.) Therefore, heuristically within each bit layer any attributes directly related in dependency graph should be placed close to each other to minimize the number of unrelated attributes in the main computation for each module.

Using the ideas presented above the transition BDD for MIHU Vortex program can be built in 10 seconds for 10 bit integer representation. This is a significant improvement from the straightforward mapping.

5   Optimization

Although the techniques presented in Section 4 enabled us to construct a BDD representation for the Vortex program in a reasonable time, the SMV model checker was not able to verify most of the properties presented in Section 3 using this transition BDD. In this section we present two techniques which enabled us to verify all the presented properties.

$$\textit{Main Computation}: r3' := (r1 \land r2) \lor (\neg r1 \land \neg r2)$$

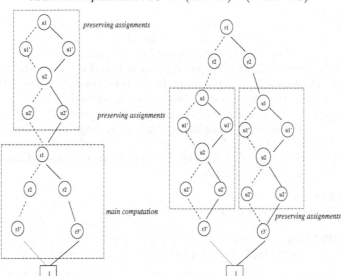

Fig. 5. Effects of Different Variable Order in Bit Layer

5.1   Variable Pruning

According to the acyclic property of Vortex, there should be no loop in the execution of any Vortex program. This means that every attribute has a "lifespan",i.e., before its first reference and after its last reference, an attribute is of no use for the computation. Note that for intermediate attributes, "first reference" is their definition; for source attributes, "first reference" is the first time they are used in computation. Naturally an attribute can be pruned outside of its life span – we can treat such variables as "don't cares" by assigning them any possible value nondeterministically. This would greatly reduce the "preserving assignments" cost in sub-BDDs for each module. For example, there are 40 integers in MIHU, so in many modules, there would be over 30 preserving assignments. But after we pruned unnecessary variables by nondeterministic assignment, at any time, there are only less than 9 preserving assignments. For image computation, the improvement is even much greater. There is no need to represent the state of inactive variables; at any time, only those active variables will be represented in image. So actually, the problem size is reduced from a huge state space over all attributes to the state space over the variables that are active. Usually the number of active variables is much smaller than the total number of variables,e.g., in MIHU the maximal number of active variables during any part of computation is 9. Therefore, after pruning inactive variables, we can achieve a much better performance than the original naive method.

5.2   Decomposition of Initial Image

Similar pruning can be applied to source attributes. They can be assigned any value nondeterministically outside their lifespan. What is more, the initial constraints can be projected to different stage of execution, which reduces the size of initial image drastically.

The process to project initial image is as follows. Suppose that the initial constraint is expressed in the conjunctive form of $\wedge f(x_i, x_j)$, where $f(x_i, x_j)$ is the logical relation between two attributes. Then for each $f(x_i, x_j)$, suppose the lifespan for the two attributes are $[a_i, b_i]$, $[a_j, b_j]$, and $a_i \geq a_j$. We can map the $f(x_i, x_j)$ into the module of step $a_i - 1$. To do this, transition $f(next(x_i), x_j)$ or $f(next(x_i), next(x_j))$ (if $a_i == a_j$) is added to module $a_i - 1$.

For example, suppose we have an initial constraint over array log[ ] that log must keep increasing, i.e. log[0] < log[1] < log[2] < log[3]. Suppose that log[2] is first referenced in module 5, and log[1] is first referenced in module 7. Then the constraint log[1] < log[2] can be mapped into module 6. The program is presented as follows.

```
MODULE No.6
//orginal assignments

TRANSITION
        next(log[1]) < log[2]
```

Notice that the "next" indicates that the next value of log[1] should satisfy this constraint in module 7. However the value of log[2] will not change, since it is already assigned before module 5.

Since the constraints over arrays can commonly arise in practical applications, (e.g., the date stored in history log should always keep increasing), this kind of constraints brings great trouble for initial image, and lead to quite large initial image size. We have three such kind of constraints over arrays in MIHU, which leads to an initial image of 65,000 BDD nodes, when integer width is 10. The time used to compute the first forward image computation takes more than one hour. After the decomposition optimization applied, the initial image shrinked from 65,000 BDD nodes to 4,000 nodes, and the first forward image computation reduces drastically to only half a second.

5.3   Execution Sequence

As we discussed above, the size of active variable set critically affects the cost of verification, i.e., the verification time would increase exponentially over the size of active variable set. The smaller the active set, the smaller the verification cost. Note that different execution sequences lead to different active variable set, e.g., the size of the largest active set in MIHU ranges from 9 to 17 according to different execution sequences. Therefore, it is important to find an optimal execution sequence which minimizes the largest active variable set.

We formalize the notion below to be used in our discussion. Let G be a given dependency graph.

Execution sequence: suppose the total number of attributes is n. For any attribute attr, it is mapped to a unique integer in range $[1..n]$. The mapping should satisfy the partial relation defined in dependency graph G.

Lifespan: For each attribute attr, its lifespan is a range $[i, j]$, where i is attr's sequence number assigned in execution sequence, j is the maximum sequence number among all its successors.

AVS_i (Active Variable Set at step i): the set of variables active at step i, i.e., $AVS_i = \{$ attr $\mid i \in$ attr's lifespan$\}$.

Minimum Active Variable Set (MAVS) problem: Find the execution sequence which minimizes the maximum value for $|AVS_i|$, $1 \le i \le n$.

Though the worst case complexity is exponential, a branch and bound algorithm can be used to solve the MAVS problem. Since the MAVS problem is actually to find out an optimal topological order for a directed acyclic graph, during the depth-first search to enumerate all possible topological sequences, we can set a bound on the optimal solution currently available and prune branches that exceed the bound. In addition, greedy search can be started first to find a "not bad" value to initialize the bound. Unfortunately, polynomial time algorithms for MAVS seems unlikely as we can show that the problem is actually NP-hard by a reduction from a known NP-complete problem called *register sufficiency problem* [7].

5.4   Experimental Results

We were able to check all properties for the MIHU example given in Section 3 using the techniques discussed above. The hardware we used is a Pentium 450MHZ PC with 128MB memory. Properties 1 and 3 were not satisfied. The errors were due to missing bounds on some of the attributes. For example, AWD_score was not bounded in the program which resulted the system assigning an agent to a customer though none were available. The experimental results are as follows.

Integer attributes: 40

Source code in Vortex program MIHU: 800 lines

Maximal active variable set: 9 attributes

Integer Width	Time (Seconds)	Transition BDD Size	Memory Used (Mb)
10	250	269,241	32
11	360	312,548	37
12	560	356,936	39
13	900	401,907	40
14	1500	446,821	42
15	4500	539,843	45

We verified the properties using forward state exploration. First we generated all the reachable states, and verified all the invariants at once. In the MIHU example the most costly computation is the sorting operations to compute sorted_vector. It could be possible to improve sorting in such cases using predicate abstraction.

6   Predicate Abstraction

It is not unusual for the complexity of verification to increase exponentially with the integer width. None of the optimization approaches mentioned above can solve this problem. However, the combination of predicate abstraction [9,5] and decision procedure can help in this problem. Any predicate can be mapped into a boolean variable, where this boolean variable will get assigned at the last module which defines its related attributes. If with the aid of a decision procedure, we can conclude that this boolean variable can be assigned deterministically 0 or 1, the abstraction on the predicate is complete. Or else we can either leave it nondeterministically assigned, or continue to generate new predicates that leads to a deterministic assignment and spread out more predicates. It is proved that for the nondeterministic abstraction [16] , ∀CTL* properties hold in all execution paths, will be preserved, which means that CTL* properties verified to be correct in abstracted version will be correct in the original version; for the deterministic abstraction, in addition to CTL* preservation, properties proved to be incorrect in the abstracted system will not hold in concrete system either.

We tried nondeterministic abstraction in MIHU, which generated 120 new boolean predicates. With this abstraction, all correct properties are verified in 10 minutes. However for the properties that were not verified, the abstraction has to be refined to eliminate false negative results in error trace. This process should be repeated until a fully deterministic abstraction is generated[16]. To generate the fully deterministic abstraction, we estimate that there will be over 500 new predicates for the MIHU.

One bottleneck in the deterministic abstraction method is that: it is required to enumerate the boolean combination over all boolean variables so that

$$InitialImage \Rightarrow R(\bigwedge f(b1, ..., bn))$$

where $f(b1, ..., bn)$ is a boolean expression on boolean variables b1,...,bn (which represent abstracted predicates), and R() is the inverse of abstraction. The goal is to generate a conjunction which is minimal and satisfies the above constraint. The best known complexity of enumeration algorithm to generate such a boolean expression is 3^k [16], where k is the number of all predicates. If k is quite large, the overhead of abstraction would be expensive.

7   Conclusions

In this paper we presented applications of model checking to verification of Vortex workflow programs. We develop techniques for mapping Vortex programs to BDDs efficiently based on the control structure and the declarative semantics of the language. Using these techniques, we were able to verify the Vortex program used for online customer support. We showed that this program did not satisfy all of the stated properties due to missing assumptions on some of the attributes.

We plan to investigate using other symbolic representations such as arithmetic constraints [3] or composite representations [2] for verification of Vortex programs. We will also do more experiments on abstraction techniques, and develop a customized model checker for Vortex language.

Acknowledgements: The work is partially supported by a faculty research grant from UCSB. The work by Bultan is also supported in part by NSF grant CCR-9970976 and NSF CAREER award CCR-9984822. The work by Su is supported in part by NSF grants IRI-9700370 and IIS-9817432.

References

1. A. Ailamaki, Y. Ioannidis, and M. Livny. Scientific workflow management by database management. In *Proc. Int. Conf. on Statistical and Scientific Database Management*, 1998.
2. T. Bultan, R. Gerber, and C. League. Composite model checking: Verification with type-specific symbolic representations. *ACM Transactions on Software Engineering and Methodology*, 9(1):3–50, January 2000.
3. T. Bultan, R. Gerber, and W. Pugh. Model-checking concurrent systems with unbounded integer variables: Symbolic representations, approximations, and experimental results. *ACM Transactions on Programming Languages and Systems*, 21(4):747–789, July 1999.
4. W. Chan, R. J. Anderson, P. Beame, S. Burns, F. Modugno, D. Notkin, and J. D. Reese. Model checking large software specifications. *IEEE Transactions on Software Engineering*, 24(7):498–520, July 1998.
5. E. M. Clarke, O. Grumberg, S. Jha, Y. Lu, and H. Veith. Counterexample-guided abstraction refinement. In *Proc. Conf. on Computer Aided Verification*, 2000.
6. C. A. Ellis. Information control nets: A mathematical model of office information flow. In *ACM Proc. Conf. Simulation, Modeling and Measurement of Computer Systems*, pages 225–240, August 1979.
7. M. Garey and D. Johnson. *Computers and Intractability A Guide to the theory of NP-Completeness*. Freeman, 1979.
8. D. Georgakopoulos, M. Hornick, and A. Sheth. An overview of workflow management: From process modeling to workflow automation infrastructure. *Distributed and Parallel Databases*, 3(2):119–154, April 1995.
9. S. Graf and H. Saïdi. Construction of abstract state graph with PVS. In *Proc. Conf. on Computer Aided Verification*, pages 72–83, 1997.
10. R. Hull, F. Llirbat, E. Simon, J. Su, G. Dong, B. Kumar, and G. Zhou. Declarative workflows that support easy modification and dynamic browsing. In *Proc. Int. Joint Conf. on Work Activities Coordination and Collaboration*, 1999.
11. N. Krishnakumar and A. Sheth. Managing heterogeneous multi-systems tasks to support enterprise-wide operations. *Distributed and Parallel Databases*, 3(2), 1995.
12. R. P. Kurshan. Program verification. *Notices of the AMS*, 47(5):534–545, May 2000.
13. K. L. McMillan. *Symbolic model checking*. Kluwer Academic Publishers, Massachusetts, 1993.
14. C. Medeiros, G. Vossen, and M. Weske. Wasa: a workflow-based architecture to support scientific database applications. In *Proc. 6th DEXA Conference*, 1995.
15. P. Muth, D. Wodtke, J. Weissenfels, G. Weikum, and A. Kotz-Dittrich. Enterprise-wide workflow management based on state and activity charts. In *Proc. NATO Advanced Study Institute on Workflow Management Systems and Interoperability*, 1997.
16. H. Saïdi. Model checking guided abstraction and analysis. In *Proceedings of Statica Analysis Symposium*, Lecture Notes in Computer Science. Springer, 2000.
17. M. Schroeder. Verification of business processes for a correspondence handling center using CCS. In *Proc. European Symp. on Validation and Verification of Knowledge Based Systems and Components*, June 1999.
18. W. M. P. van der Aalst and A. H. M. ter Hofstede. Verification of workflow task structures: A Petri-net-based approach. *Information Systems*, 25(1), 2000.
19. Workflow management coalition. http://www.aiim.org/wfmc, 2000.

Parameterized Verification of Multithreaded Software Libraries

Thomas Ball*, Sagar Chaki**, and Sriram K. Rajamani * * *

Abstract. The growing popularity of multi-threading has led to a great number of software libraries that support access by multiple threads. We present *Local/Global Finite State Machines* (*LGFSMs*) as a model for a certain class of multithreaded libraries. We have developed a tool called Beacon that does parameterized model checking of *LGFSMs*. We demonstrate the expressiveness of *LGFSMs* as models, and the effectiveness of Beacon as a model checking tool by (1) modeling a multithreaded memory manager Rockall developed at Microsoft Research as an *LGFSM*, and (2) using Beacon to check a critical safety property of Rockall.

1 Introduction

Software libraries traditionally have been designed for use by single-threaded clients. Due to the increasing use of multi-threading both on servers and clients, most libraries designed today accommodate simultaneous access by a multitude of threads. A software library typically provides its interface through a set of functions that a thread can call. In the context of the object-oriented paradigm, the library might simply export a set of classes and make its services accessible via the public methods of these classes. Furthermore, the library usually maintains internal state (using member variables of classes) which can be modified during the execution of invoked methods. Even though multiple threads can access a library simultaneously, the library provides a consistent sequential semantics to all threads.

We are interested in checking properties of multithreaded software libraries. In particular, we are interested in checking that a library is well-behaved with respect to sequences of calls made upon it by a *multitude* of client threads. For object-oriented libraries this boils down to checking if the internal state of the library is always correct irrespective of the number of threads calling it and the interleaving of the executions of the calls made by these threads. More precisely, we want to ensure that the library is *thread-safe*.

---

* Microsoft Research, tball@microsoft.com
** Carnegie Melon University, chaki+@cs.cmu.edu
* * * Microsoft Research, sriram@microsoft.com

T. Margaria and W. Yi (Eds.): TACAS 2001, LNCS 2031, pp. 158–173, 2001.
© Springer-Verlag Berlin Heidelberg 2001

We recently proposed boolean programs [BR00b, BR00a] as a model for representing abstractions of imperative programs written in languages such as C. Boolean programs are imperative programs in which all variables have boolean type. Boolean programs contain procedures with call-by-value parameter passing and recursion. Questions such as invariant checking and termination (which are undecidable in general) are decidable for boolean programs.

In order to model multi-threaded programs, we have extended the boolean program model with threads. Threads in a multi-threaded boolean program execute asynchronously, and communicate with each other using shared global variables. If B_1 and B_2 are two threads of a boolean program, we denote their asynchronous composition by $B_1 \| B_2$. Unfortunately, even for boolean programs with only two threads, invariant checking is undecidable (this can be proved along the lines of [Ram99]).

Nonetheless, in practice we believe that the interaction between threads (in boolean programs as well as programs in general) usually can be modeled by a finite state machine. Therefore, we further abstract each thread of a boolean program to a *LGFSM* (local/global finite state machine), which makes the distinction between local and (shared) global states explicit. The relationship between a boolean program B and its *LGFSM* abstraction F is one of refinement: the boolean program refines the interaction behavior specified by its *LGFSM* abstraction. We write this as $B \Rightarrow F$.

Suppose B_1 and B_2 are two threads of a boolean program B, whose interactions are described by *LGFSMs* F_1 and F_2 respectively. Then the following proof rule can be used to check if the composition of B_1 and B_2 satisfies invariant φ:

$$
\begin{array}{ll}
(1) \ B_1 & \Rightarrow F_1 \\
(2) \ B_2 & \Rightarrow F_2 \\
(3) \ F_1 \| F_2 \models \varphi \\
\hline
(4) \ B_1 \| B_2 \models \varphi
\end{array}
$$

Note that proof obligations (1) and (2) involve checking refinement between a boolean program, and an *LGFSM*, and proof obligation (3) involves checking if a composition of two *LGFSMs* satisfies an invariant. All these questions are decidable.

Now, suppose that we want to check if a boolean program with an arbitrary number of threads satisfies an invariant φ. Let B^* denote the composition of an arbitrary number of threads of a boolean program B. Then the following proof rule can be used to check if B^* satisfies invariant

φ:

$$\frac{\begin{array}{l}(5)\ B\ \Rightarrow F \\ (6)\ F^* \models \varphi\end{array}}{(7)\ B^* \models \varphi}$$

In this paper, we give an algorithm to automatically check proof obligation(6), which has been implemented in a tool called **Beacon**. We model each thread (F) of a multi-threaded library by a *local/global finite state machine*, or *LGFSM*. An arbitrary number of instances of an *LGFSM* comprise a *parameterized library system*, or *PLS* for short. We consider the question of whether or not a particular global state (a particular valuation to the global variables) is reachable in a *PLS*. We show that this problem is decidable, even when there are an arbitrary number of *LGFSMs*.

The results of this paper are four-fold:

- We formally define the *LGFSM* and *PLS* models, which can be used to model a wide class of concurrent software systems, namely those in which multiple anonymous clients require the services of a centralized library.
- Given a *PLS* system with m global states and n local states, we show that: (1) a global state is reachable in a *PLS* comprised of an arbitrary number of threads iff it is reachable in a *PLS* comprised of $2m^{n!}$ threads; (2) the global state reachability problem for a *PLS* can be decided deterministically in space $\mathcal{O}(2^{2nlog(n)+2loglog(m)})$ and time $\mathcal{O}(2^{2^{2nlog(n)+2loglog(m)}})$. These complexity results are based directly on the work of Rackoff [Rac78].
- We present an *LGFSM* model of an industrial-strength multi-threaded memory manager called **Rockall**, developed in Microsoft Research. **Rockall** is written in C++. We manually wrote a boolean program abstraction of a single thread of **Rockall**, and (automatically) inlined the procedure calls to obtain a *LGFSM*. The *LGFSM* model has $m = 2048$ global states and $n = 256$ local states. In the *LGFSM* for **Rockall**, the global states represent the internal data structures of the memory manager while the local states represent the states of the clients of the memory manager.
- We present an algorithm for checking the reachability of a global state in a *PLS* that is similar to the algorithm for computing the minimal coverability graph for Petri nets presented in [Fin93]. The algorithm has been implemented in a tool called **Beacon**. When applied to the

Rockall model, Beacon was able to prove a critical safety property of the model in about 4 hours, despite the fact that the algorithm might have had to explore a system with $2 \times 2048^{256!}$ threads, in the worst case.

The paper is organized as follows. Section 2 defines the *LGFSM* and *PLS* models, defines the global state reachability problem and shows that it is decidable. Section 3 introduces the Rockall memory manager and describes our *LGFSM* model of Rockall. Section 4 gives our algorithm for determining the reachability of a global state in a *PLS*, proves that the algorithm terminates and is sound and complete, and describes our experiences applying Beacon to Rockall. Section 5 discusses related work and Section 6 concludes the paper.

2   Modeling Multi-threaded Libraries

This section formally defines the concepts of the local/global finite-state machine (*LGFSM*) model and a parameterized library system (*PLS*), presents the reachability problem for a *PLS*, and shows that this problem is decidable. Finally it highlights some relationships between *PLS* and Petri nets.

2.1   Model

An *LGFSM* P is a 4-tuple $\langle \Lambda_P, \Gamma_P, \hat{\sigma}_P, T_P \rangle$, where

- Λ_P is a finite set of *local states*.
- Γ_P is a finite set of *global states*.
- $\hat{\sigma}_P \in \Lambda_P \times \Gamma_P$ is the *initial state*.
- $T_P \subseteq \Lambda_P \times \Gamma_P \times \Lambda_P \times \Gamma_P$ is a *transition relation* that prescribes how a pair of a local and global states transitions to another pair of local and global states.

Given an *LGFSM* P, and $f \geq 1$, the parameterized library system P_f consists of an interleaving composition of f instances of P, where all the instances share the same global states. Formally, P_f is a finite state machine $\langle \Sigma_{P_f}, \hat{\sigma}_{P_f}, T_{P_f} \rangle$, where

- Σ_{P_f} are $(f+1)$-tuples in $\Lambda_P{}^f \times \Gamma_P$. For a state $\sigma = \langle l_1, l_2, \ldots, l_f, g \rangle$ in Σ_{P_f}, we define projection operators $\sigma(i)$, for $1 \leq i \leq f+1$ to extract the components of σ.
- $\hat{\sigma}_{P_f}$ is $\langle \hat{l}, \hat{l}, \ldots, \hat{l}, \hat{g} \rangle$, where $\langle \hat{l}, \hat{g} \rangle = \hat{\sigma}_P$ and the $|\hat{\sigma}_{P_f}| = f+1$.

- $T_{P_f} \subseteq \Sigma_{P_f} \times \Sigma_{P_f}$ is a set of transitions, such that $\langle\langle l_1, l_2, \ldots, l_f, g\rangle, \langle l'_1, l'_2, \ldots, l'_f, g'\rangle\rangle$ if for some $1 \le i \le f$, we have that $\tau = \langle\langle l_i, g\rangle, \langle l'_i, g'\rangle\rangle \in T_P$, and for all j, where $1 \le j \le f$ and $i \ne j$, we have that $l_j = l'_j$. We say that the second state of the transition is the *image* of the first state under the transition. Formally, $\langle l'_1, l'_2, \ldots, l'_f, g'\rangle = Image(\langle l_1, l_2, \ldots, l_f, g\rangle, \tau)$.

A sequence $\overline{\sigma} = \sigma_0, \sigma_1, \sigma_2, \ldots, \sigma_j$ over Σ_{P_f} is a *trajectory* of P_f if (1) $\sigma_0 = \hat{\sigma}_{P_f}$, and (2) for all $0 \le i < j$, we have $\langle \sigma_i, \sigma_{i+1}\rangle \in T_{P_f}$. A state σ is *reachable* in P_f if there exists a trajectory that ends in σ. A global state $g \in \Gamma_P$ is *reachable* in P_f if there exists a reachable state σ in P_f such that $\sigma(f+1) = g$.

2.2   Decidability of the Reachability Problem

An instance of the parameterized reachability problem for software libraries consists of an *LGFSM* P and a global state $g \in \Gamma_P$. The answer to the parameterized reachability problem is "yes" if there exists some $f \ge 1$ such that g is reachable in P_f, and "no" otherwise.

We exploit two characteristics of *LGFSM* models. First, in an *PLS*, each state transition can change the local state component of at most one *LGFSM*. Because of this restriction, it is not possible for an arbitrary number of clients to change their local states in a single instant in a *PLS*.[1] Second, because the size of the global state component is bounded and the number of clients unbounded, it is not possible for clients to communicate their identity to each other through the global state.

We give an upper bound to the number of threads we need to consider, in order to to decide the global state reachability problem for *LGFSMs*. In the sequel, we denote the number of global states in a *LGFSM* ($|\Gamma_P|$) by m and the number of local states ($|\Lambda_P|$) by n. The proofs of the following theorems are presented in [BCR00] and omitted here for brevity.

Theorem 1. Let P be an *LGFSM* with m global states and n local states. Let $g \in \Gamma_P$. For all $f \ge 1$, global state g is reachable in P_f iff g is reachable by a trajectory of length at most $m^{(n+1)!}$ in P_f.

Corollary. Let P be an *LGFSM* with m global states and n local states. A global state g is reachable in P_f for some $f \ge 1$ iff g is reachable in $P_{m^{(n+1)!}}$.

Theorem 2. An instance of the parameterized reachability problem with a *LGFSM* that has m global states and n local states can be decided deterministically in space $\mathcal{O}(((n+2)!log(m))^2)$ and time $\mathcal{O}(2^{((n+2)!log(m))^2})$.

---

[1]   This is consistent with the interleaving semantics usually given to threads.

2.3   Relationship Between *PLS* and Petri Nets

The relationship between *PLS* and Petri net (PN) models of computation is underscored by the following two claims.

Claim 1. Given an LGFSM P, we can construct a Petri net PN, and a mappping γ such that for all $f \in \mathbb{N}$, γ maps every reachable state of P_f to a reachable state of PN.

Claim 2. An instance of the parameterized reachability problem for software libraries can be reduced to an instance of the coverability problem for Petri nets.

The justifications for the claims are quite simple and are left as an exercise for the reader. The decidability of the coverability problem for PNs has been known since [KM69]. Combined with claim 2, this result gives another proof for the decidability of the parameterized reachability problem for software libraries.

3   The Rockall Memory Manager

In this section, we describe the Rockall memory manager and our boolean program and *LGFSM* models of it.

3.1   A Quick Tour of Rockall

Rockall is a configurable thread-safe object-oriented memory manager. The basic data structure that Rockall uses for managing memory is the "bucket". Each bucket is responsible for allocating chunks of memory of a particular size. Buckets are arranged in a tree-like hierarchy. When a bucket runs out of memory, it requests a larger chunk of memory from its parent and then breaks up this big chunk into smaller chunks (corresponding to its own size), which it can then allocate as needed. The bucket at the root of this hierarchy gets its memory directly from the operating system. The number of buckets, their allocation sizes, and the tree hierarchy can be configured by the user at startup.

Rockall has a number of other features that are pertinent to our modeling. First, unlike most memory managers, Rockall maintains all information regarding the allocated memory chunks (two bits per chunk) separately in its own data structure (a hash table) rather than padding the memory chunk given to the user process with these bits. This prevents the user process from accidentally (or intentionally) trampling on the manager's data. This information is required for Rockall to determine which bucket a memory chunk was allocated from when memory is deallocated. Several locks are used in `Rockall` to ensure that each thread sees a consistent view of memory and also to achieve high performance.

The critical safety property of `Rockall` that we want to ascertain is the following : no memory location should be allocated or deallocated by `Rockall` twice or more in succession. In other words, allocation and deallocation of every memory location should occur alternately. Since each chunk of memory is treated independently by `Rockall`, the actual addresses of the memory chunks are not important for the verification of this property. So we do away with the address values completely. Thus, the models abstract the behavior of `Rockall` w.r.t. a single chunk of memory. Also, we consider a scenario where `Rockall` has only two buckets, $B0$ and $B1$, where $B1$ is $B0$'s parent. Even with these restrictions, the abstract models for `Rockall` are of non-trivial complexity.

A point to be noted here is that the models are conservative abstractions of `Rockall` w.r.t. sequences of allocation/deallocation of a memory location. In other words, for every sequence of allocation/deallocation of a memory location done by `Rockall`, there exists an identical sequence of allocation/deallocation done by each of the models. In particular this applies also to sequences which violate the desired safety property. Thus the fact that either of the models does not violate the safety property implies that `Rockall` does not violate it.

3.2   Boolean Program Model

We first describe an abstract Boolean Program model for `Rockall`. There are nine global boolean variables in this model:

- $B0\_lock$: locks bucket $B0$, protects variable $B0\_allocated$; must be acquired before $B0$ can allocate or deallocate a chunk ; initially free (the variable has the value **false**).
- $B1\_lock$: locks bucket $B1$, protects variables $B1\_allocated$ and $B1\_subdivided$; must be acquired before bucket $B1$ can allocate or deallocate a chunk ; initially free.
- $newpage\_lock$: must be acquired before the ownership of a chunk is transferred from one bucket to another ; protects variables $available$ and $find$; initially free.
- $find\_lock$: must be acquired before the hash table is searched to find the bucket that owns a chunk and before the ownership of a chunk is transferred from one bucket to another, as the hash table will be updated as a result ($newpage\_lock$ comes before $find\_lock$ in the lock order).

- *B0_allocated* : **true** if bucket *B0* has allocated its chunk to the user process, otherwise **false**; initially **false**.
- *B1_allocated* : **true** if bucket *B1* has allocated its chunk to bucket *B0* or to the user process, otherwise **false**; initially **false**.
- *B1_subdivided* : **true** if bucket *B1* has allocated its chunk to bucket *B0*, otherwise **false**; initially **false**.
- *available* : **true** if bucket *B1* has the right to allocate the chunk, **false** if bucket *B0* has the right to allocate it ; initially **true**.
- *find* : **true** if bucket *B1* holds the chunk, **false** if bucket *B0* holds it; models the hash table ; initially **true**.

The boolean program abstraction of `Rockall` contains seven procedures, whose behavior we summarize below:

- *B0_New()*: models the allocation of a chunk to the user by bucket *B0* ; returns **true** if a successful allocation occurs and **false** otherwise ; calls the procedure *FetchFromB1()* in the case that *B0* has no available memory and needs to get memory from *B1* before completing the allocation request.
- *FetchFromB1()* : models the allocation of *B1*'s chunk to *B0* ; returns **true** if a successful allocation occurs and **false** otherwise.
- *B1_New()* : models the allocation of *B1*'s chunk to the user ; returns **true** if a successful allocation occurs and **false** otherwise.
- *B0_Delete()* : models the deallocation of *B0*'s memory chunk ; returns **true** if a successful deallocation occurs and **false** otherwise, and calls the procedure *GiveToB1()* in case *B0* needs to return the chunk to *B1* after the deallocation.
- *GiveToB1()* : models the return of the chunk by *B0* to *B1*.
- *B1_Delete()* : models the deallocation of *B1*'s chunk ; returns **true** if a successful deallocation occurs and **false** otherwise.

3.3   Instrumented Program

Recall that we want to check if no memory location should be allocated or deallocated by `Rockall` twice or more in succession. We add the following instrumentation to our `Rockall` model, in order to reduce the problem of checking this safety property to a problem of checking an invariant.

We add two variables *safe0* and *safe1* to the boolean program. These variables summarize the allocation/deallocation behavior seen so far:

- if both variables are **false** then there have been an equal number of alternating allocations and deallocations;

- if *safe1* is **false** and *safe0* is **true** then there has been an additional allocation;
- if *safe1* is **true** and *safe0* is **false** then there has been an additional deallocation;
- finally, if both variables are **true** then there have been two or more successive allocations or deallocations (this is the error state)

Part of the instrumentation is a new procedure *UpdateState()* that updates the two shared variables *safe1* and *safe0* in accordance with the allocation/deallocation that has occurred and the above-mentioned protocol for updating these two variables. It is called every time a successful allocation/deallocation occurs.

3.4 Translation to *LGFSM*

Since the boolean model does not have any recursion, it can easily be transformed to a finite state model by inlining all procedure calls. An *LGFSM* abstraction of `Rockall` was obtained by automatically inlining the procedures of the boolean program. Local variables are used to explicitly track important control locations in the boolean program (which are implicit in the boolean program representation). The abstract *LGFSM* for `Rockall` has eleven global variables and eight local variables. Let us denote the set of global variables by γ_P and the set of local variables by λ_P. We then have $m = |\Gamma_P| = 2^{|\gamma_P|} = 2048$ and $n = |\Lambda_P| = 2^{|\lambda_P|} = 256$.

4 The `Beacon` Tool

The decidability result from Section 2 is of theoretic interest only, as it is infeasible to explicitly check all trajectories of length $2m^{n!}$ even for small values of m and n. We have implemented an algorithm which has the effect of exploring all such trajectories but employs certain key optimizations to reduce the amount of exploration required. In this section, we present the algorithm and prove that the optimizations are sound and complete. Although the algorithm could, in the worst case, still explore all trajectories of length at most $2m^{n!}$, the optimizations seem to be extremely effective in practice.

The `Beacon` tool was able to verify the desired safety property of `Rockall` for an arbitrary number of threads. It ran on a 800 MHz Pentium III machine with 512 MB of RAM and took about 240 minutes to complete. In the process it explored roughly 2 million states. The complexity result of section 2 implies that (in the worst case) the algorithm might check all trajectories of length at most $2 \times 2048^{256!}$ which is of the order of $10^{10^{600}}$. The fact that Beacon managed to verify the property indicates that the optimization techniques we employ might be quite effective in practice.[2]

4.1   The Algorithm

We start by defining an alternate representation for the states of a *PLS* P_f. As before, let $m = |\Gamma_P|$ and let $n = |\Lambda_P|$. A state σ of P_f, for any $f \geq 1$, can be represented as $(n+1)$-tuple $\theta \in \mathbb{N}^n \times \Gamma_P$. where the global states of σ and θ are the same, and for $1 \leq i \leq n$, the i-th component of θ is equal to the number of times l_i occurs in σ. Formally, we have (1) $\theta(n+1) = \sigma(f+1)$, and (2) for $1 \leq i \leq n$, $\theta(i)$ is equal to the number of occurrences of Λ_i in σ. The advantage of this alternate representation is that it provides a uniform way to represent the states of P_f for all f.

Representing Infinite Sets of States with Configurations. The number of reachable states of P_f for all f, is potentially infinite. We use the following trick to represent certain infinite sets of states. We allow a special symbol $*$ in our state representation to implicitly represent the set of all natural numbers. Formally, a *configuration* is an element of the set $\{\mathbb{N} \cup \{*\}\}^n \times \Gamma_P$. Note that every state is a configuration. A configuration θ which contains one or more occurrences of $*$, is interpreted to represent the infinite set of states obtained by replacing each occurrence of $*$ by some natural number. For example, if $n = 4$, then the configuration $\langle 3, *, 0, *, g \rangle$ represents the set of states $\{\langle 3, i, 0, j, g \rangle | i \in \mathbb{N}, j \in \mathbb{N}\}$. Note that we cannot use this trick to represent any infinite set of states compactly. For example, we cannot represent the set of states $\{\langle 3, 2i, 0, 5, g \rangle | i \in \mathbb{N}\}$ using a configuration.

We define two unary operators *Inc* and *Dec* over the domain $\mathbb{N} \cup \{*\}$. If $k \in \mathbb{N}$ then $Inc(k) = k + 1$, and $Dec(k) = k - 1$. For $k = *$, we have $Inc(*) = Dec(*) = *$. Let $\theta_1 = \langle k_1, k_2, \ldots, k_i, \ldots, k_j \ldots, k_n, g \rangle$ be a configuration. Consider i, j such that $k_i > 0$ and $\tau = \langle \langle g, l_i \rangle, \langle g', l_j \rangle \rangle \in T_P$. Then, the image of θ_1 under τ is defined as

$$Image(\theta_1, \tau) = \langle k_1, k_2, \ldots, Dec(k_i), \ldots, Inc(k_j), \ldots, k_n, g' \rangle$$

---

[2] We had initially attempted to verify the safety property for a fixed number of threads of the LGFSM using SMV [McM]. We wrote descriptions of the composition of a fixed number of threads of the LGFSM in the SMV language and tried to model check the safety property using Cadence's SMV tool. However the tool was unable to verify the property for more than 4 threads when run on the above mentioned machine.

We note that the image operator is distributive with respect to the states in a configuration. That is, $Image(\theta_1, \tau)$ exactly represents the set $\{\sigma_2 \mid \exists \sigma_1 \in \theta_1.\sigma_2 = Image(\sigma_1, \tau)\}$.

We extend the comparison operators $\leq$ and $<$ to operate over the natural numbers extended with $*$. Let $\leq^{\mathbb{N}}$ and $<^{\mathbb{N}}$ be the usual comparison operators in $\mathbb{N}$. Let i, j be in $\mathbb{N} \cup \{*\}$. We say that $i \leq j$ if (1) $j = *$, or (2) $i, j \in \mathbb{N}$ and $i \leq^{\mathbb{N}} j$. We say that $i < j$ if (1) $j = *$ and $i \in \mathbb{N}$, or (2) $i, j \in \mathbb{N}$ and $i <^{\mathbb{N}} j$.

Given two configurations Ω_1, and Ω_2 , we say that Ω_2 *covers* Ω_1 , written $\Omega_1 \leq \Omega_2$ if (1) $\Omega_1(n + 1) = \Omega_2(n + 1)$, and (2) for every $1 \leq i \leq n$, we have that $\Omega_1(i) \leq \Omega_2(i)$. We say that Ω_2 *dominates* Ω_1, written $\Omega_1 < \Omega_2$, if (1) $\Omega_1 \leq \Omega_2$, and (2) for some $1 \leq i \leq n$, we have that $\Omega_1(i) < \Omega_2(i)$. Note that if $\Omega_1 \leq \Omega_2$, then all the global states reachable from Ω_1 are also reachable from Ω_2.

Let Ω_1 and Ω_2 be two configurations such that $\Omega_1 < \Omega_2$. Then, we define $Closure(\Omega_1, \Omega_2)$ to be the configuration Ω_3 obtained in the following way:

- $\Omega_3(n + 1) = \Omega_1(n + 1) = \Omega_2(n + 1)$, and
- for every $1 \leq i \leq n$, if $\Omega_1(i) = \Omega_2(i)$, then $\Omega_3(i) = \Omega_1(i)$, otherwise $\Omega_3(i) = *$.

The Algorithm and Its Properties. Figure 1 presents our algorithm for the parameterized reachability problem. The algorithm constructs a reachability graph $\langle Reach_v, Reach_e \rangle$, where $Reach_v$ is a set of vertices, and $Reach_e$ is a set of directed edges. Each vertex in $Reach_v$ is a configuration (we use the terms "vertex", and "configuration" interchangeably in the ensuing description). We maintain a worklist of unexplored configurations. The worklist is initialized with the initial configuration. The algorithm proceeds by picking a configuration c from the worklist and investigating every transition τ enabled in c (which leads to a configuration d). If d is covered by an existing reachable configuration a then no new global states can be reached from d that could not be reached from a, so d is "dropped". Instead, if d dominates a configuration a from which d is reachable then a compression step is possible (lines [5-8]). Otherwise, d is added to the set of reachable configurations and is added to the worklist. Three properties remain to be proved about this algorithm:

- **Completeness:** Every reachable state in P_f for all f is contained in some configuration reached by the algorithm.

$WorkList := \{\theta\}$, where **let** $\hat{\sigma}_P = \langle l_i, g \rangle$ **in**

$\qquad \theta(n+1) = g,$

$\qquad \theta(i) = *$, and

$\qquad \theta(j) = 0$ for $1 \le j \le n,\ j \ne i$

$Reach_v := WorkList$

$Reach_e := \{\}$

while $(Nonempty\ (WorkList))$ **do**

$\qquad c := Remove\ (WorkList)$

$\qquad$ **foreach** transition τ enabled in c

[1] $\qquad\qquad d := Image(c, \tau)$

[2] $\qquad\qquad$ **if** there exists a vertex $a \in Reach_v$ such that $d \le a$ **then**

[3] $\qquad\qquad\qquad$ drop d and do nothing

[4] $\qquad\qquad$ **elsif** there exists a vertex $a \in Reach_v$ such that $a < d$ and

$\qquad\qquad\qquad$ there is a path from a to d through edges in $Reach_e$ **then**

[5] $\qquad\qquad\qquad e := Closure(a, d)$

$\qquad\qquad\qquad$ **let** V be the set of vertices reachable so far from a (excluding a) **in**

$\qquad\qquad\qquad$ delete vertices from V from $WorkList$ and $Reach_v$

[6] $\qquad\qquad\qquad$ delete edges connecting to/from vertices in V from $Reach_e$

[7] $\qquad\qquad\qquad$ replace a with e in $Reach_v$ and $Reach_e$

[8] $\qquad\qquad\qquad$ add e to $WorkList$

$\qquad\qquad$ **else**

[9] $\qquad\qquad\qquad Reach_v := Reach_v \cup \{d\}$

[10] $\qquad\qquad\qquad Reach_e := Reach_e \cup \langle c, d \rangle$

[11] $\qquad\qquad\qquad$ add d to $WorkList$

$\qquad\qquad$ **if**;

$\qquad$ **endfor**

endwhile

Fig. 1. Algorithm for global state reachability in a *PLS*.

– **Soundness:** Every state contained in configurations reached by the algorithm is reachable in P_f for some f.

– **Termination:** The algorithm terminates.

The proofs of these properties are similar to proofs of the minimal coverability graph algorithm for Petri Nets presented in [Fin93]. They are presented in [BCR00] and omitted here for brevity.

4.2   Implementation Details

Below we summarize some key features of the implementation of the Beacon tool:

– Beacon constructs a reachability tree instead of a graph by ensuring that the same state is not explored more than once. Maintaining a tree makes it much easier to perform the check in step [4] since there can be at most one trajectory between two vertices in a directed tree.

- The reachability tree is constructed in a depth-first manner. We are currently experimenting with a breadth-first implementation.
- We represent * by the largest unsigned integer. While computing the image in step [1] we check for overflows. In our experiments we have found that the non-zero local state counts are either * or small integers.
- The representation of * as a finite integer coupled with the overflow check automatically puts a bound on the length of any explored trajectory, and hence on the running time of Beacon. The bound on the length of the trajectory is much smaller than what is required by the result of section 2 but we have found it to be more than sufficient for Rockall. This bound can be increased to an arbitrary level simply by using a larger value for *.
- A configuration could be represented as an array of n unsigned integers. However we discovered that most of these counts are actually zero in the explored states. To reduce space requirements, we use a sparse representation where we only maintain the non-zero local state counts along with the corresponding local states.

5   Related Work

Petri nets (PNs) [Pet62] were introduced in 1962 by C. A. Petri in his doctoral dissertation. A few years later, Karp and Miller [KM69] independently proposed Vector Addition Systems (VASs) for analyzing the properties of *parallel program schemata*. Ultimately it was realized that they are mathematically equivalent. An excellent survey of PNs, VASs, and various decidability issues relating to them can be found in [EN94]. Over the years several other models were proposed for representing infinite state systems. Many of them, like *timed PNs* were extensions to PNs, and some, like VASSs, were shown to be mathematically equivalent to VASs. There has been a lot of interesting work on decidability of problems like reachability and coverability for infinite-state systems [ACJYK96, AJ97]. Very recently, there has been a remarkable attempt at trying to unify a diverse set of infinite-state systems having similar decidability properties under a single framework of *well-structured transition systems* [FS00].

The coverability problem for VASs has been known to be decidable since [KM69]. But the algorithm proposed there is notorious for its complexity. It involves the construction of a *coverability tree*, and might require non-primitive recursive space in the worst case. Lipton [Lip76] proved that deciding the coverability problem for VASs requires at least exponential space in the size of the VAS. More specifically, Lipton showed that for some constant $d > 0$, the problem cannot be decided in space $2^{d\sqrt{n}}$. His lower bounds are valid even if one only considers input whose vectors have components of value -1, 0, or 1. Nobody has been able to propose an algorithm that matches Lipton's lower bound. Rackoff [Rac78] gave a near-optimal algorithm that requires space bounded by an exponential of $nlog(n)$, where n is the size of the VAS. Unfortunately, Rackoff's algorithm is impractical for even VASs of moderate size. According to [FS00], all implemented algorithms for the coverability problem [Fin90, Fin93] use Karp and Miller's coverability tree, or the coverability graph, or some complex forward-based method. The work most related to ours is the construction of the minimal coverability graph for PNs given by Finkel [Fin93]. To the best of our knowledge, this approach has not been applied to the parameterized verification of multi-threaded software libraries, and has not succeeded on a design as large as **Rockall**. The Petri net for the PNCSA communication protocol used in [Fin93], for example, has only 31 places and 36 transitions.

The link between PNs and parameterized networks has also been known for a long time. German and Sistla investigated temporal logic model checking of parameterized networks [GS92]. Out of the two models presented by them, one is comparable to *PLS*. The algorithm they present for this model is based on Rackoff's algorithm and has double-exponential time complexity. There has also been significant research on model checking of programs written in languages like Java which support multi-threading [CDH+00, HP00]. These approaches however concentrate on general Java programs and do not consider arbitrary numbers of threads. They impose an apriori bound on the number of threads in order to do model checking.

6   Conclusion and Future Work

In this paper, we have presented a model called *LGFSM* for representing multi-threaded libraries. Using the model, we have been able to extend well-known complexity results and algorithms from the domain of PNs and VASs to multi-threaded software libraries. We have implemented our algorithm in a tool called **Beacon** and use it to verify critical safety properties of an industrial-strength memory manager called **Rockall**. Below we summarize some interesting and challenging research directions:

- The current implementation of **Beacon** could be optimized further. In particular, it would be interesting to see if data structures employed in similar algorithms for verification of cache coherence protocols [EN96, Del00] can be used in the domain of *LGFSMs*.
- As mentioned before, we believe that in most concurrent programs the interaction between threads is regular can be captured using finite state machines. One of the major challenges in software model checking is extracting this finite state behavior (sometimes called a *synchronization skeleton*) from concurrent program descriptions. Often the actual program description is too large to be verified, and the *synchronization skeleton* is sufficient to decide the property of interest. We are interested in extracting such finite state models automatically and efficiently.
- Another challenging problem is to efficiently check refinement between a *LGFSM* and a boolean program. The motive behind doing this is that if we prove a safety property about a *LGFSM* and then prove that the *LGFSM* is refined by a C program, we could conclude that the safety property holds for the C program also.
- Finally we would also like to develop parameterized verification techniques for other, slightly more relaxed models. For example we would like to model *PLS* where the threads have a sense of identity of themselves and others, say through a thread identifier.

Acknowledgement

We thank Michael Parkes for giving us access to Rockall, and for laboriously explaining its internal details. We also thank Giorgio Delzanno for useful comments and suggestions.

References

[ACJYK96]   P. A. Abdulla, K. Cerans, B. Jonsson, and T. Yih-Kuen. General decidability theorems for infinite-state systems. *LICS '96: 11th IEEE Symp. Logic in Computer Science*, pages 313–321, July 1996.

[AJ97]   P. A. Abdulla and B. Jonsson. Ensuring completeness of symbolic verificatiom methods for infinite-state systems. *Theoretical Computer Science*, 1997.

[BCR00]   Thomas Ball, Sagar Chaki, and Sriram K. Rajamani. Parameterized verification of multithreaded software libraries. Technical Report MSR-TR-2000-116, Microsoft Research, December 2000.

[BR00a]   T. Ball and S. K. Rajamani. Bebop: A symbolic model checker for boolean programs. *SPIN 00: SPIN Workshop*, Lecture Notes in Computer Science 1885, pages 113–130. Springer-Verlag, 2000.

[BR00b]   T. Ball and S. K. Rajamani. Boolean programs: A model and process
              for software analysis. Technical Report MSR-TR-2000-14, Microsoft
              Research, February 2000.

[CDH+00]   James Corbett, Matthew Dwyer, John Hatcliff, Corina Pasareanu,
              Robby, Shawn Laubach, and Hongjun Zheng. Bandera : Extracting
              finite-state models from Java source code. *ICSE 2000 : International
              Conference on Software Engineering*, 2000.

[Del00]   G. Delzanno. Automatic Verification of Parameterized Cache Coherence
              Protocols. *CAV 00: Computer Aided Verification*, Lecture Notes in
              Computer Science 1855, pages 53–68. Springer-Verlag, 2000.

[EN94]   J. Esparza and M. Nielsen. Decibility issues for petri nets - a survey.
              Journal of Informatik Processing and Cybernetics, 30(3):143–160, 1994.

[EN96]   E. A. Emerson and K. S. Namjoshi. Automatic Verification of Param-
              eterized Synchronous Systems. *CAV 96: Computer Aided Verification*,
              Lecture Notes in Computer Science 1102, pages 87–98. Springer-Verlag,
              1996.

[Fin90]   A. Finkel. Reduction and covering of infinite reachability trees. *Infor-
              mation and Computation*, 89:144–179, 1990.

[Fin93]   A. Finkel. The minimal coverability graph for petri nets. *Advances in
              Petri Nets*, Lecture Notes in Computer Sceince, 674:210–243, 1993.

[FS00]   A. Finkel and Ph. Schnoebelen. Well-structured transition systems ev-
              erywhere ! *Theoretical Computer Science*, 2000. To appear.

[GS92]   S. M. German and A. P. Sistla. Reasoning about systems with many
              processes. *JACM*, 39(3), July 1992.

[HP00]   K. Havelund and T. Pressburger. Model checking Java programs using
              JavaPathFinder. *STTT: International Journal on Software Tools for
              Technology Transfer*, 2(4), April 2000.

[KM69]   R. M. Karp and R. E. Miller. Parallel program schemata. *Journal of
              Computer and System Sciences*, 3:147–195, 1969.

[Lip76]   R. J. Lipton. The reachability problem requires exponential space. Tech-
              nical report, Department of Computer Science, Yale University, 1976.

[McM]   K.L. McMillan. `http://www-cad.eecs.berkeley.edu/~kenmcmil`.

[Pet62]   C. Petri. Fundamentals of a theory of asynchronous information flow.
              Information Processing 62, Proceedings of the 1962 IFIP Congress,
              pages 386–390, 1962.

[Rac78]   C. Rackoff. The covering and boundedness problem for vector addition
              systems. *Theoretical Computer Science*, 6:223–231, 1978.

[Ram99]   G. Ramalingam. Context sensitive synchronization sensitive analysis is
              undecidable. Technical Report RC21493, IBM T.J.Watson Research,
              May 1999.

Efficient Guiding Towards Cost-Optimality in UPPAAL*

Gerd Behrmann[1], Ansgar Fehnker[3†], Thomas Hune[2], Kim Larsen[4],
Paul Pettersson[5], and Judi Romijn[3]

[1] Basic Research in Computer Science, Aalborg University,
E-mail: behrmann@cs.auc.dk
[2] Basic Research in Computer Science, Aarhus University,
E-mail: baris@brics.dk
[3] Computing Science Institute, University of Nijmegen,
E-mail: [ansgar,judi]@cs.kun.nl
[4] Department of Computer Science, University of Twente[§],
E-mail: kgl@cs.auc.dk
[5] Department of Computer Systems, Information Technology,
Uppsala University, E-mail: paupet@docs.uu.se.

Abstract. In this paper we present an algorithm for efficiently computing the minimum cost of reaching a goal state in the model of Uniformly Priced Timed Automata (UPTA). This model can be seen as a submodel of the recently suggested model of linearly priced timed automata, which extends timed automata with prices on both locations and transitions. The presented algorithm is based on a symbolic semantics of UTPA, and an efficient representation and operations based on difference bound matrices. In analogy with Dijkstra's shortest path algorithm, we show that the search order of the algorithm can be chosen such that the number of symbolic states explored by the algorithm is optimal, in the sense that the number of explored states can not be reduced by any other search order. We also present a number of techniques inspired by branch-andbound algorithms which can be used for limiting the search space and for quickly finding near-optimal solutions.

The algorithm has been implemented in the verification tool UPPAAL. When applied on a number of experiments the presented techniques reduced the explored state-space with up to 90%.

1 Introduction

Recently, formal verification tools for real-time and hybrid systems, such as UPPAAL [LPY97], KRONOS [BDM⁺98] and HYTECH [HHWT97], have been applied

---

* This work is partially supported by the European Community Esprit-LTR Project 26270 VHS (Verification of Hybrid systems).

[§] On sabbatical from Basic Research in Computer Science, Aalborg University.

[†] Research supported by Netherlands Organization for Scientific Research (NWO) under contract SION 612-14-004.

T. Margaria and W. Yi (Eds.): TACAS 2001, LNCS 2031, pp. 174–188, 2001.
© Springer-Verlag Berlin Heidelberg 2001

to solve realistic scheduling problems [Feh99b,HLP00,NY99]. The basic common idea of these works is to reformulate a scheduling problem to a reachability problem that can be solved by verification tools. In this approach, the automata based modeling languages of the verification tools serve as the input language in which the scheduling problem is described. These modeling languages have been found to be very well-suited in this respect, as they allow for easy and flexible modeling of systems consisting of several parallel components that interact in a time-critical manner and constrain the behavior of each other in a multitude of ways.

A main difference between verification algorithms and dedicated scheduling algorithms is in the way they search a state-space to find solutions. Scheduling algorithms are often designed to find optimal (or near optimal) solutions and are therefore based on techniques such as branch-and-bound to identify and prune parts of the states-space that are guaranteed to not contain any optimal solutions. In contrast, verification algorithms do normally not support any notion of optimality and are designed to explore the entire state-space as efficiently as possible. The verification algorithms that do support notions of optimality are restricted to simple trace properties such as shortest trace [LPY95], or shortest accumulated delay in trace [NTY00].

In this paper we aim at reducing the gap between scheduling and verification algorithms by adopting a number of techniques used in scheduling algorithms in the verification tool UPPAAL. In doing so, we study the problem of efficiently computing the minimal cost of reaching a goal state in the model of *Uniformly Priced Timed Automata* (UPTA). This model can be seen as a restricted version of the recently suggested model of *Linearly Priced Timed Automata* (LPTA) [BFH+01], which extends the model of timed automata with *prices* on all transitions and locations. In these models, the cost of taking an action transition is the price associated with the transition, and the cost of delaying d time units in a location is $d \cdot p$, where p is the price associated with the location. The cost of a trace is simply the accumulated sum of costs of its delay and action transitions. The objective is to determine the minimum cost of traces ending in a goal state.

The infinite state-spaces of timed automata models necessitates the use of symbolic techniques in order to simultaneously handle sets of states (so-called symbolic states). For pure reachability analysis, tools like UPPAAL and KRONOS use symbolic states of the form (l, Z), where l is a location of the timed automaton and $Z \subseteq \mathbb{R}^{\mathbb{C}1}$ is a convex set of clock valuations called a *zone*. For the computation of minimum costs of reaching goal states, we suggest the use of *symbolic cost states* of the form (l, C), where $C : \mathbb{R}^{\mathbb{C}} \to (\mathbb{R}_{\geq 0} \cup \{\infty\})$ is a cost function mapping clock valuations to real valued costs or ∞. The intention is that, whenever $C(u) < \infty$, reachability of the symbolic cost state (l, C) should ensure that the state (l, u) is reachable with cost $C(u)$.

Using the above notion of symbolic cost states, an abstract algorithm for computing the minimum cost of reaching a goal state satisfying φ of a uniformly

---

[1] $\mathbb{C}$ denotes the set of clocks of the timed automata, and $\mathbb{R}^{\mathbb{C}}$ denotes the set of functions from $\mathbb{C}$ to $\mathbb{R}_{\geq 0}$.

Cost := ∞
Passed := ∅
Waiting := {(l_0, C_0)}
while Waiting ≠ ∅ **do**
  select (l, C) from Waiting
  if $(l, C) \models \varphi$ **and** $min(C) <$ Cost **then**
    Cost := $min(C)$
  if for all (l, C') in Passed: $C' \not\sqsubseteq C$ **then**
    add (l, C) to Passed
    for all (m, D) such that $(l, C) \rightsquigarrow (m, D)$: add (m, D) to Waiting
return Cost

Fig. 1. Abstract Algorithm for the Minimal-Cost Reachability Problem.

priced timed automaton is shown in Fig. 1. The algorithm is similar to a standard state-space traversal algorithm that uses two data-structures Waiting and Passed to store states waiting to be examined, and states already explored, respectively. Initially, Passed is empty and Waiting holds an initial (symbolic cost) state. In each iteration, the algorithm proceeds by selecting a state (l, C) from Waiting checking that none of the previously explored states (l, C') has a "smaller" cost function, written $C' \sqsubseteq C$[2], and if this is the case, adds it to Passed and its successors to Waiting In addition the algorithm uses the global variable Cost, which is initially set to ∞ and updated whenever a goal state is found that can be reached with a lower cost than the current value of Cost. The algorithm terminates when Waiting is empty, i.e. when no further states are left to be examined. Thus, the algorithm always searches the entire state-space of the analyzed automaton.

In [BFH+01] an algorithm for computing the minimal cost of reaching designated goal states was given for the full model of LPTA. However, the algorithm is based on a cost-extended version of regions, and is thus guaranteed to be extremely inefficient and highly sensitive to the size of constants used in the models. As the first contribution of this paper, we give for the subclass of UPTA an efficient zone representation of symbolic cost states based on *Difference Bound Matrices* [Dil89], and give all the necessary symbolic operators needed to implement the algorithm. As the second contribution we show that, in analogy with Dijkstra's shortest path algorithm, if the algorithm is modified to always select from Waiting the (symbolic cost) state with the smallest minimum cost, the state-space exploration may terminate as soon as a goal state is explored. This means that we can solve the minimal-cost reachability problem without necessarily searching the entire state-space of the analyzed automaton. In fact, it can even be shown that the resulting algorithm is optimal in the sense that choosing to search a symbolic cost state with non-minimal minimum cost can never reduce the number of symbolic cost states explored.

The third contribution of this paper is a number of techniques inspired by branch-and-bound algorithms [AC91] that have been adopted in making the

---

[2] Formally $C' \sqsubseteq C$ iff $\forall u. C'(u) \leq C(u)$.

algorithm even more useful. These techniques are particularly useful for limiting the search space and for quickly finding solutions near to the minimum cost of reaching a goal state. To support this claim, we have implemented the algorithm in an experimental version of the verification tool UPPAAL and applied it to a wide variety of examples. Our experimental findings indicate that in some cases as much as 90% of the state-space searched in ordinary breadth-first order can be avoided by combining the techniques presented in this paper. Moreover, the techniques have allowed pure reachability analysis to be performed in cases which were previously unsuccessful.

The rest of this paper is organized as follows: In Section 2 we formally define the model of uniformly priced timed automata and give the symbolic semantics. In Section 3 we present the basic algorithm and the branch-and-bound inspired techniques. The experiments are presented in Section 4. We conclude the paper in Section 5.

2   Uniformly Priced Timed Automata

In this section linearly priced timed automata are formalized and their semantics are defined. The definitions given here resemble those of [BFH+01], except that the symbolic semantics uses cost functions whereas [BFH+01] uses priced regions. Zone-based data-structures for compact representation and efficient manipulation of cost functions are provided for the class of uniformly priced timed automata. It is simple to extend linearly priced timed automata to networks of linearly priced timed automata, but for brevity parallel composition is omitted here.

2.1   Linearly Priced Timed Automata

Formally, linearly priced timed automata (LPTA) are timed automata with prices on locations and transitions. We also denote prices on locations as rates. Let $\mathbb{C}$ be a set of clocks. Then $\mathcal{B}(\mathbb{C})$ is the set of formulas that are conjunctions of atomic constraints of the form $x \bowtie n$ and $x - y \bowtie n$ for $x, y \in \mathbb{C}$, $\bowtie \in \{<, \leq, =, \geq, >\}$ and n being a natural number. Elements of $\mathcal{B}(\mathbb{C})$ are called clock constrains over $\mathbb{C}$. $\mathcal{P}(\mathbb{C})$ denotes the power set of $\mathbb{C}$.

Definition 1 (Linearly Priced Timed Automata). *A linearly priced timed automaton A over clocks $\mathbb{C}$ and actions Act is a tuple (L, l_0, E, I, P) where L is a finite set of locations, l_0 is the initial location, $E \subseteq L \times \mathcal{B}(\mathbb{C}) \times Act \times \mathcal{P}(\mathbb{C}) \times L$ is the set of edges, where an edge contains a source, a guard, an action, a set of clocks to be reset, and a target, $I : L \to \mathcal{B}(\mathbb{C})$ assigns invariants to locations, and $P : (L \cup E) \to \mathbb{N}$ assign prices to both locations and edges. In the case of $(l, g, a, r, l') \in E$, we write $l \xrightarrow{g,a,r} l'$.*

Clock values are represented as functions called clock valuations from $\mathbb{C}$ to the non-negative reals $\mathbb{R}_{\geq 0}$. We denote by $\mathbb{R}^{\mathbb{C}}$ the set of clock valuations for $\mathbb{C}$.

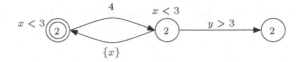

Fig. 2. An example of an LPTA with two clocks, x and y. The number in the states is the rate of the state and the number on the transitions is the cost of taking the transition. A minimal trace to the rightmost state needs to visit the initial state twice, and has cost 14.

Definition 2 (Semantics). *The semantics of a linearly priced timed automaton A is defined as a labeled transition system with the state-space $L \times \mathbb{R}^{\mathbb{C}}$ with initial state (l_0, u_0) (where u_0 assigns zero to all clocks in $\mathbb{C}$) and with the following transition relation:*

- $(l, u) \xrightarrow{\epsilon(d),p} (l, u + d)$ *if* $\forall 0 \le e \le d : u + e \in I(l)$, *and* $p = d \cdot P(l)$,
- $(l, u) \xrightarrow{a,p} (l', u')$ *if there exists* g, r *s.t.* $l \xrightarrow{g,a,r} l'$, $u \in g$, $u' = u[r \mapsto 0]$, *and* $p = P((l, g, a, r, l'))$,

where for $d \in \mathbb{R}_{\ge 0}$, $u + d$ *maps each clock x in $\mathbb{C}$ to the value $u(x) + d$, and $u[r \mapsto 0]$ denotes the clock valuation which maps each clock in r to the value 0 and agrees with u over $\mathbb{C} \setminus r$.*

The transitions are decorated with a delay-quantity or an action, together with the cost of the transition. The cost of an execution trace is simply the accumulated cost of all transitions in the trace, see Fig. 2.

Definition 3 (Cost). *Let $\alpha = (l_0, u_0) \xrightarrow{a_1, p_1} (l_1, u_1) \cdots \xrightarrow{a_n, p_n} (l_n, u_n)$ be a finite execution trace. The cost of α, $cost(\alpha)$, is the sum $\Sigma_{i=1}^{n} p_i$. For a given state (l, u) the minimum cost $mincost(l, u)$ of reaching the state, is the infimum of the costs of finite traces ending in (l, u). For a given location l the minimum cost $mincost(l)$ of reaching the location, is the infimum of the costs of finite traces ending in (l, u) for some u.*

2.2   Cost Functions

The semantics of LPTA yields an uncountable state-space and is therefore not suited for state-space exploration algorithms. To overcome this problem, the algorithm in Fig. 1 uses symbolic cost states, quite similar to how timed automata model checkers like UPPAAL use symbolic states.

Typically, symbolic states are pairs on the form (l, Z), where $Z \subseteq \mathbb{R}^{\mathbb{C}}$ is a convex set of clock valuations, called a zone, representable by *Difference Bound Matrices* (DBMs) [Dil89]. The operations needed for forward state-space exploration can be efficiently implemented using the DBM data-structure. In the priced setting we must in addition represent the costs with which individual

Table 1. Common operations on cost functions.

Operation	Cost Function ($\mathbb{R}^{\mathcal{C}} \to \mathbb{R}_{\geq 0}$)
Delay	$delay(C, p) : u \mapsto \inf\{C(v) + p \cdot d \mid d \in \mathbb{R}_{\geq 0} \wedge v + d = u\}$
Reset	$r(C) : u \mapsto \inf\{C(v) \mid u = r(v)\}$
Satisfaction	$g(C) : u \mapsto \min\{C(v) \mid v \models g \wedge u = v\}$
Increment	$C + k : u \mapsto C(u) + k, k \in \mathbb{N}$
Comparison	$D \sqsubseteq C \overset{def}{\Leftrightarrow} \forall u : D(u) \leq C(u)$
Infimum	$min(C) = \inf\{C(u) \mid u \in \mathbb{R}^{\mathcal{C}}\}$

states are reached. For this we suggest the use of *symbolic cost states*, (l, C), where C is a cost function mapping clock valuations to real valued costs. Thus, within a symbolic cost state (l, C), the cost of a state (l, u) is given by $C(u)$.

Definition 4 (Cost Function). *A cost function $C : \mathbb{R}^{\mathcal{C}} \to \mathbb{R}_{\geq 0} \cup \{\infty\}$ assigns to each clock valuation, u, a positive real valued cost, c, or infinity. The support $sup(C) = \{u \mid C(u) < \infty\}$ is the set of valuations mapped to a finite cost.*

Table 1 summarizes several operations that are used by the symbolic semantics and the algorithm in Fig. 1. In terms of the support of a cost function, the operations behave exactly as on zones; e.g. $sup(r(C)) = r(sup(C))$. The operations effect on the cost value reflect the intent to compute the minimum cost of reaching a state, e.g., $r(C)(u)$ is the infimum of $C(v)$ for all v that reset to u.

2.3 Symbolic Semantics

The symbolic semantics for LPTA is very similar to the common zone based symbolic semantics used for timed automata.

Definition 5 (Symbolic Semantics). *Let $A = (L, l_0, E, I, P)$ be a linearly priced timed automaton. The symbolic semantics is defined as a labelled transition system over symbolic cost states on the form (l, C), l being a location and C a cost function with the transition relation:*

$$- (l, C) \overset{\epsilon}{\to} \left(l, I(l)\Big(delay(I(l)(C), P(l))\Big)\right),$$

$$- (l, C) \overset{a}{\to} \left(l', I(l)(r(g(C))) + p\right) \text{ iff } l \xrightarrow{g,a,r} l', \text{ and } p = P((l, g, a, r, l')).$$

The initial state is (l_0, C_0) where $sup(C_0) = \{u_0\}$ and $C_0(u_0) = 0$.

Notice that the support of any cost function reachable by the symbolic semantics is a zone.

Lemma 1. *Given LPTA A, for each trace α of A that ends in state (l, u), there exists a symbolic trace β of A, that ends up in a symbolic cost state (l, C), such that $C(u) = cost(\alpha)$.*

Lemma 2. *Whenever (l, C) is a reachable symbolic state and $u \in sup(C)$, then $mincost(l, u) \leq C(u)$ for all u.*

Theorem 1. $mincost(l) = \min\{min(C) \mid (l, C) \text{ is reachable}\}$

Theorem 1 ensures that the algorithm in Fig. 1 indeed does find the minimum cost, but since the state-space is still infinite there is no guarantee that the algorithm ever terminates. For zone based timed automata model checkers, termination is ensured by normalizing all zones with respect to a maximum constant M [Rok93], but for LPTA ensuring termination also depends on the representation of cost functions.

2.4 Representing Cost Functions

As stated in the introduction, we provide an efficient implementation of cost functions for the class of Uniformly Priced Timed Automata (UPTA).

Definition 6 (Uniformly Priced Timed Automata). *An uniformly priced timed automaton is an LPTA where all locations have the same rate. We refer to this rate as the rate of the UPTA.*

Lemma 3. *Any UPTA A with positive rate can be translated into an UPTA B with rate 1 such that $mincost(l)$ in A is identical to $mincost(l)$ in B.*

Thus, in order to find the infimum cost of reaching a satisfying state in UPTA, we only need to be able to handle rate zero and rate one.

In case of rate zero, all symbolic states reachable by the symbolic semantics have very simple cost functions: The support is mapped to the same integer (because the cost is 0 in the initial state and only modified by the increment operation). This means that a cost function C can be represented as a pair (Z, c), where Z is a zone and c an integer, s.t. $C(u) = c$ when $u \in Z$ and ∞ otherwise. Delay, reset and satisfaction are easily implementable for zones using DBMs. Increment is a matter of incrementing c and a comparison $(Z_1, c_1) \sqsubseteq (Z_2, c_2)$ reduces to $Z_2 \subseteq Z_1 \wedge c_1 \leq c_2$. Termination is ensured by normalizing all zones with respect to a maximum constant M.

In case of rate one, the idea is to use zones over $\mathbb{C} \cup \{\delta\}$, where δ is an additional clock keeping track of the cost, s.t. every clock valuation u is associated with *exactly one* cost $Z(u)$ in zone Z^3. Then, $C(u) = c$ iff $u[\delta \mapsto c] \in Z$. This is possible because the continuous cost advances at the same rate as time. Delay, reset, satisfaction and infimum are supported directly by DBMs. Increment $C + c$ translates to $Z[\delta \mapsto \delta + k] = \{u[\delta \mapsto u(\delta) + k] \mid u \in Z\}$ and is also realizable using DBMs. For comparison between symbolic cost states, notice that $Z_2 \subseteq Z_1 \Rightarrow Z_1 \sqsubseteq Z_2$, whereas the implication in the other direction does not hold in general, see Fig. 3. However, it follows from the following Lemma 4 that comparisons can still be reduced to set inclusion provided the zone is extended in the δ dimension, see Fig. 3.

---

^{3} We define $Z(u)$ to be ∞ if u is not in Z.

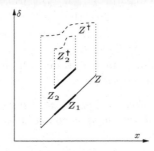

Fig. 3. Let x be a clock and let δ be the cost. In the figure, $Z \sqsubseteq Z_1 \sqsubseteq Z_2$, but only Z_1 is a subset of Z. The $()^\dagger$ operation removes the upper bound on δ, hence $Z_2^\dagger \subseteq Z^\dagger \Leftrightarrow Z \sqsubseteq Z_2$.

Lemma 4. *Let $Z^\dagger = \{u[\delta \mapsto u(\delta) + d] \mid u \in Z \wedge d \in \mathbb{R}_{\geq 0}\}$. Then $Z_1 \sqsubseteq Z_2 \Leftrightarrow Z_2^\dagger \subseteq Z_1^\dagger$.*

It is straightforward to implement the $()^\dagger$-operation on DBMs. However, a useful property of the $()^\dagger$-operation is, that its effect on zones can be obtained without implementing the operation. Let $(l_0, Z_0^\dagger)$, where Z_0 is the zone encoding C_0, be the initial symbolic state. Then $Z = Z^\dagger$ for any reachable state (l, Z) — intuitively because δ is never reset and no guards or invariants depend on δ.

Termination is ensured if all clocks except for δ are normalized with respect to a maximum constant M. It is important that normalization never touches δ. With this modification, the algorithm in Fig. 1 will essentially encounter the same states as the traditional forward state-space exploration algorithm for timed automata, except for the addition of δ.

3   Improving the State-Space Exploration

As mentioned, the major drawback of the algorithm in Fig. 1 is that it requires the entire state-space to be searched before the minimum cost of reaching a goal state can be declared. In this section we will discuss a number of possibilities for improving this in some cases.

3.1   Minimum Cost Order

In realizing the algorithm of Fig. 1, and in analogy with Dijkstra's algorithm for finding the shortest path in a directed weighted graph, we may choose always to select a (symbolic cost) state (l, C) from WAITINGfor which C has the smallest minimum cost. With this choice, we may terminate the algorithm as soon as a goal state is selected from WAITING We will refer the search order arising from this strategy as the Minimum Cost order (MC order).

Lemma 5. *Using the MC order, an optimal solution is found by the algorithm in Fig. 1 when a goal state is selected from WAITINGthe first time.*

When applying the MC order, the algorithm in Fig. 1 can be simplified since the variable COST is not needed any more. Again in analogy with Dijkstra's shortest path algorithm, the MC ordering finds the minimum cost of reaching a goal state with guarantee of its optimality, in a manner which requires exploration of a *minimum number* of symbolic cost states.

Lemma 6. *Using the algorithm in Fig. 1, it can never reduce the number of explored states to prefer exploration of a symbolic cost state of* WAITING *with non-minimal minimum cost.*

In situations when WAITING contains more than just one symbolic cost state with smallest minimum cost, the MC order does not offer any indication as to which one to explore first. In fact, for exploration of the symbolic state-space for timed automata without cost, we do not know of a definite strategy for choosing a state from WAITING such that the fewest number of symbolic states are generated. However, any improvements gained with respect to the search-order strategy for the state-space exploration of timed automata will be directly applicable in our setting with respect to the strategy for choosing between symbolic cost states with same minimum cost.

3.2   Using Estimates of the Remaining Cost

From a given state one often has an idea about the cost remaining in order to reach a goal state. In branch-and-bound algorithms this information is used both to delete states and to search the most promising states first. Using information about the remaining cost can also decrease the number of states searched before an optimal solution is reached.

For a state (l, u) let $rem((l, u))$ be the minimum cost of reaching a goal state from that state. In general we cannot expect to know exactly what the remaining cost of a state is. We can instead use an estimate of the remaining cost as long as the estimate does not exceed the actual cost. For a symbolic cost state (l, C) we require that $\text{REM}(l, C)$ satisfies $\text{REM}(l, C) \leq \inf\{rem((l, u)) \mid u \in sup(C)\}$, i.e. $\text{REM}(l, C)$ offers a lower bound on the remaining cost of all the states with location l and clock valuation within the support of C.

Combining the minimum cost $min(C)$ of a symbolic cost state (l, C) with the estimate of the remaining cost $\text{REM}(l, C)$, we can base the MC order on the sum of $min(C)$ and $\text{REM}(l, C)$. Since $min(C) + \text{REM}(l, C)$ is smaller than the actual cost of reaching a goal state, the first goal state to be explored is guaranteed to have optimal cost. We call this the MC+ order but it is also known as Least-Lower-Bound order. In Section 4 we will show that even simple estimates of the remaining cost can lead to large improvements in the number of states searched to find the minimum cost of reaching a goal state.

One way to obtain a lower bound is for the user to specify an initial estimate and annotate each transition with updates of the estimate. In this case it is the responsibility of the user to guarantee that the estimate is actually a lower bound in order to ensure that the optimal solution is not deleted. This also allows the user to apply her understanding and intuition about the system.

3.3   Heuristics and Bounding

It is often useful to quickly obtain an upper bound on the cost instead of waiting for the minimum cost. In particular, this is the case when faced with a state-space too big for the MC order to handle. As will be shown in Section 4, the techniques described here for altering the search order using heuristics are very useful. In addition, techniques from branch-and-bound algorithms are useful for improving the upper bound once it has been found. Applying knowledge about the goal state has proven useful in improving the state-space exploration [RE99,HLP00], either by changing the search order from the standard depth or breadth-first, or by leaving out parts of the state-space.

To implement the MC order, a suitable data-structure for WAITING would be a priority queue where the priority is the minimum cost of a symbolic cost state. We can obviously generalize this by extending a symbolic cost state with a new field, *priority*, which is the priority of the state used by the priority queue. Allowing various ways of assigning values to *priority* combined with choosing either to first select a state with large or small priority opens for a large variety of search orders.

Annotating the model with assignments to *priority* on the transitions, is one way of allowing the user to guide the search. Because of its flexibility it proves to be a very powerful way of guiding the search. The assignment works like a normal assignment to integer variables and allows for the same kind of expressions.

When searching for an error state in a system a *random* search order might be useful. We have chosen to implement what we call *random depth-first order* which as the name suggests is a variant of a depth-first search. The only difference between this and a standard depth-first search is that before pushing all the successors of a state on to WAITING (which is implemented as a stack), the successors are randomly permuted.

Once a reachable goal state has been found, an upper bound on the minimum cost of reaching a goal state has been obtained. If we choose to continue the search, a smaller upper bound might be obtained. During state-space exploration the cost never decreases therefore states with cost bigger than the best cost found in a goal state cannot lead to an optimal solution, and can therefore be deleted. The estimate of the remaining cost defined in Section 3.2 can also be used for pruning exploration of states since whenever $min(C) + \text{REM}(l, C)$ is larger than the best upper bound, no state covered by (l, C) can lead to a better solution than the one already found.

All of the methods described in this section have been implemented in UPPAAL. Section 4 reports on experiments using these new methods.

4   Experiments

In this section we illustrate the benefits of extending UPPAAL with heuristics and costs through several verification and optimization problems. All of the examples have previously been studied in the literature.

4.1   The Bridge Problem

The following problem was proposed by Ruys and Brinksma [RB98]. A timed automaton model of this problem is included in the standard distribution of UPPAAL[4].

Four persons want to cross a bridge in the dark. The bridge is damaged and can only carry two persons at the same time. To cross the bridge safely in the darkness, a torch must be carried along. The group has only one torch to share. Due to different physical abilities, the four cross the bridge at different speeds. The time they need per person is (one-way) 25, 20, 10 and 5 minutes, respectively. The problem is to find a schedule such that all four cross the bridge within a given time. This can be done with standard UPPAAL. With the proposed extension, one can also find the best possible time for the persons to cross the bridge, and a schedule for this.

We compare four different search orders: Breadth-First (BF), Depth-First (DF), Minimum Cost (MC) and the improved Minimum Cost (MC+) also using the estimate of the remaining cost, REM(C). In this example we choose the estimate of the remaining cost to be the time needed by the slowest person, who is still on the "wrong" side of the bridge.

Table 2 shows the number of states explored and the cost found for the first and the optimal solution. The third column shows the number of states explored and the cost when states are deleted based on the estimate of the remaining cost (this does not apply to MC and MC+ because the search stops when the first solution is found). As can be seen from the table, only about 10% of the states searched to find an initial solution using breadth first order is needed for the MC+ order to find the optimal solution.

Table 2. Bridge problem by Ruys and Brinksma.

	Initial Solution		Optimal Solution		With est. remainder	
	states	cost	states	cost	states	cost
BF	4491	65	4539	60	4493	60
DF	169	685	25780	60	5081	60
MC	1536	60	1536	60	N/A	N/A
MC+	404	60	404	60	N/A	N/A

4.2   Job Shop Scheduling

A well known class of scheduling problems are the Job Shop problems. The problem is to optimally schedule a set of *jobs* on a set of *machines*. Each job is a chain of operations, usually one on each machine, and the machines have a limited capacity, also limited to one in most cases. The purpose is to allocate starting times to the operations, such that the overall duration of the schedule, the *makespan*, is minimal.

---

[4] The distribution can be obtained at http://www.uppaal.com.

We apply UPPAAL to 25 of the smaller Lawrence Job Shop problems.[5] Our models are based on the timed automata models in [F eh99a]. In order to estimate the lower bound on the remaining cost, we calculate for each job and each machine the duration of the remaining operations. The final estimate of the remaining cost is then estimated to be the maxim um of these durations. Table 3 shows results obtained for the first 15 problems for the search orders DF, Random DF, and a com bined heuristic. The latter is based on depth-first but also takes into account the remaining operation times and the lo wer bound on the cost, via a weighted sum which is assigned to the priority field of the symbolic state. W e also tried using BF and MC order, but we did not obtain any results even if we allow MC order to searc h for more than 30 min utes using more than 2Gb of memory no solution is found. With the MC+ order w e could only find solutions to la05 and la14 exploring 9791 and 10653 states respectively. It is important to notice that the com bined heuristic used includes a clever choice between states with the same values of cost plus remaining cost. This is the reason it is able to outperform the MC+ order.

As can be seen from the table UPPAAL is handling the first 15 examples quite well. For the 10 largest problems (la16 to la25) with 10 mac hines we did not find optimal solutions though in some cases we were very close to the optimal solution. Since branch-and-bound algorithms generally do not scale too well when the number of machines and jobs increase, this is not surprising. The branch-and-bound algorithm for [A C91], who solves about 10 out the 15 problems in the same setting, faces the same problem. Note that the results of this algorithm depend sensitively on the choice of an initial upper bound. Also the algorithm used in [BJS95], who com bines a good heuristic with an efficient branch-and-bound algorithm and th us solves all of these 15 instances, does not find solutions for the larger instances with 15 jobs and 10 machines or larger.

Table 3. Results for the smaller 15 Job Shop problems with 5 mac hines and 10 jobs (la1-la5), 15 jobs (la6-la10) and 20 jobs (la11-la15). The table shows the best solution found by different search orders within 60 seconds cputime on a Pentium II 300 MHz. If the searc h terminated also the n umber of explored states is given. The last row gives the mak espan of an optimal solution.

problem instance		la01	la02	la03	la04	la05	la06	la07	la08	la09	la10	la11	la12	la13	la14	la15
DF	cost	2466	2360	2094	2212	1955	3656	3410	3520	3984	3681	4974	4557	4846	5145	5264
	states	-	-	-	-	-	-	-	-	-	-	-	-	-	-	-
RDF	cost	842	806	769	783	696	1076	1113	1009	1154	1063	1303	1271	1227	1377	1459
	states	-	-	-	-	-	-	-	-	-	-	-	-	-	-	-
comb.	cost	666	672	626	639	593	926	890	863	951	958	1222	1039	1150	1292	1289
heur	states	292	-	-	-	284	480	-	400	425	454	642	633	662	688	-
minimal makespan		666	655	597	590	593	926	890	863	951	958	1222	1039	1150	1292	1207

---

[5] These and other benchmark problems for Job Shop scheduling can be found on ftp://ftp.caam.rice.edu/pub/people/applegate/jobshop/.

4.3   The Sidmar Steel Plant

Proving schedulability of an industrial plant via a reachability analysis of a timed automaton model w as firstly applied to the SIDMAR steel plan t, which was included as case study of the Esprit-LTR Project 26270 VHS (Verification of Hybrid Systems). The plant consists of five machines placed along two tracks and a casting machine where the finished steel leaves the system. The two tracks and the casting machine are connected via two overhead cranes on one track. Each quantity of raw iron enters the system in a ladle and depending on the desired steel quality undergoes treatments in the different machines of different durations. The aim is to control the plant in particular the movement of the ladles with steel between the different machines, taking the topology of the plant into consideration.

W e use a model based on the models and descriptions in [BS99 ,Feh99b,HLP99]. A full model of the plant that includes all possible behaviors was however not imm ediate suitable for verification. Using BF or DF search it was impossible to generate a schedule for a model with only three ladles. Priorities can be used to influence the search order of the state space, and thus to improve the results. Based on a depth-first strategy, we reward transitions that are likely to serve in reaching the goal, whereas transitions that may spoil a partial solution result in lower priorities.

A schedule for three ladles was produced in [Feh99b] for a slightly simplified model using UPPAAL. In [HLP99] schedules for up to 60 ladles were produced also using UPPAAL. However, in order to do this, additional constraints were included that reduce the size of the state-space drastically, but also prune possibly sensible behavior. A similar reduced model w as used by Stobbe in [Sto00], who uses constraint programmi ng to schedule 30 ladles. All these works only consider ladles with the same quality of steel and the initial solutions cannot be improved.

Using a search order based on the priorities we can generate a schedule for ten ladles, compared to two without priorities, with varying qualities of steel within 60 seconds cputime on a Pentium II 300 MHz. The initial solution found is improved by 5% within the time limit. Importan tly, in this approach we do not rule out optimal solutions. Allowing the search to go on for longer, models with more ladles can be handled.

4.4   Pure Heuristics: The Biphase Mark Protocol

The Biphase Mark protocol is a con vention for transmitting strings of bits and clock pulses sim ultaneously as square waves. This protocol is widely used for comm unication in the ISO/OSI physical layer; for example, a version called "Manc hester encoding" is used in the Ethernet. The protocol ensures that strings of bits can be submitted and received correctly, in spite of clock drift, jitter and filtering by the channel. A formal parameterized timed automaton model of the Biphase Mark Protocol w as given in [Vaa00]. W e will use the corresponding UPPAAL models to in vestigate the benefits of heuristics in pure reachability analysis.

Table 4. Results for nine erroneous instances of the Biphase Mark protocol. The numbers are the number of state explored before reaching an error state.

	nondetection mark subcell			sampling early			sampling late		
	(16,3,11)	(18,3,10)	(32,3,23)	(16,9,11)	(18,6,10)	(32,18,23)	(15,8,11)	(17,5,10)	(31,16,23)
breadth first	1931	2582	4049	990	4701	2561	1230	1709	3035
in==1 heuristic	1153	1431	2333	632	1945	1586	725	1039	1763

The three parameters in the model are the size of the mark and code cell of the sending process and the size of the sampling distance at the receiver. Basically, for each bit send, two points needs to be read for the receiver to interpret the bit correctly. Three kinds of errors can occur: the 'middle point' (called mark subcell) is missed, the end point is sampled too early or too late. Two of the three errors occur only if input "1" is offered to the receiver, and the third error can occur in any case. Therefore we will guide the model to make a breadth first search but only in the part of the state-space where a "1" is send. Table 4 shows the number of states searched in order to find the error in three erroneous instances of the protocol. Using the heuristic almost halves the number of states searched before the error is found.

5   Conclusion

On the preceding pages, we have contributed with (1) a cost function based symbolic semantics for the class of linearly priced timed automata; (2) an efficient, zone based implementation of cost functions for the class of uniformly priced timed automata; (3) an optimal search order for finding the minimum cost of reaching a goal state; and (4) experimental evidence that these techniques can lead to dramatic reductions in the number of explored states. In addition, we have shown that it is possible to quickly obtain upper bounds on the minimum cost of reaching a goal state by manually guiding the exploration algorithm using priorities.

References

AC91.   D. Applegate and W. Cook. A Computational Study of the Job-Shop Scheduling Problem. *OSRA Journal on Computing 3*, pages 149–156, 1991.

BDM$^+$98.   M. Bozga, C. Daws, O. Maler, A. Olivero, S. Tripakis, and S. Yovine. Kronos: A Model-Checking Tool for Real-Time Systems. In *Proc. of the 10th Int. Conf. on Computer Aided Verification*, number 1427 in Lecture Notes in Computer Science, pages 546–550. Springer–Verlag, 1998.

BFH$^+$01.   G. Behrmann, A. Fehnker, T. Hune, K. G. Larsen, P. Pettersson, J. Romijn, and F. Vaandrager. Minimum-Cost Reachability for Priced Timed Automata. Accepted for Hybrid Systems: Computation and Control, 2001.

BJS95.   P. Brucker, B. Jurisch, and B. Sievers.   Code of a Branch &
            Bound Algorithm for the Job Shop Problem.   Available at url
            http://www.mathematik.uni-osnabrueck.de/research/OR/, 1995.
BS99.   R. Boel and G. Stremersch. Report for VHS: Timed Petri Net Model of
            Steel Plant at SIDMAR. Technical report, SYSTeMS Group, University
            Ghent, 1999.
Dil89.   D. Dill. Timing Assumptions and Verification of Finite-State Concurrent
            Systems. In J. Sifakis, editor, *Proc. of Automatic Verification Methods for
            Finite State Systems*, number 407 in Lecture Notes in Computer Science,
            pages 197–212. Springer–Verlag, 1989.
Feh99a.   A. Fehnker. Bounding and heuristics in forward reachability algorithms.
            Technical Report CSI-R0002, Computing Science Institute Nijmegen, 1999.
Feh99b.   A. Fehnker. Scheduling a steel plant with timed automata. In *Proceedings
            of the 6th International Conference on Real-Time Computing Systems and
            Applications (RTCSA99)*, pages 280–286. IEEE Computer Society, 1999.
HHWT97.   T. A. Henzinger, P.-H. Ho, and H. Wong-Toi. HyTech: A Model Checker
            for Hybird Systems. In Orna Grumberg, editor, *Proc. of the 9th Int. Conf.
            on Computer Aided Verification*, number 1254 in Lecture Notes in Com-
            puter Science, pages 460–463. Springer–Verlag, 1997.
HLP99.   T. Hune, K. G. Larsen, and P. Pettersson. Guided synthesis of control
            programs using UPPAAL for VHS case study 5. VHS deliverable, 1999.
HLP00.   T. Hune, K. G. Larsen, and P. Pettersson. Guided Synthesis of Control
            Programs Using UPPAAL. In Ten H. Lai, editor, *Proc. of the IEEE ICDCS
            International Workshop on Distributed Systems Verification and Valida-
            tion*, pages E15–E22. IEEE Computer Society Press, April 2000.
LPY95.   K. G. Larsen, P. Pettersson, and W. Yi. Diagnostic Model-Checking for
            Real-Time Systems. In *Proc. of Workshop on Verification and Control of
            Hybrid Systems III*, number 1066 in Lecture Notes in Computer Science,
            pages 575–586. Springer–Verlag, October 1995.
LPY97.   K. G. Larsen, P. Pettersson, and W. Yi. UPPAAL in a Nutshell. *Int. Journal
            on Software Tools for Technology Transfer*, 1(1–2):134–152, October 1997.
NTY00.   P. Niebert, S. Tripakis, and S. Yovine. Minimum-time reachability for timed
            automata. In *IEEE Mediteranean Control Conference*, 2000. Accepted for
            publication.
NY99.   P. Niebert and S. Yovine. Computing optimal operation schemes for multi
            batch operation of chemical plants. VHS deliverable, May 1999. Draft.
RB98.   T. C. Ruys and E. Brinksma. Experience with Literate Programming in
            the Modelling and Validation of Systems. In Bernhard Steffen, editor, *Pro-
            ceedings of the Fourth International Conference on Tools and Algorithms
            for the Construction and Analysis of Systems (TACAS'98)*, number 1384
            in Lecture Notes in Computer Science (LNCS), pages 393–408, Lisbon,
            Portugal, April 1998. Springer-Verlag, Berlin.
RE99.   F. Reffel and S. Edelkamp. Error Detection with Directed Symbolic Model
            Checking. In *Proc. of Formal Methods*, volume 1708 of *Lecture Notes in
            Computer Science*, pages 195–211. Springer–Verlag, 1999.
Rok93.   T. G. Rokicki. *Representing and Modeling Digital Circuits*. PhD thesis,
            Stanford University, 1993.
Sto00.   M. Stobbe. Results on scheduling the sidmar steel plant using constraint
            programming. Internal report, 2000.
Vaa00.   F. Vaandrager. Analysis of a biphase mark protocol with Uppaal. to appear,
            2000.

Linear P arametric Model Cheking
of Timed Automata*

Thomas Hune[1], Judi Romijn[2], Mariëlle Stoelinga[2], and Frits Vaandrager[2]

[1] BRICS, University of Århus, Denmark
baris@brics.dk
[2] Computing Science Institute, University of Nijmegen
[judi,marielle,fvaan]@cs.kun.nl

Abstract. We present an extension of the model checker UPPAAL capable of synthesize linear parameter constraints for the correctness of parametric timed automata. The symbolic representation of the (parametric) state-space is shown to be correct. A second contribution of this paper is the identification of a subclass of parametric timed automata (L/U automata), for which the emptiness problem is decidable, contrary to the full class where it is know to be undecidable. Also we present a number of lemmas enabling the verification effort to be reduced for L/U automata in some cases. We illustrate our approach by deriving linear parameter constraints for a number of well-known case studies from the literature (exhibiting a flaw in a published paper).

1 Introduction

During the last decade, there has been enormous progress in the area of timed model checking. Tools such as UPPAAL[11], KRONOS [5], and PMC [12] are now routinely used for industrial case studies. A disadvantage of the traditional approaches is, however, that they can only be used to verify concrete timing properties: one has to provide the values of all timing parameters that occur in the system. For practical purposes, one is often interested in deriving the (symbolic) constraints on the parameters that ensure correctness. The process of man ually finding and proving such results is very time consuming and error prone (we have discovered minor errors in the two examples we have been looking at). Therefore tool support for deriving the constraints *automatically* is very important.

In this paper, we study a parameterized extension of timed automata, as w ell as a corresponding extension of the forward reachability algorithm. W e show the theoretical correctness of our approach, and its feasibility by application to some non-trivial case studies. For this purpose, we have implemen ted a prototype extension of UPPAAL, an efficient real-time model c hecking tool [11]. The algorithm we propose and have implem ented is a semi-decision algorithm whic h will not terminate in all cases. In [2] the problem of syn thesizing values for parameters

---

* Research supported by Esprit Project 26270, Verification of Hybrid Systems (VHS), and PROGRESS Project TES4199, Verification of Hard and Softly Timed Systems (HaaST). This work was initiated during a visit of the first author to Nijmegen.

T. Margaria and W. Yi (Eds.): TACAS 2001, LNCS 2031, pp. 189–203, 2001.

such that a property is satisfied, was shown to be undecidable, so this is the best we can hope for.

A second contribution of this paper is the identification of a subclass of parameterized timed automata, called *lower bound/upper bound (L/U) automata*, which appears to be sufficiently expressive from a practical perspective, while it also has nice theoretical properties. Most importantly we show that the emptyness question for parametric timed automata shown to be undecidable in [2], is decidable for L/U automata. We also establish a number of lemmas which allow one to reduce the number of parameters when tackling specific verification questions for L/U automata. The application of these lemmas has already reduced the verification effort drastically in some of our experiments.

Our attempt at automatic verification of parameterized real-time models is not the only one. Henzinger et al. aim at solving a more general problem with HYTECH [9], a tool for model checking hybrid automata, exploring the state-space either by partition refinement, or forward reachability. The tool has been applied successfully on relatively small examples such as a railway gate controller. Experience so far has shown that HYTECH cannot cope with larger examples, such as the ones considered in this paper.

Toetenel et al. [12] have made an extension of the PMC real-time model checking tool [4] called LPMC. LPMC is restricted to linear parameter constraints as is our approach, and uses the partition refinement method, like HYTECH. Other differences with our approach are that LPMC also allows for the comparison of non-clock variables to parameter constraints, and for more general specification properties (full TCTL with fairness assumptions). Since LPMC is a quite recent tool, not many applications have been presented yet. However, a model of the IEEE 1394 root contention protocol inspired by [13] has been successfully analyzed in [4].

A more general attempt than LPMC and our UPPAAL extension has been made by Annichini et al. [3]. They have constructed and implemented a method which allows for non-linear parameter constraints, and uses heavier, third-party, machinery to solve the arising non-linear constraint comparisons. Independently, we have used the same data-structure (a direct extension of DBMs [8]) for the symbolic representation of the state space, as in [3]. For speeding up the exploration, a method for guessing the effect of control loops in the model is presented. It appears that this helps termination of the method, but it is unclear under what circumstances this technique can or cannot be used. The feasibility of this approach has been shown on a few rather small case studies.

The remainder of this paper is organized as follows. Section 2 introduces the notion of parametric timed automata. Section 3 gives the symbolic semantics, which is the basis for our model checking algorithm, presented in Section 3.5. Section 4 is an intermezzo that states some helpful lemmas and decidability results on an interesting subclass. Finally, Section 5 reports on experiments with our tool. For lack of space, some technical details and all proofs have been omitted, which can be found in the full version of this paper [10].

2   Parametric Timed Automata

2.1   Parameters and Constraints

Throughout this paper, we assume a fixed set of *parameters* $P = \{p_1, \ldots, p_n\}$. A *linear expression* e is either an expression of the form $t_1 p_1 + \cdots + t_n p_n + t_0$, where $t_0, \ldots, t_n \in \mathsf{Z}$, or ∞. We write E to denote the set of all linear expressions. A *constraint* is an inequality of the form $e \sim e'$, with e, e' linear expressions and $\sim \in \{<, \leq, >, \geq\}$. The *negation* of constraint c, notation $\neg c$, is obtained by replacing relation signs $<, \leq, >, \geq$ by $\geq, >, \leq, <$, respectively. A *(parameter) valuation* is a function $v : P \to \mathsf{R}^{\geq 0}$ assigning a nonnegative real value to each parameter. There is a one-to-one correspondence between valuations and points in $(\mathsf{R}^{\geq 0})^n$. In fact we often identify a valuation v with the point $(v(p_1), \ldots, v(p_n)) \in (\mathsf{R}^{\geq 0})^n$.

If e is a linear expression and v is a valuation, then $e[v]$ denotes the expression obtained by replacing each parameter p in e with $v(p)$. Likewise, we define $c[v]$ for c a constraint. Valuation v *satisfies* constraint c, notation $v \models c$, if $c[v]$ evaluates to true. The *semantics* of a constraint c, notation $[\![c]\!]$, is the set of valuations (points in $(\mathsf{R}^{\geq 0})^n$) that satisfy c. A finite set of constraints C is called a *constraint set*. A valuation *satisfies* a constraint set if it satisfies each constraint in the set. The *semantics* of a constraint set C is given by $[\![C]\!] := \bigcap_{c \in C} [\![c]\!]$. We write $\top$ to denote any constraint set with $[\![\top]\!] = (\mathsf{R}^{\geq 0})^n$, for instance the empty set. We use $\bot$ to denote any constraint set with $[\![\bot]\!] = \emptyset$, for instance the constraint set $\{c, \neg c\}$, for some arbitrary c.

Constraint c *covers* constraint set C, notation $C \models c$, iff $[\![C]\!] \subseteq [\![c]\!]$. Constraint set C *is split by* constraint c iff neither $C \models c$ nor $C \models \neg c$.

During the analysis questions arise of the kind: given a constraint set C and a constraint c, does c hold, i.e., does constraint c cover C? A split occurs when c holds for some valuations in the semantics of C and $\neg c$ holds for some other valuations. We will not discuss methods for answering such questions: in our implementation we use an oracle to compute the following function.

$$\mathcal{O}(c, C) = \begin{cases} \text{yes} & \text{if } C \models c \\ \text{no} & \text{if } C \models \neg c \\ \text{split} & \text{otherwise} \end{cases}$$

Observe that using the oracle, we can easily decide semantic inclusion between constraint sets: $[\![C]\!] \subseteq [\![C']\!]$ iff $\forall c' \in C' : \mathcal{O}(c', C) = \text{yes}$. The oracle that we use is a linear programming (LP) solver that was kindly provided to us by the authors of [4], who built it for their LPMC model checking tool.

2.2   Parametric Timed Automata

Throughout this paper, we assume a fixed set of clocks $X = \{x_0, \ldots, x_m\}$ and a fixed set of actions $A = \{a_1, \ldots, a_k\}$. The special clock x_0, which is called the *zero clock*, always has the value 0.

A *simple guard* is an expression f of the form $x_i - x_j \prec e$, where x_i, x_j are clocks, $\prec \in \{<, \leq\}$, and e is a linear expression. We say that f is *proper* if $i \neq j$. We define a *guard* to be a (finite) conjunction of simple guards. We let g range over guards and write G to denote the set of guards. A *clock valuation* is a function $w : X \rightarrow R^{\geq 0}$ assigning a nonnegative real value to each clock, such that $w(x_0) = 0$. We will identify a clock valuation w with the point $(w(x_0), \ldots, w(x_m)) \in (R^{\geq 0})^{m+1}$. Let g be a guard, v a parameter valuation, and w a clock valuation. Then $g[v, w]$ denotes the expression obtained by replacing each parameter p with $v(p)$, and each clock x with $w(x)$. A pair (v, w) of a parameter valuation and a clock valuation *satisfies* a guard g, notation $(v, w) \models g$, if $g[v, w]$ evaluates to true. The *semantics* of a guard g, notation $[\![g]\!]$, is the set of pairs (v, w) such that $(v, w) \models g$.

A *reset* is an expression of the form, $x_i := b$ where $i \neq 0$ and $b \in N$. A *reset set* is a set of resets containing at most one reset for each clock. The set of reset sets is denoted by R.

We now define an extension of timed automata [1,15] called parametric timed automata. Similar models ha ve been presented in [2,3,4].

Definition 1 (PTA). *A parametric timed automaton (PT A) over set of clocks X, set of actions A, and set of parameters P, is a quadruple $\mathcal{A} = (Q, q_0, \rightarrow, I)$, where Q is a finite set of locations, $q_0 \in Q$ is the initial location, $\rightarrow \subseteq Q \times A \times G \times R \times Q$ is a finite transition relation, and function $I : Q \rightarrow G$ assigns an invariant to each location. We abbr eviate a $(q, a, g, r, q') \in \rightarrow$ consisting of a source location, an action, a guard, a reset set, and a target location as $q \xrightarrow{a,g,r} q'$. For a simple guard $x_i - x_j \prec e$ to be used in an invariant it must be the case that $x_j = x_0$, that is, the simple guard represents an upper bound on a clock.*

Example 1. A parametric timed automaton with cloc ks x, y and parameters p, q can be seen in Fig. 1. The initial state is $S0$ which has invariant $x \leq p$, and the transition from the initial location to $S1$ has guard $y \geq q$ and reset set $x := 0$. There are no actions on the transitions. Initially the transition from $S0$ to $S1$ is only enabled if $p \leq q$, otherwise the system will be deadlocked.

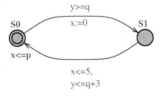

Fig. 1. A parametric timed automaton

To define the seman tics of PTAs, we require two auxiliary operations on clock valuations. For clock valuation w and nonnegative real number d, $w + d$ is the clock valuation that adds to each clock (except x_0) a delay d. For clock valuation

w and reset set r, $w[r]$ is the clock valuation that resets clocks according to r.

$$(w + d)(x) = \begin{cases} 0 & \text{if } x = x_0 \\ w(x) + d & \text{otherwise} \end{cases} \qquad (w[r])(x) = \begin{cases} b & \text{if } x := b \in r \\ w(x) & \text{otherwise.} \end{cases}$$

Definition 2 (Concrete semantics). *Let* $\mathcal{A} = (Q, q_0, \rightarrow, I)$ *be a PTA and* v *be a parameter valuation. The* concrete semantics *of* $\mathcal{A}$ *under* v, *notation* $[\![\mathcal{A}]\!]_v$, *is the labeled transition system (LTS)* $(S, S_0, \rightarrow)$ *over* $A \cup \mathsf{R}^{\geq 0}$ *where*

$$S = \{(q, w) \in Q \times (X \rightarrow \mathsf{R}^{\geq 0}) \mid w(x_0) = 0 \wedge (v, w) \models I(q)\},$$
$$S_0 = \{(q, w) \in S \mid q = q_0 \wedge w = \lambda x.0\},$$

and transition predicate $\rightarrow$ *is specified by the following two rules, for all* (q, w), $(q', w') \in S$, $d \geq 0$ *and* $a \in A$,

- $(q, w) \xrightarrow{d} (q', w')$ *if* $q = q'$ *and* $w' = w + d$.
- $(q, w) \xrightarrow{a} (q', w')$ *if* $\exists g, r : q \xrightarrow{a,g,r} q' \wedge (v, w) \models g \wedge w' = w[r]$.

2.3 The Problem

In its current version, UPPAAL is able to check for reachability properties, in particular whether certain combinations of locations and constrains on clock variables are reachable from the initial configuration. Our parameterized extension of UPPAAL handles exactly the same properties. However, rather than just telling whether a property holds or not, our tool looks for constraints on the parameters which ensure that the property holds.

Definition 3 (Properties). *The sets of* system properties *and* state formulas *are defined by, respectively,*

$$\psi ::= \forall \Box \phi \mid \exists \Diamond \phi \qquad\qquad \phi ::= x - y \prec b \mid q \mid \neg \phi \mid \phi \wedge \phi$$

where $x, y \in X$, $b \in \mathsf{N}$ *and* $q \in Q$. *Let* $\mathcal{A}$ *be a PTA,* v *a parameter valuation,* s *a state of* $[\![\mathcal{A}]\!]_v$, *and* ϕ *a state formula. We write* $s \models \phi$ *if* ϕ *holds in state* s, *we write* $[\![\mathcal{A}]\!]_v \models \forall \Box \phi$ *if* ϕ *holds in all reachable states of* $[\![\mathcal{A}]\!]_v$, *and we write* $[\![\mathcal{A}]\!]_v \models \exists \Diamond \phi$ *if* ϕ *holds for some reachable state of* $[\![\mathcal{A}]\!]_v$.

The problem that we address in this paper can now be stated as follows: *Given a parametric timed automaton* $\mathcal{A}$ *and a system property* ψ, *compute the set of parameter valuations* v *for which* $[\![\mathcal{A}]\!]_v \models \psi$.

Timed automata [1,15] arise as a special case of PTAs for which the set P of parameters is empty. If $\mathcal{A}$ is a PTA and v is a parameter valuation, then the structure $\mathcal{A}[v]$ that is obtained by replacing all linear expressions e that occur in $\mathcal{A}$ by $e[v]$ is a timed automaton.[1] It is easy to see that in general $[\![\mathcal{A}]\!]_v = [\![\mathcal{A}[v]]\!]$. Since the reachability problem for timed automata is decidable [1], this implies that, for any $\mathcal{A}$, integer valued v and ψ, $[\![\mathcal{A}]\!]_v \models \psi$ is decidable.

---

[1] Strictly speaking, $\mathcal{A}[v]$ is only a timed automaton if v assigns an integer to each parameter.

3 Symbolic State Exploration

Our aim is to use basically the same algorithm for parametric time model c hecking as for timed model c hecking. W e represent sets of states symbolically in a similar way and support the same operations used for timed model c hecking. In the nonparametrized case, sets of states can be efficien tly represented using matrices [8]. Similarly, in this paper we represent sets of states symbolically as *(constrained) parametric difference-bound matrices.*

3.1 Parametric Difference-Boun d Matrices

In the nonparametrized case, a difference-bound matrix is a $(m + 1) \times (m + 1)$ matrix whose en tries are elements from $(\mathbb{Z} \cup \{\infty\}) \times \{0, 1\}$. An entry $(c, 1)$ for D_{ij} denotes a nonstrict bound $x_i - x_j \leq c$, whereas an entry $(c, 0)$ denotes a strict bound $x_i - x_j < c$. Here, instead of using integers in the entries, we will use linear expressions over the parameters. Also, we find it convenient to view the matrix slightly more abstractly as a set of guards.

Definition 4 (PDBM). *A parametric difference-bound matrix (PDBM) is a set D which contains, for all $0 \leq i, j \leq m$, a simple guard D_{ij} of the form $x_i - x_j \prec_{ij} e_{ij}$. We r equire that, for all i, D_{ii} is of the form $x_i - x_i \leq 0$. Given a parameter valuation v, the semantics of D is defined by $[\![D]\!]_v = [\![\bigwedge_{i,j} D_{ij}]\!]_v$. We say that D is satisfiable for v if $[\![D]\!]_v$ is nonempty. If f is a proper guard of the form $x_i - x_j \prec e$ then we write $D[f]$ for the PDBM obtained from D by replacing D_{ij} by f. If i, j are indices then we write D^{ij} for the pair $(e_{ij}, \prec_{ij})$; we call D^{ij} a bound of D. Clearly, a PDBM is fully determine d by its bounds.*

Definition 5 (Constrained PDBM). *A constrained PDBM is a pair (C, D) where C is a constraint set and D is a PDBM. The seman tics of a constrained PDBM is defined by $[\![C, D]\!] = \{(v, w) \mid v \in [\![C]\!] \wedge w \in [\![D]\!]_v\}$.*

PDBMs with the tigh test possible bounds are called *canonical*. To formalize this notion, we view Boolean connectives as operations on relation symbols $\leq$ and $<$ by identifying $\leq$ with 1 and $<$ with 0. Thus we have, for instance, $(\leq \wedge \leq) = \leq$, $(\leq \wedge <) = <$ and $(\leq \implies <) = <$. Our definition of a canonical form of a constrained PDBM is essen tially equivalent to the one for standard DBMs.

Definition 6 (Canonical Form). *A constrained PDBM (C, D) is* in canonical form *iff for all i, j, k, $C \models e_{ij} (\prec_{ij} \implies \prec_{ik} \wedge \prec_{kj}) e_{ik} + e_{kj}$.*

The next important lemma, whic h basically carries over from the unparametrized case, states that canonicity of a constrained PDBM guaran tees satisfiability.

Lemma 1. *Suppose (C, D) is a constrained PDBM in c anonical form and $v \in [\![C]\!]$. Then D is satisfiable for v.*

Also the following lemma essen tially carries over from the unparametrized case, see for instance [8]. As a direct consequence, semantic inclusion of con strained PDBMs is decidable for canonical PDBMs (using the oracle function).

Lemma 2. *Suppose $(C, D), (C', D')$ are constrained PDBMs and (C, D) is canonical. Then $[\![C, D]\!] \subseteq [\![C', D']\!] \Leftrightarrow ([\![C]\!] \subseteq [\![C']\!] \wedge \forall i, j : C \models e_{ij}(\prec_{ij} \implies \prec'_{ij})e'_{ij})$.*

3.2   Operations on PDBMs

Our algorithm requires basically four operations to be implemented on constrained PDBMs: adding guards, canonicalization, resetting clocks and computing time successors.

Adding Guards In the case of DBMs, adding a guard is a simple operation. It is implemented by taking the conjunction of a DBM and the guard (which is also viewed as a DBM). The conjunction operation just takes the pointwise minimum of the entries in both matrices. In the parametric case, adding a guard to a constrained PDBM may result in a set of constrained PDBMs. We define a relation $\leadsto$ which relates a constrained PDBM and a guard to a collection of constrained PDBMs that satisfy this guard. For this we need an operation $\mathcal{C}$ that takes a PDBM and a simple guard, and produces a constraint stating that the bound imposed by the guard is larger than the corresponding bound in the PDBM, so let $D^{ij} = (e_{ij}, \prec_{ij})$ then $\mathcal{C}(D, x_i - x_j \prec e) = e_{ij} (\prec_{ij} \implies \prec) e$. Relation $\leadsto$ is defined as the smallest relation that satisfies the following rules:

$$(R1) \quad \frac{\mathcal{O}(\mathcal{C}(D, f), C) = \text{yes}}{(C, D) \overset{f}{\leadsto} (C, D)} \qquad (R2) \quad \frac{\mathcal{O}(\mathcal{C}(D, f), C) = \text{no, } f \text{ proper}}{(C, D) \overset{f}{\leadsto} (C, D[f])}$$

$$(R3) \quad \frac{\mathcal{O}(\mathcal{C}(D, f), C) = \text{split}}{(C, D) \overset{f}{\leadsto} (C \cup \{\mathcal{C}(D, f)\}, D)} \qquad (R4) \quad \frac{\mathcal{O}(\mathcal{C}(D, f), C) = \text{split, } f \text{ proper}}{(C, D) \overset{f}{\leadsto} (C \cup \{\neg\mathcal{C}(D, f)\}, D[f])}$$

$$(R5) \quad \frac{(C, D) \overset{g}{\leadsto} (C', D') , \ (C'D') \overset{g'}{\leadsto} (C'', D'')}{(C, D) \overset{g \wedge g'}{\leadsto} (C'', D'')}$$

Lemma 3. $[\![C, D]\!] \cap [\![g]\!] = \bigcup \{ [\![C', D']\!] \mid (C, D) \overset{g}{\leadsto} (C', D') \}$.

Canonicalization Each DBM can be brought into canonical form using classical algorithms for computing all-pairs shortest paths, for instance the Floyd-Warshall (FW) algorithm [6]. In the parametric case, we also apply this approach except that now we run FW *symbolically*. Below, we describe the computation steps of the symbolic FW algorithm in SOS style. Recall that the FW algorithm consists of three nested for-loops, for indices k, i and j, respectively. Correspondingly, in the SOS description of the symbolic version, we use configurations of the form (k, i, j, C, D), where (C, D) is a constrained PDBM and $k, i, j \in [0, m+1]$ record the values of indices. In the rules below, k, i, j range over $[0, m]$.

$$\frac{(C, D) \overset{x_i - x_j \ \prec_{ik} \wedge \prec_{kj} \ e_{ik} + e_{kj}}{\leadsto} (C', D')}{(k, i, j, C, D) \rightarrow_{FW} (k, i, j+1, C', D')}$$

$$(k, i, m+1, C, D) \rightarrow_{FW} (k, i+1, 0, C, D)$$

$$(k, m+1, 0, C, D) \rightarrow_{FW} (k+1, 0, 0, C, D)$$

We write $(C, D) \to_c (C', D')$ if there exists a sequence of $\to_{FW}$ steps leading from configuration $(0, 0, 0, C, D)$ to configuration $(m+1, 0, 0, C', D')$. In this case, we say that (C', D') is an *outcome* of the symbolic Floyd-Warshall algorithm on (C, D). If the semantics of (C, D) is empty, then the set of outcomes is also empty. We write $(C, D) \stackrel{g}{\leadsto}_c (C', D')$ iff $(C, D) \stackrel{g}{\leadsto} (C'', D'') \to_c (C', D')$, for some C'', D''.

The following lemma says that if we run the symbolic Floyd-Warshall algorithm, the union of the semantics of the outcomes equals the semantics of the original constrained PDBM.

Lemma 4. $[\![C, D]\!] = \bigcup \{ [\![C', D']\!] \mid (C, D) \to_c (C', D') \}$.

Resetting Clocks A third operation on PDBMs that we need is resetting clocks. Since we do not allow parameters in reset sets, the reset operation on PDBMs is essentially the same as for DBMs, see [15]. The following lemma characterizes the reset operation semantically.

Lemma 5. *Let* (C, D) *be a constrained PDBM in canonical form,* $v \in [\![C]\!]$, *and* w *a clock valuation. Then* $w \in [\![D[r]]\!]_v$ *iff* $\exists w' \in [\![D]\!]_v : w = w'[r]$.

Time Successors Finally, we need to transform PDBMs for the passage of time, notation $D\uparrow$. As in the DBMs case [8], this is done by setting the $x_i - x_0$ bounds to $(\infty, <)$, for each $i \neq 0$, and leaving all other bounds unchanged. We have the following lemma.

Lemma 6. *Suppose* (C, D) *is a constrained PDBM in canonical form,* $v \in [\![C]\!]$, *and* w *a clock valuation. Then* $w \in [\![D\uparrow]\!]_v$ *iff* $\exists d \geq 0$ $\exists w' \in [\![D]\!]_v : w' + d = w$.

3.3   Symbolic Semantics

With the four operations on PDBMs, we can describe the semantics of a parametric timed automaton symbolically.

Definition 7 (Symbolic semantics). *The symbolic semantics of PTA* $\mathcal{A} = (Q, q_0, \to, I)$ *is an LTS. The states are triples* (q, C, D) *with* q *a location from* Q *and* (C, D) *a constrained PDBM in canonical form. Let* E *be the PDBM with* $\mathsf{E}^{ij} = (0, \leq)$, *for all* i, j. *The set of initial states is* $\{(q_0, C, D) \mid (\top, \mathsf{E}\uparrow) \stackrel{I(q_0)}{\leadsto}_c (C, D)\}$. *The transitions are defined by the following rule:*

$$\frac{q \stackrel{a,g,r}{\longrightarrow} q' \ , \ (C, D) \stackrel{g}{\leadsto}_c (C'', D'') \ , \ (C'', D''[r]\uparrow) \stackrel{I(q')}{\leadsto}_c (C', D')}{(q, C, D) \to (q', C', D')}.$$

Using Lemma 3 and Lemma 4, it follows by a simple inductive argument that if state (q, C, D) is reachable in the symbolic semantics and $(v, w) \in [\![C, D]\!]$ then $(v, w) \models I(q)$. It is also easy to see that the symbolic semantics of a PTA is a finitely branching transition system. It may have infinitely many reachable states though. Our search algorithm explores the symbolic semantics in an "intelligent" manner, and for instance stops whenever it reaches a state whose semantics is contained in the semantics of a state that has been encountered before. Despite this, our algorithm need not terminate.

Each run in the symbolic semantics can be simulated by a run in the concrete semantics.

Proposition 1. *For each parameter valuation v and clock valuation w, if there is a run in the symbolic semantics of $\mathcal{A}$ reaching state (q, C, D), with $(v, w) \in [\![C, D]\!]$, then this run can be simulated by a run in the concrete semantics $[\![\mathcal{A}]\!]_v$ reaching state (q, w).*

For each path in the concrete semantics, we can find a path in the symbolic semantics such that the final state of the first path is semantically contained in the final state of the second path.

Proposition 2. *For each parameter valuation v and clock valuation w, if there is a run in the concrete semantics $[\![\mathcal{A}]\!]_v$ reaching a state (q, w), then this run can be simulated by a run in the symbolic semantics reaching a state (q, C, D) such that $(v, w) \in [\![C, D]\!]$.*

3.4   Evaluating Properties

We will now explain the relation $\overset{\phi}{\Longmapsto}$ which relates a symbolic state and a state formula ϕ to a collection of symbolic states that satisfy ϕ. For lack of space, we do not give the full formal definition.

In order to check whether a property holds, we break it down into the small basic formulas, namely checking locations and clock guards. Checking that a clock guard holds relies on the definition given earlier, of adding that clock guard to the constrained PDBM. We rely on a special normal form of the state formula, in which all $\neg$ signs have been pushed down to the basic formulas.

The following lemma gives the soundness of relation $\overset{\phi}{\Longmapsto}$.

Lemma 7. *Let $[\![\phi, q]\!]$ denote the set $\{(v, w) \mid (w, q) \models \phi\}$. Then for all properties ϕ in normal form $[\![C, D]\!] \cap [\![\phi, q]\!] = \bigcup \{[\![C', D']\!] \mid (q, C, D) \overset{\phi}{\Longmapsto} (q, C', D')\}$.*

3.5   Algorithm

We are now in a position to present our model checking algorithm for parametric timed automata. The following algorithm describes how our tool explores the symbolic state space and searches for constraints on the parameters for which a reachability formula $\exists \Diamond \phi$ holds in a PTA $\mathcal{A}$.

algorithm Reachable($\mathcal{A}$, ϕ)

$\quad$ RESULT $:= \emptyset$,PASSED $:= \emptyset$,WAITING $:= \{(q_0, C, D) \mid (\top, \mathsf{E}\uparrow) \stackrel{I(q_0)}{\rightsquigarrow}_c (C, D)\}$
$\quad$ **while** WAITING $\neq \emptyset$ **do**
$\quad\quad$ select (q, C, D) from WAITING

$\quad\quad$ RESULT $:=$ RESULT $\cup \{(q', C', D') \mid (q, C, D) \stackrel{\phi}{\mapsto} (q', C', D')\}$

$\quad\quad$ FALSE $:= \{(q', C', D') \mid (q, C, D) \stackrel{\neg\phi}{\mapsto} (q', C', D')\}$
$\quad\quad$ **for each** (q', C', D') in FALSE **do**
$\quad\quad\quad$ **if** for all (q'', C'', D'') in PASSED: $(q', C', D') \not\subseteq (q'', C'', D'')$ **then**
$\quad\quad\quad\quad$ add (q', C', D') to PASSED
$\quad\quad\quad\quad$ **for each** (q'', C'', D'') such that $(q', C', D') \to (q'', C'', D'')$ **do**
$\quad\quad\quad\quad\quad$ WAITING $:=$ WAITING $\cup \{(q'', C'', D'')\}$
$\quad$ **return** RESULT

The result returned by the algorithm is a set of symbolic states, all of which satisfy ϕ, for any valuation of the parameters and clocks in the state. For invariance properties $\forall\Box\phi$, the tool performs the algorithm on $\neg\phi$, and the result is then a set of symbolic states, none of which satisfies ϕ. The answer to the model checking problem, stated in Section 2.2, is obtained by taking the union of the constraint sets from all symbolic states in the result of the algorithm; in the case of an invariance property we take the complement of this set.

Some standard operations on symbolic states that help in exploring as little as possible, have also been implemented in our tool for parametric symbolic states. We give a short explanation here, and refer to the full version of this paper for the complete story with technical details. Before starting the state space exploration, our implementation determines the *maximal constant* for each clock. This is the maximal value to which the clock is compared in any guard or invariant in the PTA. When the clock value grows beyond this value, we can ignore its real value. This enables us to identify many more symbolic states, and helps termination.

4   Reducing the Complexity

This section introduces the class of lower bound/upper bound automata and describes several (rather intuitive) observations that simplify the model checking of PTAs in this class. Our results allow us to eliminate parameters in certain cases. Since the complexity of parametric model checking grows very fast in the number of parameters, this is a relevant issue. Secondly, our observations yield a decidability result for lower bound/upper bound automata whereas the corresponding problem for general PTAs is undecidable.

Informally, a positive occurrence of a parameter in a PTA enforces (or contributes to) an upper bound on a clock difference, for instance p in $x - y < 2p$. A negative occurrence of a parameter contributes to a lower bound on a clock difference, for instance q and q' in $y - x > q + 2q'$ ($\equiv x - y < -q - 2q'$) and in $x - y < 2p - q - 2q'$.

Definition 8. *A parameter* $p_i \in P$ *is said to* occur *in the linear expression* $e = t_0 + t_1 \cdot p_1 + \cdots t_n \cdot p_n$ *if* $t_i \neq 0$; p_i *occurs positively* in e *if* $t_i > 0$ *and*

p_i occurs negatively *in e if $t_i < 0$. A lower bound parameter of a PTA $\mathcal{A}$ is a parameter that only occurs negatively in the expressions of $\mathcal{A}$ and an upper bound parameter of $\mathcal{A}$ a parameter that only occurs positively in $\mathcal{A}$. We call $\mathcal{A}$ a lower bound/upper bound (L/U) automaton if every parameter is either a lower bound parameter or an upper bound parameter of $\mathcal{A}$, but not both.*

From now on, we work with a fixed set $L = \{l_1, \ldots l_K\}$ of lower bound parameters and a fixed set $U = \{u_1, \ldots u_M\}$ of upper bound parameters with $L \cap U = \emptyset$ and $L \cup U = P$.

We consider, apart from parameter valuations, also *extended parameter valuations*. Intuitively, an extended parameter valuation is a parameter valuation with values in $\mathsf{R}^{\geq 0} \cup \{\infty\}$, rather than in $\mathsf{R}^{\geq 0}$. We denote an extended valuation of an L/U automaton by a pair (λ, μ), which equals the function λ on the set L and μ on U and require that λ and μ do not both assign the value ∞ to a parameter. Then we can extend the notions defined for parameter valuations (Section 2) to extended valuations in the obvious way. We write 0 and ∞ for the functions assigning respectively 0 and ∞ to each parameter.

The following proposition is based on the fact that weakening the guards in $\mathcal{A}$ (i.e. decreasing the lower bounds and increasing the upper bounds) yields an automaton whose reachable states include those of $\mathcal{A}$. Dually, strengthening the guards in $\mathcal{A}$ (i.e. increasing the lower bounds and decreasing the upper bounds) yields an automaton whose reachable states are a subset of those of $\mathcal{A}$. We claim that this proposition, formulated for L/U automata, can be generalized to lower bound and upper bound parameters present in general PTAs. It is however crucial that (by definition) state formulae do not contain parameters.

Proposition 3. *Let $\mathcal{A}$ be an L/U automaton and ϕ a state formula. Then*

1. $[\![\mathcal{A}]\!]_{(\lambda,\mu)} \models \exists\Diamond\phi \iff \forall\lambda' \leq \lambda, \mu \leq \mu' : [\![\mathcal{A}]\!]_{(\lambda',\mu')} \models \exists\Diamond\phi.$
2. $[\![\mathcal{A}]\!]_{(\lambda,\mu)} \models \forall\Box\phi \iff \forall\lambda \leq \lambda', \mu' \leq \mu : [\![\mathcal{A}]\!]_{(\lambda',\mu')} \models \forall\Box\phi.$

The following example illustrates how Proposition 3 can be used to eliminate parameters from L/U automata.

Example 2. The automaton in Fig. 2 is an L/U automaton. Its location S_1 is reachable irrespective of the parameter values. By setting the parameter *min* to ∞ and *max* to 0, one checks with a non-parametric model checker that $\mathcal{A}[(\infty, 0)] \models \exists\Diamond S_1$. Then Proposition 3 (together with $[\![\mathcal{A}]\!]_v = \mathcal{A}[v]$) yields that S_1 is reachable in $[\![\mathcal{A}]\!]_{(\lambda,\mu)}$ for all extended parameter valuations $0 \leq \lambda, \mu \leq \infty$.

Clearly, $[\![\mathcal{A}]\!]_{(\lambda,\mu)} \models \exists\Diamond S_2$ iff $\lambda(min) \leq \mu(max) \land \lambda(min) < \infty$. We will see in this running example how we can verify this property completely by non-parametric model checking. Henceforth, we construct the automaton $\mathcal{A}'$ from $\mathcal{A}$ by substituting the parameter *max* by the parameter *min* yielding an (non L/U) automaton with one parameter, *min*. If we show that $[\![\mathcal{A}']\!]_v \models \exists\Diamond S_2$ for all valuations v, this essentially means that $[\![\mathcal{A}]\!]_{(\lambda,\mu)} \models \exists\Diamond S_2$ for all λ, μ such that $\mu(max) = \lambda(min) < \infty$ and then Proposition 3 implies that $[\![\mathcal{A}]\!]_{(\lambda,\mu)} \models \exists\Diamond S_2$ for all λ, μ with $\lambda(min) \leq \mu(max)$ and $\lambda(min) < \infty$.

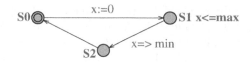

Fig. 2. Reducing parametric to non-parametric model c hecking

The question whether there exists a (non-extended) parameter valuation such that a given (final) location q is reachable, is known as the *emptiness problem* for PTAs. In [2], it is shown that the emptiness problem is undecidable for PTAs with three clocks or more. Proposition 3 implies $\exists \lambda, \mu : [\![\mathcal{A}]\!]_{\lambda,\mu} \models \exists \Diamond q$ iff $\mathcal{A}[0, \infty] \models \exists \Diamond q$. Here, (λ, μ) range over extended parameter valuations, but is not difficult to see that the statement also holds for (λ, μ) just valuations. Since $\mathcal{A}[(0, \infty)]$ is a non-parametric timed automaton and reac hability is decidable for timed automata ([1]), the emptiness problem is decidable for L/U automata. Then it follows that the dual problem is also decidable for L/U automata. This is the *universality problem* for invariance properties, asking whether an invariance property holds for all parameter valuations.

Corollary 1. *The emptiness problem is decidable for L/U automata.*

Definition 9. *A PTA $\mathcal{A}$ is fully parametric if clocks are only reset to 0 and every linear expression in $\mathcal{A}$ of the form $t_1 \cdot p_1 + \cdots + t_n \cdot p_n$, where $t_i \in \mathbb{Z}$.*

The following proposition is basically the observation in [1], that multiplication of each constant in a timed automaton and in a system propert y with the same positive factor preserves satisfaction.

Proposition 4. *Let $\mathcal{A}$ be fully parametric PTA. Then*

$$[\![\mathcal{A}]\!]_v \models \psi \iff \forall t \in \mathsf{R}^{>0} : [\![\mathcal{A}]\!]_{t \cdot v} \models t \cdot \psi,$$

where $t \cdot v$ denotes the valuation $p \mapsto t \cdot v(p)$ and $t \cdot \psi$ the formula obtained from ψ by multiplying each number in ψ by t.

Then for fully parametric PTAs with one parameter and system properties ψ without constants (except for 0), we have $[\![\mathcal{A}]\!]_v \models \psi$ for all valuations v of P if and only if both $\mathcal{A}[0] \models \psi$ and $\mathcal{A}[1] \models \psi$.

Corollary 2. *For fully parametric PTAs with one parameter and properties ψ without constants (except 0), it is decidable whether $\forall v \in [\![C]\!] : [\![\mathcal{A}]\!]_v \models \psi$.*

Example 3. The PTA $\mathcal{A}'$ mentioned in Example 2 is a fully parametric automaton and the property $\exists \Diamond S_2$ is without constants. W e establish that $\mathcal{A}'[0] \models \exists \Diamond S_2$ and $\mathcal{A}'[1] \models \exists \Diamond S_2$. Then Proposition 4 implies that $\mathcal{A}'[v] \models \exists \Diamond S_2$ for all v. As shown in Example 2, this implies that $[\![\mathcal{A}]\!]_{(\lambda,\mu)} \models \exists \Diamond S_2$ for all λ, μ with $\lambda(min) = \mu(max) < \infty$.

In the running example, we would like to use the above methods to verify that $[\![A]\!]_{(\lambda,\mu)} \not\models \exists \Diamond S_2$ if $\lambda(min) > \mu(max)$. We can in this case not fill in for $min = max$, since the bound in the constraint is strict. The following definition and result allows us to move the strictness of a constraint into the PTA.

Definition 10. *Define* $\mathcal{A}^<$ *as the automaton obtained by replacing every inequality* $x - y \le e$ *in* $\mathcal{A}$ *by a strict inequality* $x - y < e$, *provided that e contains at least one parameter.*

Proposition 5. *Let* $\mathcal{A}$ *be an* L/U *automaton. Then*

1. $[\![\mathcal{A}^<]\!]_{(\lambda,\mu)} \models \forall \Box \phi \iff \forall \lambda < \lambda', \mu' < \mu : [\![\mathcal{A}]\!]_{(\lambda',\mu')} \models \forall \Box \phi.$
2. $[\![\mathcal{A}^<]\!]_{(\lambda,\mu)} \models \exists \Diamond \phi \implies \forall \lambda' < \lambda, \mu < \mu' : [\![\mathcal{A}]\!]_{(\lambda',\mu')} \models \exists \Diamond \phi.$

We claim that we can extend the result above to a more general construction $\mathcal{A}^<_{P'}$, where we replace a guard $x - y \le e$ by $x - y < e$ by if and only if a parameter p from P' occurs in e. Then the proposition generalizes to $\mathcal{A}^<_{P'}$, provided that we replace $\lambda < \lambda'$ by $\lambda <_{P'} \lambda'$ (and similar replacements for $\lambda' < \lambda$, $\mu < \mu'$, $\mu' < \mu$). Here, $v <_{P'} v'$ is defined as $v(p) < v'(p)$ if $p \in P'$ and $v(p) = v'(p)$ otherwise.

Example 4. Consider the PTA $\mathcal{A}^<$, which equals the PTA in Fig. 2, except that $x \le max$ has been replace by $x < max$ and $x \ge min$ by $x > min$. Now, we construct the automaton $\mathcal{A}'$ from $\mathcal{A}^<$ by substituting the parameter max by min. By checking that $\mathcal{A}'[0] \models \forall \Box \neg S_2$ and $\mathcal{A}'[1] \models \forall \Box \neg S_2$, Proposition 4 yields that $\mathcal{A}'[v] \models \forall \Box \neg S_2$ for all valuations v. Then we know by Proposition 3 that $[\![\mathcal{A}']\!]_{(\lambda,\mu)} \models \forall \Box \neg S_2$ if $\infty > \lambda(min) \ge \mu(max)$. Now, Proposition 5 concludes that if $\infty > \lambda(min) > \mu(max)$ then $[\![\mathcal{A}]\!]_{(\lambda,\mu)} \models \forall \Box \neg S_2$ i.e. $[\![\mathcal{A}]\!]_{(\lambda,\mu)} \not\models \exists \Diamond S_2$. Combining the results from the examples in this section yields $[\![\mathcal{A}]\!]_{(\lambda,\mu)} \models \exists \Diamond S_2$ if and only if $\lambda(min) \le \mu(max) \land \lambda(min) < \infty$.

5   Experiments

In this section, we report on the results of experimenting with a prototype extension of UPPAAL described in the previous sections. For lack of space, we give a short impression of the experiments, which are described in greater detail in the full version [10].

The Root Contention Protocol The root contention protocol is part of a leader election protocol in the physical layer of the IEEE 1394 standard (FireWire/i-Link), which is used to break symmetry between two nodes contending to be the root of a tree, spanned in the network topology.

We use the UPPAAL models of [14,13], turn the constants used into parameters, and experiment with our prototype implementation (see Fig. 3 for results[2]).

---

[2] All experiments were performed on a 366 MHz Celeron, except the liveness property which was performed in a 333 MHz SPARC Ultra Enterprise.

In both models, there are five constants, all of which are parameters in our experiments. We have checked for safety and liveness on the parametric models, and have applied reductions as proposed in Section 4 where this was possible, to reduce the verification effort. In some cases, we could even derive the parametric conclusions by non-parametric model checking, which we have done with standard UPPAAL.

model from	initial constraints?	reduced?	property	UPPAAL	time	memory
[14]	yes	no	safety	param	2.9 h	185 Mb
[14]	yes	yes	safety	std	1 s	800 Kb
[13]	yes	no	safety	param	1.6 m	36 Mb
[13]	yes	partly	safety	param	11 s	13 Mb
[13]	yes	completely	safety	std	1 s	800 Kb
[13]	yes	no	liveness	param	2.6 h	308 Mb

Fig. 3. Experimental results for the root contention protocol

The Bounded Retransmission Protocol This protocol was designed by Philips for communication between remote controls and audio/video/TV equipment. In [7] constraints for the correctness of the protocol are derived by hand, and some instances are checked using UPPAAL. Based on the models in [7], an automatic parametric analysis is performed in [3], however, no further results are given.

model from	initial constraints	property	UPPAAL	time	memory
[7]	yes	safety1	param	1.3 m	34 Mb
[7]	no	safety2	param	11 m	180 Mb
[7]	yes	safety2	param	3.5 m	64 Mb

Fig. 4. Experimental results for the bounded retransmission protocol

For our analysis we have also used the timed automata models from [7]. In [7] three different constraints are presented based on three properties which are needed to satisfy the safety specification of the protocol. We are only able to check two of these since one of the properties contain a parameter which our prototype version of UPPAAL is not able to handle yet. The results can be found in Fig. 4[3]. Note that out of the four constants in the model which are candidates for parameters, the model checked for property 'safety1' and 'safety2' uses two and one as parameters respectively. A minor error in [7] was found while checking 'safety 1', which has been corrected by the authors of [7].

---

[3] All experiments run on a 333 MHz SPARC Ultra Enterprise.

References

1. R. Alur and D.L. Dill. A theory of timed automata. *Theoretical Computer Science*, 126:183–235, 1994.

2. R. Alur, T.A. Henzinger, and M.Y. Vardi. Parametric real-time reasoning. In *Proc. 25th Annual Symp. on Theory of Computing*, pages 592–601. ACM Press, 1993.

3. A. Annichini, E. Asarin, and A. Bouajjani. Symbolic techniques for parametric reasoning about counter and clock systems. In *Proc. 12th Int. Conference on Computer Aided Verification*, LNCS 1855, pages 419–434. Springer-Verlag, 2000.

4. G. Bandini, R. Lutje Spelberg, and H. Toetenel. Parametric verification of the IEEE 1394a root contention protocol using LPMC. http://tvs.twi.tudelft.nl/, July 2000. Submitted.

5. M. Bozga, C. Daws, O. Maler, A. Olivero, S. Tripakis, and S. Yovine. Kronos: A Model-Checking Tool for Real-Time Systems. In *Proc. 10th Int. Conference on Computer Aided Verification*, LNCS 1427, pages 546–550. Springer-Verlag, June/July 1998.

6. T.H. Cormen, C.E. Leiserson, and R.L. Rivest. *Introduction to Algorithms*. McGraw-Hill, Inc., 1991.

7. P.R. D'Argenio, J.-P. Katoen, T.C. Ruys, and J. Tretmans. The bounded retransmission protocol must be on time! In *Proc. Third Workshop on Tools and Algorithms for the Construction and Analysis of Systems*, LNCS 1217, pages 416–431. Springer-Verlag, April 1997.

8. D. Dill. Timing assumptions and verification of finite-state concurrent systems. In *Proc. Int. Workshop on Automatic Verification Methods for Finite State Systems*, LNCS 407, pages 197–212. Springer-Verlag, 1990.

9. T. A. Henzinger, P.-H. Ho, and H. Wong-Toi. HyTech: A Model Checker for Hybrid Systems. In *Proc. 9th Int. Conference on Computer Aided Verification*, LNCS 1254, pages 460–463. Springer-Verlag, 1997.

10. T.S. Hune, J.M.T. Romijn, M.I.A. Stoelinga, and F.W. Vaandrager. Linear parametric model checking of timed automata. Report CSI-R0102, CSI, University of Nijmegen, January 2001.

11. K. G. Larsen, P. Pettersson, and W. Yi. Uppaal in a Nutshell. *Int. Journal on Software Tools for Technology Transfer*, 1(1–2):134–152, October 1997.

12. R.F. Lutje Spelberg, W.J. Toetenel, and M. Ammerlaan. Partition refinement in real-time model checking. In *Proc. FTRTFT'98*, LNCS 1486, pages 143–157. Springer-Verlag, 1998.

13. D.P.L. Simons and M.I.A. Stoelinga. Mechanical verification of the IEEE 1394a root contention protocol using Uppaal2k. Technical Report CSI-R0009, CSI, University of Nijmegen, May 2000. Conditionally accepted for *STTT*.

14. M.I.A. Stoelinga and F.W. Vaandrager. Root contention in IEEE 1394. In *Proc. 5th Int. AMAST Workshop on Formal Methods for Real-Time and Probabilistic Systems*, LNCS 1601, pages 53–74. Springer-Verlag, 1999.

15. S. Yovine. Model checking timed automata. In *Lectures on Embedded Systems*, LNCS 1494, pages 114–152. Springer-Verlag, October 1998.

Abstraction in Probabilistic Process Algebra

S. Andova and J.C.M. Baeten

Department of Computing Science
Eindhoven University of Technology, The Netherlands
e-mail: {suzana, josb}@win.tue.nl, fax: +31 (0)40 247 5361

Abstract. Process algebras with abstraction have been widely used for the specification and verification of non-probabilistic concurrent systems. The main strategy in these algebras is introducing a constant, denoting an internal action, and a set of fairness rules. Following the same approach, in this paper we propose a fully probabilistic process algebra with abstraction which contains a set of verification rules as counterparts of the fairness rules in standard ACP-like process algebras with abstraction. Having probabilities present and employing the results from Markov chain analysis, these rules are expressible in a very intuitive way. In addition to this algebraic approach, we introduce a new version of probabilistic branching bisimulation for the alternating model of probabilistic systems. Different from other approaches, this bisimulation relation requires the same probability measure only for specific related processes called *entries*. We claim this definition corresponds better with intuition. Moreover, the fairness rules are sound in the model based on this bisimulation. Finally, we present an algorithm to decide our branching bisimulation with a polynomial-time complexity in the number of the states of the probabilistic graph.

1 Introduction and Motiv ation

In this work we treat the problem of abstraction from in ternal actions in fully probabilistic process algebra and its model based on branching bisimulation. One of the motives to introduce probabilities in formal methods is that they can be used to model fairness. Since the idea of fairness rules ([5]) together with abstraction (introduced by the abstraction operator τ_I and a constant τ denoting an internal action) is central to the verification techniques in process algebra we introduce verification rules in fully probabilistic process algebra that arise rather in a natural way from the ones defined in standard process algebra. These rules express the idea that due to a non-zero probability for a system to execute an external action, abstraction from in ternal steps will yield the external step(s) with probability 1 after finitely many repetitions. For example, if one process can execute external action a with probability π, external action b with probability ρ and with probability $1 - \pi - \rho$ after executing an internal action it behaves the same as initially, then it is clear that the probability to perform the internal step infinitely many times is equal to 0, or in other words, the probability to perform either a or b eventually is 1. Next, the question arises: "With what probabilit y

T. Margaria and W. Yi (Eds.): TACAS 2001, LNCS 2031, pp. 204–219, 2001.
© Springer-Verlag Berlin Heidelberg 2001

a (resp. b) occurs?". [9] gives the answer to this question as: the probability of a is $\pi/(\pi + \rho)$ and the probability of b is $\rho/(\pi + \rho)$. This corresponds to the absorption probabilities for the Markov chain given in Figure 1a. In our theory the notion that relates these two processes can be easily expressed with the following verification rule: if $X = a \uplus_\pi b \uplus_p i \cdot X$ (where i is an internal action), then $\tau \cdot \tau_{\{i\}}(X) = \tau \cdot (a \uplus_{\pi/(\pi + \rho)} b)$. (For more details of the semantics see [2] and [7].) A reader familiar with process algebra can easily see the resemblance with the $KFAR_1^b$ rule ([7]) with non-deterministic choice replaced by probabilistic choice.

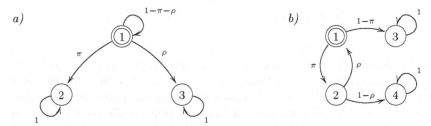

Fig. 1. Absorbing Markov chains.

Proceeding with similar reasoning for the more complex rule $KFAR_2^b$ we achieve a situation in which the definition of weak (branching) bisimulation proposed in [9] cannot abstract away the internal cycle. But working with recursive equations in our process algebra we can introduce a counterpart of this rule in the probabilistic setting in the following way:

$$X_1 = i \cdot X_2 \uplus_\pi Y_1$$
$$\frac{X_2 = i \cdot X_1 \uplus_p Y_2, \; I = \{i\}}{\tau \cdot \tau_I(X_1) = \tau \cdot (\tau_I(Y_1) \uplus_\alpha \tau_I(Y_2))} \qquad \text{(PVR2)}$$

where X_1 is the root variable and $\alpha = (1 - \pi)/(1 - \pi\rho)$. The transition systems (as defined in [9]) for these processes are given in Figure 2 (for the sake of simplicity the initial internal steps are not shown) and the corresponding Markov chain of the first process is shown in Figure 1b. The values of probabilities α and $\beta = 1 - \alpha = \pi(1 - \rho)/(1 - \pi\rho)$ are obtained as the absorption probabilities when X_1 is the root variable, that is, 1 is "the initial state of the system" (in terms of the Markov chain theory) for the Markov chain in Figure 1b. We point out that the absorption probabilities for this system differ for various initial distributions.

Further on, we define a probabilistic branching bisimulation relation on the set of fully probabilistic graphs that abstracts away internal actions in wider variety of cases than the definition in [9]. It will turn out that the set of graphs modulo this relation gives rise to a model of our process algebra. Two nodes are considered bisimilar if they have the same branching structure and if taken as roots they have the same probability measures. This means that if the system is in either of these states then the probabilities to execute a visible action and also the probabilities to enter with an internal step into a different equivalence

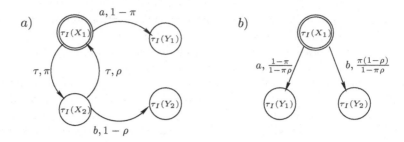

Fig. 2. Related fully probabilistic processes.

class are the same. In this definition the notion of an *entry* plays a central role (a notion to be formally defined in Definition 10 on page 212). Starting from the roots of the graphs we build a *set of entries* for which the probability measure is checked in the next stage. Informally, we can say that a node not found as an entry is just involved in (is just a part of) an internal path (or a cycle) that starts in an entry with the same branching structure as the non-entry node; the node is not involved in any other path. Also, after execution of a visible action the system never goes to the state interpreted by this non-entry node. For example, in the graph in Figure 2a, $\tau_I(X_2)$ is a non-entry node (no path from $\tau_I(Y_1)$ or $\tau_I(Y_2)$ goes back to $\tau_I(X_2)$).

Moreover, in the paper we give an algorithm which decides the probabilistic branching bisimulation in polynomial time in the number of states of the probabilistic graph.

Because parallel composition based on interleaving (see e.g. [2,3]) includes non-determinism, this algebra and semantics cannot deal with such parallel composition. However, since we define the branching bisimulation on the alternating model, and we also consider the non-deterministic (or action) nodes in our definition of bisimulation, we expect that the extension with non-deterministic choice can be achieved on the basis of the results presented here. This will enable the extension with interleaving parallel composition.

Motivating example. In order to depict the idea of our approach we give the following motivating example. An experimenter has two coins A and B. A is a fair coin with the probability distribution $\{1/2\ head, 1/2\ tail\}$, and B is biased with distribution $\{1/3\ head, 2/3\ tail\}$. First he throws coin A. If *head* turns up the throwing is over and he announces "head". If *tail* shows up then he throws coin B. If *tail* turns up then the throwing is over and he announces "tail", but if *head* turns up then he takes coin A and performs the experiment again. The process can be specified by the following recursive specification:

$A = tail_A \cdot B \boxplus_{1/2} head_A \cdot sayhead$

$B = head_B \cdot A \boxplus_{1/3} tail_B \cdot saytail$

where *sayhead* and *saytail* are atomic actions expressing the observable events of announcing "head" and "tail", respectively. Abstracting from $head_A, tail_A, head_B$ and $tail_B$ and applying the rule PVR2 we obtain that the probability to end the experiment by saying "head" or "tail", is $3/5$ and $2/5$, respectively. We point out that coin A was chosen as the initial coin. We can imagine that the throwing is performed in an isolated room and an observer can hear only the final outcome, but for her it is not clear what kind of experiment is performed in the room.

The observer will make the same observation if the experimenter performs some other experiment. Namely, instead of two coins he has only one fair die. He rolls it and if the outcome is 1 he rolls it again. If the outcome is an even number he announces "head" and if the outcome is 3 or 5 he announces "tail".   □

Related Work We have already mentioned the relation of this paper with [9]. Namely, the branching (weak) bisimulation for fully probabilistic systems presented in [9] is finer than ours. Reasoning in the process algebra which we present here, with the rules $PVR1, PRV2, \ldots$ and speaking informally, their bisimulation defines just a model of $PVR1$, not of $PVR2$ and more complex rules (see further on).

Similarities of the bisimulation defined here can be found with the branching bisimulation of Jou in [11]. The proposed probabilistic branching bisimulation in the latter work is defined on the set of finite trees. And the author's attention is more focused on the axiom: $a(\tau(x \uplus_\pi y) \uplus_\rho y) = a(x \uplus_{\pi \rho} y)$ and not on any rules that treat internal cycles. Our definition of bisimulation coincides with his one on the set of finite trees (in terms of process algebra, the set of closed terms). And the branching bisimulation presented in this paper is an extension of his branching bisimulation over infinite processes.

2   Definitions and Results

In [2] a probabilistic process algebra containing both probabilistic choice and non-deterministic choice is introduced. Our current work is based on a sub-algebra of that one for which non-deterministic choice has been excluded. Having both choices and abstraction at the same time leads to a more complex axiomatization and this extension, we think, can be achieved on the basis of the definitions we give here. Due to the absence of non-determinism the interleaving parallel composition as treated in [2] cannot be incorporated in this fully probabilistic process algebra. On the other hand, some version of synchronous parallel composition may be considered in such a process algebra (also see [6]).

In addition to the set of atomic actions A and the constant τ the fully probabilistic process algebra presented here has three operators: the probabilistic choice operator $\uplus_\pi, \pi \in \langle 0, 1 \rangle$, the sequential composition $\cdot$ and the abstraction operator τ_I for $I \subseteq A$. The axiom system is given in Table 1 and 2. Informally, process $x \uplus_\pi y$ behaves as x with probability π and as y with probability $1 - \pi$. Also, process $x \uplus_\pi y \uplus_\rho z$ behaves as x with probability π, as y with probability ρ and as z with probability $1 - \pi - \rho$. This algebra will be denoted by $prBPA_\tau$. We also add to the algebra a set of verification rules PVR1 and PVRn for $n \geq 2$:

$$\frac{X_1 = i \cdot X_1 \uplus_{\pi_1} Y_1, \tau \neq i \in I}{\tau \cdot \tau_I(X_1) = \tau \cdot \tau_I(Y_1)} \tag{PVR1}$$

$$X_1 = i_1 \cdot X_2 \,\uplus_{\pi_1} Y_1$$
$$X_2 = i_2 \cdot X_3 \,\uplus_{\pi_2} Y_2$$

.

.

. $\qquad\qquad\qquad\qquad\qquad\qquad\qquad\qquad\qquad\qquad\qquad$ (PVRn)

$$X_{n-1} = i_{n-1} \cdot X_n \,\uplus_{\pi_{n-1}} Y_{n-1}$$
$$X_n = i_n \cdot X_1 \,\uplus_{\pi_n} Y_n, I \cup \{\tau\} \supseteq \{i_1, i_2, \ldots, i_n\} \neq \{\tau\}$$

$$\tau \cdot \tau_I(X_1) = \tau \cdot (\tau_I(Y_1) \,\uplus_{\alpha_1} \tau_I(Y_2) \,\uplus_{\alpha_2} \ldots \,\uplus_{\alpha_{n-2}} \tau_I(Y_{n-1}) \,\uplus_{\alpha_{n-1}} \tau_I(Y_n))$$

where $\alpha_1 = \dfrac{1-\pi_1}{1-\pi_1\cdot\pi_2\cdot\ldots\cdot\pi_n}$, $\alpha_j = \dfrac{\pi_1\cdot\ldots\cdot\pi_{j-1}\cdot(1-\pi_j)}{1-\pi_1\cdot\ldots\cdot\pi_n}$ for $j : 1 < j \leq n$ and $\pi_k \in \langle 0, 1 \rangle$ for $k : 1 \leq k \leq n$. If we refer to the algebra extended with these rules we write $prBPA_\tau + PVR1 + PVR2 + \ldots$.

$(x \cdot y) \cdot z$	$= x \cdot (y \cdot z)$	$A5$
$x \,\uplus_\pi y$	$= y \,\uplus_{1-\pi} x$	$PrAC1$
$x \,\uplus_\pi (y \,\uplus_\rho z)$	$= (x \,\uplus_{\frac{\pi}{\pi+\rho-\pi\rho}} y) \,\uplus_{\pi+\rho-\pi\rho} z$	$PrAC2$
$x \,\uplus_\pi x$	$= x$	$PrAC3$
$(x \,\uplus_\pi y) \cdot z$	$= x \cdot z \,\uplus_\pi y \cdot z$	$PrAC4$

Table 1. Axioms for probabilistic choice and sequential composition.

$x \cdot \tau$	$= x$		$T1$
$\tau_I(\tau)$	$= \tau$		$TI0$
$\tau_I(a)$	$= a$	if $a \notin I$	$TI1$
$\tau_I(a)$	$= \tau$	if $a \in I$	$TI2$
$\tau_I(x \cdot y)$	$= \tau_I(x) \cdot \tau_I(y)$		$TI4$
$\tau_I(x \,\uplus_\pi y)$	$= \tau_I(x) \,\uplus_\pi \tau_I(y)$		$PrTI$

Table 2. Axioms for abstraction ($I \subseteq A_\tau$).

The reader has noticed that we use a set of equations of the form $X_j = P_j, j = 1, \ldots, n$, to specify recursive behaviour. In the above equations, $X_1, \ldots, X_n$ are pairwise distinct variables and $P_1, \ldots, P_n$ are guarded terms over the given signature (see e.g. [7]). Every recursive specification has a root variable. In the verification rule PVRn, X_1 is the root variable of the recursive specification.

In order to construct a model of this algebra we introduce fully probabilistic graphs. Further on, we define probabilistic branching bisimulation. We work in the alternating model with two types of nodes (processes): probabilistic nodes with probabilistic outgoing transitions only, denoted by $\rightsquigarrow$, and action nodes with action transitions only, denoted by $\xrightarrow{a}$, for $a \in A_\tau$. By allowing at most one action transition to leave an action node we obtain the alternating model of fully probabilistic process algebra.

Definition 1. *Let A be a countable set of atomic actions. A fully probabilistic graph g is a tuple $(S_p \cup S_n \cup \{NIL\}, \rightsquigarrow, \rightarrow, \mu, root)$ consisting of:*
- *a countable set S_p of probabilistic states,*
- *a countable set S_n of action states such that $S_p \cap S_n = \emptyset$ and $NIL \notin S_p \cup S_n$,*

- $root \in S_p$,
- a relation $\leadsto \subseteq S_p \times S_n$,
- a function $\rightarrow: S_n \mapsto S_p \cup \{NIL\} \times A_\tau$, and
- a partial function $\mu : S_p \times S_n \mapsto \langle 0, 1]$ such that $\mu(p, n)$ is defined iff $(p, n) \in \leadsto$ for $(p, n) \in S_p \times S_n$ and for any $p \in S_p$, $\sum_{n \in S_n} \mu(p, n) = 1$.

We denote $S = S_p \cup S_n$. If S is a finite set then we say that the probabilistic graph g is finite. NIL is called *the terminating state*. If NIL is not reachable from the root of g then it can be ignored. Function μ is called *the probability distribution function* of g.

If $(p, n) \in \leadsto$, we write $p \leadsto n$. If $\rightarrow (n) = (p, a)$ we write $n \xrightarrow{a} p$. For sake of simplicity, instead of writing the value of function μ separately, if $p \leadsto n$ we write $p \xrightarrow{\mu(p,n)}{\leadsto} n$. By **G** we denote the set of all finite fully probabilistic graphs.

Note: If $\rightarrow$ is not a function from S_n to $S_p \cup \{NIL\} \times A_\tau$, but a subset of $S_n \times S_p \cup \{NIL\} \times A_\tau$, we get the general class of probabilistic graphs, including non-determinism. In this case action nodes are rather called *non-deterministic nodes*, as we do in [2,3].

Definition 2. *Let* $g = (S \cup \{NIL\}, \leadsto, \rightarrow, \mu, root)$ *be a fully probabilistic graph. We say that* g *is* root acyclic *if there is no node* $n \in S_n$ *and* $a \in A_\tau$ *such that* $n \xrightarrow{a} root$. *Otherwise we say that* g *is* root cyclic.
We define the root unwinding map $\rho : \mathbf{G} \mapsto \mathbf{G}$ *as follows:*
- *if* g *is root acyclic, then* $\rho(g) = g$;
- *if* g *is root cyclic, then* $\rho(g) = (S \cup \{NIL\} \cup \{newroot\}, \leadsto', \rightarrow, \mu', newroot)$,
where newroot is a new node, $\leadsto' = \leadsto \cup \{(newroot, n) : root \leadsto n\}$ *and*
$$\mu'(p, n) = \begin{cases} \mu(p, n) & \text{if } p \in S \\ \mu(root, n) & \text{if } p = newroot \end{cases}$$

Proposition 1. *Let* g *be a fully probabilistic graph.*
  i. Then $\rho(g)$ *is root acyclic.*
  ii. $g \underline{\leftrightarrow} \rho(g)$, *that is,* g *and* $\rho(g)$ *are strongly bisimilar.* □

Interpretation of Constants and Operators in G

Definition 3. (Interpretation of the constants) *If* $a \in A_\tau$, *its interpretation is*
$$[a] = (\{s_p\} \cup \{s_n\} \cup \{NIL\}, \{s_p \leadsto s_n\}, \{s_n \xrightarrow{a} NIL\}, \mu(s_p, s_n) = 1, s_p).$$

Definition 4. (Interpretation of the operators) *Let* g *and* h *be graphs in* **G** *and* $g = (S_g \cup \{NIL_g\}, \leadsto_g, \rightarrow_g, \mu_g, root_g)$ *and* $h = (S_h \cup \{NIL_h\}, \leadsto_h, \rightarrow_h, \mu_h, root_h)$.

Sequential composition: $g \cdot h$ *is defined as:*
$$(S_g \cup S_h \cup \{NIL_h\}, \leadsto_g \cup \leadsto_h, \rightarrow, \mu, root_g),$$
where: $\rightarrow = (\rightarrow_g \setminus \{n \xrightarrow{a} NIL_g : n \in S_g, a \in Act_\tau\}) \cup \rightarrow_h$
$\cup \{n \xrightarrow{a} root_h : n \in S_g, a \in Act_\tau, n \xrightarrow{a} NIL_g\},$

and $\mu(p, n) = \begin{cases} \mu_g(p, n) & \text{if } p, n \in S_g \\ \mu_h(p, n) & \text{if } p, n \in S_h \end{cases}$

Probabilistic choice: $g \boxplus_\pi h$, *for* $\pi \in \langle 0, 1 \rangle$, *is defined as:*
$$(S \cup \{NIL\}, \leadsto, \to, \mu, root),$$
where: $S = (S_g \setminus \{root_g\}) \cup (S_h \setminus \{root_h\}) \cup \{root\}$, $root \notin S_g \cup S_h$,
$\leadsto \ = \ (\leadsto_g \setminus \{root_g \leadsto n \ : \ n \in S_g\}) \cup (\leadsto_h \setminus \{root_h \leadsto n \ : \ n \in S_h\})$
$\cup \{root \leadsto n \ : \ n \in S_g, root_g \leadsto n\} \cup \{root \leadsto n \ : \ n \in S_h, root_h \leadsto n\}$,
$\to \ = \ \to_g \ \cup \ \to_h$ *with the remark that* NIL_g *and* NIL_h *are identified and this node is named* NIL,

and $\mu(p, n) = \begin{cases} \mu_g(p, n) & \text{if } p, n \in S_g \setminus \{root_g\} \\ \mu_h(p, n) & \text{if } p, n \in S_h \setminus \{root_h\} \\ \pi \cdot \mu_g(root_g, n) & \text{if } p = root \ \& \ n \in S_g \ \& \ root_g \leadsto n \\ (1 - \pi) \cdot \mu_h(root_h, n) & \text{if } p = root \ \& \ n \in S_h \ \& \ root_h \leadsto n \end{cases}$

Abstraction: $\tau_I(g)$ *for* $I \subseteq A$ *is defined as:*
$$(\bar{S}_g \cup \{NIL_g\}, \leadsto_g, \to, \mu_g, root_g),$$
where: $p \overset{a}{\to} n$ *iff* $p \overset{a}{\to}_g n$ *and* $a \notin I$ *and*
$p \overset{\tau}{\to} n$ *iff* $p \overset{a}{\to}_g n$ *and* $a \in I \cup \{\tau\}$.

Similarly to the non-probabilistic version of bisimulation relations including silent steps (in particular *branching bisimulation*) we allow here an observable action a ($a \neq \tau$) to be simulated by a sequence of transitions such that exactly the last transition is an a-transition and the rest are internal transitions inside the same equivalence class. The new problem we should think about is the way we calculate the probability measure of such a sequence of transitions according to the probability distribution function μ. For that reason we sketch (repeat) the standard concept used to define a probability measure (see [8,9]), adapted for the alternating model of fully probabilistic systems.

Let $g = (S_p \cup S_n \cup \{NIL\}, \leadsto, \to, \mu, root)$ be a finite fully probabilistic graph.

Definition 5. *For* $p \in S_p$, $n \in S_n$, $C \subseteq S_p \cup \{NIL\}$ *and* $a \in A_\tau$ *we define:*

- $n \overset{a}{\to} C$ *iff* $\exists q \in C \ : \ n \overset{a}{\to} q$;
- $\mathbf{P}(p, a, C) = \sum\limits_{n: n \overset{a}{\to} C} \mu(p, n)$ *and* $\mathbf{P}(p, a, q) = \mathbf{P}(p, a, \{q\})$;
- An execution fragment *or* finite path *is a nonempty finite sequence*

$$\sigma = p_0 \leadsto n_0 \overset{a_1}{\to} p_1 \leadsto n_1 \overset{a_2}{\to} p_2 \ldots p_{k-1} \leadsto n_{k-1} \overset{a_k}{\to} p_k$$

such that $p_0, \ldots, p_k \in S_p \cup \{NIL\}$, $n_0, \ldots, n_{k-1} \in S_n$, $a_1, \ldots, a_k \in A_\tau$. *We say that* σ *starts in* p_0 *and we write* $first(\sigma) = p_0$, *and also* $trace(\sigma) = a_1 a_2 \ldots a_k$ *and* $last(\sigma) = p_k$. *If* $last(\sigma) = NIL$, *then* σ *is maximal*
- *If* $k = 0$ *we define* $\mathbf{P}(\sigma) = 1$. *If* $k \geq 1$ *we define*

$$\mathbf{P}(\sigma) = \mu(p_0, n_0) \cdot \mu(p_1, n_2) \cdot \ldots \cdot \mu(p_{k-1}, n_{k-1}).$$

- Let $Q \subseteq S_p \cup \{NIL\}$ and σ be a finite path in the form written above. If $p_0, p_1, \ldots, p_{k-1} \in Q$ then we say that σ only passes through states in Q, and we write σ_Q.

Definition 6. An execution or fullpath is either a maximal execution fragment or an infinite sequence
$$\pi = p_0 \leadsto n_0 \overset{a_1}{\rightarrow} p_1 \leadsto n_1 \overset{a_2}{\rightarrow} p_2 \ldots$$
such that $p_0, p_1, p_2, \ldots \in S_p$, $n_0, n_1, n_2 \ldots \in S_n$, $a_1, a_2, \ldots \in A_\tau$. A path is a finite path or a fullpath.

$Path_{full}(p)$ denotes the set of fullpaths starting in p. Similarly, $Path_{fin}(p)$ ($Path_{fin,Q}(p)$ for some $Q \subseteq S_p \cup \{NIL\}$) denotes the set of finite paths starting in p (that only pass through states in Q). For each process p, $\mathbf{P}$ induces a probability space on $Path_{full}(p)$ as follows.

Let $\sigma \uparrow$ denote the basic cylinder induced by σ, that is,

$$\sigma \uparrow = \{\pi \in Path_{full}(p) \ : \ \sigma \leq_{prefix} \pi\},$$

where $\leq_{prefix}$ is the usual prefix relation on sequences. We define $\sigma Field(p)$ to be the smallest sigma-field on $Path_{full}(p)$ which contains all basic cylinders $\sigma \uparrow$ where $\sigma \in Path_{fin}(p)$, that is, σ ranges over all finite paths starting in p. The probability measure $Prob$ on $\sigma Field(p)$ is the unique probability measure with $Prob(\sigma \uparrow) = \mathbf{P}(\sigma)$.

Lemma 1. ([9]) Let $p \in S_p$ and $\Sigma \subseteq Path_{fin}(p)$ such that $\sigma, \sigma' \in \Sigma$, $\sigma \neq \sigma'$ implies $\sigma \not\leq_{prefix} \sigma'$. Then, $Prob(\Sigma \uparrow) = \sum_{\sigma \in \Sigma} \mathbf{P}(\sigma)$. □

Definition 7. If $p \in S_p$, $L \subseteq A_\tau^*$ and $C \subseteq S_p \cup \{NIL\}$, then $Prob(p, L, C) = Prob(\Sigma(p)\uparrow)$, where $\Sigma(p)$ is the set of all finite paths σ starting in p with trace in L and with the last process belonging in C, that is,
$$\Sigma(p) = \{\sigma \in Path_{fin}(p) \ : \ first(\sigma) = p, trace(\sigma) \in L, last(\sigma) \in C\}.$$

$Path_{full,Q}(p)$ is defined as the set of fullpaths $\sigma \in Path_{full}(p)$ such that there is some $k_\sigma \geq 0$ and $\sigma' \in Path_{fin,Q}(p)$ such that σ' is the prefix of σ with the length k_σ. Then, in a similar way as above we define a probability space on $Path_{full,Q}(p)$, the probability measure $Prob_Q(\sigma_Q \uparrow) = \mathbf{P}(\sigma_Q)$ and $Prob_Q(p, L, C)$.

Probabilistic Branching Bisimulation The new result in our approach is a definition of probabilistic branching bisimulation that is weaker than the one in [9] and that can, we think, be extended for probabilistic processes containing non-determinism. The bisimulation on the set of fully probabilistic graphs we propose is based on the notion of a *set of entries* (a subset of the set of probabilistic nodes) and a *set of exits* (a subset of the set of action nodes).

In the following, we introduce the notion of *entries* and *exits* for a given graph with equivalence relation R defined on the set of its nodes. An *exit* of a probabilistic node is an action node that is the outgoing node of an external action transition or an internal transition that leads to a new equivalence class. Every probabilistic node has a set of exits. Having *the sets of exits* determined for each probabilistic node in the graph we can obtain *the set of entries*. First, the root of the graph is always an entry. Further, an entry in one equivalence class is a node that is first entered from an exit of some other entry by taking either an external or an internal action. In such a way each entry determines the set of its succeeding entries. In other words, a probabilistic node q is not an entry if it is reachable from entries belonging to the equivalence class of q only through internal paths passing through this equivalence class. Finally, for each entry the probabilities for reaching the equivalence classes of its succeeding entries are computed. All entries with the same probability distribution are considered bisimilar. For nodes found not to be entries the probabilities are not computed. Formal definitions follow.

Definition 8 (Entry). *If g is a fully probabilistic graph and if R is an equivalence relation on the set of states then:*

$Entry_0(g) = \{root(g)\}$,

$Entry_{i+1}(g) = \{q \ : \ \exists r \in Entry_i : \exists e \in Exit_R(r) : e \xrightarrow{a} q, a \in A_\tau \ \& \ q \notin [r]_R\}$
$\qquad\qquad \cup \{q \ : \ \exists r \in Entry_i : \exists e \in Exit_R(r) : e \xrightarrow{a} q, a \in A \ \& \ q \in [r]_R\}$,

where $Exit_R(r) = \{s \ : \ r \xRightarrow{\tau^*}_{[r]_R} \cdot \leadsto s \ \& \ \exists C \neq [r]_R : s \xrightarrow{a} C, a \in A_\tau\}$
$\qquad\qquad \cup \{s \ : \ r \xRightarrow{\tau^*}_{[r]_R} \cdot \leadsto s \ \& \ s \xrightarrow{a} [r]_R, a \in A\}$.

Finally, $Entry_R(g) = \bigcup_{i \geq 0} Entry_i(g)$.

By $\xRightarrow{\tau^*}$ *we denote the transitive and reflexive closure of* $\leadsto \cdot \xrightarrow{\tau}$ *and by* $\xRightarrow{\tau^*}_Q$ *we denote the transitive and reflexive closure of* $\{p \leadsto \cdot \xrightarrow{\tau} p' \ : \ p, p' \in Q\}$ *for* $Q \subseteq S_p \cup \{NIL\}$.

Definition 9. *If g is a fully probabilistic graph, R and $\tilde{R}$ are equivalence relations on the set of states such that $\tilde{R} \subseteq R$ and if $r \in S_p$, then:*

$NextEntry(r) = \{q \ : \ \exists e \in Exit_R(r) : e \xrightarrow{a} q, a \in A_\tau \ \& \ q \notin [r]_R\}$
$\qquad\qquad \cup \{q \ : \ \exists e \in Exit_R(r) : e \xrightarrow{a} q, a \in A \ \& \ q \in [r]_R\}$
and $NextEntryC_{\tilde{R}}(r) = \{[q]_{\tilde{R}} \ : \ q \in NextEntry(r)\}$.

Due to the fact that two entries from the same R equivalence class may have different sets of exits and sets of next entries, these sets have to be parametrized by the entry they are associated to (see Example 2).

Definition 10 (Probabilistic Branching Bisimulation). *Let g and h be fully probabilistic graphs. If R is an equivalence relation on $S_g \cup S_h \cup \{NIL_g, NIL_h\}$ such that:*

0. $(root(g), root(h)) \in R$;
1. *if $(p, q) \in R$ and $p \leadsto s$ then either*
$\quad$ *1.0 $(s, q) \in R$ or*

1.1 there are v, t such that $(p, v), (s, t) \in R$ and

$$q \overset{\tau^*}{\Longrightarrow} v \rightsquigarrow t \ \text{or} \ q \overset{\tau}{\rightarrow} \cdot \overset{\tau^*}{\Longrightarrow} v \rightsquigarrow t;$$

2. *if $(p, q) \in R$ and $p \overset{a}{\rightarrow} s$ then either*

2.0 $a = \tau$ and $(s, q) \in R$ or

2.1 there are v, t such that $(q, v), (s, t) \in R$ and

$$q \overset{\tau^*}{\Longrightarrow} \cdot \rightsquigarrow v \overset{a}{\rightarrow} t \ \text{or} \ q(\overset{\tau}{\rightarrow} \cdot \rightsquigarrow)^* v \overset{a}{\rightarrow} t;$$

3. *there is an equivalence relation $\tilde{R}$ on $Entry_R(g) \cup Entry_R(h)$ such that $\tilde{R} \subseteq R$ and*

3.0. $(root(g), root(h)) \in \tilde{R};$

3.1. if $(p, q) \in \tilde{R}$ then for any $C \in NextEntryC_{\tilde{R}}(p) \ \cup \ NextEntryC_{\tilde{R}}(q)$ and for any $a \in A$,
$$Prob_{[p]_R}(p, \tau^*, C) = Prob_{[q]_R}(q, \tau^*, C) \ and$$
$$Prob_{[p]_R}(p, \tau^* a, C) = Prob_{[q]_R}(q, \tau^* a, C);$$

then $(R, \tilde{R})$ is a probabilistic branching bisimulation relation *between g and h. We write $g \underleftrightarrow{}_{pb} h$ if there is a probabilistic branching bisimulation $(R, \tilde{R})$ between g and h.*

Using $\underleftrightarrow{}_{pb}$ we define relation $\underleftrightarrow{}_{prb}$ as follows. $g \underleftrightarrow{}_{prb} h$ if there is a probabilistic branching bisimulation $(R, \tilde{R})$ between g and h such that $\{root(g), root(h)\}$ is an R equivalence class and if $root(g) \rightsquigarrow s$ then there is t such that $root(h) \rightsquigarrow t$ and $(s, t) \in R$, and vice versa. We say that g and h are probabilistically rooted branching bisimilar. *The condition above is called* probabilistic rooted branching condition.

From now on, instead of $Prob_{[p]_R}(p, \tau^*, C)$ and $Prob_{[p]_R}(p, \tau^* a, C)$ we will write $Prob_R(p, \tau^*, C)$ and $Prob_R(p, \tau^* a, C)$, respectively. (From $Prob_R(p, \tau^*, C)$ it is clear that $[p]_R$ is the subscript set in the original notation.) Even if $[p]_{\tilde{R}}$ is not a $NextEntry$ class for p, we still take $Prob_{[p]_R}(p, \tau^*, [p]_{\tilde{R}}) = 1$.

Example 1. Let g and h be fully probabilistic graphs given in Figure 3. We define the following equivalence relation: $R = \{\{1, 2, 3, 4, 5\}, \{6, 8\}, \{7, 9\}, \{NIL\}\}$ Then $Entry_R(g \cup h) = \{1, 3, NIL\}$ and we define $\tilde{R} = \{\{1, 3\}, \{NIL\}\}$.

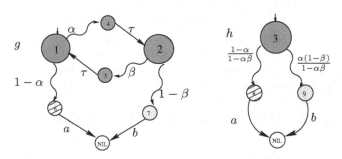

Fig. 3. Bisimilar graphs from example 1.

Probabilities of these entries to the $\tilde{R}$ equivalence classes are given in the following table. In the table we put $-$ in the (r, C) field if $C \notin NextEntryC_{\tilde{R}}(r)$. We omit the row of the NIL entry.

τ^*	$\{1,3\}$	$\{NIL\}$	τ^*a	$\{1,3\}$	$\{NIL\}$	τ^*b	$\{1,3\}$	$\{NIL\}$
1	1	0	1	$-$	$\frac{1-\alpha}{1-\alpha\beta}$	1	$-$	$\frac{\alpha(1-\beta)}{1-\alpha\beta}$
3	1	0	3	$-$	$\frac{1-\alpha}{1-\alpha\beta}$	3	$-$	$\frac{\alpha(1-\beta)}{1-\alpha\beta}$

Thus, $(R, \tilde{R})$ is a probabilistic branching bisimulation between g and h. □

Example 2. The following example shows that the root condition as it is given is sufficient.

Let g and h be graphs given in Figure 4. R=$\{\{1,3\},\{2,4,5,6\},\{NIL\}\}$ is a rooted branching bisimulation between g and h (it is the only one). But $NextEntry_R(1) = \{2\}$ and $NextEntry_R(3) = \{NIL\}$ from which we conclude that $\tilde{R}$ cannot be defined, that is, a probabilistic branching bisimulation between g and h does not exist. □

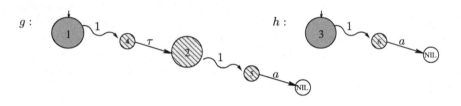

Fig. 4. Bisimilar graphs from example 2.

Example 3. Let g and h be graphs given in Figure 5. We define the following relation: $R = \{\{1,2,4,6,8,9\}, \{3,5,7,12,15,18\}, \{10,13,16\}, \{11,14,17\}\}$. Then

r	1	3	2	4	5	6	7
$Exit_R(r)$	10, 11	12	10, 11	13, 14	15	16, 17	18
$NextEntry_R(r)$	3	2	3	5	6	7	6

$Entry_R(g \cup h) = \{1,2,3,4,5,6,7\}$. If we take $\tilde{R}_0 = \{\{1,2,4,6\},\{3,5,7\}\}$, then, for instance, 1 and 2 do not have same probabilities, which means $(R, \tilde{R}_0)$ is not probabilistic branching bisimulation between g and h. But if we refine classes of $\tilde{R}_0$ into $\tilde{R}_1$ in the following way: $\tilde{R}_1 = \{\{1,4\},\{2,6\},\{3,5,7\}\}$, then it is easy to check that $\tilde{R}_1$ satisfies the third requirement in Definition 10. We conclude that $(R, \tilde{R}_1)$ is a probabilistic branching bisimulation between g and h. □

Proposition 2. *Let g be a fully probabilistic graph. Then $g \underline{\leftrightarrow}_{prb} \rho(g)$.* □

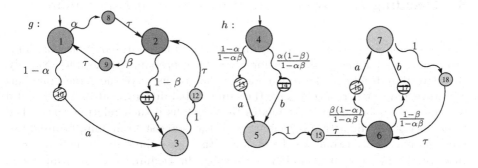

Fig. 5. Bisimilar graphs from example 3.

Proposition 3. *Let* $(R, \tilde{R})$ *be a probabilistic branching bisimulation between* g *and* h. *If* $p, q \in S_g \cup S_h$ *and* $(p, q) \in \tilde{R}$, $NextEntryC_{\tilde{R}}(p) = NextEntryC_{\tilde{R}}(q)$.   □

Corollary 1. *Let* $(R, \tilde{R})$ *be a probabilistic branching bisimulation between* g *and* h. *If* $p \in Entry_R(g)$ *then there is a node* q *in* h *such that* $(p, q) \in \tilde{R}$.   □

Proposition 4. *If* R *is an equivalence relation on the fully probabilistic graph* g *and if* C *is an* R *equivalence class containing a probabilistic node then there is an entry node in* C.   □

Using the results from the previous propositions, the Congruence theorem can be proved.

Theorem 1. $\underleftrightarrow{}_{prb}$ *is a congruence relation on* **G** *with respect to the probabilistic choice operator, the sequential composition and the abstraction operator.*

Proof. The proof about the abstraction operator is based on the relation between the set of entries in the original graph and the one obtained with abstraction. Namely, the second set is a subset of the first set. Having this in mind, a relation between probabilities of the entries in the two graphs can be established. (For more details see [4].) For the two other operators it is not difficult to construct a probabilistic bisimulation relation on composed graph from already existing relations on the components (in that composition). Namely, for the sequential composition the only interesting detail is the merging the NIL equivalence class from the first component with the equivalence class of the root of the second component. Two cases occur depending on NIL being an entry or not in the first graph. The part concerning the probabilistic choice operator can easily be proved.   □

Theorem 2 (Soundness theorem). **G**/ $\underleftrightarrow{}_{prb}$ *is a model of the presented fully probabilistic process algebra with the verification rules* $PVR1$, $PVR2$,....   □

3   Deciding the Branc hing Bisim ulation Equivalence

In this section we present an algorithm that computes a probabilistic branc hing bisimulation equivalence relation for given fully probabilistic graphs. Namely, the algorithm decides if the root nodes of the graphs have the same branching structure and, further, if they have the same probability measures. At the end it returns a pair of relations that relates these graphs if such relations exist. The basic idea of the algorithm is to start with the coarsest branching bisimulation relation that relates two nodes if and only if they have the same branching struc-ture, regardless of their probability measures. In Definition 10 one can notice that probabilistic transitions in the part which concerns the branching structure (items 0, 1 and 2) can be viewed as internal transitions. This gives us liberty to employ any algorithm that decides branching bisimulation on non-probabilistic systems. In particular, here we use the algorithm for deciding branching bisimu-lation equivalence in [10]. The original algorithm is defined on one graph in which case the output is the coarsest branching bisimulation on that graph, since it always exists. The algorithm can slightly be modified into an algorithm that works on a union of two graphs (which is what we need). In this case ($Step1$) the output is either the branching bisimulation equivalence relation R between the two graphs with roots $root_1$ and $root_2$, and it is the input of the second part of the algorithm; or it has found that the two graphs are not branching bisimilar (the root nodes are not R-related) and it returns the empty relation meaning that two graphs are not branching bisimilar. In the latter case the given graphs are not probabilistically branching bisimilar as well ($Step2$). Before the second part is run, the set of entries w.r.t. R is calculated ($Step3$). The second part of the algorithm concerns probabilities. Starting from the R equivalence classes restricted on the entries as the initial value for $\tilde{R}$ ($Step4$, where BB is the partition induced by R), the algorithm refines the $\tilde{R}$ equivalence classes by comparing the probability measures for the nodes belonging to the same class ($Step5$). If it has been found that two or more nodes from the same equiv alence class have different probabilities, then it is split into separate subclasses. Finally, if it has been detected that the roots have been split apart then the algorithm terminates ($Step6$) with the conclusion that the two graphs are not probabilis-tically bisimilar (returning the pair $(\emptyset, \emptyset)$). Otherwise, the algorithm returns the pair of relations that makes graphs g and h probabilistically branching bisimilar ($Step7$). The crucial point here is the definition of a *splitter*. (Note: many algo-rithms concerning bisim ulation are based on a notion of a splitter defined in an appropriate way for that particular relation.)

Definition 11. *Let g be a fully probabilistic graph and R an equivalence relation on g. Let $\tilde{R}$ be an equivalence relation that is a subset of R. And let Π be the par-tition induced by $\tilde{R}$. A pair (a, C) for $a \in A_\tau$ and $C \in \Pi$ is a splitter of Π if for some $E \in \Pi$ and $p, p' \in E$, if $C \in NextEntryC_\Pi(p)$ or $C \in NextEntryC_\Pi(p')$ then*

$$Prob_R(p, \tau^*a, C) \neq Prob_R(p', \tau^*a, C).$$

Thus a splitter (a, C) of a partition Π indicates a class in Π such that contains states which prevent (R, Π) from being a probabilistic branching bisimulation. Moreover, it indicates that partition Π has to be refined to Π' in such a way that (a, C) is not a splitter of Π'. And thus, we split the set of entries in finer classes, subsets of corresponding R classes, until we obtain a partition (the $\tilde{R}$ relation) that meets the third requirement in Definition 10. Formally,

Definition 12. *Let g, R and Π be defined like in the previous definition and let (a, C) be a splitter of Π. If $E \in \Pi$ we define a refinement of E w.r.t. (a, C), $Refine(E, a, C)$, in the following way:*
$$Refine(E, a, C) = \{E_n \ : \ n \in N\},$$
for some set of indices N such that
 1. $\{E_n \ : \ n \in N\}$ *is a partition of E and*
 2. $\forall n \in N : \forall s, t \in E_n : Prob_R(s, \tau^*a, C) = Prob_R(t, \tau^*a, C)$.
The refinement of Π w.r.t. splitter (a, C) is:

$$Refine(\Pi, a, C) = \bigcup_{E \in \Pi} Refine(E, a, C).$$

The probabilities $Prob_R(p, \tau^*a, C)$ can be computed by solving the linear equation system (see e.g. [8,9])

$$
\begin{aligned}
x_p &= 1 && \text{if } a = \tau \text{ and } p \in C \\
x_p &= 0 && \text{if } Path_{full,[p]_R}(p, \tau^*a, C) = \emptyset \\
x_p &= \sum_{t \in [p]_R} \mathbf{P}(p, \tau, t) \cdot x_t + \mathbf{P}(p, a, C) && \text{otherwise}
\end{aligned}
$$

The algorithm is given step-by-step in Figure 6. The input is given as a union of two graphs g and h with roots: $root_1$ and $root_2$, respectively.

Input :	finite fully probabilistic graphs g and h with $(S, \rightsquigarrow, \rightarrow, \mu, root_1, root_2)$
Output :	(R, Π) probabilistic branching bisimulation between g and h if it exists
	$(\emptyset, \emptyset)$ if g and h are not probabilistically branching bisimilar
Method :	
Step1 :	Call the coarsest branching bisimulation relation algorithm for the graphs g and h, and receive R;
Step2 :	If $R = \emptyset$ then Return $(\emptyset, \emptyset)$;
Step3 :	Compute the sets: $Entry_R$, $NextEntry_R(r)$;
Step4 :	$\Pi := \{E \cap Entry_R \ : \ E \in BB\} \setminus \{\emptyset\}$;
Step5 :	While Π contains a splitter (a, C) do $\Pi := Refine(\Pi, a, C)$;
Step6 :	If $root_1$ and $root_2$ are not Π-related then Return $(\emptyset, \emptyset)$;
Step7 :	Return (R, Π).

Fig. 6. Algorithm for computing probabilistic branching bisimulation.

Lemma 2. *The algorithm can be implemented in polynomial time in the number of states n.*

Proof. Let g and h be finite fully probabilistic graphs with n states and m transitions (total number of states and transitions for both graphs).

For the first part of the algorithm, finding the coarsest bisimulation relation we use the algorithm in [10] which has time complexity $\mathcal{O}(n \cdot m)$. In this step the probabilistic transitions are treated as internal transitions. The set of entries with respect to R can be found with a depth first search with the algorithm in [1] (with time complexity $\mathcal{O}(m)$).

The second part of the algorithm consists of solving the system of linear equations and refining the current partition with respect to a found splitter. The test whether $Path_{ful,[p]_R}(p, \tau^* a, C) = \emptyset$ can be done by a reachability analysis of the underlying directed graph. In the worst case we have to repeat the refinement step n times. And in each of them we have to solve a system of linear equations with n variables and n equations which takes $\mathcal{O}(n^{2.8})$ time with the method in [1]. Thus we obtain the time complexity of the second part of the algorithm to be in the worst case $\mathcal{O}(n^{3.8})$.

In total since $m \leq n^2 \cdot |A_\tau|$ we obtain $\mathcal{O}(n^{3.8})$ time complexity of the algorithm. □

4   Conclusion

In this paper we presented a version of fully probabilistic process algebra with abstraction which contains, in addition to the axioms for the basic operators, a set of verification rules. These rules tie in successfully the idea of abstraction in process algebra with the results from Markov chain analysis. Furthermore, we proposed a probabilistic branching bisimulation relation which corresponds to this process algebra in the sense that it gives a model for it. In such a way we obtain a model for the verification rules. One of the advantages of having such rules is that they give the probability distribution after abstraction from the internal actions, which in the model (i.e. using the bisimulation relation) should be calculated separately.

Due to the absence of non-determinism in the algebra we did not incorporate parallel composition since the model that we had used for parallel composition in the previous work requires non-determinism. Nevertheless the process algebra proposed in this paper can be widely applied. Namely, in [2,3] one can find examples of protocols for which the protocol specification does not contain non-determinism. Thus, the techniques from this paper can be applied to these specifications for the verification part, that is, for proving that these protocols behave with probability 1 as a one place buffer. Moreover, the way we presented the definitions in the paper left room for an extension with non-determinism. For example, the definition of the bisimulation relation is given for the alternating model which essentially includes non-determinism. Thus, we think that this work is good start for obtaining a probabilistic branching bisimulation relation for probabilistic processes that contain non-determinism.

References

1. A. Aho, J. Hopcroft, J. Ullman, *The design and analysis of computer algorithms*, Addison-Wesley Publishing Company, 1974.
2. S. Andova, *Process algebra with probabilistic choice (extended abstract)*, Proc. ARTS'99, Bamberg, Germany, J.-P. Katoen, ed., LNCS 1601, Springer-Verlag, pp. 111-129, 1999. Full version report CSR 99-12, Eindhoven University of Technology, 1999.
3. S. Andova, *Process algebra with interleaving probabilistic parallel composition*, Eindhoven University of Technology, CSR 99-04, 1999.
4. S. Andova, J.C.M. Baeten, *Abstraction in probabilistic process algebra (extended abstract)*, http://www.win.tue.nl/~suzana.
5. J.C.M. Baeten, J.A. Bergstra, J.W. Klop, *On the consistency of Koomen's fair abstraction rule*, Theor. Comp. Sci. 51, pp.129-176, 1987.
6. J.C.M. Baeten, J.A. Bergstra, S.A. Smolka, *Axiomatizing probabilistic processes: ACP with generative probabilities*, Information and Computation 121(2), pp. 234-255, Sep. 1995.
7. J.C.M. Baeten, W. P. Weijland, *Process algebra*, Cambridge University Press, 1990.
8. C. Baier, *On algorithmic verification methods for probabilistic systems*, Habilitation thesis, Univ. Mannheim, 1998.
9. C. Baier, H. Hermanns, *Weak bisimulation for fully probabilistic processes*, Proc. CAV'97, LNCS 1254, pp. 119-130, 1997.
10. J.F. Groote, F. Vaandrager, *An efficient algorithm for branching bisimulation and stuttering equivalence*, Proc. ICALP'90, LNCS 443, pp. 626-638, 1990.
11. C.-C. Jou, *Aspects of probabilistic process algebra*, Ph.D.Thesis, State University of New York at Stony Brook, 1990.

First Passage Time Analysis of Stochastic Process Algebra Using Partial Orders

Theo C. Ruys[1], Rom Langerak[1], Joost-Pieter Katoen[1],
Diego Latella[2], and Mieke Massink[2]

[1] University of Twente, Department of Computer Science.
PO Box 217, 7500 AE Enschede, The Netherlands.
{ruys,langerak,katoen}@cs.utwente.nl
[2] Consiglio Nazionale delle Ricerche, Istituto CNUCE.
Via Alfieri 1, S. Cataldo, Pisa, Italy.
{d.latella,m.massink}@cnuce.cnr.it

Abstract This paper proposes a partial-order semantics for a stochastic process algebra that supports general (non-memoryless) distributions and combines this with an approach to numerically analyse the first passage time of an event. Based on an adaptation of McMillan's complete finite prefix approach tailored to event structures and process algebra, finite representations are obtained for recursive processes. The behaviour between two events is now captured by a partial order that is mapped on a stochastic task graph, a structure amenable to numerical analysis. Our approach is supported by the (new) tool FOREST for generating the complete prefix and the (existing) tool PEPP for analysing the generated task graph. As a case study, the delay of the first resolution in the root contention phase of the IEEE 1394 serial bus protocol is analysed.

1 Introduction

In the classical view of system design, two main activities are distinguished: performance evaluation and validation of correctness. Performance evaluation studies the performance of the system in terms like access time, waiting time and throughput, whereas validation concentrates on the functional behaviour of the system in terms of e.g. safety and liveness properties. With the advent of embedded and multi-media communication systems, however, insight in both the functional and the real-time and performance aspects of applications involved becomes of critical importance. The seperation of these issues does not make sense anymore.

As a result, performance aspects have been integrated in various specification formalisms. A prominent example is stochastic process algebra in which features like compositionality and abstraction are exploited to facilitate the modular specification of performance models. Most of these formalisms, however, restrict delays to be governed by negative exponential distributions. The interleaving

T. Margaria and W. Yi (Eds.): TACAS 2001, LNCS 2031, pp. 220–235, 2001.

semantics typically results in a mapping onto continuous-time Markov chains (CTMC) [1,13,19], a model for which various efficient evaluation algorithms exist to determine (transient and stationary) state-based measures. Although this approach has brought various interesting results, tools, and case studies, the state space explosion problem – in interleaving semantics parallelism leads to the product of the component state spaces – is a serious drawback. Besides that, the restriction to exponential distributions is often not realistic for adequately modelling phenomena such as traffic sources or sizes of data files stored on web-servers that exhibit bursty heavy-tail distributions.

This paper proposes a partial-order semantics for a stochastic process algebra with general (continuous) distributions and combines this with techniques to compute the mean delay between a pair of events. The semantics is based on event structures [28], a well-studied partial-order model for process algebras. These models are less affected by the state space explosion problem as parallelism leads to the sum of the components state spaces rather than to their product. Moreover, these models are amenable to extensions with stochastic information [4]. A typical problem with event structures though is that recursion leads to infinite structures, whereas for performance analysis finite representations are usually of vital importance[1]. To overcome this problem we use McMillan's complete finite prefix approach [26]. This technique, originally developed for 1-safe Petri nets and recently adapted to process algebra [24], constructs an initial part of the infinite semantic object that contains all information on reachable states and transitions.

In our stochastic process algebra the advance of (probabilistic) time and the occurrence of actions is separated. This separation of discrete and continuous phases is similar to that in many timed process algebras and has been recently proposed in the stochastic setting [16,17]. Most recent proposals for incorporating general distributions into process algebra follow this approach [3,6]. As a result of this separation, interaction gets an intuitive meaning – "wait for the slowest process" – with a clear stochastic interpretation. Moreover, abstraction of actions becomes possible. We will show that due to this separation the complete finite prefix approach for process algebra [24] can be easily exploited. We use the prototype tool FOREST to automatically generate a complete finite prefix from a (stochastic) process algebraic specification.

From the finite prefixes we generate so-called stochastic task graphs, acyclic directed graphs where nodes represent tasks of which the delay is represented by a random variable and arcs denote causal dependencies between tasks. Efficient numerical analysis techniques exist for task graphs, and have been implemented. For series-parallel graphs numerical results are exact and algorithms exist to compute the distribution of the delay between a start and finish task. For arbitrary graphs various approximate techniques exist to compute (rather exact) bounds on the mean delay [21]. We use the PEPP tool suite [8,15] to analyse the task graphs generated from the complete prefixes.

---

[1] Apart from discrete-event simulation techniques and analysis techniques for regular structures (such as birth-death processes), that we do not consider here.

Most attempts to incorporate general distributions in process algebra aim at discrete-event simulation techniques [3,6,14]. To the best of our knowledge, this paper presents the first approach to analyse stochastic process algebraic specifications that may contain general distributions in a numerical manner.

The applicability of our approach is illustrated by analysing the root contention phase within the IEEE 1394 serial bus protocol [20]. In particular, we analyse the distribution of the delay between the detection of a root contention and its first resolution.

The paper is organised as follows. In Sect. 2 we present a stochastic process algebra with general distributions. In Sect. 3 we show how to obtain annotated partial orders using the FOREST tool for finite prefixes. In Sect. 4 we discuss how these partial orders can be seen as task graphs that can be analysed with the tool PEPP. In Sect. 5 we show how to combine FOREST and PEPP in order to perform a mean delay analysis of events after a specific state. Sect. 6 contains an application to the IEEE 1394 protocol, and Sect. 7 is devoted to conclusions and further work. An extended version of this paper can be found in [31].

2   A Stochastic Process Algebra

Let Act be a set of actions, $a \in Act$, $A \subset Act$, and F, G be *general* continuous probability distributions. The distinction between observable and invisible actions plays no role in this paper. The stochastic process algebra used here is a simple process algebra that contains two types of prefix processes: process $a; B$ (*action prefix*) that is able to immediately offer action a while evolving into B, and $\langle F \rangle; B$ (*timed prefix*) that evolves into process B after a delay governed by the continuous distribution F. That is, the probability that $\langle F \rangle; B$ evolves into B before t time units is $F(t)$. In the sequel such actions are called *delay* actions. The syntax of our language is given by the following grammar:

$$B ::= \text{stop} \mid a; B \mid \langle F \rangle; B \mid B + B \mid B \parallel_A B \mid \text{P}$$

The *inaction* process stop cannot do anything. The *choice* between B_1 and B_2 is denoted by $B_1 + B_2$. *Parallel composition* is denoted by $B_1 \parallel_A B_2$ where A is the set of synchronizing actions; $B_1 \parallel_\varnothing B_2$ is abbreviated to $B_1 \parallel\mid B_2$. Processes cannot synchronise on delay actions. The semantics of the parallel operator $\parallel_A$ follows the semantics of the parallel operator of LOTOS [2] and thus allows for multi-way synchronisation. Finally, P denotes *process instantiation* where a behaviour expression is assumed to be in the context of a set of process definitions of the form $\text{P} := B$ with B possibly containing process instantiations of P. In this paper, we assume that a process algebra expression has a finite number of reachable states.

A few words on $B_1 + B_2$ are in order. $B_1 + B_2$ behaves either as B_1 or B_2, but not as both. At execution the fastest process, i.e., the process that is enabled first, is selected. This is known as the race condition. If this fastest process is not uniquely determined, a non-deterministic selection among the fastest processes is made.

Example 1. In the rest of this paper we use the following stochastic process algebra expression as a running example:

$$B_{ex} := (a;\ \langle G \rangle;\ d;\ \text{stop}\ \|_{a,d}\ a;\ \langle F_1 \rangle;\ c;\ \langle F_2 \rangle;\ d;\ \text{stop})\ \|_c\ b;\ c;\ \text{stop}$$

3   Partial Orders, Finite Prefixes and FOREST

In [25,26], McMillan presents an algorithm that, for a given 1-safe Petri net, constructs an initial part of its occurrence net called *unfolding* or maximal branching process [9,28]. The so-called *complete finite prefix* of the occurrence net contains all information on reachable states and transitions. An important optimisation of the algorithm has been defined in [11]. This complete finite prefix can be used as the basis for model checking [10,34].

In [24], Langerak and Brinksma adopt the complete finite prefix approach for process algebra for a model similar to occurrence nets called *condition event structures*. In doing so, they have given an event structure semantics to process algebra. In this section, we briefly recall some definitions of [11] and [24] that are needed for the remainder of this paper. We show how to obtain partial orders from local configurations. Finally, we introduce FOREST, a prototype tool which is based on the results of [24].

Conditions and Events. A process algebra expression can be decomposed into so-called conditions, which are action prefix expressions together with information about the synchronisation context [29]. A *condition* C is defined by

$$C ::=\ \text{stop}\ \big|\ a; B\ \big|\ \langle F \rangle; B\ \big|\ C\|_A\ \big|\ \|_A C$$

where B is a process algebra expression. Intuitively, a condition of the form $C\|_A$ means that C is the left operand of a parallel operator with action set A. Similarly, a condition of the form $\|_A C$ means that C is the right operand of a parallel operator with action set C. For the construction of the complete finite prefix, the distinction between action prefix conditions and time prefix conditions plays no role; in the sequel both prefix conditions will be represented by the expression $a; B$.

A *condition event structure* is a 4-tuple $(\mathbb{C}, \mathbb{E}, \bowtie, \prec)$ with $\mathbb{C}$ a set of conditions, $\mathbb{E} = \mathbb{E}_{act} \cup \mathbb{E}_{delay}$ a set of events, $\bowtie \subset \mathbb{C} \times \mathbb{C}$, the choice relation (symmetric and irreflexive), and $\prec \subseteq (\mathbb{C} \times \mathbb{E}) \cup (\mathbb{E} \times \mathbb{C})$ the *flow* relation. The set $\mathbb{E}_{act}$ is the set of action events and $\mathbb{E}_{delay}$ is the set of delay events. Let E be a set of events, then the function $delay(E)$ returns the delay events of E, i.e. $delay(E) = \{e \in E \mid e \in \mathbb{E}_{delay}\}$. Condition event structures are closely related to Petri nets; the conditions correspond to places whereas the events correspond to transitions. In [24], actions and process instantiations are labelled with unique indices. These indices are used to create unique event identifiers. Furthermore, these indices are used to efficiently compute the finite prefix. For this paper, these indices and identifiers are not important, and therefore omitted.

States. A *state* is a tuple (S, R) with $S \subseteq \mathbb{C}$ a set of conditions, and $R \subseteq S \times S$, an irreflexive and symmetric relation between conditions called the choice relation: $R \subseteq \bowtie$. A state (S, R) corresponds to a 'global state' of the system; for each process in the system it stores the possible next condition(s). In fact, a state can always be represented by a process algebra expression. Conditions and their choice relations can be obtained by decomposing a process algebra expression. The decomposition function *dec*, which maps a process algebra expression B onto a state, is recursively defined by $dec(B) = (S(B), R(B))$ with

$$
\begin{aligned}
dec(\mathsf{stop}) &= (\{\mathsf{stop}\}, \varnothing) \\
dec(a; B) &= (\{a; B\}, \varnothing) \\
dec(B_1 \parallel_A B_2) &= (S(B_1) \parallel_A \cup \parallel_A S(B_2),\ R(B_1) \parallel_A \cup \parallel_A R(B_2)) \\
dec(B_1 + B_2) &= (S(B_1) \cup S(B_2),\ R(B_1) \cup R(B_2) \cup (S(B_1) \times S(B_2))) \\
dec(\mathsf{P}) &= dec(B) \text{ if } \mathsf{P} := B
\end{aligned}
$$

In [24] it is shown how this decomposition function can be used to construct a derivation system for condition event transitions (i.e. the $\prec$ relation).

Configurations. Let $(\mathbb{C}, \mathbb{E}, \bowtie, \prec)$ be a condition event structure. We adopt some Petri net terminology: a *marking* is a set of conditions. A *node* is either a condition or an event. The *preset* of a node n, denoted by $\bullet n$, is defined by $\bullet n = \{m \in \mathbb{C} \cup \mathbb{E} \mid m \prec n\}$, and the *postset* $n\bullet$ by $n\bullet = \{m \in \mathbb{C} \cup \mathbb{E} \mid n \prec m\}$. The *initial marking* M_0 is defined by $M_0 = \{c \in \mathbb{C} \mid \bullet c = \varnothing\}$. An event e is *enabled* in a marking M if $\bullet e \subseteq M$. Let M be a marking, then we define the function $enabled(M)$ as follows: $enabled(M) = \{e \in \mathbb{E} \mid \bullet e \subseteq M\}$.

The transitive and reflexive closure of the flow relation $\prec$ is denoted by $\leq$. The *conflict* relation on nodes, denoted by $\#$, is defined as follows: let n_1 and n_2 be two different nodes, then $n_1 \# n_2$ iff there are two distinct nodes m_1 and m_2, such that $m_1 \leq n_1$ and $m_2 \leq n_2$, with either (i) m_1 and m_2 are two conditions in the choice relation, i.e. $m_1 \bowtie m_2$, or (ii) m_1 and m_2 are two events with $\bullet m_1 \cap \bullet m_2 \neq \varnothing$. Two nodes n_1 and n_2 are said to be *independent*, notation $n_1 \asymp n_2$, iff $\neg(n_1 \leq n_2) \wedge \neg(n_2 \leq n_1) \wedge \neg(n_1 \bowtie n_2)$.

Let c be a condition, then we define $\bowtie(c)$ to be the set of conditions in choice with c, i.e. $\bowtie(c) = \{c' \in \mathbb{C} \mid c \bowtie c'\}$. Similarly for a set of conditions C: $\bowtie(C) = \{c' \in \mathbb{C} \mid \exists c \in C : c \bowtie c'\}$. For an event $e \in \mathbb{E}$, and M and M' markings, there is an *event transition* $M \xrightarrow{e} M'$ iff $\bullet e \subseteq M$ and $M' = (M \cup e\bullet) \setminus (\bullet e \cup \bowtie(\bullet e))$. An *event sequence* is a sequence of events $e_1 \ldots e_n$ such that there are markings $M_1, \ldots, M_n$ with $M_0 \xrightarrow{e_1} M_1 \longrightarrow \ldots \xrightarrow{e_n} M_n$.

We call $E_{conf} = \{e_1, \ldots, e_n\}$ a *configuration* of the condition event structure. A configuration E_{conf} must be conflict-free and backward closed with respect to the $\leq$ relation. For an event $e \in \mathbb{E}$, the *local configuration* $[e]$ is defined by $[e] = \{e' \in \mathbb{E} \mid e' \leq e\}$. The causal ordering $\leq$ restricted to $\mathbb{E} \times \mathbb{E}$ induces a *partial order* over a local configuration $[e]$ (see [22,28,30]).

A *cut* is a marking M which is maximal w.r.t. set inclusion and such that for each pair of different conditions c and c' in M the following holds: $c \asymp c'$ or $c \bowtie c'$. It can be shown [24] that each configuration corresponds to a cut which can be uniquely associated to a state. The state corresponding to the cut of a configuration E_{conf} is denoted by $State(E_{conf})$.

Unfolding. In [24], Langerak and Brinksma present an algorithm to *unfold* a process algebra expression B into a condition event structure $Unf(B)$. The representation $Unf(B)$ may be infinite for recursive processes. In order to overcome this problem they adopted McMillan's approach to compute the so-called *complete finite prefix* of a Petri net unfolding to the setting of condition event structures. The finite prefix algorithm is based on a partial order relation $\sqsubset$, called an *adequate order*. This relation is defined on finite configurations of $Unf(B)$. This adequate order $\sqsubset$ is used to identify so-called *cut-off* events which do not introduce new global states. An event e is a *cut-off event* if $Unf(B)$ contains a local configuration $[e_0]$ such that (i) $State([e]) = State([e_0])$ and (ii) $[e_0] \sqsubset [e]$. So, a cut-off event is an event of which the marking corresponds to a global state which has already been identified 'earlier' in the unfolding. Conceptually a finite prefix is obtained by taking an unfolding $Unf(B)$ and cutting away all successor nodes of cut-off events. It is clear that the finite prefix depends on the adequate order $\sqsubset$ used to compare configurations. Furthermore, the complete finite prefix approach only works for finite state processes, i.e. processes with a finite number of reachable states. In this paper we adopt the adequate order of [24]. The complete finite prefix corresponding with this adequate order is denoted by $FP(B)$.

Example 2. Fig. 1 shows the condition event structure of the unfolding $Unf(B_{ex})$ of the process algebra expression B_{ex}. As the process algebra expression B_{ex} does not contain process recursion, the unfolding $Unf(B_{ex})$ is already finite by itself. Conditions are represented by circles and events are depicted by squares. The initial marking M_0 is represented by the three conditions at the top of Fig. 1. The local configuration of event c is $[c] = \{a, \langle F_1 \rangle, b, c\}$. The state of configuration $[c]$ is formally represented by $State([c]) = (\{\langle G \rangle; d; \mathsf{stop} \|_{a,d} c, \|_{a,d} \langle F_2 \rangle; d; \mathsf{stop} \|_c, \|_c \mathsf{stop}\}, \varnothing)$. The process algebra expression corresponding with $State([c])$ is $(\langle G \rangle; d; \mathsf{stop} \|_{a,d} \langle F_2 \rangle; d; \mathsf{stop}) \|_c \mathsf{stop}$. The local configuration of event d is $[d] = \{a, b, \langle G \rangle, \langle F_1 \rangle, c, \langle F_2 \rangle, d\}$. The state of configuration $[d]$ is represented by the three leaf conditions. The partial order of the events within $[d]$ is induced by the flow relation $\prec$ which is depicted by the arrows between the conditions and events.

FOREST. FOREST[2][31] is a prototype tool that is based on the unfolding and finite prefix algorithms of [24]. Given a process algebra expression B (with a finite number of reachable states), FOREST computes the corresponding complete finite prefix $FP(B)$ as a condition event structure. The tool allows to use McMillan's original adequate ordering or the adequate ordering defined in [24]. FOREST is used as a prototype tool to experiment with several aspects of the unfolding algorithm, like alternative adequate orderings, independence algorithms, cut-off

---

[2] FOREST stands for "a tool <u>for</u> <u>e</u>vent <u>st</u>ructures".

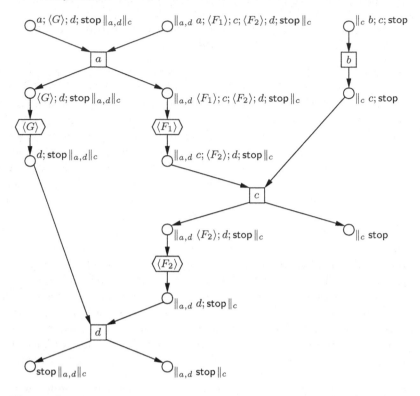

Fig. 1. Condition event structure of the unfolding $Unf(B_{ex})$.

criteria, etc. For these experimental purposes, FOREST can either export the finite prefix $FP(B)$ to a textual representation or to a format suitable as input for graph drawing tools like vcg [32] or dot [12]. Future additions to FOREST will include an interactive visual simulator and a model checking module. FOREST has been implemented in C++ (4000 lines of code) and the development took roughly eight man months.

This section has only briefly addressed the construction of the complete finite prefix $FP(B)$ of a process algebra expression B. For the remainder of this paper, the most important aspect of the unfolding algorithm is that the construction of the condition event structure induces a partial order on the events of a (local) configuration. FOREST can be used to compute such partial orders.

4   Task Graph Analysis and PEPP

The tool PEPP[3] has been developed at the University of Erlangen [8,15] in the early nineties of the previous century. The tool has a broad functionality, amongst which program instrumentation, monitoring (using the hardware

---

[3] PEPP stands for "Performance Evaluation of Parallel Programs".

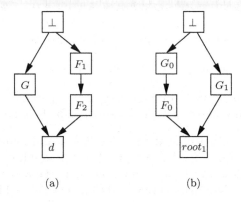

(a)   (b)

Fig. 2. Task graphs of (a) the local configuration of event d of the running example B_{ex} and (b) the local configuration of event $root_1$ of the root contention protocol (discussed in Sect. 6).

monitor ZM4) and trace analysis. In this paper, we only use the following functionality of PEPP: (i) the creation of task graphs and (ii) the automatic analysis of task graphs.

Task graphs consist of nodes connected by directed edges. Nodes, which represent tasks to be executed, can be of several types (e.g. hierarchical, cyclic and parallel nodes) but here we will only use so-called *elementary* nodes that model activities taking a certain amount of time, i.e. delay actions. The time that an activity or task takes is governed by a continuous distribution function. The dependency between tasks is modelled by the directed edges between the nodes.

PEPP supports several built-in distribution functions, like deterministic, exponential, approximate, and mixed Erlang distributions, the parameters of which can be chosen by the user. It is also possible to use general distributions in a numerical form, that can either be created by the user or by the additional tool CAPP[4] [27]. A numerical representation of a distribution is given by a text file containing the offset of the density function, the step size and the density values for each step. CAPP also allows the graphical representation of distribution and density functions. Nodes can be created interactively by the user via a graphical interface. Nodes can be connected by edges representing causal dependencies. These dependencies are required to be acyclic and the resulting graph is called a task graph. In fact a task graph can be seen as a partial ordering of nodes.

Example 3. Suppose we are interested in the running time of event d of B_{ex}, starting from the initial state. If we only consider the delay actions and the causal dependencies of $Unf(B_{ex})$ of Fig. 1, we obtain the task graph of Fig. 2 (a).

Analysis of task graphs. After a task graph has been input to PEPP, the run time distribution of the model can be analysed in several ways. The most attractive mode of analysis is via SPASS[5]. In order to analyse a task graph

---
[4] CAPP stands for "Calculation and Presentation Package".
[5] SPASS stands for "Series Parallel Structure Solver".

using SPASS it has to be in *series-parallel* reducible form. This means it can be reduced to a single node by successively applying two reduction steps:

- *Series reduction:* in this reduction step a sequence of nodes is reduced to a single node.
- *Parallel reduction:* in this reduction step several parallel nodes with the same predecessors and successors are reduced to a single node.

SPASS analysis is an exact type of analysis; the SPASS reductions preserve the performance analysis aspects. A series-parallel task graph is reduced by SPASS to a single node with a distribution that represents the first passage time of the complete task graph. This distribution function is calculated in a numerical way and can be visualised (together with its corresponding density function) using CAPP.

If a task graph is not series-parallel reducible it can be analysed using several well-known approximate (bounding) methods [15,21]. The basic idea behind these approximations is that nodes are added or deleted until the task graph becomes series-parallel reducible. This leads to upper and lower bounds of the first passage time of the task graph. PEPP offers several of these bounding techniques.

It is also possible to approximate the analysis by transforming the task graph into an interleaving transition system, and approximating the distributions by deterministic and exponential distributions. This approximation suffers heavily from state space explosion problems and does not exploit the advantages of the partial order properties; for these reasons this analysis method has not been used in this paper.

PEPP is a powerful analysis tool for stochastic task graphs. For simple examples these task graphs can easily be created in a manual way. For realistic system designs, though, developing task graphs in a direct way becomes more and more cumbersome and error prone. An effective solution to this problem, as first recognised by Herzog in [18], is to automatically generate task graphs in a compositional manner from a stochastic process algebra specification. While [18] reveals some problems in using task graphs as a semantic model for (non-recursive) stochastic process algebras, our approach – that is aimed at recursive processes – is to generate task graphs from a finite event structure semantics.

5   First Passage Time Analysis

In Sect. 3, we discussed how a partial order of events of a local configuration $[e]$ can be obtained from a finite prefix $FP(B)$ of an unfolding. In this section we discuss how the partial orders generated by FOREST can be used for first passage time analysis with PEPP.

Algorithm 1 constructs a task graph of the local configuration of an event e starting from the initial state of a process algebra expression. With PEPP we can compute the first passage time of event e to occur (starting from the initial state). If the partial order of $[e]$ happens to be series-parallel reducible, PEPP will even compute the distribution function of the runtime.

Algorithm 1. Construct the task graph for $[e]$ starting from the initial state of B.

1. Specify the target event e within the process algebra expression B.
2. Use FOREST to compute the finite prefix $FP(B)$ until event e has occurred or the complete finite prefix has been generated. If the prefix does not contain e (which means that e is not reachable), then stop; apparently the problem was not well-defined.
3. Consider the local configuration $[e]$; together with the causal ordering $\leq$ this induces a partial order P.
4. Project P onto the delay events. This yields a task graph that can be used as input to PEPP.

But the analysis is not restricted to starting from the initial state. We can also supply a set of independent events $\{e_1, \ldots, e_n\}$ as a starting point, and ask for the passage time for an event e to occur after these events. There is however a constraint involved here: if after the events $\{e_1, \ldots, e_n\}$ a delay action is enabled, then this delay action has to be causally dependent on at least one event in $\{e_1, \ldots, e_n\}$. In other words, the following should hold: $\forall e_{en} \in enabled(State([e_1] \cup \ldots \cup [e_n])) : e_{en} \in \mathbb{E}_{delay} \Rightarrow \exists e_i \in \{e_1, \ldots, e_n\} : e_i \leq e_{en}$. Otherwise there is no way to determine when such a delay event e_{en} may have started. Algorithm 2 shows how to apply PEPP when the start state is determined by a set of independent events within the finite prefix $FP(B)$. Of course, the target event e has to be causally dependent on the events in $\{e_1, \ldots, e_n\}$. If this is not the case, Algorithm 1 – started in step 5 of Algorithm 2 – will unsuccessfully terminate in step 2.

Note that the partial orders obtained by both algorithms are only useful for PEPP if the configuration between the initial event(s) and the target event e contains at least one delay event.

Example 4. Consider Fig. 1 which corresponds to the condition event structure of $Unf(B_{ex})$. Suppose we are interested in the runtime of event d. The sets $\{a\}$ and $\{a, b\}$ can both be used as input for Algorithm 2; in fact, for this example they will all yield the task graph of Fig. 2 (a). The singleton set $\{b\}$ can also be used as a starting point for Algorithm 2, as the delay events $\langle G \rangle$ and $\langle F_1 \rangle$ are not enabled in $State([b])$; only the event a is enabled in $State([b])$. Again, the task graph of Fig. 2 (a) will be computed. The singleton set $\{c\}$, however, cannot be used as a valid input for Algorithm 2 as the delay event $\langle G \rangle$, which is enabled in $State([c])$, does not depend on event c. The set $\{a, c\}$ cannot be used as input for Algorithm 2 either, because the events a and c are not independent: $a \leq c$.

6   The Root Contention Phase in IEEE 1394

This section discusses a small case study where we applied our approach to compute the mean passage time of the first resolution of the root contention phase

Algorithm 2. Construct the task graph for $[e]$ starting from $\{e_1, \ldots, e_n\}$.

1. Specify the target event e within the process algebra expression B.
2. Use FOREST to compute the finite prefix $FP(B)$ until the events $\{e_1, \ldots, e_n\}$ have all occurred or the complete finite prefix has been generated. If $FP(B)$ does not contain all events of $\{e_1, \ldots, e_n\}$, then stop; apparently the problem was not well-defined.
3. If there are conflicts among the events in $\{e_1, \ldots, e_n\}$ then stop, as apparently the problem is not well-defined; otherwise continue.
4. Calculate $S = State([e_1] \cup \ldots \cup [e_n])$.
5. Check if all enabled delay actions which causally depend on S are dependent on at least one event from $\{e_1, \ldots, e_n\}$. If not, stop; apparently the problem is not well-defined. Otherwise, apply Algorithm 1 with S as initial state and compute the partial order of the local configuration of target event e.

---

of the IEEE 1394 protocol [20]. Due to space limitations only the FOREST and PEPP models of the root contention phase are discussed here. A more thorough discussion can be found in [31].

FOREST. Fig. 3 presents the specification of the root contention protocol in our process algebra. The model itself is based on [33]. The two Node_i processes are connected to each other by two Wire_i processes, that represent the communication lines between the components. Each Node_i process has a Buf_i process which can hold a single message from the other $\mathsf{Node}_{(1-i)}$. New messages from $\mathsf{Node}_{(1-i)}$ will simply overwrite older messages. Both nodes start (via Proc_i) to wait $g_i(t)$ units of time. If after waiting, the buffer is still empty (i.e. $check\_emp_i$), the node will sent a $send\_req_i$ to its partner and will subsequently wait for an acknowledgement. If this acknowledgement (i.e. $check\_ack_i$) arrives, Node_i will declare itself a child using action $child_i$. On the other hand, if after waiting $g_i(t)$ units of time, Node_i receives a $check\_req_i$ action, it declares itself to be the leader using action $root_i$. The delay of the communication line is modelled by the delay action $\langle F_i \rangle$.

The basic idea behind the protocol is that if the waiting times $g_i(t)$ of the two nodes are different, the 'slowest' node will become root. Since with probability one the outcomes of the waiting times $g_i(t)$ will eventually be different, the root contention protocol will terminate with probability one [33].

Apart from the performance analysis of the protocol that we report on in this paper, the specification of Fig. 3 may readily be used for a functional analysis of the protocol. The condition event structure generated by FOREST for this process algebraic expression contains 57 events (of which 8 are cut off-events) and 210 conditions.

To illustrate both algorithms of Sect. 5 we have identified a start state in the process algebra expression of Fig. 3 (i.e. corresponding with the events $\{e_1, \ldots, e_n\}$) from which we want to compute the first passage time to another state (i.e. target event e). The start state is defined by the first occurrence of the

The root contention protocol is modelled by the following stochastic process algebra expression:

$$(\mathsf{Node}_0 \; ||| \; \mathsf{Node}_1) \; ||_{Glob} \; (\mathsf{Wire}_0 \; ||| \; \mathsf{Wire}_1)$$

with the following (process) definitions ($i \in \{0,1\}$) :

$$
\begin{aligned}
\mathsf{Node}_i \quad &:= \quad (\mathsf{Proc}_i \; ||_{Loc} \; \mathsf{Buf}_i) \\
\mathsf{Proc}_i \quad &:= \quad \langle G_i \rangle; \; (\mathit{check\_emp}_i; \; \mathsf{SndReq}_i + \mathit{check\_req}_i; \; \mathsf{SndAck}_i) \\
\mathsf{SndAck}_i \quad &:= \quad \mathit{send\_ack}_i; \; \mathit{root}_i; \; \mathsf{stop} \\
\mathsf{SndReq}_i \quad &:= \quad \mathit{send\_req}_i; \; (\mathit{check\_req}_i; \; \mathsf{Proc}_i + \mathit{check\_ack}_i; \; \mathit{child}_i; \; \mathsf{stop}) \\
\mathsf{Buf}_i \quad &:= \quad \mathit{check\_emp}_i; \; \mathsf{Buf}_i + \mathit{recv\_req}_i; \; \mathsf{BufReq}_i + \mathit{recv\_ack}_i; \; \mathsf{BufAck}_i \\
\mathsf{BufReq}_i \quad &:= \quad \mathit{check\_req}_i; \; \mathsf{Buf}_i + \mathit{recv\_req}_i; \; \mathsf{BufReq}_i + \mathit{recv\_ack}_i; \; \mathsf{BufAck}_i \\
\mathsf{BufAck}_i \quad &:= \quad \mathit{check\_ack}_i; \; \mathsf{Buf}_i + \mathit{recv\_req}_i; \; \mathsf{BufReq}_i + \mathit{recv\_ack}_i; \; \mathsf{BufAck}_i \\
\mathsf{Wire}_i \quad &:= \quad \mathit{send\_req}_i; \; \mathsf{WireReq}_i + \mathit{send\_ack}_i; \; \mathsf{WireAck}_i \\
\mathsf{WireReq}_i \quad &:= \quad \langle F_i \rangle; \; \mathit{recv\_req}_{(1-i)}; \; \mathsf{Wire}_i + \mathsf{Wire}_i \\
\mathsf{WireAck}_i \quad &:= \quad \langle F_i \rangle; \; \mathit{recv\_ack}_{(1-i)}; \; \mathsf{Wire}_i + \mathsf{Wire}_i \\
Glob \quad &== \quad \{\mathit{send\_req}_0, \; \mathit{send\_req}_1, \; \mathit{send\_ack}_0, \; \mathit{send\_ack}_1, \\
&\qquad \mathit{recv\_req}_0, \; \mathit{recv\_req}_1, \; \mathit{recv\_ack}_0, \; \mathit{recv\_ack}_1\} \\
Loc \quad &== \quad \{\mathit{check\_emp}_i, \; \mathit{check\_req}_i, \; \mathit{check\_ack}_i\}
\end{aligned}
$$

Fig. 3. Process algebra expression of the root contention protocol.

following actions: $\mathit{send\_req}_0$, $\mathit{recv\_req}_0$, $\mathit{send\_req}_1$ and $\mathit{recv\_req}_1$. That is, just before *both* the $\mathit{check\_req}_0$ and $\mathit{check\_req}_1$ actions are about to happen. In the root contention protocol, this corresponds to the situation in which both processes are about to receive the parent request of their contender, which will initiate a new contention resolution phase. In the graph representation of the corresponding condition event structure, this set of starting events can easily be identified, due to the flow relation $\prec$ and the induced causal order $\leq$. The complete $FP(B)$ is omitted due to its size, though.

From these four events, we are interested in the delay until the first occurrence of the event corresponding with action root_1, that is, the first resolution after the contention, which declares Node_1 to be the root. Fig. 4 shows the partial order of the events leading to this root_1 event. It is generated using the graph drawing tool dot [12]. Note that the events $\mathit{check\_req}_0$ and $\mathit{check\_req}_1$ are indeed the first events that can occur. Within FOREST, distribution events all have a $\mathit{del\_}$ prefix.

PEPP. For the runtime analysis with PEPP[6], only the delay events of the partial order are of interest. Fig. 2 (b) shows the task graph as used by PEPP containing only the delay events and the elementary start and end events; it is the projection of Fig. 4 on the delay events. For the events $\langle G_0 \rangle$ and $\langle G_1 \rangle$ we have used the same uniform distribution function $G(t)$, that is used in [5] for the

---

[6] For our experiments we used version 3.3 of PEPP (released in July 1993) [7].

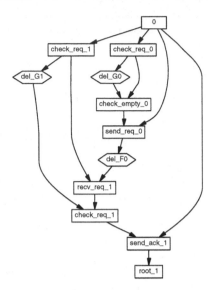

Fig. 4. Partial order of the events leading to the $root_1$ event.

transient analysis (via simulation) of the root contention protocol. A graphical representation of the distribution function $G(t)$ is given in Fig. 5. The unit of the Figures 5 and 6 is $\frac{1}{100}$ μsec as PEPP requires fixed step-size. The parameters D, N and I are parameters of the density function $g(t)$ which is defined as tuple $g = (D, N, g_0, \ldots, g_I)$, where D is the displacement between 0 and g_0 and N is the order of the distribution [15]. For the delay event $\langle F_0 \rangle$ we used an uniform distribution function $F(t)$ between $\frac{2}{198}$ and $\frac{3}{198}$, assuming that the transmission speed of the lines is $198m/\mu sec$.

We used PEPP to analyse the task graph corresponding with the local configuration of the $root_1$ event. Fig. 6 shows a graphical representation of the density function of the first passage time together with the average time (0.51 μsec) of the partial order leading to $root_1$. Note that the results obtained only relate to the time of the root contention when contention is resolved on the first attempt of the protocol. It does not provide information on the transient behaviour of the protocol.

7   Conclusions

In this paper we discussed a partial-order semantics for a stochastic process algebra that supports general (non-memoryless) distributions and combined this with an approach to numerically analyse the mean delay between two events. Based on an adaption of McMillan's complete finite prefix approach tailored to event structures and process algebra, we used FOREST to obtain finite representations for recursive processes. The behaviour between two events is now captured by a partial order of events that can be mapped on a stochastic task graph. We used PEPP for numerical analysis of such task graphs.

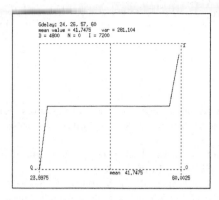

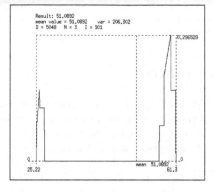

Fig. 5. Distribution function $G(t)$.   **Fig. 6.** Density function of the runtime of the configuration leading to the $root_1$ event.

The paper presents a novel application of McMillan's finite prefix algorithm. Furthermore, the work can be seen as a successor of [4] in the sense that it shows the practical feasibility of the use of event structure semantics for stochastic analysis.

A clear advantage of our approach is that we are able to reason about both the functional and non-functional aspects of systems using the same model and notation. Furthermore, as our approach uses *general* distributions, hence, it can still be used when approximations through exponential distributions are no longer realistic.

We foresee three different uses of our approach for performance modelling. First, it is possible that the first passage time between two events is simply what one is interested in, and then our approach yields the answer. Secondly, our approach might play an auxiliary role in establishing the right parameters for performance models of other types that can then be further analysed. Thirdly, our approach might be the first step in a more evolved numerical calculation exploiting more features of PEPP.

In the current setting we are able to compute the first passage time of a single event. Our next step will be to try to adopt our approach to the combined run-times of conflicting events and repetitive events. In [23], Langerak has shown how to derive a graph rewriting system from the complete finite prefix of a condition event structure. We are currently studying the use of a graph rewriting system as the basis for transient analysis with PEPP, using its more advanced node types like cyclic nodes, hierarchical nodes and probabilistic choice. This would make it possible to compare our work with discrete-event simulation approaches like ♧ [5,6]. Furthermore, we are currently working on an (user) interface to integrate FOREST and PEPP.

Acknowledgements We want to thank Markus Siegle from the University of Erlangen for kindly giving us permission to use the PEPP tool. Thanks to Holger Hermanns for support, discussions and valuable help in unravelling CAPP representations.

Boudewijn Haverkort is thanked for his helpful suggestions to improve both the contents and readability of the paper.

References

1. M. Bernardo and R. Gorrieri. A Tutorial on EMPA: A Theory of Concurrent Processes with Nondeterminism, Priorities, Probabilities and Time. *Theoretical Computer Science*, 202:1–54, 1998.
2. T. Bolognesi and E. Brinksma. Introduction to the ISO Specification Language LOTOS. *Computer Networks and ISDN Systems*, 14:25–59, 1987.
3. M. Bravetti and R. Gorrieri. Interactive Generalized Semi-Markov Processes. In J. Hillston and M. Silva, editors, *Proc. of PAPM'99*, pages 83–98, Zaragoza, Spain, September 1999.
4. E. Brinksma, J.-P. Katoen, R. Langerak, and D. Latella. A Stochastic Causality-Based Process Algebra. *The Computer Journal*, 38(7):552–565, 1995.
5. P. R. D'Argenio. *Algebras and Automata for Timed and Stochastic Systems*. PhD thesis, University of Twente, Enschede, The Netherlands, November 1999.
6. P. R. D'Argenio, J.-P. Katoen, and E. Brinksma. An Algebraic Approach to the Specification of Stochastic Systems (extended abstract). In D. Gries and W.-P. de Roever, editors, *Proc. of PROCOMET'98*, pages 126–148, Shelter Island, New York, USA, 1998. Chapman & Hall.
7. P. Dauphin, F. Hartleb, M. Kienow, V. Mertsiotakis, and A. Quick. PEPP: Performance Evaluation of Parallel Programs – User's Guide — Version 3.3. Technical Report 17/93, IMMD VII, University of Erlangen–Nürnberg, Germany, 1993.
8. P. Dauphin, R. Hofmann, R. Klar, B. Mohr, A. Quick, M. Siegle, and F. Sötz. ZM4/SIMPLE: a General Approach to Performance-Measurement and Evaluation of Distributed Systems. In T. L. Casavant and M. Singhal, editors, *Advances in Distributed Computing: Concepts and Design*. IEEE Computer Society Press, 1992.
9. J. Engelfriet. Branching Processes of Petri Nets. *Acta Informatica*, 28(6):575–591, 1991.
10. J. Esparza. Model Checking Using Net Unfoldings. *Science of Computer Programming*, 23(2):151–195, 1994.
11. J. Esparza, S. Römer, and W. Vogler. An Improvement of McMillan's Unfolding Algorithm. In T. Margaria and B. Steffen, editors, *Proc. of TACAS'96*, LNCS 1055, pages 87–106, Passau, Germany, March 1996. Springer-Verlag.
12. E. R. Gansner, E. Koutsofios, and S. C. N. an Kiem-Phong Vo. A Technique for Drawing Directed Graphs. *IEEE Transactions on Software Engineering*, 19(3):214–230, 1993.
13. N. Götz, U. Herzog, and M. Rettelbach. Multiprocessor and Distributed System Design: The Integration of Functional Specification and Performance Analysis Using Stochastic Process Algebras. In L. Donatiello and R. Nelson, editors, *Proc. of PERFORMANCE'93*, LNCS 729, pages 121–146, Rome, Italy, September 1993. Springer-Verlag.
14. P. G. Harrison and B. Strulo. Stochastic Process Algebra for Discrete Event Simulation. In F. Bacelli, A. Jean-Marie, and I. Mitrani, editors, *Quantitative Methods in Parallel Systems*, Esprit Basic Research Series, pages 18–37. Springer-Verlag, 1995. Chapter 2.
15. F. Hartleb. Stochastic Graph Models for Performance Evaluation of Parallel Programs and the Evaluation Tool PEPP. In N. Götz, U. Herzog, and M. Rettelbach,

editors, *Proc. of the QMIPS Workshop on Formalisms, Principles and State-of-the-art*, pages 207–224, Erlangen/Pommersfelden, Germany, March 1993. Arbeitsbericht Band 26, Number 14.

16. H. Hermanns. *Interactive Markov Chains*. PhD thesis, University of Erlangen, Nürnberg, Germany, 1998.

17. H. Hermanns and J.-P. Katoen. Automated Compositional Markov Chain Generation for a Plain-Old Telephone System. *Science of Computer Programming*, 36(1):97–127, 2000.

18. U. Herzog. A Concept for Graph-Based Stochastic Process Algebras, Generally Distributed Activity Times, and Hierarchical Modelling. In M. Ribaudo, editor, *Proc. of PAPM'96*, pages 1–20. C.L.U.T. Press, 1996.

19. J. Hillston. *A Compositional Approach to Performance Modelling*. Distinguished Dissertations Series. Cambridge University Press, 1996.

20. IEEE Computer Society. *IEEE Standard for a High Performance Serial Bus*, Std 1394-1995 edition, 1996.

21. R. Klar, P. Dauphin, F. Hartleb, R. Hofmann, B. Mohr, A. Quick, and M. Siegle. *Messung and Modellierung Paralleler und Verteilter Rechensysteme (in german)*. Teubner-Verlag, Stuttgart, 1995.

22. R. Langerak. *Transformations and Semantics for LOTOS*. PhD thesis, University of Twente, Enschede, The Netherlands, November 1992.

23. R. Langerak. Deriving a Graph Grammar from a Complete Finite Prefix of an Unfolding. In I. Castellani and B. Victor, editors, *Proc. of EXPRESS'99*, ENTCS 27, Eindhoven, The Netherlands, August 1999. Elsevier Science Publishers.

24. R. Langerak and E. Brinksma. A Complete Finite Prefix for Process Algebra. In N. Halbwachs and D. Peled, editors, *Proc. of CAV'99*, LNCS 1633, pages 184–195, Trento, Italy, July 1999. Springer-Verlag.

25. K. L. McMillan. *Symbolic Model Checking: An Approach to the State Explosion Problem*. Kluwer Academic Publishers, 1993.

26. K. L. McMillan. A Technique of State Space Search Based on Unfolding. *Formal Methods in System Design*, 6(1):45–65, 1995.

27. V. Mertsiotakis. Extension of the Graph Analysis Tool SPASS and Integration into the X-Window Environment of PEPP (in german). Technical report, Department of Computer Science VII, IMMD VII, University of Erlangen–Nürnberg, Germany, 1991. Internal study.

28. M. Nielsen, G. D. Plotkin, and G. Winskel. Petri Nets, Event Structures and Domains, Part 1. *Theoretical Computer Science*, 13(1):85–108, 1981.

29. E.-R. Olderog. *Nets, Terms and Formulas*, volume 23 of *Cambridge Tracts in Theoretical Computer Science*. Cambridge University Press, 1991.

30. A. Rensink. *Models and Methods for Action Refinement*. PhD thesis, University of Twente, Enschede, The Netherlands, August 1993.

31. T. C. Ruys. *Towards Effective Model Checking*. PhD thesis, University of Twente, Enschede, The Netherlands, March 2001. To be published.

32. G. Sander. Graph Layout through the VCG Tool. In R. Tamassia and I. G. Tollis, editors, *Proc. of the Int. Workshop on Graph Drawing (GD'94)*, LNCS 894, pages 194–205, Princeton, New Jersey, USA, 1994. Springer-Verlag.

33. M. I. Stoelinga and F. W. Vaandrager. Root Contention in IEEE 1994. In J.-P. Katoen, editor, *Proc. of ARTS'99*, LNCS 1601, pages 53–74, Bamberg, Germany, May 1999. Springer-Verlag.

34. F. Wallner. Model-Checking LTL using Net Unfoldings. In A. J. Hu and M. Y. Vardi, editors, *Proc. of CAV'98*, LNCS 1427, pages 207–218, Vancouver, Canada, July 1998. Springer-Verlag.

Hardware/Software Co-design Using Functional Languages

Alan Mycroft[1,2] and Richard Sharp[1,2]

[1] Computer Laboratory, Cambridge University
New Museums Site, Pembroke Street, Cambridge CB2 3QG, UK

[2] AT&T Laboratories Cambridge
24a Trumpington Street, Cambridge CB2 1QA, UK

am@cl.cam.ac.uk
rws26@cl.cam.ac.uk

Abstract. In previous work we have developed and prototyped a silicon compiler which translates a functional language (SAFL) into hardware. Here we present a SAFL-level program transformation which: (*i*) partitions a specification into hardware and software parts and (*ii*) generates a specialised architecture to execute the software part. The architecture consists of a number of interconnected heterogeneous processors. Our method allows a large design space to be explored by systematically transforming a single SAFL specification to investigate different points on the area-time spectrum.

1 Introduction

In [12] we introduced a hardware description language, SAFL (Statically Allocated Functional Language), and sketched its translation to hardware. An optimising silicon compiler for SAFL targetting hierarchical RTL Verilog has been implemented [18] and tested on a number of designs, including a small commercial processor[1]. SAFL is a first-order functional language with an ML [10] style syntax. We argue the case for functional languages over (say) Occam on the grounds of easier and more powerful program analysis, transformation and manipulation techniques. The essential features of SAFL can briefly be summarised as follows:

- programs are a sequence of function definitions;
- functions can call other defined functions but recursive calls must be tail-recursive[2]. (Section 2.5 addresses the exact technical restrictions.)

---

[1] The instruction set of Cambridge Consultants XAP processor was implemented (see www.camcon.co.uk). We did not include the SIF instruction.

[2] Section 2.6.3 shows how this restriction can be removed by mapping general recursive functions into software.

T. Margaria and W. Yi (Eds.): TACAS 2001, LNCS 2031, pp. 236–251, 2001.

This allows our SAFL silicon compiler to:

- compile SAFL in a *resource-aware* manner. That is we map each function definition into a single hardware-level *resource*; functions which are called more than once become shared resources[3].
- synthesise highly parallel hardware—referen tial transparency allows one to evaluate all subexpressions in parallel.
- statically allocate the storage (e.g. registers and memories) required by a SAFL program.

The SAFL language is designed to facilitate source-to-source transformation. Whereas traditional "blac k-box" synthesis systems synthesise hardware according to user-supplied constraints, our approach is to select a particular implementation by applying transformation rules to the SAFL source as a pre-compilation phase. We have shown that applying fold/unfold transformations [4] to SAFL specifications allows one to explore various time-area tradeoffs at the hardw are level [12,13]. The purpose of this paper is to demonstrate ho w hardware/software partitioning can be seen as a source-to-source transformation at the SAFL lev el thus providing a formal framew ork in whid to investigate hardware/software co-design. In fact we go one step further than traditional co-design since as well as partitioning a specification into hardware and software parts our transformation procedure can also synthesise an architecture tailored specifically for executing the software part. This architecture consists of any number of interconnected heterogeneous processors. There are a number of advantages to our approach:

- Synthesising an architecture specifically to execute a known piece of software can offer significant advantages over a fixed architecture [17].
- The ability to synthesise multiple processors allows a wide range of area-time tradeoffs to be explored. Not only does hardw are/software partitioning affect the area-time position of the final design, but the number of processors synthesised to execute the software part is also significant: increasing the number of processors pushes the area up whilst potentially reducing execution time (as the processors can operate in parallel).
- Resource-awareness allows a SAFL specification to represent shared resources. This increases the power of our partitioning transformation since, for example, multiple processors can access the same hardware resource (see Figure 1 for an example).

1.1   A Brief Ov erview of the SAFL Language

SAFL is a language of first order recurrence equations; a user program consists of a sequence of function definitions:

$$\texttt{fun } f_1(\vec{x}) = e_1; \ \ldots; \ \texttt{fun } f_n(\vec{x}) = e_n$$

---

[3]   All sharing issues are handled automatically by our silicon compiler: arbiters are inserted where necessary to protect shared resources and data-validity analysis is performed facilitating the generation of efficient inter-resource interface logic [18].

Programs have a distinguished function, `main`, (usually f_n) which represents an external world interface—at the hardware level it accepts values on an input port and may later produce a value on an output port. The abstract syntax of SAFL expressions, e, is as follows (we abbreviate tuples $(e_1, \ldots, e_k)$ as $\vec{e}$ and similarly $(x_1, \ldots, x_k)$ as $\vec{x}$):

- variables: x; constants: c;
- user function calls: $f(\vec{e})$;
- primitive function calls: $a(\vec{e})$—where a ranges over primitive operators (e.g. `+`, `-`, `<=`, `&&` etc.);
- conditionals: e_1 ? e_2 : e_3; and
- let bindings: `let` $\vec{x} = \vec{e}$ `in` e_0 `end`

See Figures 3 and 4 for concrete examples of SAFL code.

1.2   Comparison with Other Work

Previous work on compiling declarative specifications to hardware has centred on how functional languages themselves can be used as tools to aid the design of circuits. Sheeran's et al. muFP [19] and Lava [2] systems use functional programming techniques (such as higher order functions) to express concisely the repeating structures that often appear in hardware circuits. In this framework, using different interpretations of primitive functions corresponds to various operations including behavioural simulation and netlist generation. Our approach takes SAFL constructs (rather than gates) as primitive. Although this restricts the class of circuits we can describe to those which satisfy certain high-level properties, it permits high-level analysis and optimisation yielding efficient hardware. (A more detailed comparison of SAFL with other hardware description languages including Verilog, VHDL, ELLA and Lustre can be found in [13]).

Hardware/software co-design is well-studied and many tools have been built to aid the partitioning process [3,6,1]. Although these systems differ in their approach to co-design they are similar in so far as partitioning is a "black-box" phase performed as part of the synthesis process. By making partitioning visible at the source-level we believe our approach to be more flexible—hardware/software co-design is just one of a library of source-to-source transformations which can be applied incrementally to explore a wide range of architectural trade-offs.

The idea of converting a program into a parameterised processor and corresponding instruction memory is not new; Page described a similar transformation [17] within the framework of Handel [16] (a subset of Occam for which a silicon compiler was written). Whereas Page's transformation allowed a designer to synthesise a single parameterised processor, our method allows one to generate a much more general architecture consisting of multiple communicating processors accessing a set of (potentially shared) hardware resources.

The impact of source-to-source transformation has been investigated in the context of imperative hardware description languages [20,14]. We argue that program transformation is a more po werful technique in the SAFL domain for two reasons:

- The functional properties of SAFL allow equational reasoning and hence make a wide range of transformations applicable (as we do not have to worry about side effects).
- The resource-aware properties of SAFL give fold/unfold transformations precise meaning at the design-level (e.g. we know that duplicating a function definition in the source is guaranteed to duplicate the corresponding resource in the generated circuit).

2   Technical Details

The first step in the partitioning transformation is to define a partitioning function, π, specifying which SAFL functions are to be implem ented directly in hardware and which are to be mapped to a processor for software execution. Automated partitioning is not the subject of this paper; we assume that π is supplied by the user. For expository purposes we initially describe a transformation where all processors are variants of a stack machine: Section 2.1 describes the operation of the stack machine and Section 2.2 shows how it can be encoded as a SAFL function; a compiler from SAFL to stac k code is presented in Section 2.3. In Section 2.6 we generalise our partitioning transformation to a network of heterogenous processors.

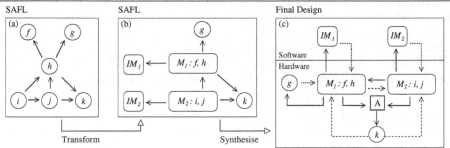

Partitioning: (a) shows the call-graph of a SAFL specification, P; (b) shows the call-graph of $\hat{\pi}(P)$, where $\pi = \{(f, M_1), (h, M_1), (i, M_2), (j, M_2)\}$. IM_1 and IM_2 are instruction memory functions (see Section 2.2); (c) shows the structure of the final circuit after compilation. The box marked 'A' represents an arbiter (inserted automatically by the SAFL compiler) protecting shared resource k; the bold arrows represent calls, the dotted arrows represent return values.

Fig. 1. A diagramm atic view of the partitioning transformation

Let $\mathcal{M}$ be the set of processor instances used in the final design. We define a (partial) partitioning function

$$\pi : SAFL\ function\ name \rightharpoonup \mathcal{M}$$

mapping the function definitions in our SAFL specification onto processors in $\mathcal{M}$. $\pi(f)$ is the processor on which function f is to be implemented. If $f \notin Dom(\pi)$ then we realise f in hardware, otherwise we say that f is *located* on machine $\pi(f)$. Note that multiple functions can be mapped to the same processor.

We extend π to a transformation function

$$\hat{\pi} : SAFL\ Program \rightarrow SAFL\ Program$$

such that given a SAFL program, P, $\hat{\pi}(P)$ is another SAFL program which respects the partitioning function π. Figure 1 shows the effect of a partitioning transformation, $\hat{\pi}$, where

$$\mathcal{M} = \{M_1, M_2\};\ \text{and}$$
$$\pi = \{(f, M_1),\ (h, M_1),\ (i, M_2),\ (j, M_2)\}$$

In this example we see that g and k are implemented in hardware since $g, k \notin Dom(\pi)$. $\hat{\pi}(P)$ contains function definitions: M_1, M_2, IM_1, IM_2, g and k where M_1 and M_2 are processor instances and IM_1 and IM_2 are instruction memories (see Section 2.2).

2.1   The Stack Machine Template

Our stack machine can be seen as a cut-down version of both Landin's SECD machine [9] and Cardelli's Functional Abstract Machine [5]. Each instruction has an op-code field and an operand field n. The following instructions are defined:

$PushC(n)$	push constant n onto the stack
$PushV(n)$	push variable (from offset n into the current stack)
$PushA(n)$	push the value of the stack machine's argument a_n (see Section 2.2) to the stack
$Squeeze(n)$	pop top value; pop next n values; re-push top value
$Return(n)$	pop result; pop link; pop n arguments; re-push result; branch to link
$Call\_Int(n)$	push address of next instruction onto stack and branch to address n
$Jz(n)$	pop a value; if it is zero branch to address n
$Jmp(n)$	jump to address n
$Alu2(n)$	pop two values; do 2-operand builtin operation n on them and push the result
$Halt$	terminate the stack machine returning the value on top of the stack

We define a family of instructions to allow the stack machine to call external functions:

Call_Ext$_f$	pop each of f's arguments from the stack; invoke the external function f and push the result to the top of the stack.

The stack machine *template, SMT*, is an abstract model of the stack machine parameterised on the code it will have to execute. Given a stack machine program, s, (i.e. a list of stack machine instructions as outlined above) $SMT\langle s \rangle$ is a stack machine *instance*: a SAFL function encoding a stack machine specialised for executing s. Our notion of a template is similar to a VHDL *generic*.

2.2 Stack Machine Instances

A stack machine instance, $SM_i \in \mathcal{M}$, is a SAFL function of the form:

$$\text{fun } SM_i(a_1, \ldots, a_{n_i}, \text{ PC, SP}) = \ldots$$
$$\text{where } n_i = max(\{arity(f) \mid \pi(f) = SM_i\})$$

Arguments PC and SP are used to store the program counter and stack pointer respectively; $a_1, \ldots, a_{n_i}$ are used to receive arguments of functions located on SM_i. Each stack machine instance is associated with an instruction memory function, IM_i of the form:

```
fun IM_i(address) =
    case address of 0 => instruction_0
                  | 1 => instruction_1
                  ... etc.
```

SM_i calls $IM_i(PC)$ to load instructions for execution.

For example, consider a stack machine instance, $SM_{f,h}$, where we choose to locate functions f (of arity 2) and h (of arity 3). Then $n_{f,h} = 3$ yielding signature: $SM_{f,h}(a_1, a_2, a_3, PC, SP)$. $IM_{f,h}$ is an instruction memory containing compiled code for f and h. To compute the value of $h(x, y, z)$ we invoke $SM_{f,h}$ with arguments $a_1 = x$, $a_2 = y$, $a_3 = z$, $PC = ext\_h_{entry}$ (h's external entry point—see Section 2.3) and $SP = 0$. Similarly to compute the value of $f(x, y)$ we invoke $SM_{f,h}$ with arguments $a_1 = x$, $a_2 = y$, $a_3 = 0$, $PC = ext\_f_{entry}$ and $SP = 0$. Note how we pad the a-arguments with 0's since $arity(f) < 3$.

The co-design of hardware and software means that instructions and ALU operations are only added to SM_i if they appear in IM_i. Parameterising the stack machine template in this way can considerably reduce the area of the final design since we remove redundant logic in each processor instance.

We can consider many other areas of parameterisation. For example we can adjust the op-code width and assign op-codes to minimise instruction-decoding delay [17]. Figure 4 gives the SAFL code for a 16-bit stack machine instance[4]. An alu2 function, and an example stack machine program which computes triangular numbers is shown in Figure 3.

---

[4] Approximately 2000 2-input equivalent gates when compiled using the SAFL silicon compiler. For simplicity we consider a simple stack machine with no Call_Ext instructions.

2.3   Compilation to Stack Code

Figure 2 gives a compilation function from SAFL to stack based code. Although the translation of many SAFL constructs is self-explanatory, the compilation rules for function definition and function call require further explanation:

Compiling Function Definitions

The code generated for function definition

$$\text{fun } f(x_1, \ldots, x_k) = e$$

requires explanation in that we create 2 distinct entry points for f: f_{entry} and ext_f_{entry}. The *internal* entry point, f_{entry}, is used when f is invoked internally (i.e. with a $\texttt{Call\_Int}$ instruction). The *external* entry point, ext_f_{entry}, is used when f is invoked externally (i.e. via a call to $\pi(f)$, the machine on which f is implemented). In this latter case, we simply execute k $\texttt{PushA}$ instructions to push f's arguments onto the stack before jumping to f's internal entry point, f_{entry}.

Compiling Function Calls

Suppose function g is in software ($g \in Dom(\pi)$) and calls function f. The code generated for the call depends on the location of f relative to g. There are three possibilities:

1. If f and g are both implemented in software on the same machine ($f \in Dom(\pi) \land \pi(f) = \pi(g)$) then we simply push each of f's arguments to the stack and branch to f's internal entry point with a $\texttt{Call\_Int}$ instruction. The $\texttt{Call\_Int}$ instruction pushes the return address and jumps to f_{entry}; the compiled code for f is responsible for popping the arguments and link leaving the return value on the top of the stack.
2. If f is implemented in hardware ($f \notin Dom(\pi)$) then we push each of f's arguments to the stack and invoke the hardware resource corresponding to f by means of a $\texttt{Call\_Ext}_f$ instruction. The $\texttt{Call\_Ext}_f$ instruction pops each of f's arguments, invokes resource f and pushes f's return value to the stack.
3. If f and g are both implemented in software but on different machines ($f, g \in Dom(\pi) \land \pi(f) \neq \pi(g)$) then g needs to invoke $\pi(f)$ (the machine on which f is located). We push $\pi(f)$'s arguments to the stack: the arguments for f possibly padded by 0s (see Section 2.2) followed by the program counter $\texttt{PC}$ initialised to ext_f_{entry} and the stack pointer $\texttt{SP}$ initialised to 0. We then invoke $\pi(f)$ using a $\texttt{Call\_Ext}_{\pi(f)}$ instruction.

Let σ, be an environment mapping variable names to stack offsets (offset 0 signifies the top of the stack). Let g be the name of the function we are compiling. Then $[\![\cdot]\!]^g\sigma$ gives an instruction list corresponding to g. (We omit g for readability in the following—it is only used to identify whether a called function is located on the same machine).

We use the notation $\sigma\{x \mapsto n\}$ to represent environment σ extended with x mapping to n. σ^{+n} represents an environment constructed by incrementing all stack offsets in σ by n—i.e. $\sigma^{+n}(x) = \sigma(x) + n$. $\emptyset$ is the empty environment. The infix operator @ appends instruction lists. $Repeat(l, n)$ is l @ ... @ l (n times); (this is used to generate instruction sequences to pad argument lists with 0s).

$$[\![c]\!]\sigma \stackrel{\text{def}}{=} [\text{PushC}(c)]$$

$$[\![x]\!]\sigma \stackrel{\text{def}}{=} [\text{PushV}(\sigma(x))]$$

$$[\![f(e_1,\ldots,e_k)]\!]\sigma \stackrel{\text{def}}{=} \begin{cases} [\![e_1]\!]\sigma \ @ \ [\![e_2]\!]\sigma^{+1} \ @ \ \ldots \ @ \ [\![e_k]\!]\sigma^{+(k-1)} \ @ \ [\text{Call\_Ext}_f] \\ \qquad \text{if } f \notin Dom(\pi) \\[2ex] [\![e_1]\!]\sigma \ @ \ [\![e_2]\!]\sigma^{+1} \ @ \ \ldots \ @ \ [\![e_k]\!]\sigma^{+(k-1)} \\ \qquad @ \ [\text{Call\_Int}(f_{entry})] \\ \qquad \text{if } f \in Dom(\pi) \wedge \pi(f) = \pi(g) \\[2ex] [\![e_1]\!]\sigma \ @ \ [\![e_2]\!]\sigma^{+1} \ @ \ \ldots \ @ \ [\![e_k]\!]\sigma^{+(k-1)} \\ \qquad @ \ Repeat([\text{PushC}(0)], arity(\pi(f)) - 2 - k) \\ \qquad @ \ [\text{PushC}(ext\_f_{entry}), \text{PushC}(0), \text{Call\_Ext}_{\pi(f)}] \\ \qquad \text{if } f \in Dom(\pi) \wedge \pi(f) \neq \pi(g) \end{cases}$$

$$[\![a(e_1, e_2)]\!]\sigma \stackrel{\text{def}}{=} [\![e_1]\!]\sigma \ @ \ [\![e_2]\!]\sigma^{+1} \ @ \ [\text{Alu2}(a)]$$

$$[\![\text{let } x = e_1 \text{ in } e_2]\!]\sigma \stackrel{\text{def}}{=} [\![e_1]\!]\sigma \ @ \ [\![e_2]\!]\sigma^{+1}\{x \mapsto 0\} \ @ \ [\text{Squeeze}(1)]$$

$$[\![e_1 \ ? \ e_2 \ : \ e_3]\!]\sigma \stackrel{\text{def}}{=} \text{let } l \text{ and } l' \text{ be new labels in}$$
$$[\![e_1]\!]\sigma \ @ \ [\text{Jz }(l)] \ @ \ [\![e_2]\!]\sigma \ @ \ [\text{Jmp }(l'), label: l]$$
$$@ \ [\![e_3]\!]\sigma \ @ \ [label: l']$$

$$[\![\text{fun } g(x_1,\ldots,x_k) = e]\!] \stackrel{\text{def}}{=} [label: g_{entry}] \ @ \ [\![e]\!]^g\emptyset\{x_k \mapsto 1, x_{k-1} \mapsto 2, \ldots, x_1 \mapsto k\}$$
$$@ \ [\text{Return}(k)]$$
$$@ \ [label: ext\_g_{entry}, \ \text{PushA}(1), \ \ldots, \ \text{PushA}(k),$$
$$\text{Call\_Int}(g_{entry}), \ \text{Halt}]$$

Fig. 2. Compiling SAFL into Stack Code for Execution on a Stack Machine Instance

2.4   The Partitioning Transformation

Having introduced the stack machine (Section 2.1) and the associated compilation function (Section 2.3) the details of the partitioning transformation, $\hat{\pi}$, are
as follows:

Let P be the SAFL program we wish to transform using π. Let f be a SAFL
function in P with definition d_f of the form

$$\texttt{fun}\ \ f(x_1, \ldots, x_k) = e$$

We construct a partitioned program $\hat{\pi}(P)$ from P as follows:

1. For each function definition $d_f \in P$ to be mapped to hardware (i.e. $f \notin Dom(\pi)$) create a variant in $\hat{\pi}(P)$ which is as d_f but for each call, $g(e_1, \ldots, e_k)$:

   If $g \in Dom(\pi)$ then replace the call $g(\vec{e})$ with a call:

$$m(e_1, \ldots, e_k, \underbrace{0, \ldots, 0,}_{arity(m)-2-k}\ ext\_g_{entry}, 0)$$

   where $m = \pi(g)$, the stack machine instance on which g is located.

2. For each $m \in \mathcal{M}$:

   (a) Compile instruction sequences for functions located on m:

$$Code_m = \{[\![d_f]\!] \mid \pi(f) = m\}$$

   (b) Generate *machine code* for m, $MCode_m$, by resolving symbols in $Code_m$,
       assigning opcodes and converting into binary representation.

   (c) Generate an *instruction memory* for m by adding a function definition,
       $\texttt{IM}_m$, to $\hat{\pi}(P)$ of the form:

   ```
   fun IM_m(address) =
       case address of 0 => instruction_0
                     | 1 => instruction_1
                     ... etc.
   ```

   where each **instruction_i** is taken from $MCode_m$.

   (d) Generate a stack machine instance, $SMT\langle Code_m\rangle$ and append it to $\hat{\pi}(P)$.

For each $m \in \mathcal{M}$, $\hat{\pi}(P)$ contains a corresponding processor instance and
instruction memory function. When $\hat{\pi}(P)$ is compiled to hardware resource-
awareness ensures that each processor definition function becomes a single processor and each instruction memory function becomes a single instruction memory. The remaining functions in $\hat{\pi}(P)$ are mapped to hardware resources as
required. Function calls are synthesised into optimised comm unication paths between the hardware resources (see Figure 1c).

2.5   Validity of Partitioning Functions

This section concerns some fine technical details—it can be skipped on first reading.

We clarify the SAFL restriction on recursion[5] given in the Introduction as follows.

In order for a SAFL program to be valid, all recursive calls, including those calls which form part of mutually-recursive cycle, may only occur in tail-context. Non-recursive calls may appear freely.

This allows storage for SAFL variables to be allocated statically as tail recursion does not require the dynamic allocation of stack frames.

Unfortunately, in general, a partitioning function, π, may transform a valid SAFL program, P, into an invalid SAFL program, $\hat{\pi}(P)$, which does not satisfy the recursion restrictions. For example consider the following program, P_{bad}:

```
fun f(x) = x+1;
fun g(x) = f(x)+2;
fun h(x) = g(x+3);
```

Partitioning P_{bad} with $\pi = \{(f, \text{SM}), (h, \text{SM})\}$ yields a new program, $\hat{\pi}(P_{bad})$, of the form:

```
fun IM(PC) = ...
fun SM(x,PC,SP) = ... let t = <top-of-stack>
                       in g(t) ...
fun g(x) = SM(x, <ext_f_entry>, 0) + 2;
```

$\hat{\pi}(P_{bad})$ has invalid recursion between g and SM. The problem is that the call to SM in the body of g is part of a mutually-recursive cycle and is not in tail-context.

We therefore require a restriction on partitions π to ensure that if P is a valid SAFL program then $\hat{\pi}(P)$ will also be a valid SAFL program. For the purposes of this paper we give the following sufficient condition:

π is a valid partition with respect to SAFL program, P, iff all cycles occurring the call graph of $\hat{\pi}(P)$ already exist in the call graph of P, with the exception of self-cycles generated by direct tail-recursion.

Thus, in particular, new functions in $\hat{\pi}(P)$—i.e. stack machines and their instructions memories—must not have mutual recursion with any other functions.

2.6   Extensions

Fine Grained Partitioning We have presented a program transformation to map function definitions to hardware or software, but what if we want to map *part* of a function definition to hardware and the rest to software? This can be achieved by applying fold/unfold transformations before our partitioning transformation. For example, consider the function

---

[5]   A more formal presentation can be found in [12].

```
f(x,y) = if x=0 then y
               else f(x-1, x*y - 7 + 5*x)
```

If we choose to map f to software our design will contain a processor and associated machine code consisting of a sequence of instructions representing multiply x and y, subtract 7, add 5 times x. However, consider transforming f with a single application of the *fold*-rule [4]:

```
i(x,y) = x*y-7 + 5*x
f(x,y) = if x=0 then y else f(x-1, i(x,y))
```

Now mapping f to software and i to hardware leads to a software representation for f containing fewer instructions and a specialised processor with a x*y-7 + 5*x instruction.

Dealing with Heterogeneous Processors So far we have only considered executing software on a network of stack machines. Although the stack machine is a familiar choice for expository purposes, in a real design one would often prefer to use different architectures. For example, specialised VLIW [8] arc hitectures are a typical choice for data-dominated em bedded systems since man y operations can be performed in parallel without the overhead of dynamic instruction scheduling. The commercial "Art Designer" tool [1] partitions a C program into hardware and software by constructing a single specialised VLIW processor and compiling code for it. In general, however, designs often consist of multiple comm unicating processors chosen to reflect various cost and performance constraints. Our framework can be extended to handle a network of heterogeneous processors as follows:

Let *Templates* be a set of processor templates (c.f. the stack machine template, *SMT*, in section 2.1).

Let *Compilers* be a set of compilers from SAFL to mac hine code for processor templates.

As part of the transformation process, the user now specifies two extra functions:

$$\delta : \mathcal{M} \rightarrow Templates$$
$$\tau : \mathcal{M} \rightarrow Compilers$$

δ maps each processor instance, $m \in \mathcal{M}$, onto a SAFL processor template and τ maps each $m \in \mathcal{M}$ onto an associated compiler. W e then modify the transformation procedure described in Section 2.4 to generate a partitioned program, $\hat{\pi}_{\delta,\tau}(P)$ as follows: for each $m \in \mathcal{M}$ we generate machine code, $MCode_m$, using compiler $\tau(m)$; we then use processor template, $MT = \delta(m)$, to generate processor instance $MT\langle MCode_m\rangle$ and append this to $\hat{\pi}_{\delta,\tau}(P)$.

Extending the SAFL Language Recall that the SAFL language specifies that all recursive calls must be in tail-context. Since only tail-recursive calls are permitted, our silicon compiler is able to statically allocate all the storage needed for a SAFL program.

As an example of these restrictions consider the following definitions of the factorial function:

```
rfact(x) = if x=0 then 1 else x*rfact(x-1)
ifact(x,a) = if x=0 then a else ifact(x-1,x*a)
```

rfact is not a valid SAFL program since the recursive call is not in a tail-context. However the equivalent tail-recursive factorial function, ifact which uses a second argument to accumulate partial results is a valid SAFL program.

Although one can sometimes transform a non-tail recursive program into an equivalent tail-recursive one, this is not always easy or natural. The transformation of factorial into its tail-recursive equivalent is only possible because multiplication is an associative operator. Thus, in general we require a way of extending SAFL to handle general unrestricted recursion. Our partitioning transformation provides us with one way to do this:

Consider a new language, SAFL+ constructed by removing the recursion restrictions from SAFL. We can use our partitioning transformation to transform SAFL+ to SAFL simply by ensuring that each function definition containing recursion other than in a tail-call context is mapped to software. Note that our compilation function (Figure 2) is already capable of dealing with general recursion without any modification.

3   Conclusions and Further Work

Source-level program transformation of a high level HDL is a powerful technique for exploring a wide range of architectural tradeoffs from an initial specification. The partitioning transformation outlined here is applicable to any hardware description language (e.g. VHDL or Verilog) given suitable compilation functions and associated processor templates. However, we believe that equational reasoning makes program transformation a particularly powerful technique in the SAFL domain.

We are in the process of deploying the techniques outlined here as part of a semi-automated transformation system for SAFL programs. The goal of the project is to develop a framework in which a SAFL program can be systematically transformed to investigate a large number of possible implementations of a single specification. So far we have developed a library of transformations which allow us to represent a wide range of concepts in hardware design including: resource sharing/duplication, static/dynamic scheduling [13] and now hardware/software partitioning. In the future we plan to investigate how partial evaluation techniques [7] can be used to transform a processor definition function and its corresponding instruction memory function into a single unit with hardwired control.

Although initial results have been promising, the project is still in its early stages. We are currently investigating ways of extending the SAFL language to make it more expressive without loosing too many of its mathematical properties. Our current ideas centre around adding synchronous communication and a restricted form of π-calculus [11] style channel passing. We believe that this will allow us to capture the semantics of I/O whilst maintaining the correspondence between high-level function definitions and hardware-level resources.

4   Acknowledgements

This work is part of a collaborative project, "Self-Timed Microprocessors", involving Cambridge University Computer Laboratory (EPSRC grant GR/L86326), AT&T Laboratories Cambridge and Cambridge Consultants Ltd.

References

1. The "Art Designer" Tool. See http://www.frontierd.com.
2. Bjesse, P., Claessen, K., Sheeran, M. and Singh, S. Lava: Hardware Description in Haskell. Proceedings of the 3rd ACM SIGPLAN International Conference on Functional Programming, 1998.
3. Balarin, F., Chiodo, M., Giusto, P., Hsieh, H., Jurecska, A., Lavagno, L., Passerone, C., Sangiovanni-Vincentelli, A., Sentovich, E., Suzuki, K., Tabbara B. Hardware-Software Co-Design of Embedded Systems: The Polis Approach. Kluwer Academic Press, June 1997.
4. Burstall, R.M. and Darlington, J. A Transformation System for Developing Recursive Programs, JACM 24(1).
5. Cardelli, L. The Functional Abstract Machine. Technical Report TR-107, AT&T Bell Laboratories, April 1983.
6. Chou, P., Ortega, R., Borriello, G., The Chinook Hardware/Software Co-Synthesis System. Proceedings of the 8th International Symposium on System Synthesis, 1995.
7. Jones, N., Gomard, C. and Sestoft, P. Partial Evaluation and Automatic Program Generation. Published by Prentice Hall (1993); ISBN 0-13-020249-5.
8. Hennessy, J., Patterson, D. Computer Architecture A Quantitative Approach. Published by Morgan Kaufmann Publishers, Inc. (1990) ; ISBN 1-55860-069-8
9. Landin, P. The Mechanical Evaluation of Expressions. Computer Journal, Vol. 6, No. 4, 1964, pages 308-320.
10. Milner, R., Tofte, M., Harper, R. and MacQueen, D. The Definition of Standard ML (Revised). MIT Press, 1997.
11. Milner, R. The Polyadic π-calculus: a tutorial. Technical Report ECS-LFCS-91-180, Laboratory for Foundations of Computer Science, University of Edinburgh, October 1991.
12. Mycroft, A. and Sharp, R. A Statically Allocated Parallel Functional Language. Proc. of the International Conference on Automata, Languages and Programming 2000. LNCS Vol. 1853, Springer-Verlag.
13. Mycroft, A. and Sharp, R. The FLaSH Project: Resource-Aware Synthesis of Declarative Specifications. Proceedings of The International Workshop on Logic Synthesis 2000. Also available as AT&T Technical Report tr.2000.6 via www.uk.research.att.com

14. Nijhar, T., and Brown, A. Source Level Optimisation of VHDL for Behavioural Synthesis. IEE Proceedings on Computers and Digital Techniques, 144, No 1, January 1997, pp1-6.

15. O'Donnell, J. Generating Netlists from Executable Circuit Specifications in a Pure Functional Language. In *Functional Programming Glasgow*, Springer-Verlag Workshops in Computing, pages 178-194, 1993.

16. Page, I. and Luk, W. Compiling Occam into Field-Programmable Gate Arrays. In Moore and Luk (eds.) FPGAs, pages 271-283. Abingdon EE&CS Books, 1991.

17. Page, I. Parameterised Processor Generation. In Moore and Luk (eds.), More FPGAs, pages 225-237. Abingdon EE&CS Books, 1993.

18. Sharp, R. and Mycroft, A. The FLaSH Compiler: Efficient Circuits from Functional Specifications. AT&T Technical Report tr.2000.3. Available from www.uk.research.att.com

19. Sheeran, M. muFP, a Language for VLSI Design. Proc. ACM Symp. on LISP and Functional Programming, 1984.

20. Walker, R. Thomas, D., Behavioral Transformation for Algorithmic Level IC Design. IEEE Transactions on CAD, Vol. 8, No.10, October 1989.

```
(* +---------------------------------------------------------------+
   | SAFL specification of simple stack processor                  |
   |    Richard Sharp and Alan Mycroft, July 2000                  |
   +---------------------------------------------------------------+ *)


(* -------------------------- ALU -------------------------------- *)

fun alu2(op:16, a1:16, a2:16):16 =
    case op of  0 => a1+a2
              ! 1 => a1-a2
              ! 2 => a1&&a2
              ! 3 => a1||a2
              ! 4 => a1^^a2
              ! 16 => a1<a2
              ! 17 => a1>a2
              ! 18 => a1=a2
              ! 19 => a1>=a2
              ! 20 => a1<=a2
              ! 21 => a1<>a2

(* ---------------- Instruction memory here  -------------------- *)

(* The following codes: f(x) = if x then x+f(x-1) else 0;   *)
(* i.e. it computes triangular numbers                      *)
fun load_instruction (address:16):24 = case address of
        0 => %000010010000000000000001 (*      pusha 1    *)
      ! 1 => %000001010000000000000011 (*      call_int f *)
      ! 2 => %000000000000000000000000 (*      halt       *)
      ! 3 => %000000100000000000000001 (* f:   pushv 1    *)
      ! 4 => %000001110000000000001100 (*      jz 11      *)
      ! 5 => %000000100000000000000001 (*      pushv 1    *)
      ! 6 => %000000100000000000000010 (*      pushv 2    *)
      ! 7 => %000000010000000000000001 (*      pushc 1    *)
      ! 8 => %000010000000000000000001 (*      alu2 sub   *)
      ! 9 => %000001010000000000000011 (*      call_int f *)
      ! 10=> %000010000000000000000000 (*      alu2 add   *)
      ! 11=> %000001100000000000001101 (*      jmp 12     *)
      ! 12=> %000000010000000000000000 (* 11: pushc 0     *)
      ! 13=> %000001000000000000000001 (* 12: return 1    *)
  default => %101010101010101010101010 (*      illop      *)

external mem_acc (address:16,data:16,write:1):16

inline fun data_read  (address:16):16 = mem_acc(address,0,0)
inline fun data_write (address:16,data:16):16 = mem_acc(address,data,1)
```

Fig. 3. The Stack Machine (Part 1 of 2)

```
(* ---------------- Stack Machine Instance -------------------- *)

fun SMachine (a1:16, PC:16, SP:16):16 =

    let var new_PC  : 16  = PC + 1
        var instr   : 24  = load_instruction(PC)
        var op_code : 8   = instr[23,16]
        var op_rand : 16  = instr[15,0]
        var inc_SP  : 16  = SP + 1
        var dec_SP  : 16  = SP - 1
    in
        case op_code of
            0 => (* halt, returning TOS *)
                    data_read(SP)
          ! 1 => (* push constant operation *)
                    data_write(dec_SP, op_rand);
                    SMachine (a1, new_PC, dec_SP)
          ! 2 => (* push variable operation *)
                    let var data:16 = data_read(SP+op_rand)
                    in  data_write(dec_SP, data);
                        SMachine (a1, new_PC, dec_SP) end
          ! 9 => (* push a-argument operation *)
                    data_write(dec_SP, a1);
                    SMachine (a1, new_PC, dec_SP)
          ! 3 => (* squeeze operation -- op_rand is how many locals to pop *)
                    let var new_SP:16 = SP + op_rand
                        var v:16 = data_read(SP)
                    in  data_write(new_SP, v);
                        SMachine (a1, new_PC, new_SP) end
          ! 4 => (* return operation -- op_rand is how many actuals to pop *)
                    let var new_SP:16 = inc_SP + op_rand
                        var rv:16 = data_read(SP)
                    in  let var r1:16 = data_read(inc_SP)
                        in  data_write(new_SP, rv);
                            SMachine (a1, r1, new_SP) end end
          ! 5 => (* call_int operation *)
                    data_write(dec_SP, new_PC);
                    SMachine (a1, op_rand, dec_SP)
          ! 6 => (* jmp (abs) operation *)
                    SMachine (a1, op_rand, SP)
          ! 7 => (* jz (abs) operation *)
                    let var v:16 = data_read(SP)
                    in  SMachine (a1, if v=0 then op_rand else new_PC, inc_SP) end
          ! 8 => (* alu2: binary alu operation -- specified by immediate field *)
                    let var v2:16 = data_read(SP)
                    in  let var v1:16 = data_read(inc_SP)
                        in  data_write(inc_SP, alu2(op_rand, v1, v2));
                            SMachine (a1, new_PC, inc_SP) end end
          default =>
              (* halt, returning 0xffff -- illegal opcode *)
                    %1111111111111111
    end
```

Fig. 4. The Stack Machine (Part 2 of 2)

Automatic Abstraction of Memories in the Formal Verification of Superscalar Microprocessors[1]

Miroslav N. Velev
mvelev@ece.cmu.edu
http://www.ece.cmu.edu/~mvelev
Department of Electrical and Computer Engineering
Carnegie Mellon University, Pittsburgh, PA 15213, U.S.A.

Abstract. A system of conservative transformation rules is presented for abstracting memories whose forwarding logic interacts with stalling conditions for preserving the memory semantics in microprocessors with in-order execution. Microprocessor correctness is expressed in the logic of Equality with Uninterpreted Functions and Memories (EUFM) [6]. Memory reads and writes are abstracted as arbitrary uninterpreted functions in such a way that the forwarding property of the memory semantics—that a read returns the data most recently written to an equal write address—is satisfied completely only when exactly the same pair of one read and one write address is compared for equality in the stalling logic. These transformations are applied entirely automatically by a tool for formal verification of microprocessors, based on EUFM, the Burch and Dill flushing technique [6], and the properties of Positive Equality [3]. An order of magnitude reduction is achieved in the number of e_{ij} Boolean variables [9] that encode the equality comparisons of register identifiers in the correctness formulas for single-issue pipelined and dual-issue superscalar microprocessors with multicycle functional units, exceptions, and branch prediction. That results in up to 40× reduction in the CPU time for the formal verification of the dual-issue superscalar microprocessors.

1 Introduction

The motivation for this work is the complexity of the formal verification of correct microprocessors. The formal verification is done with the Burch and Dill flushing technique [6] by exploiting the properties of Positive Equality [3] in order to translate the correctness formula from the logic of Equality with Uninterpreted Functions and Memories (EUFM) to propositional logic. The translation is done by a completely automatic tool [16][21]. The resulting Boolean formula can be evaluated with either BDDs [2] or Boolean Satisfiability (SAT) checkers for being a tautology, which implies that the original EUFM correctness formula is universally valid, i.e., the processor is correct under all possible conditions.

Recently we showed that errors in complex realistic microprocessors are detected in CPU time that is up to orders of magnitude smaller than the time to prove the correctness of a bug-free version of the same design [20]. The present paper aims to speed up the verification of correct microprocessors with multicycle functional units, exceptions, and branch prediction, where reads and writes of user-visible state are not reordered and occur according to their program sequence.

---

1. This research was supported by the SRC under contract 00-DC-684.

2 Background

In this work, the logic of EUFM [6] is used for the definition of high-level models of both the implementation and the specification microprocessors. The syntax of EUFM includes terms and formulas. Terms are used in order to abstract word-level values of data, register identifiers, memory addresses, as well as the entire states of memories. A term can be an Uninterpreted Function (UF) applied on a list of argument terms, a domain variable, or an *ITE* operator selecting between two argument terms based on a controlling formula, such that *ITE(formula, term$_1$, term$_2$)* will evaluate to *term$_1$* when *formula* = **true** and to *term$_2$* when *formula* = **false**. Formulas are used in order to model the control path of a microprocessor, as well as to express the correctness condition. A formula can be an Uninterpreted Predicate (UP) applied on a list of argument terms, a propositional variable, an *ITE* operator selecting between two argument formulas based on a controlling formula, or an equation (equality comparison) of two terms. Formulas can be negated and connected by Boolean connectives.

UFs and UPs are used to abstract away the implementation details of functional units by replacing them with "black boxes" that satisfy no particular properties other than that of *functional consistency*—the same combinations of values to the inputs of the UF (or UP) produce the same output value. Three possible ways to impose the property of functional consistency of UFs and UPs are Ackermann constraints [1], nested *ITEs* [3][16], and "pushing-to-the-leaves" [16]. In the nested *ITEs* scheme, the first application of some UF, $f(a_1, b_1)$, is replaced by a new domain variable c_1. A second application, $f(a_2, b_2)$, is replaced by $ITE((a_2 = a_1) \square (b_2 = b_1), c_1, c_2)$, where c_2 is a new domain variable. A third one, $f(a_3, b_3)$, is replaced by $ITE((a_3 = a_1) \square (b_3 = b_1), c_1, ITE((a_3 = a_2) \square (b_3 = b_2), c_2, c_3))$, where c_3 is a new domain variable, and so on.

The syntax for terms can be extended to model memories by means of the functions *read* and *write*, where *read* takes 2 argument terms serving as memory and address, respectively, while *write* takes 3 argument terms serving as memory, address, and data. Both functions return a term. Also, they can be viewed as a special class of (partially interpreted) uninterpreted functions in that they are defined to satisfy the forwarding property of the memory semantics, namely that *read(write(mem, aw, d), ar)* = *ITE(ar = aw, d, read(mem, ar))*, in addition to the property of functional consistency. Versions of *read* and *write* that extend the syntax for formulas can be defined similarly, such that the version of *read* will return a formula and the version of *write* will take a formula as its third argument. Both terms and formulas are called expressions.

The correctness criterion is a commutative diagram [6]. It requires that one step of the Implementation transition function followed by flushing should produce equal user-visible state as first flushing the Implementation and then using the resulting user-visible state to apply the Specification transition function between 0 and k times, where k is the issue-width of the Implementation. *Flushing* of the processor is done by feeding it with bubbles until all instructions in flight complete their execution, computing an abstraction function that maps Implementation states to a Specification state. (The difference between a bubble and a nop is that a bubble does not modify any user-visible state, while a nop increments the PC.) The correctness criterion is expressed by an EUFM formula of the form:

$$m_{1,0} \square m_{2,0} \cdots \square m_{n,0} \quad \square \quad m_{1,1} \square m_{2,1} \cdots \square m_{n,1} \quad \square \cdots \square \quad m_{1,k} \square m_{2,k} \cdots \square m_{n,k}, \qquad (1)$$

where n is the number of user-visible state elements in the implementation processor, k is the maximum number of instructions that the processor can fetch in a clock cycle, and $m_{i,j}$, $1 \leq i \leq n$, $0 \leq j \leq k$, is an EUFM formula expressing the condition that user-visible state element i is updated by the first j instructions from the ones fetched in a single clock cycle. (See the electronic version of [16] for a detailed discussion.) The EUFM formulas $m_{1,j}$, $m_{2,j}$, ..., $m_{n,j}$, $0 \leq j \leq k$, are conjuncted in order to ensure that the user-visible state elements are updated in "sync" by the same number of instructions. The correctness criterion expresses a safety property that the processor completes between 0 and k of the newly fetched k instructions.

Positive Equality allows the identification of two types of terms in the structure of an EUFM formula—those which appear only in positive equations and are called *p-terms*, and those which can appear in both positive and negative equations and are called *g-terms* (for general terms). A *positive equation* is never negated (or appears under an even number of negations) and is not part of the controlling formula for an *ITE* operator. A *negative equation* appears under an odd number of negations or as part of the controlling formula for an *ITE* operator. The computational efficiency from exploiting Positive Equality is due to a theorem which states that the truth of an EUFM formula under a maximally diverse interpretation of the p-terms implies the truth of the formula under any interpretation. The classification of p-terms vs. g-terms is done before UFs and UPs are eliminated by nested *ITEs*, such that if an UF is classified as a p-term (g-term), the new domain variables generated for its elimination are also considered to be p-terms (g-terms). After the UFs and the UPs are eliminated, a maximally diverse interpretation is one where: the equality comparison of two syntactically identical (i.e., exactly the same) domain variables evaluates to **true**; the equality comparison of a p-term domain variable with a syntactically distinct domain variable evaluates to **false**; and the equality comparison of a g-term domain variable with a syntactically distinct g-term domain variable could evaluate to either **true** or **false** and can be encoded with a dedicated Boolean variable—an e_{ij} variable [9].

In order to fully exploit the benefits of Positive Equality, the designer of a high-level processor must use a set of suitable abstractions and conservative approximations. For example, an equality comparison of two data operands, as used to determine the condition to take a branch-on-equal instruction, must be abstracted with an UP in both the Implementation and the Specification, so that the data operand terms will not appear in negated equations but only as arguments to UPs and UFs and hence will be classified as p-terms. Similarly, a Finite State Machine (FSM) model of a memory has to be employed for abstracting the Data Memory in order for the addresses, which are produced by the ALU and also serve as data operands, to be classified as p-terms. In the FSM abstraction of a memory, the present memory state is a term that is stored in a latch. Reads are modeled with an UF f_r that depends on the present memory state and the address, while producing a term for the read data. Writes are modeled with an UF f_u that depends on the present memory state, the address, and a data term, producing a term for the new memory state, which is to be stored in the latch. The result is that data values produced by the Register File, the ALU, and the Data Memory can be classified as p-terms, while only the register identifiers, whose equations control forwarding and stalling conditions that can be negated, are classified as g-terms.

We will refer to a transformation on the implementation and specification processors as a *conservative approximation* if it omits some properties, making the new processor models more general than the original ones. Note that the same transformation is applied to both the implementation and the specification processors. However, if the more general model of the implementation is verified against the more general model of the specification, so would be the original implementation against the original specification, whose additional properties were not necessary for the verification.

Proposition 1. *The FSM model of a memory, based on uninterpreted functions f_u and f_r, is a conservative approximation of a memory.*

Proof. If a processor is proved correct with the FSM model of a memory where the update function f_u and the read function f_r are completely arbitrary uninterpreted functions that do not satisfy the forwarding property of the memory semantics, then the processor will be correct for any implementation of f_u and f_r, including $f_u \equiv write$ and $f_r \equiv read$.

3   Automatic Abstraction of Memories

When abstracting memories in [19], the following transformations were applied automatically by the verification tool when processing the EUFM correctness formula, starting from the leaves of that formula:

$$read(m, a) \rightarrow f_r(m, a) \tag{2}$$

$$write(m, a, d) \rightarrow f_u(m, a, d) \tag{3}$$

$$ITE(e \ \Box \ (ra = wa), d, f_r(m, ra)) \rightarrow f_r(ITE(e, f_u(m, wa, d), m), ra) \tag{4}$$

Transformations (2) and (3) are the same as those used in the abstraction of the Data Memory, described in Sect. 2. Transformation (4) occurs in the cases when one level of forwarding logic is used to update the data read from address ra of the previous state m for the memory, where function $read$ is already abstracted with UF f_r. Accounting for the forwarding property of the memory semantics that was satisfied before function $read$ was abstracted with UF f_r, the left handside of (4) is equivalent to $read(ITE(e, write(m, wa, d), m), ra)$, i.e., to a read from address ra of the state of memory m after a write to address wa with data d is done under the condition that formula e is **true**. On the right handside of (4), functions $read$ and $write$ are again abstracted with f_r and f_u after accounting for the forwarding property. Multiple levels of forwarding are abstracted by recursive applications of (4), starting from the leaves of the correctness formula. Uninterpreted functions f_u and f_r can be automatically made unique for every memory, where a memory is identified by a unique domain variable serving as the memory argument at the leaves of a memory state term. Hence, f_u and f_r will no longer be functionally consistent across memories—a conservative approximation.

After all memories were automatically abstracted as presented above, the tool in [19] checked if an address term for an abstracted memory was still used in a negated equation, i.e., was a g-term. If so, then the abstraction for that memory was undone. Hence, abstraction was performed automatically only for a memory whose addresses are p-terms outside the memory and the forwarding logic for it. From Proposition 1, it follows that such an abstraction is a conservative approximation. The condition that address terms of abstracted memories are used only as p-terms outside the abstracted memories avoids false negatives that might result when a (negated) equation of two address terms will imply that a write to one of the addresses will (not) affect a read from the other address in the equation when that read is performed later—a property that is lost in the abstraction with UFs. In the architecture verified in [19], transformations (2) – (4) worked for the Branch-Address Register File, whose forwarding logic did not interact with stalling logic for preserving the correctness of the memory semantics for that register file, as the branch-address results were available for forwarding right after the Execute stage. However, the above abstractions were not applicable to the Integer and Floating-Point Register Files that did have stalling logic interact with their forwarding logic.

The contribution made with this paper is the idea of a *hybrid memory model*, where the forwarding property of the memory semantics is satisfied fully for only those levels of forwarding where exactly the same pair of one read and one write address is compared for equality outside the abstracted memory, i.e., in the EUFM formula resulting after the application of transformations (2) – (4). We will refer to addresses compared in general equations outside an abstracted memory as *control addresses*, and will call those general equations *control equations*. In the cases when the read address in a level of forwarding is a control address, but the write address is not or the write address is also a control address but does not appear in a control equation together with the read address, then that level of forwarding is abstracted with uninterpreted function f_{ud} (where "*ud*" stands for "update data"). UF f_{ud} takes 4 argument terms—write address wa, write data wd, read address ra, and data rd read from the previous memory state before the write—such that the functionality abstracted with $f_{ud}(wa, wd, ra, rd)$ is $ITE(ra = wa, wd, rd)$. Finally, when the read address is not a control address, the read is abstracted as before based on transformations (2) – (4).

Note that the initial state of the pipeline latches in the implementation processor consists of a domain variable for every term signal (including register identifiers) and a Boolean variable for every Boolean signal. Hence, the equality comparisons of register identifiers done in the stalling logic during the single cycle of regular symbolic simulation along the implementation side of the commutative correctness diagram will be at the level of domain variables serving as register identifiers. Furthermore, using Burch's controlled flushing [7], it is possible to flush the implementation processor without introducing additional register id equality comparisons due to the stalling logic. In controlled flushing, instructions are artificially stalled by overriding the processor stall signals with user-controlled auxiliary inputs until it is guaranteed that the stall signals will evaluate to **false**, i.e., all the data operand values can be provided correctly by the forwarding logic or can be read directly from a register file. Note that we can modify the processor logic during flushing, as all that logic does then is to complete the partially executed instructions. Mistakes in such modifications can only result in false negatives. The symbolic simulation of the non-pipelined specification processor along the specification side of the commutative correctness diagram does not result in additional control equations, as all data operands are read directly from the register files. Therefore, using controlled flushing and applying transformations (2) – (4) will result in an EUFM correctness formula with only those general (control) equations over register identifier terms that are introduced by the stalling logic in the single cycle of regular symbolic simulation in order to preserve the correctness of the memory semantics for a register file. The exact abstraction steps are presented next.

Algorithm for Applying the Hybrid Memory Model:

1. Abstract all memories:

   1.1 use rules (2) – (4) to abstract memories extended with forwarding logic;

   1.2 use UF f_{ud} to abstract levels of forwarding where the initial data is not read from a memory:

   $$ITE(e \ \square \ (ra = wa), d_1, d_0) \ \rightarrow \ ITE(e, f_{ud}(wa, d_1, ra, d_0), d_0) \tag{5}$$

   where d_0 is neither an application of UF f_r nor an ITE expression that has an application of f_r among its leaves;

   1.3 identify the control equations and control addresses.

2. For all applications of UF f_r whose address term is an ITE expression, push f_r to the leaves of the address term:

   $$f_r(m, ITE(e, ra_1, ra_2)) \ \rightarrow \ ITE(e, f_r(m, ra_1), f_r(m, ra_2)) \tag{6}$$

   until every address argument of f_r becomes a domain variable. If an address argument to f_r is an application of an UF, then use the nested ITEs scheme to eliminate it and again apply (6) recursively.

3. For those applications $f_r(m, ra)$, where the address term ra is a control address and m is of the form $ITE(e, f_u(m_0, wa, wd), m_0)$, do:

   3.1 if the write address wa is an ITE expression, $ITE(c, wa_1, wa_2)$, where some of the leaf terms are control addresses compared for equality to ra in a control equation, then apply the transformation:

   $$f_r(ITE(e, f_u(m_0, ITE(c, wa_1, wa_2), wd), m_0), ra) \ \rightarrow$$
   $$ITE(c, f_r(ITE(e, f_u(m_0, wa_1, wd), m_0), ra),$$
   $$f_r(ITE(e, f_u(m_0, wa_2, wd), m_0), ra)) \tag{7}$$

   3.2 else, if the write address wa is a control address compared for equality to ra in a control equation, then apply the transformation:

   $$f_r(ITE(e, f_u(m_0, wa, wd), m_0), ra) \ \rightarrow \ ITE(e \ \square \ (ra = wa), wd, f_r(m_0, ra)) \tag{8}$$

   3.3 else, apply the transformation:

   $$f_r(ITE(e, f_u(m_0, wa, wd), m_0), ra) \ \rightarrow$$
   $$ITE(e, f_{ud}(wa, wd, ra, f_r(m_0, ra)), f_r(m_0, ra)) \tag{9}$$

   until every memory argument of f_r becomes a domain variable, i.e., is the initial state of a memory.

Note that Step 3 relies on the assumption that every write to a memory is done under the condition that an enabling formula e is **true**. However, an unconditional write is the case when $e \equiv$ **true**. The soundness of the above transformations is proved as follows.

Proposition 2. *The hybrid memory model, based on uninterpreted functions f_w, f_r and f_{ud}, is a conservative approximation of a memory.*

Proof. If a processor is proved correct with arbitrary uninterpreted functions f_w, f_r and f_{ud}, the processor will be correct for any implementation of these uninterpreted functions, including $f_w(m, wa, wd) \equiv write(m, wa, wd)$, $f_r(m, ra) \equiv read(m, ra)$, and $f_{ud}(wa, wd, ra, rd) \equiv ITE(ra = wa, wd, rd)$ that satisfy the complete memory semantics.

Transformations (2) – (9) separate the effects of the forwarding and stalling logic, modeling conservatively their interaction. The result is a dramatic reduction in the number of e_{ij} Boolean variables required for encoding the equality comparisons of g-term domain variables, as now most of the register identifier terms are used only as inputs to uninterpreted functions, i.e., become p-terms. Indeed, only transformation (8) introduces a general equation over register identifiers. However, exactly the same equation already exists in the EUFM formula outside the abstracted memory, so that the number of general equations over register identifiers is equal to the number of equations generated by the stalling logic in the single cycle of regular symbolic simulation of the implementation processor. Hence, the translation of the EUFM correctness formula to propositional logic by applying transformations (2) – (9) will depend on significantly fewer Boolean variables and its tautology checking will be done much faster, compared to the case when these transformations are not applied.

In our previous work [16][17][19], the two final memory states reached along the two sides of the commutative diagram were checked for equality by generating a new domain variable, performing a read from that address of both final states, and comparing for equality the two resulting data terms. That scheme introduces additional e_{ij} Boolean variables encoding the equality of the final read address with each of the write addresses. The advantage of that comparison method is that it can account for the property of transitivity of equality for the register ids [4][5]. Although that property is not required for the correct benchmarks used in this paper, it is needed in order to avoid false negatives for buggy versions, as well as when verifying out-of-order superscalar processors [20]. In the present paper, the final memory states are compared for equality by applying transformation (3) to the final memory state terms, i.e., abstracting function *write* with UF f_w, and directly comparing for equality the resulting final memory state terms. Indeed, what is verified is that the same sequence of updates is performed under all conditions by both sides of the commutative diagram.

Transformations (2) – (9) are based on the assumption that reads and writes are not reordered and occur in the same sequence along the two sides of the commutative correctness diagram—the case in microprocessors with in-order execution.

4   Example

The transformation rules will be illustrated on the pipelined processor in Fig. 1. It can execute only register-register instructions and has 4 stages: Instruction Fetch (IF), Execute (EX), a Dummy stage (D), and Write-Back (WB). Since there is no forwarding logic to bypass the result of the instruction in D to the instruction in EX, a newly-fetched instruction is stalled if it has a data dependency on the preceding instruction in EX. When set to **true**, signal Flush stops the instruction fetching and inserts bubbles in the pipeline, thus flushing it by allowing partially executed instructions to complete [6]. The instruction memory, IMem, is read-only and is abstracted with 3 UFs—one for each of the instruction fields source register (SrcReg), op-code (Op), and destination register (DestReg)—and 1 UP—for the valid bit (Valid). UFs ALU and +4 abstract, respectively, the ALU in EX and the PC incrementer in IF. The register file, RegFile, is write-before-read, i.e., the newly-fetched instruction will be able to read the data written by the instruction in WB. The user-visible state elements are PC and RegFile. The processor is compared against a non-pipelined specification (not shown) that consists of the same user-visible state, UFs, and UP. It does not have the 3 pipeline latches, stalling logic, or forwarding logic.

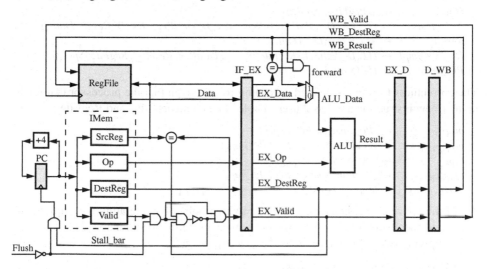

Fig. 1. Block diagram of a 4-stage pipelined processor.

Flushing the pipeline takes 3 clock cycles, as there can be up to 3 instructions in flight. In order to define the specification behavior, the implementation processor is first flushed, reaching the initial specification state $\langle PC\_Spec_0, RegFile\_Spec_0 \rangle$, as shown below. The specification processor is then exercised for 1 step from that state, reaching specification state $\langle PC\_Spec_1, RegFile\_Spec_1 \rangle$. SrcReg, DestReg, and Op are new domain variables and Valid is a new Boolean variable used to eliminate the single applications of, respectively, the three UFs and one UP that abstract the IMem. Domain variables PC and RegFile represent the initial state of the corresponding state element. Domain and Boolean variables with prefixes IF_EX_, EX_D_, and D_WB_ represent the initial state of the corresponding pipeline latch. Functions read and write are already abstracted with UFs f_r and f_u, respectively, according to (2) and (3). The left arrow "←" means assignment.

$RegFile_0$ ← $ITE(D\_WB\_Valid, f_u(RegFile, D\_WB\_DestReg, D\_WB\_Result), RegFile)$
$RegFile_1$ ← $ITE(EX\_D\_Valid, f_u(RegFile_0, EX\_D\_DestReg, EX\_D\_Result), RegFile_0)$
$forward_0$ ← $(IF\_EX\_SrcReg = D\_WB\_DestReg) \sqcap D\_WB\_Valid$
ALU_Data_0 ← $ITE(forward_0, D\_WB\_Result, IF\_EX\_Data)$
$Result_0$ ← $ALU(IF\_EX\_Op, ALU\_Data_0)$

$RegFile\_Spec_0 \leftarrow ITE(IF\_EX\_Valid, f_u(RegFile_1, IF\_EX\_DestReg, Result_0), RegFile_1)$
$PC\_Spec_0 \quad \leftarrow PC$
$Data_0 \qquad \leftarrow f_r(RegFile\_Spec_0, SrcReg)$
$Result_1 \qquad \leftarrow ALU(Op, Data_0)$
$RegFile\_Spec_1 \leftarrow ITE(Valid, f_u(RegFile\_Spec_0, DestReg, Result_1), RegFile\_Spec_0)$
$PC\_Spec_1 \quad \leftarrow +4(PC)$

The behavior of the implementation processor is captured by one cycle of regular symbolic simulation (Flush is set to **false**), followed by flushing:

$Stall\_bar \qquad \leftarrow \square(IF\_EX\_Valid \ \square \ Valid \ \square \ (IF\_EX\_DestReg = SrcReg))$
$IF\_Valid \qquad \leftarrow Valid \ \square \ Stall\_bar$
$Data_1 \qquad \leftarrow f_r(RegFile_0, SrcReg)$
$ALU\_Data_1 \leftarrow ITE(EX\_D\_Valid \ \square \ (SrcReg = EX\_D\_DestReg), EX\_D\_Result, Data_1)$
$Result_2 \qquad \leftarrow ALU(Op, ALU\_Data_1)$
$RegFile\_Impl \leftarrow ITE(IF\_Valid, f_u(RegFile\_Spec_0, DestReg, Result_2), RegFile\_Spec_0)$
$PC\_Impl \qquad \leftarrow ITE(Stall\_bar, +4(PC), PC)$

The correctness formula is defined according to (1), given that the processor can fetch up to 1 new instruction and has 2 user-visible state elements—PC and RegFile:

$m_{PC,0} \qquad \leftarrow (PC\_Spec_0 = PC\_Impl)$
$m_{RegFile,0} \quad \leftarrow (RegFile\_Spec_0 = RegFile\_Impl)$
$m_{PC,1} \qquad \leftarrow (PC\_Spec_1 = PC\_Impl)$
$m_{RegFile,1} \quad \leftarrow (RegFile\_Spec_1 = RegFile\_Impl)$
$correctness \quad \leftarrow m_{PC,0} \ \square \ m_{RegFile,0} \ \square \ m_{PC,1} \ \square \ m_{RegFile,1}$

All of the above expressions are generated by symbolically simulating the implementation and specification processors with a term-level symbolic simulator [21].

Applying rule (4) to expression ALU_Data_1, we get:

$ALU\_Data_1 \quad \leftarrow f_r(RegFile_1, SrcReg)$

This is achieved by using a unique-expression hash table [16], so that

$ITE(EX\_D\_Valid, f_u(RegFile_0, EX\_D\_DestReg, EX\_D\_Result), RegFile_0)$

is identified as the existing identical expression $RegFile_1$.

UF f_{ud} is next applied in order to abstract the one level of forwarding that affects expression ALU_Data_0 (Step 1.2 of the algorithm for the hybrid memory model):

$temp_0 \qquad \leftarrow f_{ud}(D\_WB\_DestReg, D\_WB\_Result, IF\_EX\_SrcReg, IF\_EX\_Data)$
$ALU\_Data_0 \quad \leftarrow ITE(D\_WB\_Valid, temp_0, IF\_EX\_Data)$

As a result, the only general equation left in the correctness formula is $(IF\_EX\_DestReg = SrcReg)$ in expression $Stall\_bar$, where both $IF\_EX\_DestReg$ and $SrcReg$ are addresses for the abstracted memory RegFile, i.e., they are used as address arguments in applications of f_r and f_u where the initial memory state is domain variable $RegFile$. Hence, that equation is a control equation and domain variables $IF\_EX\_DestReg$ and $SrcReg$ are control addresses.

Recursively applying Step 3 of the algorithm for the hybrid memory model to expressions $Data_0$ and ALU_Data_1, where the address term $SrcReg$ of f_r is a control address, we get:

$temp_1 \qquad \leftarrow f_r(RegFile, SrcReg)$
$temp_2 \qquad \leftarrow f_{ud}(D\_WB\_DestReg, D\_WB\_Result, SrcReg, temp_1)$
$temp_3 \qquad \leftarrow ITE(D\_WB\_Valid, temp_2, temp_1)$
$temp_4 \qquad \leftarrow f_{ud}(EX\_D\_DestReg, EX\_D\_Result, SrcReg, temp_3)$
$temp_5 \qquad \leftarrow ITE(EX\_D\_Valid, temp_4, temp_3)$
$temp_6 \qquad \leftarrow IF\_EX\_Valid \ \square \ (IF\_EX\_DestReg = SrcReg)$
$Data_0 \qquad \leftarrow ITE(temp_6, Result_0, temp_5)$
$ALU\_Data_1 \quad \leftarrow temp_5$

Now the only general equation left in the correctness formula is $(IF\_EX\_DestReg = SrcReg)$. Hence, only these two address terms will be g-terms, while the rest will be p-terms, and just one e_{ij} Boolean variable will be introduced. In contrast, there will be 8 e_{ij} variables if the hybrid memory model is not applied: 1 for encoding the above equation; 3 for the equations between $SrcReg$ and each of the destination registers used for writes within $RegFile\_Spec_0$ in order to account for the forwarding property when $read(RegFile\_Spec_0, SrcReg)$ is eliminated (see Sect. 2); and 4 for equations between a new domain variable and each of the 4 destination registers used for writes to the RegFile when its final states are compared for equality (see Sect. 3). The reduction in the number of e_{ij} variables and the speedup become dramatic for complex microprocessors, as shown in Sect. 6.

5   Rewriting Rules for Processors with Multicycle ALUs

Processors with multicycle ALUs require applying an additional transformation on the EUFM correctness formula before the rules from Sect. 3. The problem stems from the uncertain advance, as controlled by signal Done, of the instruction in the Execute stage during the single cycle of regular symbolic simulation—see Fig. 2. Multicycle ALUs are abstracted with a place holder [17][18], where an UF is used to abstract the functionality, and a new Boolean variable is introduced to express the non-deterministic completion of the computation during each cycle. The place holder is forced to complete a new computation on every cycle during flushing. As noted in Sect. 3, modifying the processor during flushing can only result in false negatives.

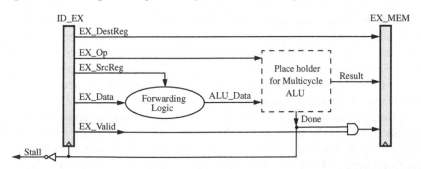

Fig. 2. The Execute stage of a pipelined processor with a multicycle ALU.

Let c be the value of signal Done during the single cycle of regular symbolic simulation. Then, on the next cycle, EX_Data will have the expression $ITE(c, read(m, ra), d_0)$, where $read(m, ra)$ is data that has been read from the register file by the next instruction, and d_0 is a domain variable for the initial value of EX_Data. Similarly, EX_SrcReg will have the expression $ITE(c, ra, a_0)$, where ra is the source register for the next instruction and a_0 is a domain variable for the initial value of that signal. Assuming one level of forwarding, ALU_Data will have an expression of the kind:

$$ITE(e \;\square\; (wa = ITE(c, ra, a_0)), d_1, ITE(c, read(m, ra), d_0)) \qquad (10)$$

where wa, d_1, and e are, respectively, the destination register, data, and enabling condition for a write in flight to the register file. Since the above expression does not exactly match either of rules (4) and (5), it is rewritten by pulling c to the top of the expression and simplifying the read address along each branch of the new top-level ITE:

$$ITE(c, ITE(e \;\square\; (wa = ra), d_1, read(m, ra)), ITE(e \;\square\; (wa = a_0), d_1, d_0)) \qquad (11)$$

Now the then-expression (selected when $c = \mathbf{true}$) of the top-level ITE can be rewritten using rule (4), while the else-expression can be rewritten using rule (5).

6   Experimental Results

The benchmarks used for the experiments are the same as in our previous work [17]:

1×DLX-C: A single-issue, 5-stage, pipelined DLX processor [10], capable of executing the 6 instruction types of register-register, register-immediate, load, store, branch, and jump. The 5 stages are Fetch, Decode, Execute, Memory, and Write-Back. Forwarding is used to bypass the data results from the Memory and Write-Back stages to the functional units in the Execute stage. However, forwarding is impossible when a load provides data for the immediately following instruction. In such cases, the data hazard is prevented by a load interlock that stalls the dependent instruction in Decode until the load completes and its result can be forwarded from Write-Back when the dependent instruction is in Execute. There are 2 stalling conditions that can trigger a load interlock—one for each of the two source registers of the instruction in Decode. Stalling due to the second source register is done only when its data value is actually used, e.g., the instruction is not of type register-immediate, so that its immediate data value will be used instead.

2×DLX-CA: A dual-issue, superscalar DLX consisting of two 5-stage pipelines. The first pipeline is complete, i.e., capable of executing the 6 instruction types, while the second pipeline can execute only arithmetic (register-register and register-immediate) instructions. Since load instructions can be executed by the complete pipeline only, there is at most 1 load destination register in the Execute stage, but 4 source registers in the Decode stage for a total of 4 possible load interlock stalling conditions. If a load interlock is triggered due to the first instruction in Decode, both instructions in that stage get stalled, so that the processor fetches 0 new instructions. Else, under a load interlock due to the second instruction in Decode, only the first instruction in that stage is allowed to proceed to Execute, while the second moves to the first slot in Decode and the processor fetches only 1 new instruction to fill the second slot in Decode. Additionally, only the first instruction in Decode is allowed to proceed when its result is used by the second instruction in that stage, or when the second instruction is not arithmetic (i.e., there is a structural hazard), in which case that instruction has to be executed by the first pipeline. Hence, 0, 1, or 2 new instructions can be fetched each cycle. This design is equivalent to Burch's processor [7].

2×DLX-CC: A dual-issue, superscalar DLX with two complete 5-stage pipelines. Now 2 load destination registers in Execute could provide data for each of the 4 source registers in Decode, for a total of 8 load interlock stalling conditions. When a load interlock is triggered for one of the two instructions in Decode, or when the second instruction in that stage depends on the result of the first, the instructions in Decode proceed as in 2×DLX-CA. However, there is no structural hazard, as both pipelines are complete. Again, 0, 1, or 2 new instructions can be fetched each cycle.

Each of the above processors also has an extension with: branch prediction, marked "**-BP**"; multicycle functional units, "**-MC**," where the Instruction Memory, the ALUs in the Execute stage, and the Data Memory can each take multiple cycles to produce a result; exceptions, "**-EX**," where the Instruction Memory, the ALUs, and the Data Memory can raise an exception; as well as combinations of these features. (For detailed descriptions of these processors and their verification see [17][18].)

The results are presented in Tables 1 and 2. The experiments were performed on a 336 MHz Sun4 with 1.2 GB of memory. The Colorado University BDD package [8], and the sifting BDD variable reordering heuristic [14] were used to evaluate the final propositional formulas. The CPU times are reported for the sequence of symbolic simulation, translation of the EUFM correctness formula to a propositional one, and evaluation of the latter with BDDs. The ratios in the last columns of the tables are of the CPU times before and after applying the automatic abstraction of the register file. Burch's controlled flushing [7] was employed for all of the designs.

The experiments with automatically abstracted register files were run with a breadth-first elimination of the UFs and UPs with the nested *ITE*s scheme (see Sect. 2) when translating the EUFM correctness formula to propositional logic. A variant of the fanin heuristic for BDD variable ordering [12] was used: all nodes in the propositional logic DAG are sorted in descending order of their fanout counts; unless already created, the BDD for each node in that order is built in a depth-first manner, such that the inputs to each AND and OR gate are sorted in descending order of their topological levels and their BDDs are built in that order. The experiments without abstracting the register file were run with various heuristics and optimizations—no single strategy performed uniformly as the best across all benchmarks—and the statistics from the experiment with the minimum CPU time for each benchmark are reported.

As Tables 1 and 2 show, the number of e_{ij} register variables is reduced to at most 10 when automatically abstracting the register file from up to 152 for the most complex benchmark, 2×DLX-CC-MC-EX-BP, before the abstraction. The e_{ij} register variables left after the abstraction are those that encode register id equality comparisons made by the stalling logic only in the single cycle of regular symbolic simulation of the implementation processor. In the case of the single-issue processors, the 2 source registers in Decode are compared with the 1 possible load destination register in Execute, for a total of 2 e_{ij} register variables. 2×DLX-CA and its variants have 4 source registers in Decode and still 1 possible load destination register in Execute (the second pipeline cannot execute load instructions). Furthermore, the 2 source registers of the

Processor	Auto. Abs. Reg. File	BDD Variables					Max. BDD Nodes	Memory [MB]	CPU Time [s]	CPU Time Ratio
		e_{ij}			Other	Total				
		Reg.	Br.	Total						
1×DLX-C		27	0	27	36	63	2,155	5.6	0.26	1.24
		2	0	2	34	36	714	5.4	0.21	
1×DLX-C-BP		27	8	35	41	76	3,408	5.7	0.36	1.24
		2	8	10	39	49	2,224	5.5	0.29	
1×DLX-C-MC		45	0	45	54	99	4,520	5.9	0.75	1.74
		2	0	2	46	48	3,095	5.6	0.43	
1×DLX-C-EX		27	0	27	64	91	7,122	6.4	1.16	1.21
		2	0	2	64	66	5,364	6.0	0.96	
1×DLX-C-MC-EX		36	0	36	77	113	18,108	6.5	4.53	2.35
		2	0	2	76	78	10,313	6.4	1.93	
1×DLX-C-MC-EX-BP		36	10	46	81	127	17,236	6.5	4.06	2.0
		2	10	12	80	92	10,839	6.3	2.03	

Table 1. Statistics for the formal verification of the single-issue pipelined processors. "Auto. Abs. Reg. File" stands for "automatically abstracted register file." The e_{ij} "Reg." variables are the ones that encode equality comparisons between register identifiers. The e_{ij} "Br." variables are the ones that encode equality comparisons between predicted and actual branch address targets.

second instruction in Decode are compared for equality with the destination register of the first instruction in that stage, in order to avoid Read-After-Write hazards [10]. Hence, there are 6 e_{ij} register variables for these benchmarks after abstracting the register file. Processor 2×DLX-CC and its extensions can additionally have a load in the Execute stage of the second pipeline, so that the load interlock logic also compares the destination register of that instruction against the 4 source registers in Decode, for a total of 10 e_{ij} register variables. As expected, most of the register ids have become p-terms after the automatic abstraction of the register file and no longer require Boolean variables for encoding their equality comparisons with other register ids.

The speedup for the single-issue pipelined processors is at most 2.0 times after applying the automatic abstraction of the register file, as these designs are relatively simple and could be verified very efficiently before the abstraction. Indeed, the extra time spent applying the transformation rules on the least complex benchmark, 1×DLX-C, is approximately equal to the time saved in the BDD-based evaluation of the resulting Boolean correctness formula, so that the CPU time was reduced with only 0.05 seconds. However, the speedup becomes dramatic for the dual-issue superscalar benchmarks and ranges from 5.7 to 43.5 times. The maximum number of BDD nodes is also reduced, ranging from 23% for 2×DLX-CA to less than 7% for 2×DLX-CC-MC, relative to the BDD node count without the abstraction.

Benchmark 1×DLX-C was first formally verified by Burch and Dill [6], who required the user to manually provide a case-splitting formula, indicating the conditions under which the processor will fetch and complete 1 new instruction. In order for

Processor	Auto. Abs. Reg. File	BDD Variables					Max. BDD Nodes	Memory [MB]	CPU Time [s]	CPU Time Ratio
		e_{ij}			Other	Total				
		Reg.	Br.	Total						
2×DLX-CA		112	0	112	58	170	17,492	6.8	4.7	5.73
		6	0	6	56	62	4,004	6.2	0.82	
2×DLX-CA-BP		112	18	130	68	198	29,397	7.2	10.5	8.14
		6	22	28	66	94	6,256	6.4	1.29	
2×DLX-CA-MC		142	0	142	76	218	68,895	8.2	21	7.19
		6	0	6	75	81	9,470	6.9	2.92	
2×DLX-CA-EX		122	0	122	92	214	143,330	12	142	21.85
		6	0	6	92	98	21,496	8.6	6.5	
2×DLX-CA-MC-EX		146	0	146	125	271	281,966	14	350	14
		6	0	6	124	130	58,847	9.3	25	
2×DLX-CA-MC-EX-BP		150	61	211	131	342	735,380	22	1,137	18.34
		6	23	29	130	159	96,346	9.3	62	
2×DLX-CC		116	0	116	69	185	40,586	7.7	20	10.2
		10	0	10	65	75	7,823	6.3	1.96	
2×DLX-CC-BP		122	25	147	82	229	74,555	8.8	43	8.21
		10	28	38	78	116	19,988	6.6	5.24	
2×DLX-CC-MC		142	0	142	94	236	315,732	14	226	37.67
		10	0	10	92	102	21,322	7.4	6	
2×DLX-CC-EX		122	0	122	103	225	413,732	18	486	17.36
		10	0	10	102	112	68,159	9.6	28	
2×DLX-CC-MC-EX		146	0	146	150	296	1,229,056	34	3,571	43.55
		10	0	10	148	158	118,216	11	82	
2×DLX-CC-MC-EX-BP		152	35	187	158	345	1,009,206	29	2,593	21.61
		10	32	42	156	198	185,249	12	120	

Table 2. Statistics for the formal verification of the dual-issue superscalar processors. "Auto. Abs. Reg. File" stands for "automatically abstracted register file." The e_{ij} "Reg." variables are the ones that encode equality comparisons between register identifiers. The e_{ij} "Br." variables are the ones that encode equality comparisons between predicted and actual branch address targets.

Hosabettu [11] to formally verify the same benchmark, he needed a month of manual work for the definition of completion functions—one per unfinished instruction, describing how that instruction would be completed, assuming all instructions ahead of it in program order have been completed. The completion functions for all instructions in flight are composed manually in order to compute the abstraction function— mapping an implementation state to a specification state—necessary for the commutative diagram. Ritter, et al. [13] could verify the same benchmark after running their symbolic simulator for 65 minutes of CPU time.

Benchmark 2×DLX-CA was first verified by Burch [7] who needed around 30 minutes of CPU time (on a slower Sun4 than the one used for the experiments in this paper) only after manually defining 28 case-splitting formulas and decomposing the commutative correctness diagram into 3 diagrams that are easier to verify. However, that decomposition was subtle enough to warrant the publication of its correctness proof as a separate paper [22]. Hosabettu [11] needed again a month of manual work for the definition of the completion functions for this design. Note that the tool [21] used for the experiments in this paper is completely automatic. It does not require manual intervention except for defining the controlled flushing of the implementation processor—something that takes a couple of minutes and has to be done just once for each design.

7   Conclusions and Future Work

An order of magnitude reduction was achieved in the CPU time for the formal verification of dual-issue superscalar microprocessors with multicycle functional units, exceptions, and branch prediction. That was possible by automatically applying a system of conservative transformation rules for abstracting the register file in a way that separates the forwarding and stalling logic, modeling completely only those levels of forwarding that directly interact with stalling conditions, but abstracting conservatively the rest. The transformation rules are based on the assumption that reads and writes of user-visible state are not reordered and occur in their program sequence.

The effectiveness of a set of conservative rewriting rules depends on accounting for variations in the description style used for the implementation and specification processors, so that false negatives are possible when certain cases are not considered. However, the potential gain from such rewriting rules is a dramatic speedup of up to orders of magnitude, as demonstrated in this paper.

The same transformation rules can be expected to speed up the checking of liveness properties for in-order microprocessors, where a design will be simulated for a fixed number of more than one clock cycles in order to prove that it will eventually complete a new instruction. Future work will extend the transformation rules for application to out-of-order microprocessors.

References

[1]   W. Ackermann, *Solvable Cases of the Decision Problem*, North-Holland, Amsterdam, 1954.

[2]   R.E. Bryant, "Symbolic Boolean Manipulation with Ordered Binary-Decision Diagrams," ACM Computing Surveys, Vol. 24, No. 3 (September 1992), pp. 293-318.

[3]   R.E. Bryant, S. German, and M.N. Velev, "Processor Verification Using Efficient Reductions of the Logic of Uninterpreted Functions to Propositional Logic,"[2] ACM Transactions on Computational Logic (TOCL), Vol. 2, No. 1 (January 2001).

[4]   R.E. Bryant, and M.N. Velev, "Boolean Satisfiability with Transitivity Constraints,"[2] *Computer-Aided Verification (CAV '00)*, E.A. Emerson and A.P. Sistla, *eds.*, LNCS 1855, Springer-Verlag, July 2000, pp. 86-98.

[5]   R.E. Bryant, and M.N. Velev, "Boolean Satisfiability with Transitivity Constraints,"[2] Tech-

---

2.   Available from: `http://www.ece.cmu.edu/~mvelev`

nical Report CMU-CS-00-101, Carnegie Mellon University, 2000.

[6] J.R. Burch, and D.L. Dill, "Automated Verification of Pipelined Microprocessor Control," *Computer-Aided Verification (CAV '94)*, D.L. Dill, *ed.*, LNCS 818, Springer-Verlag, June 1994, pp. 68-80. http://sprout.stanford.edu/papers.html.

[7] J.R. Burch, "Techniques for Verifying Superscalar Microprocessors," *33rd Design Automation Conference (DAC '96)*, June 1996, pp. 552-557.

[8] CUDD-2.3.0, http://vlsi.colorado.edu/~fabio.

[9] A. Goel, K. Sajid, H. Zhou, A. Aziz, and V. Singhal, "BDD Based Procedures for a Theory of Equality with Uninterpreted Functions," *Computer-Aided Verification (CAV '98)*, A.J. Hu and M.Y. Vardi, *eds.*, LNCS 1427, Springer-Verlag, June 1998, pp. 244-255.

[10] J.L. Hennessy, and D.A. Patterson, *Computer Architecture: A Quantitative Approach*, 2nd edition, Morgan Kaufmann Publishers, San Francisco, CA, 1996.

[11] R. Hosabettu, "Systematic Verification of Pipelined Microprocessors," Ph.D. thesis, Department of Computer Science, University of Utah, August 2000. http://www.cs.utah.edu/~hosabett.

[12] S. Malik, A.R. Wang, R.K. Brayton, and A. Sangiovani-Vincentelli, "Logic Verification Using Binary Decision Diagrams in a Logic Synthesis Environment," *International Conference on Computer-AIded Design (ICCAD '88)*, November 1988, pp. 6-9.

[13] G. Ritter, H. Eveking, and H. Hinrichsen, "Formal Verification of Designs with Complex Control by Symbolic Simulation," *Correct Hardware Design and Verification Methods (CHARME '99)*, L. Pierre and T. Kropf, *eds.*, LNCS 1703, Springer-Verlag, September 1999, pp. 234-249.

[14] R. Rudell, "Dynamic Variable Ordering for Ordered Binary Decision Diagrams," *International Conference on Computer-Aided Design (ICCAD '93)*, November 1993, pp. 42-47.

[15] M.N. Velev, and R.E. Bryant, "Exploiting Positive Equality and Partial Non-Consistency in the Formal Verification of Pipelined Microprocessors,"[2] *36th Design Automation Conference (DAC '99)*, June 1999, pp. 397-401.

[16] M.N. Velev, and R.E. Bryant, "Superscalar Processor Verification Using Efficient Reductions of the Logic of Equality with Uninterpreted Functions to Propositional Logic,"[2] *Correct Hardware Design and Verification Methods (CHARME '99)*, L. Pierre and T. Kropf, *eds.*, LNCS 1703, Springer-Verlag, September 1999, pp. 37-53.

[17] M.N. Velev, and R.E. Bryant, "Formal Verification of Superscalar Microprocessors with Multicycle Functional Units, Exceptions, and Branch Prediction,"[2] *37th Design Automation Conference (DAC '00)*, June 2000, pp. 112-117.

[18] M.N. Velev, and R.E. Bryant, "Formal Verification of Superscalar Microprocessors with Multicycle Functional Units, Exceptions, and Branch Prediction,"[2] Technical Report CMU-CS-00-116, Carnegie Mellon University, 2000.

[19] M.N. Velev, "Formal Verification of VLIW Microprocessors with Speculative Execution,"[2] *Computer-Aided Verification (CAV '00)*, E.A. Emerson and A.P. Sistla, *eds.*, LNCS 1855, Springer-Verlag, July 2000, pp. 296-311.

[20] M.N. Velev, and R.E. Bryant, "Effective Use of Boolean Satisfiability Procedures in the Formal Verification of Superscalar and VLIW Microprocessors,"[2] *submitted for publication*, 2000.

[21] M.N. Velev, and R.E. Bryant, "EVC: A Validity Checker for the Logic of Equality with Uninterpreted Functions and Memories, Exploiting Positive Equality and Conservative Transformations,"[2] *submitted for publication*, 2001.

[22] P.J. Windley, and J.R. Burch, "Mechanically Checking a Lemma Used in an Automatic Verification Tool," *Formal Methods in Computer-Aided Design (FMCAD '96)*, M. Srivas and A. Camilleri, *eds.*, LNCS 1166, Springer-Verlag, November 1996, pp. 362-376.

Boolean and Cartesian Abstraction for Model Checking C Programs

Thomas Ball   Andreas Podelski*   Sriram K. Rajamani

Software Productivity Tools
Microsoft Research

Abstract. We show how to attack the problem of model checking a
C program with recursive procedures using an abstraction that we formally define as the composition of the Boolean and the Cartesian abstractions. It is implemented through a source-to-source transformation
into a 'Boolean' C program; we give an algorithm to compute the transformation with a cost that is exponential in its theoretical worst-case
complexity but feasible in practice.

1 Introduction

Abstraction is a key issue in model checking. Much attention has been given to
Boolean abstraction (a.k.a. existential abstraction or predicate abstraction); see
e.g. [10,15,6,16,13,11]. The idea of Boolean abstraction is to map states to 'abstract' states according their evaluation under a finite set of predicates (boolean
expression over program variables) on states. The predicates induce an 'abstract'
system with a transition relation over the abstract states. An approximation of
the set of reachable concrete states (in fact, an inductive invariant) is obtained
through a fixpoint of the 'abstract' post operator.

Motivated by the fact that computing the Boolean abstraction (i.e. computing the transition relation between 'abstract' states) is prohibitively costly, we
propose a new abstraction, obtained by adding the *Cartesian abstraction* on top
of the Boolean abstraction. The Cartesian abstraction underlies the *attribute
independence* in certain kinds of program analysis (see [9]). It is used to approximate a set of tuples by the smallest Cartesian product containing this set. The
new abstraction is induced by predicates over states, but it cannot be defined by
a mapping over states (i.e., a state cannot be assigned a unique abstract value).
We use the framework of *abstract interpretation* [8] and Galois connections to
specify our abstraction as the formal composition of two abstractions.

We present an algorithm for computing the 'ideal' abstract post operator
("$\text{post}^{\#}_{\text{b-c}}$") wrt. the new abstraction (defined through a Galois connection). The
algorithm is exponential in its worst-case complexity, but it is feasible in practice;
it is the first algorithm in this context of abstract model checking that does not
compute the value explicitly for each 'abstract' state. This gain in efficiency
must, in theory, be traded with a *loss of precision*. We identify the single causes
of loss of precision under the Cartesian abstraction. To eliminate most of these,

---

* On leave from Max Planck Institute, Saarbrücken, Germany.

T. Margaria and W. Yi (Eds.): TACAS 2001, LNCS 2031, pp. 268–283, 2001.

we introduce three *refinements* of $\mathsf{post}^{\#}_{\mathsf{b.c}}$ that are based on standard concepts from program analysis. We have an implementation that combines all three refinements and that makes the loss of precision practically negligible.

The use of Cartesian abstraction allows us to represent the abstract post operator of a C program in form of a *Boolean program* [2]. Boolean program are C programs where all expressions and all variables range over the three truth values 1, 0 and $*$ (for 'unknown'). As C programs, Boolean programs have the usual update statements, and they may have procedures with call-by-value parameter passing, local variables, and recursion.

We next explain the specific context of our work. The SLAM project[1] at Microsoft Research is building processes and tools for checking temporal properties of system software written in common programming languages, such as C.

The existence of both *infinite control and infinite data* in (even sequential) software makes model checking of software difficult. Infinite control comes from procedural abstraction and recursion. Infinite data comes from the existence of unbounded data types such as integers and pointer-based data structures. Infinite control and unbounded arithmetic data has been studied in model checking in isolation, namely for pushdown systems resp. protocols, parameterized systems or timed and hybrid systems (see e.g. [17]). However, the combination of unbounded stack-based control and unbounded data has not been handled before.[2]

The SLAM project addresses this fundamental problem through a separation of concerns that abstracts infinite data domains through Cartesian and Boolean abstractions, and then uses well-known techniques [22,19] to analyze the resultant Boolean program, which has infinite control (but 'finite data'). The data are abstracted according to their evaluation under a given a set $\mathcal{P}$ of predicates on states of the C program.

Our working hypothesis is that for many interesting temporal properties of real-life system software, we can find suitable predicates such that the abstraction is precise enough to prove the desired invariant. Refinement can be accomplished by the addition of new predicates.

Given an invariant Inv to check on a C program, the SLAM process has three phases, starting with an initial set of predicates $\mathcal{P}$ and repeating the phases iteratively, halting if the invariant Inv is either proved or disproved (but possibly non-terminating):

1. construct an abstract post operator under the abstraction induced by $\mathcal{P}$;
2. model check the Boolean program that represents the abstract post operator;
3. discover new predicates and add them to the set $\mathcal{P}$ in order to refine the abstraction.

In this paper, we address the issue of abstraction in Phase (1). In principle, Phases (2) and (3) will follow the lines of other work on interprocedural program

---

[1] http://research.microsoft.com/slam/
[2] There are other promising attempts at model checking for software, of course, such as the Bandera project, for example, where *non-recursive* procedures are handled through inlining [7].

analysis [22,19], and abstraction refinement [4,15]). For more detail on Phase (2), see [2].

We note that the specific context of the SLAM project has the following consequences for the abstraction of the post operator and its computation in Phase (1):

- It is important to give a concise definition of the abstract post operator, not only to guide its implementation but also to guide the refinement process (i.e. to help identify the cause of imprecision in a given abstraction).
- The abstract post operator must be computed for its entire domain. That is, it cannot be restricted a priori to a subset of its domain. At the moment when the abstract post operator for a statement within a procedure is computed, it is generally impossible to foresee which values the statement will be applied to.

In the work on Boolean abstraction that is most closely related to ours, Graf and Saïdi [13] define an approximation of the Boolean abstraction of the post operator; our abstraction can be used to formalize that approximation in terms of a Galois connection, using a new abstract domain.

The procedure of [13] computes the image of their abstract post operator for each 'abstract state' with a linear number of calls to a theorem prover (in the number n of predicates inducing the Boolean abstraction). This is better than computing the image of the standard Boolean abstraction of the post operator, which requires exponentially many calls to a theorem prover; but still, it is only feasible if done 'on demand', i.e. for each reachable 'abstract' state (and if the number of those remains small).

In our setting, the procedure of [13] would require a fixed number $2^n \cdot 2 \cdot n$ of calls to a theorem prover. In this paper, we give a procedure with $O(2^n) \cdot 2 \cdot n$ calls; i.e., in comparison with [13], we replace the fixed (or best-case) factor 2^n by a worst-case factor $O(2^n)$, which makes all the difference for practical concerns.

2   Example C Program

In this paper, we are concerned with two SLAM tools: (1) c2bp, which takes a C program and a set of predicates, and produces an abstract post operator represented by a Boolean program [1], and (2) bebop, a model checker for Boolean programs. [2] We illustrate c2bp and bebop using a simple C program P shown in the left-hand-side of Figure 1. The property we want to check is that the assertion in line 9 is never reached, regardless of the context in which foo is called. The right-hand-side of Figure 1 shows the Boolean program B that c2bp produces from P, given the set of predicates { (z==0) , (x==y) }. The Boolean variables b1 and b2 represent the predicates (z==0) and (x==y), respectively. Each statement of the C program is translated into a corresponding statement of the Boolean program. For example, the statement, z = 0; in line 2 is translated to b1 := 1;. The translation of the statement x++; in line 5 states that if b2 is 1 before the statement, then it guaranteed to be 0 after the statement,

```
                                    decl b1, b2;
         int x, y, z, w;            /* b1 stands for predicate (z==0) and
                                        b2 stands for predicate (x==y) */
         void foo()                 void foo()
         {                          begin
[1]      do {              [1]         do
[2]          z = 0;        [2]            b1 := 1;
[3]          x = y;        [3]            b2 := 1;
[4]          if (w){       [4]            if (*) then
[5]              x++;      [5]                b2 := choose(0,b2);
[6]              z = 1;    [6]                b1 := 0;
             }                                fi
[7]      } while(x!=y)     [7]         while( b2 )
[8]      if(z){            [8]         if (!b1) then
[9]              assert(0);[9]             assert(0);
         }                             fi
         }                         end


                                    bool choose(e1,e2)
                                    begin
                           [10]        if (e1) then
                           [11]            return(1);
                           [12]        elsif (e2) then
                           [13]            return(0);
                           [14]        else
                           [15]            return(*);
                                        fi
                                    end
```

Fig. 1. An example C program, and the Boolean program produced by c2bp using predicates (z==0) and (x==y)

otherwise the value of b2 after the statement is unknown, represented by * in line 15. The Boolean program B can be now fed to bebop, with the question: "is line 9 reachable in B?", and bebop answers "no". We thus conclude that line 9 is not reachable in the C program P as well.

3   Correctness

We fix a program (e.g. a C program) generating a transition system with a set States of states $s_1, s_2, \ldots$ and a transition relation $s \longrightarrow s'$. The operator post on sets of states is defined as usual: $\mathsf{post}(S) = \{s' \mid \text{exists } s \in S : s \longrightarrow s'\}$.

In Section 7 we will use the 'weakest precondition' operator $\widetilde{\mathsf{pre}}$ on sets of states: $\widetilde{\mathsf{pre}}(S') = \{s \mid \text{for all } s' \text{ such that } s \longrightarrow s' : s' \in S'\}$.

In order to define correctness, we fix a subset init of *initial* states and a subset unsafe of *unsafe* states (its complement safe = States − unsafe is the set of *safe* states). The set of reachable states (reachable from an initial state) is the least fixpoint of post that contains init, also called the closure of init under post, $\mathsf{post}^*(\mathsf{init}) = \mathsf{init} \cup \mathsf{post}(\mathsf{init}) \cup \ldots$.

The given program is *correct* if no unsafe state is reachable; i.e., if $\mathsf{post}^*(\mathsf{init}) \subseteq \mathsf{safe}$. A *safe (inductive) invariant* is a set of states S that contains the set of initial states, is a closure under the operator post and is contained in the set of all safe states, formally: $S \subseteq \mathsf{safe}$, $S \supseteq \mathsf{post}(S)$, and $S \supseteq \mathsf{init}$.

Correctness is established by computing a safe invariant. One way to do so is to find an 'abstraction' $\mathsf{post}^\#$ of the operator post and compute the closure of $\mathsf{post}^\#$ on init (and check that it is a subset of safe). In the next section, we will make the idea of abstraction formally precise.

4   Boolean Abstraction

For the purpose of this paper, we fix a finite set $\mathcal{P}$ of state predicates $\mathcal{P} = \{p_1, \ldots, p_n\}$. A predicate p_i denotes the subset of states that satisfy the predicate, $\{s \in \mathsf{States} \mid s \models p_i\}$. The predicate is usually defined by a Boolean expression over program variables.

We distinguish the terms approximation and abstraction. The set $\mathcal{P}$ of state predicates defines the *Boolean approximation* of a set of states S as $\mathsf{Boolean}(S)$, the smallest set containing S that can be denoted by a Boolean expression over predicates in $\mathcal{P}$ (formed as usual with the Boolean operators $\land, \lor, \neg$); this set is sometimes referred as the Boolean covering of the set. This approximation can be defined through an abstract domain and two functions α_{bool} and γ_{bool} that we define below (following the abstract interpretation framework [8]); namely, the Boolean approximation of a set of states S is the set of states $\mathsf{Boolean}(S) = \gamma_{\mathsf{bool}}(\alpha_{\mathsf{bool}}(S))$. The two functions are used to directly define the operator $\mathsf{post}^\#_{\mathsf{bool}}$ on the abstract domain as an *abstraction* of the fixpoint operator post over sets of states.

Having fixed $\mathcal{P}$, we define the *abstract domain* $\mathsf{AbsDom}_{\mathsf{bool}}$ as the set of all sets V of bitvectors v of length n (one bit per predicate $p_i \in \mathcal{P}$, for $i = 1, \ldots, n$), $\mathsf{AbsDom}_{\mathsf{bool}} = 2^{\{0,1\}^n}$, together with subset inclusion as the partial ordering. The abstraction function is the mapping from the *concrete domain* 2^{States}, the set of sets of states (again with subset inclusion as the partial ordering), to the abstract domain, assigning a set of states S the set of bitvectors representing the Boolean covering of S,

$$\alpha_{\mathsf{bool}} : 2^{\mathsf{States}} \to \mathsf{AbsDom}_{\mathsf{bool}}$$
$$S \mapsto \{\langle v_1, \ldots, v_n \rangle \mid S \cap \{s \mid s \models v_1 \cdot p_1 \land \ldots \land v_n \cdot p_n\} \neq \emptyset\}$$

where $0 \cdot p_i = \neg p_i$ and $1 \cdot p_i = p_i$. The meaning function is the mapping

$$\gamma_{\mathsf{bool}} : \mathsf{AbsDom} \to 2^{\mathsf{States}},$$
$$V \mapsto \{s \mid \text{exists } \langle v_1, \ldots, v_n \rangle \in V : s \models v_1 \cdot p_1 \land \ldots \land v_n \cdot p_n\}.$$

Given $\mathsf{AbsDom}_{\mathsf{bool}}$ and the function α_{bool} (which forms a Galois connection together with the function γ_{bool}), the 'best' abstraction of the operator post is the operator $\mathsf{post}^{\#}_{\mathsf{bool}}$ on sets of bitvectors defined by

$$\mathsf{post}^{\#}_{\mathsf{bool}} = \alpha_{\mathsf{bool}} \circ \mathsf{post} \circ \gamma_{\mathsf{bool}}$$

where the functional composition $f \circ g$ of two functions f and g is defined from right to left; i.e., $f \circ g(x) = f(g(x))$.

5 Cartesian Abstraction

Given the vector domain $D_1 \times \ldots \times D_n$, the *Cartesian approximation* $\mathsf{Cartesian}(V)$ of a set of vectors V is the smallest Cartesian product of subsets of $D_1, \ldots, D_n$ that contains the set. It can be defined by the Cartesian product of the projections $\Pi_i(V)$, $\mathsf{Cartesian}(V) = \Pi_1(V) \times \ldots \times \Pi_n(V)$, where $\Pi_1(V) = \{v_1 \mid \langle v_1, \ldots, v_n \rangle \in V\}$ etc.. In order formalize the Cartesian approximation of a fixpoint operator, one uses the abstraction function from the concrete domain of sets of tuples to the abstract domain of tuples of sets (with pointwise subset inclusion as the partial ordering),

$$\alpha_{\mathsf{cartesian}} : 2^{D_1 \times \ldots \times D_n} \to 2^{D_1} \times \ldots \times 2^{D_n}$$
$$V \mapsto \langle \Pi_1(V), \ldots, \Pi_n(V) \rangle$$

and the meaning function $\gamma_{\mathsf{cartesian}}$ mapping a tuple of sets $\langle M_1, \ldots, M_n \rangle$ to their Cartesian product $M_1 \times \ldots \times M_n$. I.e., we have $\mathsf{Cartesian}(V) = \gamma_{\mathsf{cartesian}} \circ \alpha_{\mathsf{cartesian}}(V)$.

In general, one has to account formally for the empty set (i.e., introduce a special bottom element $\bot$ and identify each tuple of sets that has at least one empty component); in the context of the fixpoints considered here (we look at the smallest fixpoint that is greater than a given element, e.g. $\alpha_{\mathsf{bool}}(\mathsf{init})$), we can gloss over this issue.

We next formalize the Cartesian approximation for sets of bitvectors. The nonempty sets of Boolean values are of one of three forms: $\{0\}$, $\{1\}$ or $\{0,1\}$. It is convenient to write 0 for $\{0\}$, 1 for $\{1\}$ and $*$ for $\{0,1\}$, and thus represent a tuple of sets of Boolean values by what we call a *trivector*, which is an element of $\{1, 0, *\}^n$. We therefore introduce the *abstract domain of trivectors*, $\mathsf{AbsDom}_{\mathsf{cartesian}} = \{0, 1, *\}^n$ (again, we gloss over the issue of a special trivector $\bot$). The partial ordering $<$ is the pointwise extension of the partial order given by $0 < *$ and $1 < *$; i.e., for two trivectors $\langle v_1, \ldots, v_n \rangle$ and $\langle v'_1, \ldots, v'_n \rangle$, $\langle v_1, \ldots, v_n \rangle < \langle v'_1, \ldots, v'_n \rangle$ if $v_1 < v'_1$, $\ldots$, $v_n < v'_n$. The Cartesian abstraction $\alpha_{\mathsf{cartesian}}$ maps a set of bitvectors V to a trivector,

$$\alpha_{\mathsf{cartesian}} : \mathsf{AbsDom}_{\mathsf{bool}} \to \mathsf{AbsDom}_{\mathsf{cartesian}}, \ V \mapsto \langle v_1, \ldots, v_n \rangle$$

where, for $i = 1, \ldots, n$, (a) $v_i = 0$ if $\Pi_i(V) = \{0\}$; (b) $v_i = 1$ if $\Pi_i(V) = \{1\}$; (c) $v_i = *$ if $\Pi_i(V) = \{0, 1\}$.

The meaning $\gamma_{\text{cartesian}}(v)$ of a trivector v is the set of bitvectors that are smaller than v (wrt. the partial ordering giving on trivectors given above); i.e., it is the Cartesian product of the n sets of bit values denoted by the components of v. The meaning function $\gamma_{\text{cartesian}}$: $\mathsf{AbsDom}_{\text{cartesian}} \rightarrow \mathsf{AbsDom}_{\text{bool}}$ forms a Galois connection with $\alpha_{\text{cartesian}}$.

6 The Abstract Post Operator $\mathsf{post}^{\#}_{\text{b·c}}$ over Trivectors

We define a new Galois connection by composing the ones considered in the previous two sections,

$$\alpha_{\text{b·c}} : 2^{\mathsf{States}} \rightarrow \mathsf{AbsDom}_{\text{cartesian}}, \quad \alpha_{\text{b·c}} = \alpha_{\text{cartesian}} \circ \alpha_{\text{bool}}$$

$$\gamma_{\text{b·c}} : \mathsf{AbsDom}_{\text{cartesian}} \rightarrow 2^{\mathsf{States}}, \quad \gamma_{\text{b·c}} = \gamma_{\text{bool}} \circ \gamma_{\text{cartesian}}$$

and the abstract post operator over trivectors, $\mathsf{post}^{\#}_{\text{b·c}}$: $\mathsf{AbsDom}_{\text{cartesian}} \rightarrow \mathsf{AbsDom}_{\text{cartesian}}$, defined by $\mathsf{post}^{\#}_{\text{b·c}} = \alpha_{\text{b·c}} \circ \mathsf{post} \circ \gamma_{\text{b·c}}$.

We have thus given a formalization of the fixpoint operator that implicitly defines the invariant Inv_1 given by $\mathcal{I}_1$ in [13]; i.e., the invariant is the meaning (under $\gamma_{\text{b·c}}$) of the least fixpoint of $\mathsf{post}^{\#}_{\text{b·c}}$ that is not smaller than the abstraction of init (under $\alpha_{\text{b·c}}$), or $\mathsf{Inv}_1 = \gamma_{\text{b·c}}(\mathsf{post}^{\#}_{\text{b·c}}{}^{*}(\alpha_{\text{b·c}}(\mathsf{init})))$. The invariant Inv_1 is represented abstractly by one trivector, i.e. it is the Cartesian product of sets each described by p, $\neg p$ or $p \vee \neg p$ (i.e. true) where p is a predicate of the set $\mathcal{P}$.

7 The c2bp Algorithm to Compute $\mathsf{post}^{\#}_{\text{b·c}}$

The algorithm takes as input the transition system (defining the operators post and $\widetilde{\mathsf{pre}}$) and the set of n predicates $\mathcal{P}$; as output it produces the representation of $\mathsf{post}^{\#}_{\text{b·c}}$ in the form of a Boolean program over n 'Boolean' variables $v_1, \ldots, v_n$ (whose values range over the domain $\{0, 1, *\}$). Each statement of the Boolean program is a multiple assignment statement of the form $\langle v_1, \ldots, v_n \rangle := \langle e_1, \ldots, e_n \rangle$, where $e_1, \ldots, e_n$ are expressions over $v_1, \ldots, v_n$ that are evaluated to a value in $\{0, 1, *\}$. We write $e[v_1, \ldots, v_n]$ for e if we want to stress that e is an expression over $v_1, \ldots, v_n$. The Boolean program represents the operator $\mathsf{post}^{\#}_{\text{c2bp}}$ over trivectors by

$$\mathsf{post}^{\#}_{\text{c2bp}}(\langle v_1, \ldots, v_n \rangle) = \langle v'_1, \ldots, v'_n \rangle \ \text{ if } \ v'_1 = e_1[v_1, \ldots, v_n], \ldots, v'_n = e_n[v_1, \ldots, v_n].$$

We will now explain how the algorithm computes the expressions $e_i[v_1, \ldots, v_n]$, for each $i = 1, \ldots, n$. We first define the *Boolean under-approximation* of a set S wrt. $\mathcal{P}$ as the greatest Boolean expression over predicates in $\mathcal{P}$ whose denotation is contained in S; formally, $\mathsf{F}(S) = \nu E \in \mathsf{BoolExpr}(\mathcal{P})$. $\{s \mid s \models E\} \subseteq S$. That is, the set of states denoted by $\mathsf{F}(S)$ is $\mathsf{States} - (\gamma_{\text{bool}} \circ \alpha_{\text{bool}})(\mathsf{States} - S)$. For the purpose of defining the algorithm, the set $\mathsf{BoolExpr}(\mathcal{P})$ consists of Boolean expressions in the form of disjunctions of conjunctions of possibly negated predicates from $\mathcal{P}$. The ordering $e < e'$ is such that each disjunct of e implies some disjunct of e' (e.g., p_1 is greater than $p_1 \wedge p_2 \vee p_1 \wedge \neg p_2$).

By repeated calls to a theorem prover,[3] the algorithm computes the two Boolean expressions $E_i(0)$ and $E_i(1)$ over the predicates $p_1, \ldots, p_n$

$$E_i(0) = \mathsf{F}(\widetilde{\mathsf{pre}}(\{s \mid s \models \neg p_i\})),$$
$$E_i(1) = \mathsf{F}(\widetilde{\mathsf{pre}}(\{s \mid s \models p_i\})).$$

We define the two Boolean expressions $e_i(1)$ and $e_i(0)$ over the variables $v_1, \ldots, v_n$ by direct correspondence from the two Boolean expressions $E_i(0)$ and $E_i(1)$ over the predicates $p_1, \ldots, p_n$.

The expression e_i over the variables $v_1, \ldots, v_n$ that defines the i-th value of the successor trivector of the Boolean program is $e_i = \mathsf{choose}(e_i(1), e_i(0))$, where the symbol choose stands for an if-then–elseif-then–else combinator on two Boolean expressions; i.e., the expression $\mathsf{choose}(e, e')$ applied to two Boolean expressions e and e', each over the variables $v_1, \ldots, v_n$, evaluates as follows:

$$\mathsf{choose}(e[v_1, \ldots, v_n], e'[v_1, \ldots, v_n]) = \quad \begin{aligned} &\text{if } \langle v_1, \ldots, v_n \rangle \models e \text{ then } 1 \\ &\text{elseif } \langle v_1, \ldots, v_n \rangle \models e' \text{then } 0 \\ &\text{else } * \end{aligned}$$

The satisfaction of a Boolean expression e by a trivector $\langle v_1, \ldots, v_n \rangle$ is defined as one expects, namely $\langle v_1, \ldots, v_n \rangle \models e$ if all bitvectors in $\gamma_{\mathsf{bool}}(\langle v_1, \ldots, v_n \rangle)$ satisfy e. Thus, for example, $\langle 0, 1, * \rangle \models \neg v_1 \wedge v_2$ but $\langle 0, 1, * \rangle \not\models v_3$ and $\langle 0, 1, * \rangle \not\models \neg v_3$. (The extension of the Boolean operators to the domain $\{0, 1, *\}$ is defined accordingly.)

Proposition 1 (Correctness). *The result of the* $\mathsf{c2bp}$ *algorithm is a Boolean program representing the Boolean and Cartesian abstraction of the operator* post, *i.e.* $\mathsf{post}^{\#}_{\mathsf{c2bp}} = \mathsf{post}^{\#}_{\mathsf{b \cdot c}}$.

Proof. We define the n abstraction functions $\alpha^{(i)}_{\mathsf{b \cdot c}}$ by

$$\alpha^{(i)}_{\mathsf{b \cdot c}}(M) = \begin{cases} 1 \text{ if } M \subseteq \{s \mid s \models p_i\} \\ 0 \text{ if } M \subseteq \{s \mid s \models \neg p_i\} \\ * \text{ if neither} \end{cases}$$

and the i-th abstract post function $\mathsf{post}^{\#\,(i)}_{\mathsf{b \cdot c}}$ by $\mathsf{post}^{\#\,(i)}_{\mathsf{b \cdot c}} = \alpha^{(i)}_{\mathsf{b \cdot c}} \circ \mathsf{post} \circ \gamma_{\mathsf{b \cdot c}}$.

Since the value of any nonempty set of states S under the abstraction $\alpha_{\mathsf{b \cdot c}}$ is the trivector

$$\alpha_{\mathsf{b \cdot c}}(S) = \langle \alpha^{(1)}_{\mathsf{b \cdot c}}(S), \ldots, \alpha^{(n)}_{\mathsf{b \cdot c}}(S) \rangle,$$

---

[3] We consider the theorem prover as an oracle, which does exist for most practical concerns. It is easy to see that theoretically such an oracle does not exist and that $\mathsf{post}^{\#}_{\mathsf{b \cdot c}}$ (or $\mathsf{post}^{\#}_{\mathsf{bool}}$) cannot be computed; i.e., the problem of deciding whether an operator is equal to $\mathsf{post}^{\#}_{\mathsf{b \cdot c}}$ (or $\mathsf{post}^{\#}_{\mathsf{bool}}$) is undecidable.

we can express the abstract post operator $\text{post}^{\#}_{\text{b.c}}$ over trivectors as the tuple of the abstract post functions, each mapping trivectors to values in $\{0, 1, *\}$,

$$\text{post}^{\#}_{\text{b.c}}(\langle v_1, \ldots, v_n \rangle) = \langle \text{post}^{\# \ (1)}_{\text{b.c}}(\langle v_1, \ldots, v_n \rangle), \ldots, \text{post}^{\# \ (n)}_{\text{b.c}}(\langle v_1, \ldots, v_n \rangle) \rangle.$$

Now, we can represent the abstract post operator $\text{post}^{\#}_{\text{b.c}}$ in terms of the sets $V_i(0)$, $V_i(1)$ and $V_i(*)$, defined as the inverse images of the values 0, 1 or $*$, respectively, under the i-th abstract post functions $\text{post}^{\# \ (i)}_{\text{b.c}}$.

$$V_i(0) = \{\langle v_1, \ldots, v_n \rangle \mid \text{post}^{\# \ (i)}_{\text{b.c}}(\langle v_1, \ldots, v_n \rangle) = 0\}$$

$$V_i(1) = \{\langle v_1, \ldots, v_n \rangle \mid \text{post}^{\# \ (i)}_{\text{b.c}}(\langle v_1, \ldots, v_n \rangle) = 1\}$$

$$V_i(*) = \{\langle v_1, \ldots, v_n \rangle \mid \text{post}^{\# \ (i)}_{\text{b.c}}(\langle v_1, \ldots, v_n \rangle) = *\}$$

$$= \text{AbsDom}_{\text{cartesian}} - (V_i(0) \cup V_i(1))$$

The statement of the proposition can now be expressed by the fact that the sets $V_i(0)$, $V_i(1)$ and $V_i(*)$ are exactly the sets of trivectors that satisfy the Boolean expressions $e_i(0)$, $e_i(1)$ or neither.

$$V_i(0) = \{\langle v_1, \ldots, v_n \rangle \mid \langle v_1, \ldots, v_n \rangle \models e_i(0)\}$$

$$V_i(1) = \{\langle v_1, \ldots, v_n \rangle \mid \langle v_1, \ldots, v_n \rangle \models e_i(1)\} \tag{1}$$

$$V_i(*) = \{\langle v_1, \ldots, v_n \rangle \mid \langle v_1, \ldots, v_n \rangle \not\models e_i(0), \ \langle v_1, \ldots, v_n \rangle \not\models e_i(1)\}$$

That is, in order to prove the proposition we need to prove (1).

Since $\text{AbsDom}_{\text{bool}}$ is a complete distributive lattice, the membership of a trivector $\langle v_1, \ldots, v_n \rangle$ in $V_i(0)$ is equivalent to the condition that $\gamma_{\text{cartesian}}(\langle v_1, \ldots, v_n \rangle)$ is contained in $B_i(0)$, the largest set of bitvectors that is mapped to the value 0 by the function $\alpha^{(i)}_{\text{b.c}} \circ \text{post} \gamma_{\text{bool}}$. That is, if we define

$$B_i(0) = \nu B \in \text{AbsDom}_{\text{bool}}. \ \alpha^{(i)}_{\text{b.c}} \circ \text{post} \circ \gamma_{\text{bool}}(B) = 0$$

then

$$V_i(0) = \{\langle v_1, \ldots, v_n \rangle \in \text{AbsDom}_{\text{cartesian}} \mid \gamma_{\text{bool}}(\langle v_1, \ldots, v_n \rangle) \subseteq B_i(0)\}. \tag{2}$$

By definition of $\alpha^{(i)}_{\text{b.c}}$, we can express the set of bitvectors $B_i(0)$ as

$$B_i(0) = \nu B \in \text{AbsDom}_{\text{bool}}. \ \text{post} \circ \gamma_{\text{bool}}(B) \subseteq \{s \mid s \models \neg p_i\}.$$

The operators post and $\widetilde{\text{pre}}$ form a Galois connection, i.e. $\text{post}(S) \subseteq S'$ if and only if $S \subseteq \widetilde{\text{pre}}(S')$. Therefore, we can write $B_i(0)$ equivalently as

$$B_i(0) = \nu B \in \text{AbsDom}_{\text{bool}}. \ \gamma_{\text{bool}}(B) \subseteq \widetilde{\text{pre}}(\{s \mid s \models \neg p_i\}).$$

Thus, $B_i(0)$ is exactly the set of all bitvectors that satisfy the Boolean expression $e_i(0)$.

$$B_i(0) = \{\langle v_1, \ldots, v_n \rangle \in \{0, 1\}^n \mid \langle v_1, \ldots, v_n \rangle \models e_i(0)\}$$

This fact, together with (2), yields directly the characterization of $V_i(0)$ in (1). The other two statements in (1) follow in the similar way. $\square$

Complexity. We need to compute $\mathsf{F}(S)$ for $2n$ sets S that are either of the form $S = \widetilde{\mathsf{pre}}(\{s \in \mathsf{States} \mid s \models p_i\})$ or of the form $S = \widetilde{\mathsf{pre}}(\{s \in \mathsf{States} \mid s \models \neg p_i\})$.

In order to compute each $\mathsf{F}(S)$, we need to find all minimal implicants of S in the form of a *cube*, i.e. a conjunction $\mathcal{C} = \bigwedge_{i \in I} \ell_i$ of possibly negated predicates (i.e., ℓ_i is p_i or $\neg p_i$) such that $\{s \mid s \models \mathcal{C}\} \subseteq S$. We use some quick syntactic checks to find which of the predicates p_i can possibly influence S (i.e. such p_i or $\neg p_i$ can appear in a minimal implicant); usually, there are only few of those. 'Minimal' here means: if an implicant $\mathcal{C}$ is found, no larger conjunction $\mathcal{C} \wedge p_j$ needs to be considered. Also, if $\mathcal{C}$ is incompatible with S (i.e., $\{s \mid s \models \mathcal{C}\} \cap S = \emptyset$), no larger conjunction needs to be considered (since no conjunction $\mathcal{C} \wedge p_j$ can be an implicant).

8   Loss of Precision under Cartesian Abstraction

We will next analyze in what way precision may get lost through the Cartesian abstraction. It is important to distinguish that loss from the one that incurs from the Boolean abstraction. The latter is addressed by adding new predicates in the refinement phase.

'Loss of precision' is made formally precise in the following way (see [8,12]). Given a concrete and an abstract domain, an abstraction α and a meaning γ, we say that the operator F does not lose precision under the abstraction to $F^{\#}$ if $\gamma \circ F^{\#} = F \circ \gamma$ (i.e., does not lose precision on the abstract value a if $\gamma \circ F^{\#}(a) = F \circ \gamma(a)$).

In our setting, F will always be instantiated by $\mathsf{post}^{\#}_{\mathsf{bool}}$. In this section, the phrase 'the Cartesian abstraction does not lose precision' is short for '$\mathsf{post}^{\#}_{\mathsf{bool}}$ does not lose precision under the abstraction to $\mathsf{post}^{\#}_{\mathsf{b \cdot c}}$', i.e. $\gamma_{\mathsf{cartesian}} \circ \mathsf{post}^{\#}_{\mathsf{b \cdot c}} = \mathsf{post}^{\#}_{\mathsf{bool}} \circ \gamma_{\mathsf{cartesian}}$. We define an operator F on sets to be *deterministic* if it maps a singleton set to the empty set or another singleton set. The following observation will be used in Section 9.3:

Proposition 2. *If the operator* $\mathsf{post}^{\#}_{\mathsf{bool}}$ *is deterministic, then the Cartesian abstraction does not lose precision on trivectors* $\langle v_1, \ldots, v_n \rangle$ *such that* $v_i \neq *$, *for* $1 \leq i \leq n$.

Example 1. We take the (simple and somewhat contrived) example of the C program with one statement x = y updating x by y and the set of predicates $\mathcal{P} = \{p_1, p_2, p_2\}$ where p_1 expresses "$x > 5$", p_2 expresses "$x < 5$" and p_3 expresses "$y = 5$". Note that the conjunction of $\neg p_1$ and $\neg p_2$ expresses $x = 5$. The image of the trivector $\langle 0, 0, 0 \rangle$ under the abstract post operator $\mathsf{post}^{\#}_{\mathsf{b \cdot c}}$ is the trivector $\langle *, *, 0 \rangle$. Therefore, $\mathsf{post}^{\#}_{\mathsf{b \cdot c}}(\langle 0, 0, 0 \rangle) = \langle *, *, 0 \rangle$ because $\mathsf{post}^{\#}_{\mathsf{b \cdot c}} =$

$\alpha_{\mathsf{cartesian}} \circ \alpha_{\mathsf{bool}} \circ \mathsf{post} \circ \gamma_{\mathsf{bool}} \circ \gamma_{\mathsf{cartesian}}$ and by the following equalities.

$$
\begin{aligned}
\gamma_{\mathsf{cartesian}}(\langle 0,0,0\rangle) &= \{\langle 0,0,0\rangle\} & &\in \mathsf{AbsDom_{bool}} \\
\gamma_{\mathsf{bool}}(\{\langle 0,0,0\rangle\}) &= \{\langle x,y\rangle \mid x = 5,\ y \neq 5\} & &\in 2^{\mathsf{States}} \\
\mathsf{post}(\{\langle x,y\rangle \mid x = 5,\ y \neq 5\}) &= \{\langle x,y\rangle \mid x = y,\ y \neq 5\} & &\in 2^{\mathsf{States}} \\
\alpha_{\mathsf{bool}}(\{\langle x,y\rangle \mid x = y,\ y \neq 5\}) &= \{\langle 1,0,0\rangle, \langle 0,1,0\rangle\} & &\in \mathsf{AbsDom_{bool}} \\
\alpha_{\mathsf{cartesian}}(\{\langle 1,0,0\rangle, \langle 0,1,0\rangle\}) &= \langle *,*,0\rangle & &\in \mathsf{AbsDom_{cartesian}}
\end{aligned}
$$

The meaning of the trivector $\langle *,*,0\rangle$ is a set of four bitvectors that properly contains the image of the Boolean abstraction of the post operator $\mathsf{post}^{\#}_{\mathsf{bool}}$ applied to the meaning of the trivector $\langle 0,0,0\rangle$.

$$
\begin{aligned}
\gamma_{\mathsf{cartesian}}(\mathsf{post}^{\#}_{\mathsf{b \cdot c}}(\langle 0,0,0\rangle)) &= \{\langle 0,0,0\rangle, \langle 1,0,0\rangle, \langle 0,1,0\rangle, \langle 1,1,0\rangle\} \\
&\supset \{\langle 1,0,0\rangle, \langle 0,1,0\rangle\} \\
&= \mathsf{post}^{\#}_{\mathsf{bool}}(\gamma_{\mathsf{cartesian}}(\langle 0,0,0\rangle))
\end{aligned}
$$

That is, the Cartesian abstraction loses precision by adding the bitvector $\langle 0,0,0\rangle$ (expressing $x = 5$ through the negation of both, $x < 5$ and $x > 5$) to the two bitvectors $\langle 1,0,0\rangle$ and $\langle 0,1,0\rangle$ that form the image of the Boolean abstract post operator. (The added bitvector $\langle 1,1,0\rangle$ is semantically inconsistent and will be eliminated by standard methods in Boolean abstraction; see [13].) Note that the concrete operator post is *deterministic*; the loss of precision in the Cartesian abstraction occurs because $\mathsf{post}^{\#}_{\mathsf{bool}}$ is not deterministic ($\mathsf{post}^{\#}_{\mathsf{bool}}(\langle 0,0,0\rangle) = \{\langle 1,0,0\rangle, \langle 0,1,0\rangle\}$; as an aside, post does not lose precision under the Boolean abstraction).

Example 2. The next example is simpler than the previous one but it is not relevant in the context of C programs where the transition relation is deterministic. Nondeterminism arises in the interleaving semantics of concurrent systems. Take a program with Boolean variables x and y (standing e.g. for 'critical') and the transition relation specified by the assertion $x' = \neg y'$ (as usual, a primed variable stands for the variable's value after the transition). For simplicity of presentation, we here identify states and bitvectors. The image of every nonempty set of bitvectors under $\mathsf{post}^{\#}_{\mathsf{bool}}$ is the set of bitvectors $\{\langle 0,1\rangle, \langle 1,0\rangle\}$. The image of every trivector under $\mathsf{post}^{\#}_{\mathsf{b \cdot c}}$ is the trivector $\langle *,*\rangle$ whose meaning is the set of all bitvectors. Here again, $\mathsf{post}^{\#}_{\mathsf{bool}}$ is not deterministic. Unlike the previous example, the concrete operator post is not deterministic as well.

Example 3. The next example shows, in the setting of a deterministic transition relation, that precision can get lost if $\mathsf{post}^{\#}_{\mathsf{b \cdot c}}$ is applied to a trivector with components having value $*$. Take a program with 2 Boolean variables x_1, x_2 and the transition relation specified by the statement "assume($x_1 = x_2$)"; its post operator, defined by $\mathsf{post}(V) = \{\langle v_1, v_2\rangle \in V \mid v_1 = v_2\}$, is equal to its

Boolean abstraction. The image of the trivector $\langle *, * \rangle$ under $\mathsf{post}^{\#}_{\mathsf{b \cdot c}}$ is the trivector $\langle *, * \rangle$. The image of its meaning $\gamma_{\mathsf{cartesian}}(\langle *, * \rangle)$ under $\mathsf{post}^{\#}_{\mathsf{bool}}$ is the set of bitvectors $\{\langle 0, 0 \rangle, \langle 1, 1 \rangle\}$.

We will come back to this example in Section 9.3; there, we will also consider the general version of the same program with $n \geq 2$ Boolean variables $x_1, \ldots, x_n$ and the transition relation specified by the assertion $x_1 = x_2 \wedge x_1' = x_1 \wedge \ldots \wedge x_n' = x_n$. The image of the trivector $\langle *, \ldots, * \rangle$ under $\mathsf{post}^{\#}_{\mathsf{b \cdot c}}$ is the trivector $\langle *, \ldots, * \rangle$. The image of its meaning under $\mathsf{post}^{\#}_{\mathsf{bool}}$ is the set of all bitvectors whose first two components are equal.

9   Refinement for $\mathsf{post}^{\#}_{\mathsf{b \cdot c}}$

In this section, we apply standard methods from program analysis and propose refinements of the Cartesian abstraction; these are orthogonal to the refinement of the Boolean abstraction by iteratively adding new predicates.

9.1   Control Points

We now assume a preprocessing step on the program to be checked which introduces new control points (locations). Each conditional statement (with, say, condition ϕ) is replaced by a nondeterministic branching (each nondeterministic edge going to a different location), followed by a (deterministic) edge enforcing the condition ϕ or its negation ("assume(ϕ)" or "assume($\neg\phi$)") as a blocking invariant, followed by a (deterministic) edge with the update statement, followed by "joining" edges to the location after the original conditional statement.

Until now, we implicitly assumed predicates p_ℓ for every control point ℓ of the program (expressing that a state is at location ℓ). This would lead to a great loss of precision under the abstraction considered above. Instead, one formalizes the concrete domain as the sequence $(2^{\mathsf{States}})^{\mathsf{Loc}}$ of state spaces indexed by program locations $\ell \in \mathsf{Loc}$. Its elements are vectors $\boldsymbol{S} = \langle S[\ell] \rangle_{\ell \in \mathsf{Loc}}$ of sets of states, i.e. $S[\ell] \in 2^{\mathsf{States}}$. From now on, a state $s \in \mathsf{States}$ consists only of the environment of the data variables of the program. Accordingly, the abstract domain is the sequence $(\mathsf{AbsDom}_{\mathsf{cartesian}})^{\mathsf{Loc}}$.[4]

The post operator is now a tuple of post operators post_ℓ, one for each location ℓ of the control flow graph, $\mathsf{post} = \langle \mathsf{post}[\ell] \rangle_{\ell \in \mathsf{Loc}}$, where $\mathsf{post}[\ell]$ is defined in the standard way. We define the abstract post operator accordingly as the tuple $\mathsf{post}^{\#}_{\mathsf{b \cdot c}} = \langle \mathsf{post}^{\#}_{\mathsf{b \cdot c}}[\ell] \rangle_{\ell \in \mathsf{Loc}}$.

If ℓ is the "join" location after a conditional statement and its two predecessors are ℓ_1 and ℓ_2, then $\mathsf{post}[\ell](\boldsymbol{S}) = S[\ell_1] \cup S[\ell_2]$. We define the ℓ-th abstract

---

[4] Note that we don't need to model the procedure stack associated with the state. This is because the stack is implicitly present in the semantics of the Boolean program, and hence does not need to be abstracted by c2bp. Procedure call and return are handled essentially in the same way as assignment statements. See [1] for details.

post operator, $\mathsf{post}^{\#}_{\mathsf{b \cdot c}}[\ell](\langle \ldots, v[\ell_1], \ldots, v[\ell_2], \ldots \rangle) = v[\ell_1] \sqcup v[\ell_2]$ where $v \sqcup v'$ is the least upper bound of the two trivectors v and v' in $\mathsf{AbsDom}_{\mathsf{cartesian}}$.

In all other cases, there is a unique predecessor location for ℓ, and $\mathsf{post}[\ell]$ is defined by the transition relation for the unique edge leading into ℓ. The ℓ-th abstract post operator is then defined (and computed) as described in the preceding sections, $\mathsf{post}^{\#}_{\mathsf{b \cdot c}}[\ell] = \alpha_{\mathsf{b \cdot c}} \circ \mathsf{post}[\ell] \circ \gamma_{\mathsf{b \cdot c}}$.

Specializing the observations in Section 8, we now study the loss of precision of $\mathsf{post}^{\#}_{\mathsf{bool}}[\ell]$ under the Cartesian abstraction specifically for each kind of location ℓ. There is no loss of precision if the edge leading into ℓ is one of the two nondeterministic branches corresponding to a conditional since all data values are unchanged.

If the edge corresponds to an "assume(ϕ)" statement (its post operator is defined by $\mathsf{post}(S) = \{s \in S \mid s \models \phi\}$ for $S \subseteq \mathsf{States}$), then there is a loss of precision exactly if ϕ expresses a dependence between variables (such as $x = y$ as in Example 3); Proposition 2 applies, since the operator $\mathsf{post}^{\#}_{\mathsf{bool}}[\ell]$ is deterministic; we have $\mathsf{post}^{\#}_{\mathsf{bool}}(V) = V \cap \alpha_{\mathsf{bool}}(\{s \in \mathsf{States} \mid s \models \phi\})$.

If the edge corresponds to an update statement, then (and only then) the operator $\mathsf{post}^{\#}_{\mathsf{bool}}[\ell]$ may not be deterministic (even if the concrete operator $\mathsf{post}[\ell]$ is deterministic; see Example 1). If ℓ is a "join" location, then the loss of precision is apparent: the union of two Cartesian products gets approximated by a Cartesian product. This loss of precision gets eliminated by the refinement of the next section.

9.2 Disjunctive Completion

Following standard methods from program analysis [8], we go from the abstract domain of trivectors $\mathsf{AbsDom}_{\mathsf{cartesian}}$ to its *disjunctive completion*, which we may model as the abstract domain of *sets* of trivectors, $\mathsf{AbsDom}_{\mathsf{b \cdot c \cdot \lor}} = 2^{\{0,1,*\}^n}$ with the partial ordering $\sqsubseteq$ obtained by extending the ordering $<$ on trivectors, i.e., for two sets V and V' of trivectors, we have $V \sqsubseteq V'$ if for all trivectors $v \in V$ there exists a trivector $v' \in V'$ such that $v < v'$. For our purposes, the least element of the abstract domain $\mathsf{AbsDom}_{\mathsf{b \cdot c \cdot \lor}}$ is the set $\{\alpha_{\mathsf{cartesian}} \circ \alpha_{\mathsf{bool}}(\mathsf{init})\}$.

Note that the two domains $\mathsf{AbsDom}_{\mathsf{bool}}$ and $\mathsf{AbsDom}_{\mathsf{b \cdot c \cdot \lor}}$ are not isomorphic; we have that $V_1 = \{\langle 0, * \rangle, \langle 1, * \rangle\}$ is strictly smaller than $V_2 = \{\langle *, * \rangle\}$. The *reduced quotient* of $\mathsf{AbsDom}_{\mathsf{b \cdot c \cdot \lor}}$ (obtained by identifying sets with the same meaning, such as V_1 and V_2) is isomorphic to $\mathsf{AbsDom}_{\mathsf{bool}}$; there, the fixpoint test is exponentially more expensive than in $\mathsf{AbsDom}_{\mathsf{b \cdot c \cdot \lor}}$ (but may be practically feasible if symbolic representations are used).

The abstract post operator $\mathsf{post}^{\#}_{\mathsf{b \cdot c \cdot \lor}}$ over sets of trivectors $V \in \mathsf{AbsDom}_{\mathsf{b \cdot c \cdot \lor}}$ is the canonical extension of the abstract post operator over trivectors to a function over sets of trivectors, i.e., for $V \in 2^{\{0,1,*\}^n}$, $\mathsf{post}^{\#}_{\mathsf{b \cdot c \cdot \lor}}(V) = \{\mathsf{post}^{\#}_{\mathsf{b \cdot c}}(v) \mid v \in V\}$.

9.3 The Focus Operation

Assuming the refinement to the disjunctive completion, we now introduce the *focus* operation (the terminology stems from an—as it seems to us, related—

operation in shape analysis via 3-valued logic [20]). This operation can be used to eliminate all loss of precision under Cartesian abstraction unless the Boolean abstraction of the post operator $\mathsf{post}[\ell]$ at location ℓ is nondeterministic (as in Examples 1 and 2).

The idea of the focus operator can be explained at hand of Example 3. Here, the assertion defining the operator post associated with the "assume($x_1 = x_2$)" statement (which corresponds to the assertion "$x_1 = x_2 \wedge x_1' = x_1 \wedge x_2' = x_2$") expresses a dependence between the variables x_1 and x_2. Therefore, one defines the focus operation $\mathsf{focus}[1,2]$ that, if applied to a trivector of length $n \geq 2$, replaces the value $*$ in its first and second components; i.e.,

$$\mathsf{focus}[1,2](\langle v_1, v_2, v_3, \ldots, v_n \rangle) =$$
$$\{\langle v_1', v_2', v_3, \ldots, v_n \rangle \mid v_1', v_2' \in \{0,1\}, \ v_1' \leq v_1, \ v_2' \leq v_2\}.$$

We extend the operation from trivectors v to sets of trivectors V in the canonical way. We are now able to define the 'focussed' abstract post operator $\mathsf{post}^{\#}_{\mathsf{b \cdot c \cdot \vee \cdot}[1,2]}$ as follows (refining the operator $\mathsf{post}^{\#}_{\mathsf{b \cdot c}}$ given in the previous section).

$$\mathsf{post}^{\#}_{\mathsf{b \cdot c \cdot \vee \cdot}[1,2]}(V) = \{\mathsf{post}^{\#}_{\mathsf{b \cdot c}}(v) \mid v \in \mathsf{focus}[1,2](V)\}$$

Continuing Example 3, we have that $\mathsf{post}^{\#}_{\mathsf{b \cdot c \cdot \vee \cdot}[1,2]}(\{\langle *, * \rangle\}) = \{\langle 0,0 \rangle, \langle 1,1 \rangle\}$, which means that the operator post does not lose precision under the 'focussed' abstraction (i.e., the meaning function composed with $\mathsf{post}^{\#}_{\mathsf{b \cdot c \cdot \vee \cdot}[1,2]}$ equals post composed with the meaning function). Note that in general, the focus operation may yield trivectors with components $*$. Continuing Example 3 for the general version of the program with $n \geq 2$ Boolean variables, we have $\mathsf{post}^{\#}_{\mathsf{b \cdot c \cdot \vee \cdot}[1,2]}(\{\langle *, *, *, \ldots, * \rangle\}) = \{\langle 0, 0, *, \ldots, * \rangle, \langle 1, 1, *, \ldots, * \rangle\}$.

The definitions above generalize directly to focus operations in other than the first two and more than two components. The following observation follows directly from Proposition 2.

Proposition 3. *For every deterministic operator post, there exists a focus operation such that post does not lose precision under the 'focussed' Cartesian abstraction.*

The abstract post operator $\mathsf{post}^{\#}_{\mathsf{slam}}$ used in SLAM results from combining the three refinements presented in Sections 9.1, 9.2 and 9.3, with the *total* focus operation $\mathsf{focus}[1, 2, \ldots, n]$. I.e., for each each control point ℓ in the program, we have: $\mathsf{post}^{\#}_{\mathsf{slam}}[\ell] = \mathsf{post}^{\#}_{\mathsf{b \cdot c \cdot \vee \cdot}[1,\ldots,n]}[\ell]$.

By Proposition 3, for every ℓ such that $\mathsf{post}^{\#}_{\mathsf{bool}}[\ell]$ is deterministic, the abstraction to $\mathsf{post}^{\#}_{\mathsf{slam}}[\ell]$ does not lose precision. A symbolic model checker such as bebop can realize the disjunctive completion and the total focus operation by representing and manipulating a set of trivectors V always in its 'focussed' version, i.e. the set of bitvectors $\mathsf{focus}[1, 2, \ldots, n](V)$. In a symbolic representation, the gain of precision obtained by using the disjunctive completion and the total focus operation comes at no cost. More precisely, the two Boolean formulas representing V and $\mathsf{focus}[1, 2, \ldots, n](V)$ simplify to the same form (e.g., *true* represents $\{\langle *, \ldots, * \rangle\}$ as well as $\{0, 1\}^n$).

10 Conclusion

Abstraction is probably the single most important issue in model checking software. Our work goes beyond the standard abstraction used in model checking, the so-called Boolean abstraction. We use the abstract domain of trivectors (with a third truth value $*$) in order to define a new abstraction function $\alpha_{b \cdot c}$ in terms of Boolean and Cartesian abstraction, and an abstract post operator $\mathsf{post}^{\#}_{b \cdot c}$ in terms of a Galois connection. We present a practically feasible algorithm to compute the new abstraction, represented as a Boolean program. Previous algorithms on related Boolean abstractions were practical only when restricted to a small subset of states; that restriction is not possible in our setting, which addresses programs with recursive procedures.

We have implemented both the tools c2bp and bebop. We have used c2bp and bebop to successfully check properties of a Windows NT device driver for the serial port. The driver has a few thousand lines of C code. More details and a case study on using SLAM tools to check properties of Windows NT device drivers will appear in a forthcoming paper.

The new abstraction trades a crucial gain of efficiency with a loss of precision (by ignoring dependencies between the Boolean variables). We single out the different causes of a proper loss of precision and are able to eliminate all but one. It may be interesting to determine general conditions ensuring that no proper loss of precision can ever occur, phrased e.g. in terms of separability [18].

The formal machinery developed here has potentially other applications in designing new abstractions for model checking software, in explaining existing approaches to pointer analysis based on 3-valued logic [20], and in classifying data-flow analysis problems modeled as model checking problems [23,21]. Previous work relating the Boolean abstraction to bisimulation and temporal properties (e.g. [5,10,6,16]) should be re-examined in the light of the new abstraction, perhaps in terms of 3-valued transition systems [14].

Acknowledgements. We thank Todd Millstein and Rupak Majumdar for their work on c2bp, and Bertrand Jeannet and Laurent Mauborgne for their helpful comments.

References

1. T. Ball, R. Majumdar, T. Millstein, and S. K. Rajamani. Automatic predicate abstraction of C programs. In *Proceedings of SIGPLAN Conference on Proramming Language Design and Implementation, 2001 (to appear)*. ACM, 2001.
2. T. Ball and S. K. Rajamani. Bebop: A symbolic model checker for Boolean programs. In *SPIN 00: SPIN Workshop*, LNCS 1885, pages 113–130. Springer-Verlag, 2000.
3. E. M. Clarke and E. A. Emerson. Synthesis of synchronization skeletons for branching time temporal logic. In *Logic of Programs*, LNCS 131, pages 52–71. Springer-Verlag, 1981.

4. E. M. Clarke, O. Grumberg, S. Jha, Y. Lu, and H. Veith. Counterexample-guided abstraction refinement. In *CAV 00: Computer-Aided Verification*, LNCS 1855, pages 154–169. Springer-Verlag, 2000.
5. E. M. Clarke, O. Grumberg, and D. Long. Model checking and abstraction. In *POPL 92: Principles of Programming Languages*, pages 343–354. ACM, 1992.
6. R. Cleaveland, P. Iyer, and D. Yankelevich. Optimality in abstractions of model checking. In *SAS 95: Static Analysis*, LNCS 983, pages 51–63. Springer-Verlag, 1995.
7. J. Corbett, M. Dwyer, J. Hatcliff, C. Pasareanu, Robby, S. Laubach, and H. Zheng. Bandera: Extracting finite-state models from java source code. In *ICSE 2000: International Conference on Software Engineering*, pages 439–448. ACM, 2000.
8. P. Cousot and R. Cousot. Abstract interpretation: a unified lattice model for the static analysis of programs by construction or approximation of fixpoints. In *POPL 77: Principles of Programming Languages*, pages 238–252. ACM, 1977.
9. P. Cousot and R. Cousot. Formal language, grammar and set-constraint-based program analysis by abstract interpretation. In *FPCA 95: Functional Programming and Computer Architecture*, pages 170–181. ACM, 1995.
10. D. Dams, O. Grumberg, and R. Gerth. Abstract interpretation of reactive systems: abstractions preserving $ACTL^*$, $ECTL^*$, and CTL^*. In *PROCOMET 94: Programming Concepts, Methods, and Calculi*, pages 561–581. Elsevier Science Publishers, 1994.
11. S. Das, D. L. Dill, and S. Park. Experience with predicate abstraction. In *CAV 00: Computer-Aided Verification*, LNCS 1633, pages 160–171. Springer-Verlag, 1999.
12. R. Giacobazzi, F. Ranzato, and F. Scozzari. Making abstract interpretations complete. *Journal of the ACM*, 47(2):361–416, March 2000.
13. S. Graf and H. Saidi. Construction of abstract state graphs with PVS. In *CAV 97: Computer Aided Verification*, LNCS 1254, pages 72–83. Springer-Verlag, 1997.
14. M. Huth, R. Jagadeesan, and D. A. Schmidt. Modal transition systems: a foundation for three-valued program analysis. In *ESOP 01: European Symposium on Programming*. Springer-Verlag, 2001. To appear.
15. R. Kurshan. *Computer-aided Verification of Coordinating Processes*. Princeton University Press, 1994.
16. C. Loiseaux, S. Graf, J. Sifakis, A. Bouajjani, and S. Bensalem. Property preserving abstractions for the verification of concurrent systems. *Formal Methods in System Design Volume*, 6(1):11–44, 1995.
17. A. Podelski. Model checking as constraint solving. In *SAS 00: Static Analysis*, LNCS 1824, pages 221–37. Springer-Verlag, 2000.
18. T. Reps. Program analysis via graph reachability. *Information and Software Technology*, 40(11-12):701–726, November-December 1998.
19. T. Reps, S. Horwitz, and M. Sagiv. Precise interprocedural dataflow analysis via graph reachability. In *POPL 95: Principles of Programming Languages*, pages 49–61. ACM, 1995.
20. M. Sagiv, T. Reps, and R. Wilhelm. Parametric shape analysis via 3-valued logic. In *POPL 99: Principles of Programming Languages*, pages 105–118. ACM, 1999.
21. D. Schmidt. Data flow analysis is model checking of abstract interpretation. In *POPL 98: Principles of Programming Languages*, pages 38–48. ACM, 1998.
22. M. Sharir and A. Pnueli. Two approaches to interprocedural data dalow analysis. In *Program Flow Analysis: Theory and Applications*, pages 189–233. Prentice-Hall, 1981.
23. B. Steffen. Data flow analysis as model checking. In *TACS 91: Theoretical Aspects of Computer Science*, LNCS 536, pages 346–365. Springer-Verlag, 1991.

Finding F easible Coun ter-examples when Model Chec king Abstracted Jaτa Programs*

Corina S. Păsăreanu[1], Matthew B. Dwyer[1], and Willem Visser[2]

[1] Department of Computing and Information Sciences, Kansas State University, USA
[2] RIACS, NASA Ames Research Center, Moffett Field, USA
pcorina@cis.ksu.edu

Abstract. Despite recent advances in model checking and in adapting model checking techniques to software, the state explosion problem remains a major hurdle in applying model checking to software. Recent work in automated program abstraction has shown promise as a means of scaling model checking to larger systems. Most common abstraction techniques compute an upper approximation of the original program. Thus, when a specification is found true for the abstracted program, it is known to be true for the original program. Finding a specification to be false, however, is inconclusive since the specification may be violated on a behavior in the abstracted program which is not present in the original program. We have extended an explicit-state model checker, Java PathFinder (JPF), to analyze counter-examples in the presence of abstractions. We enhanced JPF to search for "feasible" (i.e. nondeterminism-free) counter-examples "on-the-fly", during model checking. Alternatively, an abstract counter-example can be used to guide the simulation of the concrete computation and thereby check feasibility of the counter-example. We demonstrate the effectiveness of these techniques on counter-examples from checks of several multi-threaded Java programs.

1 Introduction

In the past decade, model checking has matured into an effective technique for reasoning about realistic components of hardware systems and comm unication protocols. The past several years have witnessed a series of efforts aimed at applying model checking techniques to reason about software implemen tations (e.g., Java source code [8,12,24]). While the conceptual basis for applying model c hecking to software is reasonably well-understood, there are still unsettled questions about whether effective tool support can be constructed that allows for realistic software requirements to be checked of realistic software descriptions in a practical amount of time. Most researc hers in model checking believe that property-preserving abstraction of the state-space will be necessary to make checking

* Supported in part by NSF under grants CCR-9703094 and CCR-9708184, by NASA under grant NAG-02-1209, by DARPA/ITO's PCES program through AFRL Contract F33615-00-C-3044, and was performed for the Formal Verification of Integrated Modular Avionics Software Cooperative Agreement, NCC-1-399, sponsored by Honeywell Technology Center and NASA Langley Research Center.

T. Margaria and W. Yi (Eds.): TACAS 2001, LNCS 2031, pp. 284–298, 2001.
© Springer-Verlag Berlin Heidelberg 2001

of realistic systems practical (e.g., [6,11,19]). There are a variety of challenges in bringing this belief to reality. This paper addresses one of those challenges, namely, the problem of automating the analysis of counter-examples that have been produced from abstract model checks in order to determine whether they represent real system defects.

The work described in this paper involves the integration of two recently developed tools for model checking Java source code : Bandera [8] and Java PathFinder [24]. Bandera is a toolset that provides automated support for reducing a program's state space through the application of program slicing and the compilation of abstract definitions of program data types. The resulting reduced Java program is then fed to JPF which performs an optimized explicit-state model check for program properties (e.g., assertion violations or deadlock). If the search is free of violations then the program properties are verified. If a violation is found the situation is less clear. Bandera uses abstractions that preserve the ability to prove *all paths* properties (e.g., such as assertions or linear temporal logic formulae). To achieve state space reduction, however, the ability to disprove such properties is sacrificed. This means that a check of an abstracted system may fail either because the program has an error or because the abstractions introduce *spurious* executions into the program that violate the property. The former are of interest to a user, while the latter are a distraction to the user, especially if spurious results occur in large numbers.

Several approaches have been proposed recently for analyzing the feasibility of counter-examples of abstracted transition-system models [5,3,4]. While our work shares much in common with these approaches, it is distinguished from them in four ways: (*i*) it treats the abstraction a program's data, as well as the run-time system scheduler and the property to be checked, (*ii*) the feasibility of a counter-example is judged against the semantics of a real programming language (i.e., Java), (*iii*) we advocate multiple approaches for analyzing feasibility with different cost/precision profiles, and (*iv*) our work is oriented toward detecting defects in the presence of abstraction. We will demonstrate the practical utility of an implementation of our approaches by applying them to the analysis of counter-examples for several real multi-threaded Java applications.

Safe abstractions often result in program models where the information required to decide conditionals is lost and hence nondeterministic choice needs to be used to encode such conditionals (i.e., to account for both true and false results). Nondeterministic choice is also used to model the possible decisions that a thread (or process) scheduler would make. Such abstractions are safe for all paths properties since they are guaranteed to include all behaviors of the unabstracted system. The difficulty lies in the fact that they may introduce many behaviors that are not possible. To sharpen the precision of the abstract model (by eliminating some spurious behaviors) one minimizes the use of nondeterminism and it can be shown that the absence of nondeterminism equates to feasibility [23]. Section 3 describes how program data, the property and scheduler behavior are abstracted in Bandera/JPF using nondeterminism.

JPF can perform a state-space search that is bounded by nondeterministic-choice operations; a property violation that lies within this space has a counter-example that is free of nondeterminism and is hence feasible. JPF can also perform simulation of the concrete program guided by an abstract counter-example. If a corresponding concrete program trace exists then the counter-example is feasible. Section 4 describes these two techniques for analyzing program counter-examples that were added to JPF. Section 5 describes several defective Java applications whose counter-examples were analyzed using these techniques. In Section 6 we discuss related and future work and we conclude in Section 7. In the next section, we give some brief background on Bandera and JPF.

2   Background

Bandera [8] is an integrated collection of program analysis and transformation components that allows users to selectively analyze program properties and to tailor the analysis to that property so as to minimize analysis time. Bandera exploits existing model checkers, such as Spin [16], SMV [20], and JPF [24], to provide state-of-the-art analysis engines for checking program-property correspondence. Bandera provides support for reducing a program's state-space via *program slicing* [15] and *data abstraction*.

Data abstraction automates the reduction in size of the data domains over which program variables range [13]. A type inference algorithm is applied to ensure that a consistent set of abstractions are applied to program data. This type-based approach to abstraction is complementary to predicate abstraction approaches that reduce a program by preserving the ability to decide specific user-define predicates; JPF's companion tool implements predicate abstraction programs written in Java [25].

Java PathFinder is a model checker for Java programs that can check any Java program, since it is built on top of a custom made Java Virtual Machine (JVM), for deadlock and violations of user-defined assertions [24]. In JPF special attention is paid to reducing the number of states, rather than execution speed as is typical of commercial JVMs, since this is the major efficiency concern in explicit-state model checking. Users have the ability to set the granularity of atomic steps during model checking to: byte-codes, source lines (the default) or explicit atomic blocks (through calls to `beginAtomic()` and `endAtomic()` methods from a special class called `Verify`). A JPF counter-example indicates how to execute code from the initial state of the program to reach the error. Each step in the execution contains the name of the *class* the code is from, the *file* the source code is stored in, the *line number* of the source file that is currently being executed and the a number identifying the *thread* that is executing. Using only thread numbers in each step JPF can simulate the erroneous execution.

3   Program Abstraction

Given a concrete program and a property, the strategy of verification by using abstraction involves: *(i)* defining an abstraction mapping that is appropriate for the property being verified and using it to transform the concrete program into an abstract program, *(ii)* transforming the property into an abstract property, *(iii)* verifying that the abstract program satisfies the abstract property, and finally *(iv)* inferring that the concrete program satisfies the concrete property. In this section, we summarize foundational issues that underlie these steps.

3.1   Data Abstraction

The abstract interpretation (AI) [9] framework as described in a large body of literature establishes a rigorous semantics-based methodology for constructing abstractions so that they are *safe* in the sense that they over-approximate the set of true executable behaviors of the system (i.e., each executable behavior is covered by an abstract execution). Thus, when these abstract behaviors are exhaustively compared to a specification and found to be in conformance, we can be sure that the true executable system behaviors conform to the specification.

We present an AI, in an informal manner, as: a domain of abstract values, an abstraction function mapping concrete program values to abstract values, and a collection of abstract primitive operations (one for each concrete operation in the program). For example, to abstract from everything but the fact that integer variable x is zero or not one could use the *signs* AI [1] which only keeps track of whether an integer value is negative, equal to zero, or positive. The abstract domain is the set of tokens {*neg, zero, pos*}. The abstraction function maps negative numbers to *neg*, 0 to *zero*, and positive numbers to *pos*. Abstract versions of each of the basic operations on integers are used that respect the abstract domain values. For example, an abstract version of the addition operation for *signs* is:

$+_{abs}$	zero	pos	neg
zero	zero	pos	neg
pos	pos	pos	{zero, pos, neg}
neg	neg	{zero, pos, neg}	neg

Abstract operations are allowed to return sets of values to model lack of knowledge about specific abstract values. This imprecision is interpreted in the model checker as a nondeterministic choice over the values in the set. Such cases are a source of "extra behaviors" introduced in the abstract model due to its over-approximation of the set of behaviors of the original system.

3.2   Property Abstraction

When abstracting properties, Bandera uses an approach similar to [17]. Informally, given an AI for a variable x (e.g. *signs*) that appears in a proposition (e.g.,x>0), we convert the proposition to a disjunction of propositions of the form x==*a*, where *a* are the abstract values that correspond to values that imply the truth of the original proposition (e.g., x==*pos* implies x>0, but x==*neg* and x==*zero* do not; it follows that proposition x>0 is abstracted to x==*pos*). Thus, this disjunction under-approximates the truth of a concrete proposition insuring that the property holds on the original program if the abstracted property holds on the abstract program.

```
public class Signs {                    public static int add(int a,int b){
  public static final int NEG =0;         int r;
  public static final int ZERO=1;         Verify.beginAtomic();
  public static final int POS =2;         if(a==NEG  && b==NEG) r=NEG;
  public static int abs(int n){           else if(a==NEG  && b==ZERO)r=NEG;
    if (n < 0) return NEG;                 else if(a==ZERO && b==NEG) r=NEG;
    if (n == 0) return ZERO;               else if(a==ZERO && b==ZERO)r=ZERO;
    if (n > 0) return POS;                 else if(a==ZERO && b==POS) r=POS;
  }                                        else if(a==POS  && b==ZERO)r=POS;
                                           else if(a==POS  && b==POS) r=POS;
                                           else r=Verify.choose(2);
                                           Verify.endAtomic(); return r; }}
```

Fig. 1. Java Representation of *signs* AI (excerpts)

3.3   Scheduler Abstraction

Analyzing concurrent systems requires safe modeling of the possible scheduling decisions that are made in executing individual threads. Since software is often ported to operating system's with different scheduling policies, a property checked under a specific policy would be potentially invalid when that system is executed under a different policy. To address this, the approach taken in existing model checkers is to implement what amounts to the most general scheduling policy (i.e., nondeterministic choice among the set of runnable threads). Properties verified under such a policy will also hold under any more restrictive policy. Fairness constraints are supported in most model checkers to provide the ability to more accurately model realistic scheduling policies.

The Java language has a relatively weak specification for its thread scheduling policy. Threads are assigned priorities and a scheduler must ensure that "all threads with the top priority will eventually run" [2]. Thus, a model checker that guarantees progress to all runnable threads of the highest priority will produce only feasible schedules; JPF implements this policy.

3.4   Abstraction Implementation

In Bandera, generating an abstract program involves the following steps: the user selects a set of AIs for a program's data components, then type inference is used to calculate the abstractions for the remaining program data, then the Java class that implements each AI's abstraction function and abstract operations is retrieved from Bandera's abstraction library, and finally the concrete Java program is traversed, and concrete literals and operations are replaced with calls to classes that implement the corresponding abstract literals and operations.

Figure 1 shows excerpts of the Java representation of the *signs* AI. Abstract tokens are implemented as integer values, and the abstraction function and operations have straightforward implementations as Java methods. For Java basetypes, the definitions of abstract operations are automatically generated using a theorem prover (see [13] for details). Nondeterministic choice is specified by

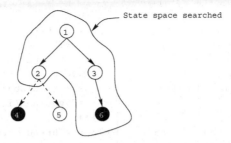

Fig. 2. Model Checking on Choose-free Paths

calls to **Verify.choose(n)**, which JPF traps during model checking and returns nondeterministic values between 0 and n inclusive. Abstract operations execute atomically (via calls to **Verify.beginAtomic()** and **Verify.endAtomic()**) since they abstract concrete byte-codes (e.g. **Signs.add()** abstracts **iadd**).

4   Finding Feasible Counter-examples

We have seen in the previous section that, if a specification is true for the abstracted program, it will also be true for the concrete program. However, if the specification is false for the abstracted program, the counter-example may be the result of some behavior in the abstracted program which is not present in the original program. It takes deep insight to decide if an abstract counter-example is feasible (i.e. corresponds to a concrete computation). We have developed two techniques that automate tests for counter-example feasibility: model checking on *choose-free* paths and abstract counter-example guided concrete simulation.

4.1   Choose-Free State Space Search

We enhanced the JPF model checker with an option to look only at paths that do not refer to instructions that introduce nondeterminism (i.e. a **Verify.choose()** call). When a *choose* occurs the search algorithm of the model checker backtracks. The approach exploits the following theorem from [23]: **Theorem.**

> *Every path in the abstracted program where all assignments are deterministic is a path in the concrete program.*

In [23], the theorem is used to judge a counter-example feasible, whereas we use it to bias the model checker to search for feasible counter-examples. The theorem ensures that paths that are free of nondeterminism correspond to paths in the concrete program (a more general definition of deterministic paths can be found in [10]). It follows that if a counter-example is reported in a *choose-free* search then it represents a feasible execution. If this execution also violates the property, then it represents a feasible counter-example.

Consider an abstracted program (whose state space is sketched in Figure 2). Black circles represent states where some assertion is violated. Dashed lines

```
       class App{                          class App{
         public static void main(...){       public static void main(...){
[1]        new AThread().start(); ...          new AThread().start(); ...
[2]        int i=0;                            int i=Signs.ZERO;
[3]        while(i<2){...                      while(Signs.lt(i,Signs.POS)){...
[4]          assert(!Global.done);              assert(!Global.done);
[5]          i++;                               i=Signs.add(i,Signs.POS);
         }}}                                 }}}
       class AThread extends Thread{        class AThread extends Thread{
         public void run(){ ...              public void run(){ ...
[6]        Global.done=true;                   Global.done=true;
       }}                                   }}
```

Fig. 3. Simple Example of Concrete (left) and Abstracted (right) Code

represent transitions that refer to *choose*, while solid lines refer to instructions other than *choose*. Model checking on choose-free paths will report only the error path 1-3-6, although path 1-2-4 leads to a state where the assertion is false (and it may correspond to an execution in the concrete program).

We also note that our technique could be implemented in any model checker, but the design of JPF made this modification particularly easy. JPF is essentially a special-purpose JVM that interprets each byte code in the compiled version of a Java program. Since *choose* operations are represented as static method calls, trapping and processing those operations specially only required modification of the code for the static method invocation byte-code. We made sure that the search on choose-free paths does not introduce deadlocks (choose instructions are interpreted as infinite self loops).

Consider checking the fragment of code on the left of Figure 3 against the assertion at line **4**, where initially **Global.done** is false; the abstracted code (using *signs* for i) is shown to the right of the original. In the abstracted program, nondeterminism is introduced through method **lt** that implements the abstract operation for <: after one pass through the **while** loop, the abstract value of i becomes *pos* and the value returned by **Signs.lt(i,Signs.POS)** can be either true or false. However, the abstract program does expose a choose-free counter-example: if the thread that is an instance of **AThread** executes line **6** before the main thread begins the execution of the **while** loop, the assertion in line **4** is violated when the body of the loop is executed for the first time (and the abstract value of i is *zero*). This counter-example does not contain nondeterministic choices, since the value returned by **Signs.lt(i,Signs.POS)**, when i is *zero*, is uniquely true.

4.2   Abstract Counter-example Guided Concrete Simulation

In Bandera, the generation of an abstracted program is automatic and is done in such a way that there is a clear correspondence between the concrete and abstracted program: for each line in the concrete program, there is a single line in the abstracted program. Since byte-codes execute atomically, for each "concrete"

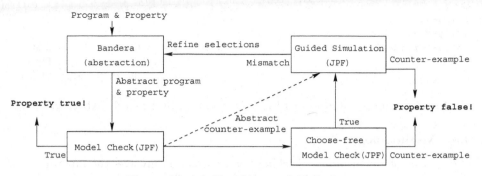

Fig. 4. Model Checking and Refinement

byte-code, there is a set of "abstract" byte-codes that execute atomically in JPF. This property of Bandera abstraction, together with the fact that all Java variables have known initial values, allows for simulation of the concrete program, based on an abstract counter-example.

This is done in JPF by executing the steps in the abstract trace. For clarity, we'll discuss the simulation in terms of the execution of lines of Java source code, but JPF can also perform simulation on a byte-code level. Each step contains information about the thread to be run next and the line of the counter-example. At each step of the concrete execution, JPF checks that the concrete line to be executed corresponds to the abstract line in the counter-example. If the lines match throughout the simulation then the abstract trace is feasible, otherwise, the abstract trace is spurious. To check whether the feasible trace is a counter-example, we have also to check if it violates the property.

Consider again the example from Figure 3 where the result of model c heck-ing the abstracted program is a counter-example where `Global.done` is set true after the loop in the main thread is executed two times. This means that the assertion is reachable (and violated) by the (abstract) trace

    `1-2-3-4-5-3-4-5-3-4`

in the main thread. While this is clearly possible in the abstract program (since, after the abstract value of `i` becomes *pos*, the condition at line `3` can be non-deterministically true or false), it is not possible in the concrete program. To see this, we simulate the steps from the abstract trace on the concrete program: after executing the loop two times, the value of `i` is 2 so the exit condition of the loop is true and the loop is exited. At this point a line mismatch is detected and the simulation stops.

It is possible to detect the infeasibility of an abstract trace earlier, using a technique similar to forward analysis (e.g.[22]): when simulating each step on the concrete program, we also check the correspondence between concrete and abstract values. This can be done in JPF by abstracting the values of variables (e.g., via calls to `Signs.abs()`) in the concrete simulation and comparing them to the abstract values in the counter-example.

```
[1] x=1;                          x=Signs.POS;
[2] y=x+1;                        y=Signs.add(x,Signs.POS);
[3] assert(x<y);                  assert((x==Signs.NEG && y==Signs.ZERO)
                                  ||(x==Signs.NEG && y==Signs.POS)
                                  ||(x==Signs.ZERO && y==Signs.POS));
```

Fig. 5. Example of Spurious Error Introduced by Property Abstraction

4.3 Methodology

Our methodology for model checking and abstraction involves the integration of the above two techniques as illustrated in Figure 4. The input (concrete) program and the specification are abstracted (using abstractions from Bandera's library) as described in Section 2 and the transformed program is fed to a model checker. If the result of model checking is true, then the specification is true for the concrete program. If the result is false, we re-run the model checker to search only choose-free paths in the model. If the model checker finds a choose-free counter-example, it is reported to the user otherwise we perform counter-example guided simulation. If the simulation succeeds, a counter-example is reported, but if a mismatch is detected then abstractions need to be refined. The refinement involves modifying the selection of abstractions guided by the counter-example reported in the first run of the model checker. For a discussion on how the abstractions could be refined, see Section 6.

4.4 Discussion

In general, the result of model checking an abstract program is false either because the concrete program does not satisfy the property (in which case the counter-example is feasible and indicates a real defect), or because the abstraction is not suitable for checking the property. In the latter case, the abstract counter-example can be one of the following:

- not feasible as a result of over-approximation of the behavior of the concrete program (e.g. the spurious counter-example of the program in Figure 3);
- feasible but not defective; as a result of the under-approximation of the property to be checked. This case is illustrated by the code in Figure 5, where both x and y are abstracted to *signs*. The predicate in the assertion is abstracted in such a way that if the assertion is true in the abstracted program, it follows that it is true in the concrete program. Abstract trace 1-2-3 violates the assertion, since after step 2, both x and y are *pos*. However, in the concrete program, the assertion is true.

In our experience this second case is rare, since in Bandera user's are guided to make abstraction selections that are able to decide both the truth and falsity of the propositions used in the property to be checked. Only when such a selection is impossible can a feasible, but not defective, counter-example arise.

We note that both choose-free model checking and abstract counter-example guided concrete simulation can be directly applied to a executable program slice.

If a trace is feasible in the sliced program, it is also feasible in the original program [15]. We also note that the techniques presented here can be applied for checking safety properties expressed in any universal temporal logic.

5   Experience with Defective Java Applications

To illustrate the potential benefits of the techniques described in the previous section, we applied them to several small to medium-size multi-threaded Java applications. These applications used both lock synchronization and condition-based synchronization (i.e., `wait/notify`). The systems are: **RAX** (Remote Agent experiment) [25], a Java version of a component extracted from an embedded spacecraft-control application, **Pipeline** [7], a generic framework for implementing multi-threaded staged calculations, **RWVSN**, Lea's [18] generic readers-writers synchronization framework, and **DEOS** [21,25], the scheduler from a real-time executive for avionics systems that was translated from C++. The following table gives some basic measures of the size of the system; *SLOC* stands for the number of source lines of code.

Program	SLOC	Classes	Methods	Fields	Threads
RAX	55	4	8	7	3
Pipeline	103	5	10	7	5
RWVSN	590	5	43	10	5
DEOS	1443	20	91	92	6

Most of these programs use the basic features of Java and its concurrency constructs, however, the **RWVSN** application uses abstract classes, inheritance, and `java.util.Vector`.

The **RAX** and **DEOS** examples had known errors that we checked for. For the **Pipeline** and **RWVSN** examples we seeded faults in the program. For example, we dropped a negation (!) in one program and changed <= into < (simulating an off-by-one error) in the other. It is interesting to note that not all seeded faults could be detected given the properties we checked for, so we altered the faults until we generated a property violation.

We now describe several model checks for these systems and the automated analysis of the resulting counter-examples. Full details for the examples and model checks is available at |http://www.cis.ksu.edu/ pcorina/case-studies—.

5.1   Description of Experiments

We model checked the **RAX** example to detect deadlocks using two different abstractions. Figure 6 shows excerpts from the original and the generated abstract Java program. The abstraction of the program was driven by our selection that the `Event.count` field should be abstracted with *signs*. Bandera's abstraction type inference determined that the local `count` variables in the `FirstTask.run()` method should also be abstracted. Running JPF on this abstracted system detects a deadlock and produces a 74 step counter-example.

```
[ 1]class Event{                                    class Event {
[ 2] int count=0;                                   int count = Signs.ZERO;
[ 3] public synchronized void wait_for_event(){     public synchronized void wait_for_event(){
[ 4]  try{wait();}                                   try {wait();}
[ 5]  catch(InterruptedException e){};               catch(InterruptedException e){};
     }                                              }
[ 6] public synchronized void signal_event(){       public synchronized void signal_event(){
[ 7]  count = count + 1;                             count = Signs.add(count,Signs.POS);
[ 8]  notifyAll();                                   notifyAll();
     }}                                             }}
[ 9]class FirstTask extends Thread{                 class FirstTask extends Thread {
[10] Event event1,event2;                           Event event1,event2;
[11] int count=0;                                   int count = Signs.ZERO;
[12] public void run(){                             public void run () {
[13]  count = event1.count;                          count = event1.count;
[14]  while(true){                                   while (true){
[15]   if(count == event1.count)                      if(Signs.eq(count,event1.count))
[16]    event1.wait_for_event();                        event1.wait_for_event();
[17]   count = event1.count;                          count = event1.count;
[18]   event2.signal_event();                         event2.signal_event();
     }}}                                            }}}
```

Fig. 6. RAX Program with Deadlock (excerpts)

Analysis of this counter-example reveals that it is spurious. After 39 steps in the counter-example the trace reaches the conditional at line **15**. In the real system, the branch condition is false, but due to the nondeterminism of Signs.eq() for positive parameters the abstract system enters the conditional. JPF is able to find a 40 step choose-free counter-example. It is clear that the presence of spurious counter-examples is closely related to the property being checked, the program and the abstraction's selected. We reran our model checks changing the abstraction for **Event.count** field to record information about the evenness or oddness of its values. This produced a 128 step counter-example, but JPF was unable to find a choose-free counter-example. At this point, we ran JPF in simulation mode guided by the 128 step counter-example and while this counter-example did contain nondeterministic choices it was shown to be feasible.

The **Pipeline** example consists of an application that uses the methods of a **Pipeline** class to manage execution of a multi-threaded staged computation. The application constructs and starts execution of a pipeline, calls stop() to end execution of the pipeline, and calls add() to provide input to the computation. We model checked a precedence property for the **Pipeline** system stating that "no pipeline stage (i.e., thread) will terminate until the stop method is called". Since JPF does not currently support checking of temporal properties, we encoded this using a boolean variable, **stopCalled**, set to true when the **stop()** method had been called and embedded assert(stopCalled) at the return point of the stage **run** methods. This example was abstracted by identifying a loop index variable that controlled the number of times the **add()** method was called and abstracting it to *signs*. Type inference determined that 5 additional fields and local variables also needed abstraction. Checking the property on the abstracted system detected an error on a 168 step counter-example. JPF found a 69 step choose-free counter-example that is similar to the example in Figure 3 in that it occurred on the first iteration of an abstracted loop.

RWVSN consists of an application that extends Lea's RWVSN class [18] to implement an object with a readers-writers synchronization policy. That object is then shared by several threads that read and write through the RWVSN interface. We checked that access by a reader excluded access by a writer by setting a boolean variable, in_writer, in the writer's critical section and resetting it upon exit, and embedding assert(!in_writer) in the reader's critical section. Abstraction was applied to 3 integer fields of the RWVSN class abstracting them to *signs*. Checking the property on the abstracted system detected an error in 179 steps. JPF found a 76 step choose-free counter-example.

The **DEOS** system has been the subject of several recent case studies in model checking code [21,25,13]; we performed the abstraction and analysis as described in [13]. The property being checked is an assertion that encodes a test for *time partitioning* in the scheduler component of the system. We used dependence analysis driven by the location of the assert statement and the data values it referenced to identify a single field (out of 92) as influencing the property. We selected the *signs* AI for that field and type inference determined that 2 more fields should be abstracted. Checking the property on the abstracted system detected an error in 471 steps. JPF found a 312 step choose-free counter-example.

5.2   Discussion

While these programs represent a range of different patterns of concurrency (e.g., clients and server, pipelines, and peer-groups) and the larger examples are real applications, we do not claim that our results generalize to a broader class of multi-threaded Java programs. We do, however, believe the results suggest that the counter-example analysis techniques we have developed have merit and can significantly reduce the burden users face when analyzing counter-examples from checks of abstracted systems.

The data clearly show that counter-examples can be reduced significantly in length; this alone makes it easier to diagnose the program fault. The fact that counter-examples are guaranteed to be feasible helps focus the user's attention on only those counter-examples for which analysis will lead to fault detection.

It should come as no surprise that a choose-free model check is faster than a typical model check since it is essentially a depth-bounded model check. Most model checkers can do depth-bounded search and in fact this often allows for detection of significantly shorter counter-examples. The key difference lies in the fact that a choose-free search uses an adaptive depth-bound that is based on encountering nondeterministic choice operators. This guarantee of not executing a choice operator is what assures counter-example feasibility. Without that a naive depth-bounded search may include execution of a choice operator.

Finally, we observe that choose-free search can be an effective way to exploit more aggressive abstraction approaches. The application of source-level predicate abstraction techniques to the **DEOS** and **RAX** is described in detail in [25]. In that work a predicate abstraction and an invariant for **DEOS** and 4 different predicate abstractions for **RAX** were used to produce abstract models that preserved both truth and falsity of the properties being checked. In contrast, the checks described in this paper sacrifice precision for more aggressive abstraction, and state-space reduction, while choose-free search enables the recovery of feasible counter-examples.

6   Related and Future Work

In our previous work [13], we focused on the specification, generation, selection and compilation of abstractions for Java programs. In this paper, we detail techniques for analyzing counter-examples and provide evidence for their usefulness on several non-trivial Java programs.

Most existing work on counter-example analysis is oriented towards the goal of verification; counter-example analysis drives abstraction refinement for the purpose of proving a property. In contrast, our work is oriented toward defect detection. Our biasing of the model checker yields a complete coverage of the sub-space of guaranteed feasible paths in the system rather than simply assessing the feasibility of a single counter-example from an unbiased model check.

Our simulation technique works because JPF maintains a correspondence between the concrete and abstracted programs and Java defines default initial values for all data (thus a program has a single initial state). It is possible to develop more general simulation techniques that handle multiple initial states, but we believe these are not necessary for Java. One such technique [5] uses forward analysis and performs a symbolic simulation of the concrete system using predicates that characterize the program data values. Since it does not keep a correspondence between concrete and abstract transitions, rather than determine the next concrete state it must compute (at each step of the simulation) the set of *all* possible next concrete states. This method, which is implemented in SMV, is limited to finite-state systems.

In SLAM [3], sequential C programs are abstracted into *boolean programs*; symbolic execution is used to map abstract counter-examples to concrete executions. INVEST [4] and interactive abstractions [22] use theorem proving to rule out spurious counter-examples. Backward analysis is used to obtain information to refine the abstractions. Unlike our approach, these tools/techniques are not concerned with property abstraction or scheduling information.

We believe that the methods described in these papers are complementary to our techniques. For example, we can use backward analysis to obtain feedback for refinement of abstractions. Backward analysis computes pre-images of the violating abstract state over the given trace. For the spurious counter-example of Figure 3, after the body of the loop is executed two times, the value of the loop condition is true, which means that the concrete value of x is believed to be less than 2. The analysis would discover that this happens because the value of x before the assignment at line 5 is believed to be less than 1 (which is not true in the concrete program, where the value of x is exactly 1). This implies that a new abstraction to be selected for variable x has to include a new token for 1 (e.g. *signs* abstraction should be replaced with *range(0..1)* abstraction [13]).

We note that both choose-free search and counter-example guided simulation techniques could be implemented in any explicit-state model checker. For example, Bandera [8] generates Promela models for Spin that can easily be adapted to perform choose-free search. Path simulation simply requires the ability to associate the steps of the concrete and abstract program and to simulate the concrete program. One can already do this by hand using Spin's simulation facilities, but automating the process would greatly ease its use. We also note that, although we set our presentation in the context of Bandera's abstraction, other forms of data abstraction, like JPF's predicate abstraction, would also be treated properly. By that we mean that a path through the predicate abstracted code that is choose-free or that can be mapped to a concrete execution is feasible.

7   Conclusion

In this paper, we have suggested two approaches for analyzing counter-examples produced by model checks of abstracted programs. These approaches have the advantage of being very fast (i.e., choose-free search is depth-bounded and the cost of simulation is related to the length of the counter-example). Based on experimentation with an implementation of these techniques in a Java model checking tool we have also found the techniques to be capable of detecting guaranteed feasible counter-examples in nearly every case. This enables aggressive abstractions to be applied without losing the ability to detect errors, thereby minimizing the need for refinement of abstractions. This implementation treats not only abstraction of program data, but also of thread scheduling policies, and the property to be checked. Finally, we believe that these techniques can be combined with other counter-example analysis methods to provide a suite of tools that vary cost and in their ability to precisely analyze counter-examples. Such a tool suite would be a useful addition to any model checking tool.

References

1. S. Abramsky and C. Hankin. *Abstract Interpretation of Declarative Languages*. Ellis Horwood Limited, 1987.
2. K. Arnold and J. Gosling. *The Java Programming Language*. Addison-Wesley, 1998.
3. T. Ball and S.K. Rajamani. Checking temporal properties of software with boolean programs. In *Proc. of the Workshop on Advances in Verification*, July 2000.
4. S. Bensalem, Y. Lakhnech, and S. Owre. Computing abstractions of infinite state systems compositionally and automatically. In *Proc. 10th International Conference on Computer-Aided Verification*, June 1998.
5. E.M. Clarke, O. Grumberg, S. Jha, Y. Lu, and H. Veith. Counterexample-guided abstraction refinement. In *Proc. 12th International Conference on Computer-Aided Verification*, July 2000.
6. E.M. Clarke, O. Grumberg, and D.E. Long. Model checking and abstraction. *ACM Transactions on Programming Languages and Systems*, 16(5):1512–1542, September 1994.

7. J.C. Corbett, M. B. Dwyer, J. Hatcliff, and Robby. Bandera : A source-level interface for model checking Java programs. In [14].
8. J.C. Corbett, M.B. Dwyer, J. Hatcliff, S. Laubach, C.S. Păsăreanu, Robby, and H. Zheng. Bandera : Extracting finite-state models from Java source code. In [14].
9. P. Cousot and R. Cousot. Abstract interpretation: A unified lattice model for static analysis of programs by construction or approximation of fixpoints. In *Conference Record of the Fourth Annual ACM Symposium on Principles of Programming Languages*, pages 238–252, 1977.
10. D. Dams, R. Gerth, G. Dhmen, R. Herrmann, P. Kelb, and H. Pargmann. Model checking using adaptive state and data abstraction. In D.L.Dill, editor, *Proc. 6th International Conference on Computer-Aided Verification*, volume 818 of *Lecture Notes in Computer Science*, pages 455–467. Springer Verlag, June 1994.
11. D. Dams, R. Gerth, and O. Grumberg. Abstract interpretation of reactive systems. *ACM Transactions on Programming Languages and Systems*, 19(2):253–291, March 1997.
12. C. Demartini, R. Iosif, and R. Sisto. A deadlock detection tool for concurrent Java programs. *Software - Practice and Experience*, 29(7):577–603, July 1999.
13. M.B. Dwyer, J. Hatcliff, R. Joehanes, S. Laubach, C.S. Păsăreanu, Robby, W. Visser, and H. Zheng. Tool-supported program abstraction for finite-state verification. In *Proceedings of the 23rd International Conference on Software Engineering*, May 2001.
14. C. Ghezzi, M. Jazayeri, and A. Wolf, editors. *Proceedings of the 22nd International Conference on Software Engineering*, June 2000.
15. J. Hatcliff, J.C. Corbett, M.B. Dwyer, S. Sokolowski, and H. Zheng. A formal study of slicing for multi-threaded programs with JVM concurrency primitives. In *Proceedings of the 6th International Static Analysis Symposium*, September 1999.
16. G.J. Holzmann. The model checker SPIN. *IEEE Transactions on Software Engineering*, 23(5):279–294, May 1997.
17. Y. Kesten and A. Pnueli. Modularization and abstraction: The keys to practical formal verification. *Lecture Notes in Computer Science*, 1450, 1998.
18. D. Lea. *Concurrent Programming in Java[tm], Second Edition: Design principles and Patterns*. The Java Series. Addison-Wesley, 2nd edition, 1999.
19. C. Loiseaux, S. Graf, J. Sifakis, A. Bouajiani, and S. Bensalem. Property preserving abstractions for the verification of concurrent systems. *Formal Methods in System Design*, 6(1):11–44, 1995.
20. K.L. McMillan. *Symbolic Model Checking*. Kluwer Academic Publishers, 1993.
21. J. Penix, W. Visser, E. Engstrom, A. Larson, and N. Weininger. Verification of time partitioning in the DEOS real-time scheduling kernel. In [14].
22. V. Rusu and E. Singerman. On proving safety properties by integrating static analysis, theorem proving and abstraction. In *Proceedings of Tools and Algorithms for the Construction and Analysis of Systems*, March 1999.
23. H. Saïdi. Model checking guided abstraction and analysis. In *Proceedings of the 7th International Static Analysis Symposium*, 2000.
24. W. Visser, G. Brat, K. Havelund, and S. Park. Model checking programs. In *Proceedings of the 15th IEEE International Conference on Automated Software Engineering*, September 2000.
25. W. Visser, S. Park, and J. Penix. Applying predicate abstraction to model check object-oriented programs. In *Proceedings of the 3rd ACM SIGSOFT Workshop on Formal Methods in Software Practice*, August 2000.

The LOOP Compiler for Java and JML

Joachim van den Berg and Bart Jacobs

Computing Science Institute, University of Nijmegen
Toernooiveld 1, 6525 ED Nijmegen, The Netherlands
{joachim,bart}@cs.kun.nl

Abstract This paper describes the architecture of the LOOP tool, which is used for reasoning about sequential Java. The LOOP tool translates Java and JML (a specification language tailored to Java) classes into their semantics in higher order logic. It serves as a front-end to a theorem prover in which the actual verification of the desired properties takes place. Also, the paper discusses issues related to logical theory generation.

1 Introduction

Being able to verify programs has always been a major topic in computer science. For this purpose many artificial, mathematically clean, programming languages have been introduced, since reasoning about real, dirty, programming languages is far from easy. Due to the progress in the field of theorem proving, and the increase in computing power, it has become feasible now to reason about real programming languages. Also, specialised tools—like theLOOP tool—contribute to this feasibility.

Using theorem provers for program verification becomes more and more common. There are numerous advantages to the use of theorem provers for doing proofs over doing proofs by hand: theorem provers are very precise, they can do lots of, often boring, proof steps in a few seconds, they keep track of the list of proof obligations which are still open, and do a lot of bureaucratic administration for the user. This is especially relevant in the area of program verification where usually many cases have to be distinguished and the proofs themselves are not so difficult (in comparison to mathematics).

Since Java is one of the most popular programming languages around, it is also of particular interest for researchers. Many research groups are focusing on specification and verification of Java programs at source-code level, using various tools, *e.g.*

- ESC/Java [23] is an extended static checker for Java (including threads), which can detect certain runtime errors at compile time, by using a built-in theorem prover. By using this checker, many (but not all) errors can be found without user interaction. ESC/Java uses a specification language which has recently been integrated with JML [15].

T. Margaria and W. Yi (Eds.): TACAS 2001, LNCS 2031, pp. 299–312, 2001.

- Jive [17] is a verification environment in which a user can write Java source-code as well as its specification. It is connected with a theorem prover, currently this is PVS [19], which is used to verify proof obligations. Jive's user interface takes care of the interaction with PVS. With Jive, one is currently able to reason about the sequential kernel of Java, but not about exceptions, a crucial part of Java.
- In the Bali project a deep embedding of a semantics for Bali, a Java subset, in Isabelle [20] has been developed, with various meta-theoretical results: formalisation of the type system to prove type-safety [18], soundness and completeness of an appropriate Hoare logic. This project is not primarily focussed on verification of concrete programs.
- The KeY project [1] aims at integrating formal specification and verification tools into the software engineering process. Within this project a dynamic logic for JavaCard, Java's subset for smart card programming, has been developed. The verification tool for this project is still under development.
- The Bandera project [5] extracts a non-finite-state model from Java source-code, and applies program analysis, abstraction and transformation techniques to it, in order to get a finite-state model. This model is abstractly represented, enabling the generation of concrete models for various model checking tools. The tools developed in this project are applied to several Java case studies.

The LOOP project [21] focuses on specification and verification of sequential Java. For this part of Java a formal semantics has been developed, based on coalgebras. JML is the language used to specify Java classes. For the kernel part of JML—in variants, behaviour specifications, including modifiable clauses—a formal semantics is being developed.

Within the LOOP project a special purpose compiler, the LOOP tool, has been built which incorporate these semantics of Java and JML. The output of the LOOP tool is a series of logical theories for the theorem provers PVS and Isabelle. This gives the verifier a choice of proof tool. Typically, when a user wants to reason about a Java class, (s)he uses the LOOP tool for the translation, and reasons about the program in the language semantics using a theorem prover. The LOOP approach makes use of existing, general purpose theorem provers, and concentrates on building a dedicated front-end for a particular application area, because developing a (dedicated) theorem prover is a project on its own. Reasoning goes via a combination of applying semantic-based Hoare logic rules and automatic rewriting. Several papers about the underlying semantics and logic have already been published [14,3,9,10,12,13]. This paper focuses on the tool itself.

Automatic translation of Java classes into a series of logical theories has several advantages above manual translation. The LOOP translation process is, boring, error-prone, and time consuming. A translated Java class is usually much larger in size than the original. A tool will do such a translation within a few seconds, without complaining, and without errors (if the translation function is implemented correctly). Another advantage is that with tool support the generated theories can be fine-tuned to achieve more efficiency in proofs, which is hardly possible when generating theories by hand.

In comparison to the projects mentioned above there are the following distinguishing features of the LOOP project.

- The ESC/Java tool involves no user interaction, is fast and easy to use, but can only detect a limited class of errors. With the LOOP tool the user has to engage in interactive program verification, using the back-end proof tool, but there are no inherent limitations to what can be (dis)proved. Thus, the ESC/Java and LOOP tools are complementary and can very well be used in combination, especially because they use the same specification language (namely JML).
- The Jive approach is closest to the LOOP approach. It differs however in its syntax-based approach, via a dedicated user interface, allowing reasoning about the actual program text (and not about its meaning). The specification language of the Jive tool resembles JML. It is too early to judge and compare these two approaches in actual examples.
- The Bandera project aims at verification of Java programs (especially involving threads) using model checkers. Similar to the LOOP project, output is generated for back-end tools that do the actual verification. However, model checkers instead of theorem provers are used. A general problem with multi-threaded Java is that the level of granularity is not well-defined.
- The Bali and KeY projects have not been used (yet) on substantial concrete examples of Java programs, making a comparison premature.

This paper is organised as follows. Section 2 describes the modular architecture of the LOOP tool. Section 3 describes some issues related to the theory generation. Section 4 briefly describes how to use the LOOP tool, and finally Section 5 gives an overview of possible application areas.

2   The Architecture of the LOOP Tool

As shown in Figure 1, the LOOP tool accepts three languages with object-oriented features, namely CCSL, Java, and JML. It serves as a front-end for a theorem prover which, in this figure, is PVS. The LOOP tool can also serve as a front-end for Isabelle. The theorem prover is used to actually prove properties about the classes in the input languages, on the basis of the logical theories generated by the LOOP tool.

2.1   Input Languages

Historically, the first input language is CCSL [7,22], short for Coalgebraic Class Specification Language. It is an experimental specification language, which is jointly developed at the University of Dresden and the University of Nijmegen. With this language one can write class specifications in an object-oriented way,

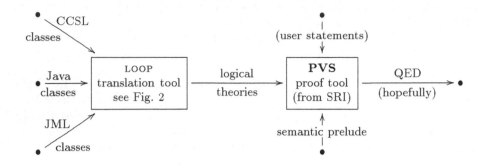

Figure 1. Overview of the LOOP project

i.e. one can write specifications with attributes, methods, and constructors. It also supports inheritance and subtyping. CCSL uses a coalgebraic semantics for classes and supports tailor-made modal operators for reasoning about class specifications. In this paper we concentrate on the input languages Java and JML, and refer to [7,22] for more information on CCSL.

The second input language is Java—one of the most popular object-orien ted programming languages. Our semantics for sequential Java, *i.e.* Java without threads, closely follows the Java Language Specification (JLS) [6]. More information about this seman tics can be found in [14,3,9,10,12].

The third input language is JML, short for Java Modeling Language. JML is a behavourial interface specification language, tailored to Java, and primarily developed at Iowa State University. It is designed to be easy to use for programmers with limited experience in logic. Therefore, it extends Java such that a user can write (class) invariants, and pre- and post-conditions for methods and constructors within the source code, making use of Java expressions (extended with various logical operators) to formulate the desired properties. All extensions of JML are enclosed bet ween Java's commen t markers, and will therefore not influence the program's behaviour. A typical JML specification for a method m looks as follows.

```
/*@ behavior
  @    requires : <precondition>
  @ modifiable : <fields>
  @     ensures : <postcondition>     // when terminating normally
  @     signals : (E) <postcondition> // when terminating abruptly
  @                                    // because of exception E
  @*/
  void m () { ... }
```

2.2 LOOP Tool Internals

In Figure 2 the view on the LOOP tool is enlarged. Here a view is considered where the tool accepts Java classes (and interfaces)[1]. The first three passes can be viewed as the first part of a standard Java compiler.

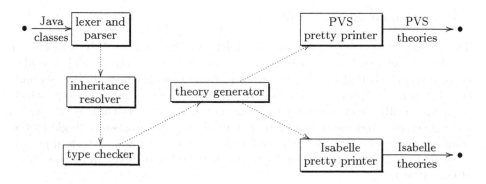

Figure 2. The "exploded" view on the LOOP tool

Standard techniques are used to build a lexer and parser, following the definition of the Java syntax in the JLS. During parsing, unknown types—class and interface types—are not resolved. These types are stored as (tagged) strings in the abstract syntax tree, and resolved in a later pass.

The inheritance resolver establishes relations between classes by resolving the unknown types. Also, in this pass overridden methods and hidden fields in Java are internally marked as overridden and hidden.

The type checker computes the type of every expression occurring in the input classes. A type checker is needed, since the overloading mechanism of Java is more powerful than the ones of PVS and Isabelle. Therefore, definitions in PVS and Isabelle are often provided with explicit types.

At this point a standard Java compiler would generate a bytecode file for each class. Instead, the LOOP tool translates each Java class into its semantics, in the form of a series of logical theories. These theories are produced internally in an abstract way using abstract logic syntax (ALS), see Subsection 3.3 below.

Finally, to come to concrete theories, a last pass, a pretty printer, is implemented to translate the ALS into concrete logic syntax. Abstract theories provide a powerful technique to produce concrete theories for different theorem

---

[1] In this paper 'Java class' may also be read as 'Java interface'. If not, it will explicitly be mentioned.

provers[2]. Implementing such a pass is fairly simple. We have implemented two of these, one for PVS and one for Isabelle.

For JML the LOOP tool works similarly. Since JML is an extension of Java, the grammar of Java is extended, and for the logic of JML, that is based upon Java expressions, also the type checker is extended. The theories for the specifications are also abstractly generated. Notably, the pretty printer components of the LOOP tool are shared with the three input languages—CCSL, Java, and JML.

2.3   Implementation Details

The OCaml language [16] is used to implement the LOOP tool. It comprises a number of tools, such as lex and yacc, a debugger, and a (native-code) compiler. OCaml is an ML dialect, supporting object-oriented features. It is a strongly typed (functional) programming language, *i.e.* every expression has a type which is automatically determined by the compiler. One great advantage of using a strongly typed language is that many potential program errors are caught by the compiler as type errors. The penalty for this is that one has to set up appropriately structured types first. This forms a non-trivial part of the implementation of the LOOP tool.

Internally, a Java/JML class and its members (fields, methods, and constructors) occurring in the input are stored as instances of certain OCaml classes. As root classes, we use two OCaml class types, **top_iface_type** for CCSL/Java/JML classes, and **top_member_type** for CCSL/Java/JML members. The "top_" class types contain common information, such as the name of the class, and the fields and methods defined in it. For each input language we introduce specialised class types, to deal with language specific properties.

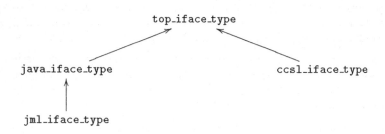

Similarly, **top_member_type** has specialised class types for CCSL, Java, and JML members. Every "iface_type" class type is mutually recursive with its "_member_type" variant. These types have a non-trivial structure, involving subtyping and mutual recursion in various forms.

---

[2] The ALS involves standard constructions from higher order logic. Thus, it is in principle easy to generate output also for any theorem prover that provides (at least) higher order logic, *e.g.* COQ [2].

Due to the object-oriented nature of the LOOP tool, it is easy to adapt the theory generation for the different input languages. Each "_iface_type" class type has a method that invokes the theory generation, which is overridden in specialised types.

Some non-technical details: the LOOP tool currently consists of over 58,000 lines of OCaml code (including documentation) of which 25,000 lines are used to implement the Java part, and 8,000 lines are used to extend it to JML. To implement CCSL 12,000 lines are used, and 13,000 lines of code are shared. Work on the LOOP tool started in 1997, and continues until this moment.

3   Generated Theories

This section focuses on some typical issues and problems related to theory generation. The contents of the theories themselves are too complicated to describe here in detail, and are not directly relevant. See [9,8] for more information.

3.1   Mutually Recursive Classes and Circular Theories

The LOOP tool translates each Java (and JML) class into its semantics in higher order logic as a series of logical theories. It is not possible to generate this semantics as one single theory, since at several places in the source-code references to other classes might occur. Having such references might lead, in that case, to circular theories, via importings. This is not allowed in PVS and Isabelle. Hence, they have to be disentangled.

In Java source-code, references to other classes can occur at three places:

1. at inheritance level, but this does not lead to circularities, since a standard Java compiler detects if a class is a subclass of itself, *e.g.* **class A extends B** and **class B extends A** is illegal;
2. at interface level. The signatures of members of class **A** contain occurrences of class **B**, and vice versa;
3. at implementation level. In a method (or constructor) body in class **A** the class **B** occurs, *e.g.* via creating an object of class **B** or a field access of an object of type **B**, and vice versa.

For a concrete (toy) example of mutual recursion between Java classes, consider classes **A** and **B** in Figure 3, where the signature of method **m** in **A** has an occurrence of class **B**, and the signatures of both methods in **B** have occurrences of class **A**. Moreover, method **m** in **A** creates an object of class **B**, and method **n** assigns a value to a field of **b** (cast to **A**).

To prevent the generated theories from being circular, the semantics of each Java class is divided into three[3] tailor-made theories:

---

[3] Actually, the semantics is spread over eight theories, but due to space restrictions only the theories generated to handle mutual recursion are presented here.

```
class A {                          class B extends A {
  int i;                             A n() { return new A(); }
  void m (B b) { b = new B(); }      void m (B b) { ((A)b).i = 1; }
}                                  }
```

Figure 3. Mutually recursive Java classes

1. the *Prelude* theory defines a special type for objects and arrays of that class. This type can be the null reference or a reference pointing to a certain memory location where an object or a (multi-dimensional) array of objects of that class is stored.

2. the *Interface* theory defines the types of fields, methods, and possibly the constructors of that class. There is also a reference to the direct superclass, and superinterfaces, if any.

3. the *Bodies and rewrites* theory gives semantics to the method and constructor bodies. Also, auto-rewrite lemmas are generated, which can be used conveniently during proofs (and hence reduce the proof interaction for a user).

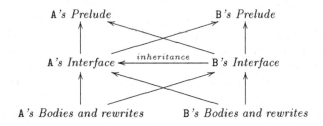

Figure 4. Generated theories and their importings for the classes A and B from Figure 3

An *Interface* theory imports all *Prelude* theories of those classes which are used in its members' signatures. Moreover, it also imports the *Interface* theory of its direct superclass, since the members of superclasses should be accessible. Importings of superclasses are transitive. A *Bodies and rewrites* theory imports all *Interface* theories from those classes of which their static type occurs in method and constructor bodies. Note that there are no circularities.

3.2   Similarity Between Theories

The kind (and number) of theories that are produced by the LOOP tool depends on the input language. Each language has its own specific properties, *e.g.* the theories for JML describe properties of implementations, whereas the theories for Java describe concrete implementations. Though there are differences between the kind of theories generated, the three input languages have theories in common. Actually, this similarity forms the reason for having one tool for the three languages.

For a JML class, possibly defining specification fields and methods, an extended *Interface* theory is generated, containing these extra fields and methods. And instead of a theory with semantics for bodies of methods and constructors, a theory with properties of implementations yielding from JML's specification constructs, such as behaviour specifications and invariants, is generated.

Also, when having both a Java implementation and a JML specification, another theory is generated to relate both of them, via a suitable translation of coalgebras, making the interface types match. This makes it possible to formulate the intended proof obligation, namely that the Java implementation satisfies the JML specification.

3.3 Abstract Theories

The LOOP tool generates logical theories for PVS and Isabelle. Both these tools offer a higher order logic but use a different syntax. The LOOP tool first generates theories as an abstract syntax tree, which abstracts away from these differences in syntax. This tree is built from types that cover common constructs used in higher order logic, such as function abstraction and application, and quantification.

```
type expression =                          and formula =
  | Expression of formula                    | True
  | Application of (expression * expression) | Not of formula
  | Tuple of expression list                 | ...
  | ...
```

Secondly, a theorem prover specific unparser, or pretty printer, is applied to the abstract theories in order to generate concrete theories. Writing such an unparser is fairly easy, as illustrated below, where it is done for PVS.

```
let rec pp_pvs_expression = function
  | Expression form -> pp_formula form
  | Application (func, arg) ->
      pp_pvs_expression func;
      print_string "(";
      pp_pvs_expression arg;
      print_string ")"
  | ...
and pp_pvs_formula = function
  | True -> print_string "TRUE"
  | Not form ->
      print_string "NOT ("; pp_formula form; print_string ")"
  | ...
```

3.4   Size and Speed

Translating the classes in the example in Subsection 3.1 leads to 12 Kb of PVS theories and 14 Kb of Isabelle theories for class A, and respectively 17 Kb and 21 Kb for class B. The main difference in size between the PVS and Isabelle theories is caused by the fact that in Isabelle each definition, when imported from another theory, has to be qualified with its theory name. A substantial part of these generated files consists of comments, explaining what is happening.

In general, the size of the generated theories strongly depends on the number of superclasses. Every inherited method is repeated in the *Interface* theory, and its body's semantics is recalculated[4] and added to the *Bodies and rewrites* theory. Thus, inheritance leads to a substantial increase in the size of the generated theories.

The LOOP tool can easily handle a large number of classes. Running the LOOP tool on the JDK 1.0.2 API (consisting of 215 classes, forming together over 1 Mb of source-code), only takes five seconds, to parse and type check. To produce the series of logical theories takes about 50 seconds longer, mainly consisting of writing the concrete theories to file[5].

4   Use Scenarios

For a successful run of the LOOP tool a Java class has to be type correct as defined by the JLS[6]. Type incorrectness of the input will lead to abrupt termination of the LOOP tool, via an error message. A successful run leads to a series of (PVS or Isabelle) type correct logical theories.

The LOOP tool requires that every Java class that is used in an implementation (and specification) occurs in the input series. This requirement is a design decision, since automatically loading of classes can lead to uncontrolled loading of too many classes. In practice it works best to cut away, for a verification, unnecessary details, *i.e.* class definitions and method definitions not used in the final program. In this way the user can restrict the size of the generated theories. It is of importance to keep this size as small as possible, to limit the time spent on loading and type checking by the theorem prover.

Once translated, the desired properties of a Java class can be verified using a theorem prover. It is up to the user how to specify these properties: either JML specifications are used (which have the advantage of automatic translation), or hand-written specifications are formulated in the language semantics (in higher order logic). The verification of these properties goes via a combination of applying (tailor-made) rewrite lemmas and definitions, and of applying Hoare logic rules [13,10].

---

[4] This recalculation is necessary in order to reason about late binding in Java, which influences the behaviour of the method execution, see [9] for details.

[5] Experiments were done on a Pentium III 500 MHz, running Linux.

[6] A JML class has to be type correct following [15].

The LOOP tool can also generate batch files. Such a batch file contains the necessary steps for a theorem prover to take for type checking the generated theories, and for rerunning proofs. Hence, batch files are useful, and reduce user interaction. They are also used for rerunning old examples after new releases (of LOOP, PVS, or Isabelle), for compatibility checks.

4.1   An Example

The example below illustrates the ease of using JML behaviour specifications. The constructor and methods all have a **normal_behavior** specification, which informally says that if precondition holds the method is only allowed to terminate normally in a state where the postcondition holds. The LOOP tool expresses the behaviour specifications in a specialised Hoare logic for JML. Reasoning about methods goes via applying suitable Hoare rules, as described in [13].

```
class A {                           class B {
  boolean b1, b2;

  /*@ normal_behavior              /*@ normal_behavior
    @     requires : true;           @     requires : true;
    @   modifiable : b1, b2;         @     ensures : \result == false;
    @       ensures : b == (b1 & b2);   @*/
    @*/                             boolean n() {
  A (boolean b) {                     A a = new A(true);
    b1 = b2 = b;                      a.m();
  }                                   return a.b1 & a.b2;
                                    }
  /*@ normal_behavior             }
    @     requires : true;
    @   modifiable : b1;
    @       ensures : b1 != b2;
    @*/
  void m() { b1 = !b2; }
}
```

In this example, it is easy to see that the constructor and the methods all terminate normally. Note that class **B** does not declare a constructor; a default constructor is created (see [6, § 8.2]) together with a default **normal_behavior** specification (see [15, p. 48]). Thus, to prove these classes correct a user has to validate four proof obligations, of which three—of the constructors of **A** and **B**, and of method **m**—are straightforward and can be established with automatic rewriting.

Proving correctness of a method containing method calls, like method **n**, can be established in two ways: (1) reasoning with their implementations, and (2) reasoning with their specifications. In general, the latter option is better, since it reduces the time spent on proving termination of the method calls and it enables modular verification.

For method **n** in class **B** the proof obligation reads like

"Spec_A holds for an *arbitrary* implementation"
$$\Longrightarrow$$
"Spec_B holds for the *given* implementation".

The specification of class A is used to obtain the specifications of its members. These specifications are used to establish the postcondition of method n. Using the composition rule from [13] also this proof is straightforward.

4.2   Strategies

Currently, most of the reasoning about JML-annotated Java programs is done in PVS. As experience is growing, more and more ingredients of the verification work are being incorporated in tailor-made proof strategies in PVS. These turn out to be extremely useful and substantially decrease the amount of interaction needed for proof construction.

5   Application Areas

The LOOP tool is applied in those areas, where the effort spent on specification and verification is justifiable. One can think of areas where economical and security aspects play an important role, such as the development of safety-critical systems, and integrated software development relying on formal methods.

Java's class library has many classes which are interesting for verification. Verifying classes from this class library can be useful, since many people use these classes to write their applications. The LOOP tool has been successfully applied to verify a non-trivial invariant property of the frequently used Vector class [11].

Also in the area of smart cards formal verification is becoming necessary, due to the higher standards the market demands. Smart cards are being issued in large numbers for security-sensitive applications, which justifies the application of formal methods: any error detected before issuing saves lots of money. The LOOP tool is used in the area of JavaCard based smart cards, especially to the JavaCard API (for specification and verification [4]), and to its applets—smart card programs—which are stored on the smart card. This work is part of a larger project, which is supported by the European Union[7].

6   Conclusions

We have presented the modular architecture of the LOOP tool, which is used to reason about Java. The LOOP tool translates the implementation and specification of Java classes into their semantics in higher order logic. Internally, this

---

[7] See: http://www.verificard.org

semantics is abstractly generated as a series of theories, which can easily be concretised as theories for different theorem provers. The actual verification is done in the theorem prover.

Doing full program verification for real-life programming languages is becoming feasible in more cases, but it still requires a major investment of time and resources. Such a verification technique can (only) be applied in areas where the presence of errors has a major impact on the money it costs to repair them. With a compiler like the LOOP tool, users can concentrate on the real work (specification and verification), without having to care about the actual modelling.

Credits

Over the past couple of years many other people (than the authors) have contributed to the implementation of the LOOP tool: Ulrich Hensel, Hendrik Tews, Marieke Huisman, Martijn van Berkum, Erik Poll, Wim Janssen, Jan Rothe, and Harco Kuppens. The authors have done most of the work for the Java and JML implementation.

Acknowledgements

Thanks are due to Erik Poll and the referees for valuable comments on an earlier version.

References

1. W. Ahrendt, T. Baar, B. Beckert, M. Giese, E. Habermalz, R. Hähnle, W. Menzel, and P.H. Schmitt. The KeY approach: Integrating object oriented design and formal verification. In G. Brewka and L.M. Pereira, editors, *Proc. 8th European Workshop on Logics in AI (JELIA)*, Lect. Notes AI. Springer, October 2000.
2. B. Barras, S. Boutin, C. Cornes, J. Courant, J.-Chr. Filliâtre, E. Giménez, H. Herbelin, G. Huet, C. Muñoz, C. Murthy, C. Parent, C. Paulin-Mohring, A. Saïbi, and B. Werner. The Coq Proof Assistant User's Guide Version 6.1. Technical Report 203, INRIA Rocquencourt, France, May 1997.
3. J. van den Berg, M. Huisman, B. Jacobs, and E. Poll. A type-theoretic memory model for verification of sequential Java programs. In D. Bert and C. Choppy, editors, *Recent Trends in Algebraic Development Techniques*, number 1827 in Lect. Notes Comp. Sci., pages 1–21. Springer, Berlin, 2000.
4. J. van den Berg, B. Jacobs, and E. Poll. Formal specification and verification of JavaCard's Application Identifier Class. Techn. Rep. CSI-R0014, Comput. Sci. Inst., Univ. of Nijmegen. Appeared in: Proceedings of the JavaCard Workshop, Cannes. INRIA Techn. Rep. Updated version will appear in: I. Attali and Th. Jensen, editors, *Proceedings of the Java Card 2000 Workshop* (Springer LNCS 2001), Sept. 2000.
5. J. Corbett, M. Dwyer, J. Hatcliff, S. Laubach, C. Pasareanu, Robby, and H. Zheng. Bandera: extracting finite-state models from Java source code. In *Proceedings 22nd International Conference on Software Engineering*, June 2000.

6. J. Gosling, B. Joy, G. Steele, and G. Bracha. *The Java Language Specification Second Edition*. The Java Series. Addison-Wesley, 2000.
7. U. Hensel, M. Huisman, B. Jacobs, and H. Tews. Reasoning about classes in object-oriented languages: Logical models and tools. In Ch. Hankin, editor, *European Symposium on Programming*, number 1381 in Lect. Notes Comp. Sci., pages 105–121. Springer, Berlin, 1998.
8. M. Huisman. *Reasoning about JAVA Programs in higher order logic, using PVS and Isabelle*. PhD thesis, Univ. Nijmegen, 2001.
9. M. Huisman and B. Jacobs. Inheritance in higher order logic: Modeling and reasoning. In M. Aagaard and J. Harrison, editors, *Theorem Proving in Higher Order Logics*, number 1869 in Lect. Notes Comp. Sci., pages 301–319. Springer, Berlin, 2000.
10. M. Huisman and B. Jacobs. Java program verification via a Hoare logic with abrupt termination. In T. Maibaum, editor, *Fundamental Approaches to Software Engineering*, number 1783 in Lect. Notes Comp. Sci., pages 284–303. Springer, Berlin, 2000.
11. M. Huisman, B. Jacobs, and J. van den Berg. A case study in class library verification: Java's Vector class. Techn. Rep. CSI-R0007, Comput. Sci. Inst., Univ. of Nijmegen. To appear in *Software Tools for Technology Transfer*, 2001.
12. B. Jacobs. A formalisation of Java's exception mechanism. Techn. Rep. CSI-R0015, Comput. Sci. Inst., Univ. of Nijmegen. To appear at ESOP'01., 2000.
13. B. Jacobs and E. Poll. A logic for the Java Modeling Language JML. Techn. Rep. CSI-R0018, Comput. Sci. Inst., Univ. of Nijmegen. To appear at FASE'01., 2000.
14. B. Jacobs, J. van den Berg, M. Huisman, M. van Berkum, U. Hensel, and H. Tews. Reasoning about classes in Java (preliminary report). In *Object-Oriented Programming, Systems, Languages and Applications*, pages 329–340. ACM Press, 1998.
15. G.T. Leavens, A.L. Baker, and C. Ruby. Preliminary design of JML: A behavioral interface specification language for Java. Techn. Rep. 98-06, Dep. of Comp. Sci., Iowa State Univ. (http://www.cs.iastate.edu/~leavens/JML.html), 1998, revised May 2000.
16. X. Leroy. *The Objective Caml system release 3.00*. Institute National de Recherche en Informatique et Automatique, 1997. Documentation and user's manual.
17. J. Meyer and A. Poetzsch-Heffter. An architecture for interactive program provers. In S. Graf and M. Schwartzbach, editors, *TACAS00, Tools ans Algorithms for the Construction and Analysis of Software*, volume 276 of *Lect. Notes Comp. Sci.*, pages 63–77, 2000.
18. D. von Oheimb and T. Nipkow. Machine-checking the Java specification: Proving type-safety. In Jim Alves-Foss, editor, *Formal Syntax and Semantics of Java*, volume 1523 of *LNCS*, pages 119–156. Springer, 1999.
19. S. Owre, J. M. Rushby, and N. Shankar. PVS: A prototype verification system. In D. Kapur, editor, *11th International Conference on Automated Deduction (CADE-11)*, number 607 in Lect. Notes Comp. Sci., pages 748–752. Springer, Berlin, 1992.
20. L.C. Paulson. *Isabelle - a generic theorem prover*. Number 828 in Lect. Notes Comp. Sci. Springer, Berlin, 1994. With contributions by Tobias Nipkow.
21. LOOP Project. http://www.cs.kun.nl/~bart/LOOP/.
22. J. Rothe, H. Tews, and B. Jacobs. The coalgebraic class specification language CCSL. Technical Report TUD-FI00-09, Dresden University of Technology, Department of Computer Science, October 2000. Available via http://wwwtcs.inf.tu-dresden.de/TU/Informatik/Fak/berichte.html.
23. Extended static checker ESC/Java. Compaq System Research Center. http://www.research.digital.com/SRC/esc/Esc.html.

Searching Powerset Automata by Combining Explicit-State and Symbolic Model Checking

Alessandro Cimatti[1], Marco Roveri[1,2], and Piergiorgio Bertoli[1]

[1] ITC-IRST, Via Sommarive 18, 38055 Povo, Trento, Italy
Phone: +39 0461 314517, Fax: +39 0461 413591.
{cimatti,roveri,bertoli}@irst.itc.it
[2] DSI, University of Milano, Via Comelico 39, 20135 Milano, Italy

Abstract. The ability to analyze a digital system under conditions of uncertainty is important in several application domains. The problem is naturally described in terms of search in the powerset of the automaton representing the system. However, the associated exponential blow-up prevents the application of traditional model checking techniques. This work describes a new approach to searching powerset automata, which does not require the explicit powerset construction. We present an efficient representation of the search space based on the combination of symbolic and explicit-state model checking techniques. We describe several search algorithms, based on two different, complementary search paradigms, and we experimentally evaluate the approach.

Keywords: Explicit-State Model Checking, Symbolic Model Checking, Binary Decision Diagrams, Synchronization Sequences

1 Introduction

The ability of analyzing digital systems under conditions of uncertainty is extremely useful in various application domains. For hardware circuits, it is important to be able to determine homing, synchronization and distinguishing sequences, which allow to identify the status of a set of circuit flip-flops. For instance, synchronization sequences, i.e. sequences that will take a circuit from an unknown state into a completely defined one [9], are used in test design and equivalence checking. Similar problems are encountered in automated test generation, e.g. to determine what sequence of inputs can take the (black-box) system under test in a known state. In Artificial Intelligence, reasoning with uncertainty has been recognized as a significant problem since the early days. For instance, the Blind Robot problem [11] requires to plan the activity for a sensorless agent, positioned in any location of a given room, so that it will be guaranteed to achieve a given objective.

Such problems are naturally formulated as search in the powerset of the space of the analyzed system [9]: a certain condition of uncertainty is represented as the set of indistinguishable system states. However, search in the powerset space

T. Margaria and W. Yi (Eds.): TACAS 2001, LNCS 2031, pp. 313–327, 2001.

yields an exponential blow-up. A straightforward application of symbolic model checking techniques is hardly viable: the symbolic representation of the powerset automaton requires exponentially more variables than needed for the analyzed system. On the other hand, approaches based on explicit-state search methods tend to suffer from the enumerative nature of the algorithms.

In this work, we propose a new approach to the problem of searching the powerset of a given nondeterministic automaton which does not require the explicit powerset automaton construction. The approach can be seen as expanding the relevant portion of the state space of the powerset automaton on demand, and allows to tackle in practice rather complex problems. The approach combines techniques from symbolic model checking, based on the use of Binary Decision Diagrams (BDDs) [3], with techniques from explicit-state model checking. We represent in a fully symbolic way sets of sets of states, and we provide for the efficient manipulation of such data structures. Using this representation, we tackle the problem of finding an input sequence which guarantees that only states in a target set will be reached for all runs, regardless of the uncertainty on the initial condition and on nondeterministic machine behaviors. We present several algorithms based on two different search paradigms. The *fully-symbolic* paradigm allows to perform a breadth-first search by representing the frontier as a single symbolic structure. In the *semi-symbolic* paradigm, search is performed in the style of explicit-state model checking, considering at each step only a (symbolically represented) element of the search space, i.e. a set of states. Both search paradigms are based on fully symbolic primitives for the expansion of the search space, thus overcoming the drawbacks of an enumerative approach.

The algorithms return with failure if and only if the problem admits no solution, otherwise a solution is returned. Depending on the style of the search, the solution can be guaranteed to be of minimal length. We also present an experimental evaluation of our algorithms, showing that the paradigms are complementary and allow to tackle quite complex problems efficiently.

The paper is structured as follows. In Section 2 we introduce the problem. In Section 3 we describe the techniques for the implicit representation of the search space, and in Section 4 we present the semi-symbolic and fully-symbolic search paradigms. In Section 5 we present an experimental evaluation of our approach. In Section 6 we discuss some related work and draw the conclusions.

2   Intuitions and Background

We consider nondeterministic finite state machines. S and A are the (finite) sets of states and inputs of the machine. $R \subseteq S \times A \times S$ is the transition relation. We use s and s' to denote states of S, and α to denote input values. In the following, we assume that a machine is given in the standard BDD-based representation used in symbolic model checking [10]. We call x and x' the vectors of current and next state variables, respectively, while α is the vector of input variables. We write $\alpha = \alpha$ for the BDD in the α variables representing the input value α. When clear from the context, we confuse the set-theoretic and symbolic

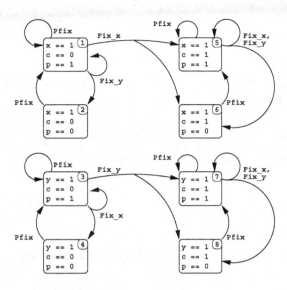

Fig. 1. The example automaton

representations. For instance, we use equivalently the *False* BDD and ∅. We write $\mathcal{R}(\boldsymbol{x}, \boldsymbol{\alpha}, \boldsymbol{x}')$ for the BDD representing the transition relation to stress the dependency on BDD variables. We say that an input α is acceptable in s iff there is at least a state s' such that $\mathcal{R}(s, \alpha, s')$ holds. The acceptability relation is represented symbolically by $\mathrm{ACC}(\boldsymbol{x}, \boldsymbol{\alpha}) \doteq \exists \boldsymbol{x}'.\mathcal{R}(\boldsymbol{x}, \boldsymbol{\alpha}, \boldsymbol{x}')$. An input sequence is an element of $\mathcal{A}^*$. We use ϵ for the 0-length input sequence, π and ρ to denote input sequences, and $\pi; \rho$ for concatenation.

In this paper we tackle the problem of finding an input sequence that, if applied to the machine from any initial state in $\mathcal{I} \subseteq \mathcal{S}$, guarantees that the machine will reach a target set of states $\mathcal{G} \subseteq \mathcal{S}$, regardless of nondeterminism. We use for explanatory purposes the simple system depicted in figure 1. A circuit is composed of two devices, x and y. The circuit is malfunctioning ($c = 0$), and the reason is that exactly one of the devices is faulty (i.e. $x = 0$ or $y = 0$). It is possible to fix either device (input Fix_x and Fix_y), but only if a certain precondition p is met. Fixing the faulty device has the effect of fixing the circuit ($c = 1$), while fixing the other one does not. Fixing either device has the uncertain effect of spoiling the fixing precondition condition (i.e. $p = 0$). $Pfix$ has the effect of restoring the fixing precondition ($p = 1$). Each state is given a number, and contains all the propositions holding in that state. For instance, state 1 represents the state where device x is the reason for the fault, and fixing is possible. Given that only one device is faulty, $x = 0$ also stands for $y = 1$, and vice versa.

The problem is finding an input sequence which fixes the circuit, taking the machine from any state in $\mathcal{I} = \{1, 2, 3, 4\}$ (where the circuit is faulty, but we don't know if the reason is in device x or y, nor if fixing is possible) to the target set $\mathcal{G} = \{5, 7\}$ (the circuit is fixed, and the fixing condition is restored).

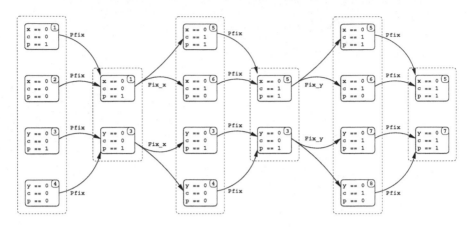

Fig. 2. A solution to for example problem

A possible solution is the input sequence: $Pfix$; Fix_x ; $Pfix$; Fix_y; $Pfix$. Figure 2 shows why this is the case. The initial uncertainty is in that the system might be in any of the states in $\{1, 2, 3, 4\}$. This set is represented in figure 2 by a dashed line. We call such a set an *uncertainty state* as in [2]. Intuitively, an uncertainty state expresses a condition of uncertainty about the system, by collecting together all the states which are indistinguishable while analyzing the system. An uncertainty state is an element of $\text{Pow}(\mathcal{S})$, i.e. the powerset of the set of states of the machine. The first input value, $Pfix$, makes sure that fixing is possible. This reduces the uncertainty to the uncertainty state $\{1, 3\}$. Despite the remaining uncertainty (i.e. it is still not known which component is responsible for the circuit fault), the following input value Fix_x is now guaranteed to be acceptable because it is acceptable in both states 1 and 3. Fix_x has the effect of removing the fault if it depends on device x, and can nondeterministically remove the precondition for further fixing ($p = 0$). The resulting uncertainty state is $\{3, 4, 5, 6\}$. The following input, $Pfix$, restores $p = 1$, reducing the uncertainty to the uncertainty state $\{3, 5\}$, and guarantees the acceptability of Fix_y. After Fix_y, the circuit is guaranteed to be fixed, but p might be 0 again (states 6 and 8 in the uncertainty state $\{5, 6, 7, 8\}$). The final $Pfix$ reduces the uncertainty to the uncertainty state $\{5, 7\}$, and guarantees that only target states are reached.

The following definition captures the intuitive arguments given above.

Definition 1. *An input α is acceptable in an uncertainty state $\emptyset \neq Us \subseteq \mathcal{S}$ iff α is acceptable in every state in Us, i.e. $\exists \boldsymbol{\alpha}.\forall \boldsymbol{x}.((Us(\boldsymbol{x}) \wedge \boldsymbol{\alpha} = \alpha) \rightarrow \text{ACC}(\boldsymbol{x}, \boldsymbol{\alpha}))$ is not $\emptyset$.*

If α is acceptable in Us, its image $Image[\alpha](Us)$ is the set of all the states reachable from Us under α, i.e. $\exists \boldsymbol{x}.(Us(\boldsymbol{x}) \wedge \exists \boldsymbol{\alpha}.(\boldsymbol{\alpha} = \alpha \wedge \mathcal{R}(\boldsymbol{x}, \boldsymbol{\alpha}, \boldsymbol{x}')))[\boldsymbol{x}'/\boldsymbol{x}]$ where $[\boldsymbol{x}'/\boldsymbol{x}]$ represents parallel variable substitution.

The image of an input sequence π in an uncertainty state, written $Image[\pi](Us)$, is defined as follows.

$$
\begin{aligned}
Image[\epsilon](Us) &\doteq Us \\
Image[\pi](\emptyset) &\doteq \emptyset \\
Image[\alpha; \pi](Us) &\doteq \emptyset, \ \textit{if } \alpha \textit{ is not acceptable in } Us \\
Image[\alpha; \pi](Us) &\doteq Image[\pi](Image[\alpha](Us)), \ \textit{otherwise}
\end{aligned}
$$

The input sequence π is a solution to the powerset reachability problem from $\emptyset \neq \mathcal{I} \subseteq \mathcal{S}$ to $\emptyset \neq \mathcal{G} \subseteq \mathcal{S}$ iff $\emptyset \neq Image[\pi](\mathcal{I}) \subseteq \mathcal{G}$.

Search in $Pow(\mathcal{S})$ can be performed either forwards (from the initial uncertainty state $\mathcal{I}$ towards the target uncertainty state $\mathcal{G}$) or backwards (from $\mathcal{G}$ towards $\mathcal{I}$). Figure 2 depicts a subset of the search space when proceeding forwards. The full picture can be obtained by considering the effect of the other input values to the uncertainty states. For instance, the input values $Pfix$ on the second uncertainty state $\{1, 3\}$ would result in a self loop, while Fix_y would lead to $\{1, 3, 7, 8\}$. The first and third uncertainty states can not be expanded further, because the input values Fix_x and Fix_y are not acceptable. When a nonempty uncertainty state $Us_i \subseteq \mathcal{G}$ is built from $\mathcal{I}$, the associated input sequence (labeling a path from $\mathcal{I}$ to Us_i) is a solution to the problem.

Figure 3 depicts the backward search space. The levels are built from the target states, on the right, towards the initial ones, on the left. At level 0 we have the pair $\langle \{5, 7\} \ . \ \epsilon \rangle$, composed of an uncertainty state and an input sequence. We call such a pair uncertainty state-input sequence (UsS) pair. The dashed arrows represent the *strong preimage* of each Us_i under the input value α_i, i.e. the extraction of the maximal uncertainty state where the α_i is acceptable, and guaranteed to result into the uncertainty state being expanded. At level 1, only the UsS pair $\langle \{5, 6, 7, 8\} \ . \ Pfix \rangle$ is built, since the strong preimage of the uncertainty state 0 for the inputs Fix_x and Fix_y is empty. At level 2, there are three UsS pairs, with (overlapping) uncertainty states Us2, Us3 and Us4, associated, respectively, with the length 2 sequences $Fix_x; Pfix$, $Pfix; Pfix$ and $Fix_y; Pfix$. (While proceeding backwards, a sequence is associated with an uncertainty state Usi if it labels a path from Usi to the target set.) Notice that Us3 is equal to Us1, and therefore deserves no further expansion. The expansion of uncertainty states 2 and 4 gives the uncertainty states 5 and 6, both obtained by the strong preimage under $Pfix$, while the strong preimage under inputs Fix_x and Fix_y returns empty uncertainty states. The further expansion of Us5 results in three uncertainty states. The one resulting from the strong preimage under $Pfix$ is not reported, as equal to Us5. Uncertainty state 7 is also equal to Us2, and deserves no further expansion. Uncertainty state 8 can be obtained by expanding both Us5 and Us6. At level 5, the expansion produces Us10, which contains all the initial states. Therefore, both the corresponding sequences are solutions to the problem.

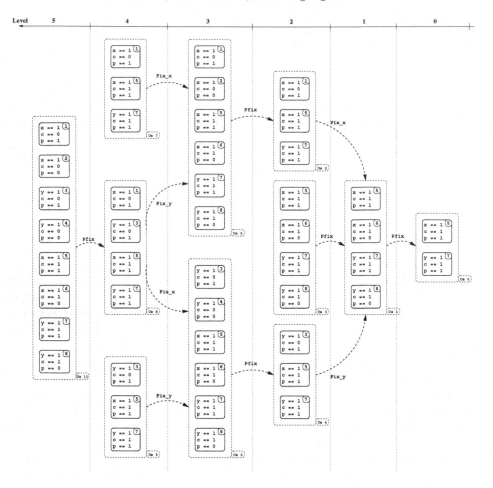

Fig. 3. The Search Space for the Example Problem

3 Efficient Representation of Pow($\mathcal{S}$)

In this section we describe the symbolic representation of the search space
Pow($\mathcal{S}$), and the primitives used in the search. Our representation mechanisms
combines elements used in symbolic and explicit-state model checking. The first
ingredient is a standard BDD package, providing for the symbolic representation mechanism. Each uncertainty state Us is directly represented by the BDD
$Us(\boldsymbol{x})$, whose models are exactly the states contained in Us. In practice, the
uncertainty state is the pointer to the corresponding BDD. The second ingredient, from explicit-state model checking, is a hash table, which is used to store
and retrieve pointers to the (BDDs representing the) uncertainty states which
have been visited during the search. The approach heavily relies on the normal form of BDD, which allow for comparison in constant time. Figure 4 gives

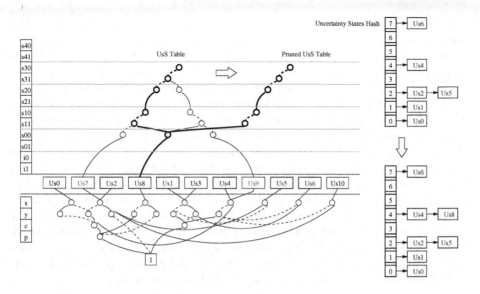

Fig. 4. The combined use of BDD and the cache

overview of the approach on the data structure built while analyzing the example. The column on the left shows the variables in the BDD package. Let us focus first on the lower part that contains the state variables, i.e. x, y, c and p. (The upper variables, including the input variables, will be clarified later in this section.) Each uncertainty state in figure 3 is represented by a (suitably labeled) BDD, shown in the picture as a subgraph. (Solid [dashed, respectively] arcs in a BDD represent the positive [negative, resp.] assignment to the variable in the originating node. For the sake of clarity, only the paths leading to $True$ are shown.) On the right hand side, two configurations of the visited uncertainty states hash are shown. The picture gives an example of the potential memory savings which can be obtained thanks to the great ability of the BDD package to minimize BDD memory occupation. Besides the uniqueness, there is a large amount of sharing among different BDDs: for instance, Us6 and Us10 share their sub-nodes with the previously constructed Us2, Us3 and Us4. Furthermore, the set-theoretic operations for the transformation and combination of uncertainty states (e.g. projection, equivalence, inclusion) can be efficiently performed with the primitives provided by the BDD package. The advantage over an enumerative representation of uncertainty states (e.g. the list of the state vectors associated to each state contained in the Us) is evident.

The exploration of Pow($\mathcal{S}$) is based on the use of UsS tables, i.e. sets of UsS pairs, of the form $UsST = \{\langle Us_1 \cdot \pi_1 \rangle, \ldots, \langle Us_n \cdot \pi_n \rangle\}$ where the π_i are input sequences of the same length, such that $\pi_i \neq \pi_j$ for all $1 \leq j \neq i \leq n$. We call Us_i the uncertainty set indexed by π_i. When no ambiguity arises, we write $UsST(\pi_i)$ for Us_i. A UsS table allows to represent a level in the search space. For instance, when proceeding backward (see figure 3), each UsS pair $\langle Us_i . \pi_i \rangle$ in the UsS table is such that Us_i is the maximal uncertainty state in which the associated input sequence is acceptable, and its image is contained in the target states. When proceeding forward, for each UsS pair, the uncertainty state is the result of the application of the corresponding input sequence to the initial set.

The key to the efficient search is the symbolic representation of UsS tables, which allows for compactly storing sets of sets of states (annotated by input sequences) and their transformations. A UsS table { $\langle \{s_1^1, \ldots, s_{n_1}^1\} . \pi_1 \rangle, \ldots,$ $\langle \{s_1^k, \ldots, s_{n_k}^k\} . \pi_k \rangle$ } is represented as a relation between input sequences of the same length and states, by associating directly to each state in the uncertainty state the indexing input sequence, i.e. { $\langle s_1^1 . \pi_1 \rangle, \ldots, \langle s_{n_1}^1 . \pi_1 \rangle, \ldots, \langle s_1^k . \pi_k \rangle,$ $\ldots, \langle s_{n_k}^k . \pi_k \rangle$ }. Given this view, the expansion can be obtained symbolically as follows. Let us consider first the UsS table $\{\langle Us . \epsilon \rangle\}$ represented by the BDD $Us(\boldsymbol{x})$. The backward step of expansion BWDEXPANDUSSTABLE constructs the UsS table containing the strong preimage of Us under each of the input values. This is the set of all state-input pairs where the input is acceptable in the state and all the successor states are in Us. Symbolically, we compute

$$\forall \boldsymbol{x}'.(\mathcal{R}(\boldsymbol{x}, \boldsymbol{\alpha}, \boldsymbol{x}') \rightarrow Us(\boldsymbol{x})[\boldsymbol{x}/\boldsymbol{x}']) \wedge \text{ACC}(\boldsymbol{x}, \boldsymbol{\alpha})$$

i.e. a BDD in the $\boldsymbol{x}$ and $\boldsymbol{\alpha}$ variables. This represents a relation between states and length-one input sequences, i.e. a UsS table where each Us_i is annotated by a length-one input sequence α_i.

The dual forward step FWDEXPANDUSSTABLE expands $\{\langle Us . \epsilon \rangle\}$ by computing the images of Us under every acceptable input:

$$(\exists \boldsymbol{x}.(Us(\boldsymbol{x}) \wedge (\forall \boldsymbol{x}.(Us(\boldsymbol{x}) \rightarrow \text{ACC}(\boldsymbol{x}, \boldsymbol{\alpha})) \wedge \mathcal{R}(\boldsymbol{x}, \boldsymbol{\alpha}, \boldsymbol{x}'))))[\boldsymbol{x}/\boldsymbol{x}']$$

The resulting BDD represents a UsS table, where each Us_i is annotated by a length-one input sequence α_i such that $\emptyset \neq Image[\alpha_i](Us) = Us_i$.

In the general case, a UsS tables can contain longer input sequences, and the vector $\boldsymbol{\alpha}$ of input variables is not enough. Therefore, we use additional variables to represent the values of the input sequence at the different steps. To represent input sequences of length i, we need i vectors of new BDD variables, called *sequence variables*. The vector of sequence variables representing the i-th value of the sequence is written $\boldsymbol{\pi}_{[i]}$, with $|\boldsymbol{\pi}_{[i]}| = |\boldsymbol{\alpha}|$. Figure 4 shows the UsS table representing the third level of backward search space depicted in figure 3. The upper variables in the order are the input variables $i0$ and $i1$ and the sequence variables. When searching forwards [backwards, respectively] $\boldsymbol{\pi}_{[i]}$ is used to encode the i-th [i-th to last, resp.] value in the sequence. The backward expansion primitive BWDEXPANDUSSTABLE can be applied in the general case to a UsS table $UsST_{i-1}(\boldsymbol{x}, \boldsymbol{\pi}_{[i-1]}, \ldots, \boldsymbol{\pi}_{[1]})$, associating an uncertainty state to plans of length $i - 1$:

$$(\forall \boldsymbol{x}'.(\mathcal{R}(\boldsymbol{x}, \boldsymbol{\alpha}, \boldsymbol{x}') \rightarrow UsST_{i-1}(\boldsymbol{x}, \boldsymbol{\pi}_{[i-1]}, \ldots, \boldsymbol{\pi}_{[1]})[\boldsymbol{x}/\boldsymbol{x}']) \wedge \text{ACC}(\boldsymbol{x}, \boldsymbol{\alpha}))[\boldsymbol{\alpha}/\boldsymbol{\pi}_{[i]}]$$

As in the length-one case, the next state variables $\boldsymbol{x}'$ in $\mathcal{R}$ and in $UsST_{i-1}$ (resulting from the substitution) disappear because of the universal quantification.

The input variables α are renamed to the newly introduced plan variables $\pi_{[i]}$, so that in the next step of the algorithm the construction can be repeated. The forward step is defined dually. Notice that the fully symbolic expansion of UsS tables avoids the explicit enumeration of input values. This can lead to significant advantages when only a few distinct uncertainty states result from the application of all possible input values.

For either search directions, every time a UsS table is built its uncertainty states have to be compared with the previously visited uncertainty states. If not present, they must be inserted in the hash of the visited uncertainty states, otherwise eliminated. This analysis is performed by a special purpose primitive, called PRUNEUSSTABLE, which operates directly on the BDD representing the UsS table. The primitive assumes that in the BDD package input and sequence variables precede state variables (see figure 4). PRUNEUSSTABLE recursively descends the UsS table, and interprets as an uncertainty state every BDD node having a state variable at its top. It accesses the hash table of the previously visited uncertainty states with the newly found Us: if it is not present, then it is stored and returned, otherwise *False* BDD is returned, and the traversal continues on different branches of the input and sequence variables. In this way, a new UsS table is built, where only the Us which had not been previously encountered are left. The pruning step also takes care of another source of redundancy: UsS tables often contain a large number of equivalent input sequences, all indexing exactly the same uncertainty state (in figure 3, two equivalent input sequences are associated with Us8). The resulting UsS table is such that, for each Us, only one (partial) assignments to the input and sequence variables is left. This simplification can sometime lead to dramatic savings.

4 Algorithms for Searching Pow($\mathcal{S}$)

In this section we present two examples of search algorithms based on the data structures and primitives described in previous section. Both algorithms take in input the problem description in form of the BDDs $\mathcal{I}(\boldsymbol{x})$ and $\mathcal{G}(\boldsymbol{x})$, while the transition relation $\mathcal{R}$ is assumed to be globally available.

Figure 5 presents the *semi-symbolic forward* search algorithm. The algorithm represents the input sequences associated with the (symbolically represented) uncertainty states visited during the search as (explicit) lists of input values. The algorithm is based on the expansion of individual uncertainty states. OpenUsPool contains the (annotated) uncertainty states which have been reached but still have to be explored, and is initialized to the first uncertainty state of the search, i.e. $\mathcal{I}$, annotated with the empty input sequence ϵ. USMARKVISITED inserts $\mathcal{I}$ into the hash table of visited uncertainty states. The algorithm loops (lines 3-11) until a solution is found or all the search space has been exhausted. First, an annotated uncertainty state $\langle Us \cdot \pi \rangle$ is extracted from the open pool (line 4) by EXTRACTBEST. The uncertainty state is expanded by FWDEXPANDUSSTABLE, computing the corresponding UsS table (with length-one sequences). The resulting UsS table is traversed as explained in previous section, accessing with each

```
      procedure SemiSymFwdSearch(I,G)
0     begin
1         OpenUsPool := {⟨I . ε⟩}; USMARKVISITED(I);
2         Solved := I ⊆ G; Solution := ε;
3         while (OpenUsPool ≠ ∅ ∧ ¬Solved) do
4             ⟨Us . π⟩ := EXTRACTBEST(OpenUsPool);
5             UsSTable := FWDEXPANDUSSTABLE(Us);
6             UsSList := PRUNELISTUSSTABLE(UsSTable);
7             for ⟨Usᵢ . αᵢ⟩ in UsSList do
8                 if Usᵢ ⊆ G then
9                     Solved := True; Solution := π; αᵢ ; break;
10                    else INSERT(⟨Usᵢ . π; αᵢ⟩, OpenUsPool) endif;
11        end while
12        if Solved then return Solution;
13        else return Fail;
14    end
```

Fig. 5. The semi-symbolic, forward search algorithm.

uncertainty state the hash table of the already visited uncertainty states, discarding all the occurrences of present uncertainty states, and marking the new ones. The primitive PRUNELISTUSSTABLE is a version of PRUNEUSSTABLE that returns the explicit list of the UsS pairs in the pruned UsS table. Each of the resulting uncertainty states is compared with the set of target states $\mathcal{G}$. If $Us_i \subseteq \mathcal{G}$, then the associated input sequence $\pi; \alpha_i$ is a solution to the problem, the loop is exited and the sequence is returned. Otherwise, the annotated uncertainty state $\langle Us_i . \alpha_i; \pi \rangle$ is inserted in OpenUsPool and the loop is resumed. If the OpenUsPool becomes empty and a solution has not been found, then a fix point has been reached, i.e. all the reachable space of uncertainty states has been covered, and the algorithm terminates with failure. Depending on EXTRACTBEST and INSERT, different search strategies (e.g. depth-first, breadth-first, best-first) can be implemented.

Figure 6 shows the *fully-symbolic, backward* search algorithm. The algorithm relies on sequence variables for a symbolic representation of the input sequences, and recursively expands the UsS tables, thus implementing a breadth-first symbolic search. The algorithm proceeds from $\mathcal{G}$ towards $\mathcal{I}$, exploring a search space built as in figure 3. The array *UsSTables* is used to store the UsS tables representing the levels of the search associated with input sequences of increasing length. The algorithm first checks (line 4) if ϵ is a solution. If not, the while loop is entered. At each iteration, input sequences of increasing length are explored (lines 5 to 8). The step at line 6 expands the UsS table in *UsSTables*[$i - 1$] and stores the resulting UsS table in *UsSTables*[i]. UsS pairs which are redundant with respect to the current search are eliminated from *UsSTables*[i] (line 7). The possible solutions contained in *UsSTables*[i] are extracted and stored in *Solutions*

```
           procedure FullySymBwdSearch(I,G)
0    begin
1        i = 0; UsMarkVisited(G);
2        UsSTables[0] := { ⟨G . ε⟩ };
3        Solutions := BwdExtractSolution(UsSTables[0]);
4        while ((UsSTables[i] ≠ ∅) ∧ (Solutions = ∅)) do
5            i := i + 1;
6            UsSTables[i] := BwdExpandUsSTable(UsSTables[i-1]);
7            UsSTables[i] := PruneUsSTable(UsSTables[i]);
8            Solutions := BwdExtractSolution(UsSTables[i]);
9        done
10       if (UsSTables[i] = ∅) then
11           return Fail;
12           else return Solutions;
13   end
```

Fig. 6. The fully-symbolic, backward search algorithm.

(line 8). The loop terminates if either a solution is found ($Solutions \neq \emptyset$), or the space of input sequences has been completely explored ($UsSTables[i] = \emptyset$).

BwdExtractSolution checks if a UsS table contains a uncertainty state Us_i such that $I \subseteq Us_i$. It takes in input the BDD representation of a UsS table $UsST_i(x, \pi_{[i]}, \ldots, \pi_{[1]})$, and extracts the assignments to sequence variables such that the corresponding set contains the initial states, by computing $\forall x.(I(x) \rightarrow UsST_i(x, \pi_{[i]}, \ldots, \pi_{[1]}))$. The result is a BDD in the sequence variables $\pi_{[i]}, \ldots, \pi_{[1]}$. If the BDD is $False$, then there are no solutions of length i. Otherwise, each of the satisfying assignments of the resulting BDD represents a solution sequence.

The algorithms described here are only two witnesses of a family of possible algorithms. For instance, it is possible to proceed forwards in the fully-symbolic search, and to proceed backwards in the semi-symbolic search.

The algorithms enjoy the following properties. First, they always terminates. This follows from the fact that the set of explored uncertainty sets (stored in the visited hash table) is monotonically increasing: at each step we proceed only if at least one new uncertainty state is generated. The newly constructed UsS table are simplified by removing the uncertainty states which do not deserve further expansion. Since the set of accumulated uncertainty states is contained in $Pow(S)$, which is finite, a fix point is eventually reached. Second, a failure is returned if and only if there is no a solution to the given problem, otherwise a solution sequence is returned. This property follows from the facts that in the semi-symbolic search uncertainty states sequences constructed are such that $\langle Us . \pi \rangle$ enjoy the property $Image[\pi](I) = Us$. Thus, π is a solution to the problem $\langle I . Us \rangle$. In the fully symbolic search uncertainty states sequences constructed are such that $\emptyset \neq Image[\pi](Us) \subseteq G$. Thus, π is a solution to the problem $\langle Us . G \rangle$. The fully symbolic algorithm is also optimal, i.e. it returns plans of minimal length. This property follows from the breadth-first style of the search.

5   Experimental Evaluation

The data structures and the algorithms (semi- and fully-symbolic forward and backward search) have been implemented on top of the symbolic model checker NuSMV [5]. An open hashing mechanism is used to store visited uncertainty states. We present a preliminary experimental evaluation of our approach. We report two sets of experiments. The first ones are from artificial intelligence planning. (The results are labeled with AI in table 1.) FIXi is the generalization of the example system of figure 1 to i devices. For lack of space, we refer to [6] for the description of the other problems. In most cases, the automaton is fully nondeterministic, and there are acceptability conditions for the inputs. The problems are specified by providing the initial and target sets.

The second class of tests is based on the ISCAS89 [7] and MCNC [16] circuit benchmarks, the problem being finding a synchronization sequence, i.e. reaching a condition of certainty (i.e. a single final state) from a completely unspecified initial condition. We ran the same test cases as reported in [12,13]. In order to tackle these problems, we extended the forward[1] search algorithms (both semi- and fully-symbolic) with an ad-hoc routine for checking if a given uncertainty state is a solution (i.e. if it contains exactly one state).

To the best of our knowledge, no formal verification system able to solve these kind of problems is available, therefore we could not perform a direct experimental comparison. In [6], a detailed comparative evaluation shows that FSB outperforms all the other approaches to conformant planning (based on a decision procedure for QBF [14], on heuristic search [1], and on planning graphs [15]). The results of our approach to searching synchronization sequences appears to be at least as good as the ones in [12,13]. Normalizing the results with respect to the platform,[2] especially for the problems with longer reset sequences (e.g. planet, sand) we obtain a significant speed up and we are able to return shorter solutions. Furthermore, our approach tackles a more complex problem. Indeed, the approach in [12,13] is tailored to synchronization problems, and the system is assumed to be deterministic, i.e. uncertainty, intended as the number of indistinguishable states, is guaranteed to be non-increasing. We deal with fully nondeterministic systems, where uncertainty can also grow. Finally, our results were obtained using a monolithic transition relation (although nothing prevents from the use of partitioning techniques).

To summarize, the experimental results seem to confirm the following intuitions. The semi-symbolic approach is often much faster than the fully-symbolic

---

[1] In order to proceed backwards when searching for a synchronization sequence, the starting point must be the set of all singletons of size $|\mathcal{S}|$. Although possible in theory, the approach seems to be unfeasible in practice.

[2] From the limited information available, we estimate that the results in [12,13] were obtained on a machine at most 15 times slower than ours.

AI Name	# FF	# I	SSF L	SSF Time	FSB L	FSB Time
fix2	3	2	5	0.001	5	0.001
fix10	6	4	21	0.001	21	0.440
fix16	6	5	33	0.010	33	56.190
bmtc102l	7	5	18	0.020	18	1.220
bmtc102m	7	5	19	0.020	19	1.190
bmtc102h	7	5	19	0.020	19	1.190
bmtc106l	11	7	18	0.100	14	62.590
bmtc106m	11	7	18	0.100	17	64.970
bmtc106h	11	7	18	0.100	17	64.970
ring2	5	2	6	0.001	5	0.001
ring10	34	2	76	0.100	29	60.940
uring2	5	2	5	0.001	5	0.001
uring10	34	2	29	0.050	29	1.260
cubec	12	3	64	0.040	60	39.210
cubes	12	3	58	0.030	54	16.140
cubee	12	3	42	0.020	42	1.350
omel50	15	3	X	4.400	X	1.380
omel100	17	3	X	67.190	X	8.130

MCNC'91 Name	#FF	#I	SSF_{Sync} L	SSF_{Sync} Time	FSF_{Sync} L	FSF_{Sync} Time
bbara	4	4	2	0.000	2	0.010
bbsse	4	7	2	0.030	2	0.010
bbtas	3	2	3	0.000	3	0.000
beecount	3	3	1	0.000	1	0.000
cse	4	7	1	0.000	1	0.010
dk14	3	3	2	0.000	2	0.000
dk15	2	3	3	0.000	1	0.000
dk16	5	2	4	0.000	4	0.010
dk17	3	2	3	0.000	3	0.010
dk27	3	1	4	0.000	4	0.000
dk512	4	1	5	0.000	4	0.000
donfile	5	2	3	0.000	3	0.000
ex1	5	9	3	0.000	3	0.160
ex2	5	2	X	0.000	X	0.000
ex3	4	2	X	0.000	X	0.000
ex4	4	6	13	0.010	10	1.150
ex5	4	2	X	0.000	X	0.000
ex6	3	5	1	0.000	1	0.000
ex7	4	2	X	0.000	X	0.000
keyb	5	7	2	0.010	2	0.010
lion9	4	2	X	0.000	X	0.000
mark1	4	5	1	0.000	1	0.000
opus	4	5	1	0.000	1	0.000
planet	6	7	20	0.110		M.O.
s1	5	8	3	0.020	3	0.800
s1a	5	8	3	0.020	3	0.810
s8	3	4	4	0.000	4	0.010
sand	5	11	19	0.190		T.O.
tav	2	4	X	0.020	X	0.000
tbk	5	6	1	0.080	1	0.000
train11	4	2	X	0.000	X	0.000

ISCAS'89 Name	#FF	#I	SSF_{Sync} L	SSF_{Sync} Time	FSS_{Sync} L	FSS_{Sync} Time
s1196	18	14	1	3.370	1	0.280
s1238	18	14	1	3.320	1	0.300
s1488	6	8	1	0.010	1	0.000
s1494	6	8	1	0.010	1	0.010
s208.1	8	10	X	0.000	X	0.000
s27	3	4	1	0.010	1	0.000
s298	14	3	2	0.010	2	0.040
s344	15	9	2	0.300	2	6.090
s349	15	9	2	0.300	2	6.100
s382	21	3	1	0.010	1	0.010
s386	6	7	2	0.040	2	0.020
s400	21	3	1	0.010	1	0.000
s420.1	16	18	X	0.120	X	0.000
s444	21	3	1	0.030	1	0.020
s510	6	19		T.O.		T.O.
s526	21	3	2	0.090	2	0.120
s641	19	35	1	1.550	1	0.150
s713	19	35	1	0.540	1	0.150
s820	5	18	1	0.150	1	0.050
s832	5	18	1	0.140	1	0.040
s838.1	32	34	X	0.430	X	0.000

The experiments were executed on an Intel 300MHz Pentium-II, 512Mb RAM, running Linux. #FF and #I are the number of boolean state variables and inputs in the system automaton. SSF and FSB are the semi-symbolic forward and the fully-symbolic backward algorithms. SSF_{Sync} and FSF_{Sync} are the semi-symbolic and fully-symbolic forward search algorithms extended with the ad-hoc termination test for synchronization sequences. Times are reported in seconds. T.O. means time out after 1 hour CPU. M.O. means memory limit of 500Mb exhausted. L is the length of the solution found. X means that the problem admits no solution.

Table 1. Experimental results

one, when a solution exists. This appears to be caused by the additional sequence variables, and by the breadth-first style of the search. However, the fully-symbolic approach appears to be superior in discovering that the problem admits no solution, and returns sequences of minimal length. Forward search (either fully- or semi-symbolic) is usually inferior to backward (with some notable exceptions).

6   Related Work and Conclusions

In this paper we have presented a new approach to the problem of searching powerset automata which tackles the exponential blowup directly related to the powerset construction. Our approach combines techniques from symbolic and explicit-state model checking, and allows for different, complementary search strategies. The work presented in this paper is based on the work in [6], developed in the field of Artificial Intelligence planning, where fully symbolic search is described. In this paper we extend [6] with semi-symbolic search techniques, and we provide a comparative evaluation of the approaches on a larger set of test cases, including synchronization sequences from the ISCAS and MCNC benchmark circuits. Besides [12,13], discussed in previous section, few other works appear to be related to ours. In SPIN [8], the idea of combining a symbolic representation with explicit-state model checking is also present: an automaton-like structure is used to compactly represent the set of visited states. In [4], an external hash table is combined with a BDD package in order to extract additional information for guided search. In both cases, however, the integration of such techniques is directed to standard model checking problems.

The work presented in this paper will be extended as follows. An extensive experimental evaluation, together with a tighter integration of optimized model checking techniques, is currently being carried on. Then, different search methods (e.g. combining forward and backward search, partitioning of UsS tables) will be investigated. Furthermore, the approach, currently presented for reachability problems, will be generalized to deal with LTL specifications. Finally, the case of partial observability (i.e. when a limited amount of information can be acquired at run time) will be tackled.

References

1. B. Bonet and H. Geffner. Planning with Incomplete Information as Heuristic Search in Belief Space. In S. Chien, S. Kambhampati, and C.A. Knoblock, editors, 5th International Conference on Artificial Intelligence Planning and Scheduling, pages 52–61. AAAI-Press, April 2000.
2. T. L. Booth. Sequential Machines and Automata Theory. J. Wiley, 1967.
3. R. E. Bryant. Graph-Based Algorithms for Boolean Function Manipulation. IEEE Transactions on Computers, C-35(8):677–691, August 1986.
4. G. Cabodi, P. Camurati, and S. Quer. Improving symbolic traversals by means of activity profiles. In Proceedings of the 31st Conference on Design Automation, pages 306–311, New York, NY, USA, June 21–25 1999. ACM Pres.

5. A. Cimatti, E.M. Clarke, F. Giunchiglia, and M. Roveri. NuSMV : a new symbolic model checker. *International Journal on Software Tools for Technology Transfer (STTT)*, 2(4), March 2000.

6. A. Cimatti and M. Roveri. Conformant Planning via Symbolic Model Checking. *Journal of Artificial Intelligence Research (JAIR)*, 13:305–338, 2000.

7. F. Brglez, D. Bryan, and K. Kozminski. Combinational profiles of sequential benchmark circuits. In *International Symposium on Circuits and Systems*, May 1989.

8. G.J. Holzmann. *Design and Validation of Computer Protocols*. Prentice Hall, 1991.

9. Zvi Kohavi. *Switching and Finite Automata Theory*. McGraw-Hill Book Company, New York, 1978. ISBN 0-07-035310-7.

10. K.L. McMillan. *Symbolic Model Checking*. Kluwer Academic Publ., 1993.

11. D. Michie. Machine Intelligence at Edinburgh. In *On Machine Intelligence*, pages 143–155. Edinburgh University Press, 1974.

12. C. Pixley, S.-W. Jeong, and G. D. Hachtel. Exact calculation of synchronization sequences based on binary decision diagrams. In *Proceedings of the 29th Conference on Design Automation*, pages 620–623, Los Alamitos, CA, USA, June 1992. IEEE Computer Society Press.

13. J.-K. Rho, F. Somenzi, and C. Pixley. Minimum length synchronizing sequences of finite state machine. In ACM-SIGDA; IEEE, editor, *Proceedings of the 30th ACM/IEEE Design Automation Conference*, pages 463–468, Dallas, TX, June 1993. ACM Press.

14. J. Rintanen. Constructing conditional plans by a theorem-prover. *Journal of Artificial Intellegence Research*, 10:323–352, 1999.

15. David E. Smith and Daniel S. Weld. Conformant graphplan. In *Proceedings of the 15th National Conference on Artificial Intelligence (AAAI-98) and of the 10th Conference on Innovative Applications of Artificial Intelligence (IAAI-98)*, pages 889–896, Menlo Park, July 26–30 1998. AAAI Press.

16. S. Yang. Logic synthesis and optimization benchmarks user guide version 3.0. Technical report, Microelectronics Center of North Carolina, Research Triangle Park, January 1991.

Saturation: An Efficient Iteration Strategy for Symbolic State–Space Generation

Gianfranco Ciardo[1], Gerald Lüttgen[2], and Radu Siminiceanu[1]

[1] Department of Computer Science, College of William and Mary
Williamsburg, VA 23187, USA {ciardo,radu}@cs.wm.edu
[2] Department of Computer Science, Sheffield University, 211 Portobello Street
Sheffield S1 4DP, U.K. g.luettgen@dcs.shef.ac.uk

Abstract. We present a novel algorithm for generating state spaces of asynchronous systems using Multi–valued Decision Diagrams. In contrast to related work, we encode the next–state function of a system not as a single Boolean function, but as cross–products of integer functions. This permits the application of various iteration strategies to build a system's state space. In particular, we introduce a new elegant strategy, called *saturation*, and implement it in the tool SMART. On top of usually performing several orders of magnitude faster than existing BDD–based state–space generators, our algorithm's required peak memory is often close to the final memory needed for storing the overall state space.

1 Introduction

State–space generation is one of the most fundamental challenges for many formal verification tools, such as model checkers [13]. The high complexity of today's digital systems requires constructing and storing huge state spaces in the relatively small memory of a workstation. One research direction widely pursued in the literature suggests the use of *decision diagrams*, usually Binary Decision Diagrams [7] (BDDs), as a data structure for implicitly representing large sets of states in a compact fashion. This proved to be very successful for the verification of synchronous digital circuits, as it increased the manageable sizes of state spaces from about 10^6 states, with traditional explicit state–space generation techniques [14], to about 10^{20} states [9]. Unfortunately, symbolic techniques are known not to work well for *asynchronous systems*, such as communication protocols, which particularly suffer from state–space explosion.

The latter problem was addressed in previous work by the authors in the context of state–space generation using *Multi-valued Decision Diagrams* [18] (MDDs), which exploited the fact that, in event–based asynchronous systems,

---

* This work was partially supported by the National Aeronautics and Space Administration under NASA Contract No. NAS1–97046 while the authors were in residence at the Institute for Computer Applications in Science and Engineering (ICASE), NASA Langley Research Center, Hampton, VA 23681, USA. G. Ciardo and R. Siminiceanu were also partially supported by NASA grant No. NAG-1-2168.

T. Margaria and W. Yi (Eds.): TACAS 2001, LNCS 2031, pp. 328–342, 2001.
© Springer-Verlag Berlin Heidelberg 2001

each event updates just a few components of a system's state vector [10]. Hence, firing an event only requires the application of *local next–state functions* and the local manipulation of MDDs. This is in contrast to classic BDD–based techniques which construct state spaces by iteratively applying a single, global next–state function which is itself encoded as a BDD [20]. Additionally, in most concurrency frameworks including Petri nets [23] and process algebras [5], next–state functions satisfy a *product form* allowing each component of the state vector to be updated somewhat independently of the others. Experimental results implementing these ideas of locality showed significant improvements in speed and memory consumption when compared to other state–space generators [22].

In this paper, we take our previous approach a significant step further by observing that the reachable state space of a system can be built by firing the system's events in any order, as long as every event is considered often enough [16]. We exploit this freedom by proposing a novel strategy which exhaustively fires all events affecting a given MDD node, thereby bringing it to its final *saturated* shape. Moreover, nodes are considered in a depth–first fashion, i.e., when a node is processed, all its descendants are already saturated. The resulting state–space generation algorithm is not only concise, but also allows for an elegant proof of correctness. Compared to our previous work [10], saturation eliminates a fair amount of administration overhead, reduces the average number of firing events, and enables a simpler and more efficient cache management.

We implemented the new algorithm in the tool SMART [11], and experimental studies indicate that it performs on average about one order of magnitude faster than our old algorithm. Even more important and in contrast to related work, the peak memory requirements of our algorithm are often close to its final memory requirements. In the case of the dining philosophers' problem, we are able to construct the state space of about 10^{627} states, for 1000 philosophers, in under one second on a 800 MHz Pentium III PC using only 390KB of memory.

2   MDDs for Encoding Structured State Spaces

State spaces and next–state functions. A discrete–state model expressed in a high–level formalism must specify: (i) $\widehat{\mathcal{S}}$, the set of *potential states* describing the "type" of states; (ii) $\mathbf{s} \in \widehat{\mathcal{S}}$, the *initial state*; and (iii) $\mathcal{N} : \widehat{\mathcal{S}} \longrightarrow 2^{\widehat{\mathcal{S}}}$, the *next–state function*, describing which states can be reached from a given state in a single step. In many cases, such as Petri nets and process algebras, a model expresses this function as a union $\mathcal{N} = \bigcup_{e \in \mathcal{E}} \mathcal{N}_e$, where $\mathcal{E}$ is a finite set of *events* and $\mathcal{N}_e$ is the next–state function associated with event e. We say that $\mathcal{N}_e(s)$ is the set of states the system can enter when event e occurs, or *fires*, in state s. Moreover, event e is called *disabled* in s if $\mathcal{N}_e(s) = \emptyset$; otherwise, it is *enabled*.

The *reachable state space* $\mathcal{S} \subseteq \widehat{\mathcal{S}}$ of the model under consideration is the smallest set containing the initial system state $\mathbf{s}$ and closed with respect to $\mathcal{N}$, i.e., $\mathcal{S} = \{\mathbf{s}\} \cup \mathcal{N}(\mathbf{s}) \cup \mathcal{N}(\mathcal{N}(\mathbf{s})) \cup \cdots = \mathcal{N}^*(\mathbf{s})$, where "*" denotes the reflexive and transitive closure. When $\mathcal{N}$ is composed of several functions $\mathcal{N}_e$, for $e \in \mathcal{E}$, we can iterate these functions in any order, as long as we consider each $\mathcal{N}_e$ often enough. In other words, $i \in \mathcal{S}$ if and only if it can be reached from **s** through zero or more event firings. In this paper we assume that $\mathcal{S}$ is finite; however, for most practical asynchronous systems, the size of $\mathcal{S}$ is enormous due to the *state–space explosion* problem.

Multi–v alued decision diagrams. One way to cope with this problem is to use efficient data structures to encode $\mathcal{S}$ that exploit the system's *structure*. W e consider a common case in async hronous system design, where a system model is composed of K *submodels*, for some $K \in \mathbb{N}$, so that a global system state is a K–tuple $(i^K, \ldots, i^1)$, where i^k is the local state for submodel k. (We use *superscripts* for submodel indices —not for exponen tiation— and *subscripts* for event indices.) Thus, $\widehat{\mathcal{S}} = \mathcal{S}^K \times \cdots \times \mathcal{S}^1$, with each *local* state space $\mathcal{S}^k$ having some finite size n^k. In Petri nets, for example, the set of places can be partitioned into K subsets, and the marking can be written as the composition of the K corresponding submarkings. When iden tifying $\mathcal{S}^k$ with the initial integer interval $\{0, \ldots, n^k{-}1\}$, for each $K \geq k \geq 1$, one can encode $\mathcal{S} \subseteq \widehat{\mathcal{S}}$ via a (*quasi–reduced ordered*) MDD, i.e., a directed acyclic edge-labelled m ulti-graph where:

- Nodes are organized into $K + 1$ *levels*. We write $\langle k.p \rangle$ to denote a generic node, where k is the level and p is a unique index for that level. Level K contains only a single *non–terminal* node $\langle K.r \rangle$, the *root*, whereas levels $K{-}1$ through 1 contain one or more non–terminal nodes. Lev el 0 consists of two *terminal* nodes, $\langle 0.\mathbf{0} \rangle$ and $\langle 0.\mathbf{1} \rangle$. (We use boldface for the node indices **0** or **1** since these have a special meaning, as w e will explain later.)
- A non–terminal node $\langle k.p \rangle$ has n^k arcs pointing to nodes at level $k - 1$. If the ith arc, for $i \in \mathcal{S}^k$, is to node $\langle k{-}1.q \rangle$, we write $\langle k.p \rangle[i] = q$. Unlike in the original BDD setting [7, 8], we allow for *redundant* nodes, having all arcs pointing to the same node. This will be con venient for our purposes, as eliminating such nodes would lead to arcs spanning multiple levels.
- A non–terminal node cannot *duplicate* (i.e., have the same pattern of arcs as) another node at the same level.

Given a node $\langle k.p \rangle$, we can recursively define the node reached from it through any integer sequence $\gamma =_{\mathrm{df}} (i^k, i^{k-1}, \cdots, i^l) \in \mathcal{S}^k \times \mathcal{S}^{k-1} \times \cdots \times \mathcal{S}^l$ of length $k - l + 1$, for $K \geq k \geq l \geq 1$, as

$$node(\langle k.p \rangle, \gamma) = \begin{cases} \langle k.p \rangle & \text{if } \gamma = (), \text{ the empty sequence} \\ node(\langle k{-}1.q \rangle, \delta) & \text{if } \gamma = (i^k, \delta) \text{ and } \langle k.p \rangle[i^k] = q. \end{cases}$$

The substates encoded by p or reaching p are then, respectively,

$$\mathcal{B}(\langle k.p \rangle) = \{\beta \in \mathcal{S}^k \times \cdots \times \mathcal{S}^1 : node(\langle k.p \rangle, \beta) = \langle 0.\mathbf{1} \rangle\} \qquad \text{``below''} \langle k.p \rangle\,;$$
$$\mathcal{A}(\langle k.p \rangle) = \{\alpha \in \mathcal{S}^K \times \cdots \times \mathcal{S}^{k+1} : node(\langle K.r \rangle, \alpha) = \langle k.p \rangle\} \qquad \text{``above''} \langle k.p \rangle\,.$$

Thus, $\mathcal{B}(\langle k.p \rangle)$ contains the substates that, prefixed by a substate in $\mathcal{A}(\langle k.p \rangle)$, form a (global) state encoded by the MDD. W e reserve the indices 0 and 1 at each level k to encode the sets $\emptyset$ and $\mathcal{S}^k \times \cdots \times \mathcal{S}^1$, respectively. In particular, $\mathcal{B}(\langle 0.\mathbf{0} \rangle) = \emptyset$ and $\mathcal{B}(\langle 0.\mathbf{1} \rangle) = \{()\}$. Fig. 1 shows a four–level example MDD and the set $\mathcal{S}$ encoded by it; only the highlighted nodes are actually stored.

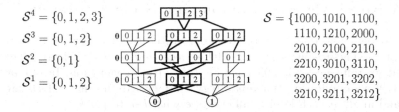

$$\mathcal{S}^4 = \{0,1,2,3\}$$
$$\mathcal{S}^3 = \{0,1,2\}$$
$$\mathcal{S}^2 = \{0,1\}$$
$$\mathcal{S}^1 = \{0,1,2\}$$

$$\mathcal{S} = \{1000, 1010, 1100,$$
$$1110, 1210, 2000,$$
$$2010, 2100, 2110,$$
$$2210, 3010, 3110,$$
$$3200, 3201, 3202,$$
$$3210, 3211, 3212\}$$

Fig. 1. An example MDD and the state space $\mathcal{S}$ encoded by it.

Many algorithms for generating state spaces using BDDs exist [20], which can easily be adapted to MDDs. In contrast to those, however, our approach does *not* encode the next–state function as an MDD over $2K$ variables, describing the K state components before and after a system step. Instead, we update MDD nodes directly, adding the new states reached through one step of the global next–state function when firing some event. For asynchronous systems, this function is often expressible as the cross–product of local next–state functions.

Product–form behavior. An asynchronous system model exhibits such behavior if, for each event e, its next–state function $\mathcal{N}_e$ can be written as a cross–product of K local functions, i.e., $\mathcal{N}_e = \mathcal{N}_e^K \times \cdots \times \mathcal{N}_e^1$ where $\mathcal{N}_e^k : \mathcal{S}^k \longrightarrow 2^{\mathcal{S}^k}$, for $K \geq k \geq 1$. (Recall that event e is disabled in some global state exactly if it is disabled in at least one component.) The product–form requirement is quite natural. First, many modeling formalisms satisfy it, e.g., any Petri net model conforms to this behavior for any partition of its places. Second, if a given model does not respect the product–form behavior, we can always coarsen K or refine $\mathcal{E}$ so that it does. As an example, consider a model partitioned into four submodels, where $\mathcal{N}_e = \mathcal{N}_e^4 \times \mathcal{N}_e^{3,2} \times \mathcal{N}_e^1$, but $\mathcal{N}^{3,2} : \mathcal{S}^3 \times \mathcal{S}^2 \longrightarrow 2^{\mathcal{S}^3 \times \mathcal{S}^2}$ cannot be expressed as a product $\mathcal{N}_e^3 \times \mathcal{N}_e^2$. We can achieve the product–form requirement by simply partitioning the model into three, not four, submodels. Alternatively, we may substitute event e with "subevents" satisfying the product form. This is possible since, in the worst case, we can define a subevent $e_{i,j}$, for each $i = (i^3, i^2)$ and $j = (j^3, j^2) \in \mathcal{N}_e^{3,2}(i)$, with $\mathcal{N}_{e_{i,j}}(i^3) = \{j^3\}$ and $\mathcal{N}_{e_{i,j}}(i^2) = \{j^2\}$.

Finally, we introduce some notational conventions. We say that event e *depends* on level k, if the local state at level k does affect the enabling of e or if it is changed by the firing of e. Let $First(e)$ and $Last(e)$ be the first and last levels on which event e depends. Events e such that $First(e) = Last(e) = k$ are said to be *local events*; we merge these into a single *macro–event* λ^k without violating the product–form requirement, since we can write $\mathcal{N}_{\lambda^k} = \mathcal{N}_{\lambda^k}^K \times \cdots \times \mathcal{N}_{\lambda^k}^1$ where $\mathcal{N}_{\lambda^k}^k = \bigcup_{\{e:First(e)=Last(e)=k\}} \mathcal{N}_e^k$, while $\mathcal{N}_{\lambda^k}^l(i^l) = \{i^l\}$ for $l \neq k$ and $i^l \in \mathcal{S}^l$. The set $\{e \in \mathcal{E} : First(e) = k\}$ of events "starting" at level k is denoted by $\mathcal{E}^k$. We also extend $\mathcal{N}_e$ to substates instead of full states: $\mathcal{N}_e((i^k, \ldots, i^l)) = \mathcal{N}_e^k(i^k) \times \cdots \times \mathcal{N}_e^l(i^l)$, for $K \geq k \geq l \geq 1$; to sets of states: $\mathcal{N}_e(\mathcal{X}) = \bigcup_{i \in \mathcal{X}} \mathcal{N}_e(i)$, for $\mathcal{X} \subseteq \mathcal{S}^k \times \cdots \times \mathcal{S}^l$; and to sets of events: $\mathcal{N}_\mathcal{F}(\mathcal{X}) = \bigcup_{e \in \mathcal{F}} \mathcal{N}_e(\mathcal{X})$, for $\mathcal{F} \subseteq \mathcal{E}$. In particular, we write $\mathcal{N}_{\leq k}$ as a shorthand for $\mathcal{N}_{\{e:First(e)\leq k\}}$.

3   A No vel Algorithm Employing Node Saturation

In the following we refer to a specific order of iterating the local next–state functions of an synchronous system model as *iteration strategy*. Clearly, the choice of strategy influences the efficiency of state–space generation. In our previous work [10] we employed a naive strategy that cycled through MDDs level–by–level and fired, at each level k, all events e with $First(e) = k$.

As main contribution of this paper, we present a novel iteration strategy, called *saturation*, which not only simplifies our previous algorithm, but also significantly improves its time *and* space efficiency. The key idea is to fire events node–wise and exhaustively, instead of level–wise and just once per iteration. Formally, we say that an MDD node $\langle k.p \rangle$ is *saturated* if it encodes a set of states that is a fixed point with respect to the firing of any event at its level or at a lower level, i.e., if $\mathcal{B}(\langle k.p \rangle) = \mathcal{N}^*_{\leq k}(\mathcal{B}(\langle k.p \rangle))$ holds; it can easily be shown by contradiction that any node below node $\langle k.p \rangle$ must be saturated, too. It should be noted that the routine for firing some event, in order to reveal and add globally reachable states to the MDD represen tation of the state space under construction, is similar to [10]. In particular, MDDs are manipulated only locally with respect to the levels on which the fired event depends, and, due to the product–form behavior, these manipulations can be carried out very efficiently. W e do not further commen t on these issues here, but concentrate solely on the new idea of node saturation and its implications.

Just as in traditional symbolic state–space generation algorithms, we use a *unique table*, to detect duplicate nodes, and *operation caches*, in particular a *union cache* and a *firing cache*, to speed–up computation. However, our approach is distinguished by the fact that only saturated nodes are checked in the unique table or referenced in the caches. Given the MDD encoding of the initial state **s**, we saturate its nodes bottom–up. This impro ves both memory and execution–time efficiency for generating state spaces because of the follo wing reasons. First, our saturation order ensures that the firing of an event affecting only the current and possibly lower levels adds as man y new states as possible. Then, since each node in the final encoding of $\mathcal{S}$ is saturated, any node we insert in the unique table has at least a chance of being part of the final MDD, while any unsaturated node inserted by a traditional sym bolic approach is *guaranteed* to be eventually deleted and replaced with another node encoding a larger subset of states. Finally, once we saturate a node at level k, we never need to fire any event $e \in \mathcal{E}^k$ in it again, while, in classic symbolic approaches, $\mathcal{N}$ is applied to the entire MDD at *every iteration*.

In the pseudo–code of our new algorithm implem enting node saturation, which is shown in Fig. 2, we use the data types *evnt* (model event), *lcl* (local state), *lvl* (level), and *idx* (node index within a level); in practice these are simply integers in appropriate ranges. W e also assume the following dynamically–sized global hash tables: (a) $UT[k]$, for $K \geq k \geq 1$, the *unique table* for nodes at level k, to retrieve p given the key $\langle k.p \rangle[0], \ldots, \langle k.p \rangle[n^k - 1]$; (b) $UC[k]$, for $K > k \geq 1$, the *union cache* for nodes at level k, to retrieve s given nodes p and q, where $\mathcal{B}(\langle k.s \rangle) = \mathcal{B}(\langle k.p \rangle) \cup \mathcal{B}(\langle k.q \rangle)$; and (c) $FC[k]$, for $K > k \geq 1$, the *firing cache*

Generate(in s:array[1..K] of *lcl*):*idx*

Build an MDD rooted at $\langle K.r \rangle$ encoding $\mathcal{N}_{\mathcal{E}}^*(\mathbf{s})$ and return r, in $UT[K]$.

declare *r,p:idx*;
declare *k:lvl*;
1. $p \Leftarrow 1$;
2. for $k = 1$ to K do
3. $r \Leftarrow NewNode(k)$; $\langle k.r \rangle[\mathbf{s}[k]] \Leftarrow p$;
4.   *Saturate*(k,r); *Check*(k,r);
5. $p \Leftarrow r$; return r;

Saturate(in *k:lvl*, *p:idx*)

Update $\langle k.p \rangle$, not in $UT[k]$, in–place, to encode $\mathcal{N}_{\le k}^*(\mathcal{B}(\langle k.p \rangle))$.

declare *e:evnt*;
declare $\mathcal{L}$:set of *lcl*;
declare *f,u:idx*;
declare *i,j:lcl*;
declare *pCng:bool*;
1. repeat
2. $pCng \Leftarrow false$;
3.   foreach $e \in \mathcal{E}^k$ do
4. $\mathcal{L} \Leftarrow Locals(e,k,p)$;
5.   while $\mathcal{L} \ne \emptyset$ do
6. $i \Leftarrow Pick(\mathcal{L})$;
7. $f \Leftarrow RecFire(e,k-1,\langle k.p \rangle[i])$;
8.   if $f \ne 0$ then
9.   foreach $j \in \mathcal{N}_e^k(i)$ do
10. $u \Leftarrow Union(k-1,f,\langle k.p \rangle[j])$;
11.   if $u \ne \langle k.p \rangle[j]$ then
12. $\langle k.p \rangle[j] \Leftarrow u$; $pCng \Leftarrow true$;
13.   if $\mathcal{N}_e^k(j) \ne \emptyset$ then
14. $\mathcal{L} \Leftarrow \mathcal{L} \cup \{j\}$;
15.   until $pCng = false$;

Union(in *k:lvl*, *p:idx*, *q:idx*):*idx*

Build an MDD rooted at $\langle k.s \rangle$, in $UT[k]$, encoding $\mathcal{B}(\langle k.p \rangle) \cup \mathcal{B}(\langle k.q \rangle)$. Return s.

declare *i:lcl*;
declare *s,u:idx*;
1. if $p = 1$ or $q = 1$ then return 1;
2. if $p = 0$ or $p = q$ then return q;
3. if $q = 0$ then return p;
4. if $Find(UC[k],\{p,q\},s)$ then return s;
5. $s \Leftarrow NewNode(k)$;
6. for $i = 0$ to $n^k - 1$ do
7. $u \Leftarrow Union(k-1,\langle k.p \rangle[i],\langle k.q \rangle[i])$;
8. $\langle k.s \rangle[i] \Leftarrow u$;
9. *Check*(k,s); *Insert*$(UC[k],\{p,q\},s)$;
10. return s;

RecFire(in *e:evnt*, *l:lvl*, *q:idx*):*idx*

Build an MDD rooted at $\langle l.s \rangle$, in $UT[l]$, encoding $\mathcal{N}_{\le l}^*(\mathcal{N}_e(\mathcal{B}(\langle l.q \rangle)))$. Return s.

declare $\mathcal{L}$:set of *lcl*;
declare *f,u,s:idx*;
declare *i,j:lcl*;
declare *sCng:bool*;
1. if $l < Last(e)$ then return q;
2. if $Find(FC[l],\{q,e\},s)$ then return s;
3. $s \Leftarrow NewNode(l)$; $sCng \Leftarrow false$;
4. $\mathcal{L} \Leftarrow Locals(e,l,q)$;
5. while $\mathcal{L} \ne \emptyset$ do
6. $i \Leftarrow Pick(\mathcal{L})$;
7. $f \Leftarrow RecFire(e,l-1,\langle l.q \rangle[i])$;
8.   if $f \ne 0$ then
9.   foreach $j \in \mathcal{N}_e^l(i)$ do
10. $u \Leftarrow Union(l-1,f,\langle l.s \rangle[j])$;
11.   if $u \ne \langle l.s \rangle[j]$ then
12. $\langle l.s \rangle[j] \Leftarrow u$; $sCng \Leftarrow true$;
13.   if $sCng$ then *Saturate*(l,s);
14.   *Check*(l,s); *Insert*$(FC[l],\{q,e\},s)$;
15. return s;

Find(in *tab*, *key*, out *v*):*bool*

If (key,x) is in hash table *tab*, set v to x and return *true*. Else, return *false*.

Insert(inout *tab*, in *key*, *v*)

Insert (key,v) in hash table *tab*, if it does not contain an entry $(key,\cdot)$.

Locals(in *e:evnt*, *k:lvl*, *p:idx*):set of *lcl*

Return $\{i \in \mathcal{S}^k : \langle k.p \rangle[i] \ne 0, \mathcal{N}_e^k(i) \ne \emptyset\}$, the local states in p locally enabling e. Return $\emptyset$ or $\{i \in \mathcal{S}^k : \mathcal{N}_e^k(i) \ne \emptyset\}$, respectively, if p is 0 or 1.

Pick(inout $\mathcal{L}$:set of *lcl*):*lcl*

Remove and return an element from $\mathcal{L}$.

NewNode(in *k:lvl*):*idx*

Create $\langle k.p \rangle$ with arcs set to 0, return p.

Check(in *k:lvl*, inout *p:idx*)

If $\langle k.p \rangle$, not in $UT[k]$, duplicates $\langle k.q \rangle$, in $UT[k]$, delete $\langle k.p \rangle$ and set p to q. Else, insert $\langle k.p \rangle$ in $UT[k]$. If $\langle k.p \rangle[0] = \cdots = \langle k.p \rangle[n^k-1] = 0$ or 1, delete $\langle k.p \rangle$ and set p to 0 or 1, since $\mathcal{B}(\langle k.p \rangle)$ is $\emptyset$ or $\mathcal{S}^k \times \cdots \times \mathcal{S}^1$, respectively.

Fig. 2. Pseudo–code for the node–saturation algorithm.

for nodes at level k, to retrieve s given node p and event e, where $First(e) > k$ and $\mathcal{B}(\langle k.s \rangle) = \mathcal{N}^*_{\leq k}(\mathcal{N}_e(\mathcal{B}(\langle k.p \rangle)))$. Furthermore, we use K dynamically–sized arrays to store nodes, so that $\langle k.p \rangle$ can be efficiently retrieved as the pth entry of the kth array. The call $Generate(\mathbf{s})$ creates the MDD encoding the initial state, saturating each MDD node as soon as it creates it, in a bottom–up fashion. Hence, when it calls $Saturate(k, r)$, all children of $\langle k.r \rangle$ are already saturated.

Theorem 1 (Correctness). *Consider a node $\langle k.p \rangle$ with $K \geq k \geq 1$ and saturated children. Moreover, (a) let $\langle l.q \rangle$ be one of its children, satisfying $q \neq \mathbf{0}$ and $l = k-1$; (b) let $\mathcal{U}$ stand for $\mathcal{B}(\langle l.q \rangle)$ before the call $RecFire(e, l, q)$, for some event e with $l < First(e)$, and let $\mathcal{V}$ represent $\mathcal{B}(\langle l.f \rangle)$, where f is the value returned by this call; and (c) let $\mathcal{X}$ and $\mathcal{Y}$ denote $\mathcal{B}(\langle k.p \rangle)$ before and after calling $Saturate(k, p)$, respectively. Then, (i) $\mathcal{V} = \mathcal{N}^*_{\leq l}(\mathcal{N}_e(\mathcal{U}))$ and (ii) $\mathcal{Y} = \mathcal{N}^*_{\leq k}(\mathcal{X})$.*

By choosing, for node $\langle k.p \rangle$, the root $\langle K.r \rangle$ of the MDD representing the initial system state $\mathbf{s}$, we obtain $\mathcal{Y} = \mathcal{N}^*_{\leq K}(\mathcal{B}(\langle K.r \rangle)) = \mathcal{N}^*_{\leq K}(\{\mathbf{s}\}) = \mathcal{S}$, as desired.

Proof. To prove both statements we employ a simultaneous induction on k. For the induction base, $k = 1$, we have: (i) The only possible call $RecFire(e, 0, \mathbf{1})$ immediately returns $\mathbf{1}$ because of the test on l (cf. line 1). Then, $\mathcal{U} = \mathcal{V} = \{()\}$ and $\{()\} = \mathcal{N}^*_{\leq 0}(\mathcal{N}_e(\{()\}))$. (ii) The call $Saturate(1, p)$ repeatedly explores λ^1, the only event in $\mathcal{E}^1$, in every local state i for which $\mathcal{N}^1_{\lambda^1}(i) \neq \emptyset$ and for which $\langle 1.p \rangle[i]$ is either $\mathbf{1}$ at the beginning of the "while $\mathcal{L} \neq \emptyset$" loop, or has been modified (cf. line 12) from $\mathbf{0}$ to $\mathbf{1}$, which is the value of f, hence u, since the call $RecFire(e, 0, \mathbf{1})$ returns $\mathbf{1}$. The iteration stops when further attempts to fire λ^1 do not add any new state to $\mathcal{B}(\langle 1.p \rangle)$. At this point, $\mathcal{Y} = \mathcal{N}^*_{\lambda^1}(\mathcal{X}) = \mathcal{N}^*_{\leq 1}(\mathcal{X})$.

For the induction step we assume that the calls to $Saturate(k-1, \cdot)$ as well as to $RecFire(e, l-1, \cdot)$ work correctly. Recall that $l = k - 1$.

(i) Unlike $Saturate$ (cf. line 14), $RecFire$ does not add further local states to $\mathcal{L}$, since it modifies "in–place" the new node $\langle l.s \rangle$, and not node $\langle l.q \rangle$ describing the states from where the firing is explored. The call $RecFire(e, l, q)$ can be resolved in three ways. If $l < Last(e)$, then the returned value is $f = q$ and $\mathcal{N}^l_{e}(\mathcal{U}) = \mathcal{U}$ for any set $\mathcal{U}$; since q is saturated, $\mathcal{B}(\langle l.q \rangle) = \mathcal{N}^*_{\leq l}(\mathcal{B}(\langle l.q \rangle)) = \mathcal{N}^*_{\leq l}(\mathcal{N}_e(\mathcal{B}(\langle l.q \rangle)))$. If $l \geq Last(e)$ but $RecFire$ has been called previously with the same parameters, then the call $Find(FC[l], \{q, e\}, s)$ is successful. Since node q is saturated and in the unique table, it has not been modified further; note that in–place updates are performed only on nodes not yet in the unique table. Thus, the value s in the cache is still valid and can be safely used. Finally, we need to consider the case where the call $RecFire(e, l, q)$ performs "real work." First, a new node $\langle l.s \rangle$ is created, having all its arcs initialized to $\mathbf{0}$. We explore the firing of e in each state i satisfying $\langle l.q \rangle[i] \neq \mathbf{0}$ and $\mathcal{N}^e_l(i) \neq \emptyset$. By induction hypothesis, the recursive call $RecFire(e, l-1, \langle l.q \rangle[i])$ returns $\mathcal{N}^*_{\leq l-1}(\mathcal{N}_e(\mathcal{B}(\langle l-1.\langle l.q \rangle[i] \rangle)))$. Hence, when the "while $\mathcal{L} \neq \emptyset$" loop terminates, $\mathcal{B}(\langle l.s \rangle) = \bigcup_{i \in \mathcal{S}^l} \mathcal{N}^l_e(i) \times \mathcal{N}^*_{\leq l-1}(\mathcal{N}_e(\mathcal{B}(\langle l-1.\langle l.q \rangle[i] \rangle))) = \mathcal{N}^*_{\leq l-1}(\mathcal{N}_e(\mathcal{B}(\langle l.q \rangle)))$ holds. Thus, all children of node $\langle l.s \rangle$ are saturated. According to the induction hypothesis, the call

$Saturate(l, s)$ correctly saturates $\langle l.s \rangle$. Consequently, we have $\mathcal{B}(\langle l.s \rangle) = \mathcal{N}^*_{\leq l}(\mathcal{N}^*_{\leq l-1}(\mathcal{N}_e(\mathcal{B}(\langle l.q \rangle)))) = \mathcal{N}^*_{\leq l}(\mathcal{N}_e(\mathcal{B}(\langle l.q \rangle)))$ after the call.

(ii) As in the base case, $Saturate(k, p)$ repeatedly explores the firing of each event e that is locally enabled in $i \in \mathcal{S}^k$; it calls $RecFire(e, k-1, \langle k.p \rangle[i])$ that, as shown above and since $l = k-1$, returns $\mathcal{N}^*_{\leq k-1}(\mathcal{N}_e(\mathcal{B}(\langle k-1.\langle k.p \rangle[i] \rangle)))$. Further, $Saturate(k, p)$ terminates when firing the events in $\mathcal{E}^k = \{e_1, e_2, \ldots, e_m\}$ does not add any new state to $\mathcal{B}(\langle k.p \rangle)$. At this point, the set $\mathcal{Y}$ encoded by $\langle k.p \rangle$ is the fixed–point of the iteration

$$\mathcal{Y}^{(m+1)} \Leftarrow \mathcal{Y}^{(m)} \cup \mathcal{N}^*_{\leq k-1}(\mathcal{N}_{e_1}(\mathcal{N}^*_{\leq k-1}(\mathcal{N}_{e_2}(\cdots \mathcal{N}^*_{\leq k-1}(\mathcal{N}_{e_m}(\mathcal{Y}^{(m)})) \cdots)))),$$

initialized with $\mathcal{Y}^{(0)} \Leftarrow \mathcal{X}$. Hence, $\mathcal{Y} = \mathcal{N}^*_{\leq k}(\mathcal{X})$, as desired. □

level	event: l_1	event: l_2	event: l_3	event: e_{21}	event: e_{321}
3	*	*	$1 \to 0$	*	$0 \to 1$
2	*	$0 \to 1, 2 \to 1$	*	$0 \to 1$	$0 \to 2$
1	$0 \to 1, 1 \to 2, 2 \to 0$	*	*	$1 \to 0$	$0 \to 1$

Fig. 3. Example of the execution of the $Saturate$ and $RecFire$ routines.

Fig. 3 illustrates our saturation–based state–space generation algorithm on a small example, where $K = 3$, $|\mathcal{S}_3| = 2$, $|\mathcal{S}_2| = 3$, and $|\mathcal{S}_1| = 3$. The initial state is $(0, 0, 0)$, and there are three local events l_1, l_2, and l_3, plus two further events, e_{21} (depending on levels 2 and 1) and e_{321} (depending on all levels). Their effects, i.e., their next–state functions, are summarized in the table at the top of Fig. 3; the symbol "*" indicates that a level does not affect an event. The

MDD encoding $\{(0,0,0)\}$ is displayed in Snapshot (a). Nodes $\langle 3.2 \rangle$ and $\langle 2.2 \rangle$ are actually created in Steps (b) and (g), respectively, but we show them from the beginning for clarity. The level lvl of a node $\langle lvl.idx \rangle$ is given at the very left of the MDD figures, whereas the index idx is shown to the right of each node. We use dashed lines for newly created objects, double boxes for saturated nodes, and shaded local states for substates enabling the event to be fired. We do not show nodes with index $\mathbf{0}$, nor any arcs to them.

- *Snapshots (a–b):* The call $Saturate(1,2)$ updates node $\langle 1.2 \rangle$ to represent the effect of firing l_1^*; the result is equal to the reserved node $\langle 1.1 \rangle$.
- *Snapshots (b–f):* The call $Saturate(2,2)$ fires event l_2, adding arc $\langle 2.2 \rangle[1]$ to $\langle 1.1 \rangle$ (cf. Snapshot (c)). It also fires event e_{21} which finds the "enabling pattern" $(*, 0, 1)$, with arbitrary first component, and starts building the result of the firing, through the sequence of calls $RecFire(e_{21}, 1, \langle 2.2 \rangle[0])$ and $RecFire(e_{21}, 0, \langle 1.1 \rangle[1])$. Once node $\langle 1.3 \rangle$ is created and its arc $\langle 1.3 \rangle[0]$ is set to $\mathbf{1}$ (cf. Snapshot (d)), it is saturated by repeatedly firing event l_1. Node $\langle 1.3 \rangle$ then becomes identical to node $\langle 1.1 \rangle$ (cf. Snapshot (e)). Hence, it is not added to the unique table but deleted. Returning from $RecFire$ on level 1 with result $\langle 1.1 \rangle$, arc $\langle 2.2 \rangle[1]$ is updated to point to the outcome of the firing (cf. Snapshot (f)). This does not add any new state to the MDD, since $\{1\} \times \{0\}$ was already encoded in $\mathcal{B}(\langle 2.2 \rangle)$.
- *Snapshots (f–o):* Once $\langle 2.2 \rangle$ is saturated, we call $Saturate(3,2)$. Local event l_3 is not enabled, but event e_{321} is, by the pattern $(0, 0, 0)$. The calls to $RecFire$ build a chain of nodes encoding the result of the firing (cf. Snapshots (g–i)). Each of them is in turn saturated (cf. Snapshots (h–j)), causing first the newly created node $\langle 1.4 \rangle$ to be deleted, since it becomes equal to node $\langle 1.1 \rangle$, and second the saturated node $\langle 2.3 \rangle$ to be added to the MDD. The firing of e_{321} (cf. Snapshot (k)) not only adds state $(1, 2, 1)$, but the entire subspace $\{1\} \times \{1, 2\} \times \mathcal{S}^1$, now known to be exhaustively explored, as node $\langle 2.3 \rangle$ is marked saturated. Event l_3, which was found disabled in node $\langle 3.2 \rangle$ at the first attempt, is now enabled, and its firing calls $Union(2, \langle 3.2 \rangle[1], \langle 3.2 \rangle[0])$. The result is a new node which is found by $Check$ to be the reserved node $\langle 2.1 \rangle$ (cf. Snapshot (m)). This node encoding $\mathcal{S}_2 \times \mathcal{S}_1$ is added as the descendant of node $\langle 3.2 \rangle$ in position 0, and the former descendant $\langle 2.2 \rangle$ in that position is removed (cf. Snapshot (n)), causing it to become disconnected and deleted. Further attempts to fire events l_3 or e_{321} add no more states to the MDD, whence node $\langle 3.2 \rangle$ is declared saturated (cf. Snapshot (o)). Thus, our algorithm terminates and returns the MDD encoding of the overall state space $(\{0\} \times \mathcal{S}^2 \times \mathcal{S}^1) \cup (\{1\} \times \{1, 2\} \times \mathcal{S}^1)$.

To summarize, since MDD nodes are saturated as soon as they are created, each node will either be present in the final diagram or will eventually become disconnected, but it will never be modified further. This reduces the amount of work needed to explore subspaces. Once all events in $\mathcal{E}^k$ are exhaustively fired in some node $\langle k.p \rangle$, any additional state discovered that uses $\langle k.p \rangle$ for its encoding benefits in advance from the "knowledge" encapsulated in $\langle k.p \rangle$ and its descendants.

4 Garbage Collection and Optimizations

Garbage collection. MDD nodes can become disconnected, i.e., unreachable from the root, and should be "recycled." Disconnection is detected by associating an *incoming–arc counter* to each node $\langle k.p \rangle$. Recycling disconnected nodes is a major issue in traditional symbolic state–space generation algorithms, where usually many nodes become disconnected. In our algorithm, this phenomenon is much less frequent, and the best runtime is achieved by removing these nodes only at the end; we refer to this policy as LAZY policy.

We also implemented aSTRICT policy where, if a node $\langle k.p \rangle$ becomes disconnected, its "delete–flag" is set and its arcs $\langle k.p \rangle[i]$ are re–directed to $\langle k-1.0 \rangle$, with possible recursive effects on the nodes downstream. When a hit in the union cache $UC[k]$ or the firing cache $FC[k]$ returns s, we consider this entry stale if the delete–flag of node $\langle k.s \rangle$ is set. By keeping a per–level count of the nodes with delete–flag set, we can decide in routine $NewNode(k)$ whether to (a) allocate new memory for a node at level k or (b) recycle the indices and the physical memory of all nodes at level k with delete–flag set, after having removed all the entries in $UC[k]$ and $FC[k]$ referring to them. The threshold that triggers recycling can be set in terms of number of nodes or bytes of memory. The policy using a threshold of one node, denoted as STRICT(1), is optimal in terms of memory consumption, but has a higher overhead due to more frequent clean–ups.

Optimizations. First, observe that the two outermost loops in *Saturate* ensure that firing some event $e \in \mathcal{E}^k$ does not add any new state. If we always consider these events in the same order, we can stop iterating as soon as $|\mathcal{E}^k|$ consecutive events have been explored without revealing any new state. This saves $|\mathcal{E}^k|/2$ firing attempts on average, which translates to speed–ups of up to 25% in our experimental studies. Also, in *Union*, the call $Insert(UC[k], \{p, q\}, s)$ records that $\mathcal{B}(\langle k.s \rangle) = \mathcal{B}(\langle k.p \rangle) \cup \mathcal{B}(\langle k.q \rangle)$. Since this implies $\mathcal{B}(\langle k.s \rangle) = \mathcal{B}(\langle k.p \rangle) \cup \mathcal{B}(\langle k.s \rangle)$ and $\mathcal{B}(\langle k.s \rangle) = \mathcal{B}(\langle k.s \rangle) \cup \mathcal{B}(\langle k.q \rangle)$, we can, optionally, also issue the calls $Insert(UC[k], \{p, s\}, s)$, if $s \neq p$, and $Insert(UC[k], \{q, s\}, s)$, if $s \neq q$. This *speculative union heuristic* improves performance by up to 20%.

5 Experimental Results

In this section we compare the performance of our new algorithm, using both the STRICT and LAZY policies, with previous MDD–based ones, namely the traditional RECURSIVE MDD approach in [22] and the level–by–level FORWARDING–arcs approach in [10]. All three approaches are implemented in SMART [11], a tool for the logical and stochastic–timing analysis of discrete–state systems. For asynchronous systems, these approaches greatly outperform the more traditional BDD–based approaches [20], where next–state functions are encoded using decision diagrams. To evaluate our saturation algorithm, we have chosen a suite of examples with a wide range of characteristics. In all cases, the state space sizes depend on a parameter $N \in \mathbb{N}$.

- The classic *N queens problem* requires to find a way to position N queens on a $N \times N$ chess board such that they do not attack each other. Since there will be exactly one queen per row in the final solution, we use a *safe* (i.e., at most one token per place) Petri net model with $N \times N$ transitions and N rows, one per MDD level, of $N + 1$ places. For $1 \leq i, j \leq N$, place p_{ij} is initially empty, and place p_{i0} contains the token (queen) still to be placed on row i of the chess board. Transition t_{ij} moves the queen from place p_{i0} to place p_{ij}, in competition with all other transitions t_{il}, for $l \neq j$. To encode the mutual exclusion of queens on the same column or diagonal, we employ *inhibitor arcs*. A correct placement of the N queens corresponds to a marking where all places p_{i0} are empty. Note that our state space contains *all* reachable markings, including those where queens n to N still need to be placed, for any n. In this model, locality is poor, since t_{ij} depends on levels 1 through i.
- The *dining philosophers* and *slotted ring models* [10, 25] are obtained by connecting N identical safe subnets in a circular fashion. The MDD has $N/2$ MDD levels (two subnets per level) for the former model and N levels (one subnet per level) for the latter. Events are either local or synchronize adjacent subnets, thus they span only two levels, except for those synchronizing subnet N with subnet 1, which span the entire MDD.
- The *round–robin mutex protocol* model [17] also has N identical safe subnets placed in a circular fashion, which represent N processes, each mapped to one MDD level. Another subnet models a resource shared by the N processes, giving raise to one more level, at the bottom of the MDD. There are no local events and, in addition to events synchronizing adjacent subnets, the model contains events synchronizing levels n and 1, for $2 \leq n \leq N + 1$.
- The *flexible manufacturing system* (FMS) model [22] has a fixed shape, but is parameterized by the initial number N of tokens in some places. We partition this model into 19 subnets, giving rise to a 19–level MDD with a moderate degree of locality, as events span from two to six levels.

Fig. 4 compares three variants of our new algorithm, using the LAZY policy or the STRICT policy with thresholds of 1 or 100 nodes per level, against the RECURSIVE algorithm in [22] and the FORWARDING algorithm in [10]. We ran SMART on a 800 MHz Intel Pentium III PC under Linux. On the left column, Fig. 4 reports the size of the state space for each model and value of N. The graphs in the middle and right columns show the peak and final number of MDD nodes and the CPU time in seconds required for the state–space generations, respectively.

For the models introduced above, our new approach is up to two orders of magnitude faster than [22] (a speed–up factor of 384 is obtained for the 1000 dining philosophers' model), and up to one order of magnitude faster than [10] (a speed–up factor of 38 is achieved for the slotted ring model with 50 slots). These results are observed for the LAZY variant of the algorithm, which yields the best runtimes; the STRICT policy also outperforms [22] and [10]. Furthermore, the gap keeps increasing as we scale up the models. Just as important, the saturation algorithm tends to use many fewer MDD nodes, hence less memory. This is most apparent in the FMS model, where the difference between the peak and

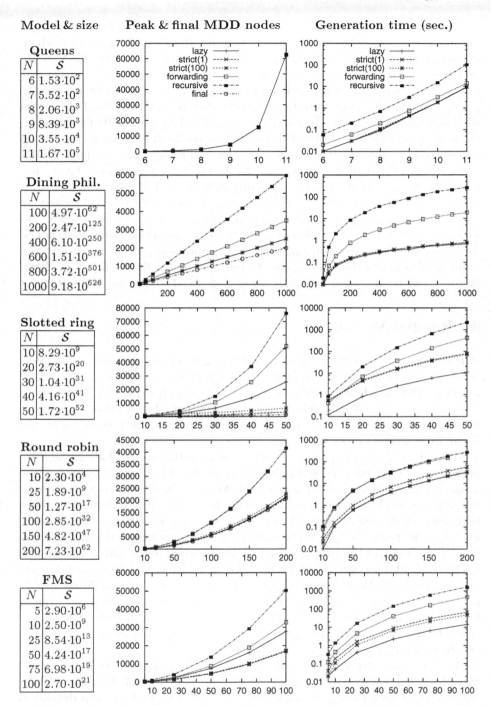

Fig. 4. State–space sizes, memory consumption, and generation times (a logarithmic scale is used on the y-axis for the latter). Note that the curves in the upper left diagram are almost identical, thus they visually coincide.

the final number of nodes is just a constant, 10, for any STRICT policy. Also notable is the reduced memory consumption for the slotted ring model, where the STRICT(1) policy uses 23 times fewer nodes compared to [22], for $N = 50$. In terms of absolute memory requiremen ts, the number of nodes is essentially proportional to bytes of memory. For reference, the largest memory consumption in our experiments using saturation was recorded at 9.7MB for the FMS model with 100 tokens; auxiliary data structures required up to 2.5MB for encoding the next–state functions and 200KB for storing the local state spaces, while the caches used less than 1MB. Other SMAR T structures account for another 4MB.

In a nutshell, regarding generation time, the best algorithm is LAZY, followed by STRICT(100), STRICT(1), FORWARDING, and RECURSIVE. With respect to memory consumption, the best algorithm is STRICT(1), followed by STRICT(100), LAZY, FORWARDING, and RECURSIVE. Thus, our new algorithm is consistently faster and uses less memory than previously proposed approac hes. The worst model for all algorithms is the queens problem, whic h has a very large number of nodes in the final representation of $\mathcal{S}$ and little locality. Even here, however, our algorithm uses slightly fewer nodes and is substantially faster.

6   Related W ork

W e already pointed out the significant differences of our approach to symbolic state–space generation when compared to traditional approaches reported in the literature [20], which are usually deployed for model checking [12]. Hence, for a fair comparison, we should extend our algorithmic implemen tation to that of a full model checker first. Doing this is out of the scope of the present paper and is currently work in progress.

The following paragraphs briefly survey some orthogonal and alternative approaches to improving the scalability of symbolic state–space generation and model–checking techniques. Regarding *synchronous hardware systems*, symbolic techniques using BDDs, which can represent state spaces in sublinear space, have been thoroughly investigated. Several implemen tations of BDDs are available; we refer the reader to [27] for a survey on BDD packages and their performance. To improve the time efficiency of BDD–based algorithms, breadth–first BDD–manipulation algorithms [4] have been explored and compared against the traditional depth–first ones. However, the results show no significant speed–ups, although breadth–first algorithms lead to more regular access patterns of hash tables and caches. Regarding space efficiency, a fair amount of work has concentrated on choosing appropriate variable orderings and on dynamically re–ordering variables [15].

For *asynchronous software systems*, symbolic techniques have been investigated less, and mostly only in the setting of P etri nets. For safe Petri nets, BDD–based algorithms for the generation of the reachability set have been developed in [25] via encoding each place of a net as a Boolean variable. These algorithms are capable of generating state spaces of large nets within hours. Recently, more efficient encodings of nets have been introduced, which take place invariants into account [24], although the underlying logic is still based on Boolean variables. In contrast, our work uses a more general version of decision diagrams, namely MDDs [18, 22], where more complex information is carried in eac h node of a diagram. In particular, MDDs allo w for a natural encoding of asynchronous system models, such as distributed embedded systems.

For the sake of completeness, we briefly mention some other BDD–based techniques exploiting the component–based structure of many digital systems. They include partial model checking [3], compositional model c hecking [19], partial–order reduction [2], and conjunctive decompositions [21]. Finally, also note that approaches to symbolic verification have been developed, which do not rely on decision diagrams but instead on arithmetic or algebra [1, 6, 26].

7   Conclusions and Future W ork

W e presented a novel approach for constructing the state spaces of asynchronous system models using MDDs. By a voiding to encode the global next–state function as an MDD, but splitting it in to several local next–state functions instead, we gained the freedom to choose the sequence of event firings, which controls the fixed–point iteration resulting in the desired global state space. Our central contribution is the development of an elegant iteration strategy based on saturating MDD nodes. Its utilit y is proved by experimental studies which show that our algorithm often performs sev eral orders of magnitude faster than most existing algorithms. Equally importan t, the peak size of the MDD is usually k ept close to its final size.

Regarding future work, we plan to employ our idea of saturation for implementing an MDD–based CTL model c hecker within SMART [11], to compare that model checker to state–of–the–art BDD–based model checkers, and to test our tool on examples that are extracted from real soft ware.

Acknowledgmen ts. We would like to thank the anonymous referees for their valuable commen ts and suggestions.

References

[1] P. Aziz Abdulla, P. Bjesse, and N. Eén. Symbolic reachability analysis based on SAT-solvers. In *TA CAS 2000*, vol. 1785 of *LN CS*, pp. 411–425. Springer-Verlag, 2000.

[2] R. Alur, R.K. Brayton, T.A. Henzinger, S. Qadeer, and S.K. Rajamani. Partial-order reduction in symbolic state-space exploration. In *CAV '97*, vol. 1254 of *LN CS*, pp. 340–351. Springer-Verlag, 1997.

[3] H.R. Andersen, J. Staunstrup, and N. Maretti. Partial model checking with RO-BDDs. In *TA CAS '97*, vol. 1217 of *LN CS*, pp. 35–49. Springer-Verlag, 1997.

[4] P. Ashar and M. Cheong. Efficient breadth–first manipulation of binary decision diagrams. In *ICCAD '94*, pp. 622–627. Computer Society Press, 1994.

[5] J.A. Bergstra, A. Ponse, and S.A. Smolka. *Handbook of Process Algebra*. Elsevier Science, 2000.

[6]   A. Biere, A. Cimatti, E.M. Clarke, and Y. Zhu. Symbolic model checking without
      BDDs. In *TACAS '99*, vol. 1579 of *LNCS*, pp. 193–207. Springer-Verlag, 1999.
[7]   R.E. Bryant. Graph-based algorithms for Boolean function manipulation. *IEEE
      Trans. on Comp.*, 35(8):677–691, 1986.
[8]   R.E. Bryant. Symbolic Boolean manipulation with ordered binary-decision dia-
      grams. *ACM Comp. Surveys*, 24(3):393–418, 1992.
[9]   J.R. Burch, E.M. Clarke, K.L. McMillan, D.L. Dill, and L.J. Hwang. Symbolic
      model checking: 10^{20} states and beyond. *Inform. & Comp.*, 98(2):142–170, 1992.
[10] G. Ciardo, G. Lüttgen, and R. Siminiceanu. Efficient symbolic state–space con-
      struction for asynchronous systems. In *ICATPN 2000*, vol. 1639 of *LNCS*, pp.
      103–122. Springer-Verlag, 2000.
[11] G. Ciardo and A.S. Miner. SMART: Simulation and Markovian Analyzer for
      Reliability and Timing. In *IPDS '96*, p. 60. IEEE Computer Society Press, 1996.
[12] A. Cimatti, E. Clarke, F. Giunchiglia, and M. Roveri. NuSMV: A new symbolic
      model verifier. In *CAV '99*, vol. 1633 of *LNCS*, pp. 495–499. Springer-Verlag,
      1999.
[13] E.M. Clarke, O. Grumberg, and D. Peled. *Model Checking*. MIT Press, 1999.
[14] R. Cleaveland, J. Parrow, and B. Steffen. The Concurrency Workbench: A
      semantics-based tool for the verification of finite-state systems. *TOPLAS*,
      15(1):36–72, 1993.
[15] M. Fujita, H. Fujisawa, and Y. Matsunaga. Variable ordering algorithms for or-
      dered binary decision diagrams and their evaluation. *IEEE Trans. on Computer–
      Aided Design of Integrated Circuits and Systems*, 12(1):6–12, 1993.
[16] A. Geser, J. Knoop, G. Lüttgen, B. Steffen, and O. Rüthing. Chaotic fixed point
      iterations. Techn. Rep. MIP-9403, Univ. of Passau, 1994.
[17] S. Graf, B. Steffen, and G. Lüttgen. Compositional minimisation of finite state
      systems using interface specifications. *Formal Asp. of Comp.*, 8(5):607–616, 1996.
[18] T. Kam, T. Villa, R.K. Brayton, and A. Sangiovanni-Vincentelli. Multi-valued
      decision diagrams: Theory and applications. *Multiple-Valued Logic*, 4(1–2):9–62,
      1998.
[19] K. Larsen, P. Pettersson, and W. Yi. Compositional and symbolic model-checking
      of real-time systems. In *RTSS '95*, pp. 76–89. Computer Society Press, 1995.
[20] K.L. McMillan. *Symbolic Model Checking: An Approach to the State-explosion
      Problem*. PhD thesis, Carnegie-Mellon Univ., 1992.
[21] K.L. McMillan. A conjunctively decomposed Boolean representation for symbolic
      model checking. In *CAV '96*, LNCS, pp. 13–24. Springer-Verlag, 1996.
[22] A.S. Miner and G. Ciardo. Efficient reachability set generation and storage using
      decision diagrams. In *ICATPN '99*, vol. 1639 of *LNCS*, pp. 6–25. Springer-Verlag,
      1999.
[23] T. Murata. Petri nets: Properties, analysis and applications. *Proc. of the IEEE*,
      77(4):541–579, 1989.
[24] E. Pastor and J. Cortadella. Efficient encoding schemes for symbolic analysis of
      Petri nets. In *DATE '98*, pp. 790–795. IEEE Computer Society Press, 1998.
[25] E. Pastor, O. Roig, J. Cortadella, and R.M. Badia. Petri net analysis using
      Boolean manipulation. In *ICATPN '94*, vol. 815 of *LNCS*, pp. 416–435. Springer-
      Verlag, 1994.
[26] M. Sheeran and G. Stålmarck. A tutorial on Stålmarck's proof procedure for
      propositional logic. *Formal Methods in System Design*, 16(1):23–58, 2000.
[27] B. Yang, R.E. Bryant, D.R. O'Hallaron, A. Biere, O. Coudert, G. Janssen, R.K.
      Ranjan, and F. Somenzi. A performance study of BDD–based model checking. In
      FMCAD '98, vol. 1522 of *LNCS*, pp. 255–289. Springer-Verlag, 1998.

Automated Test Generation from Timed Automata

Brian Nielsen and Arne Skou

Aalborg University
Department of Computer Science
Fredrik Bajersvej 7E
DK-9220 Aalborg, Denmark
E-mail: {bnielsen | ask}@cs.auc.dk

Abstract. Testing is the most dominating validation activity used by industry today, and there is an urgent need for improving its effectiveness, both with respect to the time and resources for test generation and execution, and obtained test coverage. We present a new technique for automatic generation of real-time black-box conformance tests for non-deterministic systems from a determinizable class of timed automata specifications with a dense time interpretation. In contrast to other attempts, our tests are generated using a coarse equivalence class partitioning of the specification. To analyze the specification, to synthesize the timed tests, and to guarantee coverage with respect to a coverage criterion, we use the efficient symbolic techniques recently developed for model checking of real-time systems. Application of our prototype tool to a realistic specification shows promising results in terms of both the test suite size, and the time and space used for test generation.

1   Background

Testing consists of executing a program or a physical system with the intention of finding undiscovered errors. In typical industrial projects, as much as a third of the total development time is spent on testing, and it therefore constitutes a significant portion of the cost of the product. Since testing is the most dominating validation activity used by industry today, there is an urgent need for improving its effectiveness, both with respect to the time and resources used for test generation and execution, and obtained coverage.

A potential improvement that is being examined by researchers is to make testing a formal method, and to provide tools that automate test case generation and execution. This approach has experienced some level of success: Formal specification and automatic test generation are being applied in practice [7, 20, 23, 26], and commercial test generations tools are emerging [17, 24]. Typically, a test generation tool inputs some kind of finite state machine description of the behavior required of the implementation. A formalized *implementation relation* describes exactly what it means for an implementation to be correct with respect to a specification. The tool interprets the specification or transforms it to a data structure appropriate for test generation, and then computes a set of test sequences. Since exhaustive testing is generally infeasible, it must select only a subset of tests for execution. Test selection can be based on manually stated test purposes, or on a coverage criterion of the specification or implementation.

T. Margaria and W. Yi (Eds.): TACAS 2001, LNCS 2031, pp. 343–357, 2001.

However, these tools do not address real-time systems, or only provide a limited support of testing the timing aspects. They often abstract away the actual time at which events are supplied or expected, or does not select these time instances thoroughly and systematically. To test real-time systems, the specification language must be extended with constructs for expressing real-time constraints, the implementation relation must be generalized to consider the temporal dimension, and the data structures and algorithms used to generate tests must be revised to operate on a potentially infinite set of states. Further, the test selection problem is worsened because a huge number of time instances are relevant to test. It is therefore necessary to make good decisions of *when* to deliver an input to the system, and *when* to expect an output. Since real-time systems are often safety critical, the time dimension must be tested thoroughly and systematically. Automated test generation for real-time systems is a fairly new research area, and only few proposals exist that deal with these problems.

This paper presents a new technique for automatic generation of timed tests from a restricted class of dense timed automata specifications. We permit both non-deterministic specifications and (black-box) implementations. Our implementation relation is therefore based on Hennessy's classical testing theory [21] for concurrent systems, which we have generalized to take time into account. We propose to select test cases by partitioning the state space into coarse grained equivalence classes which preserve essential timing and deadlock information, and select a few tests for each class. This approach is inspired by sequential black-box testing techniques frequently referred to as domain- or partition testing [3]. We regard the clocks of a timed specification as (oddly behaving) input parameters.

We present an algorithm and data structure for systematically generating timed Hennessy tests. The algorithm ensures that the specification will be covered such that the relevant Hennessy tests for each reachable equivalence class will be generated. To compute and cover the reachable equivalence classes, and to compute the timed test sequences, we employ efficient symbolic reachability techniques based on constraint solving that have recently been developed for model checking of timed automata [15, 6, 28, 4, 18].

In summary, the contributions of the paper are:

- We propose a *coarse* equivalence class partitioning of the state space and use this for *automatic* test selection.
- Other work on test generation for real-time systems allows deterministic specifications only, and use trace inclusion as implementation relation. We permit both *non-deterministic* specifications and (black-box) implementations, and use an implementation relation based on Hennessys testing theory that takes *deadlocks* into account.
- Application of the recently developed *symbolic reachability techniques* has to our knowledge not previously been applied to test generation.
- Our techniques are implemented in a prototype *test generation tool*, RTCAT.
- We provide *experimental data* about the efficiency of our technique. Application of RTCAT to one small and one larger case study results in encouragingly small test suites.

The remainder of the paper is organized as follows. Section 2 summarizes the related work. Section 3 introduces Hennessy tests, the specification language, and the symbolic reachability methods. Section 4 presents the test generation algorithm. Section 5 contains our experimental results. Section 6 concludes the paper and suggests future work.

2 Related Work

Springintveld et al. proved in [27] that *exhaustive* testing wrt. *trace equivalence* of *deterministic* timed automata with a *dense time* interpretation is theoretically possible, but highly infeasible in practice. Another result generating checking sequences for a discretized *deterministic* timed automaton is presented by En-Nouaary et al. in [16]. Although the required discretization step size $(1/(|X| + 2)$, where $|X|$ is the number of clocks) in [16] is more reasonable than [27], it still appears to be too small for most practical applications because too many tests are generated. Both of these techniques are based on the so called *region* graph technique due to Alur and Dill [1]. Clock regions are very fine-grained equivalence classes of clock valuations. We argue that coarser partitions are needed in practice. Further, our equivalence class partitioning as well as the used symbolic techniques are much less sensitive to the clock constants and the number of clocks appearing in the specification compared to the region construct.

Cardell-Oliver and Glover showed in [9] how to derive checking sequence from a *discrete time*, *deterministic*, timed transition system model. Their approach is implemented in a tool which is applied to a series of small cases. Their result indicates that the approach is feasible, at least for small systems, but problems arise if the implementation has more states than the specification. No test selection wrt. the time dimension is performed, i.e., an action is taken at all the time instances it is enabled.

Clarke and Lee [11, 12] also propose domain testing for real-time systems. Although their primary goal of using testing as a means of approximating verification to reduce the state explosion problem is different from ours, their generated tests could potentially be applied to physical systems as well. Their technique appear to produce much fewer tests than region based generation. The time requirements are specified as directed acyclic graphs called *constraint graphs*. Compared to timed automata this specification language appear very restricted, e.g., since their constraint graphs must be acyclic this only permits specification of finite behaviors. Their domains are "nice" linear intervals which are directly available in the constraint graph. In our work they are (convex) polyhedra of a dimension equal to the number of clocks.

Braberman et al. [8] describe an approach where a structured analysis/structured design real-time model is represented as a timed Petri net. Analysis methods for timed Petri nets based on constraint solving can be used to generate a symbolic *timed reachability tree* up to a predefined time bound. From this, specific timed test sequences can be chosen. This work shares with ours the generation of tests from a symbolic representation of the state space. We *guarantee coverage* according to a well defined criterion without reference to a predefined or explicitly given upper time bound. The paper also proposes other selection criteria, mostly based on the type and order of the events in the trace. However, they are concerned with generating *traces only*, and not on deadlock properties as we are. The paper describes no specific data structures or algorithms for constraint solving, and states no results regarding their efficiency. Their approach does not appear to be implemented.

Castanet et al. presents in [10] an approach where timed test *traces* can be generated from timed automata specifications. Test selection must be done *manually* through engineerer specified test purposes (one for each test) themselves given as deterministic acyclic timed automata. Such explicit test selection reduces the state explosion problem during test generation, but leaves a significant burden on the engineer. Further, the test sequences appear to be synthesized from paths available directly in an intermediate timed automaton formed by a synchronous product of the specification and the test purpose, and not from a (symbolic) interpretation thereof. This approach therefore risks generating tests which need not be passed by the implementation, or not finding a test satisfying the test purpose when one in fact exists.

Finally, test generation from a discrete time temporal logic is investigated by [20].

3 Preliminaries

3.1 Hennessy Tests

In Hennessy's testing theory [21] specifications $\mathcal{S}$ are defined as finite state labelled transition systems over a given finite set of actions Act. Also, it assumes that implementations $\mathcal{I}$ (and specifications) can be observed by finite tests $\mathcal{T}$ via a sequence of synchronous CCS-like communications. So, the execution of a test consists of a finite sequence of communications forming a so–called *computation* — denoted by $Comp(\mathcal{T} \parallel \mathcal{I})$ (or $Comp(\mathcal{T} \parallel \mathcal{S})$). A test execution is assigned a verdict (pass, fail or inconclusive), and a computation is *successful* if it terminates after an observation having the verdict pass.

Hennessy tests have the following abstract syntax $\mathcal{L}_{\text{tlts}}$: (1) **after** σ **must** A, (2) **can** σ, and (3) **after** σ **must** $\emptyset$, where $\sigma \in Act^*$ and $A \subseteq Act$. Informally, (1) is successful if at least one of the observations in A (called a *must set*) can be observed whenever the trace σ is observed, (2) is successful if σ is a prefix of the observed system, and (3) is successful is this is not the case (i.e. σ is not a prefix).

Definition 1. *The Testing Preorder* $\sqsubseteq_{\text{te}}$:

1. $\mathcal{S}$ **must** $\mathcal{T}$ *iff* $\forall \Sigma \in Comp(\mathcal{T} \parallel \mathcal{S}).$ Σ is successful.
2. $\mathcal{S}$ **may** $\mathcal{T}$ *iff* $\exists \Sigma \in Comp(\mathcal{T} \parallel \mathcal{S}).$ Σ is successful.
3. $\mathcal{S} \sqsubseteq_{\text{must}} \mathcal{I}$ *iff* $\forall \mathcal{T} \in \mathcal{L}_{\text{tlts}}.$ $\mathcal{S}$ **must** $\mathcal{T}$ *implies* $\mathcal{I}$ **must** $\mathcal{T}$
4. $\mathcal{S} \sqsubseteq_{\text{may}} \mathcal{I}$ *iff* $\forall \mathcal{T} \in \mathcal{L}_{\text{tlts}}.$ $\mathcal{S}$ **may** $\mathcal{T}$ *implies* $\mathcal{I}$ **may** $\mathcal{T}$
5. $\mathcal{S} \sqsubseteq_{\text{te}} \mathcal{I}$ *iff* $\mathcal{S} \sqsubseteq_{\text{must}} \mathcal{I}$ and $\mathcal{S} \sqsubseteq_{\text{may}} \mathcal{I}$

$\square$

Specifications and implementations are compared by the tests they pass. The must (may) preorder requires that every test that must (may) be passed by the specification must (may) also be passed by the implementation. In non-deterministic systems these notions do not coincide. The testing preorder defined formally in Definition 1 requires satisfaction on both the must and may preorders.

A must test **after** σ **must** A can be generated from a specification by 1) finding a trace σ in the specification, 2) computing the states that are reachable after that trace, and 3) computing a set of actions A that must be accepted in these states. To facilitate and ease systematic generation of all relevant tests, the specification can be converted to a success graph (or acceptance graph [13]) data structure. A success graph is a *deterministic* state machine trace equivalent to the specification, and whose nodes are labeled with the must sets holding in that node, the set of actions that are possible, and the actions that must be refused.

We propose a simple timed generalization of Hennessy's tests. In a timed test **after** σ **must** A (or **after** σ **must** $\emptyset$), σ becomes a timed trace (a sequence of alternating actions and time delays), after which an action in A must be accepted immediately. Similarly, a test **can** σ (**after** σ **must** $\emptyset$) becomes a timed trace satisfied if σ is (is not) a prefix trace of the observed system. A test will be modelled by an executable timed automaton whose locations are labelled with pass, fail, or inconclusive verdicts.

3.2 Event Recording Automata

Two of the surprising undecidability results from the theoretical work on timed languages described by timed automata is that 1) a non-deterministic timed automaton cannot in general be converted into a deterministic (trace) equivalent timed automaton, and 2) trace (language) inclusion between two non-deterministic timed automata is undecidable [2]. Thus, unlike the untimed case, deterministic and non-deterministic timed automata are not equally expressive. The Event Recording Automata model (ERA) was proposed by Alur, Fix, and Henzinger in [2] as a determinizable subclass of timed automata, which enjoys both properties.

Definition 2. *Event Recording Automaton:*

1. An ERA $\mathcal{M}$ is a tuple $\langle Act, N, l_0, E \rangle$ where Act is the set of actions, N is a (finite) set of locations, $l_0 \in N$ is the initial location, and $E \subseteq N \times G(X) \times Act \times N$ is the set of edges. We use the term *location* to denote a node in the automaton, and reserve the term *state* to denote the semantic state of the automaton also including clock values.
2. $X = \{x_a \mid a \in Act\}$ is the set of clocks. The guards $G(X)$ are generated by the syntax $g ::= \gamma \mid g \wedge g$ where γ is a constraint of the form $x_1 \sim c$ or $x_1 - x_2 \sim c$ with $\sim \in \{\leq, <, =, >, \geq\}$, c a non-negative integer constant, and $x_1, x_2 \in X$.

$\square$

Like a timed automaton, an ERA has a set of clocks which can be used in guards on actions, and which can be reset when an action is taken. In ERAs however, each action a is uniquely associated with a clock x_a, called the *event clock* of a. Whenever an action a is executed, the event clock x_a is automatically reset. No further clock assignments are permitted. The event clock x_a thus *records* the amount of time passed since the last occurrence of a. In addition, no internal τ actions are permitted. These restrictions are sufficient to ensure determinizability [2]. We shall finally also assume that all observable actions are *urgent* meaning that synchronization between the environment and automaton takes place immediately when the parties have enabled a pair of complementary actions. With non-urgent observable actions this synchronization delay would be unbounded.

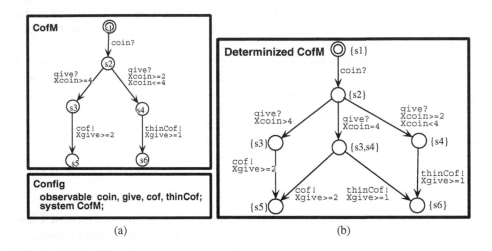

Fig. 3. *ERA specification of a coffee vending machine (a), and determinized machine (b).*

Figure 3a shows an example of a small ERA. It models a coffee vending machine built for impatient users such as busy researchers. When the user has inserted a coin (`coin`), he must press the give button (`give`) to indicate his eager to get a drink. If he is very eager, he presses `give` soon after inserting the coin, and the vending machine outputs thin coffee (`thinCof`); apparently, there is insufficient time to brew good coffee. If he waits more than four time units, he is certain to get good coffee (`cof`). If he presses `give` after exactly four time units, the outcome is non-deterministic.

In a *deterministic* timed automata, the choice of the next edge to be taken is uniquely determined by the automaton's current location, the input action, and the time the input event is offered. The determinization procedure for ERAs is given by [2], and is conceptually a simple extension of the usual subset construction used in the untimed case, only now the guards must be taken into account. Figure 3b illustrates the technique. Observe how the guards of the `give` edges from $\{s2\}$ become mutually exclusive such that either both are enabled, or only one of them is.

3.3 Symbolic Representation

Timed automata with a dense time interpretation cannot be analyzed by finite state techniques, but must rather be analyzed symbolically. Efficient symbolic reachability techniques have been developed for model checking of timed automata [15, 6, 28, 4, 18]. Specifically, we shall employ similar techniques as those developed for the UPPAAL tool [28, 4, 18].

The state of a timed automaton can be represented by the pair $\langle \bar{l}, \bar{u} \rangle$, where $\bar{l}$ is the automaton's current location (vector), and where $\bar{u}$ is the vector of its current clock values. A *zone* z is a conjunction of clock constraints of the form $x_1 \sim c$ or $x_1 - x_2 \sim c$ with $\sim \in \{\leq, <, =, >, \geq\}$, or equivalently, the solution set to these constraints. A symbolic state $[\bar{l}, z]$ represents a (infinite) set of states: $\{\langle \bar{l}, \bar{u} \rangle \mid \bar{u} \in z\}$. Forward reachability analysis starts in the initial state, and computes the symbolic states that can be reached by executing an action or a delay from an existing one. When a new symbolic state is included in one previously visited, no further exploration of the new state needs to take place. Forward reachability thus terminates when no new states can be reached. A concrete timed trace to a given state or set of states can be computed by back propagating its constraints along the symbolic path used to reach it, and by choosing specific time points along this trace.

Zones can be represented and manipulated efficiently by the *difference bound matrix* (DBM) data structure. DBMs were first applied to represent clock differences by Dill in [15]. A DBM represents clock difference constraints of the form $x_i - x_j \prec c_{ij}$ by a $(n + 1) \times (n + 1)$ matrix such that c_{ij} equals matrix element (i, j), where n is the number of clocks, and $\prec \in \{\leq, <\}$.

4   A Test Generation Algorithm

Our equivalence class partitioning and coverage criterion are introduced in Section 4.1. An algorithm for constructing the equivalence classes of a specification is provided in Section 4.2. The test generation algorithm is presented in Section 4.3.

4.1   State Partitioning

Since exhaustive testing is generally infeasible, it is important to systematically select and generate a limited amount of tests. A test *selection criterion* (or coverage criterion) is a rule describing what behavior or requirements should be tested. *Coverage* is a metric of completeness with respect to a test selection criterion. In industrial projects it is highly desirable that there is such a well defined metric of the testing thoroughness, and that this can be measured.

We propose a criterion based on partitioning the state space of the specification into coarse equivalence classes, and requiring that the test suite for each class makes a set of required observations of the implementation when it is expected to be in a state in that class. These observations are used to increase the confidence that the equivalence classes are correctly implemented. The partitioning and observations can be done in numerous ways, and some options are explored and formally defined in [22]. Given the partitioning stated in the following, the *stable edge set criterion* implemented in RTCAT requires that all relevant *simple deadlock* observations of the forms **after** ϵ **must** A (a *must* property), **after** a **must** $\emptyset$ (a *refusal* property), and **can** a (a *may* property) are made at least once in each class.

From each control location L (recall that a location in a deterministic automaton is the set of locations of the original automaton that the automaton can possibly occupy after a given trace), the clock valuations are partitioned such that two clock valuations belong to the same equivalence class iff they enable precisely the same edges from L, i.e. the states are equivalent wrt. the enabled edges. An equivalence class will be represented by a pair $[L, p]$, where L is a set of location vectors, and p is the inequation describing the clock constraints that must hold for that class, i.e., $[L, p]$ is the set of states $\{\langle L, \bar{u} \rangle \mid \bar{u} \in p\}$. Further, to obtain contiguous convex equivalence classes, and to reuse the existing efficient symbolic techniques, this constraint is rewritten to its disjunctive normal form. Each disjunct is treated as its own equivalence class. The partitioning from a given set of locations is defined formally in Definition 4.

Definition 4. *State partitioning* $\Psi(L)$:
Let L be a set of location vectors, $E(L)$ the set of edges starting in a location vector in L, E a set of edges, and $\Gamma(E) = \{g \mid \bar{l} \xrightarrow{g,a} \bar{l}' \in E\}$. Recall from Definition 2 that $G(X)$ denotes the guards generated by the syntax $g ::= \gamma \mid g \wedge g$ where γ is a basic clock constraint of the form $x_1 \sim c$ or $x_1 - x_2 \sim c$.

Let P be a constraint over clock inequations γ composed using *any* of the logical connectives $\wedge, \vee,$ or $\neg$. Let $\mathrm{DNF}(P)$ denote a function that rewrites constraint P to its equivalent disjunctive normal form, i.e., such that $\bigvee_i \bigwedge_j \gamma_{ij} = P$. Each conjunct in the disjunctive form can be written as a guard g in $G(X)$ by appropriately negating basic clock constraints where required. The disjunctive normal form can therefore be interpreted as a disjunction of guards such that $\bigvee_i g_i = \bigvee_i \bigwedge_j \gamma_{ij}$. The *set* of guards g_i whose disjunction equals the disjunctive normal form is denoted GDNF, i.e, $\mathrm{GDNF}(P_E) = \{g_i \in G(X) \mid \bigvee_i g_i = \mathrm{DNF}(P_E)\}$.

1. $\Psi(L) = \{P_E \mid E \in 2^{E(L)}\}$, where $P_E = \bigwedge_{g \in \Gamma(E)} g \wedge \bigwedge_{g \in \Gamma(E(L)-E)} \neg g$

2. $\Psi_{\mathrm{dnf}}(L) = \bigcup_{P_E \in \Psi(L)} \mathrm{GDNF}(P_E)$

$\square$

Our partitioning is based on the guards that actually occur in a specification, and is therefore much coarser than e.g., the region partitioning which is based on the guards that could possibly occur in an automaton according to the syntax in Definition 2. It also has the nice formal property that the states in the same equivalence class are also equivalent with respect the previously stated *simple deadlock* properties. This follows from the absence of τ actions, and since only enabled edges, and not the precise clock values, affects the satisfaction of these properties. In contrast, different equivalence classes typically satisfy different simple deadlock properties. It is therefore natural to check that the implementation matches these properties for each equivalence class. Using an even coarser partitioning is therefore likely to leave out significant timing and deadlock behavior.

Each equivalence class $[L, p]$ can now be decorated with the action sets M, C, R defined in Definition 5.

Definition 5. *Decorated Equivalence Classes*:
Define $\text{Must}([L, p]) = \{A \mid \exists \langle L, \bar{u} \rangle \in [L, p]. \langle L, \bar{u} \rangle \models \textbf{after } \epsilon \textbf{ must } A\}$
$\text{Sort}([L, p]) = \{a \mid \exists \langle L, \bar{u} \rangle \in [L, p]. \langle L, \bar{u} \rangle \xrightarrow{a}\}$

1. $M([L, p]) = \text{Must}[L, p]$.
2. $C([L, p]) = \text{Sort}([L, p])$.
3. $R([L, p]) = Act - \text{Sort}([L, p])$.

$\square$

M contains the sets of actions necessary to generate the must tests, C the may tests, and R the refusal tests for that class. Specifically, if σ is a timed trace leading to class $[L, p]$, and $A \in M([L, p])$ then **after** σ **must** A is a test to be passed for that class. So is **after** $\sigma \cdot a$ **must** $\emptyset$ if $a \in R([L, p])$, and **can** $\sigma \cdot a$ if $a \in C([L, p])$. The number of generated tests can be further reduced by removing tests that are logically passed by another test. The must sets can be reduced to $M([L, p]) = min_{\subseteq} \text{Must}[L, p]$. The actions observed during the execution of a must test can be removed from the may tests, i.e., $C([L, p]) = \text{Sort}([L, p]) - \bigcup_{A \in M([L, p])} A$.

4.2 Equivalence Class Graph Construction

We view the state space of the specification as a graph of equivalence classes. A node in this graph contains an equivalence class. An edge between two nodes are labeled with an observable action, and represents the possibility of executing an action in a state in the source node, waiting some amount of time, and thereby entering a state in the target node. The graph is constructed by starting from an existing node $[L, p]$ (initially the equivalence classes of the initial location), and then for each enabled action a, by computing the set of locations L' that can be entered by executing the a action from the equivalence class. Then the partitions p' of location L' can be computed according to Definition 4 (2). Every $[L', p']$ is then an a successor of $[L, p]$. It should be noted that only equivalence classes whose constraints have solutions need to be represented. The equivalence class graph is defined inductively in Definition 6. This definition can easily be turned into an algorithm for constructing the equivalence class graph.

Definition 6. *Equivalence Class Graph*:
The nodes and edges are defined inductively as:

1. The set $\{[L_0, p] \mid L_0 = \{\bar{l}_0\}, \ p \in \Psi_{\text{dnf}}(L_0), \text{ and } p \neq \emptyset\}$ are nodes.
2. if $[L, p]$ is a node, so is $[L', p']$, and $[L, p] \xrightarrow{a} [L', p']$ is an edge if $p' \neq \emptyset$, where $L' = \{\bar{l}' \mid \exists \bar{l} \in L. \bar{l} \xrightarrow{g,a} \bar{l}'\}$, and $p' \in \Psi_{\text{dnf}}(L')$.

$\square$

The construction algorithm implicitly determinizes the specification. The equivalence class graph preserves all timed traces of the specification, and furthermore preserves the required deadlock information for our timed Hennessy tests of the specification by the M, C, and R action sets stored in each node. The non-determinism found in the original specification is therefore not lost, but is represented differently, and in a way that is more convenient for test generation: A test is composed of a trace, a deadlock observation possible in the specification thereafter, and associated verdicts, and this information can be found simply by following a path in the equivalence class graph. All timed Hennessy tests that the specification passes can thus be generated from this graph. The explicit graph also makes it easy to ensure coverage according to the coverage criterion by marking the visited parts of the graph during test generation. The equivalence class graph for the coffee machine is depicted in Figure 7.

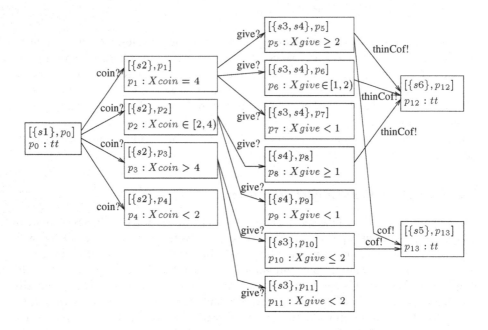

Fig. 7. *Equivalence class graph for the coffee machine.*

4.3   Overall Algorithm

The equivalence class graph preserved the necessary information for generating timed Hennessy tests. However, it also contains behavior and states *not* found in the specification, and using such behavior will result in irrelevant and unsound tests. An unsound test may produce the verdict fail even when the implementation conforms to the specification. According to the testing preorder only tests passed by the specification should be generated. To ensure soundness, only the traces and deadlock properties actually contained in the specification may be used in a generated test. To find these, we therefore interpret the specification symbolically, and generate the timed Hennessy tests from a representation of only the reachable states and behavior. Moreover, the use of reachability analysis gives a termination criterion for this interpretation; when completed it guarantees that every reachable equivalence class is represented by some symbolic state. Thus, we are able to guarantee coverage by inspecting the reached symbolic states.

Algorithm 8 presents the main steps of our generation procedure. Step 1 constructs the equivalence class graph as described in Section 4.1. The result of step 2 is a *symbolic reachability graph*. Nodes in this graph consist of symbolic states $[L, z/p]$ where L is a set of location vectors, and where z is a constraint characterizing a set of reachable clock valuations also in p, i.e., $z \subseteq p$. An edge represents that the target state is reachable by executing an action from the source state and then waiting some amount of time.

The nodes in the reachability graph are decorated according to Definition 5 in step 3. The boolean flag *toBeTested* indicates whether test cases should be made for this symbolic state or they should be omitted. If no tests should be made, the only actions executed from this state will be those necessary to reach other symbolic states. Normally this flag would be set only the first time an equivalence class is reached during the forward reachability analysis in the previous step. Subsequent passes over the same class would hence be ignored. This ensures that each simple deadlock property is only generated once per equivalence class, and thus reduces the number of produced test cases. Different settings of this flag permit other strategies to be easily implemented. Other strategies could be to test all reached symbolic states, or only test certain designated locations deemed critical by the user.

Algorithm 8. *Overall Test Case Generation Algorithm*:
input: ERA specification S.
output: A complete covering set of timed Hennessy tests to be passed.

1. Compute $S_p =$ Equivalence Class Graph(S).
2. Compute $S_r =$ Reachability Graph(S_p).
3. Label every $[L, z/p] \in S_r$ with the sets M, C, R, and boolean flag *toBeTested*.
4. Traverse S_r. For each $[L, z/p]$ in S_r:
   if *toBeTested*($[L, z/p]$) then enumerate tests:
   (a) Choose $\langle \bar{l}, \bar{u} \rangle \in [L, z/p]$
   (b) Compute a concrete timed trace $\sigma \in S_r$ from $\langle \bar{l}_0, \bar{0} \rangle$ to $\langle \bar{l}, \bar{u} \rangle$.
   (c) Make test cases to be passed:
       if $A \in M([L, p])$ then **after** σ **must** A is a test.
       if $a \in C([L, p])$ then **can** $\sigma \cdot a$ is a test.
       if $a \in R([L, p])$ then **after** $\sigma \cdot a$ **must** $\emptyset$ is a test.

$\square$

Step 4 contains the generation process itself. If a particular point in the symbolic state is of interest, such as an extreme value, this must be computed (step 4a). When a point has been chosen, a trace leading to it from the initial state is computed (step 4b). Finally, in step 4c, a test case can be generated for each of the must, may, and refusal properties holding in that symbolic state, and can finally be output as a test automaton in whatever output format is desired.

It should be noted that the above algorithm generates individual timed Hennessy tests. In general, it is desirable to compose several of these properties into fewer tree structured tests. To facilitate test composition, the traversal and construction of test cases in step 4 should be done differently. A composition algorithm is implemented in RTCAT. Furthermore, the graphs in steps 1 and 2 can be constructed on-the-fly. Since not all equivalence classes may be reachable, this could result in a smaller graph and less memory use during its construction.

5   Experimental Results

RTCAT accepts ERA specifications in AUTOGRAPH format [25]. A specification may consist of several ERAs operating in parallel, and communicating via shared clocks and integer variables, but no internal synchronization is allowed as stated in Section 3.2. Other features are described in [22]. RTCAT occupies about 22K lines of C++ code, and is based on code from a simulator for timed automata (part of an old version of the UPPAAL toolkit [19]). Its AUTOGRAPH file format parser was reused with some minor modifications to accommodate the ERA syntax. Also its DBM implementation was reused with some added operations for zone extrapolation and clock scaling.

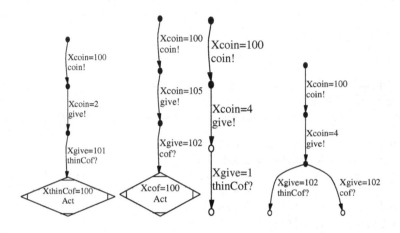

Fig. 9. Example tests generated from the coffee machine in Figure 3. Filled states are **fail** states, and unfilled states are **pass** states. Diamonds contain actions to be refused at the time indicated at the its top. Act is an acronym for all actions.

Figure 9 shows some examples of generated test cases from the coffee machine specification in Figure 3a. RTCAT has been configured to select test points in the interior of the equivalence classes. To analyze the feasibility of our techniques we have created an ERA version of the frequently studied Philips audio protocol [5, 4] and a simple token passing protocol, applied RTCAT, and measured the number and length of the generated tests, the number of reached (convex) equivalence classes and symbolic states, and the space and time needed to generate the tests and output them to a file. The ERA models can be found in [22]. The platform used in the experiment consists of a Sun Ultra-250 workstation running Solaris 5.7. The machine is equiped with 1 GB RAM and 2x400 MHz CPU's. No extra compiler optimizations was done to the code. The results are tabulated in Table 10.

The size of the produced test suites is in all combinations quite manageable, and constitute test suites that could easily be executed in practice. There is thus a large margin allowing for more test points per equivalence class, or longer tests. Moreover, coverage of even larger specifications can also be obtained. Since the reached symbolic states are labeled *toBeTested* during construction of the reachability graph, the construction order may influence the number and length of tests. Our results show that depth first construction generates slightly fewer tests than breadth first, but also considerably longer test suites. This suggests that breadth first should be used when the most economic covering test suite is desired, and that depth first should be used when a covering test suite is desired that also checks longer sequences of interactions.

	Breadth First				Depth First			
Specification	CofM	Phil (R)	Phil (S)	Token^7	CofM	Phil (R)	Phil (S)	Token^7
Equivalence Classes	14	60	47	42	14	60	47	42
Symbolic States	17	71	97	15427	17	85	98	7283
Time (s)	1	1	2	541	1	2	2	158
Memory (MB)	5	5	5	40	5	5	5	24
C-Number of Tests	16	97	68	71	16	86	67	60
C-Total Length	45	527	393	574	45	1619	487	5290
I-Number of Tests	22	118	85	84	22	118	85	84
I-Total Length	58	614	467	665	58	2103	587	6321

Table 10. *Experimental results from generating tests from the coffee machine, the Philips audio protocol receiver component, sender component with collision detection, and 7-node token passing protocol. I=individually generated tests (algorithm 8), C=composed tests.*

The tabulated figures on the space and time consumption is the maximum observed; generally test composition takes slightly longer and uses a little extra space. For the first three specifications, the space and time consumption is quite low, and indicates that fairly large specifications can be handled. However, we have also encountered a problem with our current implementation which occurs for some specifications (such as the token passing protocol), where our application of the symbolic reachability techniques becomes a bottleneck. When the specification uses a large set of active clocks (one per node to measure the token holding time for that node plus one auxiliary in the example), we experience that a large number of symbolic states is constructed in order to terminate the forward reachability analysis. Consequently, an extreme amount of memory is used to guarantee complete coverage. It is important to note that the size of the produced test suite is still quite reasonable. We believe that this problem can be alleviated by applying the reachability analysis on the original specification automaton rather than as presently done on the equivalence class graph. This should result in larger and fewer symbolic states. Further, more sophisticated clock reduction algorithms could be applied [14], e.g., in the token passing protocol only one node may hold the token at a time, and thus one clock suffices.

6 Conclusions and Future Work

This paper presented a new technique for generating real-time tests from a restricted, but determinizable class of timed automata. The underlying testing theory is Hennessy's tests lifted to include timed traces. A principal problem is to generate a sufficiently small test suite that can be executed in practice while maintaining a high likelihood of detecting unknown errors and obtaining the desired level of coverage. In our technique, the generated tests are selected on the basis of a coarse equivalence class partitioning of the state space of the specification. We employ the efficient symbolic techniques developed for model checking to synthesize the timed tests, and to guarantee coverage with respect to a coverage criterion. The techniques are implemented in a prototype tool. Application thereof to a realistic specification shows promising results. The test suite is quite small, and is constructed quickly, and with a reasonable memory usage. Our experiences, however, also indicate a problem with our application of the symbolic reachability analysis, which should be addressed in future implementation work. Compared to previous work based on the region graph technique, our approach appear advantageous.

Much other work remain to be done. In particular we are examining the possibilities for generalizing our specification language. It will be important to allow specification and effective test of timing uncertainty, i.e., that an event must be produced or accepted at some (unspecified) point in an interval. Further, it should be possible to specify environment assumptions and to take these into account during test generation. Finally, our techniques should be examined with real applications, and the generated test should be executed against real implementations.

References

[1] Rajeev Alur and David L. Dill. A Theory of Timed Automata. *Theoretical Computer Science*, 126(2):183–235, 25 April 1994.

[2] Rajeev Alur, Limor Fix, and Thomas A. Henzinger. Event-Clock Automata: A Determinizable Class of Timed Automata. In *6th Conference on Computer Aided Verification*, 1994. Also in LNCS 818.

[3] Boris Beizer. *Software Testing Techniques*. International Thompson Computer Press, 1990. 2nd edition, ISBN 1850328803.

[4] Johan Bengtsson, W. O. David Griffioen, Kåre J. Kristoffersen, Kim G. Larsen, Fredrik Larsson, Paul Petterson, and Wang Yi. Verification of an Audio Protocol with Bus Collision using UppAal. In *9th Intl. Conference on Computer Aided Verification*, pages 244–256, 1996. LNCS 1102.

[5] Doeko Bosscher, Indra Polak, and Frits Vaandrager. Verification of an Audio Protocol. TR CS-R9445, CWI, Amsterdam, The Netherlands, 1994. Also in LNCS 863, 1994.

[6] Ahmed Bouajjani, Stavros Tripakis, and Sergio Yovine. On-the-fly Symbolic Model-Checking for Real-Time Systems. In *1997 IEEE Real-Time Systems Symposium, RTSS'97*, San Fransisco, USA, December 1996. IEEE Computer Society Press.

[7] Marius Bozga, Jean-Claude Fernandez, Lucian Ghirvu, Claude Jard, Thierry Jéron, Alain Kerbrat, Pierre Morel, and Laurent Mounier. Verification and Test Generation for the SS-COP Protocol. *Science of Computer Programming*, 36(1):27–52, 2000.

[8] V. Braberman, M. Felder, and M. Marré. Testing Timing Behaviors of Real Time Software. In *Quality Week 1997. San Francisco, USA.*, pages 143–155, April-May 1997 1997.

[9] Rachel Cardell-Oliver and Tim Glover. A Practical and Complete Algorithm for Testing Real-Time Systems. In *5th international Symposium on Formal Techniques in Real Time and Fault Tolerant Systems (FTRTFT'98)*, pages 251–261, September 14–18 1998. Also in LNCS 1486.

[10] R. Castanet, Ousmane Koné, and Patrice Laurençot. On the fly test generation for real-time protocols. In *International Conference in Computer Communications and Networks*, Lafayette, Lousiana, USA, October 12-15 1998. IEEE Computer Society Press.

[11] Duncan Clarke and Insup Lee. Testing Real-Time Constraints in a Process Algebraic Setting. In *17th International Conference on Software Engineering*, 1995.

[12] Duncan Clarke and Insup Lee. Automatic Test Generation for the Analysis of a Real-Time System: Case Study. In *3rd IEEE Real-Time Technology and Applications Symposium*, 1997.

[13] Rance Cleaveland and Matthew Hennessy. Testing Equivalence as a Bisimulation Equivalence. *Formal Aspects of Computing*, 5:1–20, 1993.

[14] Conrado Daws and Sergio Yovine. Reducing the Number of Clock Variables of Timed Automata. In *1996 IEEE Real-Time Systems Symposium, RTSS'96*, Washington, DC, USA, december 1996. IEEE Computer Society Press.

[15] David L. Dill. Timing Assumptions and Verification of Finite-State Concurrent Systems. In *International Workshop on Automatic Verification Methods for Finite State Systems*, pages 197–212, Grenoble, France, June 1989. LNCS 407.

[16] Abdeslam En-Nouaary, Rachida Dssouli, and Ferhat Khendek. Timed Test Cases Generation Based on State Characterization Technique. In *19th IEEE Real-Time Systems Symposium (RTSS'98)*, pages 220–229, December 2–4 1998.

[17] Alain Kerbrat, Thierry Jéron, and Roland Groz. Automated Test Generation from SDL Specifications. In *Ninth SDL Forum*, 21-25 June 1999. Montral, Qubec, Canada.

[18] Kim G. Larsen, Fredrik Larsson, Paul Petterson, and Wang Yi. Efficient Verification of Real-Time Systems: Compact Data Structures and State-Space Reduction. In *18th IEEE Real-Time Systems Symposium*, pages 14–24, 1997.

[19] Kim G. Larsen, Paul Pettersson, and Wang Yi. UppAal in a Nutshell. *International Journal on Software Tools for Technology Transfer*, 1(1):134–152, 1997.

[20] Dino Mandrioli, Sandro Morasca, and Angelo Morzenti. Generating Test Cases for Real-Time Systems from Logic Specifications. *ACM Transactions on Computer Systems*, 13(4):365–398, 1995.

[21] R. De Nicola and M.C.B Hennessy. Testing Equivalences for Processes. *Theoretical Computer Science*, 34:83–133, 1984.

[22] Brian Nielsen. *Specification and Test of Real-Time Systems*. PhD thesis, Department of Computer Science, Aalborg University, Denmark, april 2000.

[23] Jan Peleska and Bettina Buth. Formal Methods for the International Space Station ISS. In E.-R. Olderog and B. Steffen, editors, *Correct System Design*, pages 363–389, 1999. Springer LNCS 1710.

[24] Jan Peleska and Cornelia Zahlten. Test Automation for Avionic Systems and Space Technology. In *GI Working Group on Test, Analysis and Verification of Software*, 1999. Munich, Extended Abstract.

[25] Annie Ressouche, Robert de Simone, Amar Bouali, and Valérie Roy. The FCTOOLS User Manual. Technical Report ftp://ftp-sop.inria.fr/meije/verif/fc2.userman.ps, INRIA Sophia Antipolis.

[26] Holger Schlingloff, Oliver Meyer, and Thomas Hülsing. Correctness Analysis of an Embedded Controller. In *Data Systems in Aerospace (DASIA99). ESA SP-447, Lisbon, Portugal*, pages 317–325, 1999.

[27] J. Springintveld, F. Vaandrager, and P.R. D'Argenio. Testing Timed Automata. TR CTIT 97-17, University of Twente, 1997. To appear in *Theoretical Computer Science*.

[28] Wang Yi, Paul Pettersson, and Mats Daniels. Automatic Verification of Real-Time Communicating Systems by Constraint Solving. In *7th Int. Conf. on Formal Description Techniques*, pages 223–238, 1994. North-Holland.

Testing an Intentional Naming Sheme Using Genetic Algorithms

Sarfraz Khurshid

Laboratory for Computer Science
Massachusetts Institute of Technology
Cambridge, MA 02139
khurshid@lcs.mit.edu

Abstract. Various attempts have been made to use genetic algorithms
(GAs) for software testing, a problem that consumes a large amount
of time and effort in software development. We demonstrate the use of
GAs in automating testing of complex data structures and methods for
manipulating them, which to our knowledge has not been successfully
displayed before on non-trivial software structures. We evaluate the effectiveness of our GA-based test suite generation technique by applying
it to test the design and implementation of the Intentional Naming System (INS), a new scheme for resource discovery and service location in a
dynamic networked environment. Our analysis using GAs reveals serious
problems with both the design of INS and its inventors' implementation.

1 Introduction

Genetic algorithms [7] are a family of computational models inspired b y biological evolution. These algorithms encode a potential solution to a specific problem
on a simple chromosome-like data structure and apply recombination operators
to these structures so as to preserve critical information. Genetic algorithms are
often viewed as function optimizers, although the range of problems to which
they have been applied is quite broad [19].

There have been various attempts ([3], [6], [10], [14], [16], [18], [20]) to use
genetic algorithms in software testing, a problem that is very labor intensive
and expensive [2]. In this paper we explore the use of genetic algorithms in
automating testing of complex data structures used in naming infrastructures
for dynamic networks of computers and devices.

Naming is a fundamental issue in distributed systems that is growing in
importance as the number of directly accessible systems and resources grows to
the point that it is difficult to discover the (names of) objects of interest. The
difference between a true confederation of computing services and a collection of
networked centralized computing systems lies in the system's abilit y to provide
a uniform and location independent way of accessing and naming resources.

Testing architectures that provide service location and resource discovery
using location independent names in a worldwide internetwork is clearly a challenging task.

T. Margaria and W. Yi (Eds.): TACAS 2001, LNCS 2031, pp. 358–372, 2001.
© Springer-Verlag Berlin Heidelberg 2001

1.1   Software Testing

Studies indicate that software testing consumes more than fifty percent of the cost of software development [2]. This percentage is even higher for critical software, such as that used for avionics systems. As software becomes more pervasive and is used more often to perform critical tasks, it will be required to be of higher quality. Unless we can find more efficient ways to perform effective testing, the percentage of development costs devoted to testing will increase significantly.

Generation of test data to satisfy testing requirements is a particularly labor-intensive component of the testing process. For a given testing requirement, test data generation techniques try to identify a program input that will satisfy the selected testing criteria. If the process of test data generation is automated, significant reductions in the cost of software development could be achieved.

Various test data generation techniques have been automated. *Goal-oriented* test data generators select inputs to execute the selected goal irrespective of the path taken (e.g. [13]). *Random* test data generators use some distribution to select random inputs (e.g. [15]). *Structural* or *path-oriented* test data generators make use of the program's control flow graph to select a particular path, and use a technique such as symbolic evaluation to generate test data for the selected path (e.g. [5], [17]). *Intelligent* test data generators typically guide the search for new test data using complex analyses of the code (e.g. [4], [14]).

In this paper we present a technique for automating test data generation using a genetic algorithm, that aims at testing structural properties of the data structures involved in the program and their associated methods. The genetic algorithm conducts its search by constructing new test data (*next generation*) from previously generated test data (*current generation*) that are evaluated as good candidates. The algorithm evaluates the candidate test data based on the code coverage achieved, the control points of interest executed or avoided, and the required properties satisfied.

Our GA-based testing technique has four essential components. The first part is to identify methods to test and global properties of interest concerning these methods. The second part is to determine a genetic encoding such that *each* test datum encodes a *sequence* of operations of interest and their parameters.

The third component involves computing the fitness of test data and has three subparts. First, we trivially modify the methods identified in the first part to reward test data that access them by incrementing their score per line of code executed in a method of interest. Second, we identify control points in code that are of particular interest and either add a bonus score or a penalty for executing that point. The rationale for doing so is explained in Section 3.2. Third, we award bonus points to test data that possess the properties identified in part one. This bonus or penalty is considerably greater than the score given per statement of execution in the first part.

The final component of our framework is to apply standard genetic operators of evaluation, crossover, and mutation on the genetic representation of test data in the current generation and move onto the next generation.

An advantage of our approach is that since the genetic representation of each test datum represents a *sequence* of operations of interest, it is straightforward to test the behavior of a program when such operations are interleaved.

Another benefit is due to the idea of using *barriers* (i.e. awarding a large negative penalty for executing certain control points) as this induces new test data to evolve and identify bugs that have not already been discovered, without having to fix the ones previously found.

Our framework applied to generate automated test data for the Intentional Naming System (INS) [1] (Section 2), a new scheme for resource discovery and service location in a dynamic networked environment, reveals serious flaws in both the design and implementation [21] of INS. These flaws, to our knowledge, were not previously known to the INS inventors. In particular, we establish that in the INS naming architecture, addition of a new service can cause a situation where the system makes valid services inaccessible to clients seeking them.

In the next section, the background on INS is given. Then, the genetic algorithm for test data generation is described. Following that, the results from testing the INS implementation are presented. Next, the technique presented is compared to related work. Finally, conclusions and future work are given.

2   INS Background

One particular service discovery solution in dynamic networked environments is the *Intentional Naming System* (INS) [1], which allows services to describe and refer to each other using names which are *intentional*. These names describe a set of properties that the services should have rather than specify a low-level network location. The idea is to allow applications to refer to *what* service they want rather than *where* in the network topology the service resides. It also allows applications to communicate seamlessly with end-nodes, despite changes in the mapping from name to end-node addresses during the session.

INS comprises applications and *intentional name resolvers* (INRs). Applications may be clients or services with services providing the functionality or data required by clients. Like IP routers or conventional name servers, INRs route requests from clients to appropriate locations, using a database that maps service descriptions to their physical network locations.

An INR provides a few fundamental operations. When a service wants to advertise itself – because, for example, it has come online after being down, or because its functionality has been extended – it calls the *Add-Name* operation to register the service against an advertisement describing it. Applications make queries by calling the resolvers *Lookup-Name* operation.

Intentional names are implemented in INS using *name-specifiers* that represent both queries and advertisements. A name-specifier (Figure 1) is an arrangement of alternating levels of *attributes* and *values* in a tree structure. In Figure 1, hollow circles identify attributes and filled circles identify values. Attributes represent categories in which an object can be classified. Each attribute has a

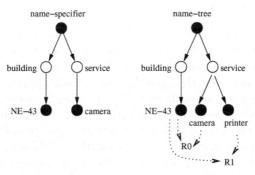

Lookup-Name (name-tree, name-specifier) = {R0}

Fig. 1. Example of a *Lookup-Name* operation

corresponding value that is the objects classification within that category. A wild-card may be used in place of a value to show that any value is acceptable.

An attribute together with its value form an *av-pair*; each av-pair has a set of child av-pairs that specialize it to further describe the object. Orthogonal av-pairs specializing the same av-pair are siblings in the tree. The name-specifier in Figure 1 describes an object in building NE-43 that provides a camera service.

An INR stores its information in a database called a *name-tree* (Figure 1). A name-tree resembles a super-positioning of several name-specifiers, and stores the correspondence between name-specifiers and *name-records*, which include the IP addresses of services advertising the name.

A name-tree also has two fundamental building blocks, an *attribute-node* and a *value-node*. A value-node can have several attribute-nodes as children. Similarly, an attribute-node can have several value-nodes as children, each representing a distinct value the name-tree knows.

A value-node that corresponds to a leaf av-pair of an advertised name-specifier also contains a pointer to the relevant name-record. In Figure 1 this is represented by broken arrows, and the name-tree shown stores two objects, one (i.e. R0) that provides a camera service in NE-43 and the other one (i.e. R1) that provides a printer service in the same building.

The name-records for a name-specifier are retrieved from a name-tree using the *Lookup-Name* operation. An algorithm for this operation is given in pseudo-code in the published description of INS [1], and is replicated in Appendix A. When it is invoked on the name-specifier and name-tree in Figure 1, R0 is returned since the value of attribute 'service' sought by the client (i.e. camera) does not match that provided by R1 (i.e. printer).

An implementation of the naming architecture of INS appears in [21]. About 1400 lines of Java code implement *Lookup-Name* and *Add-Name* and the relevant data structures and methods, and another 900 lines constitute the testing code used by INS inventors.

3   The Stochastic Approach

A *genetic algorithm* is an optimization heuristic that emulates natural processes like selection and mutation in natural evolution. It evolves solutions to problems that have large solution spaces and are not amenable to traditional search or optimization techniques. Genetic algorithms have been applied to a broad range of learning and optimization problems [19] since their inception by Holland [7].

Typically a genetic algorithm starts with a random population of solutions (*chromosomes*). Through a *recombination* process and *mutation* operators it evolves the population toward an optimal solution. Achieving an optimal solution is not guaranteed and the task is to design the process to maximize the likelihood of generating such a solution. The first step is the evaluation of *fitness* of solutions in the current population to act as parents in the next generation. Solutions are considered more fit than others if they are closer to an optimal.

Upon evaluation, several solutions are selected and solutions with a higher value of fitness are more likely to get selected. After selection, the parents are recombined and mutated to generate offsprings. The new population is thus formed and the cycle is repeated.

The processes of evaluation, selection, recombination and mutation are usually performed many times in a genetic algorithm. Selection, recombination, and mutation are generic operations in any genetic algorithm and have been throughly investigated in literature. On the other hand, evaluation is problem specific and relates directly to the structure of the solutions. Therefore, in a genetic algorithm a major issue is to design the structure of solutions and the method of evaluation. Among other issues are size of the population, portion of population taking part in recombination, and mutation rate.

Our GA-based testing technique has four essential components:

· identification of methods to test and their global properties of interest;
· framing a genetic encoding such that each chromosome represents a *sequence* of operations of interest and their parameters;
· formulation of the fitness function, which has three subparts:
    ·· (trivial) modification of the methods identified in part one to reward chromosomes that access them by incrementing the score of a chromosome per line of code it executes in such a method;
    ·· identification of control points of interest in code and addition of either a bonus score or a penalty for causing execution of that point;
    ·· awarding bonus points to chromosomes that possess the properties identified in part one. The bonus or penalty is considerably greater than the score given per statement of execution in the first part;
· application of standard evaluation, crossover, and mutation operators on the chromosomes in the current generation and move onto the next generation.

An optimal chromosome would therefore encode a test suite that invokes a sequence of operations of interest, and satisfies the desired properties with regards to that sequence, executes or avoids executing control points of interest as required, and gives maximal code coverage. The following sections explain these notions in detail.

Name–Specifier 0	Name–Specifier 1	Name–Specifier 2	Name–Specifier 3	Name–Specifier 4

0   170

Fig. 2. Representation of a test suite

3.1   Genetic Encoding

As a very first step of our testing technique we identify methods that we want
to test. The most interesting operations in the naming architecture of INS are
Lookup-Name and *Add-Name*. These methods in turn determine the genetic encoding and fitness function that evaluates the chromosomes.

The most obvious way to test the behavior of operations is to have a chromosome represent which operation to perform along with its parameters. So if
we were to test name resolution of INS, a chromosome could encode a *Lookup-
Name* or *Add-Name* operation along with the name-tree and the name-specifier
on which to perform that operation.

A problem with this representation is that it is not immediate how to observe
the combined effect of a sequence of *dependent* operations. For example, in INS,
if for a given name-tree we want to determine the effect of repeated additions
on the resolution of a fixed name-specifier in the resulting name-trees, it would
not be feasible to do so.

An alternative representation is to have a chromosome denote a sequence
of operations with some parameter having an implicit representation. In the
case of INS, a chromosome could then encode successive *Lookup-Name* and *Add-
Name* operations with only *one* parameter. It represents that sequence of operations starting from an empty name-tree. So for example it could encode[1]

$$add\ \mathcal{N}_1,\ lookup\ \mathcal{N}_2,\ add\ \mathcal{N}_3,\ add\ \mathcal{N}_4,\ lookup\ \mathcal{N}_5$$

to represent a sequence of operations that starts with a new name-tree $\mathcal{T}_0$, adds
$\mathcal{N}_1$ to $\mathcal{T}_0$ to result in name-tree $\mathcal{T}_1$, resolves $\mathcal{N}_2$ with respect to $\mathcal{T}_1$, and so on.
This way we could evaluate how a chromosome performs based on the results
generated by each of the *Add-Name* or *Lookup-Name* operation that it induces.

We use a slight modification of this representation in our framework for
testing INS. In particular, a chromosome denotes five name-specifiers, last four of
which are to be inserted in an empty name-tree one by one, and the first one is to
be resolved following each insertion. So, for example, the chromosome in Figure
2 would start execution by creating a new name-tree, then $\mathcal{N}_1$ would be added
to the name-tree, followed by resolution of $\mathcal{N}_0$, addition of $\mathcal{N}_2$, resolution of $\mathcal{N}_0$,
and so on. Notice that this structure is particularly well suited for investigating
the effect that addition has on resolution, and there is no need to have an explicit
encoding for a name-tree.

---

[1] For convenience, we write $\mathcal{N}_i$ for Name-Specifier i

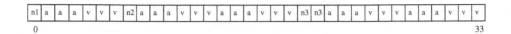

0   33

Fig. 3. Genetic representation of a name-specifier

In order to represent a name-specifier we need to determine a suitable number of bits that capture the behavior of methods under scrutiny. Due to the recursive nature of *Lookup-Name* and *Add-Name* it is necessary to have a representation that induces some recursive calls. We use two way branching at the top level and allow one of the children to branch two way, while the other child may only have one further child.

The name-specifier in the top right corner of Figure 5 depicts a *full* name-specifier that can be encoded like this. Moreover, we select the attributes and values from a pool of 8 attributes, {a0,...,a7}, and 8 values, {v0,...,v7}. This gives us sufficient freedom to perform our testing using diverse test cases.

We use 34 bits (Figure 3) to represent a name-specifier and thus, a chromosome can be represented using 170 bits as is shown in Figure 2. In Figure 3, 'n1' represents 1 or 2 way branching at top level, 'n2' determines whether the first child has a child, 'n3n3' determines whether the second child has 0,1, or 2 children. The sequence 'aaa' contains an attribute and 'vvv' contains a value.

Figure 4 illustrates a sample chromosome and presents the results of the test sequence it would induce. Name-specifiers1–4 are inserted one by one into an empty name-tree to get the name-tree shown in the bottom right corner. Name-specifier0 is resolved after each addition and the resulting name-records are displayed in the bottom line. Notice that during this execution as more advertisements are added to the name-tree, resolution returns more name-records[2].

3.2   Fitness Function

To evaluate the performance of a chromosome, we define our fitness function to have two components. The first component, $\mathcal{F}_s$, only computes the number of statements that are executed while simulating the sequence of operations encoded in a chromosome. In the case of INS, we add a statement of the form **score++;** with every statement of the *Lookup-Name* procedure. This step can easily be automated. Notice, that based solely on this fitness function we can start our experimentation and the fittest chromosomes would try to maximize code coverage of this method.

However, simply achieving maximal code coverage is not our goal. The second component of our fitness function, $\mathcal{F}_d$, is determined by the kind of tests we would like to perform. It uses two simple ideas.

Firstly, in order to induce chromosomes to explore certain aspects of the system being tested, we award *bonus* reward to chromosomes that do so. This could

---

[2] The result of *Lookup-Name* is treated empty if it is {} or {*}

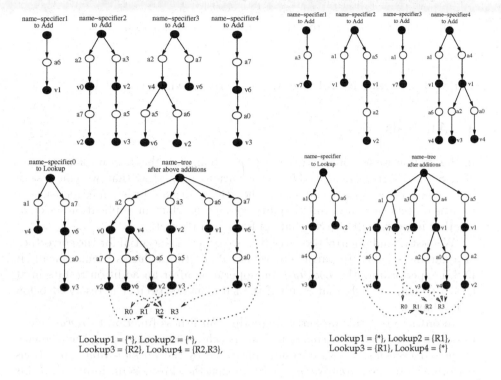

Fig. 4. Visualisation of a sample chromosome to test INS. Lookupi denotes the result of ith call to *Lookup-Name* .

Fig. 5. Revealing a flaw in the INS implementation

involve control points in the code that are more susceptible to lead to run-time errors, or global properties of the test sequence represented by a chromosome like for example, rewarding chromosomes that result in differing results of *Lookup-Name* operation. The chromosome presented in Figure 4 was in fact produced by rewarding 10 extra points per pairwise different *Lookup-Name* results that it produced.

Secondly, we introduce *barriers* in the form of penalty points for chromosomes that execute parts of the code that we have already determined no longer to be interesting from the point of view of further testing. This concept of using barrier functions turns out to be a very powerful idea as we demonstrate in the next section.

The fact that we can use it to evolve chromosomes that do *not* visit certain parts of the code means that once we discover a bug, we do not have to fix it immediately in order to proceed with our testing. Instead we can just introduce a *negative* score at that control point and the testing system would evolve to test other parts of the code that can be executed independently of this buggy point.

These two components together form our fitness function

$$\mathcal{F} = \mathcal{F}_s + \mathcal{F}_d$$

and we demonstrate its utility in the next section where we test INS.

4 Analysis

In this section we use our testing technique to analyze the Java implementation of INS that is given in [21]. There are various properties that we can test of a naming scheme. For example, whether the name resolution mechanism ever returns objects that have functionality conflicting what an application seeks, or whether it returns all objects that conform to a request.

W e test a fundamental property that we believe is essential for the correctness of a naming scheme. In particular, we see if addition behaves monotonically in INS, i.e. performing the *Lookup-Name* operation after an addition results in at least the name-records that result if the same name-specifier is resolv ed before that addition.

In order to test this property we modify our fitness function to *reward* chromosomes that are able to *violate* it. This is achieved by comparing the elements of the sequence $\mathcal{R}_1, \ldots, \mathcal{R}_4$ of results produced by the *Lookup-Name* operations performed after each *Add-Name* operation that the chromosome induces[3]. If this sequence is found to have elements $\mathcal{R}_i$ and $\mathcal{R}_j$ for $i > j$ such that $\mathcal{R}_i \subset \mathcal{R}_j$, we reward such a chromosome with an additional score of 100 poin ts for each such pair.

After incorporating this change we execute our system and let it evolve to see if any of the chromosomes can actually result in such behavior. The evolution stabilizes in about 110 generations and the highest scoring chromosome represents the name-specifiers illustrated in Figure 5. As we see from the results of *Lookup-Name* operations, the last *Lookup-Name* operation produces no name-records, despite the fact that before the final addition was performed, a valid service, namely R1, w as returned.

Careful examination of the INS code reveals that the inventors of INS use a (boolean) flag to indicate whether a set contains all elements of a domain, instead of actually inserting those elements into it at the time of its creation (line 1 of pseudo-code in the Appendix). This flag representation later causes problems when set unions are performed, and results in loss of information. In Figure 5 this happens after the final addition when an attribute corresponding to a4 in the name-specifier to lookup is searched in the name-tree. This is an extremely subtle flaw, and our system quickly evolves to detect it and generates our first counterexample.

W e next explore the question if this violation of a fundamental propert y is solely due to the use of this flag based representation. Our task now is to induce

---

[3] We write $\mathcal{R}_i$ for Lookupi, to represent a set of name-records resulting by an execution of *Lookup-Name* after the ith addition

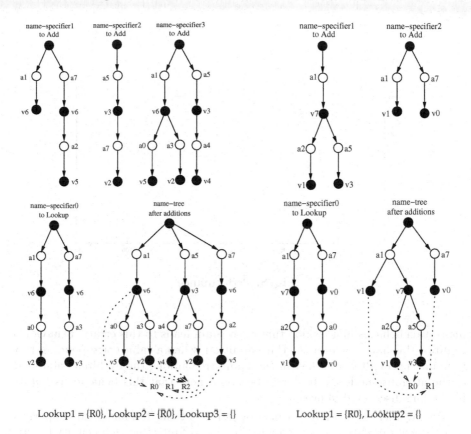

Lookup1 = {R0}, Lookup2 = {R0}, Lookup3 = {}   Lookup1 = {R0}, Lookup2 = {}

Fig. 6. Another flaw in the INS implementation

Fig. 7. Non-monotonicity of the Add-Name operation in INS

our system to evolve *away* from using any union operation that leads to this effect. To achieve this, we introduce a *negative* reward for any chromosome that causes an execution of the union operation when exactly one of the sets involved has its flag set and the other one is non-empty. We subtract 200 points from the score of such a chromosome.

Having set the parameters this way, we restart the evolution of our testing system and observe the behavior of the highest ranked chromosome. Around generation number 98 the system stabilizes and the best chromosome in that state is presented in Figure 6. We only illustrate the first four name-specifiers since the desired effect is observed then. Notice that the third addition contradicts the monotonicity property.

An analysis of the behavior of *Lookup-Name* on this test suite reveals that the INS implementation does not handle a value mismatch correctly. When attributes match at a certain level but no corresponding value matches, the imple-

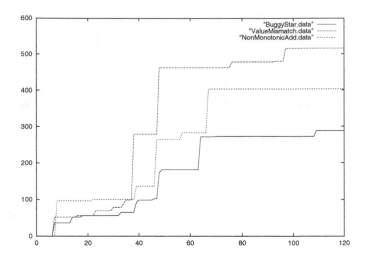

Fig. 8. Performance

mentation behaves in a fashion that once again leads to this erratic behavior. In Figure 6 this happens after the third addition, when a value corresponding to v2 in name-specifier0 is searched in the name-tree among the children value-nodes of the attribute-node a0. It should be noted here that this behavior is *not* due to the bug discovered above.

Having identified another cause of failure of the fundamental property of monotonicity in INS we once again use the idea of introducing a penalty function to discourage chromosomes from causing execution paths that lead to already discovered bugs. We now add an additional penalty of 100 points at the control point in *Lookup-Name* that handles a value mismatch.

This time our system evolves to a stable state in about 65 generations. Figure 7 displays part of the highest scoring chromosome in that generation. The second addition triggers off the required effect. It is interesting to note that this behavior is independent of the bugs discovered above with the INS inventors implementation.

In fact, this problem is due to a flaw in the semantics of INS. INS inventors defined missing attributes to act as wild-cards [1] and the *Lookup-Name* algorithm tries to incorporate that feature. However, this leads to INS displaying this highly undesirable behavior and there is no consistent notion of what it means for a name-record to conform to a name-specifier.

Figure 8 shows the performance of our testing system in producing each of the three counterexamples discussed in this section. We plot the score of the best test suite in a generation (on the vertical axis) against the generation number. "BuggyStar.data" shows the results of experiment that resulted in the chromosome in Figure 5, "ValueMismatch.data" for that in Figure 6, and "NonMonotonicAdd.data" for the chromosome in Figure 7.

All the tests took less than 1 minute on an Intel Celeron 400 MHz processor. Throughout the experiments our genetic algorithm used a population size of 200 chromosomes with the fittest 100 parenting offsprings, mutation rate of 0.05 and a single-point crossover. It took fewer than 120 generations for the system to stabilize in each testing scenario.

5 Related W ork

Other researchers have investigated the use of genetic algorithms for automating test data generation, but most work has focused on achieving maximal code or branch coverage.

McGraw et al. [14] explore their use in dynamic test data generation where the problem of test data generation is reduced to one of minimizing a function. They provide an implementation of Korel's function minimization approach to test data generation using a genetic algorithm. A stated goal of their approach is to cover all branches in a program.

Pargas et al. [16] present a goal-oriented technique for automatic test data generation using a genetic algorithm that is guided by the control dependencies in the program. They aim at achieving statement and branch coverage.

The GA-based framework of Roper et al. [18] tests C programs by instrumenting them with probes that provide feedback on the coverage achieved.

Jones et al. [10] have used genetic algorithms to generate test sets automatically that satisfy the requirements for test data set adequacy of structural testing. A recent paper by Bueno et al. [3] builds on their work and presents a tool for the automation of test data generation and infeasible path identification. Their focus is also to perform structural software testing.

Grob [6] argues that genetic algorithms make Dynamic Timing Analysis of systems feasible, and give accurate predictions of a system's run-time behavior through their analysis of the interactions of the program's input parameters.

Schultz et al. [20] apply GA-based machine learning techniques to the general problem of evaluating an intelligent controller for an autonomous vehicle. Their approach subjects a vehicle controller to an adaptively chosen set of fault scenarios within a vehicle simulator, and searches for combination of faults, using genetic algorithms, that produce noteworthy performance by the controller.

Our approach contrasts with these in several ways. First, we aim to test complex data structures and methods for manipulating them, and our primary concern is not to get the maximal code or branch coverage. Second, we use the idea of barrier functions (negative reward) which allows us to identify new bugs without having to fix the ones that we have already discovered. Third, we are able to test properties concerning interleaving of operations in a real world system.

Recently [12], we created an object model of the naming infrastructure of INS in Alloy [8] and analyzed it with the Alloy Analyzer [9] to disprove a published claim made by the inventors of INS about the equivalence of wild-cards and missing attributes. Using that model, we also discovered that the published

Lookup-Name algorithm [1] failed to handle certain boundary conditions and gave erratic results. Private communication with the INS inventors revealed that those boundary cases were fixed in their Java implementation given in [21].

The most important advance over our work in [12] is that the analysis presented here discovers bugs in the proposed fixes of the inventors, and, moreover, identifies a major flaw in the design of the naming semantics of INS and its name resolution algorithm. In [11] we extend our original Alloy model to reveal the flaws discussed here using the Alloy Analyzer.

Using a model checker to verify properties about a structure of the complexity of INS requires a thorough understanding of the algorithms involved and changing them necessitates remodeling. A model checker, however, typically guarantees to find a bug if one exists in (small) finite scope, provided the model is sound. Also, a model can be constructed without an actual implementation.

Our analysis using genetic algorithms only needs elementary knowledge of the implementation details of INS. Moreover, since our GA-based framework manipulates the implementation code directly, the same framework can be used to incorporate any future changes to the code being tested.

6   Conclusions

We have presented and successfully demonstrated an automated test data generation framework based on genetic algorithms that can be adapted to test complicated software structures and methods for manipulating them. Our approach is especially well suited to evaluating other naming schemes in which the correspondence between names and objects is non-trivial.

Care, however, needs to be taken in order to adjust the parameters, especially the fitness function, so as to induce the chromosomes to evolve to test the desired features. We decided to set the bonus or penalty points two orders of magnitude more than the reward for executing a statement of the code, after some experimentation.

Designing a suitable genetic representation of the test data required some care. A cursory examination of the description of the data structures involved would lead to an inefficient encoding. The use of a representation that never encodes a name-tree directly makes it more versatile.

We believe that the use of genetic algorithms in testing has great benefits, as they not only generate quality test data quickly but also can identify structural flaws that are particularly hard to detect otherwise. We view them as complementary to other standard testing tools. A static analysis tool, for example, might be used to assist in computing a suitable fitness function.

It is our goal to identify a set of properties that encapsulates the correctness of a general naming scheme. This would be a first step in creating a framework for testing an arbitrary naming scheme using our GA-based testing technique.

We would also like to explore the possibility of using these ideas in program slicing and detection of infeasible program paths. The concept of using barriers while evaluating fitness seems especially promising.

Acknowledgement

This research was funded by an Information Technology Research grant from the National Science Foundation (#0086154), and by a grant from the NTT Corporation. We would like to thank William Adjie-Winoto for discussions on INS. We are also grateful to Daniel Jackson, Viktor Kuncak, and Alexandru Salcianu for detailed comments on earlier drafts of this paper. Ahmad Kamal, Mehreen Naseem, and Maimoon Nasim kindly helped with the final draft while the author was in Lahore.

References

1. W. Adjie-Winoto, E. Sc hwartz, H. Balakrishnan, and J. Lilley. The design and implementation of an intentional naming system. In *17th ACM Symposium on Operating Systems (SOSP 99)*, Kiawah Island, December 1999.
2. B. Beizer. *Software Testing Techniques*. International Thomson Computer Press, 1990.
3. P. M. S. Bueno and M. Jino. Identification of potentially infeasible program paths by monitoring the search for test data. In *Proceedings of the Fifteenth IEEE International Conference on Automated Software Engineering (ASE 2000)*, Grenoble, France, September 2000.
4. K-H. Chang, J. H. Cross, W. H. Carlisle, and D. B. Bro wn. A framework for intelligent test data generators. In *Journal of Intelligent and Robotic Systems – Theory and Applications*, July 1991.
5. L. A. Clarke. A system to generate test data and symbolically execute programs. In *IEEE Transactions on Software Engineering*, September 1976.
6. H. Grob. Intelligent timing analysis of real-time software. Internal Report, University of Glamorgan, U.K.
7. J. Holland. Adaption in natural and artificial systems. In *Ann Arbor: The University of Michigan Press*, 1975.
8. D. Jackson. Alloy: A lightweight object modelling notation. Technical Report 797, MIT Laboratory for Computer Science, Cambridge, MA, February 2000.
9. D. Jackson, I. Schechter, and I. Shlyakhter. Alcoa: the alloy constraint analyzer. In *Proceedings of the International Conference on Software Engineering*, Limerick, Ireland, June 2000.
10. B. F. Jones, H. H. Sthamer, and D. E. Eyres. Automatic structural testing using genetic algorithms. *Software Engineering Journal*, pages 299–306, Sep 1996.
11. S. Khurshid. Exploring the design of an intentional naming scheme with an automatic constraint analyzer. Masters Thesis, MIT Laboratory for Computer Science, Cambridge, MA, May 2000.
12. S. Khurshid and D. Jackson. Exploring the design of an intentional naming scheme with an automatic constraint analyzer. In *Proc. 15th IEEE International Conference on Automated Software Engineering (ASE 2000)*, Grenoble, France, September 2000.
13. B. Korel. Automated software test data generation. In *IEEE Transactions on Software Engineering 16(8):870 – 879*, August 1990.
14. G. McGraw, C. Michael, and M. Schatz. Generating software test data by evolution. Technical Report RSTR-018-97-01, RST Corporation, Sterling, VA, February 1998.

15. H. D. Mills, M. D. Dyer, and R. C. Linger. Cleanroom software engineering. In *IEEE Software 4(5): 19-25*, September 1999.
16. R. P. Pargas, M. J. Harrold, and R. P. Peck. Test-data generation using genetic algortihms. In *Journal of Software Testing, Verification, and Reliability*. Wiley, 1999.
17. C. V. Ramamoorthy, S. F. Ho, and W. T. Chen. On the automated generation of program test data. In *IEEE Transactions on Software Engineering 2(4):293 – 300*, December 1976.
18. M. Roper, I. Maclean, A. Brooks, J. Miller, and M. W ood. Genetic algorithms and the automatic generation of test data. Technical Report RR/95/195 [EFoCS-19-95], University of Strathclyde, Glasgow, U.K., 1995.
19. P. Ross and D. Brown. Applications of genetic algorithms. *AISB Quaterly on Evolutionary Computation*, (89):23–30, Autumn 1994.
20. A. C. Schultz, J. J. Grefenstette, and K. A. De Jong. Learning to break things: adaptive testing of intelligent controllers. In *Handbook of Evolutionary Computing*. IOP Publishing Ltd and Oxford University Press, 1995.
21. E. Schwartz. Design and implementation of intentional names. Masters Thesis, MIT Laboratory for Computer Science, Cambridge, MA, May 1999.

A   Pseudo-code for *Lookup-Name*

The following pseudo-code description of *Lookup-Name* is taken from [1].

```
Lookup-Name(T,n)
   S <- the set of all possible name-records
   for each av-pair p := (na, nv) in n
      Ta <- the child of T such that
            Ta's attribute = na's attribute
      if Ta = null
         continue
      if nv = *         // wild card matching
         S' <- empty-set
         for each Tv which is a child of Ta
            S' <- S' union (all of the name-records in the
                            subtree rooted at Tv)
         S <- S intersection S'
      else              // normal matching
         Tv <- the child of Ta such that
               Tv's value = nv's value
         if Tv is a leaf node or p is a leaf node
            S <- S intersection (the name-records of Tv)
         else
            S <- S intersection Lookup-Name(Tv, p)
   return S union (the name-records of T)
```

Fig. 9. *Lookup-Name* algorithm

Building a Tool for the Analysis and Testing of Web Applications: Problems and Solutions

Filippo Ricca and Paolo Tonella

ITC-irst
Centro per la Ricerca Scientifica e Tecnologica
38050 Povo (Trento), Italy
{ricca, tonella}@itc.it
tel. +39.0461.314592, fax +39.0461.314591

Abstract. Web applications are becoming increasingly complex and important for companies. Their design, development, analysis and testing need therefore to be approached by means of support tools and methodologies. In this paper we consider the problems related to building tools for the analysis and testing of Web applications and we try to provide some indications on possible solutions, based upon our experience in the development of the tools ReWeb and TestWeb.

The definition of a proper reference model will be discussed, as well as the impact of dynamic pages during Web site downloading and subsequent model construction. Visualization techniques addressing the large amount of extracted data will be presented, while infeasibility problems will be considered with reference to the testing phase.

1 Introduction

In the last years, Web applications have become important assets for several companies, being a convenient and inexpensive way to provide product information, e-commerce and services on-line. Since a software bug in a Web application could interrupt an entire business and cost millions of dollars, there is a strong demand for methodologies, tools and models that can improve the web site quality and reliability [7,8]. For example, tools can support developers understanding the abstract structure of a Web application by means of views and analyses, ensuring that the requirement specifications are satisfied by the application, and they can help in the testing phase. Developing a tool that extracts a model of a Web application, implements some static analyses and supports the developers in the testing phase is not easy. Main problems are related to: modeling the abstract structure of Web applications, adapting known analysis and testing techniques to the characteristics of Web based systems, and visualizing large graphs [6,10]. Only few works have insofar considered the problems related to Web site static analysis, maintenance, testing and to building the associated tools. One of the first systematic studies on Web maintenance is [12], where the authors recognize the similarity between software systems and web based systems and the importance of the maintenance phase. They have built a tool called SiteSeer

T. Margaria and W. Yi (Eds.): TACAS 2001, LNCS 2031, pp. 373–388, 2001.

that downloads web sites and computes some metrics on them. The paper [9] describes SPHINX, a Java toolkit and interactive development environment for Web spiders. SPHINX consists of two parts: the Spider workbench, a customizable spider that supports a graphical user interface and visualizes the web site recovered as a graph, and the WebSPHINX class library, that provides support for writing Web spiders in Java. The CAPBAK/Web tool, explained in [8], is a web testing tool that supports functional testing and regression testing. In [7] an approach to data flow testing of Web applications is presented.

In this paper we consider the problems related to building tools for the analysis and testing of Web applications and we try to provide some indications on possible solutions, based upon our experience in the development of the tools **ReWeb** and **TestWeb**. **ReWeb** downloads and analyzes the pages of a Web application with a twofold purpose: building a model of the application and supplying some views and analyses to the developer. **TestWeb**, a structural testing tool, generates and executes a set of test cases for a Web application whose model was computed by **ReWeb**.

The remainder of this paper is organized as follows: the next section describes a generic Web application infrastructure, Section 3 introduces the general architecture of our tools and presents the adopted analysis model for Web applications, Sections 4 and 5 explain problems encountered and solutions adopted in the development of the tools **ReWeb** and **TestWeb**. Finally, Section 6 concludes the paper.

2 Web Applications

A typical generic Web Application infrastructure is shown in Figure 1 (a similar schema is proposed in [13]).

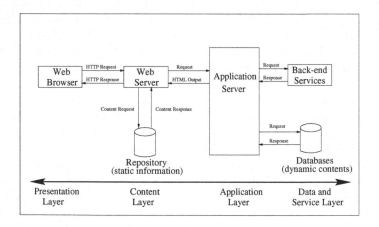

Fig. 1. Web application infrastructure.

The browser sends the requests via HTTP to the server for an interactive view of Web pages. Web pages can be static or dynamic. While the content of a static page is fixed and stored in a repository, the content of a dynamic page is computed at run-time by the application server and may depend on the information provided by the user through input fields (a similar distinction is proposed in [4] and [5]). The programs that generate dynamic pages at run-time, as for example CGI scripts and servlets, run on the application server and can use information stored in databases and other resources. The Web server and the application server can be located on the same machine or on different machines.

Similarly to [5], we classify Web applications according to a taxonomy, ordered by growing complexity, which is characterized by dynamism, page decomposition and data flow.

- Level 0: static pages without frames.
- Level 1: static pages with frames.
- Level 2: dynamic pages without data transfer from client.
- Level 3: dynamic pages with data transfer from client.

The difficulties and problems in the construction of a tool, that supports developers in the phases of analysis and testing of Web applications, grow with increasing levels in the taxonomy. Applications at levels 2 and 3 typically exploit information stored inside a database to build the content of the dynamic pages. All four levels are in the scope of the proposed techniques.

3   Tool Architecture

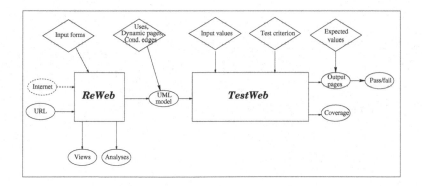

Fig. 2. *Roles of Reweb and TestWeb.*

The two tools **ReWeb** and **TestWeb** have been developed to support analysis and testing of Web applications. Their relative roles are schematized in

---

[1] Although some authors distinguish between Web sites and applications, using the latter term only in presence of dynamic pages (our levels 2 and 3), we will use them interchangeably in the following if the distinction is not important.

Figure 2. **ReW eb** downloads and analyzes the pages of a W eb application with the purpose of building a model of it and producing some analyses and views. **TestW eb** generates and executes a set of test cases for a W eb application whose model w as computed by **ReW eb** The whole process is semi-automatic, and the interventions of the user are indicated within diamonds in Figure 2. Explanations on the manual interventions will be given in the following sections.

Both tools perform their operations on an abstraction of the W eb applications, indicated in Figure 2 as UML model. UML, the Unified Modeling Language [3], was exploited to express such a model. Let us consider the key requirements on the model. W e are interested in a model that can be directly abstracted from the implemen tation. Some importart characteristics that it should have can be summarized as follo ws:

- The focus should be on the navigational features of the site;
- It should be complete i.e. the most important entities as, for example links, frames, forms and dynamic pages must be explicitly represented in the model;
- It should be possible to provide (partial) automatic support for its extraction;
- It should be possible to apply to it some static analyses and testing techniques derived from those used with traditional software systems.
- It should be possible to derive some views from it that represent the W eb site in an intuitive mode;

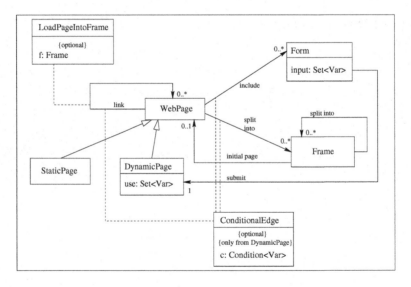

Fig. 3. *Meta model of a generic W eb application structure.*

Figure 3 shows our meta model used to describe the elemen ts in the model of a W eb application. It satisfies all key requiremen ts given above. The central entity in a Web site is the *WebPage*. A Web page contains the information to be displayed to the user, and the navigation links toward other pages. It also includes organization and interaction facilities (e.g., frames and forms).

The two subclasses of *WebPage* model the static and dynamic pages. When the content of a dynamic page depends on the value of a set of input variables, the attribute *use* of class *DynamicPage* contains them.

A *frame* is a rectangular area in the current page where navigation can take place independently. Moreover the different frames into which a page is decomposed can interact with each other, since a link in a page loaded into a frame can force the loading of another page into a different frame. This can be achieved by adding a `target` to the hyperlink. Organization into frames is represented by the association *split into*, whose target is a set of *Frame* entities. Frame subdivision may be recursive (auto-association *split into* within class *Frame*), and each frame has a unary association with the Web page initially loaded into the frame (absent in case of recursive subdivision into frames). When a link in a Web page forces the loading of another page into a different frame, the target frame becomes the data member of the (optional) association class *LoadPageIntoFrame*.

In HTML user input can be gathered by exploiting *forms*. A Web page can include any number of forms (association *include*). Each form is characterized by the input variables that are provided by the user through it (data member *input*). Values collected by forms are submitted to the Web server via the special link *submit*, whose target is always a dynamic page. Since links, frames and forms are part of the content of a Web page, and for dynamic pages the content may depend on the input variables, even the organization of a page is, in general, not fixed and depends on the input. This is the reason for the association class *ConditionalEdge*, which optionally adds a boolean condition, function of the input variables, representing the existence condition of the association (which can in turn be a *link*, an *include* or a *split into*). The target, page, form or frame, is referenced by the source dynamic page only when the input values satisfy the condition in the *ConditionalEdge*.

4   ReWeb

The **ReWeb** tool consists of three modules: a Spider, an Analyzer and a Viewer. The Spider downloads all pages of a target web site, starting from a given URL and providing the input required by dynamic pages, and it builds a model of the downloaded site. Each page found within the site host is downloaded and marked with the date of downloading. The HTML documents outside the web site host are not considered. The user has to specify the set of inputs for each page that contains Forms. The Analyzer uses the UML model of the web site and the downloaded pages to perform several analyses, presented in the following, some of which are exploited during static verification. The Viewer provides a Graphical User Interface (GUI) to display the Web application model as well as the output of the static analyses. The graphical interface supports a rich set of navigation and query facilities. W eb Spider and Analyzer are written in Java, while the Viewer is based on Dotty[2].

4.1 Spider

```
SPIDER(target_url)
1    UML_Model ← ∅
2    Error_urls ← ∅
3    Pages_already_visited ← ∅
4    Urls_found ← ∅
5    S ← {target_url}
6    while (S ≠ ∅)
7        choosen_url ← chooseElement(S)
8        S ← S \ {choosen_url}
9        if not (choosen_url ∈ P agesalready_visited) then
10           if (choosen_url is OK) then
11               P agesalready_visited ← P agesalready_visited ∪ {choosen_url}
12               if (choosen_url is a HTML page) then
13                   Download(choosen_url)
14                   Urls_found ← scanPage(c hoosenurl)
15                   S ← S ∪ Urls_found
16                   AddElementsT oModel(UMLModel, choosen_url, Urls_found)
17               endif
18           else
19               Error_urls ← Error_urls ∪ {choosen_url}
20           endif
21       endif
22   endwhile
```

Fig. 4. *Pseudo-code of the Spider.*

W eb pages are not actually written using a single language. They can be rather regarded as multilanguage documents, where code fragments in languages different from HTML can be loaded (e.g. Applets) or in terpreted (e.g. Javascript). Libraries for the construction of Spider programs are available for programming languages such as Perl, C/C++, or Java. An example is the W ebSPHINX class library [9]. W e decided to implem ent our W eb Spider just exploiting the Java language and its standard library, starting from scratch, in order to have to-tal control on the multilingual aspects of the downloaded pages. W e developed a parser which recognizes both HTML and Ja vascript code fragments, and extracts the needed information (links, forms, frames, etc.) from them.

Figure 4 shows the pseudo-code of our Spider. The procedure *SPIDER* takes a given URL in input and builds the associated UML model. The body of the command *while* (contained in lines 6-22) is executed until there are elements in the set S. The function *chooseElement* (line 7) chooses an element in the set S while the condition *chosen_url is OK* (line 10) is true if chosen_url is well-formed and the corresponding page exists in the W eb site. The condition *chosen_url is*

---
[2] Dotty is a customizable graph Editor developed at AT&T Bell Laboratories by Eleftherios Koutsofios and Stephen C. North.

an HTML page (line 12) is true if the content type of the document connected to chosen_url is HTML. In line 13 the procedure *Download* is called to store the retrieved page in the file-system. The function *scanPage* (line 14) scans the page and returns the set of URLs found within it and contained in the site host. The procedure *AddElementsToModel* (line 16) adds nodes and edges to the model in accordance with our meta model. If the set S is implemen ted as a stack, the algorithm visits the W eb site in depth-first way, while using a queue produces a breadth-first visit.

Problems encoun tered in the construction of the Spider are due to irregularities and am biguities present in HTML code, also noted in [12], and to the current state of the W eb technology, offering a large spectrum of alternatives to implem ent a web site. Our solution was to improve the robustness of the parser, so that it could accept a superset of HTML including the main irregularities commonl y recognized and properly interpreted by available browsers.

Dynamic pages pose additional problem to the activit y of the Spider. Since the content of these pages is decided at run time, it ma y in general depend on the input previously provided by the user. In particular, the structure of a dynamic page may change when it is encountered in a different interaction. Since the model of a W eb site encompasses all possibilities, the Spider has to recover all variants of a dynamic page, and has to merge them in to a single representative object. This can be achieved by specifying the input values to be provided before downloading the dynamic page of in terest. Moreo ver, the same dynamic page has to be downloaded several times, with different inputs, when the different conditions generate a different page structure. All sequences of input values to be provided before each page download are specified in a file which is read by the Spider. All dynamic pages specified in the file are do wnloaded after providing the W eb server with the given inputs. Finally, all versions of the same page are merged. Although the n umber of inputs to be provided may explode com binatorially, out experience suggests that in practice few alternatives are sufficient to cover all variants.

An additional input that may affect the content displayed in a dynamic page is the *cookie* that the browser provides to the W eb server. A *cookie* is a user identifier that is stored by the browser in the local file system and is pro vided to the W eb server to allow user identification each time a new connection with a given server is established. After recognizing the user, the W eb server can provide a customized v ersion of the dynamic pages in the site. Since their structure ma y depend on the cookie, the Spider needs the ability to send a cookie to the W eb server, in order to obtain also the pages that are generated when the user is identified.

4.2   Analyzer

The UML model of a W eb site can be interpreted as a graph by associating objects with nodes and associations with edges. Some simple analyses ma y determine the presence of **unreachable pages**, i.e., pages that are available at the server site but cannot be reached along any path starting from the initial

```
FLOW_ANALYSIS(graph G = (N, E))
1    for each (n ∈ N)
2        initialize IN_n and OUT_n
3    endfor
4    change ← true
5    while (change)
6        change ← false
7        for each (n ∈ N)
8            IN_n ← ⊕_{p∈pred(n)} OUT_p
9            OLDOUT_n ← OUT_n
10           OUT_n ← GEN_n ∪ (IN_n − KILL_n)
11           if OUT_n ≠ OLDOUT_n then
12               change ← true
13           endif
14       endfor
15   endwhile
```

Fig. 5. *Pseudo-code of the flow analysis algorithm.*

page. They are obtained as the difference between the pages available in the Web server file system and those downloaded by the Spider. **Ghost pages** are associated with pending links, which reference a non existing page.

More advanced analyses [11] can be derived from the general framework of flow analysis [1], described by the algorithm in Figure 5. The algorithm propagates flow information inside a graph until the fix-point is reached. The kind of flow information to be propagated depends on the purpose of the analysis being performed. Some examples are given below. Moreover, the confluence operator exploited at line 8 to collect outgoing information from predecessor nodes is also dependent on the analysis, and is typically either the intersection or the union. After initializing the input and output sets of each node (IN_n and OUT_n, lines 1-3) with the initial flow information, propagation is achieved inside a fix-point loop (line 5) by subtracting the destroyed information ($KILL_n$ set) and adding the generated information (GEN_n set) to the incoming information (line 10) for each node n in the graph.

An example of analysis which specializes the algorithm in Figure 5 is the computation of the **reaching frames**, which determines the set of frames in which each page can appear. When a page is loaded into a frame as its initial page or is reachable through an edge decorated with a *LoadPageIntoFrame* association class instance, it *generates* the name of the frame as flow information. By propagating such information along the site graph until the fix-point is reached, the reaching frames of each page are determined. The outcome of the reaching frames analysis is useful to understand the assignment of pages to frames. The presence of undesirable reaching frames is thus made clear. Examples are the possibility to load a page at the top level, while it was designed to always be loaded into a given frame, or the possibility to load a page into a frame where it should not be.

Flow analyses can be employed in a more traditional fashion to determine the **data dependences**. Nodes of kind *Form* generate a definition of each variable in the *input* set. Such definitions are propagated along the edges of the Web site graph. If a definition of a variable reaches a node where the same variable is used (*use* attribute of a dynamic page), there is a data dependence between defining node and user node. Data dependences are useful to represent the information flows in the application. They may reveal the presence of undesirable possibilities, such as using a variable not yet defined or using an incorrect definition of a variable. Data dependences are also extremely important for dynamic validation, when data flow testing techniques are adopted.

When the pages of a site are traversed, it is impossible to reach a document without traversing a set of other pages, called its **dominators**. Sites in which traversing a given page is considered mandatory, e.g., because it contains important information, will have it in the dominator set of every node. Dominator analysis, also derived from the algorithm in Figure 5, automates the check.

The evolution of web sites [10,12] is another interesting object of investigation. Such an analysis requires the ability to compare successive versions of its pages and to graphically display the differences. Given two versions of a web site, downloaded at different dates, their comparison aims at determining which pages were added, modified, deleted or left unchanged. It can be combined with the static analyses described above, since their re-computation over time allows controlling the evolution of the application quality.

4.3   Viewer

The *graph view* of a Web application is a graph, whose nodes correspond to the objects in the model and whose edges correspond to the associations between objects. Labeled edges are used for the links having a *LoadPageIntoFrame* or *ConditionalEdge* relation specifier. In the *graph view*, to intuitively suggest decomposition into frames, we adopt the convention of joining horizontally the nodes of type frame contained in the same page, and collapsing the edges of type "split into" into a single edge. An example of decomposition into frames is shown in Figure 6. Page madmaxpub/index.html (the main page) is divided into two frames with identifiers a and b, and frame a is used as a menu to force the loading of pages into the other frame.

The *graph view* of a web application can be enriched with information about its history [10], by coloring the nodes and associating different colors to different time points (see Figure 6). In particular, a scale of colors ranging from the blue, going through the green and reaching the red can be employed to represent nodes added/modified in the far past, in the medium past or more recently.

The Viewer is based on Dotty, and uses the algorithm explained in [6] for drawing directed graphs. The aesthetic principles followed by the algorithm are: to expose hierarchical structure (if any) in the graph, to avoid edge crossings (if possible) and sharp bends, to keep edges short, to favor symmetry and balance. The layout algorithm of the *graph view* of a web site is very important to understand its structure, especially when the site is very complex.

Another problem connected with the visualization of a web site is the fact that also small sites (e.g. with 100 pages) can have an entangled structure difficult to understand. A way to improve the Viewer display is to use techniques to

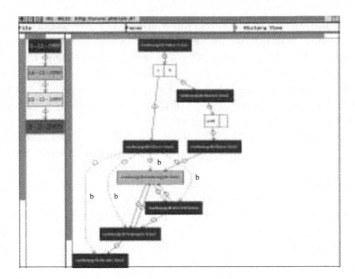

Fig. 6. *Colored graph view of the site www.ubicum.it/madmaxpub at date 3-2-2000.*

abstract, to simplify, to extract a portion of, or to see only a part of the *graph view*. Another possibility can be to add other views of a web site as for example the birdeye and overview diagrams or to display only the depth-first tree without return edges (solution adopted in [9]). The views and facilities we propose follow. The *system view* represents the organization of pages into directories; the *data flow view* displays the read/write accesses of pages to variables, respectively through incoming/outgoing edges linking pages to variables; the *history representation with percentage bars* describes, in compact way, the percentages of nodes with the same color. Among the provided facilities, the viewer supports zoom, search, deletion of incoming or outgoing edges, and focus. The facilities for focusing on and searching a node are useful when the visualized graphs are very large. By exploiting the focusing facility it is possible to display only a limited neighborhood of a selected node. Another possibility to access the *graph view*, not yet implemented, is the identification and extraction of a portion of a web site by means of pattern matching techniques. Recurrent patterns are expected to be used in the design of web sites (for example *tree, hierarchy, full connectivity, indexed-sequence*).

5   TestWeb

Web sites can involve a complex interaction among Web browser, operating systems, plug-in applications, communicating protocols, Web servers, databases, server programs (for example CGI programs) and firewalls. Such complexity makes the test of Web Sites a great challenge [8]. Ideally all components and functionality of a Web site on both client and server sides should be completely tested. However, this is rarely possible in modern Web site projects because of the extreme time pressure under which Web systems are developed. Available testing techniques [8] differ on the features of the Web site we want to test. For example it is possible to execute link testing, HTML validation, performance testing, and security testing. We are interested in *dynamic validation* using our UML model as a base for this type of testing. In general, dynamic validation methods aim at exercising the system by supplying a vector of input data (*test case*) and comparing the expected outputs with the actual ones after execution. In particular, we considered *white box testing* of Web Applications: the internal structure of a Web application is accessed to measure the coverage that a given *test suite* (collection of test cases) reaches, with respect to a given *test criterion* (stating the features to be tested). Some white box testing criteria, derived from those available for traditional software [2], are: Page testing, Hyperlink testing, Definition-use testing, All-uses testing, All-paths testing. A *test case* for a Web application is a triple: URL, input (a sequence of variable-value assignments separated by the character '&'), type of parameter passing (GET or POST). Execution consists of requesting the Web server for the URL in the triple with the associated input and storing the output pages. Satisfaction of any of the white box testing criteria involves selecting a set of paths in the Web site graph and providing input values. Since path selection is independent (conditional edges excluded) from input values, it can be automated.

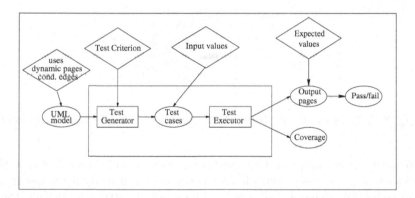

Fig. 7. *Architecture of the tool TestWeb.*

TestWeb(see Figure 7) contains a test case generation engine (Test generator), able to generate test cases from the UML model of a Web application. The user has to add some information to the model produced by **ReWeb** to complete it for testing purposes and furthermore the user has to choose a test criterion. The user specifies the page type when the distinction between static and dynamic pages cannot be obtained automatically (e.g., dynamic pages with no input). The user also provides the set of used variables, *use*, for each dynamic page whose content depends on some input value. Finally, the user has to attach conditions to the edges whose existence depends on the input values.

Additional manual interventions, related to state unrolling, will be described in the following on an example. Generated test cases are sequences of URLs which, once executed, grant the coverage of the selected criterion. Input values in each URL sequence are left empty by the Test generator, and the user has to fill in them, possibly exploiting the techniques traditionally used in black box testing (boundary values, etc.). **TestWeb**'s Test executor can now provide the URL request sequence of each test case to the Web server, attaching proper inputs to each form. The output pages produced by the server are stored for further examination. After execution, the test engineer intervenes to assess the pass/fail result of each test case. A second, numeric output of test case execution is the level of coverage reached by the current test suite.

Regression testing highly benefits from the automation in test case execution, since each test case can be re-executed unattended on a new version of the Web application, and its output pages can be automatically compared with those obtained from a run of the previous version.

5.1   Test Generator

Given the graph representation of a Web application, a *reduced graph* can be computed for the purposes of white box testing: each static page without forms is removed from the graph by a Cross-Term step described in [2] (see Figure 8).

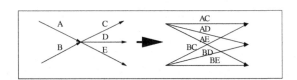

Fig. 8. *Step of the Cross-Term algorithm at a node selected for removal.*

In the resulting graph, a fictitious *entry* node is added, connected with all nodes with no predecessor, and a fictitious *exit* node is directly reachable from all *output* nodes, i.e., dynamic nodes with non empty *use* attribute. In fact, the end of a computation is reached, in a Web application, when some result is displayed to the user, but no intrinsic notion of termination for a navigation session exists.

Differently from the flow-graph of a structured program, the *graph view* of a Web application can contain horrible-loops [2], i.e., there may be nodes jumping into or out of a loop and/or there may be more than one iterating node for the same loop. In presence of horrible-loops the usual strategies used to cover nested-loops and concatenated-loops do not work. We have chosen a general solution: a test case generation technique based on the computation of the path expression [2] of the reduced Web site graph. A *path expression* is an algebraic representation of all paths in a graph. Variables in a path expression are edge labels. They can be combined through operators + and *, associated respectively with selection and loop. Brackets can be used to group subexpressions.

```
REDUCTION(graph)
1    Combine all serial links by multiplying their expressions
2    Combine all parallel links by adding their path expressions
3    Remove all self-loops by replacing them this a link of the form X*
4    while (number of nodes in the graph > 2)
5         n ← choose a node of the graph different from initial or final node
6         Apply Cross-Term elimination to n
7         Combine any remaining serial links as in step 1
8         Combine all parallel links as in step 2
9         Remove all self-loops as in step 3
10   endwhile
```

Fig. 9. *Reduction algorithm.*

Computation of the path expression for a site can be performed by means of the Reduction algorithm described in [2] and depicted in Figure 9.

The lines 1-3 of the Reduction algorithm initialize the process and put the graph in normal form. The body of the command *while* is executed until the number of nodes in the graph is greater than 2. Line 5 assigns a node of the graph different from the initial or final node to variable n, while line 6 executes a Cross-Term step on node n. This step eliminates the node n and transforms the graph according to the diagram shown in Figure 8. Lines 7-10 combine all serial and parallel links and remove self-loops. At the end of the execution, the path-expression of the input graph is obtained.

```
P A THGENERATION(path_expression)
1    while criterion not satisfied
2         for each alternative from inner to outer nesting
3              choose one never considered before, if any
4              or randomly choose one
5         endfor
6         if computed path increases coverage then
7              add it to the resulting paths
8         endif
9    endwhile
```

Fig. 10. *The heuristic technique adopted to obtain the paths satisfying a criterion.*

Since the path expression directly represents all paths in the graph, it can be employed to generate sequences of nodes (test cases) which satisfy any of the coverage criteria. Determining the minimum number of paths, from a path expression, satisfying a given criterion is in general a hard task. However, heuristics can be defined to compute an approximation of the minimum. The heuristic technique adopted for this work is based on the scheme of Figure 10 (the alternative at line 2 for a loop is whether to re-iterate or not). Definition-use and all-uses testing can be achieved by considering, for each data dependence, the definition as *entry* node and the use as *exit* of the subgraph to be tested. Criteria

such as definition-use and all-paths testing, for which the coverage of possibly
infinite paths should be achieved, could require that only independent paths be
considered or that loops be k-limited.

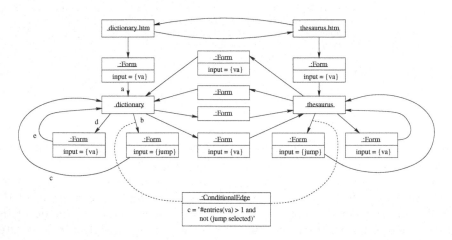

Fig. 11. *Model of a portion of* www.m-w.com, *including two conditional edges.*

Figure 11 shows the portion of the W eb site www.m-w.com which provides on
line access to the Merriam-W ebster English dictionary and thesaurus. A word
can be entered in the initial page (either `dictionary.htm` or `thesaurus.htm`).
A dynamic page `dictionary` is then composed in response to the input word,
stored in variable `va`. The content of the resulting page depends on the number
of entries found in the dictionary. If there are more than one entry, a selection
list is displayed to the user, together with an explanation of the main entry. The
user can choose among the alternatives – the selection is stored in variable `jump`
– and move to a page, still named `dictionary`, with an explanation of such an
entry. The model of the site represents the conditional existence of the list of
alternatives with a ConditionalEdge object associated with the edge labelled b.
The site offers the possibility to enter a new word from both the dynamic pages
`dictionary` and `thesaurus`, and allows switching from dictionary to thesaurus
and vice versa from the initial and result pages.

In order to determine a set of paths to be exercised during white box testing,
the path expression is computed. Let us consider the portion of the site devoted
to the extraction of entries from the dictionary (symmetric considerations can
be made for the thesaurus). The path expression associated with the labelled
edges of Figure 11 is $a(bc + de)^*$. Some of the paths generated from it can be
traversed only if proper inputs are provided, while some other paths are infeasible
for every input. For example, the path abc can be traversed only if the input
word has more than one entry in the dictionary. This condition is quite easy
to achieve and requires only a careful selection of input data. A path whose
infeasibility does not depend on the input is $abcbc$. In fact, if one of the entries is

selected from the list displayed to the user, the next dynamic page `dictionary` that is obtained will not include the list of alternative entries any longer. This condition is represented as `'not (jump selected)'` in Figure 11: if a selection was performed by the user, edge *b* does not exist. As a consequence the path expression cannot be easily exploited for path generation.

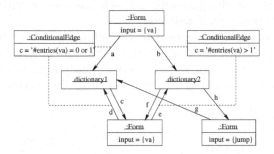

Fig. 12. *Page* `dictionary` *was unrolled into* `dictionary1` *and* `dictionary2`.

The problem highlighted above derives from the possibility to use a same dynamic page for different purposes. Actually, some Web sites consist of just one dynamic page which displays different information according to an internally recorded state of the interaction. In other words, while for static sites the Web page is coincident with the state of the interaction, this is not necessarily true with dynamic sites. A possible solution to this problem is to perform an operation of state unrolling on the dynamic pages that are used to display different contents under different conditions. In the example of Figure 11, page `dictionary` is used for two purposes: to propose a list of alternative dictionary entries and to provide the final result of the search, once a single entry is identified. Such two purposes may be represented explicitly by the two pages `dictionary1` and `dictionary2` into which the initial page is unrolled (see Figure 12). The conditions in the *ConditionalEdge* objects are now simplified and verify only the number of dictionary entries. The path expression of such site portion becomes $(ac + bf + bhgc)(dc + ef + ehgc)^*$ and all the paths that can be generated from it are feasible, provided that an input word with the appropriate number of dictionary entries is selected.

6   Conclusions and Future Work

We proposed some analysis and testing techniques working on Web applications. The starting point for their definition is a model of Web sites, designed to include all characteristics that are relevant from an architectural point of view. Page downloading and model construction were achieved by providing input values for the forms in the site. Moreover, the site model was enriched with information about conditional edges and variable uses, exploited during testing.

Facilities for the display of the resulting model are provided by the analysis
tool **ReW eb** while test generation and execution is automated by **TestW eb**
Our experience with **ReW eb**and **TestW eb**suggests that the choice of a good
model is fundamental for both analysis and testing. W e showed some views
and facilities of **ReW eb**on a real example (`www.ubicum.it`). Path testing in
presence of an internal representation of the interaction state can be simplified
by means of a state unrolling operation, which was also described with reference
to a real world example (`www.m-w.com`).

Our future work will be devoted to extending the set of analyses available
(to include, for example, pattern matching), adding abstraction techniques to
support a high level view of the site, (partially) automating input selection during
testing in presence of conditional edges and providing better support to state
unrolling.

References

1. A. V. Aho, R. Sethi, and J. D. Ullman. *Compilers. Principles, Techniques, and
   Tools.* Addison-Wesley Publishing Company, Reading, MA, 1985.
2. B. Beizer. *Software Testing Techniques, 2nd edition.* International Thomson Computer Press, 1990.
3. G. Booch, J. Rumbaugh, and I. Jacobson. *The Unified Modeling Language – User
   Guide.* Addison-Wesley Publishing Company, Reading, MA, 1998.
4. J. Conallen. *Building Web Applications with UML.* Addison-Wesley Publishing
   Company, Reading, MA, 2000.
5. D. Eichmann. Evolving an engineered web. In *Proc. of the International Workshop
   on Web Site Evolution*, Atlanta, GA, USA, October 1999.
6. E.R. Gasner, E. Koutsofios, S. North, and Kiem-Phong Vo. A technique for drawing
   directed graphs. In *IEEE-TSE 1993*, March 1993.
7. Chien-Hung Liu, David C.Kung, Pei Hsia, and Chih-Tung Hsu. Structural testing
   of web applications. In *Proc. of ISSRE 2000, International symposium on software
   reliability engineering, San Jose, California*, pages 84–96, October 2000.
8. Edward Miller. The web site quality challenge. - companion paper: "website testing". In *Proc. of QW1998 conference*, 901 Minesota street San Francisco, CA 94107
   USA, 1998.
9. Robert C. Miller and Krishna Bharat. Sphinx: A framework for creating personal,
   site-specific web-crawlers. In *Proc. of WWW7, Brisb ane Australia*, April 1998.
10. F. Ricca and P. Tonella. Visualization of web site history. In *Proc. of the In-
    ternational Workshop on Web Site Evolution*, pages 30–33, Zurich, Switzerland,
    2000.
11. F. Ricca and P. Tonella. Web site analysis: Structure and evolution. In *Proceedings
    of the International Conference on Software Maintenance*, pages 76–86, San Jose,
    California, USA, 2000.
12. P. Warren, C. Boldyreff, and M. Munro. The evolution of websites. In *Proc. of the
    International Workshop on Program Comprehension*, pages 178–185, Pittsburgh,
    PA, USA, May 1999.
13. Y. Zou and K. Kontogiannis. Enabling technologies for web-based legacy sys-
    tem integration. In *Proc. of the International Workshop on Web Site Evolution*,
    Atlanta, GA, USA, October 1999.

TATOO: *T*esting and *A*nalysis *T*ool for *O*bject-*O*riented Software

Amie L. Souter[1], Tiffany M. Wong[2], Stacey A. Shindo[1], and Lori L. Pollock[1]

[1] Department of Computer and Information Sciences
University of Delaware, Newark, DE 19716
{souter, pollock, shindo}@cis.udel.edu
[2] Department of Computer Science
Dartmouth College, Hanover, NH 03755
Tiffany.M.Wong@dartmouth.edu

Abstract. Testing is a critical component of the software development process and is required to ensure the reliability, robustness and usability of software. Tools that systematically aid in the testing process are crucial to the development of reliable software. This paper describes a code-based testing and analysis tool for object-oriented software. TATOO provides a systematic approach to testing tailored towards object behavior, and particularly for class integration testing. The underlying program analysis subsystem exploits combined points-to and escape analysis developed for compiler optimization to address the software testing issues.

1   Introduction

Testing is a critical component of the software development process and is required to ensure the reliability, robustness and usability of software. Unfortunately, testing, and in particular ad hoc testing, is labor and resource intensive, accounting for 50%-60% of the total cost of software development[13]. Therefore, it is imperative that testing techniques be developed that provide as much automation and ease of use as possible. In particular, tools that systematically aid in the testing process are crucial to the development of reliable software.

Object-oriented features enable the programmer to design and develop software that is reusable and modular. Encapsulation, inheritance, and polymorphism are extremely useful to the programmer, but create difficulties for the tester. Encapsulation allows the programmer to create classes with state and functionality. All instantiated classes possess different state at different times through a program's execution, requiring many different test cases in order to adequately test the states of different objects. Complex class interactions are introduced through inheritance and class composition. These interactions also need to be tested, requiring test cases to exercise the complexities of these class relationships. Dynamic binding caused by polymorphism creates additional complexities when testing object-oriented software. A single polymorphic call site represents potential calls to one of a number of different methods with the same

T. Margaria and W. Yi (Eds.): TACAS 2001, LNCS 2031, pp. 389–403, 2001.

name. Each possible receiver type must be executed in order to adequately test a program.

In this paper, we present a **T**esting and **A**nalysis **T**ool for **O**bject-Oriented programs, *TATOO*, which embodies our novel code-based testing method focused on object manipulations[16]. Our tool establishes an environment to systematically test programs by providing: (1) automatically generated test tuples based on object manipulations, (2) test coverage information through code instrumentation and test coverage identification, (3) feedback about external influences that may affect the correctness of the testing runs, and (4) visualization of the underlying program representation that shows the interactions of objects in a program.

TATOO is composed of two subsystems: *program analysis* and *testing*. The program analysis subsystem's main objective is to produce the program representation needed for the testing subsystem. The testing subsystem generates the test tuples needed for generating test cases as well as provides test coverage information. In addition, the testing subsystem controls the user interface environment.

TATOO is a prototype tool implemented in Java, consisting of several components:

- The extended FLEX compiler infrastructure[11], which translates the source program into a program representation useful for testing.
- A test tuple generator that generates paths based on object manipulations.
- A Java graphical user interface that displays the source code and information corresponding to the component under test.
- The daVinci toolkit[8], which displays the program representation in a high quality manner, and facilitates communication with the Java GUI, allowing interaction between the graphical program representation and the source code and testing information.
- A code instrumentation tool.
- A trace analyzer, which provides coverage information about an executed program based on a given set of test tuples.

The major contribution of this work is a systematic framework for integration testing. The framework is based on a testing technique that focuses on object manipulations, and is capable of analyzing incomplete programs. Unlike previous work, the technique addresses the common situation of instance variables being objects and not primitive types.

The remainder of this paper is organized as follows. Section 2 provides background information on testing and object manipulations. An overview of *TATOO* is given in Section 3. Sections 4 and 5 describe the details of the *TATOO* subsystems. In Section 6, we evaluate the overhead attributed to the use of the program representation. Finally, we conclude with possible extensions to the tool.

2 Underlying Testing and Analysis Technique

There are two main testing philosophies, namely, *black-box* and *white-box* testing. *Black-box* testing [2] does not use any knowledge of the internals of a program. The program is a black-box in which information about the source code is unknown; we only know what is provided from a program specification. Black-box tests are designed to uncover errors, but the focus of such testing is on verifying that a specified function operates according to the specification. Black-box testing has also been referred to as *functional* testing or *specification-based* testing.

White-box, *structural*, or *code-based* testing techniques are based on knowledge of the code. White-box testing is not an alternative to black-box testing; in fact, they complement each other and both should be performed. Test cases are derived through examining the program code and using well-defined data flow or control flow information about the program. Control flow-based techniques are motivated by the intuition that covering different control-flow paths would exercise a large proportion of program behaviors. For example, *branch testing* [7] is a control flow based testing method, which is based on exercising all the true and false outcomes of every branch statement. The general idea behind *data flow testing* [14,10], is to generate test data based on the pattern of data used throughout a program.

Data flow testing is based on the premise that testing paths that read and write values stored into the same memory locations tests the behavior of a program in terms of its manipulation of data. More specifically, data flow testing is based on def-use pairs in a program, where a *def* of a variable is an assignment of a value to the variable via a read or assignment operation, and a *use* of a variable is a reference to the variable, either in a predicate or a computation. A def-use pair for variable v is an ordered pair (d,u) where d is a statement in which v is defined and u is a statement that is reachable by some path from d, and u uses v or a memory location bound to v. Data flow testing uses def-use pairs in order to generate paths through the definition and use statements in the code. Then test data is generated based on those paths. The idea is that for each definition in the program, we want to exercise all of the uses of the definition.

Systematic testing techniques are categorized into different levels of testing. First, *unit testing* of object-oriented programs focuses on validating individual classes. As classes are combined or integrated together, *integration testing* is performed to validate that the classes function appropriately when combined together. Our research has focused on extending data flow testing to the object-oriented domain with special concern for testing instance variables that are objects and code-based integration testing of object-oriented components.

2.1 Object Manipulation-Based Testing

Our approach to code-based testing of object-oriented software seeks to provide coverage in terms of the elemental read and write actions, which is similar to data flow testing. We call our approach the *OMEN* approach, because it is based on covering basic *O*bject *M*anipulations in addition to using *E*scape i*N*formation to provide helpful feedback to the tester in an interactive testing tool environment.[1]

Object-oriented programming focuses on the data to be manipulated rather than the procedures that do the manipulating. An object-oriented program achieves its goals by creating objects of specific classes. The state of an object is encapsulated as a copy of all of the fields of data that are defined in the corresponding class definition. Actions are performed on an object by invoking methods defined in the class definition, often called sending a message to the object. A method invocation can modify and/or read the data stored in the particular object.

Table 1. Basic object manipulations.

Object-related Statements	Object Manipulations
copy $r_1 = r_2$	read of reference r_2 write to reference r_1
load $r_1 = r_2.f$	read of reference r_2 read of field $r_2.f$ write to reference r_1
store $r_1.f = r_2$	read of reference r_2 read of reference r_1 write to field $r_1.f$
global load $r = cl.f$	read of class variable f write to reference r
global store $cl.f = r$	read of reference r write class variable cl.f
return r	read of reference r
object creation $r = $ new Object(....)	create a new object write to reference r MOD and USE
method invocation $r = r_0.methodname(r_1,..., r_n)$	write to reference r read of references r_0-r_n MOD and USE of r_0's fields

In order to better understand the possible behaviors of an object-oriented program in terms of object manipulations, we identify the most elemental object manipulation as either a read or write action. The actions that a particular statement or method performs on an object can be decomposed into a sequence of these elemental actions. Table 1 depicts the elemental object manipulations performed by each object-related statement. We assume that the program has been preprocessed such that all statements that perform object manipulations

---

[1] In addition, we view the test cases and the results of executing the test cases as an *omen* to predicting the behaviors of the executing program in the production environment.

have been expressed in the form of these basic statements. Due to aliasing and polymorphism, we may have a set of objects potentially referenced by each reference, but for these descriptions, we use the singular form. However, our analysis addresses the potential for a set of objects being referenced.

We extrapolate the concept of data flow testing to the testing of elemental object manipulations by defining a *(write, read)* association of a given object's state, extending this association to include object creation points. From Table 1, we can see that the statement that reads an object field is the load statement, while the store statement writes to an object field. To ensure that we do not miss any viable *(write, read)* pairs, we assume that a given load/store statement may read/write the field of any object which the reference is potentially referencing at that program point. Because objects are instantiated at run-time through executable statements, we extend *(write, read)* pairs to triples of the form *(write, read, object creation)* to reflect the fact that a test case should cover the creation of the object before any writes or reads to that object.

2.2   Using Escape Analysis Information

Escape analysis is a relatively new technique used for optimizing object-oriented codes, particularly Java codes[17,6,3,4]. The analysis is used to determine which synchronization operations are unnecessary and could be eliminated, as well as for reducing the number of objects that are unnecessarily allocated on the heap when they could be allocated on the stack.

We use escape analysis for testing, in order to provide useful feedback to the tester. For example, when a program is being tested and errors are uncovered, the tester or developer needs to find the cause of the error, i.e., debug the code. Our key insight is that the escape information will provide useful feedback to the tester about possible problem areas, where objects interact with outside code, which may be causing inadvertent changes to an object.

3   TATOO System Architecture

TATOO provides a tester with an interactive testing environment to systematically test software using the OMEN testing technique. The prototype testing tool allows the tester to visualize a graphical representation of the program, which characterizes how objects interact with other objects. In addition, the testing tool provides the tester with both visual and report-based coverage information about the program under test. *TATOO* also provides information about how objects interact with unanalyzed portions of code, as well as where objects may potentially escape through method calls or return statements. This information is useful in determining potentially fault prone sections of code.

The tool architecture is composed of two main subcomponents, namely the program analysis subsystem and the testing subsystem, as shown in figure 1. The program analysis subsystem performs the required analysis to obtain the annotated points-to escape (ape) graph program representation described in section

4.1. In addition, a term representation used to view the ape graph, and an annotation table which maintains the required information necessary for the testing subsystem are generated. After program analysis is performed, the testing subcomponent computes test tuples for testing the program component under test. In addition, the testing subcomponent provides a graphical user interface environment that supports two primary features: test coverage identification and program representation visualization. The test coverage identifier provides an environment that lets the user execute the program and then visualize coverage information. Alternatively, the primary purpose of the program representation visualizer is to allow the user to visualize object interactions.

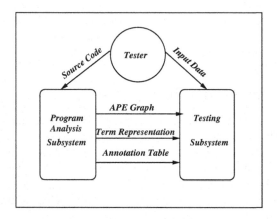

Fig. 1. Overall tool architecture.

4   Program Analysis Subsystem

Figure 2 depicts the subcomponents of the program analysis subsystem. Java bytecode produced from any Java source compiler is the input to the program analysis subsystem. The FLEX static analyzer [11] translates the Java byte code into an intermediate format based on object manipulations, and then performs points-to analysis to construct the *A*nnotated *P*oints-to *E*scape (ape) graph [16]. Annotations necessary for calculating read-write relationships between fields of objects are an important aspect of the ape graph.

The ape graph object, produced by the FLEX static analyzer, is then parsed to construct a graphical term representation needed to visually display the ape graph. In addition, a textual representation of the annotation table is generated, which consists of the annotations for each edge in the ape graph. The final output of the program analysis subsystem is the ape graph object, the ape graph graphical representation, and the annotation table.

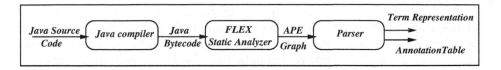

Fig. 2. Program analysis subsystem.

4.1   Ape Graph Program Representation

To develop the ape graph program representation, we extended and modified the points-to escape graph program representation [17] to exploit its ability to mimic object manipulations. The points-to escape graph representation combines points-to information about objects with information about which object creations and references occur within the current analysis region versus outside this program region. For our purposes, the current analysis region is the current component under test (CUT), where a component is not necessarily a class or method, but any grouping of methods. The points-to information characterizes how local variables and fields in objects refer to other objects. The escape information can be used to determine how objects allocated in one region of the program can escape and be accessed by another region of the program.

In the points-to escape graph, nodes represent objects that the program manipulates and edges represent references between objects. Each kind of object that can be manipulated by a program is represented by a different set of nodes in the points-to escape graph. There are two distinct kinds of nodes, namely, inside and outside nodes. An inside node represents an object creation site for objects created and reached by references created inside the current analysis region of the program. In contrast, an outside node represents objects created outside the current analysis region or accessed via references created outside the current analysis region. There are several different kinds of outside nodes, namely, parameter nodes, load nodes, and return nodes.

The distinction between inside and outside nodes is important because it is used to characterize nodes as either captured or escaped. A *captured* node corresponds to the fact that the object it represents has no interactions with unanalyzed regions of the program, and the edges in the graph completely characterize the points-to information between objects represented by these nodes. On the other hand, an *escaped* node represents the fact that the object escapes to unanalyzed portions of the program. An object can escape in several ways. A reference to the object was passed as a parameter to the current method, a reference to the object was written into a static class variable, a reference was passed as a parameter to an invoked method and there is no information about the invoked method, or the object is returned as the return value of the current method.

There are also two different kinds of edges. An *inside edge* represents references created inside the current analysis region. An *outside edge* represents references created outside the current analysis region.

We have extended the points-to escape graph by adding annotations to edges in the graph. The annotations provide information about where basic object manipulations i.e., loads and stores of objects, occur within a program. Using the annotations, we are able to compute store-load i.e., (write-read) pairs for the objects in the program, which can be used in a manner similar to data flow testing.

For each method in the CUT, we build one ape graph per method. For each load/store of the reference represented by a particular edge e in an ape graph, we maintain:

- a sequence of statement numbers, $(s_1, s_2, ..., s_n)$, where s_n is the unique statement number of the load/store statement; $s_1, s_2, ...s_{n-1}$ contains the statement numbers of the call sites where this edge was merged into the caller's ape graph during interprocedural analysis performed during construction of the current method's ape graph. Statement s_1 is the statement number of the call site within the current analysis method which eventually leads to the load/store statement.
- a corresponding sequence of statement numbers, $(evs_1, evs_2, ...evs_n)$, where each evs_i is the unique number of the earliest statement at which the statement s_i could have an effect on other statements. We call this the earliest visible statement for s_i, evs_i. The earliest visible statement $evs_i = s_i$ when the statement s_i is not inside a loop; otherwise $evs_i =$ the statement number of the header of the outermost loop containing s_i.

4.2   Example Annotation Construction

Figure 3 shows an example set of annotations added to a single edge of an ape graph. The nodes in this graph represent objects created within the current analysis region; therefore, they are both inside nodes. The edge labeled top represents a reference from a field named top of the object of type Stack, annotated with both a load and store annotation. The annotations indicate that there exist both a load and store of the field top. Further, the location where the load and store occurs is maintained through the annotations. The annotation, (store 25-13-3), represents two calls, one invoked on line 25 of the program. The second call invoked on line 13 can lead to a store of an object into the field top at line 3. Similarly, the load of the field top occurs at line 7, following a chain of calls from lines 27 and 14. The above example does not include *evs* statement numbers, but they would be maintained in the same manner.

The annotation chains are easily constructed because the ape graphs for individual methods of the CUT are built during a reverse topological traversal over the call graph. Therefore, a callee's graph is always constructed before its callers' graphs. When constructing a caller's graph, the callees' annotations are simply merged into the caller's graph at the appropriate call site.

To emphasize the expressiveness of the ape graph, we include a complete ape graph for a simple method. Figure 4 illustrates the ape graph for method push. The black nodes represent outside nodes and the white nodes represent inside

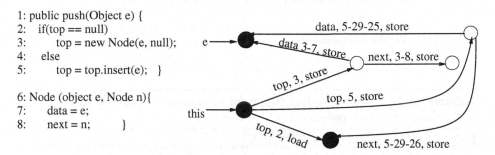

Fig. 3. Illustration of ape graph annotation.

```
1: public push(Object e) {
2:   if(top == null)
3:       top = new Node(e, null);
4:   else
5:       top = top.insert(e);   }

6: Node (object e, Node n){
7:     data = e;
8:     next = n;        }
```

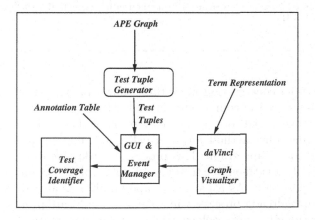

Fig. 4. Example of complete ape graph for a single method.

nodes. The graph was built by processing each statement in the method push. The constructor call to Node on line 3 maps the nodes from the Node graph into the ape graph for push, creating the edges (data, 3-7, store) and (next, 3-8, store). The annotations 3-7 and 3-8 indicate that a store occurred on lines 7 and 8, through a call at line 3. A similar mapping occurs at line 5, through the call to insert creating the other data and next edges. Due to space limitations, the code for the method insert does not appear.

Fig. 5. Testing subsystem.

5   Testing Subsystem

The testing subsystem, shown in figure 5, takes as input the ape graph object, the term representation necessary for graphically viewing the ape graph, and the annotation table, all generated from the program analysis subsystem. The following subsections describe the components of the testing subsystem, namely the test tuple generator and the test coverage identifier.

5.1   Test Tuple Generator

Algorithm 1. Compute testing tuples for a component represented by a set of call graphs, each with possibly multiple roots.

Input: set of call graphs and ape graphs for the CUT;
Output: set of test tuples for the CUT and feedback on potential influences from outside the CUT;

```
 1: /* Process each method's ape graph */
 2: foreach node n in a topological ordering of call graph nodes do
 3:    Let m = method represented by node n;
 4:    foreach edge e labeled STORE in m's ape graph  do
 5:       /* Create tuples from stores in ape graph */
 6:       Identify associated loads, labeling e, occurring after the STORE
 7:       /* Using node type and escape information create tuple or report feedback */
 8:       if source node of e is an inside node then
 9:          Replace tuple (store,load) by (cs_{sn},store,load);
10:       else /*source node is an outside node*/
11:          Feedback(object for (store,load) is potentially created outside CUT);
12:       if source node not escaped and target node is escaped then
13:          Feedback(value loaded in (cs_{sn},store,load)
                   is potentially changed by method outside CUT, but l is indeed referencing object created
                   at cs_{sn});
14:    endfor
15:    foreach edge e in ape graph labeled only by LOAD do
16:       if target node is a load node in APE graph then
17:          Feedback(load at statement cs_{l} in method m has potentially reaching references from
                   outside CUT);
18:    endfor
19: endfor
```

The test tuple construction algorithm, shown in Algorithm 1, computes a set of test tuples for the component under test(CUT), based on object manipulations. Starting at the root of each call graph of the CUT and proceeding in topological order, the method for each call graph node is processed once, by analyzing the node's ape graph. This processing order avoids creating duplicate tuples potentially identified due to subgraphs of invoked methods also appearing in a caller's ape graph. As a particular ape graph is analyzed, only unmarked edges (those not already processed in a caller's graph) are processed.

The algorithm processes each edge in a method's ape graph. For each annotation on an ape graph edge representing a store, the associated loads potentially occurring after the store are identified, and a *(store,load)* tuple is created. The annotations reflect the results of the flow sensitive points-to escape analysis used

to build the ape graph. Thus, the *evs* and *cs* statement numbers on these annotations are adequate to identify the reachable loads from a particular store. The
object creation site associated with the *(store,load)* tuple is determined by the
source node of the edge being analyzed. If the source node is an inside node, then
the source node is the object creation site and the node number of the source
node is used to complete the tuple for the *(store,load)* tuple. If the source node
is an outside node, then the object is not created inside CUT, and feedback is
given depending on the kind of the source node and whether it is interior or root
of the call graph. Additionally, feedback is given when the target node of the
ape graph edge being analyzed is escaped from CUT.

The algorithm also provides feedback for load nodes when a corresponding
store is not present in CUT. This is represented by an ape graph edge that
is labeled only with load annotations and no store annotations. The feedback
provides the tester with information about the fact that an object creation site
could have potentially occurred outside CUT, as well as the possibility that the
load in CUT has potentially reaching references from outside CUT.

5.2   Test Coverage Identifier

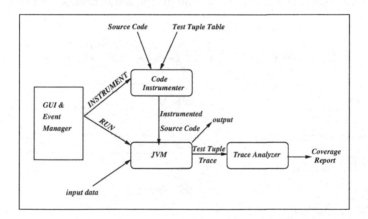

Fig. 6. Test Coverage Identifier.

The test coverage identifier provides an environment useful for providing
test coverage information about the component under test. Figure 6 illustrates
the subcomponents of the test coverage identifier. There are two user events,
INSTRUMENT and *RUN*, which the event manager understands. An *INSTRU-
MENT* event invokes the code instrumenter, which takes the program source
code and test tuple table as input. The source line numbers corresponding to
the store-load-object creation site form the entries of the test tuple table, providing all the information necessary to instrument the source code. Simple print
statements are inserted into the source code to produce instrumented code. The

second event, *RUN*, invokes the component under test, prompting the user, if necessary, for input data, running the program on the JVM, and generating a test tuple trace file, in addition to the normal output of the program. The test tuple trace file is generated by running the instrumented source code, which provides information about the test tuples covered during the program execution.

Currently, we maintain coverage information for one run of the program. In the future, we will maintain information for multiple runs of the program, therefore providing more coverage information for the test suite of programs running on the component under test. The trace analyzer currently provides visual coverage information by analyzing the test tuple trace file and highlighting the source code and the corresponding test tuples that were covered during the program execution.

5.3   Ape Graph and Test Tuple Visualizer

The primary function of *TATOO*s ape graph and test tuple visualizer is for visualizing the ape graph representation of the CUT, which graphically displays object interactions. This subsystem is composed of the daVinci toolkit[8], a graphical user interface, and an event manager that communicates with daVinci, providing interaction between the source code, ape graph, annotations, and test tuples.

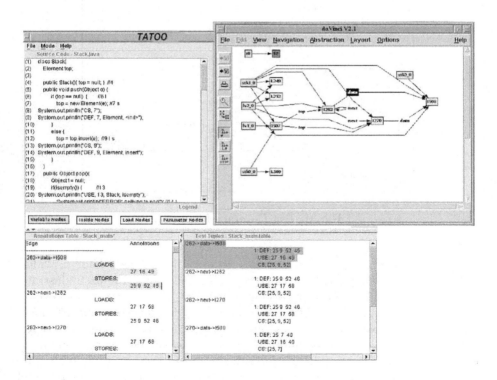

Fig. 7. The *TATOO* user interface including daVinci.

Visualization of the ape graph is achieved through the daVinci graph drawing tool, which is an X-Window visualization tool for drawing high quality directed graphs automatically[8]. The term representation, produced by the program analysis subsystem, is the graphical representation used as input to daVinci. DaVinci not only displays the graph, but allows interaction between the graph and an external program. Our event manager communicates with daVinci through the API defined by the daVinci toolkit.

The graph visualizer interface of *TATOO* is shown in figure 7. A user can view the source code for a class, the annotations and test tuples produced for that class, and a graphical representation of the ape graph. In addition, the user is able to selectively view the ape graph and the source code, annotations, and test tuples corresponding to the selected graph segment. For example, a user can click on an edge in the daVinci graph window, and the source code, annotations, and test tuples corresponding to the selected edge are highlighted in their respective windows. The graph visualizer allows for a fine grain level of detail corresponding to how objects interact with other objects in a program. Its usefulness stems from the ability to statically visualize an object's fields and the points-to relationships constructed throughout the program. The escape information could also be visualized in a similar fashion, allowing for the user to click on the escape information, which would identify the region of code and the section of the graph that an object could escape through. The escape information is available to us, but this capability has not been included in our current prototype testing tool.

6   Implementation and Evaluation

TATOO has been implemented in Java and evaluated with a set of Java programs. Table 2 shows some general characteristics of the benchmark programs we have used with *TATOO*, as well as the storage requirements necessary for the ape graph. The characteristics include the number of lines of user code, the number of JVM instructions, the number of classes analyzed, and the number of methods analyzed. We have reported these numbers separately for user and library sizes in order to show that a relatively small program may rely heavily on libraries; therefore, analysis of the user program depends not only on the user code, but on the library code as well.

Table 2. Program characteristics and storage requirements.

Name	Problem Domain	# of lines	jvm instr User	Lib	classes User	Lib	methods User	Lib	ave size(Kb) User	Lib	max size(Kb)
compress	text compression	910	2500	7070	17	90	50	301	6.1	1.1	43.0
db	database retrieval	1026	2516	11648	9	100	240	306	14.5	0.9	98.6
mpeg	audio decompr	3600	12019	7188	49	92	58	383	5.9	1.0	201
jlex	scanner generator	7500	11000	7250	19	72	106	264	22.6	1.0	379
jess	expert system	9734	15200	13005	108	105	468	436	13.9	1.1	668

One concern in developing a code-based testing tool is the overhead of the underlying static analysis. We have experimentally evaluated the space overhead of our static analysis. The last three columns of table 2 show the average storage requirements of the ape graph per method (user and library), and the maximum ape graph storage requirement per benchmark. We computed the storage requirements by computing the sum of two products. The first product is the total number of nodes over all the ape graphs times the size of an ape graph node, and the second product is the total number of edges over all the ape graphs times the size of an edge. The storage requirement per ape graph is relatively small. The compositional nature of the ape graphs avoids the requirement of keeping all ape graphs in memory at once. The maximum ape graph represents the size needed to maintain the main method of the program. Essentially, the maximum ape graph contains the graphs from all of its callees, which were merged into itself.

The test tuple construction algorithm takes one pass over the call graphs representing the CUT. For each node in the call graph, it processes each unmarked edge of the ape graph for that method exactly once. The ape graph is easily extendible and the computation of additional test tuples can be performed in a demand-driven way as clients are added.

7   Related Work

Two proposed code-based testing tools based on data flow testing techniques include the Coupling Based Coverage Tool (CBCT)[1] and Orso's testing tool[12]. CBCT is a coverage-based testing tool that reports coverage metrics to the user, by instrumenting the source code. CBCT is based on a coupling-based testing technique, which is a data flow method based on coupling relationships that exist among variables across call sites, and is useful for integration testing. To our knowledge, CBCT has not been implemented. Orso's testing technique for integration testing is based on a data flow testing technique used for integration testing, in particular for polymorphic test coverage[12]. His tool is similar to ours, but uses a different program representation, which does not provide testing feedback to the user. There is also no mention of how they deal with references or instance variables that are objects of different types in Java code.

Previous work on structural testing of object-oriented software has concentrated on data flow analysis for computing def-use associations for classes[9], testing of libraries in the presence of unknown alias relationships between parameters and unknown concrete types of parameters, dynamic dispatches, and exceptions[5], and developing a set of criteria for testing Java exception handling constructs[15].

8   Conclusions and Future Work

We have presented *TATOO*, a testing and analysis tool for object-oriented software. The primary benefits of this tool are its ability to automatically generate code-based test tuples for testing, to determine test coverage through code instrumentation and test coverage notification, to provide feedback to the tester about external object interactions that could affect their result, and to visually display object interactions through the daVinci graph drawing tool.

In the future, we plan on extending this work in several ways. First, we plan on designing and implementing a new component to *TATOO* which automatically or semi-automatically generates test cases from the test tuples. Then, we plan to perform an experimental evaluation on different variations of the OMEN approach. Finally, we plan on designing and implementing a regression testing component for *TATOO* which will indicate portions of code that need to be re-tested after modifications have been made to the original code.

References

1. R. Alexander. Testing the polymorphic relationships of object-oriented components. Technical report, George Mason University, 1999.
2. B. Beizer. *Software Testing Techniques*. Van Nostrand Reinhold, 2nd edition, 1990.
3. B. Blanchet. Escape analysis for object oriented languages. Application to Java. In *Proceedings of OOPSLA*, November 1999.
4. J. Bodga and U. Hoelzle. Removing unnecessary synchronization in Java. In *Proceedings of OOPSLA*, November 1999.
5. R. Chatterjee and B. Ryder. Data-flow-based Testing of Object-Oriented Libraries. Technical Report 382, Rutgers University, March 1999.
6. J. Choi, M. Gupta, M. Serrano, V. Sreedhar, and S. Midkiff. Escape analysis for Java. In *Proceedings of OOPSLA*, November 1999.
7. T. Chusho. Test Data Selection and Quality Estimation Based on the Concept of Essential Branches for Path Testing. *IEEE Transaction on Software Engineering*, 13(5):509–517, May 1987.
8. M. Fröhlich and M. Werner. The Graph Visualization System daVinci. Technical report, Universität Bremen, Germany, September 1994.
9. M.J. Harrold and G. Rothermel. Performing Data Flow Testing on Classes. In *Proceedings of the Symposium on the Foundations of Software Engineering*, 1994.
10. M.J. Harrold and M.L. Soffa. Interprocedural Data Flow Testing. In *Proceedings of the ACM Symposium on Testing, Analysis, and Verification*, 1989.
11. M. Rinard et. al. FLEX. www.flex-compiler.lcs.mit.edu, 2000.
12. A. Orso. *Integration Testing of Object-Oriented Software*. PhD thesis, Politecnico Di Milano, 1999.
13. W. Perry. *Effective Methods for Software Testing*. John Wiley Inc, 1995.
14. S. Rapps and E. Weyuker. Selecting Software Test Data Using Data Flow Information. *IEEE Transactions on Software Engineering*, 11(4):367–375, April 1985.
15. S. Sinha and M.J. Harrold. Criteria for Testing Exception-Handling Constructs for Java Programs. In *Proceedings on Software Maintenance*, January 1999.
16. A. Souter and L. Pollock. OMEN: A Strategy for Testing Object-Oriented Software. In *Proceedings of the International Symposium on Software Testing and Analysis*, August 2000.
17. J. Whaley and M. Rinard. Compositional Pointer and Escape Analysis for Java Programs. In *Proceedings of OOPSLA*, November 1999.

Implementing a Multi-valued Symbolic Model Checker

Marsha Chechik, Benet Devereux, and Steve Easterbrook

Department of Computer Science, University of Toronto,
Toronto, ON M5S 3G4, Canada.
{chechik,benet,sme}@cs.toronto.edu

Abstract. Multi-valued logics support the explicit modeling of uncertainty and disagreement by allowing additional truth values in the logic. Such logics can be used for verification of dynamic properties of systems where complete, agreed upon models of the system are not available. In this paper, we present an implementation of a symbolic model checker for multi-valued temporal logics. The model checker works for any multi-valued logic whose truth values form a quasi-boolean lattice. Our models are generalized Kripke structures, where both atomic propositions and transitions between states may take any of the truth values of a given multi-valued logic. Properties to be model checked are expressed in CTL, generalized with a multi-valued semantics. The design of the model checker is based on the use of MDDs, a multi-valued extension of Binary Decision Diagrams. We describe MDDs and their use in the model checker. We also give its theoretical time complexity and some preliminary empirical performance data.

1 Introduction

Multi-valued logics provide an interesting alternative to classical boolean logic for modeling and reasoning about systems. By allowing additional truth values in the logic, they support the explicit modeling of uncertainty and disagreement. For these reasons, they have been explored for a variety of applications in databases [12], knowledge representation [13], machine learning [17], and circuit design [15].

A number of specific multi-valued logics have been proposed and studied. For example, Łukasiewicz [16] first introduced a three-valued logic to allow for propositions whose truth values are 'unknown', while Belnap [1] proposed a four-valued logic that also introduces the value 'both' (i.e. "true *and* false"), to handle inconsistent assertions in database systems. Each of these logics can be generalized to allow for different levels of uncertainty or disagreement. In practice, it is useful to be able to choose different multi-valued logics for different modeling tasks.

The motivations that led to the development of these logics clearly apply to the modeling of software behaviour, especially the exploratory modeling used in the early stage of requirements engineering and architectural design:

- We need to allow for *uncertainty* – for example, we may not yet know whether some behaviours should be possible;
- We need to allow for *disagreement* – for example, different stakeholders may disagree about how the systems should behave;
- We need to represent *relative importance* – for example, in the case where some behaviours are essential and others may or may not be implemented.

T. Margaria and W. Yi (Eds.): TACAS 2001, LNCS 2031, pp. 404–419, 2001.

For reasoning about dynamic properties of systems, existing modal logics can be extended to the multi-valued case. Fitting [10] suggests two different approaches for doing this: the first extends the interpretation of atomic formulae in each world to be multi-valued; the second also allows multi-valued accessibility relations between worlds. The latter approach is more general, and can readily be applied to the temporal logics used in automated verification [6].

Some automated tools for reasoning with multi-valued logics exist. In particular, the work of Hähnle and others [14,19] has led to the development of several theorem-provers for first-order multi-valued logics. However, as yet the question of model checking for multi-valued modal logics has not been addressed.

In this paper we describe our implementation of a multi-valued symbolic CTL model checker, Xchek. Xchek is generalized for an entire family of multi-valued logics, known as the quasi-boolean logics. It takes as its input a description of a particular quasi-boolean logic, represented as a lattice of truth values, a state machine model, represented as a multi-valued Kripke structure, and a temporal logic property expressed in CTL. It returns the truth value that the property has in the initial state(s).

The paper is structured as follows. Section 2 motivates the work with an example of a multi-valued state machine model. Section 3 describes the family of quasi-boolean multi-valued logics, and shows how these are specified as lattices of truth values. Section 4 explains our approach, describing our multi-valued extension of Kripke structures and our multi-valued extension of CTL. Section 5 presents the design of the model checker and analyses its performance. Section 6 presents our conclusions.

2   Motivation

To motivate the development of our model checker, and to illustrate its application, we present an example state machine model expressed in a multi-valued logic. The model captures an early draft of the requirements for a simple coffee dispenser. We distinguish behaviours that *must* be true (are required), behaviours that *should* be true (are desired, but not required), behaviours that *should not* be true (are undesirable), and behaviours that *must not* be true (are prohibited). We use two types of unknown: *Don't Know* for things that will be controlled by the system, where we do not yet know what behaviours we want; and *Don't Care* for things that are controlled by the environment, where the value does not matter. We represent these six possibilities in a 6-valued logic, arranged as a lattice in Figure 1(a), using the partial order 'more true than'.

Figure 1(b) shows the model. Each variable is assigned a truth value in each state. Each transition between states is also labeled with a truth value. The coffee dispenser starts in state OFF. In this state, it is irrelevant whether there is a cup in the machine, so that variable has the value 'DC' ("don't care"). The specification team *have not yet decided* whether they need a power-saving standby mode. They model their uncertainty by including the state IDLE, but label the transitions into it 'S', indicating these *may be* desirable. They also use the value 'DK' ("Don't Know") for the state of the power in IDLE, and for the transition from OFF to IDLE. However, the transition from OFF to READY is labeled 'T', indicating that when the power is switched on, the machine *must* enter the READY state. From there, it *must* be able to deliver coffee, and it *should* then

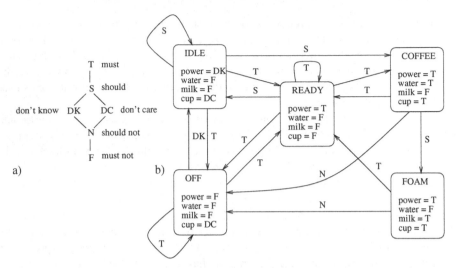

Fig. 1. (a) A lattice of truth values; (b) The coffee dispenser model that uses it.

be able to deliver foam. The transitions from COFFEE and FOAM to OFF are labeled 'N'. These are undesirable, but we cannot prohibit them because the machine has no direct control over the power supply. Note that by convention we omit all 'F' transitions. Hence there is an 'F' self-loop for COFFEE and FOAM, indicating we *must not* stay in either state, and an 'F' transition from READY to FOAM, indicating this *must not* occur.

We can now write properties that ought to be true of the model, even though it contains some uncertainties. For example:

1. The machine must always be able to make coffee.
2. It is desirable that the machine make foam.
3. Coffee cannot be dispensed if there is no cup.
4. Once coffee is dispensed, we cannot get coffee again until the cup is changed.

We formalize these properties in Section 4 and give results of model checking them on the coffee dispenser model in Table 1 of Section 5.

In this example, the use of a 6-valued logic allows us to distinguish two levels of priority for requirements, and two different types of unknown. We could choose different multi-valued logics if we wanted to distinguish further levels of priority, or different types of 'unknown'. We are also interested in modeling disagreement, and have developed a method for reasoning about whether disagreements between stakeholders' views affect various system properties. In [9] we outline a general framework for combining inconsistent state machine models into a single model using multi-valued logics to capture levels of (dis)agreement. We eventually plan to use the model checker described below as a negotiation tool for constructing and reasoning about such models.

3   Specifying the Logics

Our approach to modeling makes use of an entire family of multi-valued logics. Rather than giving a complete axiomatization for each logic, we simply give a semantics by defining conjunction, disjunction and negation on the truth values of the logic, and restrict ourselves to logics where these operations are well-defined, and satisfy commutativity, associativity etc. Such properties can be easily guaranteed if we require that the truth values of the logic form a lattice. In this section we describe the types of lattices used in our logics.

Definition 1. *A lattice is a partial order* $(\mathcal{L}, \sqsubseteq)$ *for which a unique greatest lower bound and least upper bound, denoted* $a \sqcap b$ *and* $a \sqcup b$, *respectively, exist for each pair of elements* (a, b).

$a \sqcap b$ and $a \sqcup b$ are referred to as *meet* and *join*, respectively. The partial order operation $a \sqsubseteq b$ means "*b* is at least as true as *a*". The following properties hold for all lattices:

$$a \sqcup a = a \qquad\qquad a \sqcap a = a \qquad\qquad \text{(idempotence)}$$
$$a \sqcup b = b \sqcup a \qquad\qquad a \sqcap b = b \sqcap a \qquad\qquad \text{(commutativity)}$$
$$a \sqcup (b \sqcup c) = (a \sqcup b) \sqcup c \quad a \sqcap (b \sqcap c) = (a \sqcap b) \sqcap c \quad \text{(associativity)}$$

Definition 2. *A lattice is* complete *if it includes a meet and a join for every subset of its elements. Every complete lattice has a top* $(\top)$ *and a bottom* $(\bot)$.

$$\bot = \sqcap \mathcal{L} \quad (\bot \text{ characterization}) \qquad \top = \sqcup \mathcal{L} \quad (\top \text{ characterization})$$

For example, in the lattice of Figure 1(a), $\top$ is labeled 'T' and $\bot$ is labeled 'F'. We adopt the convention of labeling $\top$ and $\bot$ in this way in all our lattices. Also, we only use lattices that have a finite number of elements. Every finite lattice is complete.

Definition 3. *A finite lattice* $(\mathcal{L}, \sqsubseteq)$ *is* quasi-boolean *[2] if there exists a unary operator* $\neg$ *defined for it, with the following properties* $(a, b$ *are elements of* $\mathcal{L})$:

$$\neg(a \sqcap b) = \neg a \sqcup \neg b \quad \text{(De Morgan)} \qquad \neg\neg a = a \qquad (\neg \text{ involution})$$
$$\neg(a \sqcup b) = \neg a \sqcap \neg b \qquad\qquad a \sqsubseteq b \Leftrightarrow \neg a \sqsupseteq \neg b \quad (\neg \text{ antimonotonic})$$

Thus, $\neg a$ *is a* quasi-complement *of* a.

The family of multi-valued logics we use are exactly those logics whose truth values form a quasi-boolean lattice. Meet and join in the lattice of truth values define conjunction and disjunction operators, respectively, and we assume that an appropriate negation operation is defined with the properties required by Definition 3. The identification of a suitable negation operator is greatly simplified by the observation that quasi-boolean lattices are symmetric about their horizontal axes:

Definition 4. *A lattice* $(\mathcal{L}, \sqsubseteq)$ *is* horizontally-symmetric *if there exists a bijective function* $H : \mathcal{L} \to \mathcal{L}$ *such that for every pair* $a, b \in \mathcal{L}$,

$$a \sqsubseteq b \Leftrightarrow H(a) \sqsupseteq H(b) \quad (\text{order} - \text{embedding}) \quad H(H(a)) = a \quad (\text{H involution})$$

Theorem 1. *[6] Horizontal symmetry is a necessary and sufficient condition for a lattice to be quasi-boolean with* $\neg a = H(a)$ *for each element of the lattice.*

The negation of each element is then defined as its image through horizontal symmetry[1]. For example, in Figure 1(a) we have $\neg$T=F, $\neg$S=N, $\neg$DK=DK, $\neg$DC=DC, etc. Finally, we define an operator $\to$ as follows:

$$a \to b \equiv \neg a \sqcup b \quad (\text{definition of } \to)$$

---

[1] Note that we still have to choose how to negate any elements that fall *on* the axis of symmetry.

4   Multi-valued Model Checking

CTL model checking on two-valued logics was introduced by Clarke and his colleagues in [8]. CTL is a branching-time temporal logic that allows quantification over individual paths in a tree of computations exhibited by a model. There are five basic pairs of operators: AX and EX ("next"), AF and EF ("eventually" or "in the future"), AG and EG ("globally"), AU and EU ("until"), AR and ER ("release"). Models are represented as Kripke structures, which are finite-state machines that guarantee that there is a transition out of every state. See [7] for a detailed account of CTL model checking.

In this section we describe our multi-valued extension of Kripke structures, which we call χKripke structures, and we give the semantics of multi-valued CTL [6].

4.1   Defining the Model

A state machine M is a χ*Kripke structure* if $M = (S, S_0, R, I, A, L)$, where:

- L is a quasi-boolean logic represented by a lattice $(\mathcal{L}, \sqsubseteq)$.
- A is a (finite) set of atomic propositions, otherwise referred to as variables (e.g. power or milk in the example in Figure 1(b)).
- S is a (finite) set of states. States are not explicitly labeled – each state is uniquely identified by its variable/value mapping. Thus, two states cannot have the same mapping. However, we sometimes use state labels as a shorthand for the respective vector of values, as we did in the coffee dispenser example.
- $S_0 \subseteq S$ is the non-empty set of initial states.
- Each transition (s, t) in M has a logical value in $\mathcal{L}$. Thus, $R : S \times S \rightarrow \mathcal{L}$ is a total function assigning a truth value from the logic L to each possible transition between states, including self-loops. Note that a χKripke structure is a completely connected graph. We also require that each state has at least one non-false transition coming out of it.
- $I : S \times A \rightarrow \mathcal{L}$ is a total function that maps a state s and an atomic proposition (variable) a to a truth value ℓ of the logic. For simplicity we assume that all our variables are of the same type, ranging over the values of the logic. For a given variable a, we will write I as $I_a : S \rightarrow \mathcal{L}$. For symbolic model checking, we compute *partitions* of the state space w.r.t. a variable a using $I_a^{-1} : \mathcal{L} \rightarrow 2^S$. A partition has the following properties:

$$\forall a \in A, \forall \ell_1, \ell_2 \in \mathcal{L} : \ell_1 \neq \ell_2 \Rightarrow (I_a^{-1}(\ell_1) \cap I_a^{-1}(\ell_2) = \emptyset) \quad \text{(disjointness)}$$
$$\forall a \in A, \forall s \in S, \exists \ell \in \mathcal{L} : s \in I_a^{-1}(\ell) \quad \text{(cover)}$$

4.2   Multi-valued CTL

Here we give semantics of CTL operators on a χKripke structure M over a quasi-boolean logic L. We will refer to this language as *multi-valued CTL, or χCTL*. L is described by a finite, quasi-boolean lattice $(\mathcal{L}, \sqsubseteq)$, and thus the conjunction $\sqcap$, disjunction $\sqcup$ and negation $\neg$ operations are available. In extending the CTL operators, we want to ensure that the expected CTL properties, given in Figure 2, are still preserved. Note that the AU fixpoint is somewhat unusual because it includes an additional conjunct,

$$\begin{array}{ll}
\neg AX\varphi = EX(\neg\varphi) & \text{(negation of ``next'')} \\
A[\bot U\varphi] = E[\bot U\varphi] = \varphi & (\bot \text{ ``until''}) \\
A[\varphi U\psi] = \psi \vee (\varphi \wedge AXA[\varphi U\psi] \wedge EXA[\varphi U\psi]) & (AU \text{ fixpoint}) \\
E[\varphi U\psi] = \psi \vee (\varphi \wedge EXE[\varphi U\psi]) & (EU \text{ fixpoint})
\end{array}$$

Fig. 2. Properties of CTL operators.

$EXA[fUg]$. This additional term preserves a "strong until" semantics for states that have no outgoing T transitions [4].

We first give the semantics of the propositional operators. We extend the domain of the interpretation function I to any CTL formula φ. For a model M, we use $P_\varphi^M(s)$ to denote the truth value that formula φ takes in state s. We omit M if it is clear from context. If $s \in S$ is a state, $a \in A$ is a variable, and φ and ψ are CTL formulae:

$$\begin{array}{ll}
P_a(s) \equiv I(s, a) & P_{\varphi\wedge\psi}(s) \equiv P_\varphi(s) \wedge P_\psi(s) \\
P_{\neg\varphi}(s) \equiv \neg P_\varphi(s) & P_{\varphi\vee\psi}(s) \equiv P_\varphi(s) \vee P_\psi(s)
\end{array}$$

We proceed by defining the EX operator. In standard CTL, EX is defined using existential quantification over next states. We extend the notion of quantification for multi-valued reasoning by using conjunction and disjunction for universal and existential quantification, respectively. This treatment of quantification is standard [1,18]. The semantics of the EX operator is

$$P_{EX\varphi}(s) \equiv \bigvee_{t \in S}(R(s, t) \wedge P_\varphi(t))$$

The definitions of AU, EU and AX are given using the properties in Figure 2:

$$\begin{array}{l}
P_{AX\varphi}(s) \equiv \neg P_{EX\neg\varphi}(s) \\
P_{E[\varphi U\psi]}(s) \equiv P_\psi(s) \vee (P_\varphi(s) \wedge P_{EXE[\varphi U\psi]}(s)) \\
P_{A[\varphi U\psi]}(s) \equiv P_\psi(s) \vee (P_\varphi(s) \wedge P_{AXA[\varphi U\psi]}(s) \wedge P_{EXA[\varphi U\psi]}(s))
\end{array}$$

The remaining CTL operators, $AF(\varphi)$, $EF(\varphi)$, $AG(\varphi)$, $EG(\varphi)$, $A[\varphi R\psi]$, $E[\varphi R\psi]$ are the abbreviations for $A[\top U\varphi]$, $E[\top U\varphi]$, $\neg EF(\neg\varphi)$, $\neg AF(\neg\varphi)$, $\neg E[\neg\varphi U\neg\psi]$, $\neg A[\neg\varphi U\neg\psi]$, respectively.

The properties of the coffee dispenser in Figure 1(b), given in Section 2, can be formalized in $\mathcal{X}$CTL as follows [2]:

1. $EF(\text{water})$ The expected answer is T.
2. $EF(\text{milk})$ The expected answer is S.
3. $AG(\text{water} \to \text{cup})$ The expected answer is T.
4. $AG(\text{water} \to AXA[\neg\text{water} \ \mathcal{W} \ (\neg\text{cup} \wedge \neg\text{water})])$ The expected answer is T.

5 Symbolic Multi-valued Model Checker

In this section we describe the implementation of our symbolic multi-valued model checker, $\mathcal{X}$chek. The architecture of $\mathcal{X}$chek is shown in Figure 3. $\mathcal{X}$chek takes as input a model M with variable and transition values from a lattice $\mathcal{L}$, and a $\mathcal{X}$CTL formula φ. It outputs a total mapping from $\mathcal{L}$ to the set S of states, indicating in which states φ takes

---

[2] We use the operator *while* defined as $A[x \ \mathcal{W} \ y] = \neg E[\neg y \ U \ (\neg x \wedge \neg y)]$.

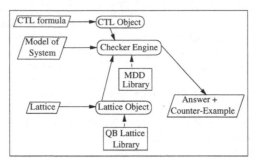

Fig. 3. Architecture of $\mathcal{X}$chek.

each value ℓ. This is simply P_φ^{-1}, the inverse of the valuation function defined above. Thus, the task of the model checker is to compute P_φ given the transition function R.

Since states are assignments of values to the variables, an arbitrary ordering imposed on A allows us to consider a state as a vector in $\mathcal{L}^n$, where $n = |A|$. Hence P_φ and R can be thought of as functions of type $\mathcal{L}^n \to \mathcal{L}$ and $\mathcal{L}^{2n} \to \mathcal{L}$ respectively. Such functions are represented within the model checker by multi-valued decision diagrams (MDDs), a multi-valued extension of the binary decision diagrams (BDDs) [3].

As an example, consider the coffee dispenser shown in Figure 1(b). Using the variable ordering (`power`, `water`, `milk`, `cup`), the state labeled `COFFEE` is just the vector $s = (T, T, F, T)$, the one labeled `FOAM` is $t = (T, F, T, T)$, and the existence of a T-valued transition between them is expressed by the fact that $R = (T, T, F, T, T, F, T, T) = T$ or, more compactly, $R(s, t) = T$.

$\mathcal{X}$chek uses two supplementary libraries: a library for handling quasi-boolean lattices and an MDD library. The former includes functions to compute unions and intersections of sets of logical values, determine whether given lattices have some desired properties, e.g., distributivity, and to support various lattice-based calculations. Our library is based on Freese's Lisp lattice library [11]. The MDD library is described below.

5.1 Data Structures

There is an extensive literature dealing with MDDs [21], mostly in the field of circuit design. To our knowledge, the logics used in that literature are given by total orders (such as the integers modulo n) and not by arbitrary quasi-boolean lattices, but we concede that this is a minor difference. Also, as far as we know, they have not been used in formal verification before, so for the purposes of this paper we will describe them briefly. We will assume a basic knowledge of BDDs [3].

The basic notion in the construction of binary decision diagrams is the Shannon expansion. A boolean function f of n variables can be expressed relative to a variable a_0, by computing f on $n-1$ variables with a_0 set to $\top$, and the same function with a_0 set to $\bot$. These functions are referred to as $f_\top$ and $f_\bot$, respectively. We write this expansion as $f(a_0, \ldots, a_{n-1}) \to f_\top(a_1, \ldots, \ldots, a_{n-1}), f_\bot(a_1, \ldots, a_{n-1})$ This notion is generalized as follows:

Definition 5. *[21] Given a finite domain D, the generalized Shannon expansion of a function $f : D^n \to D$, with respect to the first variable in the ordering, is:*

$$f(a_0, a_1, \ldots, a_{n-1}) \rightarrow f_0(a_1, \ldots, a_{n-1}), \ldots, f_{|D|-1}(a_1, \ldots, a_{n-1})$$

where $f_i = f[a_0/d_i]$, the function obtained by substituting the literal $d_i \in D$ for a_0 in f. These functions are called cofactors.

Definition 6. *Assuming a finite set D, and an ordered set of variables A, a multi-valued decision diagram (MDD) is a tuple $(V, E, \mathrm{var}, \mathrm{child}, \mathrm{image}, \mathrm{value})$ where:*

- $V = V_t \cup V_n$ *is a set of nodes, where V_t and V_n indicate a set of terminal and non-terminal nodes, respectively;*
- $E \subseteq V \times V$ *is a set of directed edges;*
- $\mathrm{var} : V_n \rightarrow A$ *is a variable labeling function.*
- $\mathrm{child} : V_n \rightarrow D \rightarrow V$ *is an indexed successor function for nonterminal nodes;*
- $\mathrm{image} : V \rightarrow 2^D$ *is a total function that maps a node to a set of values reachable from it;*
- $\mathrm{value} : V_t \rightarrow D$ *is a total function that maps each terminal node to a logical value.*

We describe constraints on the elements of an MDD below. Although D may be any finite set, for our purposes we are interested only in lattices; so instead of D we will refer to elements of the finite lattice $(\mathcal{L}, \sqsubseteq)$ modeling a logic.

Consider the function $f = x_1 \wedge x_2$, with $\ell_0 = \mathrm{F}, \ell_1 = \mathrm{M}, \ell_2 = \mathrm{T}$. The MDD for this expression is shown in Figure 4b. The diagram is constructed by Shannon expansion, first with respect to x_1, and then (for each cofactor of f) with respect to x_2. The dashed arrows indicate f and its cofactors, and also the cofactors of the cofactors.

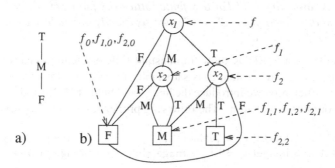

a)   b)

Fig. 4. (a) A three-valued lattice. (b) The MDD for $f = x_1 \wedge x_2$ in this lattice.

The following properties hold for all MDDs:

$$\forall u_0 \in V_n : \mathrm{out}(u_0) = |\mathcal{L}| \quad \wedge \quad \forall u_1 \in V_t : \mathrm{out}(u_1) = 0 \qquad \text{(semantics of nodes)}$$
$$\forall u_0, u_1 \in V, \exists \ell \in \mathcal{L} : (u_0, u_1) \in E \Rightarrow \mathrm{child}_\ell(u_0) = u_1 \qquad \text{(semantics of edges)}$$

where $\mathrm{out}(u)$ stands for the number of non-null children of u. Several further properties are required for the data structure to be usable:

$$\forall u_0, u_1 \in V_n : (u_0, u_1) \in E \wedge \mathrm{var}(u_0) = a_i \wedge \mathrm{var}(u_1) = a_j \Rightarrow i < j \qquad \text{(orderedness)}$$
$$\forall u_0, u_1 \in V : f^{u_0} = f^{u_1} \Rightarrow u_0 = u_1 \qquad \text{(reducedness)}$$
$$\forall u_0, u_1 \in V_n, \ell \in \mathcal{L} :$$
$$(\mathrm{var}(u_0) = \mathrm{var}(u_1)) \wedge (\mathrm{child}_\ell(u_0) = \mathrm{child}_\ell(u_1)) \Rightarrow u_0 = u_1 \qquad \text{(uniqueness 1)}$$
$$\forall u_0, u_1 \in V_t : (\mathrm{value}(u_0) = \mathrm{value}(u_1)) \Rightarrow u_0 = u_1 \qquad \text{(uniqueness 2)}$$

In general, the efficiency of decision diagrams, binary or multi-valued, comes from the properties of reducedness and orderedness (defined above). Orderedness is also required for termination of many algorithms on the diagrams. Uniqueness implies reducedness [21] – MDDs will be unique by construction, and thus reduced.

Note that in general we do not distinguish between a single node in an MDD and the subgraph rooted there, referring to both indiscriminately as u. The function computed by an MDD is denoted $f^u : \mathcal{L}^n \to \mathcal{L}$, and is defined recursively as follows:

$$u \in V_t \Rightarrow f^u(s_0, \dots, s_{n-1}) = \mathsf{value}(u) \qquad \text{(terminal constants)}$$
$$u \in V_n \Rightarrow f^u(s_0, \dots, s_{n-1}) = f^{\mathsf{child}_{s_i}(u)}(s_0, \dots, s_{i-1}, s_{i+1}, \dots, s_{n-1}),$$
$$\text{where } a_i = \mathsf{var}(u) \text{ and } s \in \mathcal{L}^n \qquad \text{(cofactor expansion)}$$

Consider the MDD in Figure 4. To compute $f = x_1 \wedge x_2$ with $x_1 = \mathrm{T}$ and $x_2 = \mathrm{F}$ using this diagram, we want to find $f(s)$ where $s = (\mathrm{T}, \mathrm{M})$. We begin at the root node. Its var is x_1, so we pick out s_1, which is T, and descend to the node $\mathsf{child}_\mathrm{T}(f)$, indicated by the arrow to f_2 (which represents the function $\mathrm{T} \wedge x_2$). Now we compute $f_2(\mathrm{M})$ by choosing $\mathsf{child}_\mathrm{M}(f_2)$, which is a node in V_t, so we stop and return M. Thus, we conclude that $f(\mathrm{T}, \mathrm{F}) = \mathrm{M}$.

We will be calculating equality, conjunction, disjunction, negation, and existential quantification on the functions represented by MDDs. MDDs have the same useful property as BDDs: given a variable ordering, there is precisely one MDD representation of a function. This allows for constant-time checking of function equality.

Theorem 2. Canonicity [21] *For any finite lattice (or finite set) $\mathcal{L}$, any nonnegative integer n, and any function $f : \mathcal{L}^n \to \mathcal{L}$, there is exactly one reduced ordered MDD u such that $f^u = f(a_0, \dots, a_{n-1})$.*

In the boolean case, BDDs allow for constant-time existential quantification, since any node which is not a constant $\bot$ is satisfiable. In order to implement multi-valued quantification efficiently, we introduce the image attribute of MDD nodes, which stores the possible outputs of functions. The following properties hold for image:

$$u \in V_t \Rightarrow \mathsf{image}(u) = \{\mathsf{value}(u)\} \qquad \text{(image property 1)}$$
$$u \in V_n \Rightarrow \mathsf{image}(u) = \bigcup_{\ell \in \mathcal{L}} \mathsf{image}(\mathsf{child}_\ell(u)) \qquad \text{(image property 2)}$$

Definition 7. *A function f is ℓ-satisfiable if some input yields ℓ as an output, or, equivalently, $f^{-1}(\ell) \neq \emptyset$:*

$$(f^u)^{-1}(\ell) \neq \emptyset \ \Leftrightarrow \ \ell \in \mathsf{image}(u) \qquad \text{(correctness of image)}$$
$$(\exists s \in \mathcal{L}^n : f^u(s)) = \left(\bigvee_{s \in \mathcal{L}^n} f^u(s) \right) = \left(\bigvee_{\ell \in \mathsf{image}(u)} \ell \right) \qquad \text{(existential quantification)}$$

To demonstrate how existential quantification works, we refer again to the example in Figure 4, and compute $\exists x_2 : x_1 \wedge x_2$. There are two nodes labeled with x_2 to be dealt with. By inspection we see that $\mathsf{image}(f_1) = \{\mathrm{F}, \mathrm{M}\}$ and $\mathsf{image}(f_2) = \{\mathrm{F}, \mathrm{M}, \mathrm{T}\}$. So f_1 is replaced with the terminal node $\mathrm{F} \vee \mathrm{M} = \mathrm{M}$, and f_2 with the terminal node $\mathrm{F} \vee \mathrm{M} \vee \mathrm{T} = \mathrm{T}$.

In general, algorithms for manipulating BDDs are easily extensible to the multi-valued case, provided they do not use any optimizations that depend on a two-valued boolean logic (e.g. complemented edges [20]). The differences are discussed below.

```
function MakeUnique(name, children)
    find (create if not found) a node u s.t.
        var(u) = name ∧
        ∀ℓ, childₗ(u) = children(ℓ)
    return u


function Quantify(u, i)
// existentially quantifies over all variables aⱼ with j ≥ i.
    if var(u) < i
        then foreach ℓ ∈ L
            children(ℓ) := Quantify(childₗ(u), i)
        return MakeUnique(var(u), children)
        else return Lattice.bigOR(image(u))


function Apply(op, u₁, u₂)
// applies the lattice operation op to the MDDs u₁ and u₂
    global G = |u₁| × |u₂| array of int
    Apply'(op, u₁, u₂)


function Apply'(op, u₁, u₂)
// helper function for Apply which actually does the work
    if G[u₁][u₂] non-empty
        then return G[u₁][u₂]
    else
        if u₁ ∈ L ∧ u₂ ∈ L
            then u := Lattice.doOp(u₁, u₂, op)
        else if var(u₁) = var(u₂)
            then foreach ℓ ∈ L
                children(ℓ) := Apply'(op, childₗ(u₁), childₗ(u₂))
            u := MakeUnique(var(u₁), children)
        else if var(u₁) < var(u₂)
            then foreach ℓ ∈ L
                children(ℓ) := Apply'(op, childₗ(u₁), u₂)
            u := MakeUnique(var(u₁), children)
        else
            foreach ℓ ∈ L
                children(ℓ) := Apply'(op, u₁, childₗ(u₂))
            u := MakeUnique(var(u₁), children)
        G[u₁][u₂] := u
        return u
```

Fig. 5. The MDD algorithms MakeUnique, Quantify and Apply for binary operators. Apply for unary operators is defined similarly.

The most-used method in an MDD (or BDD) library is MakeUnique, defined in Figure 5. This guarantees uniqueness and thus reducedness [21]. MakeUnique is not a public method, but it is used by most of the public methods.

The public methods required for model checking are: Build, to construct an MDD based on a function table; Apply, to compute ∧, ∨ and ¬ of MDDs; Quantify, to existentially quantify over the primed variables; and AllSat to retrieve the computed par-

---

function $EX(P_\varphi)$
   return $\text{Quantify}(\text{Apply}(\wedge, R, \text{Prime}(P_\varphi)), n)$

function $\text{QUntil}(\text{quantifier}, P_\varphi, P_\psi)$
   $QU_0 = P_\psi$
   repeat
      if (quantifier is A)
         $\text{AXTerm}_{i+1} := \text{Apply}(\neg, EX(\text{Apply}(\neg, QU_i)))$ // $AX(QU_i)$
         $\text{EXTerm}_{i+1} := EX(QU_i))$
      else
         $\text{AXTerm}_{i+1} := P_\varphi$
         $\text{EXTerm}_{i+1} := EX(\text{Apply}(\neg, QU_i)))$
      $QU_{i+1} := \text{Apply}(\vee, P_\psi, (\text{Apply}(\wedge, P_\varphi, \text{Apply}(\wedge, \text{EXTerm}_{i+1}, \text{AXTerm}_{i+1})))))$
   until $QU_{i+1} = QU_i$
   return QU_n

procedure $\text{Check}(p, M)$
Case
   $p \in A$:   **return** $\text{Build}(p)$
   $p = \neg\varphi$:   **return** $\text{Apply}(\neg, \text{Check}(\varphi, M))$
   $p = \varphi \wedge \psi$:   **return** $\text{Apply}(\wedge, \text{Check}(\varphi, M), \text{Check}(\psi, M))$
   $p = \varphi \vee \psi$:   **return** $\text{Apply}(\vee, \text{Check}(\varphi, M), \text{Check}(\psi, M))$
   $p = EX\varphi$:   **return** $EX(\text{Check}(\varphi, M))$
   $p = AX\varphi$:   **return** $\text{Apply}(\neg, EX(\text{Apply}(\neg, \text{Check}(\varphi, M))))$
   $p = E[\varphi U\psi]$: **return** $\text{QUntil}(E, \text{Check}(\varphi, M), \text{Check}(\psi, M))$
   $p = A[\varphi U\psi]$: **return** $\text{QUntil}(A, \text{Check}(\varphi, M), \text{Check}(\psi, M))$

Fig. 6. The multi-valued symbolic model checking algorithm.

tition $P_\varphi^{-1}(\mathcal{L})$. Build ensures orderedness of MDDs while they are being constructed, and Apply preserves it. Apply and Quantify are shown in Figure 5. Note how each interfaces with the lattice library: Apply calls the method Lattice.doOp to compute $\wedge$ or $\vee$ of two terminal nodes, while Quantify requires Lattice.bigOR to compute the disjunction of an MDD's image-set.

An additional function, Prime, primes all of the variables in an MDD. In general, primed and unprimed variables may be mixed in the variable ordering, but for the purposes of this presentation, primed variables are always higher in the ordering. For instance, (a, c, b, a', c', b') is an acceptable variable ordering, but (a, a', b, b', c, c') is not. Quantify will still work in the more general case, but some preliminary variable reordering will be needed.

5.2   The Model Checker

Symbolic model checkers for boolean logic [7,4] are naturally extended to the multi-valued case. The model checker presented here is a symbolic version of the multi-valued model checker described in [6].

The full model checking algorithm is described in Figure 6. The function $EX(P_\varphi)$ computes $P_{EX\varphi}$ symbolically; QUntil carries out the fixed-point computation of both AU and EU. $AX\varphi$ is computed as $\neg EX\neg\varphi$. EG, AG, EF, AF, ER and AR are not

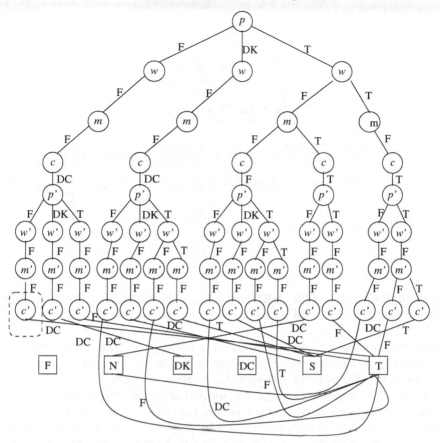

Fig. 7. MDD for R, representing the transition relation for the coffee dispenser.

shown in this Figure, but could be added as cases and defined in terms of calls to EX, QUntil, and Apply.

Proposition 1 *The function* EX(P_φ) *computes* $EX\varphi$. *That is, a state vector s ℓ-satisfies* Quantify$(R \wedge P_{\varphi'}, n)$ *if and only if* $(\bigvee_{t \in S} R(s, t) \wedge P_\varphi(t)) = \ell$.

To illustrate the algorithm, we compute the partition given by the $\mathcal{X}$CTL formula $EX(\text{cup})$ in the coffee dispenser example in Figure 1(b). This computation is equivalent, in symbolic terms, to computing $\exists v'$, s.t. $R \wedge P_{\text{cup}'}$, where v' is a *primed state vector*; the intuition here is the quantification over all possible next states. This is implemented in the model checker by the expression

$$\text{Quantify}(\text{Apply}(\wedge, R, \text{Prime}(P_\varphi)), n)$$

Not every n-ary function over an arbitrary quasi-boolean lattice can be written in the relatively economical form of a propositional formula, and so we need to show either an MDD or a function-table representation. We will use MDDs. The MDD for the transition relation of the model (R) is shown in Figure 7. For clarity and to save space, we used the following conventions: (a) all state variables are abbreviated to their initial

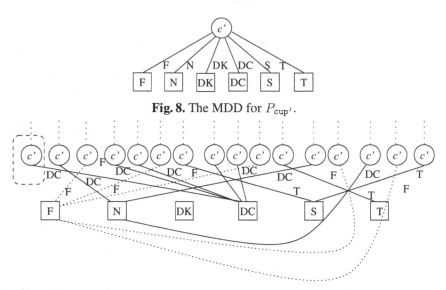

Fig. 8. The MDD for $P_{\mathrm{cup}'}$.

Fig. 9. The lowest level of the MDD for $R \wedge P_{\mathrm{cup}'}$. Dotted lines indicate the transitions which existed in Figure 7 and are now set to F.

letters; e.g., m stands for milk, w for water, etc; (b) the MDD is not reduced; (c) the transitions to the terminal node F are not shown. Note that there are no transitions to node DC in this diagram. The MDD for $P_{\mathrm{cup}'}$ is given in Figure 8.

We start by computing $R \wedge P_{\mathrm{cup}'}$. The top part of the MDD is the same as shown in Figure 7. The bottom row is given in Figure 9. The conjunction of two MDDs with the same variable in the root node is carried out by pairwise conjunction of their children; for instance, consider the leftmost node in Figure 7 labeled with cup′, indicated by the dashed box; its child$_{\mathrm{DC}}$ is T, and its other children are F. The MDD for cup′ has child$_\ell = \ell$ for all $\ell \in \mathcal{L}$. Their conjunction, then, has child$_\ell = \ell$ for any $\ell \in \mathcal{L}$ except for DC; DC $\wedge$ T = DC, so the child is DC, as shown by the dashed box in Figure 9.

To complete the computation, the model checker needs to existentially quantify over the primed variables. Quantify replaces all primed-variable nodes u which are immediate children of unprimed-variable nodes, with the constant node $\bigvee \mathrm{image}(u)$. For instance, we can see by inspection that the leftmost subgraph with power′ at the root (which corresponds to the successor states of OFF) has DC, N, F in its image-set, so it is replaced by the terminal node $\bigvee\{\mathrm{DC}, \mathrm{N}, \mathrm{F}\} = \mathrm{DC}$; from this we conclude that EX cup has the value DC in state OFF, the model's initial state.

The properties of the coffee dispenser example given in Section 2 and formalized in Section 4 can be model checked with the results given in Table 1.

Num	Property	Result	Comment
1.	$EF(\mathrm{water})$	T	as expected
2.	$EF(\mathrm{milk})$	S	as expected
3.	$AG(\mathrm{water} \rightarrow \mathrm{cup})$	T	as expected
4.	$AG(\mathrm{water} \rightarrow AXA[\neg\mathrm{water}\ \mathcal{W}\ (\neg\mathrm{cup}\wedge\neg\mathrm{water})])$	S	as $R(\mathrm{COFFEE}, \mathrm{FOAM}) = \mathrm{S}$

Table 1. Results of model checking the coffee dispenser.

MDD Method	Running Time	Notes
MakeUnique(var, child)	$O(1)$	Hash-table lookup.
Build(f)	$O(|\mathcal{L}|^n)$	O(size of the function table to convert to MDD).
Apply(op, u_1, u_2)	$O(|u_1||u_2|)$	The worst-case is pairwise conjunction of every node in u_1 with every node in u_2.
Quantify(u, i)	$O(|u|)$	Depth-first traversal of the graph.
Prime(u)	$O(|u|)$	Same as above.

Table 2. MDD methods used for model checking, and their running times.

5.3   Analysis

Table 2 shows the running times of MDD operations used by the model checker in terms of $|u|$, the size of the MDD. In the worst case, this size is $O(|\mathcal{L}|^n)$ [21].

The running times of MDD methods Build and Apply critically depend on the sizes of MDD structures. In order to form a rough estimate of these sizes in the average case, we ran the MDD library on several test sets, with results shown in Figure 10. Each data point in the graph stands for a set of 200 MDDs, each representing a function generated by filling in a random value (chosen from a uniform distribution) from $\mathcal{L}$ for each possible input. We generated one such set for 3, 4, and 5 variables for lattices ranging in size from 3 to 8 (the x-axis of the graph), and took the average size of the MDDs representing the functions. The figure shows the *worst-case* size $|\mathcal{L}|^n$, and our *experimental* results, for $n = 4$ and $n = 5$; $n = 3$ is similar.

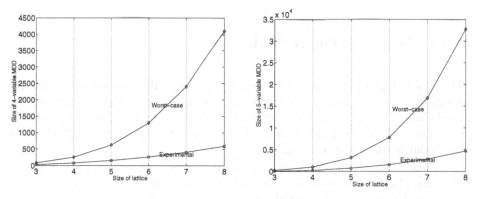

Fig. 10. Worst-case and experimental average-case sizes of MDDs plotted against lattice size. (a) $n = 4$, (b) $n = 5$.

The results show the average size of the generated MDDs to be roughly $|\mathcal{L}|^{n-1}$, a linear improvement over the worst-case $O(|\mathcal{L}|^n)$. We recognize the weakness of this methodology: that it does not give a good idea of how the structure of the problem affects the size of MDDs. We suspect that the structure of the model checking problem results in a somewhat better improvement, but do not yet have adequate benchmarks with which to test this hypothesis. In the future, we would like to perform the same test for an appropriate test suite of multi-valued models, to check whether the structure of the model checking task has an impact on the size of MDDs.

The running time of $\mathcal{X}$chek is dominated by the fixpoint computation of QUntil. The proof of termination of this algorithm is based on each step of QUntil being a monotonic lattice operator; a detailed proof can be found in [6]. The total number of steps is bounded above by $|\mathcal{L}|^n \times h$ (h is the height of the lattice $\mathcal{L}$), and the time of each step is dominated by the time to compute the EXTerm and AXTerm, which is $O(|\mathcal{L}|^{2n})$; so the worst-case running time for $\mathcal{X}$chek is $O(|\mathcal{L}|^{3n} \times h)$, where h is the height of the lattice. The results of Figure 10 suggest that in the average case, each step's running time is $O(|\mathcal{L}|^{2n-2})$, for an average termination time of $O(|\mathcal{L}|^{3n-2} \times h \times |p|)$, where $|p|$ is the size of the $\mathcal{X}$CTL formula.

At first glance, MDDs appear to be performing significantly worse than BDDs ($O(|\mathcal{L}|^n)$ versus $O(2^n)$ in the worst case). However, our multi-valued logics compactly represent incompleteness in a model. For example, suppose we have a model with n states and wish to differentiate between p of those states ($p \ll n$) by introducing an extra variable a. In classical model checking this uncertainty can only be handled by duplicating each of $n - p$ states (one for each value of a). In fact, most of these states are likely to be reachable; thus, the size of the state space nearly doubles. In the multi-valued case, the reachable state-space will increase at most by p states. This computation did not take into an account the presence of "unknown" transitions; these could also be encoded into the binary representation, but would lead to a further state-space increase. Thus, we expect that often our model checker would perform as well as the classical one, and on some problems even better.

Finally, the scope of the applicability of an MDD-based model checker includes reasoning about inconsistent models.

6   Conclusion and Future Work

Multi-valued logics can be useful for describing models that contain incomplete information or inconsistency. In this paper we presented an extension of classical CTL model checking to reasoning about arbitrary quasi-boolean logics. We also described an implementation of a symbolic multi-valued model checker $\mathcal{X}$chek and illustrated it using a simple coffee dispenser example.

We plan to extend the work presented here in a number of directions to ensure that $\mathcal{X}$chek can effectively reason about non-trivial systems. We will start by addressing some of the limitations of our $\mathcal{X}$Kripke structures. In particular, so far we have assumed that our variables are of the same type, with elements described by values of the lattice associated with that machine. We need to generalize this approach to variables of different types. We are also working on generalizing our algorithm to verification of properties expressed in CTL*.

In this paper we concentrated our attention on a purely symbolic model checker. The union, intersection, and quantification were computed using MDD operations. Alternatively, one can build a table-driven model checker, where such operations are table lookups. This model checker has the same running time as the MDD-based one. However, lattice-theoretic results can be used to significantly optimize the table-driven model checker. Our report on this work is forthcoming [5].

Acknowledgments

We thank the members of the University of Toronto formal methods reading group for many interesting discussions and for comments on earlier drafts of this paper. Special thanks go to Albert Lai, Victor Petrovykh, Mark Pichora, Arie Gurfinkel, Christopher Thompson-Walsh and Ric Hehner. We are also grateful to Ralph Freese of the University of Hawaii for the lattice library. This work was funded by NSERC and CITO.

References

1. N.D. Belnap. "A Useful Four-Valued Logic". In Dunn and Epstein, editors, *Modern Uses of Multiple-Valued Logic*, pages 30–56. Reidel, 1977.
2. L. Bolc and P. Borowik. *Many-Valued Logics*. Springer-Verlag, 1992.
3. R. E. Bryant. "Symbolic Boolean manipulation with ordered binary-decision diagrams". *Computing Surveys*, 24(3):293–318, September 1992.
4. T. Bultan, R. Gerber, and C. League. "Composite Model Checking: Verification with Type-Specific Symbolic Representations". *ACM Trans. on Software Engineering and Methodology*, 9(1):3–50, Jan 2000.
5. M. Chechik, B. Devereux, S. Easterbrook, A. Lai, & V. Petrovykh. "Efficient Multiple-Valued Model-Checking Using Lattice Representations". submitted for publ. Jan 2001.
6. M. Chechik, S. Easterbrook, and V. Petrovykh. "Model-Checking Over Multi-Valued Logics". In *Proc. Formal Methods Europe (FME'01)*, March 2001.
7. E. Clarke, O. Grumberg, and D. Peled. *Model Checking*. MIT Press, 1999.
8. E. M. Clarke, D. E. Long, and K. L. McMillan. "Compositional Model Checking". In *Proc. 4th Ann. Symp. on Logic in Computer Science*, pages 464–475, June 1989.
9. S. Easterbrook and M. Chechik. "A Framework for Multi-Valued Reasoning over Inconsistent Viewpoints". In *Proc. 23rd Int. Conf. on Software Engineering (ICSE'01)*, May 2001.
10. M. Fitting. Many-Valued Modal Logics. *Fundamenta Informaticae* 15(3-4):335–350, 1991.
11. R. Freese, J. Ježek, and J. B. Nation. *Free Lattices*. Amer. Math. Soc., Providence, 1995. Mathematical Surveys and Monographs, vol. 42.
12. B. R. Gaines. "Logical Foundations for Database Systems". *Int. J. of Man-Machine Studies*, 11(4):481–500, 1979.
13. M. Ginsberg. "Multi-valued logic". In M. Ginsberg, editor, *Readings in Nonmonotonic Reasoning*, pages 251–255. Morgan-Kaufmann, 1987.
14. R. Hähnle. *Automated Deduction in Multiple-Valued Logics*, volume 10 of *International Series of Monographs on Computer Science*. Oxford U. Press, 1994.
15. S. Hazelhurst. *Compositional Model Checking of Partially Ordered State Spaces*. PhD thesis, Dept of Computer Science, U. of British Columbia, 1996.
16. J. Łukasiewicz. *Selected Works*. North-Holland, Amsterdam, Holland, 1970.
17. R. S. Michalski. "Variable-Valued Logic and its Applications to Pattern Recognition and Machine Learning". In D. C. Rine, editor, *Computer Science and Multiple-Valued Logic: Theory and Applications*, pages 506–534. North-Holland, Amsterdam, 1977.
18. H. Rasiowa. *An Algebraic Approach to Non-Classical Logics. Studies in Logic and the Foundations of Mathematics*. Amsterdam: North-Holland, 1978.
19. V. Sofronie-Stokkermans. Automated theorem proving by resolution for finitely-valued logics based on distributive lattices with operators. *Multiple-Valued Logic: An International Journal* 5(2), 2000.
20. F. Somenzi. "Binary Decision Diagrams". In Manfred Broy and Ralf Steinbrüggen, editors, *Calculational System Design*, vol 173 of *NATO Science Series F: Computer and Systems Sciences*, pp 303–366. IOS Press, 1999.
21. A. Srinivasan, T. Kam, S. Malik, and R.E. Brayton. "Algorithms for Discrete Function Manipulation". In *IEEE Int. Conf. on Computer-Aided Design*, pages 92–95, 1990.

Is There a Best Symbolic Cycle-Detection Algorithm?

Kathi Fisler[1,4], Ranan Fraer[2], Gila Kamhi[2], Moshe Y. Vardi[1]*, and Zijiang Yang[1,3]

[1] Department of Computer Science, Rice University, Houston, TX, USA
[2] Intel Development Center, Haifa, Israel
[3] CCRL, NEC, Princeton, NJ, USA
[4] Worcester Polytechnic Institute, Worcester, MA, USA

Abstract. Fair-cycle detection, a core problem in model checking, is solvable in linear time in the size of the design model using an explicit-state representation. Existing cycle-detection algorithms for symbolic model checking are quadratic or $n \log n$ time in the worst case and often inefficient in practice. Which default symbolic cycle-detection algorithm to implement in model checkers remains an open question. We compare several such algorithms based on the numbers of external and internal iterations and the numbers of image operations that they perform on both randomly-generated and real examples. Unlike recent work by Ravi, Bloem, and Somenzi, we conclude that model checkers need to implement at least two generic cycle-detection algorithms: the traditional Emerson-Lei algorithm and one that evolved from our study, originally due to Hojati *et al.* We demonstrate that these two algorithms are complementary, as the latter algorithm is provably incomparable to Emerson-Lei's and often dominates it in practice.

1 Introduction

Model checking, whether for LTL, CTL, or ω-automata, has linear time complexity in the size of the design model. This well-known result follows from two facts: first, that most model checking techniques reduce to the problem of locating cycles through a given set of nodes in a graph [3,18]; second, that cycle detection is solvable in linear time using a depth-first search that identifies strongly-connected components (cf. [4]). This depth-first strategy provides a suitable approach to cycle detection in explicit-state model checking, and has been implemented in several tools [7,11].

Depth-first approaches to cycle detection are not suitable for BDD-based symbolic model checking because BDDs represent sets of states while depth-first search examines individual states. Efficient BDD-based model checking requires efficient breadth-first, set-based cycle-detection algorithms. Most modern symbolic model checkers employ some variant of Emerson and Lei's symbolic cycle-detection algorithm [5]. CTL model checkers use the Emerson-Lei algorithm

---

* Work partially supported by NSF Grant CCR-9988322 and a grant from the Intel corporation.

T. Margaria and W. Yi (Eds.): TACAS 2001, LNCS 2031, pp. 420–434, 2001.

(henceforth EL) to process formulas of the form EG φ, which specify infinite paths on which every state satisfies φ. Linear-time model checkers compose the design model with an automaton representing the negation of the property, then check for cycles in the product automaton using the CTL formula EG **true**. Unfortunately, EL's time complexity is not linear in the size of the design model: the algorithm contains a doubly-nested fixpoint operator, and hence requires time quadratic in the design size in the worst case. The algorithm is also often slow in practice. EL is a so-called *SCC-hull* algorithm [16]. SCC-hull algorithms compute the set of states that contains all fair cycles. In contrast, SCC-enumeration algorithms enumerate all the strongly connected components of the state graph. While SCC-enumeration algorithms have a better worst-case complexity than SCC-hull algorithms [1], their performance in practice seems to be inferior to that of SCC-hull algorithms [16]. This paper focuses on SCC-hull algorithms.

Researchers have proposed several alternatives to EL [8,10,14]. Ravi, Bloem, and Somenzi have presented both a classification scheme for such algorithms and an experimental comparison of several algorithms with EL [16]. They concluded that no algorithm consistently outperforms EL for cycle detection, and, consequently, there is no reason to "dethrone" EL as the default cycle-detection algorithm. Their comparison, however, is based primarily on running times, and secondarily on numbers of image operations. This approach has two significant drawbacks: it provides no useful feedback on *why* the algorithms behave as observed, and it suggests no techniques for predicting when one algorithm might outperform another. Furthermore, their comparison considers some algorithms that are based on post-image operations and some that are based on pre-image operations (as is EL), making it rather difficult to draw firm conclusions.

This paper demonstrates a methodology that both addresses these concerns and identifies a symbolic cycle-detection algorithm that provides a viable alternative to EL. Ravi *et al.* present bounds on the number of image operations performed by various cycle-detection algorithms. We argue that to understand the performance of SCC-hull algorithms one needs to measure both the number of image computations as well as the number of external iterations (defined in Section 2). Our methodology focuses on the number of external iterations performed as a basis for comparing and refining symbolic cycle-detection algorithms. In aiming to balance the numbers of external and internal iterations performed, we have identified an algorithm that, as we argue, should join EL as a generic cycle-detection algorithm. We demonstrate that this algorithm is incomparable to EL, dominating it in many cases. Our conclusion is that, as in many other aspects of model checking, there is no "best" cycle-detection algorithm and model checkers need to implement at least both EL and our algorithm.

Section 2 describes our analyses of three existing symbolic cycle-detection algorithms and shows how the competitive algorithm evolved from these analyses. Section 3 presents experimental results on randomly generated and real examples for both the special case of terminal and weak systems and more general examples. Section 4 compares the competitive algorithm to a specialized cycle-detection algorithm for terminal and weak systems. Section 5 concludes.

2   Symbolic Cycle-Detection Algorithms

Cycle-detection algorithms in the context of model checking search for "bad" cycles in a directed graph representing a transition system modeling a design undergoing verification. Two parameters specify which cycles are considered bad: the invariant and the fair sets. The invariant specifies a condition, such as a propositional formula, that must be true of every state on a bad cycle. The fair sets specify sets of states that every bad cycle must pass through. We write $EG_{fair}\varphi$ to indicate a search for cycles satisfying invariant φ and passing through fair sets fair. We will omit the fair annotation when all states are considered fair.

Cycle detection in BDD-based model checking is challenging because the BDDs co-mingle information about different paths through a design. Symbolic cycle-detection algorithms maintain a set of states that may lead to bad cycles; this set is conservative, in that it contains all states that do lead to bad cycles. We call this the *approximation set*. The algorithms repeatedly refine the approximation set by locating and removing states that cannot lead to a bad cycle; we call this the *pruning* step. If a state lies on a bad cycle, then it must have a successor and a predecessor on that same cycle (and thus also in the approximation set). Cycle-detection algorithms use this information in different ways.

Formally, these algorithms search for cycles in nondeterministic transition systems. A transition system is a tuple $\langle Q, R, Q_0, \mathcal{F} \rangle$, where Q is a set of states, $Q_0 \subseteq Q$ is the initial state set, $R \subseteq Q \times Q$ is the transition relation, and $\mathcal{F} \subseteq Q$ is the set of fair states. A transition system is *weak* iff (1) there exists a partition of Q into sets $Q_1, \ldots, Q_n$ such that each Q_i is either contained in $\mathcal{F}$ or is disjoint from it, and (2) the Q_i's are partially ordered so that there is no transition from Q_i to Q_j unless $Q_i \leq Q_j$. If the Q_i's contained in $\mathcal{F}$ are the maximal elements of the partial order, a weak system is called *terminal*. This definition of weak and terminal transition systems is due to Bloem, Ravi, and Somenzi [2], as refined from Kupferman and Vardi [15]. In model checking, designs commonly have several fair sets, and bad cycles must pass through each fair set. Such designs are outside the scope of weak systems, whose definition is only meaningful for one fair set.[1]

EL appears in Figure 1 (left).[2] At each iteration through the **while** loop, EL computes the set of states that can reach every fair set via a non-trivial path contained in the approximation set, b. We call these iterations *external*; the reachability computations (the EU formula) form the *internal* iterations. EL does most of its work in the internal iterations: each external iteration performs only one preimage computation per fair set outside of the internal iterations.

Hardin *et al.* attempted to reduce the number of external iterations that EL performs as a means of achieving an improved algorithm [8]. Their algorithm, called Catch-Them-Young (henceforth CTY), aggressively prunes the set

---

[1] LTL-to-automaton translation algorithms may yield multiple fair sets when one would suffice, rendering an otherwise weak system non-weak. Thus, minimizing the number of fair sets is an important optimization.

[2] Figure 1 shows VIS' implementation of EL; in SMV, the final image computation ($b := b \wedge EX\ d$) is outside the **for** loop.

$b :=$ invariant ;
while b changes **do**
  for each fair set $\mathcal{F}_i$ **do**
    $d := \mathsf{E}[b \; \mathsf{U} \; (\mathcal{F}_i \wedge b)]$;
    $b := b \wedge \mathsf{EX} \; d$;

$b :=$ invariant ;
while b changes **do**
  for each fair set $\mathcal{F}_i$ **do**
    $\mathcal{F}_i := \mathcal{F}_i \wedge b$;
    $b := \mathsf{E}[true \; \mathsf{U} \; \mathcal{F}_i] \wedge \mathsf{E}[true \; \mathsf{S} \; \mathcal{F}_i]$
  while b changes **do**
    $b := b \wedge \mathsf{EX} \; b \wedge \mathsf{EY} \; b$;
  $res := \mathsf{EF} \; b;$

$b :=$ invariant ;
while b changes **do**
  for each fair set $\mathcal{F}_i$ **do**
    $\mathcal{F}_i := \mathcal{F}_i \wedge b$;
    $b := \mathsf{E}[b \; \mathsf{U} \; (b \wedge \mathsf{EX} \; \mathcal{F}_i)]$;
  while b changes **do**
    $b := b \wedge \mathsf{EX} \; b$;

Fig. 1. The EL (left), CTY (middle), and OWCTY (right) cycle-detection algorithms. In CTY, $\mathsf{EP} \; \mathcal{F}_i$ denotes all states that can reach $\mathcal{F}_i$ and $\mathsf{EY} \; b$ denotes the successors of b. A variant of CTY, CTY+, replaces "true" with b in the EU and ES computations. Each algorithm initializes the approximation set to states satisfying the invariant.

of states potentially lying on bad cycles during the internal iterations (a closely related algorithm was proposed in [10]). This can reduce the number of external iterations by removing states during an external iteration that a later external iteration would otherwise handle in EL.[3] The original CTY algorithm does cycle detection only; it does not compute EG as EL does. For consistency, Figure 1 (middle) provides a version of CTY that can be used to compute EG; this entails one difference from the original algorithm: the extra EF computation in the last step of the algorithm.

The external iterations in CTY perform two steps: first, compute the set of states that are both reachable from and can reach every fair set (the internal iterations); second, repeatedly prune the approximation set until it is closed under both successors and predecessors. In contrast, EL prunes the approximation set only once and removes only states which have no successor in the approximation set; EL does not iterate the pruning step within one external iteration. CTY can eliminate states from the approximation set earlier than can EL, hence the name "Catch-Them-Young". Like EL, CTY has quadratic time complexity with respect to the size of the design. Hardin *et al.*'s experimental results, conducted over a large set of randomly-generated designs, were mixed; CTY tended to outperform EL when there was no bad cycle, but performed worse than EL in the presence of cycles [8]. CTY's aggressive pruning strategy succeeded in reducing the number of external iterations, but nevertheless incurred a noticeable performance penalty.

In order to understand *why* CTY fails to outperform EL, we must examine each algorithm's actual computations. This paper studies patterns of image computations and external iterations, as the former are the most expensive operations in a BDD-based setting and the latter greatly impact the performance of cycle detection algorithms. Section 3 presents numeric data from this analysis. In summary, while CTY performs significantly fewer external iterations than EL, it does not reduce the number of image computations. In essence, EL does too little work outside the internal iterations whereas CTY does too much work overall. Engineering a better balance between the iterations might yield an algorithm that consistently outperforms both EL and CTY. One key difference between EL

---

[3] Though EL may eliminate states in earlier iterations than CTY.

and CTY is that EL prunes based only on successors, whereas CTY considers both successors and predecessors. An intermediate approach could perform CTY's repeated pruning, but using only pre-image computations, as in EL [19]. This could greatly reduce the number of image computations of CTY, though perhaps at the expense of some additional external iterations. The resulting algorithm, called One-Way-Catch-Them-Young (henceforthowCTY), appears in Figure 1 (right).[4] owCTY is essentially the pre-image version of Hojati *et al.*'s EL2 algorithm (sans an initial reachability computation) [10]; its pruning strategy is similar in spirit to that of Kesten *et al.*'s algorithm for cycle detection in the presence of strong fairness [14] (which uses forward instead of backward image operations).

How do owCTY and EL compare? Hojati *et al.*'s experiments on a small set of small examples discussed only running time and were inconclusive for these two algorithms. Ravi *et al.*'s experiments compared EL and the forward-operator version of EL2/owCTY; this is not too meaningful, since the issue of forward vs. backward reachability [9] is orthogonal to the balance between external and internal iterations (indeed, the upper bounds obtained in [16] for EL and forward-EL2 are incomparable). owCTY's worst-case running time has only a linear overhead (see below) over the $\mathcal{O}(|\mathcal{F}|dh)$ worst-case upper bound that Ravi *et al.* identified for EL [16] (where $|\mathcal{F}|$ is the number of fairness constraints, d is the diameter of the state graph, and h is the length of the longest reachable path in the SCC quotient graph). A worst-case analysis as done in [16] provides, however, only a very coarse comparison between the two algorithms. First, the overhead of owCTY over EL is not very significant. Second, the worst-case instances for EL may be different than those for owCTY, which means that the comparison of worst-case running times does not tell us how the two algorithms compare on a given input instance. A more meaningful analysis would compare how the two algorithms perform on concrete instances. Analysis at this level shows that the two algorithms are incomparable. Figure 2 illustrates the differences between the EL and owCTY pruning strategies; owCTY outperforms EL on the first transition system, while EL outperforms owCTY on the second.

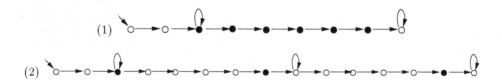

Fig. 2. Two transition systems that illustrate the differences between EL and owCTY. Black circles denote fair states. All states satisfy the invariant.

Consider the first transition system. Both algorithms eliminate the rightmost state in the first iteration and capture the remaining states in the approximation set. During the first iteration, owCTY eliminates all but the leftmost fair state;

---

[4] A variant of owCTY performs pruning inside the **for** loop; in practice, neither version consistently outperforms the other.

EL eliminates only the rightmost fair state. EL requires an additional iteration to eliminate each of the four middle fair states. Each iteration involves a reachability computation that OWCTY does not perform. If the chain of fair states in the first system contained n fair states, OWCTY would perform $\mathcal{O}(n)$ image computations while EL would perform $\mathcal{O}(n^2)$ image computations. Thus, EL has a quadratic overhead relative to OWCTY on such systems.

Now consider the second transition system. In the first iteration, both algorithms eliminate the rightmost state and retain the remaining states in the approximation set. During the first iteration, EL throws away the rightmost fair state. The reachability computation in the second external iteration begins at the middle fair state; thus, EL eliminates the non-fair states between the right two fair states without traversing them explicitly again. OWCTY, in contrast, uses an additional image computation to eliminate each of those non-fair states. The second system currently contains two copies of a chain of states consisting of four non-fair states, followed by a fair state, followed by a non-fair state with a self loop. If the system had k consecutive copies of this chain, each with m states in the initial non-fair chain, EL would perform $\mathcal{O}(k^2 m)$ image computations as compared to OWCTY's $\mathcal{O}(k^2 m + km) = \mathcal{O}(k^2 m)$ image computations. That is, the overhead of OWCTY relative to EL is only linear.

In general, the two algorithms are incomparable with respect to their numbers of image computations. As OWCTY *provably* performs no more external iterations than EL, OWCTY's overhead (if it exists at all) is caused by the last line of the algorithm, which prunes the approximation set. Thus, OWCTY's overhead is at most linear relative to EL, while, as we saw, EL can have a quadratic overhead relative to OWCTY.

To gain a better picture on the comparative performance of EL, CTY, and OWCTY, the experimental analyses in Section 3 gather data on the numbers of external iterations across several randomly generated and real examples; to complement the Ravi *et al.* study [16], we also include running time, memory usage, and BDD size statistics. Our analyses show that OWCTY requires almost the same number of external iterations as CTY with far fewer image computations; in practice, OWCTY almost always matches or improves on EL's performance.

3   Comparative Analysis of the Algorithms

3.1   Experiments on Random Systems

Our first set of experiments compares the algorithms on random systems. We generate random systems by generating random directed graphs. We would like to obtain directed graphs with non-uniform out-degree and linear density (*i.e.*, a linear number of edges in the number of nodes); linear density prevents cycle detection from becoming trivial due to an excess or paucity of edges. The following model of random graphs, due to Karp [13], satisfies these criteria:

Definition 1 *For each positive integer n and each p with $0 < p < 1$, the sample space consists of all labeled digraphs $D_{n,p}$ with n vertices and edge probability p.*

Given a graph G with vertices V and edges E, the *order* of G is $|V|$ and the *density* of G is $|E|/|V|$. We will use n and d to represent a graph's order and density, respectively. We wish to generate graphs in the space $D_{n,d/n}$. Generating the graphs directly based on this model becomes time consuming as n grows larger: the procedure must decide whether to include each of the possible $n(n-1)$ edges based on the probability d/n. Instead, we fix the number of edges to be the expected number dn, and choose dn distinct edges from the $n(n-1)$ candidates. This approach provides a very good approximation to the given model [19].

Our experiments compare four algorithms: EL, CTY, CTY+, and OWCTY. CTY+ is a variant of CTY that restricts the reachability computations to consider only paths through the approximation set, rather than through the entire state space as in CTY [19]; in other words, CTY+ replaces line 5 of CTY with $b :=$ $E[b \ U \ \mathcal{F}_i] \wedge E[b \ S \ \mathcal{F}_i]$, where S is the past-time operator *since*. We present two sets of results. The first measures the number of external iterations that each algorithm performs, the next measures the number of image computations that each algorithm performs.[5] The experiments use graphs with order 2^{12} and densities varying over 1.2, 1.6, 2.0, and 2.4. This order is large enough to explore the behavior of the algorithms, yet small enough to analyze in a reasonable amount of time. We define a single fair set for each graph, with size varying over $.01n$, $.1n$, $.3n$, $.5n$, $.7n$, and $.9n$ where n is the digraph order. Each experiment fixes either the density or the size of the fair set and varies the other. The figures reported in the rest of this section are averaged over 100 individual experiments.

	$|\mathcal{F}|$			
	.01n	.1n	.5n	.9n
CTY	2.18	2.41	2.09	2.00
CTY+	2.18	2.41	2.09	2.00
OWCTY	2.17	2.37	2.07	2.00
EL	2.66	5.36	13.20	20.89

	d			
	1.2	1.6	2.0	2.4
CTY	2.00	2.00	2.00	2.00
CTY+	2.00	2.00	2.00	2.00
OWCTY	2.00	2.00	2.00	2.00
EL	20.89	10.37	7.02	5.09

Table 1. Average number of external iterations on digraphs with order 2^{12}. The left table fixes the density at 1.2 and varies the fair set size. The right table fixes the fair set size at $.9 \times 2^{12}$ and varies the density.

Table 1 shows the number of external iterations on digraphs with order $n = 2^{12}$. One set of experiments fixes the density at 1.2 and varies the fair set size; the other fixes the fair set size at $.9 \times 2^{12}$ and varies the density. The tables indicate that CTY, CTY+ and OWCTY perform far fewer external iterations than EL. Furthermore, OWCTY performs essentially the same number of external iterations as CTY; thus pruning based on predecessors as well as successors, as CTY does, does not significantly reduce the number of external iterations over a pruning strategy based only on successors. We therefore expect OWCTY to consume considerably fewer resources than CTY in practice. EL requires significantly

---

[5] We refer to post- and pre-image computations collectively as image computations.

more external iterations as the fair set grows larger, and significantly fewer external iterations as the density increases. In contrast, CTY, CTY+, and OWCTY perform fairly consistent numbers of external iterations in both cases.

The data in Table 1 do not indicate that CTY and OWCTY are more efficient than EL because the former algorithms may do more work in the internal iterations. The number of image computations offers a more precise efficiency comparison. Image computations are the most computationally expensive operations in each of the cycle-detection algorithms. The cost of these operations depends on the density and order of the underlying graphs [19]. Since we analyze the four algorithms over the same randomly generated graphs, the cost of individual image computations is comparable across the algorithms. The number of image computations is therefore a fair parameter for comparing the algorithms.

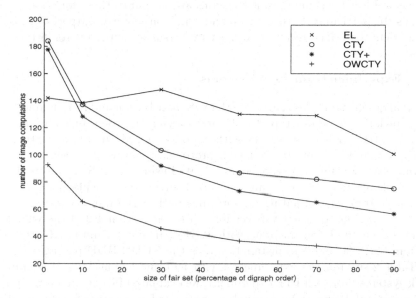

Fig. 3. Number of image computations for EL, CTY, CTY+ and OWCTY.

Figure 3 shows the number of image computations performed over graphs with order $n = 2^{12}$, density $d = 1.2$, and fair set size ranging over $.01n$, $.1n$, $.3n$, $.5n$, $.7n$, and $.9n$. For CTY, CTY+ and OWCTY the number of image computations decreases as the fair set gets larger. CTY performs more image computations than CTY+ because CTY+ restricts reachability computations to the approximation set, which allows the computation to converge faster. OWCTY performs fewer image computations than either CTY or CTY+ because it does not perform forwards reachability. Separate data (not shown) show that the backwards reachability computations in OWCTY and CTY perform almost the same numbers of image computations; furthermore, the pruning step in OWCTY performs roughly half as many image computations as that in CTY+ [19]. Thus, eliminating the forward image computations makes OWCTY less computationally expensive without adversely affecting the number of external iterations required.

Separate experiments (not shown) show that the number of image computations decreases sharply as the density increases [19]. In the case of EL, the number of image computations drops because the algorithm performs fewer external iterations as density increases, as discussed previously. For the remaining three algorithms, our experimental data shows that the size of the approximation set after each iteration becomes larger as the density increases. The approximation set determines the base set for subsequent reachability computations. The larger the base set, the faster reachability computations converge [19]. Therefore, fewer image computations are needed when the digraph density increases. Although each pruning step removes fewer vertices, the final approximation set is also larger, so the algorithms perform fewer image computations as density increases. Plots for running time statistics are similar to those for image computations. In particular, both OWCTY and CTY consistently outperform EL. This contradicts the mixed results in other CTY versus EL experiments [8,16].

3.2   Experiments on Real Systems

Our real design examples come from the VIS distribution and from Fabio Somenzi. They include an ethernet protocol with varying numbers of collisions before failure, a tree-structured arbiter with 8 nodes, a gcd circuit, a floating point multiplier, and two mutual exclusion protocols (bakery and eisenberg). These examples are written in Verilog and evaluated using the VIS model checker [17]. We implemented OWCTY within the VIS framework by replacing the original (EL) algorithm for evaluating EG formulas with OWCTY in a copy of VIS. We ran the experiments using VIS version 1.3 (with version 1.2 of the vl2mv compiler), on an Intel 686 machine with 1GB of memory running RedHat Linux version 2.2.12-20; our VIS installation uses the CUDD BDD package.

Table 2 summarizes experiments with LTL model checking of terminal and weak systems. For each LTL experiment, we evaluated EG_{fair}**true** on the product of the original design and a manually-constructed automaton for the negation of the property. Table 3 covers examples with multiple fair sets in the context of CTL model checking. Table 4 covers LTL model checking under multiple fairness constraints. In each table, stars on experiment names denote that the models contained cycles or that the property failed. The EX/EY and EU/ES figures count the number of image and reachability computations performed, respectively[6].

The tables show that OWCTY generally matches or outperforms EL, while CTY and CTY+ are clearly not competitive. In many cases, OWCTY outperforms EL dramatically; in contrast, we have not yet found an example on which EL significantly outperforms OWCTY. The benefits of OWCTY are particularly evident on the ethernet and gcd examples in Table 2. As expected, OWCTY uses fewer external iterations than EL; however, OWCTY sometimes performs more image computations than EL.

---

[6] The EU/ES counts do not include trivial computations of the form $[\varphi \cup \varphi]$.

Experiment	Procedure	Ext. Iter.	EX or EX/EY	Time (sec)	Mem (MB)	peak live BDD nodes
ethernet 1	EL	51	2179	356.6	13.6	339932
	CTY	2	42/43	187.9	14.6	398280
	CTY+	2	41/42	184.8	14.6	398280
$G(p \to Fq)$	OWCTY	3	57	5.5	11.7	175118
ethernet 2	EL	107	6506	10656.1	14.4	367135
	CTY	2	67/68	1893.6	33.6	1365367
	CTY+	2	66/67	1887.6	33.6	1365755
$G(p \to Fq)$	OWCTY	3	113	59.6	14.1	404723
ethernet 3	EL	171	11914	4371.3	13.7	279823
	CTY	2	95/96	1962.2	35	1456597
	CTY+	2	94/95	1938.0	35	1456597
$G(p \to Fq)$	OWCTY	3	177	24.6	13.8	290593
ethernet 4	EL	-	-	(30H)	-	-
	CTY	2	130/131	5859.7	53.6	2320201
	CTY+	2	130/2	5895	53.6	2320201
$G(p \to Fq)$	OWCTY	3	245	491.4	14.1	368225
treearb 8*	EL	8	75	6.2	13.6	234021
	CTY	-	-	(20M)	(23)	-
	CTY+	-	-	(20M)	(23)	-
$G(p \to Fq)$	OWCTY	2	24	4.2	12.7	206640
gcd	EL	-	-	(37H)	-	-
	CTY	2	15/3	1384.2	59.3	2298351
	CTY+	2	14/2	1383.0	59.3	2298351
$G(p \to XFq)$	OWCTY	2	24	2497.5	130.9	6285856
fpmult	EL	2	18	18345.8	363	17667058
	CTY	2	26/3	33089.7	369	17619441
	CTY+	2	18/2	21994.7	368	17619441
$G(p \to XXXq)$	OWCTY	2	17	22457.2	369	17422253

Table 2. LTL model checking on weak and terminal systems. Parenthesized times indicate terminated computations; M indicates minutes instead of seconds.

Experiment	Procedure	Num Fair	Ext. Iter.	EX / EU or EX/EY/EU/ES	Time (sec)	Mem (MB)	peak live BDD nodes
bakery1*	EL	6	18	554 / 91	1.3	6.2	34447
	CTY	6	11	1371/650/67/66	10	13.3	176492
	CTY+	6	12	344/299/51/50	7.0	13	182755
AG$(p \to$ AF$q)$	OWCTY	6	18	516 / 75	1.6	6.1	36962
bakery2	EL	6	18	490 / 92	1.3	6.0	29524
	CTY	6	11	1239/614/67/66	9.4	13.3	176492
	CTY+	6	11	282/246/47/46	6.0	12.7	180657
AG$(p \to$ AF$q)$	OWCTY	6	18	444 / 72	1.4	5.8	28849
treearb8*	EL	8	15	382 / 106	14.8	13.6	328115
	CTY	8	-	-	(194M)	(112)	-
	CTY+	8	-	-	(170M)	(123)	-
AG$(p \to$ AF$q)$	OWCTY	8	13	416 / 104	13.1	13.4	309449
eisenberg2	EL	6	27	669 / 124	1.6	5.5	17352
	CTY	6	23	2159/2031/139/138	7.8	11.2	180311
	CTY+	6	16	252/506/56/55	3.8	8.6	148353
AG$(p \to$ AF$q)$	OWCTY	6	27	631 / 102	1.4	5.4	18504
elevator*	EL	8	12	849/97	498.2	13.8	275914
	CTY	8	-	-	(104M)	(38)	-
	CTY+	8	-	-	(104M)	(43)	-
AG$(p \to$ AF$q)$	OWCTY	8	12	861/79	536.8	13.6	275914

Table 3. CTL model checking on systems with multiple fairness constraints.

Experiment	Procedure	Num Fair	Ext. Iter.	EX / EU or EX/EY/EU/ES	Time (sec)	Mem (MB)	peak live BDD nodes
treearb8*	EL	9	15	1021 / 135	1397.8	13.8	239731
	CTY	9	-	-	(186M)	(44)	-
	CTY+	9	-	-	(207M)	(157)	-
G$(p \to$ F$q)$	OWCTY	9	14	1000 / 126	911.6	13.9	369062
eisenberg2	EL	7	24	1332 / 161	5.7	7.2	47704
	CTY	7	24	5114/5486/169/168	60.3	13.7	240028
	CTY+	7	15	229/399/53/52	4.7	8.8	147763
G$(p \to$ F$q)$	OWCTY	7	24	1197 / 109	5.3	7.1	59802
elevator3*	EL	3	2	7 / 1	1164.7	87.5	4062730
	CTY	-	-	-	(60M)	(270)	-
	CTY+	-	-	-	(60M)	(270)	-
Gp	OWCTY	3	2	13 / 1	1167.3	87.5	4062730
elevator4*	EL	1	2	3 / 1	16192.4	282	13308496
	CTY	1	-	-	(365M)	(278)	-
	CTY+	1	-	-	(367M)	(278)	-
Gp	OWCTY	1	2	5 / 1	16388.0	282	13308496

Table 4. LTL model checking on systems with multiple fairness constraints.

Exp.	Proc.	Num Fair	Ext. Iter.	EX	Time (sec)
A*	EL	2	6	203	65.49
	OWCTY	2	2	77	32.58
D*	EL	6	2	147	16.26
	OWCTY	6	2	149	16.33
E*	EL	4	3	125	6.89
	OWCTY	4	2	87	6.39
F*	EL	2	10	50	870.0
	OWCTY	2	2	27	897.7
H1*	EL	2	8	40	633.8
	OWCTY	2	2	23	495.7
H3*	EL	2	8	40	550.5
	OWCTY	2	2	23	592.7

Exp.	Proc.	Num Fair	Ext. Iter.	EX	Time (sec)
I*	EL	2	2	40	1004.5
	OWCTY	2	2	23	692.9
J1*	EL	2	8	40	521.9
	OWCTY	2	2	23	426.6
J2*	EL	2	8	40	447.9
	OWCTY	2	2	23	347.7
K*	EL	2	7	25	220.3
	OWCTY	2	2	20	165.3
L*	EL	2	6	24	129.4
	OWCTY	2	2	19	129.4
M1*	EL	2	7	35	81.5
	OWCTY	2	2	21	53.9

Table 5. Results from Intel on checking EG_{fair}**true** on systems that have (and require) multiple fairness constraints.

Finally, we compared OWCTY and EL on Intel designs using internal Intel tools (Table 5). All the table entries reflect the composition of actual designs with linear-time properties, using multiple fairness constraints. OWCTY performed significantly better than EL in all examples except F and H3, where EL slightly outperformed OWCTY.

4 OW CTY V ersus Specialized Algorithms

Our experimental results show that OWCTY generally outperforms EL on terminal and weak systems. Bloem, Ravi, and Somenzi have presented an algorithm that is specialized to verify terminal and weak systems efficiently [2]. Linear-time model checkers detect bad cycles by using the EL algorithm to check EG **true** over the product of the design and the negation of the desired property. Bloem et al. observed that for terminal and weak systems, CTL formulas capture the search for bad cycles. Specifically, the formulas EF fair and EF EG fair are true of terminal and weak systems, respectively, when they contain infinite fair cycles. Accordingly, their algorithm (henceforth BRS) checks one of the formulas EF fair, EF EG fair, or EG_{fair}**true** based on the structure of the input system. This structure follows from the structure of the property being tested: if a property corresponds to a weak (resp. terminal) system, the product of that property and a design model is also a weak (resp. terminal) system. Bloem et al. showed that BRS significantly outperforms EL in practice on terminal and weak systems.

Table 6 compares OWCTY to BRS.[7] For the examples from Table 2, we checked both EG_{fair}**true** and the appropriate formula from BRS using OWCTY. The statis-

---

[7] The gcd and fpmult examples are the same as Bloem et al. used in their paper [2]. Our resource usage on these examples differs widely from theirs due to differences between our two versions of the compiler from Verilog to BLIF, the VIS input language.

Experiment	Procedure	EX	Time (sec)	Mem (MB)	peak BDD nodes
ethernet 1	¬EF EG fair	53	4.2	11.2	151306
$G(p \to Fq)$	$EG_{fair}true(\text{OWCTY})$	57	5.5	11.7	175118
ethernet 2	¬EF EG fair	109	24.4	13.7	381839
$G(p \to Fq)$	$EG_{fair}true(\text{OWCTY})$	113	59.6	14.1	404723
ethernet 3	¬EF EG fair	173	13.3	13.6	287787
$G(p \to Fq)$	$EG_{fair}true(\text{OWCTY})$	177	24.6	13.8	290593
ethernet 4	¬EF EG fair	241	145.6	14.0	373531
$G(p \to Fq)$	$EG_{fair}true(\text{OWCTY})$	245	491.4	14.1	368225
treearb 8*	¬EF EG fair	22	4.1	12.6	200529
$G(p \to Fq)$	$EG_{fair}true(\text{OWCTY})$	24	4.2	12.7	206640
gcd	¬EF EG fair	20	3351.6	193	8204281
$G(p \to XFq)$	$EG_{fair}true(\text{OWCTY})$	24	2497.5	130.9	6285856
fpmult	¬EF fair	8	5565.5	329	16109729
$G(p \to XXXq)$	$EG_{fair}true(\text{OWCTY})$	17	22457.2	369	17422253

Table 6. Comparison between the OWCTY and BRS algorithms.

tics on $EG_{fair}true$ are reproduced from Table 2. The specialized approach outperforms OWCTY on most of these examples (except the gcd example). This is due to the difference between checking $EG_{true}fair$ (BRS) and $EG_{fair}true$ (OWCTY). The former restricts the search for a bad cycle to the fair states; the latter looks for a cycle that intersects the fair states. As a result, both EL and OWCTY can have non-fair states in their approximation sets, while BRS' approximation set contains only fair states. This restriction usually allows BRS to converge faster.

This comparison demonstrates how exploiting structural information about systems can lead to more efficient verification algorithms. Note, however, that BRS is not a generic cycle-detection algorithm. Furthermore, we must also consider the cost of determining whether a system is weak or terminal, which is not included in our paper or in Bloem *et al.*'s. In theory, this operation can be done symbolically in $\mathcal{O}(n \log n)$ time [1], but experimental results are not yet available. For the simple properties considered by Bloem *et al.* and here, this overhead is insignificant; for more complicated properties (such as those including complex environmental assumptions) it could be rather substantial. OWCTY, which is a generic algorithm, performs well in practice without the overhead of specialized analyses as required in BRS.

5 Conclusions

Symbolic model checking remains a heuristic process, as metrics do not yet exist to predict BDD behavior under differing algorithms. As a result, comparative analyses of algorithms are extremely useful in helping tool developers choose which algorithms to implement. In the name of good science, these analyses need to be reproducible and portable to the greatest extent possible. Such analyses provide not only firm data, but a foundation for future algorithm development.

This paper compares three symbolic cycle-detection algorithms (and a variant on one of them) based on the number of iterations they take through their outermost fixpoint operator, as well as the number of image operations they perform. Each algorithm employs a slightly different strategy for pruning the set of states potentially lying on cycles. Our analysis shows that the original Emerson-Lei (EL) algorithm [5] performs too little work outside of its internal iterations, while Hardin et al.'s Catch-Them-Young (CTY) algorithm [8] performs too much. In contrast, Hojati's EL2 algorithm [10], which we view as a one-way version of CTY (OWCTY) does seem to balance the work inside and outside the internal iterations. On random examples and on terminal and weak systems, OWCTY dominates EL, while on general systems, OWCTY is competitive with EL, dominating it significantly in many cases. We have also shown that the two algorithms are incomparable with respect to the number of image computations they perform: EL can have a quadratic overhead over OWCTY, while OWCTY can have a linear overhead over EL. These results support our conclusion that model checkers need to contain both EL and OWCTY.

In the course of this project, we have identified two desired features for verification tools. First, we want tools to implement multiple algorithms for common problems such as cycle-detection. Both our analysis and the recent one by Ravi et al. [16] indicate that no algorithm consistently outperforms the others; indeed, verification tasks may be tractable with one algorithm and intractable with another. Tools providing multiple algorithms afford human verifiers opportunities to experiment and find algorithms that work on their applications. A similar conclusion in the context of semi-exhaustive reachability analysis was reached in [6]. Second, we want tools to provide visualizations of computational patterns during model checking. Intel's Palette [12] does some of this; we wish we had such a tool to augment VIS and other publicly-available tools. Testbeds supporting multiple algorithms and better data collection would provide strong support for more disciplined approaches to algorithm comparisons in verification.

Acknowledgements

We thank Kavita Ravi, Fabio Somenzi, and Roderick Bloem for their very helpful comments on this paper, and the Rice PLT group for access to their large-memory server.

References

1. Bloem, R., H. N. Gabow and F. Somenzi. An algorithm for strongly connected component analysis in $n \log n$ symbolic steps. In *Intl. Conf. on Formal Methods in Computer-Aided Verification*, Lecture Notes in Computer Science. Springer-Verlag, 2000.

2. Bloem, R., K. Ravi and F. Somenzi. Efficient decision procedures for model checking of linear time logic properties. In *Intl. Conf. on Computer-Aided Verification*, Lecture Notes in Computer Science, pages 222–235. Springer-Verlag, 1999.
3. Clarke, E. M., E. A. Emerson and A. P. Sistla. Automatic verification of finite-state concurrent systems using temporal logic specifications. *ACM Transactions on Programming Languages and Systems*, 8(2):244–263, January 1986.
4. Courcoubetis, C., M. Y. Vardi, P. Wolper and M. Yannakakis. Memory efficient algorithms for the verification of temporal properties. *Formal Methods in System Design*, 1:275–288, 1992.
5. Emerson, E. A. and C. L. Lei. Efficient model checking in fragments of the propositional model mu-calculus. *Proceedings of LICS 1986*, pages 267–278, 1986.
6. Fraer, R., G. Kamhi, L. Fix and M. Y. Vardi. Evaluating semi-exhausting verification techniques for bug hunting. In *Proceedings of the 1st Intl. Workshop on Symbolic Model Checking*. Electronic Notes in Theoretical Computer Science, 1999.
7. Hardin, R. H., Z. Har'El and R. P. Kurshan. COSPAN. In *Intl. Conf. on Computer-Aided Verification*, number 1102 in Lecture Notes in Computer Science, pages 423–427. Springer-Verlag, 1996.
8. Hardin, R. H., R. P. Kurshan, S. K. Shukla and M. Y. Vardi. A new heuristic for bad cycle detection using BDDs. In *Proc. Conf. on Computer-Aided verification (CAV'97)*, pages 268–278. Springer-Verlag. LNCS 1254, 1997.
9. Henzinger, T., O. Kupferman and S. Qadeer. From *pre*historic to *post*modern symbolic model checking. In Hu, A. and M. Vardi, editors, *Intl. Conf. on Computer-Aided Verification*, volume 1427 of *Lecture Notes in Computer Science*, pages 195–206. Springer-Verlag, 1998.
10. Hojati, R., H. Touati, R. Kurshan and R. Brayton. Efficient ω-regular language containment. In *Intl. Conf. on Computer-Aided Verification*, number 663 in Lecture Notes in Computer Science. Springer-Verlag, 1992.
11. Holzmann, G. and D. Peled. The state of SPIN. In *Intl. Conf. on Computer-Aided Verification*, number 1102 in Lecture Notes in Computer Science, pages 385–389. Springer-Verlag, 1996.
12. Kamhi, G., L. Fix and Z. Binyamini. Symbolic model checking visualization. In *Intl. Conf. on Formal Methods in Computer-Aided Verification*, number 1522 in Lecture Notes in Computer Science, pages 290–303. Springer-Verlag, 1998.
13. Karp, R. M. The transitive closure of a random digraph. *Random Structures and Algorithms*, 1(1), 1990.
14. Kesten, Y., A. Pnueli and L. on Raviv. Algorithmic verification of linear temporal logic specifications. In *Intl. Colloquium on Automata, Languages, and Programming*, number 1443 in Lecture Notes in Computer Science. Springer-Verlag, 1998.
15. Kupferman, O. and M. Y. Vardi. Freedom, weakness, and determinism: From linear-time to branching-time. In *IEEE Symp on Logic in Computer Science*, 1998.
16. Ravi, K., R. Bloem and F. Somenzi. A comparative study of symbolic algorithms for the computation of fair cycles. In *Intl. Conf. on Formal Methods in Computer-Aided Verification*, Lecture Notes in Computer Science. Springer-Verlag, 2000.
17. The VIS Group. VIS: A system for verification and synthesis. In Alur, R. and T. Henzinger, editors, *Intl. Conf. on Computer-Aided Verification*, volume 1102 of *Lecture Notes in Computer Science*. Springer-Verlag, July 1996.
18. Vardi, M. Y. and P. Wolper. An automata-theoretic approach to automatic program verification. In *IEEE Symposium on Logic in Computer Science*, 1986.
19. Yang, Z. Performance analysis of symbolic reachability algorithms in model checking. Master's thesis, Rice University, Department of Computer Science, 1999. Available at http://www.cs.rice.edu/CS/Verification/.

Combining Structural and Enumerative Techniques for the Validation of Bounded Petri Nets

Rubén Carvajal-Schiaffino, Giorgio Delzanno, and Giovanni Chiola

Dipartimento di Informatica e Scienze dell'Informazione
Università di Genova
via Dodecaneso 35, 16146 Genova
{ruben,giorgio,chiola}@disi.unige.it

Abstract. We propose a new *validation* algorithm for *bounded* Petri Nets. Our method combines *state enumeration* and *structural techniques* in order to compute *under-approximations* of the reachability set and graph of a net. The method is based on *two heuristics* that exploit properties of T-semiflows to detect acyclic behaviors. T-semiflows also give us an heuristic estimation of the number of levels of the reachability graph we have to keep in memory during forward exploration. This property allows us to organize the space used to store the reachable markings as a circular array, reusing all markings outside a *sliding window* containing a fixed number of the last levels of the graph. We apply the method to examples taken from the literature [ABC+95,CM97,MCC97]. Our algorithm returns *exact* results in all the experiments. In some examples, the circular memory allow us to save up to 98% of memory space, and to scale up to 255 the number of tokens in the specification of the initial marking.

1   Introduction

Bounded Petri Nets (PNs) are finite-state concurrent systems in which the maximal number of processes (tokens) in any possible state (place) is bounded by a constant. Though decidable, the verification of safety and liveness properties of bounded PNs is a very hard problem in practice. Following the literature in the field [STC98,Val98], the techniques used to attack this problem can be distinguished into the following classes.

State Enumeration Techniques. The *reachability graph* of a finite-state system built using an *exhaustive search* algorithm [Hol88] is a complete tool for the *verification* of safety and liveness properties. This technique suffers from the *state explosion problem*, i.e., the explosion of the size of the reachability graph compared to the size of the specification [BCB+90,Val98]. *Partial search* [Hol88] can be used as heuristics to *validate* large finite-state systems. In general, partial search returns under-approximations of the reachability graph. Therefore,

T. Margaria and W. Yi (Eds.): TACAS 2001, LNCS 2031, pp. 435–449, 2001.

it cannot be used for verification purposes, but only for *simulation* and *testing*. When incorporated in searc h algorithms, efficien t data structures likehash tables [Hol88], *BDDs* [BCB+90], and *Sharing Trees* [GGZ95] represent other important *heuristics* to alleviate state explosion.

Structural Techniques. While state en umeration is a general-purpose technique for validation of finite-state systems, v erification techniques based on *structural properties* are a distinguishing feature of PNs [STC98]. These techniques work without explicitly computing the reachability graph. They rely on *linear pro- gramming* (synonymous of *efficiency*) usually returning *approximated* answers. For instance, the *state equation* [Rei86] can be used to over-approximate the reachability set of a PN, and thus to verify safety properties [STC98]. Other techniques like *traps* can be used to improve the precision of the state equation [EM00].

Our Contribution. In contrast with traditional uses of structural theory, in this paper we investigate the *combination* of *enumerative* and *structural* techniques for *validating* and *debugging* systems modeled as bounded PNs. Specifically, we use structural properties as *heuristics* to guide the *search* during state explo- ration. In order to attack state explosion we incorporate our heuristics within a *partial search* algorithm, and w e leave open the possibility of using efficient data structures for storing intermediate results.

   More precisely, the algorithm we propose explores part of the state-space of a PN using properties of *minimal T-semiflows* in order to detect *acyclic* occurrence sequences without having to search for visited markings. Minimal T-semiflo ws form a system of *generators* (the fundamental set) for all the positive integer solutions of the system of equalities

$$\mathbf{C} \cdot \boldsymbol{x} = 0, \ \mathbf{C} \text{ being the } token \ flow \text{ matrix.}$$

To apply our heuristics, we require the fundamental set to be *integral*, i.e., T- semiflows must be non-negative *integer* com binations of minim al T-semiflows. This conditions is satisfied by several case-studies we have found in the liter- ature (see Section 5). Integrality is a new property we introduce on the basis of classical notions of *linear programming* [Sch94]. Our algorithm returns an under-approximation of the reachability graph, while automatically measuring the quality of the approximation. Specifically, a flag is raised whenever the re- turned graph is an *equivalent* representation of the reachability graph. Thus, in an ideal situation our *validation* method can also be used as a complete tool for *verification*. At any momen t during the execution, the algorithm works on a *sliding window* that covers the last levels of the partially constructed graph. The num ber of levels included in the sliding window is computed statically, using again minim al T-semiflows. This property gives us an *estimation* of the number of levels of the reachability graph we need to keep in memory during forw ard exploration. W e exploit these information to build the followinggarbage collec- tion procedure: we organize the main memory as a *circular array*, and we re-use the memory allocated to all markings outside the windo w.

In order to test the *applicability* of our assumptions and the *quality* of our heuristics, we run a prototype implementation of the algorithm (without use of dedicate data structures to store the markings) on several examples taken from [ABC+95,CM97,MCC97]. Our aim was to check safety properties and compute the reachability set. The preliminary results seem very promising. In some of the examples, we were able to scale up the number of tokens in the initial marking to 255, and to handle the resulting PN using only 25Mbytes of main memory (within the range of the RAM memory of a personal computer, see Section 5). Without sliding window the same examples would have required approximatively 1,300 Mbytes of memory, i.e., our heuristics can save up to 98% of memory space. Finally, we obtained an exact representation of the reachability set in all our experiments, i.e., with our method we were able to *verify all* safety properties taken into consideration.

Plan of the paper. In Section 2, we recall the main properties of the Structural Theory of Petri Nets. In Section 3, we introduce the notions necessary to our algorithm. In Section 4, we present the heuristics and the validation algorithm. In Section 5, we discuss our experimental results. Finally, in Section 6 and 7 we discussed related works and future directions of research, respectively. The extended version of this paper (containing the proofs of all results) is available as technical report [CDC00].

2   Structural Theory for Petri Nets

Following [STC98], a PN N is a tuple $\langle P, T, \mathbf{Pre}, \mathbf{Post}, m_0 \rangle$, where P is the finite set of *places*, T is the finite set of *transitions*, $\mathbf{Pre}$ and $\mathbf{Post}$ are the $|P| \times |T|$ sized, incidence matrices, and m_0 is the *initial marking*. The matrix $\mathbf{C} = \mathbf{Post} - \mathbf{Pre}$ is called *token flow matrix*. A *marking* $m = \langle m_1, \ldots, m_n \rangle$ is a vector of natural numbers of dimension $n = |P|$. We will use $\mathbf{0}$ to denote the *null vector* $\langle 0, \ldots, 0 \rangle$. Given two vectors $m = \langle m_1, \ldots, m_n \rangle$ and $m' = \langle m'_1, \ldots, m'_n \rangle$, we define $m \geq m'$ if and only if $m_i \geq m'_i$ for $i : 1, \ldots, n$. Similarly, we can define $m = m'$, whereas $m > m'$ holds if and only if $m \geq m'$ and $m \neq m'$.

Occurrence sequences, and Parikh vectors. Let N be a PN with token flow matrix $\mathbf{C}$, n places, and m transitions $t_1, \ldots, t_m$. A transition $t \in T$ is *enabled* at marking m if $m \geq \mathbf{Pre}[P, t]$, i.e., there are enough tokens to fire t. The *firing* of the transition t, namely $m \overset{t}{\to} m'$, yields a new marking $m' = m + \mathbf{C}[P, t]$. An *occurrence sequence* from m is a sequence of transitions $\sigma = s_1 \ldots s_k$ such that $m \overset{s_1}{\to} \ldots \overset{s_k}{\to} m_k$. The *reachability set* is denoted by $\mathcal{R}(N, m_0)$. The *reachability graph* is denoted by $\mathcal{G}(N, m_0)$. The *state equation* is defined as the system of equalities

$$m' = m_0 + \mathbf{C} \cdot x,$$

where m' and x are vectors of variables that range over positive integers. The *Parikh vector* p_σ associated to a finite *occurrence sequence* σ is defined as follows:

$$p_\sigma = \langle Occ_{t_1}(\sigma), \ldots, Occ_{t_m}(\sigma) \rangle,$$

where $Occ_{t_i}(\sigma)=$number of occurrences of t_i in σ. In the following we will use $\boldsymbol{x}, \boldsymbol{y}, \ldots$ to denote vectors of natural numbers with dimension $= |T|$ (for clarity, always referred to as Parikh vectors).

T-semiflows, and Fundamental Set. An integer vector $\boldsymbol{x}$ of dimension m is called a *T-flow* if and only if

$$\mathbf{C} \cdot \boldsymbol{x} = 0, \text{ where } \mathbf{C} \text{ is the token flow matrix.}$$

The following proposition relates T-flows and cyclic sequences.

Proposition 1 (From [STC98]). *Let N be a PN, and let $\boldsymbol{m} \overset{\sigma}{\to} \boldsymbol{m}'$. Then, the Parikh vector p_σ associated to σ is a T-flow if and only if $\boldsymbol{m} = \boldsymbol{m}'$.*

A *T-semiflow* is a T-flow $\boldsymbol{x}$ such that $\boldsymbol{x} \geq \boldsymbol{0}$. A *minimal* T-semiflow is a T-semiflow $\boldsymbol{x}$ such that: *the greatest common divider of all its positive components is equal to 1, and there are no T-semiflow $\boldsymbol{y}$ such that the set of non-zero components of $\boldsymbol{y}$ are contained in that of $\boldsymbol{x}$.* The *fundamental set of T-semiflows*, say $\mathcal{F}$, of N is the set of minimal T-semiflows of N. The fundamental set can be computed using a variation of the Gaussian elimination method. The number of minimal T-semiflows of a PN N could be exponential in the size of N [STC98]. T-semiflows enjoy the following properties.

Theorem 1 (From [STC98]). *Let N be a PN with fundamental set $\mathcal{F} = \{\boldsymbol{x_1}, \ldots, \boldsymbol{x_k}\}$. Every T-semiflow $\boldsymbol{y}$ can be obtained as a non-negative linear combination with rational coefficients of the minimal T-semiflows, i.e., $\boldsymbol{y} = c_1 \boldsymbol{x_1} + \ldots + c_k \boldsymbol{x_k}$, where $\boldsymbol{x_i} \in \mathcal{F}$, $c_i \in \mathbf{Q}$, and $c_i \geq 0$ for $i : 1, \ldots, k$.*

In the following we will call $Lin_{\mathbf{Q}+}(\mathcal{F})$ ($Lin_{\mathbf{Z}+}(\mathcal{F})$) the set of vectors obtained as non-negative linear combinations with rational (integer) coefficients of vectors in $\mathcal{F}$. From Theorem 1 and Prop. 1, we obtain the following corollary.

Corollary 1 (Cycle $\Rightarrow$ T-semiflow [STC98]). *Let N be a PN, and let $\boldsymbol{m} \overset{\sigma}{\to} \boldsymbol{m}'$. If $\boldsymbol{m} = \boldsymbol{m}'$, i.e., σ is a cycle in $\mathcal{G}(N, \boldsymbol{m})$, then $p_\sigma \in Lin_{\mathbf{Q}+}(\mathcal{F})$.*

The reverse implication might not hold. A counterexample of a PN in which a T-semiflow is not realizable (all paths denoted by the T-semiflow are not valid occurrence sequences) is given by Reisig in [Rei86]. Note that for *Free-choice* PNs [DE95] minimal T-semiflows are always realizable. Unfortunately, this class does not permit to model interesting examples of mutual-exclusion algorithms.

3   Towards the Combination with State Enumeration

Our starting point consists in a reformulation of the standard exhaustive search algorithm using Parikh vectors. The unique goal of this preliminary step is to simplify the integration of our *structural* heuristics in the enumerative approach.

ALGORITHM ES($N, \mathcal{P}$) : Boolean.
$N = \langle P, T, \mathbf{Pre}, \mathbf{Post}, \boldsymbol{m}_0 \rangle$: PN;
$\mathcal{P}$: the *safety* property;

Old:=$\emptyset$;
New:=$\{\boldsymbol{m}_0\}$;
while (**New** nonempty) do
  $\boldsymbol{m}$ = element from **New**;
  if not($\mathcal{P}(\boldsymbol{m})$) then return(false);
  for every $\mathbf{t}_i \in T$ enabled at $\boldsymbol{m}$ do
    $\boldsymbol{m}' = \boldsymbol{m} + \mathbf{C}[P, \mathbf{t}_i]$;
    if ($\boldsymbol{m}' \notin$ **Old** $\cup$ **New**) then
      add $\boldsymbol{m}'$ to **New**;
  endf;
  add $\boldsymbol{m}$ to **Old**;
  delete $\boldsymbol{m}$ from **New**;
endw;
return(true).

ALGORITHM DES($N, \mathcal{P}$) : Boolean.
$N = \langle P, T, \mathbf{Pre}, \mathbf{Post}, \boldsymbol{m}_0 \rangle$: PN;
$\mathcal{P}$: the *safety* property;
$\boldsymbol{y}_0 := \mathbf{0}$;

OLD := $\emptyset$;
NEW := $\{\boldsymbol{y}_0\}$;
while (NEW nonempty) do
  $\boldsymbol{y}$ = element from NEW;
  if not($\mathcal{P}(M(\boldsymbol{y}))$) then return(false);
  for every $\mathbf{t}_i \in T$ enabled at $M(\boldsymbol{y})$ do
    $\boldsymbol{y}' = \boldsymbol{y}[y_i := y_i + 1]$;
    if ($M(\boldsymbol{y}') \notin M($OLD $\cup$ NEW$)$) then
      add $\boldsymbol{y}'$ to NEW;
  endf;
  add $\boldsymbol{y}$ to OLD;
  delete $\boldsymbol{y}$ from NEW;
endw;
return(true).

Fig. 1. Two formulations of the **Type 1** Reachability Algorithm for PNs.

3.1   An Encoding Based on Parikh Vectors

Let N be a PN with n places, m transitions, token flow matrix $\mathbf{C}$, and initial marking $\boldsymbol{m}_0$. Following [Hol88], the *exhaustive search* procedure ES (*exhaustive search*) of Fig. 1 builds the complete reachability set (graph) storing the set of visited markings in the variable **Old**. The procedure ES can be reformulated using a representation of a reachable marking $\boldsymbol{m}$ via the Parikh vector p_σ associated to the path σ such that $\boldsymbol{m}_0 \xrightarrow{\sigma} \boldsymbol{m}$. In fact, from the state equation we know that

$$\boldsymbol{m} = \boldsymbol{m}_0 + \mathbf{C} \cdot p_\sigma.$$

A Parikh vector $\boldsymbol{x}$ can be used as a concise representation for *all realizable* paths σ starting from $\boldsymbol{m}_0$ such that $p_\sigma = \boldsymbol{x}$. Given a Parikh vector $\boldsymbol{y}$ we define the *marking* $M(\boldsymbol{y})$ associated to $\boldsymbol{y}$ as

$$M(\boldsymbol{y}) = \boldsymbol{m}_0 + \mathbf{C} \cdot \boldsymbol{y}.$$

Note that $M(\boldsymbol{y}_0) = \boldsymbol{m}_0$ whenever $\boldsymbol{y}_0 = \mathbf{0}$. Furthermore, given a set of Parikh vectors S we define

$$M(S) = \{\boldsymbol{m} \mid \boldsymbol{m} = M(\boldsymbol{y}), \ \boldsymbol{y} \in S\}.$$

Using the mapping $M(\cdot)$, we can reformulate the forward reachability algorithm representing explicitly the Parikh vectors underlying every marking, as shown in the *dual exhaustive search* procedure DES (*dual exhaustive search*) of Fig. 1. In the algorithm DES (the *skeleton* of ES), firing a transition t_i enabled at $M(\boldsymbol{y})$ modifies a vector $\boldsymbol{y} = \langle y_1, \ldots, y_n \rangle$ as follows

$$\boldsymbol{y}[y_i := y_i + 1] = \langle y_1, \ldots, y_{i-1}, y_i + 1, y_{i+1}, \ldots, y_n \rangle.$$

Suppose we run the two algorithms of Fig. 1 in parallel, then the following properties hold at any step: $m' = M(y')$, $\mathbf{Old} = M(\text{OLD})$, and $\mathbf{New} = M(\text{NEW})$. From now on, we will use the algorithm DES as a platform to include the set of heuristics based on properties of T-semiflows described in the following section.

3.2 Sufficient Conditions for Detecting Acyclic Behaviors

As shown next, the *contraposed* form of Cor. 1 of Section 2 can be used to devise *sufficient conditions* for detecting acyclic occurrence sequences without having to search for visited markings.

Corollary 2 (Not-T-semiflo w⇒ Not-Cycle). *Let N be a PN, and let $m \xrightarrow{\sigma} m'$. If $p_\sigma \notin Lin_{\mathbf{Q}+}(\mathcal{F})$ then σ is a not a cycle in $\mathcal{G}(N, m)$.*

This property goes well together with our formulation of the forward reachability algorithm using Parikh vectors. Before entering in more details, let us first analyze the cost needed to check the condition $p_\sigma \notin Lin_{\mathbf{Q}+}(\mathcal{F})$ of Cor. 2. To test this condition, we must solve a *linear problem* with *rational* solutions (polynomial in the size of $\mathcal{F}$). Are there more efficient sufficient conditions (e.g. linear in $\mathcal{F}$) we can use? To answer this question, let us introduce the following *new* notion.

Definition 1 (Integral Fundamental Set). *We say that the fundamental set $\mathcal{F}$ is integral whenever $x \in Lin_{\mathbf{Q}+}(\mathcal{F})$ implies that $x \in Lin_{\mathbf{Z}+}(\mathcal{F})$, i.e. all T-semiflows can be computed using non-negative combinations with integer coefficients.*

Under the assumption that $\mathcal{F}$ is integral, the following theorem can be used as a sufficient condition for detecting acyclic behaviors.

Theorem 2 (Sufficien t Condition for Not-T-semiflo w) *Let N be a PN with m transitions, and integral fundamental set $\mathcal{F} = \{x_1, \ldots, x_k\}$, where $x_i = \langle x_{i,1}, \ldots, x_{i,m} \rangle$. Furthermore, let $m \xrightarrow{\sigma} m'$, and $p_\sigma = \langle y_1, \ldots, y_m \rangle$ be the Parikh vector associated to σ. If for all $i : 1, \ldots, k$ there exists $j \in \{i, \ldots, m\}$ such that $x_{i,j} > y_j$, then for all non-empty subpath σ' of σ, $p'_\sigma \notin Lin_{\mathbf{Q}+}(\mathcal{F})$.*

The cost of checking the condition of Theorem 2 is *linear* in the cardinality of $\mathcal{F}$. The cardinality of $\mathcal{F}$ is potentially *exponential* in the size of N, but it is often linear in practice (see Section 5). As a remark, note the difference between the hypotheses of Theorem 2, and those of Prop 1, namely $\mathbf{C} \cdot p_\sigma \neq \mathbf{0}$. If Theorem 2 holds, then *all subpaths* contained in the path σ from m to m' are acyclic. Contrary, if $\mathbf{C} \cdot p_\sigma \neq \mathbf{0}$, then we deduce that *only* the paths from m to m' are acyclic. However, it is easy to build a Petri Net for which there exist three markings m, m' and m'' such that $m \xrightarrow{\sigma_1} m'' \xrightarrow{\sigma_2} m'$, $\mathbf{C} \cdot p_{\sigma_1 + \sigma_2} \neq \mathbf{0}$, and $\mathbf{C} \cdot p_{\sigma_2} = \mathbf{0}$.

3.3 Checking the Integrality of $\mathcal{F}$

To check the integrality of the fundamental set, we can use the notion of *total unimodularity* [Sch94]. A matrix $\mathbf{A}$ with integer coefficients is totally unimodular if every subdeterminant of $\mathbf{A}$ is 0, 1 or -1. From [Sch94], we know that if $\mathbf{A}$ is totally unimodular, then the extreme points of the set of solutions of $\mathbf{A} \cdot \boldsymbol{x} = \boldsymbol{b}$ are integer numbers for any vector $\boldsymbol{b}$. Furthermore, to check the total unimodularity of $\mathcal{F}$, we can use the following (polynomial-time) criterion on the matrix with minimal T-semiflows as *rows*.

Theorem 3 (From [Sch94]). *Let $\mathbf{A}$ be matrix with two non-zero coefficient in each column. $\mathbf{A}$ is totally unimodular iff its rows can be split into two classes such that for each column: if the nonzero in the column have the same sign then they are in different classes, and if they have opposite signs they are both in the same class.*

Thus, if $\mathcal{F}$ forms a totally unimodular matrix, then $\boldsymbol{x} \in Lin_{\mathbf{Q}+}(\mathcal{F})$ if and only if $\boldsymbol{x} \in Lin_{\mathbf{Z}+}(\mathcal{F})$. Perhaps surprisingly, several examples taken from the literature satisfy the integrality requirement on $\mathcal{F}$. We will turn back to this point in Section 5.

4   Partial Search with Structural Heuristics

We come now to the definition of our partial search algorithm. Basically, the idea is to replace the core of the reachability algorithm DES of Fig. 1 with two heuristics selected on the basis of a preliminary comparison of Parikh vectors with minimal T-semiflows. The first heuristics exploits Theorem 2 to add markings to the set of visited states. The second heuristics applies sufficient conditions to *localize* the search for back-edges in the reachability graph. A Boolean flag (we will call **complete**) is used to estimate the *quality* of the approximation computed by the heuristics. The resulting *partial search* PS algorithm is shown in Fig. 2. To explain it in detail, in the rest of the section we will use the predicate SFC defined as

$$\text{SFC}(\boldsymbol{y}) \doteq \quad \text{for all } \boldsymbol{x} = \langle x_1, \ldots, x_m \rangle \in \mathcal{F} \text{ exists } i \in \{i, \ldots, m\} \text{ s.t. } y_i < x_i.$$

to denote the comparison between a Parikh vector $\boldsymbol{y} = \langle y_1, \ldots, y_m \rangle$ and the minimal T-semiflows of $\mathcal{F}$. Now, let $\boldsymbol{y}'$ be the new Parikh vector generated during the execution of forward reachability, and let OLD and NEW denote the set of visited markings.

The First Structural Heuristics. Suppose $\text{SFC}(\boldsymbol{y}')$ holds. From Theorem 2 and Cor. 2, we can deduce that the marking $M(\boldsymbol{y}')$ is not present in *all paths* σ, $p_\sigma = \boldsymbol{y}'$, going from $\boldsymbol{m_0}$ to $M(\boldsymbol{y}')$. Under this hypothesis, our heuristics is defined as follows: without further checks on OLD we instruct the algorithm to immediately add $\boldsymbol{y}'$ to NEW. The advantage of the heuristics is that we avoid the cost of searching for (a possible occurrence of) $M(\boldsymbol{y}')$ in the whole graph. The drawback is that it could introduce redundant markings. In fact, the marking $M(y')$ may occur in paths unrelated to y' (not captured by Cor. 2). This fact does not influence the termination of the resulting algorithm, as stated in Theorem 4. We postpone the practical evaluation of the first heuristics to Section 5.

The Second Structural Heuristics. Suppose that $\mathrm{SFC}(y')$ does not hold. Then, there exists some $x \in \mathcal{F}$ such that $y' \geq x$. In other words, all paths σ such that $p_\sigma = y'$ contain a subpath that is a minimal T-semiflow. Furthermore, since by definition $\mathbf{C} \cdot x = 0$, if we apply the state equation we obtain that

$$M(y') \;=\; m_0 + \mathbf{C} \cdot (y' - x).$$

Our idea is to use the *normalized* Parikh vector $y' - x$ to guide the search for a marking $m \in \mathrm{OLD}$ such that $m = M(y')$. Formally, let the *rank* of a Parikh vector y be defined as

$$rank(\langle y_1, \ldots, y_n \rangle) = y_1 + \ldots + y_n.$$

Furthermore, given a set of Parikh vectors S, let the k-th *level* of S be defined as

$$\mathrm{S}[k] = \{ y \mid y \in \mathrm{S},\ rank(y) = k \}.$$

Then, if $\mathrm{SFC}(y') = false$, we first search for a marking m such that $m = M(y')$ in all levels $\mathrm{OLD}[rank(y' - x)]$ with $x \in \mathcal{F}$ and $y' \geq x$. If we find the node we draw a back-edge. The edge will be part of a cycle. If the previous *local* search fails, we discharge the vector y', while setting the Boolean flag **complete** to *false*. This way, we inform the user that the algorithm is computing an *under-approximation* of the reachability graph. Basically, we substitute the *full termination test* $y \in \mathrm{OLD}$ of the algorithm DES of Fig. 1 with a sufficient condition. If the flag **complete** is true when the algorithm terminates the exploration of the state space, then the resulting reachability graph is exact. The following theorem formalizes these properties.

Theorem 4. *Let N be a bounded PN with integral fundamental set $\mathcal{F}$, $\mathcal{P}$ a safety property and let C be the value of the flag **complete** when the algorithm PS of Fig. 2 returns. Then, (1) the computation of $\mathrm{PS}(N,\mathcal{P})$ always terminates (returning true or false); (2) if $\mathrm{PS}(N,\mathcal{P}) = true$ and $C = true$, then $\mathcal{P}$ holds for N; (3) if $\mathrm{PS}(N,\mathcal{P}) = false$, then $\mathcal{P}$ does not hold for N.*

The second heuristics gives us a bound on the number of levels we have to keep in memory during the exploration of the reachability graph. The bound WS (window size) is the maximum between the *ranks* of the minimal T-semiflows in $\mathcal{F}$, namely

$$WS \;=\; max\{ \, rank(x) \mid x \in \mathcal{F} \, \}.$$

Thus, our algorithm works only on a *window* of dimension WS that covers the last levels of the current reachability set. We will present a memory management based on this property in the next section.

ALGORITHM PS($N, \mathcal{P}$): Boolean
$N = \langle P, T, \mathbf{Pre}, \mathbf{Post}, \boldsymbol{m}_0 \rangle$;
$\mathcal{F}$: *integral* fundamental set of N;
$\mathcal{P}$: the *safety* property;

$\boldsymbol{y}_0 := \mathbf{0}$; **complete**:=true;
NEW := $\{\boldsymbol{y}_0\}$; OLD := $\emptyset$;
while (NEW nonempty) do
   $\boldsymbol{y}$ = element from NEW;
   if not($\mathcal{P}(M(\boldsymbol{y}))$) then return(false);
   for every $\mathbf{t}_i \in T$ enabled at $M(\boldsymbol{y})$ do
     $\boldsymbol{y}' = \boldsymbol{y}[y_i := y_i + 1]$;
      if for all $\boldsymbol{x} \in \mathcal{F}$ exist $i \in \{1, \ldots, m\}$ s.t. $y_i' - x_i < 0$ then
         if ($M(\boldsymbol{y}')$ is not in $M(\text{NEW})$) then add $\boldsymbol{y}'$ to NEW;
      else if ($M(\boldsymbol{y}')$ is not in $M(\text{OLD}[rank(\boldsymbol{y}' - \boldsymbol{x})])$ for some $\boldsymbol{x} \in \mathcal{F}, \boldsymbol{y}' \geq \boldsymbol{x}$) then
         complete:=false;
           else add the back-edge;
   endfor;
   add $\boldsymbol{y}$ to OLD; delete $\boldsymbol{y}$ from NEW;
endw;
if **complete** write('Exact RS') else write('Approximated RS');
return(true).

Fig. 2. A **Type 2** Reachability Algorithm.

5   Experim ental Results

We have implemen ted a prototype version of the algorithm DFR of Fig. 2, borrowing the graphical interface and the library for computing structural properties from GreatSPN [CFGR95], and using the following specialized memory managem ent.

5.1   Organizing the Memory as a Circular Arra y

W e consider PNs where transitions can be fired at most 255 times. W e organize the available memory (RAM + sw ap area) as a *circular array*, where each slot in the array contains m bytes and stores a Parikh vector (m=number of transitions). Our representation does not depend on the bound on the number of tokens in the places. If TM is the size of allocated memory in b ytes, the number of available slots AS is then $AS = TM/m$. Furthermore, if NS is the num ber or reachable vectors, then the *virtual* memory required to store them is $MS = NS * m$ bytes. A table maintains the initial and final address of the set of Parikh vectors of each level. Each level is stored as an ordered list. A *sliding window* covering the last WS levels of the reachability graph mo ves around the circular array (we defined WS in the previous section). The global size of the sliding window is the sum of the n umber of states in each of its levels. By construction of PS, we can always reuse the states outside the window in successive

CASE-STUDY	T	P	SF	ET	WS	I?
Kanban [CM97]	16	16	5	0.01s	8	√
Flexible Manufacturing System (FMS) [CM97]	20	22	4	0.04s	13	√
Multipoll [MCC97]	21	18	8	0.06s	5	√
Central Server Model (CSM)[ABC$^+$95] Fig. 76 pp. 154	13	14	4	0.03s	5	√
Readers-Writers [ABC$^+$95] Fig. 11 pp. 17	7	7	2	0.02s	4	√
2x2 Mesh [ABC$^+$95] Fig. 130 pp. 256	32	32	8	0.07s	5	√

Fig. 3. Profile of the case-studies: T=number of transitions; P=number of places; SF(size of $\mathcal{F}$)=number of minimal T-semiflows; ET=CPU execution time to compute $\mathcal{F}$ using GSPN on a Pentium 133Mhz; WS=size of the sliding windo w; I?=is the *fundamental set* integral?

iterations. An *overflow exception OF* is raised as soon as the algorithm adds a slot of the last level of the window to its first level (i.e. the window covers all memory). NR will indicates the number of times the *last* slot of the sliding window goes beyond the rightmost limit of the array ($NR = 0$ means $MS \leq TM$). Finally, the ratio R defined as $1 - TM/MS$ give us an estimation of the saving of memory occupancy w e obtain with our heuristics.

5.2   Practical Evaluation

At this stage of our work, the purposes of the experiments were: (1) testing the *applicability* of the assumptions under which the algorithm works (the existence of an integral fundamental set); (2) testing the *quality* and *efficiency* of our heuristics; (3) testing the *scalability* of the specialized memory managem ent.

Applicability. To make the tests more interesting, we considered models of concurrent and productions systems taken from [ABC$^+$95,CM97,MCC97]. Furthermore, in order to study the scalability of our approach we restricted ourselves to consider systems with *parametric* initial markings, where the parameter is the number of *initial tokens* in some given places of the net. For these examples, we were interested in computing the set of reachable states, so as to prove safety properties like mutual exclusion. As shown in Fig. 3, most of the examples in [ABC$^+$95,CM97,MCC97] with the previous characteristics turned out to have *integral* fundamental set. W e computed$\mathcal{F}$ using the structural library of GSPN within negligible execution times (see again Fig. 3). W e remark that only the Kanban system of [CM97] is a *free choice* net, all the other examples heavily rely on the use of *semaphores*.

Quality and Efficiency. In order to test the *quality* and *efficiency* of our heuristics, we compared the execution times of our protot ype with those of GreatSPN [CFGR95], one of the more efficien t tools for the generation of the reachability graph of a PN. W e performed all experimen ts on a Pentium with a clock speed

CASE-STUDY	NT	ET-**Prot**	NS-**Prot**	CF	ET-**GSPN**	NS-**GSPN**
Kanban	2	1.530s	4,600	true	0.860s	4600
	4	229.070s	454,475	true	158.700s	454,475
	5	1464.270s	2,546,432	true	$\checkmark$	$\checkmark$
	6	$\checkmark$	$\checkmark$	—		
FMS	2	1.270s	3,444	true	0.460s	3,444
	4	249.170s	438,600	true	117.770s	438,600
	5	$\checkmark$	$\checkmark$	—	$\checkmark$	$\checkmark$
Multipoll	2	5.210s	11,328	true	2.190s	11,328
	4	56.280s	106,280	true	27.030s	106,280
	9	1164.750s	1,943,160	true	$\checkmark$	$\checkmark$
	10	$\checkmark$	$\checkmark$	—		
Mesh	2	178.870s	200,544	true	46.150s	200,544
	3	$\checkmark$	$\checkmark$	—	$\checkmark$	$\checkmark$
CSM	2	0.020s	76	true	0.010s	76
	32	23.180s	95,876	true	27.920s	95,876
	75	311.530s	1,170,704	true	538.450s	1,170,704
	115	1156.240s	4,162,544	true	$\checkmark$	$\checkmark$
	116	$\checkmark$	$\checkmark$	—		
Reader-Writers	4	0.030s	90	true	0.010s	90
	32	7.170s	64,889	true	10.250s	64,889
	62	94.350s	762,384	true	175.300s	762,384
	114	1069.020s	7,927,295	true	$\checkmark$	$\checkmark$
	115	$\checkmark$	$\checkmark$	—		

NT=Number of Tokens in the initial marking;
ET=CPU Execution Time on a Pentium 133Mhz;
NS=Number of reachable markings;
CF=value of the Complete Flag when PS returns;
$\checkmark$=memory overflow;
-**Prot**=executed on our prototype;
-**GSPN**=executed on GreatSPN [CFGR95].

Fig. 4. First serie of experimental evaluations.

of 133Mhz, RAM memory of 32Mb ytes, and swap area of 34Mbytes, allocating a priori 55Mbytes of memory to store the reachability set. The table in Fig. 4 summarizes the results of a first serie of experiments. Surprisingly, the algorithm returned an *exact* representation (without redundancies) of the reachability set in all the examples (and different values for the parameter=number of tokens in the initial marking). In all the experiments of Fig. 4 we never had to exploit the circularity of our memory organization: 55Mb ytes where enough to store the reachability set. The cost of our heuristics and of the localized search turned out to be comparable to that of the efficient search of GreatSPN (despite the fact that GreatSPN makes also use of simplification rules). However, on examples like Reader-Writers GreatSPN was not able to compute the reachability graph for nets with more than 62 tokens in the initial marking (as indicated by the over-

| \multicolumn{9}{c}{Readers-Writers (No. trans. m= 7) executed on our **prototype**} | | | | | | | | |
NT	TM	NS	MS	NR	R	ET	CF	OF
255	45 Mb	185,977,536	1,302 Mb	28	96%	27,981s	true	
255	35 Mb	185,977,536	1,302 Mb	37	97%	27,996s	true	
255	25 Mb	185,977,536	1,302 Mb	52	98%	27,991s	true	
255	21 Mb	66,252,650	463 Mb	22	95%	9,719s	true	√
128	45 Mb	12,440,544	87.1 Mb	1	48%	1,723s	true	
128	35 Mb	12,440,544	87.1 Mb	2	60%	1,722s	true	
128	25 Mb	12,440,544	87.1 Mb	3	71%	1,721s	true	
128	15 Mb	12,440,544	87.1 Mb	5	82%	1,722s	true	
128	5 Mb	12,440,544	87.1 Mb	17	94%	1,723s	true	
128	3 Mb	5,631,404	40 Mb	13	92%	766.6s	true	√
64	1 Mb	860,145	6 Mb	6	83%	108.3s	true	
64	500 Kb	860,145	6 Mb	12	91%	108.5s	true	
64	250 Kb	169,728	1.2 Mb	4	25%	19.6s	true	√
32	300 Kb	64,889	455 Kb	1	34%	7.33s	true	
32	75 Kb	64,889	455 Kb	6	83%	7.38s	true	
32	50 Kb	23,099	162 Kb	3	69%	2.38s	true	√

NT=number of tokens in the initial marking;
TM=total allocated memory;
NS=number of reachable states;
MS=NS*m;
NR=number of rounds in the circular memory;
R=1-(TM/MS) (saving ratio in pct);
ET=CPU execution time on a Pentium, 133Mhz;
CF=complete flag;
OF=overflow flag.

Fig. 5. Second serie of experimental evaluations.

flow flag √). This fact is due to the overhead of a more sophisticated encoding of markings and to the organization of visited markings as a tree structure [Chi89] (trade-off between efficient search operations and memory requirements). Both our prototype and GreatSPN store the edges of the reachability graph on disk.

Scalability. In order to test the scalability of our method, we performed a second serie of experiments in which we successively reduced the quantity of memory allocated for storing the reachability set. The aim was to test the efficacy of the circular implementation of the memory. The results were quite surprising. For instance, as shown in Fig. 5 we were able to scale up to 255 the number of tokens in the initial marking of Readers-Writers. In this case the net has approximatively 185 millions of reachable states. It would take approximatively 1300 Mbytes of memory to store the entire reachability set. With our heuristics, we were able to run the example using *only* 25 Mbytes of memory, hence saving 98% of memory space. The memory manager returned an overflow exception (indicated again with $\sqrt{}$) when we tried to use 21Mb of memory. Furthermore, for an initial marking with 128, 64, and 32 tokens we were able to compute the reachability set saving (approximatively) 94% (TM=5Mb ytes), 92% (TM=0.5Mb ytes), and 84% (TM=75Kb) of memory space, respectiv ely We obtained similar results for the CSM example. The results on the other examples w ere less appealing, though we also managed to scale up FMS to an initial marking with 5 tok ens. However, we believe that more results will be obtained by using efficient data structures to store sets of markings.

6   Related W orks

As mentioned in the introduction, structural techniques are traditionally used to compute over-approximations of the reachability set, see e.g. [STC98]. In [EM00], *traps* are used to improve the quality of the approximation. *Place* invariants can also be used to over-approximate the reachability set. Place invariants are the dual notion of T-semiflows, i.e., the solution of the system $y \cdot C = 0$. Let P be the matrix of minim al P-semiflows. As shown in [STC98], the solution of the equation $P \cdot x = P \cdot m_0$ over-approximates the set of solutions of the state equation $m = m_0 + C \cdot \sigma$, i.e., over-approximates the reachability set. Contrary, in our approach we have used T-semiflows to find under-approximations (useful for debugging) and to derive conditions to establish the quality of the approximation. Furthermore, differently from [EM00 ,STC98], our approach is incorporated in state enumeration. W e are not aware of other approaches where T-semiflows are used for under-approximating the reachability set. In [MC99], Miner and Ciardo use MDDs (Multi-v alued Decision Diagrams) to store the reachability set; whereas, Pastor et al. [PCP99] use P-invariants (semiflows) to improve a BDD-based encoding of the reachability set. Other compact data structures (like Sharing Trees) are tested on reachability problems of bounded PNs in [GGZ95,ST99]. As mentioned in the introduction, our heuristics could be incorporated, e.g., in a BDD-based framew ork. Our use of heuristics shares some similarities with *depth-first* search algorithms [Hol88,Val98] for state enumeration, an approach used to compute an under-approximation of the *reachability graph*. In fact, our heuristics gives us conditions to detect acyclic paths of the reachability graph that go from the initial marking to the curren t marking. However, note that the use of Parikh vectors allows us to check the absence of cycles on *collections* of paths (all paths and related subpaths represented by the vector). Furthermore, the use of the second heuristics allows us to obtain more accurate information w.r.t. a generic depth-first search where only the current paths is memoized. Depth-first search algorithms com bined with methods for storing visited markings have been proposed in [JJ91,MK96]. As heuristics for garbage collection, in [JJ91] Jard and Jéron propose to discharge states selected randomly from the set of visited markings, whereas Miller and Katz in [MK96] select the states to discharge using their *revisiting degree*. Differently from [JJ91,MK96], our method is based on a breadth-first search, in which we use the *rank* of minim al T-semiflo ws (i.e., heuristics peculiar of Petri Nets) to guide garbage collection.

7 Conclusions

We have presented a new algorithm for validating concurrent systems modeled as bounded Petri Nets. Our method is combines forward state exploration with two structural heuristics based on the properties of T-semiflows. One of the main feature of our heuristics is that they give us an estimation on the number of levels of the reachability graph we need to keep in memory. Using this measure, we can organize main memory as a *circular array*, so as to garbage collect states outside the current working window. In our prototype, information for computing error traces are stored on disk. In this preliminary work, we were mainly interested in evaluating the applicability of the method (are there interesting examples that fulfill our assumptions?), and the efficacy of the specialized memory management (can we save memory?). In this respects, we think that our results are quite promising (see Section 5). For a better evaluation of the approach (e.g. to compare its scalability w.r.t. BDD-based approaches like [MC99,PCP99]), we plan to integrate efficient data structures within our preliminary *naive* implementation of the algorithm (in which vectors are stored as sequences of slots, as described in Section 5). Finally, it would be interesting to study the applicability of similar techniques for the validation of *infinite-state* systems, e.g., integrated in approaches like [DR00].

Acknowledgements. The authors would like to thank Javier Esparza for having pointed out to us several important references, Jean-Francois Raskin for fruitful discussions, and the anonymous reviewers for useful suggestions and the pointers to [JJ91,MK96].

References

ABC⁺95. M. Ajmone Marsan, G. Balbo, G. Conte, S. Donatelli, and G. Franceschinis. *Modelling with Generalized Stochastic Petri Nets.* Series in Parallel Computing. John Wiley & Sons, 1995.

BCB⁺90. J. R. Burch, E. M. Clarke, K. L. McMillan, D. L. Dill, and J. Hwang. Symbolic Model Checking: 10^{20} States and Beyond. In *Proc. LICS '90*, pages 428-439, 1990.

Chi89. G. Chiola. Compiling Techniques for the Analysis of Stochastic Petri Nets. In *Modelling Techniques and Tools for Computer Performance Evaluation*, pages 11–24, 1989.

CFGR95. G. Chiola, G. Franceschinis, R. Gaeta, and M. Ribaudo. GreatSPN 1.7: Graphical Editor and Analyzer for Timed and Stochastic Petri Nets. In *Performance Evaluation*, 24(1-2):47–68, 1995.

CM97. G. Ciardo and A. S. Miner. Storage Alternatives for large structured state spaces. In *Proc. Modelling Techniques and Tools for Computer Performance Evaluation*, LNCS 1245, pages 44-57. Springer, 1997.

CDC00. R. Carvajal-Schiaffino, G. Delzanno, and G. Chiola. Combining Structural and Enumerative Techniques for the Validation of Bounded Petri Nets: A New 'Type 2' Validation Algorithm. Technical Report, DISI-00-10, Dipartimento di Informatica e Scienze dell'Informazione dell'Università di Genova, October 2000.

DR00.   G. Delzanno and J. F. Raskin. Symbolic Representation of Upward-closed
           Sets. In *Proc. TACAS 2000*, LNCS 1785, pages 426-440. Springer, 2000.
Des98.   J. Desel. Basic Linear Algebraic Techniques for Place/Transition Nets. In
           Reisig and Rozenberg [RR98], pages 257-308, 1998.
DE95.   J. Desel and J. Esparza. Free Choice Petri Nets. Cambridge University
           Press, 1995.
DR98.   J. Desel and W. Reisig. Place/Transition Petri Nets. In Reisig and Rozen-
           berg [RR98], pages 122-173, 1998.
EM00.   J. Esparza and S. Melzer. Verification of safety properties using integer pro-
           gramming: Beyond the state equation. Formal Methods in System Design,
           16:159-189, 2000.
GGZ95.   F. Gagnon, J.-Ch. Grégoire, and D. Zampuniéris. Sharing Trees for 'On-
           the-fly' Verification. In *Proc. FORTE '95*, 1995.
Gra97.   B. Grahlmann. The PEP Tool. In *Proc. CAV'97*, LNCS 1254, pages 440-
           443. Springer, 1997.
Hol88.   G. Holzmann. Algorithms for Automated Protocol Verification. AT&T
           Technical Journal 69(2):32-44, 1988.
JJ91.   C. Jard and Th. Jéron. Bounded-memory Algorithms. In *Proc. CAV'91*,
           LNCS 575, pages 192-202. Springer, 1991.
MCC97.   P. Marenzoni, S. Caselli, and G. Conte. Analysis of Large GSPN Mod-
           els: A Distributed Solution Tool. In *Proc. Int. Work. on Petri Nets and
           Performance*, 1997.
McM93.   K. L. McMillan. *Symbolic Model Checking: An Approach to the State Ex-
           plosion Problem*. Kluwer Academic, 1993.
MK96.   H. Miller and S. Katz. Saving Space by Fully Exploiting Invisible Transi-
           tions. In *Proc. CAV '96*, LNCS 1102, pages 336-347. Springer, 1996.
MC99.   A. Miner and G. Ciardo. Efficient Reachability Set Generation and Storage
           using Decision Diagrams. In *Proc. ICATPN '99*, LNCS 1639, pages 6-25.
           Springer, 1999.
PCP99.   E. Pastor, J. Cortadella, and M. A. Peña. Structural Methods to Improve
           the Symbolic Analysis of Petri Nets. In *Proc. ICATPN '99*, LNCS 1639,
           pages 26-45. Springer, 1999.
Rei86.   W. Reisig. P etri Nets. An introduction. EATCS Monographs on Theoretical
           Computer Science, Springer 1986.
RR98.   W. Reisig and G. Rozen berg, editors. Lectures on Petri Nets I: Basic
           Models. *Advances in Petri Nets*, LNCS 1491. Springer, 1998.
Sch94.   A. Schrijver. Theory of Linear and Integer Programming, Wiley & Sons,
           1994.
STC98.   M. Silva, E. Teruel, and J. M. Colom. Linear Algebraic and Linear Pro-
           gramming Techniques for Analysis of Place/Transition Net Systems. In
           Reisig and Rozenberg [RR98], pages 308-309, 1998.
ST99.   K. Strehl and L. Thiele. Interval Diagram Techniques For Symbolic Model
           Checking of Petri Nets. In *Proc. DATE'99*, pages 756-757, 1999.
Val98.   A. Valmari. The State Explosion Problem. In Reisig and Rozenberg [RR98],
           pages 308-309, 1998.
Wim97.   G. Wimmel. A BDD-based Model Chec ker for the PEP Tool. Technical
           Report, University of Newcastle upon Tyne, 1997.

A Sweep-Line Method for
State Space Exploration

Søren Christensen[1], Lars Michael Kristensen[1,2]*, and Thomas Mailund[1]

[1] Department of Computer Science, University of Aarhus
IT-parken, Aabogade 34, DK-8200 Aarhus N., DENMARK,
{schristensen,lmkristensen,mailund}@daimi.au.dk
[2] School of Electrical and Information Engineering, University of South Australia
Mawson Lakes Campus, SA 5095, AUSTRALIA
lars.kristensen@unisa.edu.au

Abstract. We present a state space exploration method for on-the-fly verification. The method is aimed at systems for which it is possible to define a measure of progress based on the states of the system. The measure of progress makes it possible to delete certain states on-the-fly during state space generation, since these states can never be reached again. This in turn reduces the memory used for state space storage during the task of verification. Examples of progress measures are sequence numbers in communication protocols and time in certain models with time. We illustrate the application of the method on a number of Coloured Petri Net models, and give a first evaluation of its practicality by means of an implementation based on the DESIGN/CPN state space tool. Our experiments show significant reductions in both space and time used during state space exploration. The method is not specific to Coloured Petri Nets but applicable to a wide range of modelling languages.

1 Introduction

State space exploration has proven to be powerful for investigating the correctness of concurrent systems. The basic idea behind state space exploration is to construct a directed graph, called the *state space*, in which the nodes correspond to the set of reachable states of the system, and the arcs correspond to the state changes. Such a state space represents all possible executions of the system, and can be used to algorithmically verify and analyse an abundance of properties about the system under consideration.

The main disadvantage of using state spaces is the *state explosion problem*: even relatively small systems may have an astronomical number of reachable states, and this is a serious limitation to the use of state space methods in the analysis of real-life systems. This has led to the development of many different reduction methods for alleviating the state explosion problem. Examples of reduction methods are partial order reduction methods [19, 21, 22], the symmetry

---

* Supported by the Danish Natural Science Research Council.

T. Margaria and W. Yi (Eds.): TACAS 2001, LNCS 2031, pp. 450–464, 2001.

method [5, 6, 14], and the unfolding method [7, 17]. Reduction methods represent the full state space in a compact or condensed form, or represent only a subset of the full state space. The reduction is done such that the answer to the verification questions can still be determined from the reduced state space.

Reduction methods typically exploit certain characteristics of the system, and hence work well for systems possessing these characteristics, but fail to work well for systems which do not have these characteristics. An example of this is the symmetry method which exploits the symmetry present in many concurrent systems, but fails to work on systems which do not possess symmetry. This paper presents a *sweep-line method* for state space exploration. The method is aimed at systems for which it is possible to define a measure of progress based on the states of the system. Examples of such progress measures are sequence numbers in communication protocols and time in certain systems with time. The key property of a progress measure is that for a given state s, all states reachable from s have a progress measure which is greater than or equal to the progress measure of s. The progress measure will often be specific for the system under consideration. However, for some modelling languages a progress measure can be defined based on only the modelling language itself. The progress measure then applies to all models of systems constructed in that modelling language. Time in Coloured Petri Nets [13, 16] is an example of such a progress measure.

A progress measure makes it possible to delete certain states on-the-fly during state space generation, since it ensures that these states can never be reached again. Since we only delete states that can never be reached again, we never risk processing the same state twice. The sweep-line method therefore ensures that the generation terminates for finite-state systems after having visited all reachable states. Intuitively, the idea is to drag a *sweep-line* through the full state space, calculate the reachable states in front of the sweep-line and delete states behind the sweep-line.

The sweep-line method makes it possible to investigate a number of interesting properties of systems, such as deadlocks, reachability, and safety properties. Practical experiments with a prototype implementation of the sweep-line method show significant savings in both time and space for finite state systems. For infinite-state systems the sweep-line method can be used to explore and analyse larger prefixes of the state space than can be done with ordinary state space exploration.

Deleting and/or throwing state information away on-the-fly during state space generation, is also the underlying idea of the *bit-state hashing method* [10, 11] and the *state space caching method* [9, 12]. The basic idea of state space caching is to make a depth-first generation of the state space, keep the states of the depth-first search stack in memory, and allow for deletion of states during the state space generation which are not on the depth-first search stack. An advantage of the sweep-line method compared to state space caching is that states are only generated and processed once. With the state space caching method, the same state may be regenerated and processed several times leading to an increase in run-time. As shown in [8] this run-time penalty can be fought against by combining state space caching and partial order methods. The bit-state hashing method always keeps the states of the depth-first search stack in memory, but reduces (in its simplest form) the information stored about a single state to a hash value (index value). This hash value is then stored using a single bit in a bit-vector. A main difference between bit-state hashing and the sweep-line method is that with the sweep-line method full coverage of the state space is guaranteed. This is not the case with bit-state hashing, since two different states may be mapped to the same hash value due to hash collisions.

The idea of using a system specific progress measure to improve state space analysis is due to Kurt Jensen. The detailed realisation presented in this paper is the responsibility and work of the authors alone. The idea of utilising a measure of progress to delete states during on-the-fly verification is intriguingly simple, but to the best of our knowledge it has never been documented before.

The rest of this paper is organised as follows. Section 2 gives an informal introduction to the sweep-line method using a small Coloured Petri Net model as an example. Section 3 formalises the concept of progress measure. Section 4 gives the generic state space construction algorithm for the sweep-line method. Section 5 shows how this generic algorithm can be tailored for on-the-fly verification. Section 6 contains additional examples of progress measures and gives some numerical data on the performance of the sweep-line method using these examples. Section 7 contains the conclusions and a further discussion of related work.

2   The Sweep-Line Method

In this section we informally introduce the sweep-line method using a small example of a sliding window communication protocol [1]. The protocol makes efficient use of the network by sending a certain number of packets, called the window size, before it waits for an acknowledgement from the receiver. The packets transmitted on the network include a cyclic sequence number used to order the packets received from the network correctly at the receiver. For efficiency reasons the number of bits reserved for this counter must be kept at a minimum, but reserving too few bits can result in erroneous acceptance of packets by the receiver. We assume that the network allows both overtaking and loss of packets. The purpose of the analysis is to investigate whether the design of the protocol is sufficiently robust to work correctly under these conditions.

We have modelled the sliding window protocol using Coloured Petri Nets (CP-nets or CPNs) [13, 16], but the sweep-line method is not specific to this formalism. Our aim here is not to explain the CPN model of the sliding window protocol in great detail, but just to use it for introducing the basic ideas of the sweep-line method.

Figure 1 gives an overview of the CPN model of the sliding window protocol. It consists of three modules corresponding to a Sender, a Network, and a Receiver. In the CPN model we have supplemented the cyclic sequence number with a non-cyclic counter specifying the *generation* of the cyclic counter. This allows us to detect if the receiver ever is in a situation where a faulty acceptance of a packet occurs.

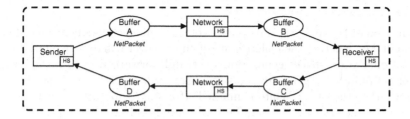

Fig. 1. Module overview of the sliding window protocol.

The left-hand side of Fig. 2 shows the sender module which has a single counter (NextSend) specifying the sequence number of the next packet to be sent. The idea of the window mechanism is that it allows the sender to send a number of packets without receiving an acknowledgement. Whenever the sender receives an acknowledgement from the receiver, the window is updated accordingly.

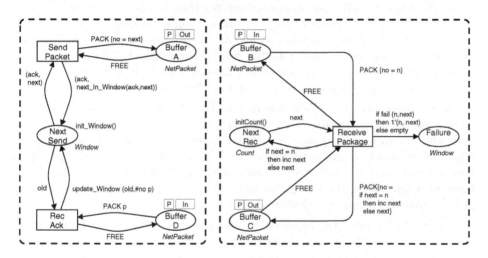

Fig. 2. Sender module (left) and Receiver module (right).

The right-hand side of Fig. 2 shows the receiver module, which has a counter (NextRec) specifying the next packet which can be accepted. NextRec is a counter on the form (gen, seq), where gen is an integer giving the current generation, and seq is the sequence number of the packet within the generation. If the expected packet arrives, the counter is increased and an acknowledgement with the sequence number of the next packet is sent back to the sender. If a packet arrives out of order, the receiver will respond with an acknowledgement containing the sequence number of the packet it was expecting to receive. In the CPN model a check has been inserted to inspect the validity of the packets being successfully received. This means that the Failure state will be marked if and only if the receiver ever accepts an invalid packet.

The aim of the analysis is to check whether the cyclic sequence numbers are too small, i.e., whether the Failure state of the receiver will ever be marked. Using conventional state spaces generation, a straightforward way to investigate this property would be to generate the state space and check for each newly created state whether the place Failure is marked. If a state is detected where the place Failure is marked, generation can be terminated and an error reported. For the sliding window protocol example it is, however, possible to exploit the NextRec counter in the receiver to reduce the memory used for state space storage during the search. The basic observation is that the NextRec counter has the property that as the protocol executes, generation numbers are increasing and so are the sequence numbers within each generation. This in turn makes it possible to define a *progress measure* on the states by means of which the progress of the sliding window protocol can be quantified, and which makes it possible to compare states wrt. their progress measure. Let for a state s, (gen_s, seq_s) denote the value of the receiver's NextRec counter in s. We can then talk about a state s representing a state where the protocol has progressed further than in another state s' (written $s' \leq s$) if and only if $(gen_{s'} < gen_s) \vee ((gen_{s'} = gen_s) \wedge (seq_{s'} \leq seq_s))$. Since generation numbers are increasing and so are the sequence numbers within each generation, the above progress measure has the property that for all successors s'' of a state s, $s \leq s''$. This means that from a state s, it is never possible to reach a state s'' with a progress measure less than the progress measure of s.

In conventional state space generation, the states are kept in memory to recognise already examined states. However, states which have a progress measure which is strictly less than the minimal progress measure of those states for which successors have not yet been calculated can never be reached again. It is therefore safe to delete such states. Saving memory by deleting such states is the basic idea underlying the sweep-line method. The role of the progress measure is to be able to recognise such states.

Figure 3 illustrates the intuition behind the sweep-line method. s_0 denotes the initial state of the system. The two gray areas show the states kept in memory. Some of these have been processed (light gray), i.e., their successor states have been calculated, and some have only been calculated (dark gray). There is a *sweep-line* through the stored states separating the states with a progress measure which is strictly less than the minimal progress measure among the unprocessed states, from the states which have progressed further than the minimal unprocessed states. States strictly to the left of the sweep-line can never be reached from the unprocessed states and can therefore safely be deleted. As the state space generation proceeds, the sweep-line will move from left to right. We drag the sweep-line through the state space, calculating the reachable states in front of the sweep-line and deleting states behind the sweep-line. All states on the sweep-line have the same progress measure.

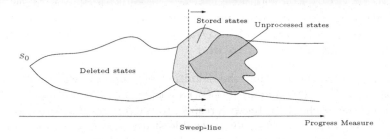

Fig. 3. The sweep-line method.

The full state space of the sliding window protocol with 5 packets has $28,438$ nodes. If the sweep-line method is applied, using our prototype implementation, then at most $8,622$ nodes are stored at any moment during state space generation. This means that the memory consumption measured in the number of nodes is reduced by almost 70%. Moreover, the time used for keeping track of progress measures and deleting states on-the-fly is more than compensated for by the time gained in faster insertion of new states in the state space. We will provide further statistics for the application of the sweep-line method on the sliding window protocol in Sect. 6, where we also give other examples of applications of the sweep-line method.

3 Progress Measures

In this section we formalise the notion of *progress measure* which is the fundamental concept underlying the sweep-line method. We assume that the systems we are considering can be characterised as a tuple $\mathcal{M} = (\mathbb{S}, T, \Delta, s_0)$, where $\mathbb{S}$ is the set of *states*, T is the set of *transitions*, $\Delta \subseteq \mathbb{S} \times T \times \mathbb{S}$ is the *transition relation*, and s_0 is the *initial state*. Most models of concurrent systems including CPN models, fall into this category of systems.

Let $s, s' \in \mathbb{S}$ be two states and $t \in T$ a transition. If $(s, t, s') \in \Delta$ we say that t is *enabled* in s, and that the *occurrence* of t in the state s leads to the state s'. This is also written $s \xrightarrow{t} s'$. A state s_n is *reachable* from a state s_1 iff there exists states $s_2, s_3, \ldots, s_{n-1}$ and transitions $t_1, t_2, \ldots t_{n-1}$ such that $(s_i, t_i, s_{i+1}) \in \Delta$ for $1 \leq i \leq n - 1$. If a state s' is reachable from a state s we write $s \rightarrow^* s'$. For a state s, $reach(s) = \{\, s' \in \mathbb{S}, \mid s \rightarrow^* s' \,\}$ denotes the set of states reachable from s. The set of *reachable states* of $\mathcal{M}$ is then $reach(s_0)$. The *state space* of a system is the directed graph (V, E) where $V = reach(s_0)$ and $E = \{(s, t, s') \in \Delta \mid s, s' \in V\}$.

A *progress measure* specifies a *partial order* $(O, \sqsubseteq)$ on the states of the system. A partial order $(O, \sqsubseteq)$ consists of a set O and a relation $\sqsubseteq \subseteq O \times O$ which is reflexive, transitive, and antisymmetric. Moreover, the partial order is required to preserve the reachability relation $\rightarrow^*$ of the system:

Definition 1. *A **progress measure** is a tuple* $\mathcal{P} = (O, \sqsubseteq, \psi)$ *such that* $(O, \sqsubseteq)$ *is a partial order and* $\psi : \mathbb{S} \rightarrow O$ *is a mapping from states into* O *satisfying:* $\forall s, s' \in reach(s_0) : s \rightarrow^* s' \Rightarrow \psi(s) \sqsubseteq \psi(s')$. □

It is worth noting that the definition of progress measure implicitly states that for all $s \in reach(s_0) : \psi(s_0) \sqsubseteq \psi(s)$, i.e., the initial state is minimal among the reachable states with respect to the progress measure. We only require $s \rightarrow^* s' \Rightarrow \psi(s) \sqsubseteq \psi(s')$ for reachable states $s, s' \in reach(s_0)$. In general we cannot determine whether $s \in reach(s_0)$ for arbitrary states $s \in \mathbb{S}$ without calculating the full state space. Hence in practice, a conservative approach is to ensure the property for all states in $\mathbb{S}$. In general we cannot determine whether $s \rightarrow^* s'$ either, without calculating the state space, but for some systems it is possible to determine statically from the model that for all transitions t and all states $s, s' \in \mathbb{S}$ we have $s \xrightarrow{t} s' \Rightarrow \psi(s) \sqsubseteq \psi(s')$ and hence by transitivity that $s \rightarrow^* s' \Rightarrow \psi(s) \sqsubseteq \psi(s')$. Since progress measures in the general case will be user-specified, they can be erroneous. The mapping $\psi : \mathbb{S} \rightarrow O$ could violate $s \rightarrow^* s' \Rightarrow \psi(s) \sqsubseteq \psi(s')$. However, since $s \rightarrow^* s' \Rightarrow \psi(s) \sqsubseteq \psi(s')$ for all $s, s' \in reach(s_0)$ iff $s \xrightarrow{t} s' \Rightarrow \psi(s) \sqsubseteq \psi(s')$ for all $s, s' \in reach(s_0)$ and all $t \in T$, this property can easily be checked during the state space exploration. When we process the enabled transitions in a state s, we check that all successor states have a progress measure greater than or equal to s.

All models have progress measures. A trivial progress measure is $O = \{\bot\}$ (the one-point set), $\sqsubseteq = \{(\bot, \bot)\}$ (the order on that set), and $\psi(s) = \bot$ for all $s \in \mathbb{S}$. However, this progress measure offers no reduction of the state space. Another progress measure is $O = \mathbb{S}_{SCC}$, the set of *strongly connected components* of the state space, $\sqsubseteq = \rightarrow^*_{SCC}$, the reachability relation between the strongly connected components, and $\psi(s) = SCC(s)$, i.e., ψ maps a state into the strongly connected component to which it belongs. This progress measure offers maximal reduction for the sweep-line method, but since in general we cannot compute the strongly connected component to which a state belongs without calculating the state space, this progress measure is of little practical interest. What is needed is a non-trivial progress measure that can be computed based on the individual states alone, i.e., no knowledge of the state space is required. One example of this is the progress measure of the sliding window protocol defined in the previous section.

4   State Space Exploration

Exploring the state space with the sweep-line method is based on the algorithm used for conventional state space construction. Figure 4 shows the standard algorithm for constructing a state space. It works on three sets: NODES, the set of nodes/states in the state space; EDGES, the set of edges in the state space; and UNPROCESSED the set of states that has been reached so far, but which have not been further processed, i.e., their successor states have not been calculated.

The sweep-line state space generation algorithm is derived from the standard algorithm by adding *garbage collection*. At certain intervals we delete all states

```
 1: UNPROCESSED.ADD(s₀)
 2: NODES.ADD(s₀)
 3: while ¬ UNPROCESSED.EMPTY() do
 4:    s ← UNPROCESSED.GETNEXT()
 5:    for all (t, s') such that s ⟶ᵗ s' do
 6:       EDGES.ADD(s, t, s')
 7:       if ¬ NODES.CONTAINS(s') then
 8:          NODES.ADD(s')
 9:          UNPROCESSED.ADD(s')
10:       end if
11:    end for
12: end while
```

Fig. 4. Generic algorithm for state space exploration.

that have a progress measure which is strictly less than all states in UNPRO-CESSED, and at the same time we delete all edges connecting deleted states. If the order is total, as was the case in Sect. 2, there will be one minimal progress measure among the unprocessed states, and it suffices to compare the progress measure of a state to that minimal progress measure. Since in general $\sqsubseteq$ is only required to be a partial order, it is possible for all unprocessed states to have different, incomparable progress measures. Hence, in worst case the progress measure of a state needs to be compared to each of them in order to determine whether it can be deleted or not.

When to garbage collect can be decided in different ways. Garbage collecting in each loop is likely to be too time consuming and the number of states that can be deleted in each iteration is likely to be small. Collecting at fixed intervals can suffer from the same problems, but it is less likely. If the intervals are chosen to be too large, however, there may not be sufficient memory to store all states calculated between two collections. This tradeoff can be adjusted dynamically, by determining when to collect based on available memory and/or the amount of memory reclaimed in previous collections. When memory is scarce, the interval should be decreased, when little memory is reclaimed per collection, the interval should be increased. In our prototype implementation (see Sect. 6), garbage collection is done whenever a fixed, user specified, number of nodes have been added to the state space. The results obtained with this simple strategy were quite satisfactory for our experiments, so we have not yet experimented with other strategies.

To maximise the number of states that can be deleted in each garbage collection, the minimal unprocessed states should have progressed as much as possible. Therefore, the method GETNEXT on UNPROCESSED (which return the next state to process) should preferably always return a state with a minimal progress measure. If the progress measure maps to a total order, as has been the case for all our applications, then UNPROCESSED can be implemented as a priority queue using the progress measure as the priority, and $\sqsubseteq$ as the ordering. In this case a breadth-first generation based on progress measure is obtained. With other progress measures, other data structures might be needed to implement UNPROCESSED efficiently.

It is worth observing that the progress measure ensures that all states of a strongly connected component will be garbage collected at the same time. The reason for this is that nodes in the same strongly connected component have the same progress measure as a consequence of Def. 1. This means that an efficient way to capture strongly connected components is to do this as an integrated part of the garbage collection algorithm. This is interesting since strongly connected components are used to check certain properties of systems in an efficient way.

5   Checking Properties

The sweep-line method garbage collects nodes shortly after having created them. Hence, to obtain verification results, properties must be checked on-the-fly. In this section we show how the sweep-line method can be used to verify a number of standard behavioural properties of systems. The properties considered do not represent an exhaustive list of properties which can be verified with the sweep-line method. Here, we have chosen a set of behavioural properties which in our experience constitute properties which are often of interest for the analysis of systems. Combining the sweep-line method with more general temporal logic model checking is beyond the scope of this paper.

A *deadlock* is a state in which no transitions are enabled. Using the algorithm in Fig. 4, the state s could be examined between line 4 and line 5, and if there are no enabled transitions in s it should be reported as a deadlock.

Checking if a state satisfying a given predicate is *reachable* is straightforward. The sweep-line method guarantees that each reachable state is visited at some point. If one of the visited states satisfies the predicate we answer "yes", if none satisfy the predicate we answer "no". Checking a *safety property* means checking that all reachable states satisfy a given predicate. This amounts to checking that the negation of the predicate is not reachable.

Checking that a given predicate is a *home predicate* means checking that from all reachable states, it is possible to reach a state where the predicate holds. A typical predicate could check if a given transition is enabled. Home predicates can be decided using the strongly connected components, i.e., a predicate is a home predicate iff each terminal strongly connected component contains at least one state satisfying the predicate. Since all states in a strongly connected component have the same progress measure, no part of a strongly connected component can be garbage collected before the entire strongly connected component has been computed. Checking this kind of property requires only that terminal strongly connected components are analysed before they are deleted. When we garbage collect, we calculate the strongly connected components of the states we are about to delete, isolate the terminal strongly connected components and check whether they contain a state satisfying the predicate.

When a deadlock or a violation of some property is detected, a trace leading to the deadlock or a state violating the property should be reported. With the sweep-line method, reporting such a trace is complicated by the fact that states between the initial state and the state at the end of the trace might have been garbage collected. These states need to be re-computed. In some cases it is possible to calculate transitions "backwards", i.e., from a state s it is possible to calculate all states s' and transitions t such that $s' \xrightarrow{t} s$. In such cases, a trace can be found by searching backwards for the initial state. Since all reachable states have a progress measure greater than or equal to the initial state, searching can be stopped along a given path if the progress measure drops below this value.

In many cases, however, it is not possible to search backwards. In such cases, the following scheme can be used. When garbage collecting, we make sure that for any unprocessed state s we have at least one predecessor s' with a progress measure strictly less than that of s among the states we do not garbage collect. In this way, when we need to calculate a trace leading to state s, the intersection between NODES and the set of predecessors of s is non-empty. In this intersection, there is a set of minimal states. We can start a search for one of these, using the sweep-line method. When one is found, we construct the last part of the trace as the path from this state to s. The state we find will have a set of predecessors stored in NODES, and we can start a search for one of these. This can then be iterated until we have built a path from s_0 to s. In each iteration, the distance to s_0 is shortened by at least one, so the algorithm is guaranteed to terminate.

6   Experimental Results

A prototype of the sweep-line method has been implemented based on the state space tool of DESIGN/CPN [4]. In this section we give a first evaluation of the practicality of the sweep-line method by applying this prototype on three examples. The first example is the sliding window protocol from Sect. 2. The second example is a stop-and-wait communication protocol taken from [16]. The third example is taken from the industrial case-study [3] in which state spaces of timed CP-nets and the DESIGN/CPN tool were used to validate vital parts of the B&O BeoLink system. All results in this section were obtained using a Pentium II 166 Mhz PC with 160 Mb of memory.

The prototype implementation uses a simple algorithm for initiating a garbage collection during the sweep: Whenever n new states have been added to the state space, a garbage collection is initiated. The garbage collection is implemented as a copying collector: when collecting, the states that should not be deleted are copied into a new state space. This new state space then becomes the current state space, and the old state space is deleted. This scheme was chosen for its simplicity, but it has the drawback that it requires space for two copies of the states that are not deleted. This problem can be avoided using other garbage collection techniques, but for our experiments the copy collection proved sufficient.

Sliding Window Protocol. Table 1 lists statistics for the application of the sweep-line method for different configurations of the sliding window protocol from

Table 1. Experimental results – Sliding Window Communication Protocol.

Packets	Full State Spaces		Sweep-Line Method		Reduction	
	States	Time	States	Time	States	Time
5	28,438	0:02:39	8,622	0:01:26	69.7 %	45.9 %
10	60,013	0:08:48	8,622	0:03:26	85.6 %	61.0 %
15	91,588	0:21:15	8,622	0:05:26	90.6 %	74.4 %
20	123,163	0:33:16	8,622	0:07:36	93.0 %	77.7 %
25	154,738	0:51:10	8,622	0:09:22	94.4 %	77.9 %

Sect. 2. The results were obtained by garbage collecting for each 2000 new states. The table consists of four main columns. The Packets column gives the configuration under consideration, i.e., the number of packets that the sender is requested to send to the receiver. The Full State Spaces column gives the number of states in the full state space and the CPU seconds it took to generate it. The Sweep-Line Method column gives the maximal number of states stored during the sweep, and the time it took to make the sweep through the state space. The Reduction column compares the sweep-line method to full state spaces by giving the reduction obtained in terms of states which had to be stored, and the reduction in run-time. E.g., for 5 packets a reduction of 69.7 % is obtained in the number of states, and a reduction of 45.9 % in run-time.

Table 1 shows that the use of the sweep-line method saves both memory and time. Moreover, the savings obtained grew with the system configuration. It was to be expected that the sweep-line method would reduce the memory consumption since states are being deleted during generation of the state space. However, from the results listed in Table 1 it follows that for the sliding-window protocol the sweep-line method is also faster than full state spaces. Hence, in this case the overhead added by having to delete states is accounted for by having significantly fewer states to compare with in the hash collision list when a new state has been generated and is to be inserted in the state space.

Stop-and-wait Communication Protocol. The stop-and-wait protocol contains a single sender and a single receiver. Data packets are to be transmitted from sender to receiver such that each packet is received exactly once, and in the right order. Each packet contains a sequence number. This number is increased for each new packet and the sequence number is never reset. Thus the sequence number of the packet currently being transmitted by the sender can be used as a progress measure.

Table 2 lists statistics for the application of the sweep-line method for different configurations of the stop-and-wait protocol. The results were obtained when garbage collecting after each 2000 new states. The table consists of the same four main columns as the table for the sliding window protocol.

BeoLink System. The BANG & OLUFSEN BeoLink system makes it possible to distribute audio and video throughout a home via a network. The state space

Table 2. Experimental results – Stop-and-Wait Communication Protocol.

Packets	Full State Spaces States	Time	Sweep-Line Method States	Time	Reduction States	Time
10	2,576	0:00:04	2,002	0:00:04	22.3%	0.0%
50	13,416	0:00:29	2,278	0:00:21	83.0%	27.6%
100	26,966	0:01:20	2,278	0:00:43	91.6%	46,2%
200	54,066	0:04:04	2,281	0:01:29	95.8%	63.5%
300	81,166	0:08:36	2,282	0:02:17	97.2%	73.4%
400	108,266	0:14:23	2,282	0:03:05	97.9%	78.6%
500	135,366	0:21:57	2,282	0:03:58	98.4%	81.9%
1000	270,866	1:21:10	2,284	0:08:51	99.2%	89.1%

analysis in [3] focused on the *lock management protocol* of the BeoLink system. This protocol is used to grant devices exclusive access to various services in the system. The exclusive access is implemented based on the notion of a *key*. A device is required to possess the key in order to access services. When the system boots no key exists, and the lock management protocol is (among other things) responsible for ensuring that a key is generated when the system starts. It is the obligation of the so-called *video* or *audio master* device to ensure that new keys are generated when needed. Timed CP-nets were applied in [3] since timing is crucial for the correctness of the lock management protocol. Here we used the sweep-line method to verify that when the BeoLink system starts eventually a key is generated by the lock management protocol.

The progress measure used for the CPN model of the BeoLink system is based on the time concept of CP-nets. The progress measure is based on the fact that timed CP-nets have a global clock giving the current model time, and that time cannot go backwards in a timed CP-net. That time always progresses is a general property of the time concept of CP-nets, and as a consequence, time can be used as a progress measure on timed CPN models of systems. This is an example of a progress measure being given by the formalism, rather than being specific to individual models.

Table 3 lists statistics for the verification of the initialization phase of the BeoLink system for different configurations of the BeoLink system. The Config column specifies the configuration in question. Configurations with one video master are written on the form VM: n, where n is the total number of devices in the system. Configurations with one audio master are written on the form AM: n. The results were obtained when garbage collecting after each 3000 new states.

7 Conclusion

In this paper we have presented a sweep-line method for alleviating the state explosion problem. The method relies on the notion of progress measure combined with breadth-first state space generation. The experimental results ob-

Table 3. Experimental results – BeoLink System.

Config	Full State Spaces States	Time	Sweep-Line Method States	Time	Reduction States	Time
VM: 3	1,130	0:00:06	1,130	0:00:06	0.0 %	0.0 %
AM: 3	1,839	0:00:11	1,839	0:00:11	0.0 %	0.0 %
VM: 4	13,421	0:02:40	5,170	0:02:50	61.5 %	-6.0 %
AM: 4	22,675	0:05:32	5,170	0:04:39	77.2 %	16.0 %
VM: 5	164,170	2:30:27	35,048	1:08:28	78.7 %	54.5 %
AM: 5	282,399	5:03:53	35,048	1:59:39	87.6 %	60.6 %

tained with a prototype implementation of the method have been encouraging, and demonstrated significant savings in memory as well as in time.

The aim of this paper has been to develop and specify a basic version of the sweep-line method, and we have shown how the basic sweep-line generation algorithm can be adapted to allow on-the-fly verification. Investigating how other model checking algorithms can be combined with the sweep-line method is a topic of future work. The constraint is that the sweep-line method relies inherently on breadth-first generation of the state space. The model checking procedure therefore needs to be breadth-first based in order to be compatible with the sweep-line method. Future work also includes investigating the combination of the sweep-line method and other state space reduction methods such as partial order reduction methods [21, 19, 22] and the symmetry method [6, 14, 5].

The sweep-line method is geared towards systems for which it is possible to quantify its progress based on the states. The method does not work well for fully or almost fully reactive systems, where most of the state space is strongly connected, i.e., the state space has very few strongly connected components. In fact, the number of nodes in the largest strongly connected component gives a lower bound on the memory consumption of the sweep-line method. The examples contained in this paper demonstrate, however, that there exists many interesting and non-trivial systems for which a progress measure can be specified, and where the sweep-line method is a very efficient way of analysing these systems. A measure of progress seems likely to be present also in other systems.

A disadvantage of the sweep-line method is that when a violation of a property has been detected, a run-time expensive backwards search is required in order to provide an execution/counter example showing why the property does not hold. With other similar methods such as state space caching [9,12] and bit-state hashing [10,11], the counter example is immediately available on the depth-first search stack. With state space caching, state space generation is expensive and counter example generation is inexpensive, whereas with the sweep-line method the opposite is true. On the other hand, since the sweep-line method relies on breadth-first generation it is more geared towards finding short counter examples which is not the case for the state space caching method.

Two other methods for deleting states during state space generation have been given in [18] and [15]. The observation behind [18] is that a state can be deleted once all its predecessor states have been explored. The method in [18] relies on being able to compute the number of predecessor states. This is for instance possible when the transition relation of the system can be represented using BDDs [2]. The method in [15] combines partial-order reduction and bit-state hashing with the idea of deleting states which are invisible to the LTL-X temporal logic property to be verified. Invisible states are deleted on-the-fly during state space generation, and to alleviate the problem of revisiting states, a preprocessing phase based on bit-state hashing is used to compute approximative information about the number of predecessors of states. This makes it possible to avoid blindly deleting states which could possibly be visited again. The sweep-line method and the methods in [18] and [15] all exploit different information to obtain the criteria for deleting states. The sweep-line method exploits a progress measure which is typically a property of the system to be verified, [18] exploits semantic information about the predecessors of each state, whereas [15] exploits the temporal logic property to be verified.

We have seen that for timed CP-nets it is possible to define a progress measure based on the modelling formalism and which, as a consequence, is applicable to all timed CPN models of systems. In other cases the user is required to provide the progress measure as input to the sweep-line generation algorithm. It is therefore relevant to ask how difficult it is to come up with a progress measure. We claim that if there is progress present in the system, then the modeller has in most cases an intuition about this which can be formalised into a progress measure and provided to the tool. In the prototype implementation of the sweep-line method in the DESIGN/CPN state space tool, the full STANDARD ML [20] programming language is available to the user for specifying progress measures, and hence offers great flexibility for specifying progress measures. The provided progress measure is also required to fulfill the property that all successors of a state s have a progress measure which is greater than or equal to the progress measure of s. If the user specifies a progress measure as input to the tool which does not have the required property, i.e., the progress is not actually present in the system, then this is not disastrous. Violations against the required property can be detected fully automatically by the tool during state space generation. In case a violation is detected, the state space generation can be stopped and a state and one of its successor states reported back to the user demonstrating why the provided progress measure does not fulfill the required property.

References

1. D. Bertsekas and R. Gallager. *Data Networks*. Prentice-Hall, Inc., 1992.
2. R.E. Bryant. Graph Based Algorithms for Boolean Function Manipulation. *IEEE Transactions on Computers*, C-35(8):677–691, 1986.
3. S. Christensen and J.B. Jørgensen. Analysis of Bang and Olufsen's BeoLink Audio/Video System Using Coloured Petri Nets. In P. Azéma and G. Balbo, editors,

Proceedings of ICATPN'97, volume 1248 of *Lecture Notes in Computer Science*, pages 387–406. Springer-Verlag, 1997.

4. S. Christensen, J.B. Jørgensen, and L.M. Kristensen. Design/CPN - A Computer Tool for Coloured Petri Nets. In E. Brinksma, editor, *Proceedings of TACAS'97*, volume 1217 of *Lecture Notes in Computer Science*, pages 209–223. Springer-Verlag, 1997.

5. E.M. Clarke, R. Enders, T. Filkorn, and S. Jha. Exploiting Symmetries in Temporal Logic Model Checking. *Formal Methods in System Design*, 9, 1996.

6. E.A. Emerson and A.P. Sistla. Symmetry and Model Checking. *Formal Methods in System Design*, 9, 1996.

7. J. Esparza. Model Checking using Net Unfoldings. *Science of Computer Programming*, 23:151–195, 1994.

8. P. Godefroid. *Partial-Order Methods for the Verification of Concurrent Systems, An Approach to the State-Explosion Problem*, volume 1032 of *Lecture Notes in Computer Science*. Springer-Verlag, 1996.

9. G.J. Holzmann. Tracing protocols. *AT&T Technical Journal*, 64(10):2413–2433, December 1985.

10. G.J. Holzmann. *Design and Validation of Computer Protocols*. Prentice-Hall International Editions, 1991.

11. G.J. Holzmann. An Analysis of Bitstate Hashing. *Formal Methods in System Design*, 13(3):287–305, November 1998. Extended and revised version of Proc. PSTV95, pp. 301-314.

12. C. Jard and T. Jeron. Bounded-memory Algorithms for Verification On-the-fly. In *Proceedings of CAV'91*, volume 575 of *Lecture Notes in Computer Science*. Springer-Verlag, 1991.

13. K. Jensen. *Coloured Petri Nets. Basic Concepts, Analysis Methods and Practical Use. Volume 1, Basic Concepts*. Monographs in Theoretical Computer Science. Springer-Verlag, 1992.

14. K. Jensen. Condensed State Spaces for Symmetrical Coloured Petri Nets. *Formal Methods in System Design*, 9, 1996.

15. S. Katz and H. Miller. Saving Space by Fully Exploiting Invisible Transitions. *Formal Methods in System Design*, 14:311–332, 1999.

16. L.M. Kristensen, S. Christensen, and K. Jensen. The Practitioner's Guide to Coloured Petri Nets. *International Journal on Software Tools for Technology Transfer*, 2(2):98–132, 1998.

17. K. L. McMillan. A Technique of State Space Search Based on Unfolding. *Formal Methods in System Design*, 6(1):45–65, 1995.

18. A. N. Parashkevov and J. Yantchev. Space Efficient Reachability Analysis Through Use of Pseudo-Root States. In *Proceedings of TACAS'97*, volume 1217 of *Lecture Notes in Computer Science*, pages 50–64. Springer-Verlag, 1997.

19. D. Peled. All from One, One for All: On Model Checking Using Representatives. In *Proceedings of CAV'93*, volume 697 of *Lecture Notes in Computer Science*, pages 409–423. Springer-Verlag, 1993.

20. J.D. Ullman. *Elements of ML Programming*. Prentice-Hall, 1998.

21. A. Valmari. A Stubborn Attack on State Explosion. In *Proceedings of CAV'90*, volume 531 of *Lecture Notes in Computer Scienc*, pages 156–165. Springer-Verlag, 1990.

22. P. Wolper and P. Godefroid. Partial Order Methods for Temporal Verification. In *Proceedings of CONCUR'93*, volume 715 of *Lecture Notes in Computer Science*. Springer-Verlag, 1993.

Assume-Guarantee Based Compositional Reasoning for Synchronous Timing Diagrams

Nina Amla[1], E. Allen Emerson[1], Kedar Namjoshi[2], and Richard Trefler[3]

[1] Department of Computer Sciences, University of Texas at Austin [†]
{namla,emerson}@cs.utexas.edu
[2] Bell Laboratories, Lucent Technologies
kedar@research.bell-labs.com
[3] AT&T Research
trefler@research.att.com

Abstract. The explosion in the number of states due to several interacting components limits the application of model checking in practice. Compositional reasoning ameliorates this problem by reducing reasoning about the entire system to reasoning about individual components. Such reasoning is often carried out in the assume-guarantee paradigm: each component guarantees certain properties based on assumptions about the other components. Naïve applications of this reasoning can be circular and, therefore, unsound. We present a new rule for assume-guarantee reasoning, which is sound and complete. We show how to apply it, in a fully automated manner, to properties specified as synchronous timing diagrams. We show that timing diagram properties have a natural decomposition into assume-guarantee pairs, and liveness restrictions that result in simple subgoals which can be checked efficiently. We have implemented our method in a timing diagram analysis tool, which carries out the compositional proof in a fully automated manner. Initial applications of this method have yielded promising results, showing substantial reductions in the space requirements for model checking.

1 Introduction

Compositional reasoning [7] – reducing reasoning about a system to reasoning about its components – has been an active area of research for nearly three decades. Recently, it has gained further importance as a way of ameliorating the state explosion problem in model checking. For example, given programs P_1, P_2 and specification T, we would like to check whether the composed system satisfies T (written as $P_1//P_2 \models T$). Since reasoning about $P_1//P_2$ directly only exacerbates the state explosion problem, compositional reasoning techniques are designed to reason about P_1 in isolation from P_2 (and vice versa) to draw conclusions about $P_1//P_2$. There are, however, several difficulties which must be overcome, foremost among them are the task decomposition problem, the generation of auxiliary assertions and the general applicability of the compositional method to the task at hand.

[†] Partially supported by NSF 980-4736, TARP 003658-0650-1999 and SRC 98-DP-388.

T. Margaria and W. Yi (Eds.): TACAS 2001, LNCS 2031, pp. 465–479, 2001.
© Springer-Verlag Berlin Heidelberg 2001

Firstly, *task decomposition* is necessary since it is unlikely that P_1 by itself satisfies all of T: we would like to decompose T into T_1 and T_2 such that $T = T_1 \wedge T_2$ and then show that $P_1 \models T_1$ and $P_2 \models T_2$. Secondly, auxiliary assertions are usually necessary, since P_1 may satisfy T_1 only when its environment behaves like P_2. To solve this problem, *assume-guarantee* style reasoning adds auxiliary assertions, Q_2 (respectively Q_1) which represent assumptions about the behavior of P_2 (P_1) as an environment for P_1 (P_2). Such auxiliary assertions must often be generated by hand, however. Finally, naïve compositional rules based on this style of reasoning, for instance, $P_1 // P_2 \models T$ holds if $P_1 // Q_2 \models T_1$ and $P_2 // Q_1 \models T_2$, are sound only for safety properties.

In this paper, we first present a new rule for assume-guarantee reasoning, which generalizes several earlier rules (cf. [15,1,3,12,13]), by removing the sources of incompleteness in some of these rules, by using processes, instead of temporal logic formulas, as specifications, and by allowing more general forms of process definition and composition. The new rule extends the naïve rule above with a check for soundness. As it deals uniformly with processes, it fits in well with a top-down refinement approach to designing systems. We show that this rule is also complete, in that if $P_1 // P_2 \models T$, then it is possible to prove this fact with our rule.

Next, we explore the benefits of applying this rule in the case where T is specified as a timing diagram. Timing diagrams are visual descriptions of process behavior that are widely used in the hardware industry. We show that not only is task decomposition a relatively simple problem for timing diagrams, but also that it is possible to automatically generate auxiliary assertions directly from the specification. Furthermore, we identify a large class of timing diagrams for which the soundness check of the rule is always satisfied, and the auxiliary assertion generation and, therefore, the model checking process is efficient – linear in the size of the diagram and the structure. We have implemented our method in a timing diagram analysis tool, RTDT [4], which uses the tool COSPAN [8] to discharge model checking subgoals. We report here on its application to a memory controller and a PCI Interface Core; in both cases, we obtain substantial reduction in the space used for model checking.

The organization of the paper is as follows: we describe our new rule and prove its soundness and completeness in Section 2. The theory behind the application of this rule to timing diagrams is presented in Section 3. Our experiments with applying this rule are described in Section 4. We conclude the paper with a description of related work in Section 5.

2   Assume-Guarantee Based Compositional Reasoning

In this section, we first present the naïve compositional reasoning rule and explain why it is unsound. We then present our new rule, and show that it is both sound and complete. We begin by defining some basic concepts: processes, composition, and closure. Although the eventual application of our rule is to finite state processes, we develop it in a more general setting.

2.1   Preliminaries

For a non-empty set of typed variables V, an assignment of values to variables in V is called a *V-state*. A *V-sequence* $x = x_0, x_1, \ldots$ is a non-empty sequence (finite or infinite) of V-states. The length of x (number of states in x) is written as $|x|$. We write $x[i..j]$, for $j \geq i$, to denote the subsequence $x_i, \ldots, x_j$ and $x; y$ to denote concatenation of a finite sequence x to y. A *language* L over V is a set of finite or infinite sequences of V-states. A *W-sequence* x, where $V \subseteq W$, *satisfies* L iff x projected on to V belongs to L. The term $(\exists W : L)$ defines a language over $V \backslash W$. A $(V \backslash W)$-sequence x satisfies $(\exists W : L)$ iff there exists a sequence y, with the same length as x, such that y is in L and x and y differ only on the values of variables in W. For a language L over V, let $[L]$ mean that every V-sequence (finite or infinite) satisfies L. Thus, for L_1 and L_2 over V, $[L_1 \Rightarrow L_2]$ denotes $L_1 \subseteq L_2$.

A *process* P is specified by a tuple (V, I, R, F). V is a non-empty set of typed *variables*, partitioned into three sets: *private* variables V^p, *interface* variables V^i, and *external* variables V^e. The variables V', which are in 1-1 correspondence with V, represent values for V in the next state. The set of *modifiable* variables, V^m, is $V^p \cup V^i$. $I(V^m)$ is an *initial condition*, $R(V, (V^m)')$ is a *transition relation* and $F(V)$ is a *fairness* condition. A V-sequence x is an *execution* of P iff $I(x_0)$ and for all i such that $i + 1 < |x|$, $R(x_i, x_{i+1})$ holds. The set of finite executions is denoted by *finexec*(P). The *language* of P, $\mathcal{L}(P)$, is the set of finite executions of P together with those infinite executions of P that satisfy F. The *observable language* of P, denoted by $\mathcal{L}^{\mathcal{O}}(P)$, is the projection of its language on $V^i \cup V^e$. In the rest of the paper, we assume that private variables of a process are distinct from the variables of all other processes, since this does not affect the observable language.

For processes P and A, the relationship "*P implements A*", denoted by $P \models A$, is defined only if $V^i(A) \subseteq V^i(P)$, and is defined as $[\mathcal{L}^{\mathcal{O}}(P) \Rightarrow \mathcal{L}^{\mathcal{O}}(A)]$, which can be written as $[\mathcal{L}(P) \Rightarrow (\exists V^p(A) : \mathcal{L}(A))]$. This matches the usual definition when A is an automaton, since a sequence over $V^p(A)$ is a run of the automaton.

For a language L on variables V, the *closure* of L, denoted by $cl(L)$, is a language consisting of V-sequences x where, for every $i < |x|$, there exists a sequence y such that $x[0..i]; y \in L$. For any process P, there is a process $CL(P)$ with the property $[\mathcal{L}^{\mathcal{O}}(CL(P)) \equiv cl(\mathcal{L}^{\mathcal{O}}(P))]$. If P is finite-state, $CL(P)$ is formed from P by changing the fairness condition of P to *true*.

A process Q *does not block* process P iff (i) any initial state of P can be extended to an initial state of $P//Q$, and (ii) for any reachable state of $P//Q$, any transition of P from that state can be extended to a joint transition of $P//Q$. A process is *machine closed* iff every finite execution can be extended to an infinite fair execution.

The *composition* of the processes $P_1 = (V_1, I_1, R_1, F_1)$ and $P_2 = (V_2, I_2, R_2, F_2)$, denoted by $P_1//P_2$, is the process $P = (V, I, R, F)$, where $V = V_1 \cup V_2$, $V^p = V_1^p \cup V_2^p$, $V^i = V_1^i \cup V_2^i$, $I = I_1 \wedge I_2$, $R = R_1 \wedge R_2$, and $F = F_1 \wedge F_2$. The *disjunction* of the processes P_1 and P_2, denoted by $P_1 + P_2$, is defined as the process $P = (V, I, R, F)$, where $V = V_1 \cup V_2 \cup \{c\}$, $V^p = V_1^p \cup V_2^p \cup \{c\}$,

$V^i = V_1^i \cup V_2^i$, $I = (c \wedge I_1) \vee (\neg c \wedge I_2)$, $R = (c' = c) \wedge ((c \wedge R_1) \vee (\neg c \wedge R_2))$, and $F = (\mathsf{FG}(c) \wedge F_1) \vee (\mathsf{FG}(\neg c) \wedge F_2)$. The private variable c serves to choose initially between the two processes. The following proposition summarizes the properties of these constructions needed for the later proofs.

Proposition 0. For processes P_1, P_2, P,
(a) $[\mathit{finexec}(P_1//P_2) \equiv \mathit{finexec}(P_1) \wedge \mathit{finexec}(P_2)]$,
$[\mathcal{L}(P_1//P_2) \equiv \mathcal{L}(P_1) \wedge \mathcal{L}(P_2)]$, and $[\mathcal{L}^{\mathcal{O}}(P_1//P_2) \equiv \mathcal{L}^{\mathcal{O}}(P_1) \wedge \mathcal{L}^{\mathcal{O}}(P_2)]$
(b) $[(\exists\{c\} : \mathcal{L}(P_1 + P_2)) \equiv \mathcal{L}(P_1) \vee \mathcal{L}(P_2)]$
(c) $[\mathcal{L}^{\mathcal{O}}(CL(P)) \equiv cl(\mathcal{L}^{\mathcal{O}}(P))]$

This definition of processes and of composition is quite general: it includes Moore and Mealy styles of definition as special cases, and processes in a composition can modify shared variables. Interleaving composition can be defined by adding a shared "turn" variable.

2.2   Compositional Reasoning Rules

To show that $P_1//P_2 \models T_1//T_2$ holds, one may attempt to show that $P_1 \models T_1$ and $P_2 \models T_2$. This "non-circular" proof often does not work if the components are tightly coupled, since P_1 may satisfy T_1 only in the presence of P_2. Hence, several so-called "circular" proof rules have been proposed, of which this is an example: to show $P_1//P_2 \models T_1//T_2$, show that (i) $P_1//T_2 \models T_1$, and (ii) $P_2//T_1 \models T_2$. This rule can be shown to be sound for non-blocking safety properties (i.e., for finite computations). It is, however, *unsound* for liveness properties. To see this, consider the following instantiation.

```
process P1: var x: boolean; initially x=true or x=false; transition x'=y
process P2: var y: boolean; initially y=true or y=false; transition y'=x
property T1: eventually(x) , property T2: eventually(y)
```

Although both hypotheses hold, it is not true that $P_1//P_2 \models T_1//T_2$, as the computation where x and y are always *false* is a valid computation of $P_1//P_2$. In an attempt to fix this problem, several proposed rules (cf. [1,3]) replace hypothesis (ii) with, say, $P_2//CL(T_1) \models T_2$. Using the safety closure of T_1 prevents any possibility of circular reasoning amongst liveness properties. On the other hand, this makes it difficult to apply the rule when liveness properties are needed as assumptions. We adopt a different strategy to fixing the problem: we use an additional hypothesis that checks if the circular reasoning is sound. For simplicity, we present this rule for the composition of two processes; it can be easily extended to apply to any finite composition.

Rule: To show that $P_1//P_2 \models T$, find Q_1 and Q_2 such that the following conditions are satisfied.

C0 $V^i(Q_1) \subseteq V^i(P_1)$, Q_1 does not block P_2, and symmetrically for Q_2.
C1 $P_1//Q_2 \models Q_1$, and $P_2//Q_1 \models Q_2$
C2 $Q_1//Q_2 \models T$
C3 Either $P_1//CL(T) \models (T + Q_1 + Q_2)$, or $P_2//CL(T) \models (T + Q_1 + Q_2)$

Note: Notice that hypothesis C3 need not be checked when T is a safety property, as $[\mathcal{L}^{\mathcal{O}}(CL(T)) \Rightarrow \mathcal{L}^{\mathcal{O}}(T)]$ holds in this case.

Theorem 0 (Soundness). The rule is sound for arbitrary P_1, P_2 and T.

Proof. We have to show that $P_1 // P_2 \models T$ follows from the conditions C0-C3. This, by definition, is equivalent to showing that $[\mathcal{L}(P_1 // P_2) \Rightarrow \mathcal{L}^{\mathcal{O}}(T)]$. By the results in [2], any language L can be can be written as a conjunction of the safety property $cl(L)$ and the liveness property $(cl(L) \Rightarrow L)$. Based on this characterization, we break up the proof into the following two parts.

Safety $[\mathcal{L}(P_1 // P_2) \Rightarrow cl(\mathcal{L}^{\mathcal{O}}(T))]$, and
Liveness $[\mathcal{L}(P_1 // P_2) \wedge cl(\mathcal{L}^{\mathcal{O}}(T)) \Rightarrow \mathcal{L}^{\mathcal{O}}(T)]$

In the following, let W be the private variables of $Q_1 // Q_2$.

Lemma 0. $[finexec(P_1 // P_2) \Rightarrow (\exists W : finexec(Q_1 // Q_2))]$
Proof Sketch. This follows from conditions C0 and C1 by induction on the length of executions. $\square$

First, we show the safety part by proving the equivalent (as $cl(\mathcal{L}(P))$ is the set of executions of P) statement $[finexec(P_1 // P_2) \Rightarrow cl(\mathcal{L}^{\mathcal{O}}(T))]$. Let U be the private variables of T.

$\qquad finexec(P_1 // P_2)$
$\Rightarrow \qquad$ (by Lemma 0)
$\qquad (\exists W : finexec(Q_1 // Q_2))$
$\Rightarrow \qquad$ (as $cl(\mathcal{L}(P))$ includes $finexec(P)$)
$\qquad (\exists W : cl(\mathcal{L}(Q_1 // Q_2)))$
$\Rightarrow \qquad$ (by C2; monotonicity of cl)
$\qquad (\exists W : cl(\mathcal{L}^{\mathcal{O}}(T)))$
$\Rightarrow \qquad$ (W contains private variables not occurring in T)
$\qquad cl(\mathcal{L}^{\mathcal{O}}(T))$

Next, we show the liveness part.

$\qquad \mathcal{L}(P_1) \wedge \mathcal{L}(P_2) \wedge cl(\mathcal{L}^{\mathcal{O}}(T))$
$\Rightarrow \qquad$ (by Proposition 0(c))
$\qquad \mathcal{L}(P_1) \wedge \mathcal{L}(P_2) \wedge \mathcal{L}^{\mathcal{O}}(CL(T))$
$\Rightarrow \qquad$ (by condition C3)
$\qquad \mathcal{L}(P_1) \wedge \mathcal{L}(P_2) \wedge \mathcal{L}^{\mathcal{O}}(T + Q_1 + Q_2)$
$\Rightarrow \qquad$ (by Proposition 0(b); $W \cup U \cup \{c\}$ consists of private variables)
$\qquad (\exists W \cup U \cup \{c\} : \mathcal{L}(P_1) \wedge \mathcal{L}(P_2) \wedge (\mathcal{L}(T) \vee \mathcal{L}(Q_1) \vee \mathcal{L}(Q_2)))$
$\Rightarrow \qquad$ (distributing $\wedge$ over $\vee$; Proposition 0(a) and condition C1)
$\qquad (\exists W \cup U \cup \{c\} : \mathcal{L}(T) \vee \mathcal{L}^{\mathcal{O}}(Q_1 // Q_2))$
$\Rightarrow \qquad$ (distributing $\exists$ over $\vee$; condition C2)
$\qquad (\exists W \cup U \cup \{c\} : \mathcal{L}(T)) \vee (\exists W \cup U \cup \{c\} : \mathcal{L}^{\mathcal{O}}(T))$
$\Rightarrow \qquad$ ($W \cup \{c\}$ consists of private variables not in T)
$\qquad \mathcal{L}^{\mathcal{O}}(T)$
$\square$

Theorem 1 (Completeness-1). The rule is complete for non-blocking processes P_1, P_2 that have disjoint interface variables.

Proof. Suppose that $P_1//P_2 \models T$ holds. Let $Q_1 = P_1$ and $Q_2 = P_2$. As Q_1 is non-blocking and has disjoint interface variables from P_2, it satisfies the condition C0; similarly for the symmetric case. Condition C1 is satisfied as $P_1//P_2 \models P_1$ and $P_1//P_2 \models P_2$ holds trivially. Condition C2 is $P_1//P_2 \models T$, which is true by assumption. Condition C3 holds as $P_1 \models (T + P_1 + P_2)$ by weakening. □

Theorem 2 (Completeness-2). The rule is complete for arbitrary processes.

Proof. Suppose that P_1, P_2, T are processes such that $P_1//P_2 \models T$. Each P_i can be made non-blocking by adding a transition for each blocking condition to a special state that has a self-loop. If P_1, P_2 have shared interface variables V, then rename the variables V to W_1 and W_2 in the processes P_1 and P_2 respectively, and modify T to T', which also accepts computations that diverge from T by differing on the values of W_1 and W_2 or by entering a blocking state. The result of the $\models$ check is unchanged with the new processes. From the previous theorem, therefore, there is a proof of $P_1//P_2 \models T$. □

3   Compositional Reasoning with Timing Diagrams

In the previous section, we gave a sound and complete rule for assume-guarantee based compositional reasoning. In this section we show how to apply that rule to specifications in the form of timing diagrams. By focusing on timing diagrams, which are a highly regular specification formalism, we obtain several benefits. Firstly, for a large class of timing diagrams the soundness check C3 in the rule follows directly as a consequence of the expressiveness of the formalism and so can be dispensed with. Secondly, we take advantage of the fact that many timing diagrams have efficient model checking procedures. Finally, we also show that the generation of helper assertions is not only automatic but efficient for a large class of timing diagrams.

Timing diagrams are a graphical notation commonly used to specify timing behavior of hardware systems. Synchronous Regular Timing Diagrams (SRTD's) [4] are a class of timing diagrams that correspond to a subset of the ω-regular languages. SRTD's have a formal syntax and semantics and there are efficient, polynomial time algorithms for model checking SRTD's (see [4] for details). These facts make SRTD's an effective formal specification notation.

An SRTD is specified by describing a number of waveforms with respect to a given clock. The clock waveform is a sequence of boolean values ($\{0, 1\}$), where the value toggles at consecutive points. A change in the clock value from 0 to 1 is called a *rising* edge, while a change from 1 to 0 is called a *falling* edge. The waveforms are sequences of values over $\{0, 1, X, D\}$, where X indicates a don't-care value, and D a don't-care transition. A change in value of a waveform (e.g., $0 \to 1$) must occur at rising or falling edges of the clock. The waveforms of an SRTD are partitioned into an initial *precondition* part that does not contain any don't-care transitions and the following *postcondition* part. In turn, the post-condition may be partitioned using *pause* markers. For example, in the SRTD of Figure 1, there are three signals, $A.p$, $B.q$ and $A.r$, the clock, a precondition marker, etc.

A don't care value (X) is used to specify that the value at a point is unknown, unspecified or unimportant. A maximal sequence of don't-care transition values (D) on a waveform must be preceded by a definite boolean value b, and followed by the value $\neg b$. The sequence of D values indicates that the transition from b to $\neg b$ occurs exactly once in the specified interval. A pause specifies that there is a break in explicit timing at that point, i.e. the value of the signals, except the clock, remains unchanged for an arbitrary but finite period of time. At each pause point, there must be at least one signal whose waveform has a definite change of value relative to the following point. This signal indicates the end of the pause. One such signal is designated as the "owner" of the pause.

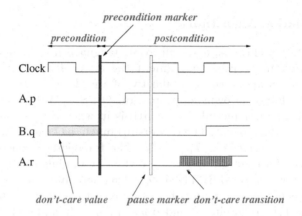

Fig. 1. Annotated Synchronous Regular Timing Diagram

An SRTD defines an ω-regular language. In [4], it is shown that we can construct regular expressions for the precondition T_{pre} and the postcondition T_{post} of an SRTD T. In the remainder of the paper, we use T_{pre} (T_{post}) to denote both the syntactical definition of precondition (postcondition) and its associated regular expression.

An infinite computation σ satisfies an SRTD T (written $\sigma \models T$) if and only if every finite segment of σ that satisfies the precondition is immediately followed by a segment that satisfies the postcondition of the diagram. The precondition, however, may be satisfied in an overlapping manner, which leads to two distinct notions of satisfaction, overlapping and non-overlapping semantics.

Definition 0 (Overlapping Semantics). An infinite computation σ satisfies an SRTD T under the overlapping semantics $(\sigma \models_o T)$ iff every occurrence of T_{pre} in σ is followed by an occurrence of T_{post}. Formally, this is true iff $\sigma \notin (\Sigma^* ; T_{pre} ; \neg T_{post})$, where Σ is the set of valuations to the signals in T.

To define non-overlapping semantics, it is convenient to assume that there is an auxiliary proposition p such that for all sequences σ, p is true at the ith point iff T_{pre} is satisfied by a prefix of the suffix sequence starting at point i.

Definition 1 (Non-overlapping Semantics). An infinite computation σ satisfies an SRTD T under the non-overlapping semantics ($\sigma \models_n T$) iff every occurrence of T_{pre} that does not overlap an occurrence of T_{pre} or T_{post} is immediately followed by an occurrence of T_{post}. This is true iff $\sigma \in ((\neg p)^* ; T_{pre} ; T_{post})^\omega + ((\neg p)^* ; T_{pre} ; T_{post})^* ; (\neg p)^\omega$.

Proposition 1. For any SRTD T, $\sigma \models_o T$ implies $\sigma \models_n T$.

3.1   Translation Algorithms

In order to use SRTD's as a specification language in a compositional model checking paradigm we need to augment the above definitions of SRTD's with some information about the modularit y of the design being verified. This is achieved by defining an ownership function $O : S \to N$ that maps each signal to the implemen tation module that con trols it, where S is the set of signals and N is a set of module names. The o wnership function O can be used to partition the SRTD T into *fragments*, $T_1, \ldots, T_n$. The fragment T_i consists of T_{pre}, and only those waveforms in T_{post} that are owned by module i. An SRTD fragment may not be a well-formed SRTD since a fragmet may contain a pause whose pause owner is in another fragmen t. In Figure 1, the ownership function O maps signals $A.p$ and $A.r$ to module A and $B.q$ to module B, and we have one fragmen t consisting of waveforms p and r and another with waveform q.

W e present an algorithm that translates an SRTD into a non-deterministic ω-automaton (ω-NFA) for the *complement* of the SRTD property under the non-overlapping semantics – the construction for the overlapping case is similar and is described in [4]. Then, we give an algorithm that constructs a process that generates the non-overlapping language of the SRTD fragmen ts.

To construct an ω-NFA $A_{\bar{T}}$ for the complemen t of the timing diagram language of T, we proceed as follows. First, we construct a deterministic automaton A_{pre} from T_{pre} that accepts at the first point on a string where the precondition holds. We do so by creating a non-deterministic automaton that accepts the language $\Sigma^* ; T_{pre}$ and determinizing it, so that it en ters an accepting state at every point on an input string where T_{pre} holds. W e then eliminate outgoing edges from accepting states of this automaton. The n umber of reachable states in the resulting DFA can be exponential in the length of the precondition if the precondition has don't-care values. Otherwise, there are only linearly many reachable states, as the reachable part of the DFA is just the automaton for the string matching problem, which can be constructed efficiently (cf. [6]).

Next, for each signal i, we construct an ω-DFA $A_{\overline{post(i)}}$ that tracks the waveform for signal i over the length of the postcondition. This automaton checks at each clock point that the waveform has the specified value. For a don't-care transition, the automaton maintains an extra bit that records whether the transition has occurred. For a pause, the automaton goes into a "waiting" state, where it checks that the value of the signal remains unchanged, and which it leaves when the pause owner signal changes value. The automaton for signal i accepts a computation iff either the waveform pattern is incorrect at some point, or if signal i is the owner of the kth pause in T and the automaton stays in the waiting state for pause k forever.

The automaton $A_{\overline{T}}$ works in the following manner: from the initial state, it runs A_{pre} on the input until this accepts; then it guesses a failing postcondition signal i and runs $A_{\overline{post(i)}}$, accepting if this accepts. If $A_{\overline{post(i)}}$ terminates (so the postcondition holds for signal i), $A_{\overline{T}}$ returns to its initial state.

Theorem 3. (Correctness) For any SRTD T and infinite sequence σ, $\sigma \models_n T$ iff $\sigma \notin L(A_{\overline{T}})$.

The *size* of an SRTD T is product of the number of signals and the number of clock points.

Theorem 4. (Model Checking Complexity) For a process M and an SRTD T, under the non-overlapping semantics, the time complexity of model checking is linear in the size of M and T_{post}, and exponential in the size of T_{pre}.

Theorem 5. For a process M and an SRTD T such that T_{pre} does not contain don't-care values the time complexity of model checking under the non-overlapping semantics is linear in the size of M and T.

Theorem 6. For a process M and an SRTD T, the time complexity of model checking under the overlapping semantics is linear in the size of M and T.

These constructions can be modified easily to construct similar automata for SRTD fragments; the modification consists of choosing the failing postcondition signal only amongst the postcondition signals of the fragment.

3.2   Automatic Construction of Helper Processes

We now present an algorithm that constructs a helper processes Q_j that generates the non-overlapping language corresponding to the fragment T_j of the diagram. The process Q_j works as follows. It sets each signal i in T_j nondeterministically until the precondition holds, then it generates values for the signals of T_j as specified in the postcondition. For a don't-care value, the output is chosen nondeterministically. For a don't-care transition, the point at which the transition occurs is chosen nondeterministically as well. If the process is the owner of a pause, it non-deterministically decides when to generate this event and maintains the current value till that point. The process has a fairness constraint that forces this event to occur within a finite period. Otherwise, it maintains its value until the event that signals the end of the pause occurs, without any requirement for termination.

Proposition 2. (Correctness) For any SRTD fragment T_j, the corresponding helper process Q_j is non-blocking, and σ is a computation of $(//j : Q_j)$ iff $\sigma \models_n T$.

The key feature of this construction is that, for every pause k, only the process that includes the signal owning the pause has a fairness constraint enforcing the occurrence of the pause breaking event. This ensures non-interference between the fairness conditions, which is the essence of the soundness check in our compositional rule.

Theorem 7. (Non-in terference) For SRTD T under the non-overlapping semantics, the corresponding processes $Q_1, \ldots, Q_n$, where $n > 1$, and computation σ, $\sigma \in cl(\mathcal{L}^O(Q_1 // \ldots // Q_n))$ implies $\sigma \in \mathcal{L}^O(Q_1 + \ldots + Q_n)$.

Proof Idea. If σ is in $cl(\mathcal{L}^O(Q_1 // \ldots // Q_n))$, it must satisfy the waveform pattern at each point. If it is not in $\mathcal{L}^O(Q_1 + \ldots + Q_n)$, this can only be because σ never produces the pause breaking event of a pending pause. But such a pause is owned by a particular Q_i; hence, σ is a computation of the Q_j's, $j \neq i$. $\square$

Theorem 8. For SRTD T with corresponding processes $Q_1, \ldots, Q_n$, the number of states of $Q_1 // \ldots // Q_n$ can be exponential in the size of T.

For linear timing diagrams, those with no o verlapping don't-care transitions, no don't-care values at any pause and no don't-care values in the precondition, we have the following theorem.

Theorem 9. For linear SRTD T and the corresponding processes $Q_1, \ldots, Q_n$, the number of states of $Q_1 // \ldots // Q_n$ is bounded by $\mathcal{O}(|T|)$.

3.3   Compositional Model Chec king of SRTD's

In this section, we will describe a proof methodology that uses SRTD's as the property T in the proof rule in Section 2. We would like to show that $P_1 // P_2 \models_n T$, where T is an SRTD (respectively, $P_1 // P_2 \models_o T$). By our construction in Section 3.2, we know that any SRTD T can be automatically decomposed into helper processes Q_1 and Q_2 relative to an ownership function. In order to apply the compositional rule with these choices for the Q_i's, we need only check condition C1 and C3, as conditions C0 and C2 are true by construction. In the non-overlapping case, condition C3 need not be checked, as it follows from Theorem 7. Thus, the only condition to be checked is C1. The details of this check are described in the following section.

4   Applications

We have incorporated the algorithms described in the previous sections into the RTDT tool [4]. RTDT has a user-friendly editor that allows a designer to create and edit SRTD's and a translator that complies the SRTD's into ω-automata. RTDT forms an easy to use interface to the verification tool COSPAN [8]. COSPAN is based on the automata-theoretic, language containment approach to model checking, where both the implementation and the specification are specified as ω-automata.

COSPAN checks $A \models B$ by considering only the infinite fair executions. In order to check inclusion for the finite executions as well, we utilize machine closure. If A is machine closed, any finite execution x of A can be extended to an infinite fair execution; thus, if the COSPAN check is successful, x matches some finite computation of B. The alternative is to use COSPAN's facilities for checking finite computations, but this requires the product of A and B to be constructed twice – once for each check. The machine closure method turns out to be better, as in some of our examples, processes are trivially machine closed. We added the ability to check machine closure to COSPAN.

In our current implementation, we use the non-overlapping semantics since it requires that we only check condition C1. We would like to take advantage of the linear-time (Theorems 5,6) model checking algorithms to discharge the obligation $P_1//Q_2 \models Q_1$ (similarly for the other obligation) in C1. We use Proposition 1 to replace the more expensive check $P_1//P_2 \models_n T$ by the computationally cheaper check $P_1//P_2 \models_o T$.

We used RTDT in conjunction with COSPAN to verify two systems. The first is a synchronous memory access controller and the second is Lucent's Synthesizable PCI Interface Core.

4.1   Memory Access Controller

The memory access controller system has an arbiter that provides arbitration between two user processes and a memory controller that controls three target processes. The user processes may non-deterministically request a transaction and the arbiter grants one user permission to initiate the transaction. That user process may then issue a memory instruction by asserting either the read or write line and setting the address bus. The target whose tag matches the address awakens, services the request, then asserts the ack line on completion.

We verified that this system satisfied both read and write memory transactions formulated as SRTD's. Table 1 presents the verification statistics of both the compositional and non-compositional approaches. In Table 1, Arb and Mem refer to the arbiter and memory controller implementation processes and Arb' and Mem' are the automatically generated helper processes. $mc(Arb/Mem')$ and $mc(Arb'//Mem)$ refer to the machine closure check performed by COSPAN. T_a (T_m) is the SRTD fragment that corresponds to process Arb (Mem). Table 1 indicates that the compositional checks are more efficient than model checking $Arb//Mem \models T$ directly. The cost of checking $Arb//Mem' \models T_a$ is more

Model Checking Task	Number of Variables	Number of Reachable States	Bdd Size	Space (MBytes)	Time (seconds)
SRTD for the read transaction					
Arb//Mem $\models$ T	260	2.5e+06	50084	22	73
mc(Arb//Mem')	114	1.9e+06	14772	0	2
mc(Arb'//Mem)	86	1.9e+04	14793	0	3
Arb'//Mem $\models$ Tm	129	1.1e+05	17993	6	23
Arb//Mem' $\models$ Ta	201	1.1e+06	34861	14	46
SRTD for the write transaction					
Arb//Mem $\models$ T	258	2.6e+06	54834	22	77
mc(Arb//Mem')	112	1.0e+06	14551	0	2
mc(Arb'//Mem)	99	3.8e+04	15432	0	4
Arb'//Mem $\models$ Tm	106	1.1e+05	16854	2	11
Arb//Mem' $\models$ Ta	220	7.3e+05	42844	17	67

Table 1. Verification Statistics for Memory Access Controller Design

than checking $Arb'//Mem \models T_m$ and this is because most of the signals in the SRTD's for both the read and write transactions belonged to the arbiter.

4.2   Lucent's PCI Synthesizable Core

The second example is the Lucent Technologies PCI Interface Core, which is a set of building blocks that bridges an industry standard PCI Bus interface to a high performance F-Bus. The F-Bus supports multiple masters and slaves and there are separate master and slave interfaces to the PCI Bus. The PCI Interface Core is designed to be fully compatible with the PCI Local Bus specification [14].

In previous work [4], we used Lucent's PCI Bus Functional Model [5], which is a sophisticated environment that was developed to test the PCI Interface Core for functionality and compliance with the PCI specification. The Functional Model consists of the PCI Core blocks and abstract models for both the PCI Bus and the F-Bus. This model has about 1500 bounded state variables and was too large for model checking directly. We, therefore, restricted our verification efforts to a part of this design called *pcim-core* that deals with basic

PCI functionality. The *pcim-core* process consists of a master controller *mcntrl*, a slave controller *scntrl*, a configuration process *config* and an address multiplexer *admux*. In addition there is an environment process *pcim-ENV* that contains all the inputs to the *pcim-core* process. We added a number of constraints on *pcim-ENV* to reduce the size of the state space. These constraints were property specific and were different for each property we checked.

Model Checking Task	Number of Variables	Number of Reachable States	Bdd Size	Space (MBytes)	Time (seconds)
SRTD Burst Property 1					
MC'//SC//Env $\models$ Ts	293	5.2e+05	158490	14	302
MC//SC'//Env $\models$ Tm	79	1.2e+07	44066	3	40
MC//SC//Env $\models$ T	335	4.4e+08	273140	20	511
SRTD Burst Property 2					
MC'//SC//Env $\models$ Ts	291	3.8e+05	115488	9	124
MC//SC'//Env $\models$ Tm	74	9.9e+06	42436	3	40
MC//SC//Env $\models$ T	331	1.8e+08	241792	18	430
SRTD Non Burst Property 1					
MC'//SC//Env $\models$ Ts	127	2.5e+28	587771	93	5281
MC//SC'//Env $\models$ Tm	58	1.4e+09	77411	3	74
MC//SC//Env $\models$ T *	–	–	6725219	342	138110

* did not complete due to shortage of space

Table 2. Verification Statistics for PCI Synthesizable Core Design

We formulated a number of properties as SRTD's by looking at the timing diagrams found in the PCI specification [14] and the PCI Core User's manual [5]. These SRTD's were defined over signals controlled by *mcntrl* and *scntrl*. We used RTDT to automatically construct the helper processes MC' and SC' and the property automata T_m and T_s. In Table 2, *ENV* refers to the composition of *pcim-ENV*, *config* and *admux*, while *MC* and *SC* refer to *mcntrl* and *scntrl* respectively. Machine closure was trivially satisfied since the *pcim-core* process did not contain any fairness.

The basic bus transfer on the PCI is a burst, which is composed of an address phase followed by one or more data phases. In the non-burst mode, each address phase is followed by exactly one data phase. The data transfers in the PCI protocol are controlled by three signals *PciFrame*, *PciIrdy* and *PciTrdy*. The master of the bus drives the signal *PciFrame* to indicate the start and end of a transaction. *PciIrdy* is asserted by the master to indicate that it is ready to transfer data. Similarly the slave uses *PciTrdy* to signal that it is ready for data transfer. Data is transferred between master and slave when both *PciIrdy* and *PciTrdy* are asserted on a rising clock edge. The *PciStop* signal is used by the slave to indicate termination of the transaction and the *PciDevsel* signal is used to indicate the chosen device. The first property in Table 2 stated that "in an ongoing transaction, once the *PciStop* signal is asserted, the *PciTrdy* and *PciDevsel* signals remain constant until the data phase completes (*PciIrdy* is deasserted)". The second property specified that "if *PciFrame* is deasserted when both *PciIrdy* and *PciTrdy* are asserted then the data phase completes successfully ". The final property specified the non-burst mode, "if *PciFrame* is asserted for exactly one clock cycle and *PciIrdy*, *PciDevsel* and *PciTrdy* are eventually asserted then in the next clock cycle the transaction ends". Table 2 indicates that the compositional checks are far more efficient than the corresponding non-compositional checks. The non-compositional check for the non-burst property ran out of memory, the numbers shown in Table 2 are the BDD size, space and time just before memory exhaustion. The slave controller *scntrl* has a lot of interaction with both *config* and *admux* processes and this resulted in these processes being pulled into the cone of influence. This is reflected in the significant disparity in the numbers for the two compositional checks.

5   Related Work and Conclusions

As mentioned in the introduction, compositional reasoning for concurrently active processes has been the subject of much work over the past three decades. Our first contribution in this paper is the development of a sound and complete rule for reasoning about arbitrary processes, including those with fairness constraints. Earlier work (cf. [15,1,3,12,13]) either applies only to restricted kinds of processes or temporal logic formulas, or proposes incomplete rules. Our rule extends a simple reasoning rule that is known to be sound for safety properties with an additional soundness check for liveness properties. Thus, in a sense, the rule isolates the difficulties with reasoning about liveness in the soundness check.

The possibility of using timing diagrams for compositional verification appears to have been first recognized in a paper by Josko [10] on modular reasoning. This paper, however, uses timing diagrams only for illustrative purposes. In later work (cf. [9]), a compositional verification methodology proposed in [11] is used to verify timing diagrams. This work uses timing diagrams as a convenient notation for expressing temporal properties – the assume-guarantee reasoning is left to the verifier. In contrast, our work shows how assume-guarantee pairs can be generated mechanically from timing diagram specifications, resulting in a completely automated compositional v erification method.

In our work, we show that timing diagram specifications in the form of SRTD's are naturally decomposable into assume-guarantee properties about the components of the system. W e also show that, although timing diagrams can express liveness properties, the naïve compositional reasoning rule can be applied safely, as the additional soundness check always succeeds for the non-overlapping semantics. W e show how to apply the compositional rule in a fully automated manner. Our experiments with the memory controller and the PCI interface core show that compositional reasoning can indeed be done successfully in this w ay, producing substantial savings in the time and space required for the verification. Although, in these examples, the natural decomposition of the timing diagram property suffices for generating the helper process, it is possible that this will not true in some cases. Th us, heuristics for automatically generating helper processes may be needed – which we leave for future work.

References

1. M. Abadi and L. Lamport. Conjoining specifications. *ACM Trans. on Programming Languages and Systems (TOPLAS)*, May 1995.
2. B. Alpern and F. Schneider. Defining liveness. *Information Processing Letters*, 21(4), 1985.
3. R. Alur and T. Henzinger. Reactive modules. In *IEEE LICS*, 1996.
4. N. Amla, E.A. Emerson, R.P. Kurshan, and K.S. Namjoshi. Model checking synchronous timing diagrams. In *FMCAD*, volume 1954 of *LNCS*, 2000.
5. Bell Laboratories, Lucent Technologies. PCI Core User's Manual (Version 1.0). Technical report, July 1996.
6. T.H. Cormen, C.E. Leiserson, and R.L. Rivest. *Introduction to Algorithms*, chapter 34. MIT Press and McGraw-Hill, 1990.
7. W.P. de Roever, F. de Boer, U. Hannemann, J. Hooman, Y. Lakhnech, M. Poel, and J. Zwiers. *Concurrency Verification: Introduction to Compositional and Noncompositional Proof Methods*. 1999. Draft book.
8. R.H. Hardin, Z. Har'el, and R.P. Kurshan. COSPAN. In *CAV*, volume 1102 of *LNCS*, 1996.
9. J. Helbig, R. Schlor, W. Damm, G. Dohmen, and P. Kelb. VHDL/S - integrating statecharts, timing diagrams, and VHDL. *Microprocessing and Microprogramming*, 38, 1993.
10. B. Josko. Model checking of CTL formulae under liveness assumptions. In *ICALP*, volume 267 of *LNCS*, 1987.
11. B. Josko. *Modular Specification and Verification of Reactive Systems*. Universität Oldenburg, 1993.
12. K.L. McMillan. Circular compositional reasoning about liv eness. In *CHARME*, volume 1703 of *LNCS*, 1999.
13. K.S. Namjoshi and R.J. Trefler. On the completeness of compositional reasoning. In *CAV*, volume 1855 of *LNCS*. Springer-Verlag, 2000.
14. PCI Special Interest Group. PCI Local Bus Specification Rev 2.1. Technical report, June 1995.
15. A. Pnueli. In transition from global to modular reasoning about programs. In *Logics and Models of Concurrent Systems*, NATO ASI Series, 1985.

Sim ulation Revisited

Li Tan and Rance Cleaveland

Department of Computer Science
State University of New York at Stony Brook
Stony Brook, NY 11790 USA
{tanli, rance}@cs.sunysb.edu

Abstract. This paper develops an efficient algorithm for determining when one system is capable of simulating the behavior of another. The method combines an iterative algorithm for computing behavioral pre-orders with an algorithm that simultaneously computes the bisimulation equivalence classes of the systems in question. Experimental data indicate that the new routine dramatically outperforms the best-known algoritm for computing simulation, even when the systems are minimized with respect to bisimulation before the simulation algorithm is invoked.

1 Introduction

A traditional problem in the verification of concurrent systems is the following: given two processes A and B, does B *simulate* A [Mil71]? The resulting *simulation ordering* has numerous practical motivations, both in its own right as a *refinement / approximation ordering* [BBLS92,DGG97,Jon91,LV95] and as a vehicle on which to base the definitions of other refinement orderings [BHR84,DNH83]. Indeed, efficient algorithms for computing the sim ulation ordering underpin algorithms for computing relations such as trace inclusion and the failures/must preorder [CH93].

Despite its utility, not much attention has been paid to algorithms for computing the simulation ordering for finite-state systems. Bloom and Paige [BP95] present a global routine that runs in time $O(m_1 n_2 + m_2 n_1)$, where m_i and n_i represent the number of states and transitions in the two systems being checked. Essentially the same algorithm was discovered independently in [HHK95], and similar ideas may be found in [CC95,CS90]. Celikkan [Cel95] defines an on-the-fly algorithm of comparable complexity.

This paper develops a new technique for computing the sim ulation ordering that combines the fixpoint calculation techniques of [BP95] with the fast *bisimulation-minimization* algorithm due to Paige and Tarjan [PT87,Fer90]. One well-known way to improve the performance of a simulation checker is first to minimize the systems in question with respect to bisimulation in order to reduce the number of states that must be considered. By intertwining the computation of the bisimulation equivalence classes with the simulation relation, our approach exploits the benefits of minimization while avoiding the complete computation of equivalence classes if this is unnecessary.

T. Margaria and W. Yi (Eds.): TACAS 2001, LNCS 2031, pp. 480–495, 2001.
© Springer-Verlag Berlin Heidelberg 2001

2   Background

In this paper systems will be modeled as *labeled transition systems* (LTSs).

Definition 1. *A labeled transition system is a triple $\langle S, A, \longrightarrow \rangle$, where S is a set of states, A a set of actions, and $\longrightarrow \subseteq S \times A \times S$ the transition relation.*

States may be seen as "configurations" the system may enter, while actions represent system activities that can cause state changes. We write $s \xrightarrow{a} s'$ in lieu of $\langle s, a, s' \rangle \in \longrightarrow$, and we sometimes abuse terminology by referring to a tuple $\langle S, A, \longrightarrow, s_I \rangle$, where $s_I \in S$ is the *start state*, as a labeled transition system.

As we make extensive use of binary relations, we introduce some terminology here. If $R \subseteq S \times S$ is a binary relation over set S then we write $R^{-1} = \{\langle s', s \rangle \mid \langle s, s' \rangle \in R\}$ for the inverse of R. Also, if $s \in S$ then we use $R(s)$ to represent the set $\{s' \mid \langle s, s' \rangle \in R\}$, and if $T \subseteq S$ we define $R(T) = \bigcup_{s \in T} R(s)$.

Definition 2. *Let $\langle S, A, \longrightarrow \rangle$ be a LTS, and let $R \subseteq S \times S$ be a relation. Then:*

1. *R is a* simulation *if for every $\langle s_1, s_2 \rangle \in R$ and $a \in A$, whenever $s_1 \xrightarrow{a} s_1'$ then there is a s_2' such that $s_2 \xrightarrow{a} s_2'$ and $\langle s_1', s_2' \rangle \in R$.*
2. *R is a* bisimulation *if both R and R^{-1} are simulations.*

It is easy to establish that for any LTS there is a maximal simulation, $\preceq$, and bisimulation, $\sim$, and that the former is a preorder while the latter is an equivalence relation. The following states an obvious connection between $\preceq$ and $\sim$.

Theorem 1. *Let $\langle S, A, \longrightarrow \rangle$ be a LTS, with $s_1, s_2, s_3 \in S$. Then:*

1. *If $s_1 \sim s_2$ and $s_2 \preceq s_3$ then $s_1 \preceq s_3$.*
2. *If $s_1 \preceq s_2$ and $s_2 \sim s_3$ then $s_1 \preceq s_3$.*

This result has practical implications for computing $\preceq$, since it indicates that LTSs may be minimized with respect to $\sim$ before calculating $\preceq$.

The notion of simulation may be extended to two LTSs as well. Let $T_1 = \langle S, A_1, \longrightarrow_1 \rangle$ and $T_2 = \langle S_2, A_2, \longrightarrow_2 \rangle$ be LTSs. Then a *simulation from T_1 to T_2* is relation $R \subseteq S_1 \times S_2$ satisfying the following for every $\langle s_1, s_2 \rangle \in R$ and $a \in A$:

if $s_1 \xrightarrow{a}_1 s_1'$ then there is a s_2' such that $s_2 \xrightarrow{a}_2 s_2'$ and $\langle s_1', s_2' \rangle \in R$.

A maximal simulation $\preceq$ from T_1 to T_2 exists, and if $s_1 \in S_1$ and $s_2 \in S_2$ then we write $s_1 \preceq s_2$ when these states are in this relation. If $S_1 \cap S_2 = \emptyset$ then it is easy to show that $s_1 \preceq s_2$ in the sense just described if and only if s_1 and s_2 are related by the maximal simulation in the single transition systems $T = \langle S_1 \cup S_2, A_1 \cup A_2, \longrightarrow_1 \cup \longrightarrow_2 \rangle$. If $T_1 = \langle S_1, A_1, \longrightarrow_1, s_1 \rangle$ and $T_2 = \langle S_2, A_2, \longrightarrow_2, s_2 \rangle$ have start states s_1 and s_2 indicated, then we write $T_1 \preceq T_2$ if $s_1 \preceq s_2$.

3   The Relational Coarsest KA-Partition Problem

We are interested in determining algorithmically whether $T_1 \preceq T_2$, where $T_1 = \langle S_1, A, \longrightarrow_1, s_1 \rangle$ and $T_2 = \langle S_2, A, \longrightarrow_2, s_2 \rangle$ are LTSs. To simplify the presentation, we consider a restricted version of the problem in which transition systems are *unlabeled*. In what follows a(n unlabeled) transition system is a pair $\langle S, E \rangle$ where S is a set of states and $E \subseteq S \times S$ is the transition relation. On occasion, we designate a start state $s_I \in S$ and call $\langle S, E, s_I \rangle$ a transition system. Transition systems may be seen as labeled transition systems whose action set A contains a single action. Note that in $\langle S, E \rangle$ E is a binary relation over S.

In this section we show how calculating $\preceq$ can be reduced to solving the *Relational Coarsest KA-Partition Problem*. To define this problem, we first review the Relational Coarsest Partition Problem [PT87], whose solution corresponds to computing the equivalence classes of $\sim$ over a single transition system.

The Relational Coarsest Partition Problem (RCPP). The statement of the RCPP uses the following terminology.

Definition 3. *Let $\langle S, E \rangle$ be a transition system.*

1. *A* partition *of S is a collection $\{B_1, \ldots, B_n\}$ of disjoint nonempty subsets of S such that $S = \bigcup_{i=1}^{n} B_i$. Each B_i in a partition P is called a* block *of P.*
2. *A partition P refines a partition P' ($P \trianglelefteq P'$) if for every $B_i \in P$ there is a $B'_j \in P'$ such that $B_i \subseteq B'_j$. In this case we say that P' is coarser than P.*
3. *Let $S_1, S'_1 \subseteq S$. Then S_1 is* stable *with respect to S'_1 if either $S_1 \cap E^{-1}(S'_1) = \emptyset$ or $S_1 \subseteq E^{-1}(S'_1)$. A partition P of S is stable with respect to a set $S' \subseteq S$ if each $B_i \in P$ is stable with respect to S'. A partitition P is stable with respect to another partition P' if every $B_i \in P$ is stable with respect to every $B'_j \in P'$. A partition P is* self-stable *if it is stable with respect to itself.*

Intuitively, a set S_1 is stable with respect to S'_1 if either no state in S_1 has a transition into S'_1 ($S_1 \cap E^{-1}(S'_1) = \emptyset$) or every state in S_1 has at least one transition into S'_1 ($S_1 \subseteq E^{-1}(S'_1)$). It is easy to see that $\trianglelefteq$ defines a partial order over the set of partitions of S and that a coarsest self-stable partition of S is guaranteed to exist. The RCPP may now be defined as follows.

Given: Transition system $\langle S, E \rangle$ with $|S| < \infty$.
Compute: The coarsest self-stable partition P of S.

One may show that any self-stable partition of S is a bisimulation and that the blocks in the largest self-stable partition of S are the equivalence classes of $\sim$.

The Relational Coarsest KA-Partition Problem. Theorem 1 suggests one way to improve the efficiency of computing whether or not $T_1 \preceq T_2$: minimize both T_1 and T_2 with respect to $\sim$ before calculating $\preceq$ using e.g. the algorithm in [BP95]. Doing so entails using a preprocessing step to compute the equivalence classes of $\sim$ for each of T_1 and T_2. Our goal is to find an way to compute bisimulation classes and a simulation relation simultaneously, thereby eliminating the need for fully computing equivalence classes when this is unnecessary. Our method involves associating *auxiliary information* in the form of a set of "potentially simulating states" with each equivalence class of states in the "lower" transition system. This auxiliary information will also be recorded in terms of equivalence classes of states in the "upper" transition system. When a lower equivalence class is split, auxiliary information must be altered appropriately. To make these notions precise, we define the *Relational Coarsest KA-Partition Problem*, which is an alteration of the RCPP introduced above.

Definition 4. *Let $T_1 = \langle S_1, E_1 \rangle$ and $T_2 = \langle S_2, E_2 \rangle$ be transition systems.*

1. *A kernel-auxiliary pair (KA-pair) has form $\langle B, X \rangle$, where $B \subseteq S_1$ and $X \subseteq S_2$. We write $\langle B, X \rangle \subseteq \langle B', X' \rangle$ if $B \subseteq B'$ and $X \subseteq X'$. We often refer to B as the kernel set of $\langle B, X \rangle$ and X as the auxiliary set.*
2. *A set P of KA-pairs is a kernel-auxiliary partition (KA-partition) from T_1 to T_2 if $P_1 = \{B \mid \langle B, X \rangle \in P\}$ is a partition of S_1.*
3. *A KA-partition P refines KA-partition P' ($P \trianglelefteq P'$) if for every $\langle B, X \rangle \in P$ there is a $\langle B', X' \rangle \in P'$ such that $\langle B, X \rangle \subseteq \langle B', X' \rangle$.*
4. *KA-pair $\langle B, X \rangle$ is stable with respect to KA-pair $\langle B', X' \rangle$ if either $B \cap E_1^{-1}(B') = \emptyset$, or $B \subseteq E_1^{-1}(B')$ and $X \subseteq E_2^{-1}(X')$. A KA-partition P is stable with respect to KA-pair $\langle B', X' \rangle$ if every $\langle B, X \rangle \in P$ is stable with respect to $\langle B', X' \rangle$. KA-partition P is stable with respect to KA-partition P' if P is stable with respect to every KA-pair in P'. KA-partition P is self-stable if it is stable with respect to itself.*

Note that if P is a self-stable KA-partition from T_1 to T_2 and $\langle B, X \rangle, \langle B', X' \rangle \in P$, then either no state in B has a transition into B', or every state in B has a transition into B' and every state in X has a transition into X'. When P is a self-stable KA-partition, the set $\{B \mid \langle B, X \rangle \in P\}$ is a self-stable partition.

Every KA-partition P defines a relation $R(P) \subseteq S_1 \times S_2$ given by: $\langle s_1, s_2 \rangle \in R(P)$ if and only if there exists $\langle B, X \rangle \in P$ such that $s_1 \in B$ and $s_2 \in X$. The following is an easy consequence of Definition 4 and Theorem 1.

Theorem 2. *Let $T_1 = \langle S_1, E_1 \rangle$ and $T_2 = \langle S_2, E_2 \rangle$ be transition systems with $s_1 \in S_1$ and $s_2 \in S_2$. Then there is a unique coarsest self-stable KA-partition $P_{\max}$ from T_1 to T_2, and $s_1 \preceq s_2$ if and only if $\langle s_1, s_2 \rangle \in R(P_{\max})$.*

The Relational Coarsest KA-Partition Problem may now be stated as follows.

Given: Transition systems $T_1 = \langle S_1, E_1 \rangle$, $T_2 = \langle S_2, E_2 \rangle$, with $|S_1|, |S_2| < \infty$.
Compute: The coarsest self-stable partition P from T_1 to T_2.

The statement of this problem does not mention partitions of the state set of the "upper" transition system. The following corollary indicates that auxiliary sets can be efficiently represented as unions of bisimulation-equivalence classes.

Corollary 1. *Let $T_1 = \langle S_1, E_1 \rangle$ and $T_2 = \langle S_2, E_2 \rangle$ be transition systems, let $P_{\max}$ be the coarsest self-stable KA-partition on T_1 and T_2. and let Q be the coarsest self-stable partition over S_2. Then for any $\langle B, X \rangle \in P_{\max}$ and $C \in Q$, either $X \subseteq C$ or $X \cap C = \emptyset$.*

4   Computing the Relational Coarsest KA-Partition

This section presents two approaches to constructing the relational coarsest KA-partition on two systems. The first is based on the "naive" relational coarsest partition algorithm of [PT87], and we include it here to illustrate the basic operations that both algorithms must perform. The second builds on the sophisticated "three-way splitting" approach also found in [PT87].

4.1   A Naive Approach

The naive algorithm uses a *partition-refinement* strategy. Starting with the coarsest possible KA-partition, KA-pairs are repeatedly "split" until the KA-partition becomes self-stable. The basic operation in the algorithm involves splitting the KA-pairs in a KA-partition P with respect to a KA-pair $C' = \langle B', X' \rangle$.

$split(C' = \langle B', X' \rangle, P')$
1    $P' := \emptyset$
2   **for** every $\langle B, X \rangle \in P$ **do**
3   **if** $B \cap E_1^{-1}(B') \neq \emptyset$ **then**
4   **if** $B \not\subseteq E_1^{-1}(B')$ **then**
5                $\langle B_1, X_1 \rangle := \langle B \cap E_1^{-1}(B'), X \cap E_2^{-1}(X') \rangle$
6                $\langle B_2, X_2 \rangle := \langle B - E_1^{-1}(B'), X \rangle$
7                $P' := P' \cup \{\langle B_1, X_1 \rangle, \langle B_2, X_2 \rangle\}$
8   **else**
9                $\langle B_1, X_1 \rangle := \langle B, X \cap E_2^{-1}(X') \rangle$
10                $P' := P' \cup \{\langle B_1, X_1 \rangle\}$
11   **else** $P' := P' \cup \{\langle B, X \rangle\}$
return(P')

The crucial insight underlying this operation occurs in lines 5–6. In this situation the kernel set, B, of KA-pair $\langle B, X \rangle$ must be split because it is not stable with respect to B', the kernel set of C'. Because states in B_1 have transitions into B', the "auxiliary set", X_1, of states that potentially simulate those in B_1 must also have transitions into X'. The auxiliary set X_2 of B_2 does not have to satisfy this requirement, since states in B_2 do not have transitions into B'. Note that both $\langle B_1, X_1 \rangle$ and $\langle B_2, X_2 \rangle$ are stable with respect to C'.

We call C' a *splitter* for P if $P \neq split(C', P)$ (note this means that P is not stable with respect to C'). The naive algorithm works as follows.

---

1    $P := \{\langle S_1, S_2 \rangle\}$
2   **while** P is not stable with respect to some $C' = \langle B', X' \rangle \in P$ **do**
3        $P := split(C', P)$

It will be convenient in what follows to view the execution of our KA-partition algorithms in terms of a tree whose nodes are labeled with KA-pairs. A node has children if the KA-pairs labeling the children are the result of applying a *split* operation to the label of the node. Thus a node may have two children (if its kernel set is split in lines 5–6) or one child (if its kernel set remains unchanged but its auxiliary set is *pruned* in line 9). If a node labeled by $\langle B, X \rangle$ has two children, we assume the left child is labeled by $\langle B_1, X_1 \rangle$ (line 6) and the right by $\langle B_2, X_2 \rangle$. An invariant in this tree is that the right child of every two-child node has the same auxiliary set as its parent. We refer to such a tree as a *partition tree*. Note that the leaves of this tree represent the current KA-partition; when the algorithm terminates the leaves constitute the coarsest self-stable KA-partition.

The correctness of the naive algorithm relies on the following observations, which are adaptations of similar ones found in [PT87].

1. If $P' \trianglelefteq P$ and P is stable with respect to C', then so is P'.
2. If P is self-stable, then P is stable with respect to any P' such that $P \trianglelefteq P'$.
3. If $P \trianglelefteq P'$ then $split(C', P) \trianglelefteq split(C', P')$ for any C'.
4. *split* is commutative: $split(C_1, split(C_2, P)) = split(C_2, split(C_1, P))$.

To analyze the complexity of this procedure we first introduce the following notation. Let S refer to the set of bisimulation-equivalence classes of transition system $\langle S, E \rangle$; thus $|S|$ represents the number of such equivalence classes.

The loop in the naive algorithm executes at most $|S_1| \cdot |S_2|$ times, since each bisimulation-equivalence class has an auxiliary set that can only decrease $|S_2|$ times. Furthermore, each execution of the loop can be performed in $|E_1| + (|S_1| \cdot |E_2|)$. The first term counts the total amount of time over all splitters for updating kernel sets in the KA-pairs, while the second reflects the time for updating the auxiliary sets. In addition, only the current KA-partition needs to be stored. This leads to the following.

Theorem 3. *The naive algorithm computes the relational coarsest KA-partition in* $O(|S_1| \cdot |S_2| \cdot (|E_1| + (|S_1| \cdot |E_2|)))$ *time and* $O(|S_1| \cdot |S_2|)$ *space.*

4.2 An Improved Algorithm

The algorithm just given uses the "naive" partition-refinement strategy of [PT87] as a basis for computing the coarsest self-stable KA-partition; it also makes no attempt to exploit bisimulation equivalence in the "upper" transition system. These observations suggest two avenues for an improved routine.

1. Use the "three-way splitting" partition-refinement algorithm of [PT87].
2. Maintain equivalence classes of states in the auxiliary sets of KA-pairs.

This section shows how these ideas may be combined into a single efficient procedure. We begin by briefly reviewing the three-way splitting idea of [PT87].

Partition-refinement and three-way splitting. Paige and Tarjan [PT87] exploit Hopcroft's "process the smaller half" strategy for minimizing deterministic state machines [AHJ74] to give a more efficient algorithm for solving the RCPP. The main idea is to split a partition with respect to two splitters by only processing the transitions entering the smaller of the two. This approach may split equivalence classes into three pieces, and we thus refer to it as "three-way splitting."

The key insight behind three-way splitting is as follows. Let $T = \langle S, E \rangle$, and consider block B in partition P of S. Suppose B is stable with respect to a set (former block) $C \subseteq S$, and suppose further that C has been split into C_1 and C_2 and B must now be split with respect to these. If $B \subseteq E^{-1}(C)$, then splitting B with respect to both C_1 and C_2 yields (up to) three new equivalence classes.

$$B_{11} = B \cap E^{-1}(C_1) \cap E^{-1}(C_2)$$
$$B_{12} = (B \cap E^{-1}(C_1)) - E^{-1}(C_2)$$
$$B_2 = (B - E^{-1}(C_1)) \cap E^{-1}(C_2)$$

B_{11} contains states from B having transitions into both C_1 and C_2, B_{12} contains states from B having transititions into C_1 but not C_2, while B_2 contains states from B with no transitions into C_1 but transitions into C_2. Note that $B = B_{11} \cup B_{12} \cup B_2$.

Algorithmically, [PT87] gives a way to compute B_{11}, B_{12} and B_2 by scanning the smaller of C_1 and C_2. To achieve this one must know, for each state s in B, how many of s's transitions lead to states in C. One can then construct similar counts for each state in B and the smaller of C_1 and C_2 (call it C_{small}) by processing each transitions leading into C_{small}. That is,

$$B_{11} = \{s \in B \mid 0 < |E(s) \cap C_{\mathsf{small}}| < |E(s) \cap C|\}$$
$$B_{12} = \{s \in B \mid 0 = |E(s) \cap C_{\mathsf{small}}|\}$$
$$B_2 = \{s \in B \mid |E(s) \cap C_{\mathsf{small}}| = |E(s) \cap C|\}$$

To exploit this observation the three-way splitting algorithm maintains a list of *compound splitters*, which are trees of splitters with respect to whose roots the current partition is stable. In the previous example, C would be the root of a compound splitter, while C_1 and C_2 would be the children of C. When three-way splitting is done with respect to C_1 and C_2, C_1 and C_2 become the roots of new compound splitters if they have themselves been previously split. More details may be found in [PT87,Fer90].

Adapting three-way splitting to KA-partitions. To adapt three-way splitting to KA-partitions it is convenient to recall how our algorithms construct "partition trees" labeled by KA-pairs. As was the case in the previous algorithm, we maintain the following invariant in this tree: the right child of a two-child node has the same auxiliary set as its parent. The leaves of the tree constitute the current KA-partition, and a compound splitter is a subtree with the property that the current KA-partition is stable with respect to the label of the subtree's root.

Let $\langle B, X \rangle$ be a KA-pair in the current KA-partition, and let C be the root node of compound splitter having two subtrees. Assume further that the KA-pair labeling C is $\langle B', X' \rangle$ and that the label of C's left child, C_1, is $\langle B'_1, X'_1 \rangle$ and that the label of its right child, C_2, is $\langle B'_2, X' \rangle$. (Recall that the right child's auxiliary set is the same as its parent's.) Then the result of splitting $\langle B, X \rangle$ with respect to both C_1 and C_2 will in general be the following.

$$\langle B_{11}, X_1 \rangle = \langle B \cap E_1^{-1}(B_1') \cap E_1^{-1}(B_2'), X \cap E_2^{-1}(X) \rangle$$
$$\langle B_{12}, X_1 \rangle = \langle ((B \cap E_1^{-1}(B_1')) - E_1^{-1}(B_2'), X \cap E_2^{-1}(X) \rangle$$
$$\langle B_2, X \rangle = \langle ((B - E_1^{-1}(B_1')) \cap E_1^{-1}(B_2'), X \rangle$$

The characterizations of the kernel sets B_{11}, B_{12} and B_2 follows from the discussion of the Paige-Tarjan algorithm above, but the associated auxiliary sets deserve further comment. Regarding $\langle B_2, X \rangle$, recall that since C is a node in the partition tree whose right child is C_2, the auxiliary sets labeling C and C_2 are the same. Since $\langle B, X \rangle$ is stable with respect to C, it follows that every state in X has a transition into X', the auxiliary set of C and hence of C_2. Since B_2 consists of the states of B with no transitions into C_1, it follows that every state in X is a candidate for simulating every state in B_2.

On the other hand, states in B_{12} have transitions into C_2 but not C_1. Since the auxiliary set of C_1 is a subset of the auxiliary set of C, not every state in X, the auxiliary set of B, can safely simulate states in B_{12}: only those with a transition into X' $(X \cap E_2^{-1}(X'))$ can. A similar line of reasoning holds for $\langle B_{11}, X_2 \rangle$. Note (suprisingly)that the auxiliary sets of B_{11} and B_{12} are the same.

Figure 1 shows the resulting tree structure rooted at B. Node $\langle B_1, X_1 \rangle$ is inserted so that the partition tree is binary; implicitly, $B_1 = B_{11} \cup B_{12}$. Note that the invariant regarding right children is maintained.

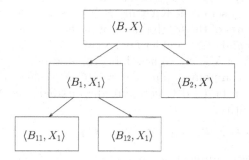

Fig. 1. Three-way splitting.

An additional subtlety in KA-partitions is that compound splitters can have one child rather than two. This arises when a node's auxiliary set is pruned without its kernel set being split. Such splitters can be treated as special cases of two-child splitters in which the right child's kernel set is empty. A KA-pair split by such a splitter will only have one child, as its kernel set cannot be split.

To implement these ideas efficiently we use several data structures. For each KA-pair $D = \langle B, X \rangle$ in the current partition (i.e. at the leaves of the partition tree) we use doubly-linked lists $D.B$ and $D.K$ to represent B and X, respectively.

This ensures constant-time insertions and deletions. Internal tree nodes do not have their kernel and auxiliary sets represented explicitly; rather, they may be reconstructed from the leaves that are descendants of the node. We also use the following data structure for efficiency reasons.

Kernel count table. To each compound splitter $C = \langle B', X' \rangle$ we associate a hash table $C.K$ that, for each state $s \in S_1$ in the "lower" transition system, maintains $|B' \cap E_1(s)|$ (i.e. the number of transitions from s into the kernel set of C). We use $C.K(s)$ to stand for the count associated with state $s \in S_1$. In three-way splitting, it suffices to compute $C_{\mathsf{small}}.K$, where C_{small} is the smaller child of C, in order to compute B_{11}, B_{12}, B_2 and $C_{\mathsf{big}}.K$, where C_{big} is the larger of C's children.

Auxiliary count table. In analogy with $C.K$, $C.A$ records, for each $s \in S_2$ in the "upper" transition system, the quantity $|C.X \cap E_2(s)|$. So $C.A(s)$ is the number of transitions s has into the set stored in $C.X$.

Incoming node lists. For each potential compound splitter $C = \langle B', X' \rangle$, $C.F$ records the list of KA-pairs whose kernel states have transitions to B'. This information is needed to ensure that auxiliary sets are refined properly when nodes are split with respect to C. In particular, if C's right child, C_2, has a smaller kernel set than its sibling C_1, and KA-pair $D = \langle B, X \rangle$ is such that B only has transitions into C_1, then the auxiliary set of D's (only) child, which would be $X \cap E_2^{-1}(X')$, will not be computed if only blocks with transitions into C_2 are analyzed.

For leaf nodes C, $C.X$ stores the auxiliary set associated with the node. For internal nodes D, in contrast, we use $D.X$ to store *difference sets*. More specifically, rather than storing the entire auxiliary set of the KA-pair $\langle B, X \rangle$ associated with D in $D.X$, we store only those elements of the set that are not in the auxiliary set of D's left child. Let D_1 be the left child of D, and let $\langle B_1, X_1 \rangle$ be D_1's KA-pair. Then the set of states stored in $D.X$ is $X - X_1$. When doing three-way splitting on KA-pair $\langle B, X \rangle$ with respect to compound splitter $C = \langle B', X' \rangle$ whose left child C_1 is labeled $\langle B_1', X_1' \rangle$, $C.X$ can be used to compute the auxiliary set X_1 of $\langle B_{11}, X_1 \rangle$ using the following identity.

$$X \cap E_2^{-1}(X') = X - \{s \in X \mid E_2(s) \subseteq (X' - X_1')\} \tag{1}$$

The use of difference sets has efficiency ramifications; in particular, the amortized analysis of the complexity of the algorithm relies on the use of difference sets.

Special care must be taken for partition-tree nodes having only one child. Since only leaves store KA-pairs, calculating the kernel set of an internal node D requires gathering all the kernel sets of the leaves in D's subtree. In the Paige-Tarjan algorithm [PT87], this may be done in time proportional to the size of D's kernel set, since every internal node has two children and kernel sets are disjoint. Because of the existence of single-child chains in our tree, this does not immediately apply. To solve this problem, we use *path compression*: we add a field $D.root$ that points to the first node on a single-child chain that D may be part of. For nodes that are the roots of such chains, we add an additional field, $D.end$, that points to the end of its single-child chain.

Bisimulation equivalence in auxiliary sets. The second direction for improving the algorithm involves the exploitation of bisimulation equivalence classes in auxiliary sets. The basic approach is to maintain a current partition for states in the "upper" transition system, $T_2 = \langle S_2, E_2 \rangle$. Each block represents an approximation to the bisimulation equivalence classes of T_2. The fields $D.X$ then point to lists of these equivalence classes rather than to states.

More specifically, we use *auxiliary list tables (ALTs)* to store auxiliary sets. An ALT has two kinds of entries.

Base entries point to lists of states in the upper transition system. Taken together, the base entries form a partition of the state space.

List entries point to lists of base entries. These entries will in turn be pointed to by the auxiliary set components $C.X$ of a node C in the partition tree.

The lists in ALT are implemented as doubly-linked lists in order to support $O(1)$ insertions and deletions. In addition, for $s \in S_2$, $baseOf(s)$ retrieves the base entry s belongs to; this can be implemented in constant time by maintaining an array storing each auxiliary state's base entry b and position in the state list of b. We also associate with each base entry b a field $b.t$, which is used for splitting b, and a hash table $b.R$ indexed by the list entries it belongs to; $b.R$ stores the positions of b in these list entries so that b can be quickly deleted. Together $baseOf$ and $b.R$ allow the query $s \in l?$, where l is a list entry, to be answered in $O(1)$ time: first look up the base entry b that s belongs to, then look in $b.R$ to see if there is an entry for l. $mkListEntry(l)$ is an initialization function; it creates a list entry for a set of states by first creating a new base entry for this set and then a new list entry containing only this base entry. $addBaseToList(b, l)$ adds a base entry b to a list entry l and saves b's position in the doubly-linked list of l to $b.R$. $removeBaseFromList(b, l)$ removes b from l and adjusts $b.R$ accordingly. $duplicate(l)$ returns a new list entry whose doubly-linked list contains the same bases as l.

During the execution of the algorithm base entries will periodically require splitting, since states in the same base entry may be determined not to be bisimulation equivalent. For example, this happens when auxiliary sets are "pruned" during three-way splitting: some states in a base entry b may be determined to have transitions to a given auxiliary set (which may be shown always to be a union of bisimulation equivalence classes in the upper system), while others do not. In this case the former states are moved to $b.t$. Then operation *processSplitBases* splits bases whose $b.t$ list is non-empty; such base entries are called *split bases*. For a given split base b, *processSplitBases* creates a new base entry b' for the states in $b.t$ if b itself is non-empty and moves $b.t$ to b'. The procedure then updates list entries appropriately: it takes another parameter, a list of pairs of list entries, with the first list of each pair representing an "old home" of b and the second representing the "new home" for b'. (In general, the former list will be the auxiliary list of a node and the later an auxiliary list of a left child. The former should be turned into a difference list, while the latter is expecting to be populated with base entries.) No pair shares the same "old list" component, so this list of pairs can be organized as hash table, enabling membership queries to be done in $O(1)$ time. For all other list entries that are not in an "old list", the routine adds the new base entry b' to those already containing b so that the states they contain remain unchanged.

The algorithm in detail. Our algorithm computes the Relational Coarsest KA-Partition from $T_1 = \langle S_1, E_1 \rangle$ to $T_2 = \langle S_2, E_2 \rangle$ in several stages. It starts by building a KA-partition containing one KA-pair, $\langle S_1, S_2 \rangle$: every state in S_2 is assumed to simulate every state in S_1, and all states in S_1 and S_2 are assumed to be bisimulation equivalent.

The first step in the algorithm is to stabilize the KA-partition with respect to the single KA-pair $\langle S_1, S_2 \rangle$. After creating a node C and initializing $C.B$ to S_1 and $C.X$ to S_2, $C.B$ is split into states having transitions and those that do not; the former are assigned to $C_1.B$, where C_1 is the left child of C, while the latter are assigned to $C_2.B$, the right child of C. The counters in $C.K$ are also initialized to the number of transitions each state has (except that states without transitions are not touched). Then the auxiliary list of C is copied into $C_2.X$, and $C_1.X$ computed by scanning the transitions leading into $C.X$. This procedure may also induce a split in the base entry containing S_2, since states without transitions cannot be bisimilar to those that do. The latter states are assigned to a base entry that becomes part of $C_1.X$, while those that do not become the elements of $C.X$, which is now a difference list. At the end, there is a single compound splitter, C, with left child C_1 and right child C_2.

The algorithm then loops, repeatedly removing splitters from a list of splitters, performing the split, and potentially adding new splitters, until the list of splitters is empty. Given a (compound) splitter C, the kernel sets of the current partition (leaves in the partition tree) are split by processing the child containing the smaller splitter. This entails decrementing $C.K(s)$ and incrementing $C_{\text{small}}.K(s)$, where C_{small} is the smaller child of C. Then each KA-pair D that is touched in this process is examined and split using three-way splitting. Temporary fields $D.B_0$ and $D.B_1$ are used for this purpose.

Following the three-way splitting operations, the auxiliary sets for KA-pairs with transitions into C are created. Right children are given copies of the auxiliary sets of their parents by copying list entries in the ALT, and base entries are split when some states are determined to have transitions into some sets that others cannot match. Finally, splitter lists are updated; C_1 and C_2 are added as compound splitters if they have children, as well as other nodes that were split and yet were not part of any splitter.

Theorem 4. *The algorithm converges, and the leaf KA-pairs form the relational coarsest KA-partition when the algorithm terminates.*

The next theorems characterize the complexity of our algorithm. Recall that for transition system $T = \langle S, E \rangle$, $\mathcal{S}$ refers to the set of bisimulation equivalence classes T. We also use $\mathcal{E}$ to refer to the transition relation on $\mathcal{S}$ defined by: $\langle h, h' \rangle \in \mathcal{E}$ if and only if there exist $s_1 \in h_1, s_2 \in h_2$ such that $E(s_1, s_2)$.

Theorem 5. *The overall running time of the three-way splitting algorithm with path compression is* $O(|S_1| \cdot |S_2| + |E_1| \cdot log(|S_1|) + |S_1| \cdot |E_2| + |\mathcal{E}_1| \cdot |S_2|)$.

Theorem 6. *The space required by the three-way splitting algorithm is bounded by* $O(|T_1| + |T_2| + |S_1| \cdot |S_2|)$.

We conclude this section by comparing our time and space efficiency with the simulation algorithm in [BP95]. That procedure ran in $O(|S_1| \cdot |S_2| + |S_1| \cdot |E_2| + |S_2| \cdot |E_1|)$ time and $O(|T_1| + |T_2| + |S_1| \cdot |S_2|)$ space. Our complexity results replace many occurences of E_i and S_i with $\mathcal{E}_i$ and S_i; indeed, the only worst-case penalty our procedure pays is the $|E_1| \cdot log(|S_1|)$ factor, which is due to the three-way splitting our procedure performs. The experimental results in the next section nevertheless indicate that our procedure works better in practice.

5   Experimental Results

To assess the practical performance of our algorithm we implemented it in the Concurrency Workbench of the New Century (CWB-NC), a verification tool for finite-state systems (see www.cs.sunysb.edu/~cwb to obtain the system). The CWB-NC analysis routines work on labeled transition systems, so we adapted our algorithm to this setting by adding an action parameter to the splitting operation and then splitting a partition with respect to all actions, given a splitter. The approach followed is similar to that presented in [Fer90] for adapting the Paige-Tarjan algorithm [PT87] to labeled transition systems. The implementation of our algorithm involves 2,045 lines of Standard ML of New Jersey, with approximately a quarter of this total being devoted to maintaining ALT tables.

We then tested four different simulation algorithms on case studies included in the CWB-NC release. The four simulation algorithms checked included: the implementation of the Bloom-Paige algorithm [BP95,CC95] included in the CWB-NC release; our naive algorithm; our algorithm with the ALT data structure but without path compression; and our full algorithm. In all cases *early termination* is used: when two start states are found to be unrelated, the algorithm terminates. We ran the implementations on two different classes of systems.

Railway-signaling schemes. Three models of the British Rail Slow-Scan communications protocol as modeled in [CLNS96] were compared to each other. The systems are implemented in a version of CCS with priorities.
Alternating-bit protocols. Different versions of the alternating-bit protocol were compared, including ones that deadlocked and chains of cells.

All testing was done on a Sun Ultra SparcIIi with two 336 MHz processors and 3 GB of main memory. All times are reported in seconds of CPU time.

The results for the railway models are reported in Table 2, while those for the alternating bit protocol may be found in Table 4. The columns headed "Bloom-Paige" present times for the Bloom-Paige algorithm, "Naive KA-part" for our naive algorithm, "Sim-ALT" for our more sophisticated algorithm without path compression, and "Sim-ALT-PC" for our algorithm with path compression. W e also compared the performance of Sim-AL T and the Bloom-P aige algorithm when the systems are first minim ized with respect to strong bisimulation. Tables 1 and 3 give the sizes of the systems before and after minim ization. In all case "# states / # trans" refers to the n umber of reachable states and transitions.

Table 1. Railway system sizes before and after minimi zation.

	# states	# trans	# bisim classes	# of bisim trans
basicSS	312	801	287	713
recoverySS	1100	2801	789	2233
ftolerantSS	11905	33760	7485	26165

Table 2. Railway simulation results.

Agent 1 Agent 2	ans	Bloom- Paige	min + Bloom-Paige	Naive KA-Part	Sim-ALT	Sim-ALT -PC	min + Sim-ALT
basicSS recoverySS	T	124.74	7.14+ 62.91	24.22	7.52	9.62	7.14+ 2.44
basicSS ftolerantSS	F	N/A^1	131.48+ 2109.90	330.78	139.80	139.02	131.48+ 26.63
recoverySS ftolerantSS	F	N/A^1	137.21 + N/A^1	634.10	278.05	273.99	137.21 + 32.15
recoverySS basicSS	F	186.23	7.14 + 157.28	28.67	14.95	13.60	7.14 + 1.39
ftolerantSS basicSS	F	10831.63	131.48 + 1724.00	284.85	192.50	194.12	131.48 + 23.99
ftolerantSS recoverySS	F	N/A^1	137.21 + 31104.24	192.95	256.73	267.59	137.21 + 17.91

1. Memory allocation error after > 4 hour

Based on the times presented one may draw the following conclusions.

1. *Our algorithms dramatically outperform the Bloom-Paige algorithm in time and space.* Even the naive algorithm substan tially outperforms Bloom-P aige. The degrees of improvement are often quite startling, ranging up to a factor of 100 and beyond; we believe this is due to the space efficiency of our algorithms, which causes them to use less virtual memory .
2. *When there are few equivalence classes, minimizing and then running Bloom-Paige can be competitive with our algorithms running on unminimized sys-*

Table 3. ABP system sizes before and afterminimi zation.

	# states	# trans	# bisim classes	# bisim trans
ABP-lossy	57	130	15	32
ABP-safe	49	74	18	32
Two-link-netw	1589	6819	197	791
Three-link-netw	44431	280456	2745	16188
Two-link-netw-safe	1171	3153	196	662

Table 4. ABP simulation results.

Agent 1 Agent 2	ans	Bloom-Paige	min+ Bloom-Paige	Naive KA-Part	Sim-ALT	Sim-ALT -PC	min+ Sim-ALT
ABP-lossy Two-link-netw	F	11.07	2.00+ 0.20	4.21	2.78	5.57	2.00+ 0.12
ABP-lossy Three-link-netw	F	7104.53	89.91+ 14.60	185.00	443.48	476.82	89.91+ 2.66
Two-link-netw Three-link-netw	F	N/A	91.81+ 232.10	4320.63	662.97	625.84	91.81+ 6.71
Two-link-netw ABP-lossy	F	18.34	2.00+ 0.24	5.52	6.31	5.30	2.00+ 0.13
Three-link-netw ABP-lossy	F	1116.19	89.91+ 5.79	231.63	137.63	135.59	89.91+ 2.31
Three-link-netw Two-link-netw	F	N/A[1]	91.81+ 160.25	4966.73	473.28	561.37	91.81+ 88.47
ABP-safe ABP-lossy	T	0.16	0.08 + 0.02	0.20	0.09	0.11	0.08+ 0.02
Two-link-netw-safe Two-link-netw	T	432.58	1.99 + 3.82	84.27	5.60	5.68	1.99 + 0.95

1. Memory allocation error after > 1 hour

tems. The ABP results suggest this in particular: minimization can dramatically improve the performance of Bloom-P aige. This also leads us to believe that paging is a major source of inefficiency in Bloom-P aige.

3. *Sim-ALT substantially outperforms Bloom-Paige when both are run on minimized systems.* This result may seem surprising, given that our algorithm is intended to combine the benefits of minimization with those of simulation checking. Howevever, as Theorem 5 shows, our algorithm's time complexit y still contains factors involving the number of transitions in the input systems.

4. *Path compression is a net loss for our algorithm.* In order to obtain the complexity result in Theorem 5 it was necessary to introduce path compression. However, the performance figures suggest that this impro vement does not materialize in practice.

6   Conclusions and Future W ork

This paper has presented an algorithm for determining whether or not one transition system can sim ulate another. The procedure com bines ideas from traditional simulation algorithms with notions found in bisim ulation-equivalence procedures; the resulting routine has asymptotic time- and space-complexities that approach those of the best-known algorithm [BP95,CC95]. In practice, our approach dramatically outperforms the existing routines, o wing to the fact that our procedure exploits bisim ulation equivalence to reduce both time and space consumption.

As future work we plan to investigate the use of our ideas to impro ve mucalculus model checking. It is known that bisimilar systems satisfy the same mu-calculus formulas; consequently, com bining a bisimulation-equivalence algorithm with a model c hecker could also yield potentially dramatic performance impro vements in practice. W e also wish to investigate adaptations of our algorithm in the computation of other relations, including the so-called "w eak" simulation ordering in which transitions labeled by internal actions are allowed to be "absorbed" into transitions labeled by external actions. It should also be noted that our algorithm is *global*: the transition system m ust be built before the routine may be run. It would be interesting to investigate com bining our ideas with on-the-fly approaches to system minim ization in order to avoid the *a priori* construction of the system state spaces [BFH+92].

Related work. Bloom [Blo89] proposed an algorithm for *ready simulation* that runs in $\theta((|E_1|+|E_2|)\cdot(|S_1|+|S_2|)^6)$ time. Bloom and P aige impro ved this result to $O(|S_1|\cdot|T_2|+|S_2|\cdot|T_1|)$ in [BP95]; similar ideas ma y also be found in [CS90], where preorder-checking is reduced to model checking, and in [CC95,HHK95].

References

AHJ74.   A.Aho, J. Hopcroft, and J.Ullman. *Design and Analysis of Algorithms.* Addisom W esley, 1974.

BBLS92.   S. Bensalem, A. Bouajjani, C. Loiseaux, and J. Sifakis. Property-preserving simulations. In G.v. Bochmann and D.K. Probst, editors, *Computer Aided Verification (CAV '92)*, volume 663 of *Lecture Notes in Computer Science*, pages 260–273, Montréal, June/July 1992. Springer-Verlag.

BFH+92.   A. Bouajjani, J.C. Fernandez, N. Halbwachs, C. Ratel, and P. Raymond. Minimal state graph generation. *Science of Computer Programming*, 18(3):247–271, June 1992.

BHR84.   S. D. Brookes, C. A. R. Hoare, and A. W. Roscoe. A theory of comm unicating sequential processes. *Journal of the ACM*, 31(3):560–599, July 1984.

Blo89.   B. Bloom. *Ready Simulaton, Bisimulation, and the Semantics of CCS-Like languages.* PhD thesis, Massachusetts Institute of Technology, Aug. 1989.

BP95.   B. Bloom and R. Paige. Transformational design and implementation of a new efficient solution to the ready simulation problem. *Science of Computer Programming*, 24(3):189–220, June 1995.

CC95.   U. Celikkan and R. Cleaveland. Generating diagnostic information for be-
           havioral preordering. *Distributed Computing*, 9:61–75, 1995.
Cel95.   U. Celikkan. *Semantic Preorders in the Automated Verification of Concur-
           rent Systems*. PhD thesis, North Carolina State University, Raleigh, 1995.
CH93.   R. Cleaveland and M. C. B. Hennessy. Testing equivalence as a bisimulation
           equivalence. *Formal Aspects of Computing*, 5:1–20, 1993.
CLNS96.   R. Cleaveland, G. Luettgen, V. Natarajan, and S. Sims. Modeling and ver-
           ifying distributed systems using priorities: A case study. *Software Concepts
           and Tools*, 17:50–62, 1996.
CS90.   R. J. Cleaveland and B. Steffen. When is 'partial' adequate? a logic-based
           proof technique using partial specifications. In *Proceedings of 5th Annual
           IEEE Symposium on Logic in Computer Science*, Philadelphia, PA, June
           1990.
DGG97.   D. Dams, R. Gerth, and O. Grumberg. Abstract interpretation of reac-
           tive systems. *ACM Transactions on Programming Languages and Systems*,
           19(2):253–291, March 1997.
DNH83.   R. De Nicola and M. C. B. Hennessy. Testing equivalences for processes.
           Theoretical Computer Science, 34:83–133, 1983.
Fer90.   J.-C. Fernandez. An implementation of an efficient algorithm for bisimula-
           tion equivalence. *Sicence of Computer Programming*, 13:219–236, 1989/90.
HHK95.   M. Henzinger, T. Henzinger, and P. Kopke. Computing simulations on finite
           and infinite graphs. In 36th *Annual IEEE Syposium on Foundations of
           Computer Science*, pages 453–462. Computer Society Press, 1995.
Jon91.   B. Jonsson. Simulations between specifications of distributed systems. In
           J.C.M. Baeten and J.F. Groote, editors, *CONCUR '91*, volume 527 of *Lec-
           ture Notes in Computer Science*, pages 346–360, Amsterdam, August 1991.
           Springer-Verlag.
LV95.   N. Lynch and F. Vaandrager. Forward and backward simulations—part i:
           Untimed systems. *Information and Computation*, 121(2):214–233, Septem-
           ber 1995.
Mil71.   R. Milner. An algebraic definition of simulation between programs. In
           *Proceedings of the Second International Joint Conference on Artificial Intel-
           ligence*. BCS, 1971.
PT87.   R. Paige and R. E. Tarjan. Three partition refinement algorithms. *SIAM
           Journal of Computing*, 16(6):973–989, December 1987.

Compositional Message Sequence Charts

Elsa L. Gunter[1], Anca Muscholl[2], and Doron A. Peled[1]

[1] Bell Laboratories
600 Mountain Ave.
Murray Hill, NJ 07974, USA
[2] Université Paris 7
2, place Jussieu, case 7014
75251 Paris Cedex 05, France

Abstract. Message sequence charts (MSCs) is a standard notation for describing the interaction between communicating objects. It is popular among the designers of communication protocols. MSCs enjoy both a visual and a textual representation. High level MSCs (HMSCs) allow specifying infinite scenarios and different choices. Specifically, an HMSC consists of a graph, where each node is a finite MSC with *matched* send and receive events, and vice versa. In this paper we demonstrate a weakness of HMSCs, which disallows one to model certain interactions. We will show, by means of an example, that some simple finite state and simple communication protocol cannot be represented using HMSCs. We then propose an extension to the MSC standard, which allows HMSC nodes to include unmatched messages. The corresponding graph notation will be called HCMSC, which stands for High level *Compositional* Message Sequence Charts. With the extended framework, we provide an algorithm for automatically constructing an MSC representation for finite state asynchronous message passing protocols.

1 Introduction

Visual notations are useful in the design of large and complicated systems. They allow a more intuitive understanding of the behavior of the system and the relation between its components. They often allow abstracting away parts of the system that are less relevant for a particular view. Message sequence charts are among the most frequently used formalism for designing communication protocols. Recently, they have been also used in the development of object oriented systems, e.g. in UML. In the recent years, we observe the development of a growing number of tools and algorithms for the manipulation of MSC based designs [1,2,3,7,11,12].

The standard visual and textual notation [9] by ITU allows representing a single execution scenario, as well as a collection of scenarios, including choices and repetition. This is achieved by a notation called HMSC (High Level Message Sequence Chart), which consists of a graph, where each node contains a single MSC. The system behavior can follow the paths on that graph, starting from some initial node. In this paper we show, by means of an example, a limitation

T. Margaria and W. Yi (Eds.): TACAS 2001, LNCS 2031, pp. 496–511, 2001.
© Springer-Verlag Berlin Heidelberg 2001

of HMSCs. This limitation stems from the constrain t that each MSC node in an HMSC m ust have only *matched* send and receive events, i.e., each MSC m ust be labeled by message arrows. W e show examples where one cannot break a possibly infinite computation of a finite state system in to finitely many nodes with matched comm unication events. (A finite execution can always be represented as a single node.) W e demonstrate that such undecomposable beha viors are not merely a theoretical result, but can represent the execution of real protocols.

To circum vent the problem, we suggest an extension to the MSC standard, titled *compositional message sequence charts* (CMSC and HCMSC). This extension allows specifying MSCs with unmatc hed sends and receives. The seman tics of the new construct prescribes how to com bine such MSC nodes together. W e use the extended notation to suggest an algorithm for the automatic generation of HCMSC represen tations for finite state systems. W e show that basic properties of HCMSCs become undecidable, e.g. the question whether a message will be received in at least one computation. W e propose to use a restriction of HCMSCs, called *realizable* HCMSCs. W e show how to test whether an HCMSC is realizable in an efficient way. The notion of realizable HCMSC is quite natural, as our algorithm for the HCMSC generation already yields HCMSCs of this kind.

The deficiency of the original MSCs w as also recognized in [10]. The solution suggested there is a different extension to HMSCs. According to this extension, one can use parallel components of MSCs, and allow intercomm unication between them, using a mec hanism called 'gates'. Our solution differs from that of [10], as we study the effect of allowing comm unication between sequentially composed CMSCs. That is, a comm unication that starts in one CMSC and ends in a subsequent one. Notice that our solution is more canonical, since it does not make use of special message names for the purpose of binding b y name identifiers, as in [10]. Further papers considering this issue are [8,13]. These papers look at the problem of checking whether a finite state protocol can be translated into an HMSC. In the first of these papers, it is sho wn that this question is decidable, whereas the second paper shows that for a natural class of finite state protocols one can efficiently check whether the translation into an equivalent HMSC is possible.

2   Preliminarie s

Each MSC describes a scenario where some processes comm unicate with each other. Such a scenario includes a description of the messages sen t, messages received, the local events, and the ordering between them. In the visual description of MSCs, each process is represented as a vertical line, while a message is represented by a horizontal or slanted arrow from the sending process to the receiving one, as in Figure 1. The corresponding ITU Z120 textual representation of the MSC appears on the righ t side part of Figure 1.

Definition 1. *An MSC M is a tuple* $\langle V, <, \mathcal{P}, \mathcal{N}, L, T, N, m \rangle$.

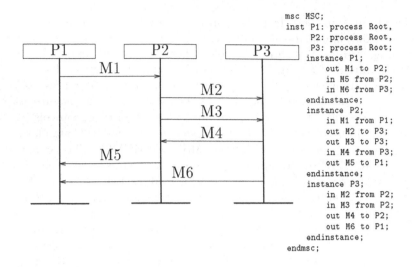

```
msc MSC;
inst P1: process Root,
     P2: process Root,
     P3: process Root;
instance P1;
    out M1 to P2;
    in M5 from P2;
    in M6 from P3;
endinstance;
instance P2;
    in M1 from P1;
    out M2 to P3;
    out M3 to P3;
    in M4 from P3;
    out M5 to P1;
endinstance;
instance P3;
    in M2 from P2;
    in M3 from P2;
    out M4 to P2;
    out M6 to P1;
endinstance;
endmsc;
```

Fig. 1. Visual and textual representation of an MSC

- V is a (finite or infinite) set of events,
- $< \subseteq V \times V$ is an acyclic relation,
- $\mathcal{P}$ is a set of processes,
- $\mathcal{N}$ is a set of message names,
- $L : V \to \mathcal{P}$ is a mapping that associates each event with a process,
- $T : V \to \{s, r, l\}$ is a mapping that describes each event as send, receive or local, respectively.
- $N : V \to \mathcal{N}$ maps every event to a name.
- $m \subseteq V \times V$ is a partial function called matching that pairs up send and receive events. Each send is paired up with exactly one receive and vice versa. Events v_1 and v_2 can be paired up with each other, only if $N(v_1) = N(v_2)$.

A message consists of a pair of matched send and receive events. For two events e and f, we have $e < f$ if and only if one of the following holds:

- e and f are a matching send and receive events, respectively.
- e and f belong to the same process P, with e appearing before f on the process line.

We assume fifo (first in first out) message passing, i.e.,

$$(T(e_1) = T(e_2) = s \wedge T(f_1) = T(f_2) = r \wedge m(e_1, f_1) \wedge m(e_2, f_2) \wedge$$
$$L(e_1) = L(e_2) \wedge L(f_1) = L(f_2) \wedge N(e_1) = N(e_2) \wedge e_1 < e_2) \to f_1 < f_2$$

An MSC with a finite (an infinite, respectively) set of events is called a finite (infinite, respectively) MSC.

Denote by $e \longrightarrow f$ the fact that $e < f$ and either e and f are a matching send and receive events, or e and f belong to the same process and there is no event between e and f on some process line. That is, e immediately precedes f. The transitive closure of the relation $<$ is a partial order called the *visual ordering* of events and it is obtained from the syntactical representation of the chart (e.g. represented according to the standard syntax ITU-Z120 [9]). Clearly, the visual ordering can be defined equivalently as the transitive closure of the relation $\longrightarrow$. A *linearization* of an MSC $M = \langle V, <, \mathcal{P}, \mathcal{N}, L, T, N, m \rangle$ is a total order on V, which extends the relation $(V, <)$.

Example 1. Let us denote in the example MSC given in Figure 1 by e_i the send event and by f_i the receive event of message Mi, $1 \le i \le 6$. Then we have $V = \{e_1, \ldots, e_6, f_1, \ldots, f_6\}$, $\mathcal{P} = \{P1, P2, P3\}$, $\mathcal{N} = \{M1, \ldots, M6\}$ and $N(e_i) = N(f_i) = Mi$ for all i. The events located on $P1$ are $\{e_1, f_5, f_6\} = L^{-1}(P1)$, with $T(e_1) = $ s, $T(f_5) = T(f_6) = $ r, and $e_1 < f_5 < f_6$. This ordering is the time ordering of events on $P1$. We also have $m(e_i, f_i)$ and $e_i < f_i$ for all i (message ordering). In particular, $e_1 < f_1 < e_2 < f_2$ and e_1 is the minimal event of the MSC w.r.t. visual ordering.

A *type* is a triple (i, j, C), including two processes P_i and P_j, and a message name $C \in \mathcal{N}$. Each *send* or *receive* event has a type, according to the origin and destination of the message, and the label of the message. Matching events have the same type.

The partial order between the send and receive events of Figure 1 is shown in Figure 2. In this figure, only the 'immediately precedes' order $\longrightarrow$ is shown. Notice for example that the *send* events of the two messages, $M5$ and $M6$, are unordered.

Definition 2. *The* concatenation *of two MSCs* $M_1 = \langle V_1, <_1, \mathcal{P}, \mathcal{N}_1, L_1, T_1,$ $N_1, m_1 \rangle$ *and* $M_2 = \langle V_2, <_2, \mathcal{P}, \mathcal{N}_2, L_2, T_2, N_2, m_2 \rangle$ *over the same set of processes* $\mathcal{P}$ *and disjoint sets of events* $V_1 \cap V_2 = \emptyset$ *(we can always rename events so that the sets become disjoint), denoted* $M_1 M_2$, *is* $\langle V_1 \cup V_2, <, \mathcal{P}, \mathcal{N}_1 \cup \mathcal{N}_2, L_1 \cup L_2, T_1 \cup T_2, N_1 \cup N_2, m_1 \cup m_2 \rangle$, *where*

$$< \; = \; <_1 \cup <_2 \cup \{(p, q) \mid L_1(p) = L_2(q) \wedge p \in V_1 \wedge q \in V_2\}.$$

That is, the events of M_1 precede the events of M_2 for each process, respectively. If $M = M_1 M_2$, we say that M_1 is a *prefix* of M. Notice that there is no synchronization of the different processes when moving from one node to the other. Hence, it is possible that one process is still involved in some actions of one node, while another process has advanced to a different node. The infinite concatenation of finite MSCs is defined in a similar way.

Definition 3. *Let* $M_1, M_2, \ldots, \ldots$ *be an infinite sequence of finite MSCs,* $M_i = \langle V_i, <, \mathcal{P}, \mathcal{N}_i, L_i, T_i, N_i, m_i \rangle$. *Then the infinite concatenation* $M_1 M_2 \ldots$ *is defined as the MSC* $\langle V, <, \mathcal{P}, \mathcal{N}, L, T, N, m \rangle$ *where* $V = \cup_{i \ge 1} V_i$ *is the disjoint union of the* V_i, $\mathcal{N} = \cup_{i \ge 1} \mathcal{N}_i$, $L|_{V_i} = L_i$, $T|_{V_i} = T_i$, $N|_{V_i} = N_i$, $m = \cup_{i \ge 1} m_i$ *and*

$$< \; = \; \bigcup_{i \ge 1} <_i \; \cup \; \{(p, q) \mid L_i(p) = L_j(q) \wedge p \in V_i \wedge q \in V_j \wedge i < j\}.$$

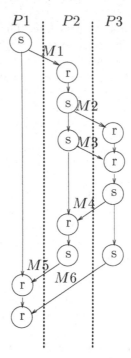

Fig. 2. The partial order between the events of the MSC in Figure 1.

Since a communication system usually includes many (or even infinitely many) such scenarios, a high level description is needed for combining them together. The standard description consists of a graph called HMSC (high level MSC), where each node contains one MSC as in Figure 3. Each maximal path in this graph (i.e., a path that is either infinite or ends with a node without outgoing edges) that starts from a designated initial state corresponds to a single *execution* or *scenario*. Such an execution can be used to denote the communication structure of a typical (aka 'sunny day') or an exceptional (aka 'rainy day') behavior of a system, or a counterexample found during testing or model checking.

Definition 4. *An HMSC N is a 4-tuple $\langle \mathcal{S}, \tau, s_0, c \rangle$ where $\mathcal{S}$ is a finite set of states, each labeled by some finite MSC over the same set of processes, and with sets of events disjoint from one another. The mapping c associates the state s with an MSC $c(s)$. By $\tau \subseteq \mathcal{S} \times \mathcal{S}$ we denote the edge relation and the initial state is $s_0 \in \mathcal{S}$. An execution of N is a (finite or infinite) MSC $c(s_0) c(s_1) c(s_2) \ldots$ associated with a maximal path of N that starts with the initial state s_0.*

Figure 3 shows an example of an HMSC where the node in the upper left corner is the starting node. The executions of this system are either finite or infinite. Note that according to HMSC semantics, process $P2$ in Figure 3 may send its **Report** message after process $P1$ has progressed into the next node and has sent its **Req_service** message.

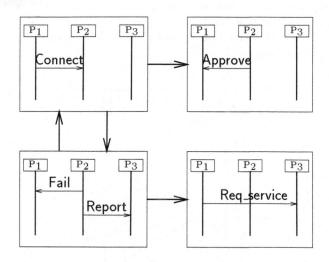

Fig. 3. An HMSC graph

3 MSC Decomposition

The HMSC model com bines the visual notation of message sequence charts with the ability to describe repetitions and alternative computations. In this section we will show that this, seemingly powerful model, cannot describe some basic finite state comm unication protocols. The main problem lies within the requirement that the *send* and *receive* events in each node must be matched.

We want to exemplify that there are finite state protocols that do not allow a finite HMSC representation. To do that, we show an infinite execution ξ of a finite state protocols with the following property: There is no way to write ξ as an infinite concatenation of finite MSCs. Given the above property, it is not possible to construct an HMSC such that ξ would correspond to a traversal of one of the HMSC paths. Th us, we cannot represent such a system using HMSCs.

As an example, consider the infinite MSC whose prefix appears in Figure 4. W e assume that $P1$ repeatedly sends a message m to $P2$, and $P2$ repeatedly sends m' to $P1$. W e omit the message labels m, m' below. W e can model for example each of the processes $P1$ and $P2$ by a finite state machine. Here, $P1$ starts by sending twice message m to $P2$, then he alternates between receiving m' from $P2$ and sending back m to $P2$. Process $P2$ alternates between sending m' to $P1$ and receiving m from $P1$. W e show that this infinite MSC cannot be decomposed into a product of finite MSCs. W e start with the *send* event e_1 and *receive* event f_1. Obviously, because of the compulsory matc hing in HMSCs, they must belong to the same MSC node. We have the *send* event g_1 preceding f_1, on the same process line, while its corresponding *receive* event h_1 succeeds the *send* e_1. Thus, the events g_1 and h_1 must be in the same node with e_1 and f_1. For the same reason, we have that e_2 and f_2 must belong to the same node with g_1, and h_1, and so forth.

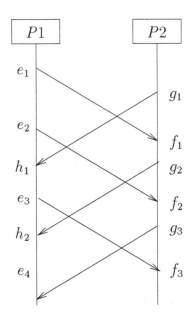

Fig. 4. A prefix of an MSC execution that cannot be decomposed .

While the repeated crossing of message edges seems to be un typical for MSCs, the above behavior ξ describes a possible execution of an actual protocol [15], where messages and acknowledgments are being sent between two processes, with (bounded) buffering.

4   Compositional MSCs

In order to represent comm unication protocols, whose description could only be approximated using standard MSCs, w e suggest an extension of the MSC stan-dard. Intuitively, a *compositional MSC*, or CMSC, ma y include *send* events that are not matched by corresponding *receive* events and vice versa. An unmatched *send* event may be matched in future HCMSC nodes (on some path). Simi-larly, an unmatched *receive* event may be matched in previous HCMSC nodes. The definition of a CMSC is hence similar to an MSC, except that unmatc hed *send* and *receive* messages are allowed. (For its similarity to Definition 1, we will omit repeating the formal definition with the corresponding change.)

We denote an unmatched *send* by a message arrow, where the *receive* end (the target of the arrow) appears within an empty circle. Similarly, an unmatched *receive* is denoted by an arrow where the *send* part (the source of the arrow) appears within a circle. CMSC arrows where both the send and the receive are unmatched events are forbidden. Moreover, we also disallow an unmatched *receive* event to be followed by a matched *receive* event of the same type in the same CMSC node. Similarly, we disallow an unmatched *send* event to be preceded by a matched *send* event of the same type in the same CMSC node. In Figure 5, we can see an HCMSC that represents the execution that is approximated in Figure 4.

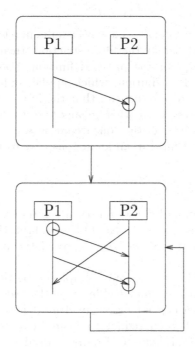

Fig. 5. A decomposition of the execution in Figure 4.

Before defining the concatenation of CMSCs let us denote a CMSC as *left-closed*, if it does not contain unmatched *receive* events.

Definition 5. *The* concatenation $M_1 M_2$ *of two CMSCs* $M_1 = \langle V_1, <_1, \mathcal{P}, \mathcal{N}_1, L_1, T_1, N_1, m_1 \rangle$ *and* $M_2 = \langle V_2, <_2, \mathcal{P}, \mathcal{N}_2, L_2, T_2, N_2, m_2 \rangle$ *over disjoint events sets, is defined when the following conditions hold:*

1. M_1 is left-closed.

2. *For any type t, the number of unmatched receive events of type t in M_2 is at most equal to the number of unmatched send events of type t in M_1.*
3. *If M_2 contains a matched send event of type t then the number of unmatched r̃eceive events of type t in M_1 is equal to the number of unmatched send events of type t in M_1.*

Define a matching function m that pairs up unmatched send events of M_1 with unmatched receive events of M_2 according to their order on their process lines. That is, the ith unmatched send in M_1 is paired up with the ith unmatched receive event of the same type in M_2. Notice that the function m is uniquely defined.

The concatenation $M_1 M_2$ is then defined as $\langle V_1 \cup V_2, <, \mathcal{P}, \mathcal{N}_1 \cup \mathcal{N}_2, L_1 \cup L_2, T_1 \cup T_2, N_1 \cup N_2, m_1 \cup m_2 \cup m \rangle$, where

$$< \; = \; <_1 \cup <_2 \cup \{(p,q) \mid L(p) = L(q) \wedge p \in V_1 \wedge q \in V_2\} \cup \{(p,q) \mid (p,q) \in m\}.$$

It is easy to see that a concatenation always results in a left-closed CMSC. Moreover, if M_1 and M_2 both satisfy the fifo restriction, then $M_1 M_2$ also does. This follows from the last requirement in the definition. Note that this requirement is consistent with our fifo definition, which applies only to messages with the same name. Thus, if we require instead that the fifo condition is satisfied by *all* messages from one process to another means that we have to modify the last requirement of the definition of the concatenation accordingly. Infinite concatenation and HMSCs are defined in an analogous way to Definitions 3, 4.

5   Undecidability

Extending the MSC standard allows representing the execution of a bigger class of protocols than what is allowed by the ITU standard. However, unsurprisingly, with the added expressiveness we loose some of the power of analyzing such systems.

Unlike simple HMSC, where some simple properties can be checked, see e.g., [12], in HCMSC one cannot decide even the trivial property of whether a particular message can be sent or received in at least one computation. The undecidability proof will be a reduction from Post Correspondence Problem (PCP). An instance of PCP is a set of pairs of words

$$C = \{(v_1, w_1), (v_2, w_2), \ldots, (v_m, w_m)\}$$

over some mutual alphabet Σ. We want to find out if there is some integer $n > 0$ and some sequence of indexes $i_1, i_2, \ldots, i_n$ such that $v_{i_1} v_{i_2} \ldots v_{i_n} = w_{i_1} w_{i_2} \ldots w_{i_n}$. We require in addition that the PCP solution is such that $i_n = 1$. This is not a restriction, since we can use a suitable encoding so that whenever $w_{i_1} w_{i_2} \ldots w_{i_{n-1}} w_1$ is a prefix of $v_{i_1} v_{i_2} \ldots v_{i_{n-1}} v_1$, then these two words are equal. We need this variant of PCP for technical reasons which will become clear in the proof below.

We will construct a HCMSC with five processes P_1 to P_5, and with CMSC nodes $E_1, E_2, \ldots, E_m, E_1', E_2', \ldots, E_m', F, F'$.

- Messages from P_1 to P_2 correspond to the letters of Σ. Each CMSC E_i contains a sequence of unmatched *send* events from P_1 to P_2, representing the sequence of messages of v_i. Each CMSC E_i' contains a sequence of unmatched *receive* events from P_1 to P_2, representing the sequence of messages of w_i.
- Messages from P_3 to P_4 correspond to the index of the PCP word being sent. Each CMSC E_i contains also a single unmatched *send* from P_3 to P_4 representing the current index i. Each CMSC E_i' contains the corresponding unmatched *receive* event.

The HCMSC N has the form $F(E_1 + \cdots + E_m)^*(E_1' + \cdots + E_m')^*E_1'F'$. That is, N starts at some initial node F, which contains only one unmatched *send* from P_1 to P_5. Then one can repeatedly take nodes of the form E_i, any number of times. Then one can take any number of nodes of the form E_i', followed by the nodes E_1', F'. The sink node F' contains a message from P_2 to P_5, then a message from P_4 to P_5 and finally an unmatched *receive* (matching the *send* from node F) from P_1 to P_5. Notice that whenever the message from P_1 to P_5 is received, the sequence $w_{i_1} \cdots w_{i_n}$ corresponding to the unmatched *send* events on the path in N is a prefix of $v_{i_1} \cdots v_{i_n}$, corresponding to the unmatched *receive* events, and $i_n = 1$. Under our assumption about PCP words this means equality, i.e., $v_{i_1} \ldots v_{i_n} = w_{i_1} \ldots w_{i_n}$, and we obtained a solution. Notice that we might have unmatched sends on P_1 and P_3 in the CMSC associated with the path in N. This explains why we obtain only the prefix relation and why we need the particular PCP encoding. Thus, the message from P_1 to P_5 is received if and only if there is a nonempty solution to the PCP instance.

6   Realizable HCMSCs

The way we defined HCMSCs makes that not all executions correspond to CMSC scenarios. We define *realizable HCMSCs*, a subclass where all maximal executions define left-closed CMSC. Note that we explicitly allow executions with unmatched *send* events. For example, the HCMSC of Figure 5 is such that every finite execution is a left-closed CMSC with unmatched sends. However, the (unique) infinite execution corresponds to an infinite MSC.

Definition 6. *An HCMSC is* realizable *if the execution of every finite path starting with the initial state is a left-closed CMSC.*

We will show that one can efficiently test whether an HCMSC is realizable. Consider the CMSC $M = c(s_0)c(s_1) \cdots c(s_n)$ associated with a finite path $\chi = s_0, s_1, \ldots, s_n$ of the HCMSC N with initial state s_0. Let t be a type, then the t-*deficit* $D_t(\chi)$ of χ is the difference between the number of send events and the number of receive events of type t in χ. A necessary condition for N to be realizable is that $D_t(\chi) \geq 0$ for every loop χ and every type t. More generally, an HCMSC $N = \langle \mathcal{S}, \tau, s_0, c \rangle$ is realizable if and only if every node s which is accessible from the initial node satisfies the following conditions. Assume that node s contains x unmatched receives of type t. Then $D_t(\chi) \geq x$ for all paths χ from s_0 to s' with $(s', s) \in \tau$. Moreover, if node s also contains a matched *send* of type t, then $D_t(\chi) = x$ for all paths χ from s_0 to s' with $(s', s) \in \tau$.

We describe below the algorithm for checking that an HCMSC N is realizable. We define for each state s and each type t the t-deficit $d_t(s)$ of s as the difference between unmatched sends of type t and unmatched receives of type t in s. We can view N as a weighted directed graph $G_t(N) = \langle S, \tau, \gamma \rangle$, with edges weighted by $\gamma(s', s) = d_t(s')$. That is, each edge is labeled by the t-deficit of its source node. Then all we have to do is the following:

1. Check that $G_t(N)$ has no cycle with negative weight.
2. Check for all states s, s' such that $(s', s) \in \tau$: the minimal weight d of a path from s_0 to s' satisfies $d \geq x$, where x is the number of unmatched receives of type t in s.
3. Check for all states s, s' such that $(s', s) \in \tau$ and s' contains a matched *send* of type t: the *maximal* weight d of a path from s_0 to s' satisfies $d \leq x$, where x is the number of unmatched receives of type t in s.

For the first two items above we can apply a dynamic programming algorithm (Warshall's algorithm) for computing the shortest paths between all pairs of nodes in time $O(|S|^3)$. That is, assuming that $S = \{s_1, \ldots, s_n\}$ we compute the minimal weight of paths from state s_i to state s_j by allowing as intermediate nodes $\emptyset$, then $\{s_1\}$, $\{s_1, s_2\}$ up to S. Alternatively, we can use the Bellman-Ford algorithm, [4]. This algorithm computes in time $O(|S||\tau|)$ all shortest paths from a given source in a graph G with negative weights, provided that G contains no negative cycle (detecting such a cycle, if one exists). Combining the second and the third item above we need to check for all states s containing a matched *send* of type t and all nodes s' where $(s', s) \in \tau^*$ that all paths from s_0 to s' have the same t-deficit, say $D(s')$. This means that we first compute the t-deficits along one path χ from s_0 to s. Let $D(s) = D_t(\chi)$. Then we compute backwards, from *state* s on, the deficits $D(s')$ for all nodes s' belonging to paths from s_0 to s. It remains to check for each pair s', s'' of nodes between s_0 and s with $(s', s'') \in \tau$ that we have $D(s') + d_t(s'') = D(s'')$. The last step can be done edge by edge. The overall complexity is in $O(|\tau|)$. Doing all this for all graphs $G_t(N)$ yields an $O(|\mathcal{P}|^2|S||\tau|)$ algorithm for checking whether N is realizable.

We conclude this section with a remark on the regularity of the set of executions of an HCMSC. Note that a realizable HCMSC N has bounded message queues if and only if $D_t(\chi) = 0$ for every loop χ in N and every type t. It is not difficult to see that bounded message queues do not ensure that the set of linearizations of executions in an HMSC or an HCMSC is regular. In the case of HMSCs a syntactic restriction which is sufficient for regularity has been proposed in [3,11]. This condition states that the communication graph of every loop in the HMSC must be strongly connected. The *communication graph* of an MSC M is a directed graph with vertex set consisting of all processes which occur in M. There is an edge from process P to process Q if P sends a message to Q in M. The communication graph of a path π in an HMSC is the communication graph of the MSC associated with π. We show in the following a similar syntactic condition for HCMSC which is sufficient for obtaining a regular set of linearizations, provided that the message queues are bounded. For this we define the communication graph of an CMSC M as follows. As before, vertices are those processes with events occurring in M. We have an edge from P to Q if there is a (matched or unmatched) send event on P with target process Q. As for HMSCs we require that the communication graph of any loop in the HCMSC is strongly connected.

Proposition 1. *Let N be an HCMSC with bounded message queues, i.e., the deficit of every execution χ of N is such that $D_t(\chi) \leq k$, for some constant k depending on N and for any type t. Assume that the communication graph of any loop in N is strongly connected. Then the set of linearizations of N is regular.*

The proposition above can be shown using the same ideas as for HMSCs (see [3,11]). We can show that for any linearization of an execution $c(s_0)c(s_1)\cdots c(s_m)$ of N it suffices to store a polynomial number of prefixes of CMSCs $c(s_i)$. We use the fact that the deficit $D_t(\chi)$ of any path χ is at most equal to the size of the HCMSC N.

7 An HCMSC Representation for Finite State Systems

The HCMSC extension suggested in this paper broadens the scope of HMSCs and allows us to capture many more protocols. We present now an automatic translation from finite state systems with asynchronous message passing to (realizable) HCMSC.

We are given a finite state space $G = (S, S_0, E, \Sigma)$, with states S, initial states $S_0 \subseteq S$, and edges $E \subseteq S \times \Sigma \times S$, labeled over a set of actions Σ. The actions in Σ are *send, receive* and *local* actions. The states in S contain information about the system, including the contents of the various interprocess message queues.

We start with a trivial translation, which establishes the theoretic possibility of performing such a translation for a class of finite state systems with asynchronous message passing. We later proceed to suggest a more informative translation. The trivial translation is performed by constructing the dual graph $H = (N, N_0, F)$ of G as follows:

- The *nodes* N of H correspond to the *edges* of G. That is, $N = E$. The label of a node e is the label of e in G.
- The *initial nodes* $N_0 \subseteq N$ of H correspond to the edges of G that exit from an initial state of S_0.
- The edges F of H correspond to pairs of edges of G such that the target of the first edge is the source of the second.

The above trivial construction does not provide any new insight, since the HCMSC graph follows closely the state space and each CMSC node includes a single local or unmatched event. We thus look into a translation that would construct more reasonable HCMSCs. The translation aims at optimizing the following goals:

1. Minimize the number of unmatched events appearing in the individual CMSC nodes, if possible obtaining an HCMSC without any unmatched events (however, recall from Section 3 that this is not always achievable).
2. Present relatively long scenarios with the CMSCs, in order to obtain an intuitive understanding of the interprocess interaction.
3. Minimize the number of individual CMSC blocks, so that the HCMSC would not become too big.

Notice that the second and third goal may contradict each other in some systems. The above 'trivial' translation gives a rather reasonable solution to the third goal, while providing unacceptable solution for the second goal. Notice further that the size of an HCMSC graph can easily get prohibitively large. Thus, in practice, the HCMSC construction algorithm should be applied only to small parts of communication protocols, rather than to complete protocols.

It is easy to see that different execution paths in the state space may correspond to a single CMSC. For example, consider an execution path in which we have a *send* from $P1$ to $P2$, then the matching *receive*, then another *send* of the same type, and finally another matching *receive*. Consider now another execution path, in which we have first the two *send* transitions, and then the two *receive* transitions. These two paths obviously correspond to the same MSC. The *partial order reduction* algorithms were constructed for this particular reason. The *sleep set* method of Godefroid, adapted to our case, is in particular appropriate.

The Algorithm

Definition 7. *For a letter $e \in \Sigma$ (an event), define the set of events $dep(e)$ that include exactly events f such that either e and f are from the same process, or e and f are a matching pair.*

Notice that this definition is tailored for a message passing communication system and need to be adapted when using other kinds of concurrency (e.g., with shared variables).

Let '$\prec$' be a total order over the events in Σ satisfying that all the *receive* events precede the *send* events. Denote by $en(s)$ the set of transitions that are enabled at a state s.

1. Make a first guess of a set of nodes such that every cycle must pass through one of these nodes. One possibility is to set $Z \subseteq S$ to include every node in which all the queues are empty. Another possibility is to start with the single set that includes the initial node. One heuristics is to perform simple DFS on the state space and include in Z every node in the target of a back edge. Notice that this is not optimal (finding a minimal set of such nodes is an NP-complete problem). The nodes in Z are new cutpoints for the finite state space in the sense that every cycle must pass at least one of these points. Thus, the paths from Z to Z contain no cycles.

2. Start a *minimized DFS* from nodes in Z or at an initial state. The search stops at nodes in Z (after progressing at least one step) or to a terminating node. The minimization algorithm, related to Godefroid's sleep set algorithm [5], and to the variant of that algorithm presented in [14] is shown in Figure 6. This version allows removing nodes that have an empty number of successors under the reduction.[1]

3. Construct CMSCs for the paths from the nodes in Z according to the paths generated during the reduced DFS of the previous step. Since the number of paths can be enormous, one can split the reduced graph further, e.g., at points that have a relatively large number of incoming or outgoing edges. In this way, we generate shorter paths, but possibly more of them. The matching algorithm at the end of the section can be used to match corresponding *send* and *receive* events in the same CMSC.

4. Connect the separate CMSCs in the following way: If one CMSC ends at some state $s \in Z$ and another CMSC starts with that state, make an edge from the former to the latter.

```
function expand_node(s, sleep);
local explored, working_set, new_sleep, fixed;
    explored := ∅;
    fixed := false;
    if en(s) = ∅ then return true fi;
    working_set := en(s) \ sleep ;
    while working_set ≠ ∅ do
        α := biggest action in working_set according to '≺';
        working_set := working_set\{α};
        s' := α(s);
        new_sleep := (sleep ∪ explored ) \ dep(α);
        explored := explored ∪ {α};
        if s' ∈ Z orelse s' is terminal orelse exists_node(s', new_sleep)
            orelse expand_node(s', new_sleep) then
            fixed := true;
            create_edge((s, sleep), α, (s', new_sleep)) fi;
        fi
    end while;
    if fixed then store_node_in_hash(s, sleep);
    return fixed;
end expand_node.
```

Fig. 6. A reduced state space generation algorithm

Properties of the Algorithm. Define the relation '$\longrightarrow$' between strings over Σ by $\sigma \longrightarrow \rho$ if $\sigma = v e f w$ and $\rho = v f e w$, where v, w are sequences of

---

[1] Another change from the original algorithm is that the new nodes are pairs of a state and a sleep set, and two states that are paired with different sleep sets are considered different nodes.

transitions and f, e are individual transitions and $f \notin dep(e)$. Let $\xrightarrow{*}$ be the transitive and reflexive closure of $\longrightarrow$.

The relation '$\sqsubseteq$' between strings over Σ is such that $v \sqsubseteq w$ when

- v is smaller than w according to the alphabetical order based on '$\prec$'.
- $w \xrightarrow{*} w'$, and v is a prefix of w'.

Lemma 1. *If $v \sqsubseteq w$, then a CMSC with a linearization v is a prefix of a CMSC with a linearization w.*

Sketch of proof. We can show that the transitions of each process in v are a prefix of the transitions of the same process in w. ∎

Lemma 2. *If $v \sqsubseteq w$, v is not a prefix of w, and w is generated during the reduced DFS, then v is not generated by the algorithm.*

Sketch of proof. Take the longest common prefix u of v and w (u can be empty). Let b be the first letter after u in w, and a the first letter after u in v. Then from the definition of the relation '$\sqsubseteq$', we have that $a \prec b$, $a \notin dep(b)$, and b appears in v after u, following some sequence of transitions u' that are not included in $dep(b)$. According to the algorithm, during the DFS, $u\,b$ is reached before $u\,a$. When the search backtracks from u, it has b in its sleep set, since $a \notin dep(b)$. If the search reaches $u\,u'$, then b is still in the sleep set, since b is independent of all the events in u'. Because of this, $u\,u'\,b$ is not generated. ∎

Lemma 3. *If v is not generated during the search, then there is some w such that $v \sqsubseteq w$, and w is generated.*

Sketch of proof. First, observe that '$\sqsubseteq$' is a reflexive and transitive relation. The proof is by an induction on the order '$\sqsubseteq$'. Suppose that v is not generated. This is because $v = u\,u'\,a\,w$ for some sequences u, u' and w, and a transition a, and a was in the sleep set paired with the state obtained after the reduced DFS has searched u. Furthermore, the transition a was taken after u, and is independent of the transitions in u' and is bigger according to '$\prec$' than the first letter in u'. Thus, we have that $v \sqsubseteq u\,a\,u'\,w$. Then, by the induction hypothesis, either $u\,a\,u'\,w$ is expanded, or a string w' such that $u\,a\,u'\,w \sqsubseteq w'$ is expanded. But by the transitivity of $\sqsubseteq$, we have the result. ∎

The Matching Algorithm. Consider an CMSC node M constructed by the above algorithm. By construction, each path from the initial node to M has the same t-deficit, for every type t (since the states of the original finite state machine refer to the contents of queues). Notice also that every loop in the HCMSC thus generated has zero t-deficit, for any type t. Suppose now that the t-deficit of paths from the initial MSC M_0 to the predecessors of M is equal to d. Then we match the events in M as follows.

1. Mark the first d *receive* events of type t in M as 'unmatched' (there may be fewer than d such messages).
2. Of the remaining *send* and *receive* events of type t, pair the ith *send* with the ith *receive*.
3. If there are *send* events of type t that are unpaired in the previous step, mark them 'unmatched'.

8   Conclusion and Implementation

HMSCs are a useful and standard notation for describing executions of communication protocols. We showed that the requirement of pairing up *send* and *receive* events in each MSC node prohibits the representation of a simple finite state protocol. We presented an extension of the HMSC notation, which we call HCMSC. This notation circumvents this problem. With the extension, w e presented an algorithm for automatically generating the HCMSC structure for finite state communication protocols. We have implemented this algorithm as an extension of the PET system [6]. The implementation is written using 800 lines of SML/NJ code, and in addition exploits the C code of the MSC/POGA [2] system for generating the HCMSC visual structure.

Acknowledgment. We would like to thank Mihalis Yannakakis, who suggested the counterexample in Figure 4, which is simpler than our original counterexample.

References

1. R. Alur, K. Etessami, and M. Yannakakis. Inference of message sequence charts. In *Proc. of the 22nd Int. Conf. on Software Engineering*, pp. 304–313, ACM, 2000.
2. R. Alur, G. H. Holzmann, and D. A. Peled. An analyzer for message sequence charts. *Software Concepts and Tools*, 17(2):70–77, 1996.
3. R. Alur and M. Yannakakis. Model checking of message sequence charts. In *Proc. of CONCUR'99*, LNCS no. 1664, 1999.
4. T. H. Cormen, C. E. Leiserson, and R. L. Rivest. *Introduction to algorithms.* MIT Press, Cambridge, Massachusetts, 1999.
5. P. Godefroid and P. Wolper. A partial approach to model checking. *Information and Computation*, 110(2):305–326, 1994.
6. E. Gunter and D. Peled. Path exploration tool. In *Proc. of Tools and Algorithms for the Construction and Analysis of Systems (TACAS'99), Amsterdam, The Netherlands*, LNCS 1579, pages 405–419, 1999. Springer.
7. L. Hélouët and P. Le Maigat. Decomposition of Message Sequence Charts. In *Proc. of the 2nd Workshop on SDL and MSC (SAM2000)*, pp. 46–60, 2000.
8. J. G. Henriksen, M. Mukund, K. Narayan Kumar, and P. Thiagarajan. On message sequence graphs and finitely generated regular MSC languages. In *Proc. of ICALP'00, 2000*, LNCS no. 1853, pp. 675-686, 2000.
9. ITU-T Recommendation Z.120, Message Sequence Chart (MSC), 1996.
10. S. Mauw and M. Reniers. High-level message sequence charts. In *SDL'97: Time for Testing - SDL, MSC and Trends. Proc. of the SDL Forum'97*, pp. 291–306, 1997.
11. A. Muscholl and D. Peled. Message sequence graphs and decision problems on Mazurkiewicz traces. In *Proc. MFCS'99*, LNCS no. 1672, pp. 81–91, 1999.
12. A. Muscholl, D. Peled, and Z. Su. Deciding properties of message sequence charts. In *Proc. of FoSSaCS'98*, LNCS no. 1378, pp. 226–242, 1998.
13. A. Muscholl and D. Peled. High-level message sequence charts and finite-state communication protocols. Submitted.
14. D. Peled. All from One, One for All: on Model Checking Using Representatives. In *Proc. of CAV '93*, LNCS no. 697, pp. 409–423, 1993.
15. A. Tanenbaum, Computer Networks, Prentice Hall, 1988.

An Automata Based Interpretation of Live Sequence Charts*

Jochen Klose[1] and Hartmut Wittke[2]

[1] University of Oldenburg
Jochen.Klose@Informatik.Uni-Oldenburg.de
[2] OFFIS
Wittke@Offis.de

Abstract. The growing popularity of sequence charts, first of all Message Sequence Charts and UML Sequence Diagrams, for the description of communication behavior has evoked criticism regarding the semantics of the charts which led to extensions of these standardized visual formalisms. One such extension are Live Sequence Charts which allow to distinguish mandatory and possible behavior in protocol specifications. In the original language definition for LSCs the semantics are only described informally, although a sketch for a possible formalization has been provided as well. In this paper we intend to fill in the semantic blanks of the original LSC definition. Following the sketched path we define the semantics of an LSC by deriving a Timed Büchi Automata from it. We also consider qualitative and quantative timing aspects. We finally show how LSCs are integrated into a verification tool set for STATEMATE designs.

1 Introduction

In recent years the use of Embedded Control Units (ECUs) has become more and more widespread in industry, especially in automotive and avionics applications. Many of these ECUs have to satisfy safety critical requirements. Developing such systems requires non-trivial effort to ensure correctness of the design. Therefore many companies have come to realize the usefulness of (semi-)formal methods in the development process of safety critical ECUs.

One example of a semi-formal specification technique are Message Sequence Charts (MSCs), a graphical formalism which is concerned with the communication behavior of protocols. MSCs have been standardized by the ITU (International Telecommunications Union) in Recommendation Z.120 ([IT96b]). Designed to capture protocol scenarios in the telecommunication area, MSCs can also be used to sketch scenarios of general interprocess communication.

Notwithstanding the fact that there exists a formal semantics [IT96a], we consider MSCs only a semi-formal specification technique, because there are

---

* Research in part supported by the German Research Council (DFG) within the USE project as part of the SPP Integration of Specification Techniques with Engineering Applications

T. Margaria and W. Yi (Eds.): TACAS 2001, LNCS 2031, pp. 512–527, 2001.

still a lot of questions unanswered. For example, one MSC only specifies one scenario, i.e. one possible communication sequence of the system. But: What does a collection of MSCs for some system mean? Is progress along the instance axis enforced? What happens when a condition is evaluated to false? These and other open questions have been identified by several researchers (see e.g. [Krü99], [DH99]).

We follow the Live Sequence Charts (LSC) approach of [DH99][1] which is an conservative extension of standard MSCs. As explained in [DH99] LSCs can be used to distinguish between accepted and non-accepted sequences of variable valuations of systems (*runs*). LSCs extend the formalism of MSCs along the following lines:

- conditions are interpreted, they are not only treated as comments as in MSCs
- distinction between possible (standard MSC) and mandatory behavior. This includes the ability to
  - enforce progress along each instance axis,
  - specify if a message has to be received or not,
  - distinguish between LSCs which show only one possible communication (existential interpretation) and LSCs which show mandatory communication, i.e. it has to be exhibited by all system runs (universal interpretation),
  - distinguish between conditions that have to be satisfied and those that may be violated without generating an error.
- specification of activation conditions guarding the activation point of the LSC, and whether an LSC should be activated only at system start (*initial* activation mode) or whenever the activation condition evaluates to true (*invariant* activation mode)

The parts of an LSC which may be interpreted either as mandatory or possible are assigned a temperature, *hot* for mandatory and *cold* for possible elements. Thus we have messages, conditions and instance locations with temperatures. Graphically cold elements are depicted by dashed lines whereas hot ones are represented as solid lines (see figure 1).

We will substantiate the original paper [DH99] in two ways: We will on one hand provide a more concrete semantics for a subset of the original features using Timed Büchi Automata. On the other hand we will introduce timing annotations which are not covered by [DH99]. Our notion of time is discrete as we base our time model on the steps of a system exhibiting time-discrete behavior.

Before we go into the details of the process of transforming the LSC into an automata format (which we call *unwinding*) we need to explain the context in which we want to use LSCs. At the University of Oldenburg/OFFIS[2] the STATEMATE Verification Environment (STVE) has been developed over the last years which allows to verify safety-critical properties of STATEMATE designs (see [BBea99], [DDK99] or [DK01] for details). The STATEMATE tool from i-Logix

---

[1] A newer version of this paper is to appear this year: [DH01]

[2] Oldenburger Forschungs- und Entwicklungsinstitut für Informatik-Werkzeuge und -Systeme

is a commercial case tool which is based on Harel's statecharts [HP96] and is widely used in industry. The STVE translates the STATEMATE design into the input format of the underlying symbolic modelchecker and also lets the designer specify the properties to be verified in a graphical way. For this purpose *Symbolic Timing Diagrams* (STDs) are used, which have been developed at OFFIS as well. STDs allow to state constraints on the changes of values of inputs and outputs of the system under design; see [Fey96], [FJ97] for more information. The STD specification is translated into propositional temporal logic (see [Fey96]) which serves as input for the modelchecker.

The algorithm of unwinding LSCs explained in this paper is already implemented in a tool (cf. section 5), which is integrated into the STVE at the moment of writing. The roles of LSCs and STDs are complementary, STDs talk about one component (*black box view*) whereas LSCs are obviously much better suited to express properties about the interactions of components (*white box view*).

The paper is structured as follows: In section 2 we define the subset of LSC features considered here. Section 3 describes how the unwinding structure for an LSC is constructed and section 4 shows the subsequent transformation into a Timed Büchi Automaton. In section 5 we give an overview about the tool environment for verification of STATEMATE designs against LSC specifications. We give a summary and identify directions of further research in section 6.

2   LSC Subset

LSCs as presented in [DH99] provide a rich set of features. We will only treat a subset of these in the present paper in order to focus on the core concepts. The integration of LSCs into the STVE entails some other restrictions which are caused by STATEMATE. But we also add two features which were not covered in the original paper: *timing annotations* which allow to specify a lower and an upper bound between two subsequent locations on one instance. We borrow the interval notation used in both STDs [Fey96] and MSCs [AHP96]. Timer durations are consequently interpreted as a multiple of our discrete base time unit. Our interpretation of timing annotations and timers allows the user to specify runs of a system not only in a qualitative manner, but also to constrain event sequences by quantitative time bounds. The second new concept are *simultaneous regions*, which allow to specify the simultaneous observation of several events. In contrast, the non-deterministic symbolic transition system presented in [DH99], implements a pure interleaving interpretation of LSCs: only a single instance is allowed to proceed at a time. We feel that such an interpretation is not powerful enough in the context of STATEMATE, where the communicating activities run in parallel and can change arbitrary many variable values at the same time. Besides explicit simultaneous regions, our interpretation considers unordered events of a coregion or of different instances observable in any order including *simultaneity*.

In this paper we do not treat existential LSCs, because the universal interpretation seems to be the natural choice for formal verification as we want to prove that the entire system fulfills the specification. We feel that the intention of using an existential LSC is to get a satisfying run as a witness. This would entail a modified unwinding algorithm which is out of scope for the present paper. Our algorithm can also handle sub-charts, the details of which we omit here due to limited space.

The following concepts are contained in our approach (see figure 1 for the graphical representation of the concepts): Hot and cold locations, hot and cold messages, hot and cold conditions, coregions, *simultaneous regions*, timer, *timing annotations*.

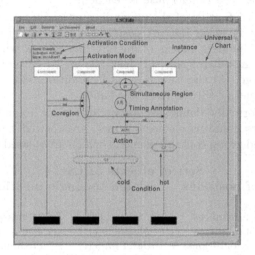

Fig. 1. LSC example

We restrict the setting of a timer to be bound (via a simultaneous region) to some sort of event. This is what we feel is the intention which was so far not expressible in MSCs: A timer is set when some event is observed and we then wait for some subsequent event.

3   Constructing the Unwinding Structure

In order to generate the unwinding structure from an LSC we first need to identify its building blocks. They are those elements of the chart which have to happen simultaneously, i.e which are indivisible. In our case the simultaneous region construct covers the majority of these elements since it encompasses both regular messages and regular conditions. The other two elements left, the instance head and the instance end, are of a more auxiliary nature. They are not unwound explicitly but the set of all instance heads/instance ends forms the start state/end state for the unwinding structure. The other elements of our LSC subset are either irrelevant for the structure or can be stated using the simultaneous region. Timer and timing annotations are not treated in the unwinding, as their timing information is considered later when transforming the unwinding structure into an automaton. Actions are disregarded because they hold no information relevant for the run. Coregions are not treated as constructs of their own but as the separate simultaneous region constructs of which they are comprised. Neither do sub-charts form a separate construct as they can be expressed by their enclosed simultaneous region constructs as well.

The construction of the unwinding structure borrows the basic technique from the unwinding of Symbolic Timing Diagrams (cf. [Fey96]) using *Phases*. Informally a *Phase* shows how far the unwinding of the LSC has progressed. Starting with the *Initial Phase* all possible successor *Phases* are computed and this is iterated until the *Final Phase* is reached.

For the formal definition of the unwinding procedure we first introduce the concept of a *position* in an LSC: A *position* is simply a graphical point in an LSC. The atomic building blocks of an LSC are *events* which may be one of the following: (1) instance head , (2) instance end, (3) sending a message, (4) receiving a message, (5) the valuation of a condition, (6) setting a timer, (7) expiration of a timer or (8) the reset of a timer

In order to formally define events we introduce a number of sets. The first group of sets contains elements which are related to sets of positions, whereas the second group contains elements which are related to single positions.

Sets of objects of LSC l

related to sets of positions	related to single positions	
$Instances(l)$ set of instances	$Msgsend(l)$	set of message sendings
$Messages(l)$ set of messages	$Msgrecv(l)$	set of message receipts
$Conditions(l)$ set of conditions	$Set\_Timer(l)$	set of timer settings
	$Reset\_Timer(l)$	set of timer resets
	$Timeouts(l)$	set of timeouts
	$Timer(l)$	$Set\_Timer(l) \cup Reset\_Timer(l)$ $\cup Timeouts(l)$

Analogously to the chart-oriented sets of the second group we define the same sets for each instance i of the LSC l. For conditions we define the set of condition valuations which are local to instance i as the restriction of the shared condition for the whole chart to instance i: $Conds(i) := Conditions(l) \downarrow i$. We write $Conds(l)$ for $\bigcup_{i \in Instances(l)} Conds(i)$. We denote the instance head of instance i by $\perp_i$ and the instance end of i by $\top_i$.

Events Given these basic definitions we now formalize events:

For LSC l :
$Events(l) :=$
$\{ \perp_i \mid i \in Instances(l) \} \cup$
$Msgsend(l) \cup Msgrecv(l) \cup$
$Timer(l) \cup Conds(l) \cup$
$\{ \top_i \mid i \in Instances(l) \}$

For instance i :
$Events(i) :=$
$\{ \perp_i \} \cup$
$Msgsend(i) \cup Msgrecv(i) \cup$
$Timer(i) \cup Conds(i) \cup$
$\{ \top_i \}$

With each event $e \in Events(i)$ we associate its position given by the function $position(e)$. In order to handle simultaneous observation of multiple events we introduce for instance i the maximal set:

$$Sim\_Regions(i) := \{ sr \subseteq Events(i) \mid \forall x, y \in sr : position(x) = position(y) \}.$$

We also associate a position with each $sr \in Sim\_Regions(i)$ by the function $position(sr)$. Note that simultaneous regions are sets of *basic events*. Single events are treated as singleton simultaneous regions. Positions along one instance axis are totally ordered.

We now consider the set $Coregions(i)$ of coregions of instance i. A coregion $cr \in Coregions(i)$ starts at the graphical position x of instance i and ends at graphical position y. We define for $cr : startpos(cr) := x$ and $endpos(cr) := y$ and $position(cr) := startpos(cr)$. For each $cr \in Coregions(i)$ we then define $contents(cr) := \{sr \in Sim\_Regions(i) \mid position(cr) \leq position(sr) \leq endpos(cr)\}$.

In addition to a graphical position we associate a logical position with each simultaneous region which is used to determine the order along the instance axis. We call this logical position the *location* of the simultaneous region. For $sr \in Sim\_Regions(i)$ we define :

$$location(sr) := \begin{cases} position(sr), & if \ \neg\exists \ cr \in Coregions(i) : sr \in contents(cr) \\ position(cr), & if \ \exists \ cr \in Coregions(i) : sr \in contents(cr) \end{cases}$$

Let $Locations(i) := \{ location(sr) \mid sr \in Sim\_Regions(i)\}$ be the set of locations of instance i. Note that for distinct $sr, sr' \in Sim\_Regions(i)$ not located in the same coregion either $location(sr) < location(sr')$ or $location(sr') < location(sr)$ holds. Moreover, for distinct $sr, sr' \in Sim\_Regions(i)$ located in the same coregion: $location(sr) = location(sr')$. Thus, with respect to coregions locations along one instance axis are ordered only partially. Concerning simultaneous regions and coregions we formulate the following well-formedness rules:

- Simultaneous regions located in a coregion must be singleton sets, or in other words, must be single events, because otherwise they would impose an order (simultaneity) on some of the events in the coregion.
- At most one condition valuation may be located in a simultaneous region. Several condition valuations can always be merged into one.
- Timer settings must only occur in simultaneous regions together with at least one non-timer setting event, because there has to be some reference point for the timer.

For the unwinding procedure we furthermore need to know the *predecessors* of each simultaneous region which are determined by the following function $(sr \in Sim\_Regions(i))$[3]:

$$predecessor(sr) := \begin{cases} \emptyset & ,if \ sr = \{\bot_i\} \\ \{sr' \mid sr' \in Sim\_Regions(i) \wedge \\ \quad location(sr') < location(sr) \wedge \\ \quad \neg\exists f \in Sim\_Regions(i) : \\ \quad location(sr') < location(f) \\ \quad < location(sr)\} & ,else \end{cases}$$

---

[3] Note that the set of predecessors usually contains just one element. Only a coregion as predecessor produces a set containing several elements.

This definition of a predecessor set for each location allows us to determine sets of legal event sequences along one instance axis. But simultaneous regions of one instance can be bound to other simultaneous regions on other instances. For example, shared conditions involve a simultaneous region on each instance sharing the condition. If one of the simultaneous regions of this set occurs, the other simultaneous regions of the set must occur simultaneously. This leads to the definition of

Simultaneous Classes Let $\leftrightarrow_{LSC}$ denote the equivalence relation "*has to happen simultaneously*", then:

$Sim\_Classes(l) :=$
$$\{scl \subseteq \bigcup_{i \in Instances(l)} Sim\_Regions(i)|\ \forall sr, sr' \in scl : sr \leftrightarrow_{LSC} sr'\}$$
The simultaneous classes impose the ordering between different instances. Here the constructs that satisfy $\leftrightarrow_{LSC}$ are

- shared condition valuations $c \in Conditions(l)$ which form a synchronization barrier, since c has to be evaluated *simultaneously* at each involved instance
- sending and receiving a message $m \in Messages(l)$. This is only legal for models with zero delay communication like STATEMATE. For delayed (synchronous or asynchronous) communications sending and receipt of a message have to be treated separately. For simplicity's sake we only consider non-delayed communication in the remainder of this paper.
- a singleton simultaneous region

Note that $\forall sr \in \bigcup_{i \in Instances(l)} Sim\_Regions(i) \exists^1 scl \in Sim\_Classes(l) :$ $sr \in scl$. For $scl \in Sim\_Classes(l)$ we now define the set of simultaneous classes which have to be unwound before scl. We call this set the *prerequisites* for scl.

$$prerequisite(scl) := \begin{cases} \emptyset & , if\ scl \in \{\wp(\bigcup_{i \in Instances(l)}\{\perp_i\})\} \\ \{scl' \mid scl' \in Sim\_Classes(l) \wedge \exists sr \in scl \, \exists\, sr' \in scl' : \\ \quad sr' \in predecessor(sr)\ \}, else \end{cases}$$

With these definitions we are now fully equipped to formally define the unwinding procedure. The procedure unwinds a LSC step by step by constructing sets of *simultaneous classes*.

Unwinding Sets Each step in the unwinding process is characterized by three sets:

- $History \subseteq Sim\_Classes(l)$, the set of simultaneous classes which have already been unwound
- $Ready \subseteq Sim\_Classes(l)$, the set of simultaneous classes whose prerequisites have already been unwound:
- $Fired \in \wp^+(Ready)$, the set of simultaneous classes which are unwound in the current phase[4]

---

[4] $\wp^+$ denotes the power set without the empty set.

In addition to these three sets we introduce the *Cut* through the LSC which keeps track of the progress of the unwinding, i.e. the Cut identifies the border line between elements which have already been unwound and those that still have to be considered. A cut can be visualized as a piece of rope lying across the LSC touching exactly one location of each instance. More formally we define the set of all cuts of an LSC l as:

$$Cuts(l) := \{(x_1, .., x_n) \mid x_j \in Sim\_Regions(j), 1 \leq j \leq n = |Instances(l)| \}$$

An unwinding phase $Phase_i$ consists of the sets $Ready_i$, $History_i$ and the vector Cut_i. Each phase is represented as a node in the unwinding structure which is therefore annotated with the the triple $(Ready_i, History_i, Cut_i)$; the phases are connected by edges annotated with elements of $Fired$. Thus we have the following sets:

- $Phases(l)$ - set of all possible phases for LSC l
- $Fireds(l)$ - set of all possible fired-sets for LSC l
- $Cuts(l)$ - set of all possible cut-vectors for LSC l

Computing the Phases Each unwinding step entails the computation of the successor phase(s) from the present one starting with the initial phase and ending with the final phase. The ready set of the initial phase contains all simultaneous classes, which have only instance heads as prerequisites, its history and cut contain all instance heads:

$Phase_0 = (Ready_0, History_0, Cut_0)$, where
$Ready_0 = \{a \in Sim\_Classes(l) \mid prerequisite(a) \in \{\wp^+(\bigcup_{i \in Instances(l)}\{\perp_i\})\}$
$History_0 = \{\bigcup_{i \in Instances(l)}\{\{\perp_i\}\}\}$
$Cut_0 = (\perp_1, .., \perp_n)$, where n is the Number of instances of LSC l

A non-initial and non-final phase $Phase_j$ is characterized by

$Phase_j = (Ready_j, History_j, Cut_j)$, where
$Ready_j = \{a \in Sim\_Classes(l) \mid$
$\qquad\qquad \forall b \in prerequisite(a) : b \in History_j \wedge a \notin History_j\}$
$History_j \subseteq Sim\_Classes(l)$
$Cut_j = (x_1, .., x_n), \forall k \in Instances(l) : x_k \in Sim\_Regions(k)$

The final phase $Phase_{final}$ is characterized by

$Phase_{final} = (Ready_{final}, History_{final}, Cut_{final})$, where
$Ready_{final} = \{\bigcup_{i \in Instances(l)}\{\{\top_i\}\}\}$
$History_{final} = Sim\_Classes(l) \setminus \{\bigcup_{i \in Instances(l)}\{\{\top_i\}\}\}$

An unwinding-step from $Phase_i$ to $Phase_j$ is thus defined by the function

$$Step : Phases(l) \times \wp^+(Sim\_Classes(l)) \rightarrow Phases(l)$$

where $Step((Ready_i, History_i, Cut_i), Fired_i) =$
$$(Ready_j, History_i \cup Fired_i, upd(Cut_i, Fired_i)), \text{ with}$$

$upd : Cuts(l) \times Fireds(l) \rightarrow Cuts(l)$ and

$upd(Cut_i, Fired_i) := (x_1, .., x_n)$, where

$$x_k = \begin{cases} x_k' & \exists\, z \in Fired_i\ \exists\, scl \in z : x_k' \in scl \\ x_k & else \end{cases}, k = 1, .., n$$

For each subsequent unwinding step first a subset of the ready set is selected. This subset represents the simultaneous classes which are unwound in the current step. All possible subsets except the empty set are considered to determine the set of next nodes in the unwinding structure. The source node is connected to all its successor nodes by an edge annotated with the set of simultaneous classes unwound in this step. The new ready set is then computed for all successor nodes in the following manner: First the simultaneous classes which have just been unwound have to be removed from the ready set, then all simultaneous classes whose prerequisites are now fulfilled are added. In the history the just unwound simultaneous classes are recorded, whereas for the Cut the simultaneous classes that have just been unwound are added and the ones just left are removed. The unwinding structure concludes with the final node. Notice that the resulting structure contains one path for each possible ordering — including simultaneity! — of unordered events.

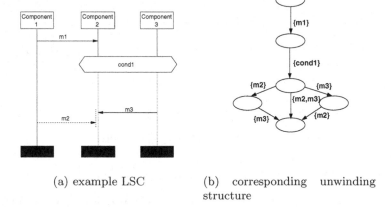

(a) example LSC

(b) corresponding unwinding structure

Fig. 2. Simple unwinding example

Figure 2 shows a simple unwinding example. We have omitted the node annotations to increase readability. m2 and m3 are located in a coregion - they may be observed in any order and in our interpretation also simultaneously[5].

Optimizing the Structure The unwinding structure for an LSC can become very broad if the LSC contains large coregions or many elements which may be executed in parallel. As a consequence it may contain identical substructures in different branches. In order to streamline the structure these identical substructures should be merged. But this merge may only be performed if the substructures represent the same unwinding step, i.e. they must have the same history and ready sets.

Temperatures Each location is annotated with a temperature indicating if progress is enforced along the instance axis. When the events associated with a location are observed, a hot temperature at the location requires the events located at the following location to occur eventually. A cold temperature allows the events located at the following location not to occur at all, but if they are observed they must be observed after the events of the previous location.
Let $temp(i, x) \rightarrow \{hot, cold\}$ be the temperature of location x at instance i. We now define the temperature of a cut by

$$temp(Cut_j) = \begin{cases} hot, & if \; \exists \; i \in Instances(l) \; \exists \; x_i \in Locations(i) : x_i \in Cut_j \\ & \wedge \; temp(i, location(x_i)) = hot \\ cold, & else \end{cases}$$

The temperature of a phase is defined to be the temperature of its Cut. We can now define the set of cold phases of LSC l:

$ColdPhases(l) := \{ph \in Phases(l) \mid ph = (Ready_{ph}, History_{ph}, Cut_{ph}) \wedge temp(Cut_{ph}) = cold\}$. By definition: $temp(Phase_{final}) = cold$.

4   From the Unwinding Structure to a Timed Büchi Automaton

The unwinding structure is an intermediary data structure which is incomplete since it cannot express time. This motivates the following transformation of the unwinding structure into a Timed Büchi Automaton (TBA) which serves as intermediate format to the STVE. There exists a translation of the TBA format into propositional temporal logic (for details see [Fey96]).

Before we formally introduce Timed Büchi Automata we describe how timing information is added, since this is the key procedure in transforming the unwinding structure into a TBA.

---

[5] For delayed communication we would have to put the send and receive events of the messages in separate simultaneous classes.

4.1 Adding Timing Information

Hot locations can be annotated by *timing annotations* which are interval notations of the form $[n, m]$, where n, m are non-negative integers and $n \leq m$. The
notation is similar to the one used for constraint intervals in STDs [Fey96] or
for specifying delays in MSCs [AHP96]. The meaning of a timing annotation is:
After having observed the events located at the annotated location at least n and
at most m steps later the events located at the following location are observed.

For each location of the LSC an integer clock is introduced. This clock is
reset when the location is unwound, i.e. when an event located at this location is
observed. A boolean expression constrains the clock value to be in the specified
range when the next location along the instance axis is entered (i.e. when an
event located at the following location is observed). The boolean expression is
simply **true** if the location does not have a timing annotation. For treatment of
timing annotations we therefore define:

- For $i \in Instances(l)$ and $x \in Locations(i)$ let $clk(i, x)$ be the unique clock
  identifier denoting the clock associated with the location x of instance i
- The set of clock names is given by
  $Clocks(l) := \bigcup_{i \in Instances(l)} \bigcup_{x \in Locations(i)} clk(i, x)$.
- For $i \in Instances(l)$ and $x \in Locations(i)$ let $t\_ann(i, x)$ be the timing
  annotation for location x of instance i. Note that $t\_ann(i, x) = \epsilon$ if location x
  of instance i is not annotated with a timing annotation. Otherwise $t\_ann(i, x)$
  is of the form $[n, m]$, with $n \leq m$, n, m integers.
- Let $clk\_resets(Fired_j) := \{ clk(i, x) \mid \exists z \in Fired_j \exists scl \in z \exists sr \in$
  $scl : location(sr) = x \land x \in Locations(i)\}$, $scl \in Sim\_Classes(l)$, $sr \in$
  $Sim\_Regions(i)$ be the set of names of clocks which are reset when $Fired_j$
  is unwound. I.e. for each location reached with $Fired_j$ the corresponding
  clocks are reset.
- Let $Clk\_Resets(l) := \bigcup_{f \in Fireds(l)} clk\_resets(f)$ be the set of all clocks which
  are reset in LSC l.
- Let $clk\_conds(Fired_j) := \{ t\_ann(i, x) \mid \exists z \in Fired_j \exists scl \in z \exists sr \in$
  $scl : x \in predecessor(location(sr))\}$, $scl \in Sim\_Classes(l)$, $sr \in$
  $Sim\_Regions(i)$ be the set of timing annotations to be considered when
  unwinding $Fired_j$.
- Let $Clk\_Conds(l) := \bigcup_{f \in Fireds(l)} clk\_conds(f)$ be the set of all timing annotations in LSC l.

Finally let us note that timers may be treated in a way quite similar to timing
annotations. Figure 3 shows an example; note that we are dealing with a TBA
instead of an unwinding structure here. The TBA definition as well as the exact
treatment of clocks will be demonstrated in section 4.2.

4.2 Timed Büchi Automaton Definition

A Timed Büchi Automaton ([Alu98],[AD92]) A is a tuple
$A = (\Sigma, S, s_0, C, \longrightarrow_{TBA}, F)$, where

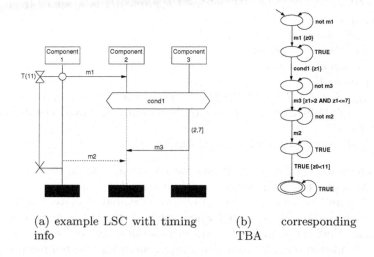

(a) example LSC with timing info   (b)   corresponding TBA

Fig. 3. Unwinding timing annotations and timers

- Σ is the alphabet
- S is the set of states
- $s_0 \in S$ is the initial state
- C is a set of clocks
- $\longrightarrow_{TBA}: S \times Pred \times \wp^+(C) \times \wp(Conds(C)) \to S$ is the transition function. *Pred* are predicates ranging over Σ. $Conds(C)$ are predicates constraining clocks of C. A transition $(s, p, c, cond) \longrightarrow_{TBA} s'$ represents the change from state s to state s' for observation p. The clocks in c are reset when taking the transition and the transition can only be taken if the clock constraints in *cond* hold.
- Finally $F \subseteq S$ is the set of accepting states

Informally the TBA for an LSC is derived from its unwinding structure by

- renaming the nodes with a fresh set of phase names
- changing the edge annotation to the conjunction of the elements of the corresponding fired set
- adding a dedicated *Exit* state for violated cold conditions
- determining the set of accepting states according to the Büchi acceptance condition
- adding self loops on each state and labeling them with the condition which has to hold while the TBA stays in the associated state[6].

A TBA A_{LSC} for an LSC is a tuple $A_{LSC} = (\Sigma, S, s_0, C, \longrightarrow_{TBA}, F)$, where

- $\Sigma := Sim\_Classes(l)$

---

[6] The self loops are needed because time only passes when a transition is taken. Otherwise time could not progress in a state.

- $S := Ph\_names(l) \cup \{Exit\}$, where $Ph\_names(l)$ is a set of fresh identifiers and $phname$ is the function that associates a name from $Ph\_names(l)$
  with each phase of the unwinding structure, i.e. $\forall\, p \in Phases(l)\; \exists^1 p' \in$
  $Ph\_names(l) : p' = phname(p)$.
- $s_0 := phname(Phase_0)$
- $C := Clocks(l)$
- $\longrightarrow_{TBA}\colon S \times Pred \times \wp^+(Clk\_Resets(l)) \times \wp(Clk\_Conds(l)) \;\to\; S$, where
  the $Pred$ is built from $f \in Fireds(l)$ by conjunction (and negation) of the
  elements of f.
- $F := \{\, phname(cph) \mid cph \in ColdPhases(l)) \}$

Up to here we did not mention how we handle activation mode and activation condition of a LSC. The language definition [DH99] provides the activation
modes *initial* and *invariant*. An initial LSC is activated at system initialization,
while an invariant LSC is activated whenever its activation condition evaluates
to true; note that the kernel automata are identical in both cases. Activation
mode and condition must be regarded when generating the temporal logic formulae from the TBAs[Fey96]. Thus we need to preserve this information in the
TBA format and extend the it with an activation predicate.

4.3   Determinism in the TBA

Adding the self loops for each state in the TBA raises the question of what
annotation should be put on the self loop. This is closely related to the question
of determinism of the TBA. There are three options of what the transition
annotation should be: First, the annotation could be omitted altogether – this
would be equivalent to a *true* annotation – resulting in a very non-deterministic
TBA. The *true* annotation does not require the TBA to take a transition when
the corresponding message has been observed. This non-deterministic behavior
is obviously too weak, so we need a stronger interpretation.

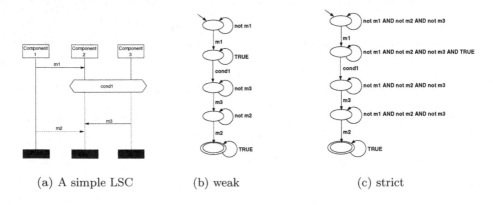

(a) A simple LSC   (b) weak   (c) strict

Fig. 4. Different annotation types for self loops

The interpretation corresponding to [DH99], where each occurrence of a message has to be explicitly noted in the LSC and no other occurrence is allowed, we call *strict*. This is achieved by annotating each self loop with the conjunction of the negation of all messages appearing in the LSC (cf. figure 4(c)). This interpretation may be too strong in certain cases where we do not care if messages visible in the LSC occur anytime else, as long as the ordering imposed by the LSC is satisfied. This leads to the *weak* interpretation where the self loop annotation only contains the negation of the next message(s). This forces the TBA to react to the first occurrence of the message that is expected next, but does not restrain the occurrence of this message at other times (cf. figure 4(b)).

These different degrees of determinism only concern messages. For conditions we always annotate the self loop with *true* (cf. figures 4(c) and 4(b)), because we do not know when to evaluate a condition. This problem is inherent in the LSCs where there is only the possibility to specify if a condition has to be reached – and therefore evaluated – at all. Even if all locations before a condition are hot this does not tell us anything about when exactly the condition is evaluated. The designer would have to use a timing annotation to force a condition to be evaluated at a certain time or within a certain time interval.

5   Integration with STVE

The further incorporation of LSCs into the STVE is currently under way. The transformation of LSCs into TBAs described above is only one issue when connecting LSCs to the tool set. We have also developed an editor and a mapping tool for LSCs. Since LSCs should not only be used in the context of STATEMATE, the LSC identifiers for instances, messages and those used in conditions are only symbolic names, i.e. place holders for concrete identifiers of the model to be verified. Based on the internal representation of STATEMATE designs in the STVE (cf. [BBea99]) the mapping tool allows the user to associate the activities of the STATEMATE design with the instances of a LSC. The interfaces of the selected activities are computed and also offered to the user for identification of messages and conditions with certain variables and their valuations. The mapping of LSC objects to design items yields boolean expressions as atomic propositions of the temporal logic formulae.

Figure 5 gives an overview over the LSC tools in the STATEMATE context. For a given STATEMATE design LSC requirements are created with the LSC editor. The requirements thus created are then translated by the LSC compiler which implements the unwinding procedure described in this paper into the intermediate TBA format from which the temporal logic formula is generated. Since only symbolic names are used in LSCs, the TL formula only contains propositions which regard these symbolic names. Therefore we need the LSC mapper to relate the STATEMATE identifiers to the LSC identifiers. The result is a table which gives for each proposition (which consists of symbolic names) the concrete model elements. This table together with the formula generated from the LSC form the input for the modelchecker (Φ in figure 5). The STVE also translates the STATEMATE model into the input format for the modelchecker which then determines, if the model satisfies the requirement.

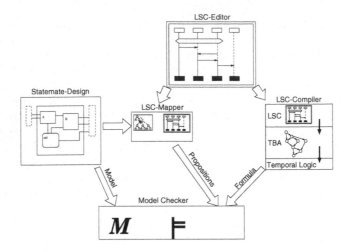

Fig. 5. Integration of LSCs with STVE

6   Conclusion

We have shown in this paper how the rather high-level semantics for LSCs presented in [DH99] can be elaborated. We only considered a subset of LSC features, which consists of what we feel are the LSC core concepts. We made some further restrictions either for simplicity's sake or due to limitations imposed by STATEMATE (zero-delay messages). We then demonstrated how this subset may be efficiently transformed into an automaton with the focus on the technical procedure of unwinding the LSC. Having arrived at the TBA format the gateway to the STVE is wide open. This format is also used for code generation from STDs in conjunction with a STATEMATE design and to synthesize state charts from STDs. These routes are possible for LSCs as well, although at the moment we have only used LSCs for formal verification as described in section 5.

The verification of STATEMATE models against LSCs has at the moment of writing not been tested extensively, so that more experience is needed in this respect. Especially the issue of complexity needs further investigation. While STDs are used to specify properties of components in a black box view, the benefit of LSCs is the ability to specify protocols in a glass box view of the system. Therefore it is quite natural to consider the whole model at once, while STDs allow the user to scale down the verification task by system verification (cf. [BBea99]). To verify large models against LSC specifications we will need powerful abstraction techniques to reduce the state space for the verification. Complexity also has to be investigated on the requirement side, where the formula may become very large depending on the size of the LSC and the degree of parallelism it contains.

In the future we plan to extend both LSCs and the verification tool set to also cope with UML models. In this respect not only the concept of synchronous and asynchronous communication has to be reflected in LSCs, but we will also need to develop strategies for verification in the object-oriented world.

Acknowledgments We would like to thank Werner Damm and David Harel for their comments on the first version of this paper and the following discussions. We also thank Uwe Higgen, Rainer Koopmann and Olaf Bär, who played a major role in implementing the tools described here.

References

[AD92]   R. Alur and D. Dill. The Theory of Timed Automata. In de Bakker, Henzinger, and de Roever, editors, *Proceedings of Rex 1991: Real Time in Theory and Practice*, number 600 in LNCS. Springer Verlag, 1992.

[AHP96]   R. Alur, G. J. Holzmann, and D. Peled. An analyzer for Message Sequence Charts. In T. Margaria and B. Steffen, editors, *Tools and Algorithms for the Construction and Analysis of Systems (TACAS'96)*, volume 1055 of *Lecture Notes in Computer Science*, pages 35–48, Passau, Germany, 1996. Springer-Verlag.

[Alu98]   R. Alur. Timed Automata. In *NATO-ASI 1998 Summer School on Verification of Digital and Hybrid Systems*, 1998.

[BBea99] Tom Bienmüller, Udo Brockmeyer, and Werner Damm et. al. Formal Verification of an Avionics Application using Abstraction and Symbolic Model Checking. In Felix Redmill and Tom Anderson, editors, *Towards System Safety – Proceedings of the Seventh Safety-critical Systems Symposium, Huntingdon, UK*, pages 150–173. Safety-Critical Systems Club, Springer Verlag, 1999.

[DDK99]   W. Damm, G. Döhmen, and J. Klose. Secure Decentralized Control of Railway Crossings. In S. Gnesi and D. Latella, editors, *Fourth International ERCIM Workshop on Formal Methods in Industrial Critical Systems*, 1999.

[DH99]   W. Damm and D. Harel. LSCs: Breathing Life into Message Sequence Charts. In *FMOODS'99 IFIP TC6/WG6.1 Third International Conference on Formal Methods for Open Object-Based Distributed Systems*, 1999.

[DH01]   W. Damm and D. Harel. LSCs: Breathing Life into Message Sequence Charts. *Formal Methods in System Design*, 2001. to appear.

[DK01]   Werner Damm and Jochen Klose. Verification of a Radio-based Signaling System Using the Statemate Verification Environment. *Formal Methods in System Design*, 2001. to appear.

[Fey96]   Konrad Feyerabend. Realtime Symbolic Timing Diagrams. Technical report, Carl von Ossietzky Universität Oldenburg, 1996.

[FJ97]   Konrad Feyerabend and Bernhard Josko. A visual formalism for real time requirement specifications. In *Proceedings of the 4th International AMAST Workshop on Real-Time Systems and Concurrentand Distributed Software, ARTS'97, Lecture Notes in Computer Science 1231*, pages 156–168, 1997.

[HP96]   David Harel and Michal Politi. *Modeling Reactive Systems with Statecharts: The STATEMATE Approach*. Part No. D–1100–43. i-Logix Inc., Three Riverside Drive, Andover, MA 01810, June 1996.

[IT96a]   ITU-T. *ITU-T Annex B to Recommendation Z.120 Formal Semantics of Message Sequence Charts*. ITU-T, Geneva, 1996.

[IT96b]   ITU-T. *ITU-T Recommendation Z.120: Message Sequence Chart (MSC)*. ITU-T, Geneva, October 1996.

[Krü99]   Ingolf Krüger. Towards the Methodical Usage of Message Sequence Charts. In Katharina Spies and Bernhard Schätz, editors, *Formale Beschreibungstechniken für verteilte Systeme (FBT99)*, 9. GI/ITG Fachgespräch, pages 123–134. Herbert Utz Verlag, June 1999.

Coverage Metrics for Temporal Logic Model Checking

Hana Chockler[1], Orna Kupferman[1], and Moshe Y. Vardi[2]*

[1] Hebrew University, School of Engineering and Computer Science, Jerusalem 91904, Israel
Email: {hanac,orna}@cs.huji.ac.il,   URL: http://www.cs.huji.ac.il/{~hanac,~orna}
[2] Rice University, Department of Computer Science, Houston, TX 77251-1892, U.S.A.
Email:vardi@cs.rice.edu,   URL: http://www.cs.rice.edu/~vardi

Abstract. In formal verification, we verify that a system is correct with respect to a specification. Even when the system is proven to be correct, there is still a question of how complete the specification is, and whether it really covers all the behaviors of the system. In this paper we study coverage metrics for model checking. Coverage metrics are based on modifications we apply to the system in order to check which parts of it were actually relevant for the verification process to succeed. We introduce two principles that we believe should be part of any coverage metric for model checking: a distinction between state-based and logic-based coverage, and a distinction between the system and its environment. We suggest several coverage metrics that apply these principles, and we describe two algorithms for finding the uncovered parts of the system under these definitions. The first algorithm is a symbolic implementation of a naive algorithm that model checks many variants of the original system. The second algorithm improves the naive algorithm by exploiting overlaps in the variants. We also suggest a few helpful outputs to the user, once the uncovered parts are found.

1   Introduction

In *model checking* [CE81,QS81,LP85], we verify the correctness of a finite-state system with respect to a desired behavior by checking whether a labeled state-transition graph that models the system satisfies a specification of this behavior, expressed in terms of a temporal logic formula or a finite automaton. Beyond being fully-automatic, an additional attraction of model-checking tools is their ability to accompany a negative answer to the correctness query by a counterexample to the satisfaction of the specification in the system. Thus, together with a negative answer, the model checker returns some erroneous execution of the system. These counterexamples are very important and they can be essential in detecting subtle errors in complex designs [CGMZ95]. On the other hand, when the answer to the correctness query is positive, most model-checking tools terminate with no further information to the user. Since a positive answer means that the system is correct with respect to the specification, this at first seems like a reasonable policy. In the last few years, however, there has been growing awareness of the importance of suspecting the system of containing an error also in the case model checking

---

* Supported in part by NSF grant CCR-9700061, NSF grant CCR-9988322, and by a grant from the Intel Corporation.

succeeds. The main justification of such suspects are possible errors in the modeling of the system or of the behavior, and possible incompleteness in the specification.

There are various ways to look for possible errors in the modeling of the system or the behavior. One direction is to detect *vacuous satisfaction* of the specification [BBER97,KV99], where cases like antecedent failure [BB94] make parts of the specification irrelevant to its satisfaction. For example, the specification $\varphi = AG(req \rightarrow AF\,grant)$ is vacuously satisfied in a system in which *req* is always **false**. A similar direction is to check the validity of the specification. Clearly, a valid specification is satisfied trivially, and suggests some problem. A related approach is taken in the process of constraint validation in the verification tool FormalCheck [Kur98], where sanity checks for constraint validation include a search for enabling conditions that are never enabled, and a replacement of all or some of the constraints by **false**. FormalCheck also keeps track of variables and values of variables that were never used in the process of model checking.

It is less clear how to check completeness of the specification. Indeed, specifications are written manually, and their completeness depends entirely on the competence of the person who writes them. The motivation for such a check is clear: an erroneous behavior of the system can escape the verification efforts if this behavior is not captured by the specification. In fact, it is likely that a behavior not captured by the specification also escapes the attention of the designer, who is often the one to provide the specification.

This direction, of checking whether the specification describes the system exhaustively, has roots in simulation-based verification techniques, where *coverage metrics* are used to improve the quality of test vectors. For example, *code coverage* [CK93] measures the fraction of HDL statements executed during simulation, *transition coverage* [HYHD95,HMA95] measures the fraction of transitions executed, and *tag coverage* [DGK96] attributes variables with tags that are used to detect whether assigning a forbidden value to a variable leads to an erroneous behavior of the system. In [FDK98,FAD99], Fallah et al. compute the tag coverage achieved by simulation and generated simulation sequences that cover a given tagged variable. Of a similar nature is the *tour-generation algorithm* in [HYHD95], which generates test vectors that traverse all states of the system. Ho and Horowitz [HH96] define test coverage in terms of *control events*. Each control event identifies an interesting subset of the control variables, and the test vectors have to cover all the events. They also define *design coverage* by means of the states and edges covered by the test vectors (see also [MAH98]). In order to circumvent the state-explosion problem in these methods, Bergmann and Horowitz develop the technique of *projection directed state exploration*, which allows to compute the above coverage metrics for small portions of the design [BH99]. Coverage metrics are helpful as an indicator whether the simulation process has been exhaustive. Still, simulation-based verification techniques lack of a uniform definition of coverage.

Following the same considerations, analyzing coverage in model checking can discover parts of the system that are not relevant for the verification process to succeed. Low coverage can point to several problems. One possibility is that the specification is not complete enough to fully describe all the possible behaviors of the system. In this case, the output of a coverage check is helpful in completing the specification. Another possibility is that the system contains redundancies. In this case, the output of the coverage check is helpful in simplifying the system.

Two approaches for defining and developing algorithms for coverage metrics in temporal logic model checking are studied in the literature. The first approach, of Katz et al. [KGG99], is based on a comparison of the system with a tableau of the specification. Essentially, a tableau of a universal specification φ is a system that satisfies φ and subsumes all the behaviors allowed by φ. By comparing a system with the tableau of φ, Katz et al. are able to detect parts of the systems that are irrelevant to the satisfaction of the specification, to detect different behaviors of the system that are indistinguishable by the specification, and to detect behaviors that are allowed by the specification but not generated by the system. Such cases imply that the specification is incomplete or not sufficiently restrictive. The tableau used in [KGG99] is reduced: a state of the tableau is associated with subformulas that have be true in it, and it induces no obligations on the other, possibly propositional, subformulas. This leads to smaller and less restrictive tableaux. Still, we found the approach in [KGG99] too strict. Indeed, a system passes the criteria in [KGG99] iff it is bisimilar to the tableau of the specification, but we want specifications to be much more abstract than their implementations[1].

The second approach, of Hoskote et al. [HKHZ99], is to define coverage by examining the effect of modifications in the system on the satisfaction of the specification. Given a system modeled by a Kripke structure K, a formula φ satisfied in K, and a signal (atomic proposition) q, a state w of K is q-covered by φ if the Kripke structure obtained from K by flipping the value of q in w no longer satisfies φ (the signal q corresponds to a boolean variable that is **true** if w is labeled with q and is **false** otherwise, so when we say that we flip the value of q, we mean that we switch the value of this variable). Indeed, this indicates that the value of q in w is crucial for the satisfaction of φ in K. The signal q is referred to as the *observable signal*. Let us denote by $\tilde{K}_{w,q}$ the Kripke structure obtained from K by flipping the value of q in w, and denote by q-$cover(K, \varphi)$ the set of states q-covered by φ in K. It is easy to see that q-$cover(K, \varphi)$ can be computed by a naive algorithm that performs model checking of φ in $\tilde{K}_{w,q}$ for each state w of K. By [HKHZ99], a state is covered if it belongs to q-$cover(K, \varphi)$ for some observable signal q.

Hoskote et al. describe an algorithm for computing the set of states that are q-covered by a formula φ in the logic *acceptable ACTL*. Acceptable ACTL is a restriction of the universal fragment ACTL of CTL in which no disjunctions are allowed and all the implications $\alpha \rightarrow \beta$ are such that α is propositional. The algorithm in [HKHZ99] is applied to φ after an *observability transformation*. The restricted syntax of acceptable ACTL together with the observability transformation lead to a symbolic algorithm that, like CTL model-checking, requires linear time [2]. On the other hand, the set of states designated as q-covered by the algorithm is not q-$cover(K, \varphi)$. It is claimed in

---

[1] The approach in [KGG99] also has some technical and computational drawbacks: the specification considered is the (big) conjunction of all the properties the system should satisfy, the complexity of the algorithm is exponential in the specification (for φ in ACTL), and it is restricted to universal safety specifications whose tableaux have no fairness constraints.

[2] The restricted syntax of acceptable ACTL and the observability transformation force $\tilde{K}_{w,q}$, for all states w, to satisfy φ in exactly the same way K does. For example, if a path in K

[HKHZ99] that the set found by the algorithm meets better the intuition of coverage. One can argue whether this is indeed the case; we actually found several performances of the algorithm in [HKHZ99] quite counter-intuitive (for example, the algorithm is syntax-dependent, thus, equivalent formulas may induce different coverage sets; in particular, the set of states q-covered by the tautology $q \rightarrow q$ is the set of states that satisfy q, rather than the empty set, which meets our intuition of coverage). Anyway, this is not the point we want to make here — there are many possible ways of defining coverage sets, each way has its advantages, and there need not be a best way. The point we want to make in this paper is that there are two important principles that should be part of any coverage metric for temporal logic model checking: a distinction between state-based and logic-based approaches, and a distinction between the system and its environment. These principles, which we explain below, are not applied in [HKHZ99] and in other work on coverage hitherto.

The first principle, namely a distinction between state-based and logic-based approaches, is based on the observation that there are several ways to model a system, and the different ways should induce different references to the observability signal and its modification. Recall [HKHZ99]'s definition of coverage. Hoskote et al. model systems by Kripke structures and the observable signal q is one of the atomic propositions that label the states of the structure and encode the system's variables. For every state w, the truth value of q is flipped in $\tilde{K}_{w,q}$. This approach is *state based*, as it modifies q in each of the states. When the system is modeled as a circuit and its state space is 2^V, for the set V of signals, transitions are given as relations between current and next values to the signals in V [MP92]. Then, flipping the value of a signal in a state changes not only the "label" of the state but also the transitions to and from the state. So, in the state-based approach, we consider modifications that refer to a single state of the system and to the adjacent transitions. When the system is modeled as a circuit, we can also take the *logic-based* approach, where we do not flip the value of a signal in a particular state, but rather, fix the signal to 0, 1, or "don't care" everywhere in the circuit, and check the effect of these fixes on the satisfaction of the specification.

In order to explain the second principle, namely a distinction between a system and its environment, assume a definition of coverage in which a state is covered iff its removal violates the specification. Since universal properties are preserved under state removal, no state would be covered by a universal specification in such a definition. So, is this a silly definition? The definition makes perfect sense in the context of closed systems. There, universal properties can be satisfied by the empty system, and if a designer wants the system to do something (more than just being correct), this something should be specified by an existential specification. On the other hand, in an open system, which interacts with its environment, the above definition makes sense only if we restrict it to states whose removal leaves the system responsive to all the behaviors of the environment and does not deadlock the interaction between the system and its environment. Indeed, we cannot remove a state if the environment can force a visit to it. Likewise, it makes no sense to talk about q-coverage for a signal q that corresponds to an input variable. Indeed, it is the environment that determines the value of q, we cannot flip its

---

satisfies $\alpha U \beta$ by fulfilling β in the present, this path is expected to satisfy β in the present also in $\tilde{K}_{w,q}$. This restriction is what makes the algorithm so efficient.

value, and anyway we cannot talk about states being q-covered or not: all the values of q should be around simply since the environment can force them all. Hence, in the definition of coverage metrics, in both the design and implementation levels, there should be a distinction between input and output variables, and coverage should be examined only with respect to elements the system has control on.

The contribution of our paper is as follows. We introduce the above two principles in the definition of coverage, and we give several coverage metrics that apply them. Our definitions are similar to the one in [HKHZ99] in the sense that they consider the influence of local modifications of the system on the satisfaction of the specification (in fact, [HKHZ99] can be viewed as a special case of our state-based approach, for a closed system, with $C \cap O = \emptyset$, and with only output variables being observable). Hence, the naive algorithm, which finds the set of covered states (in the state-based approach) or signals (in the logic-based approach) by model checking each of the modified systems is applicable. We describe two alternatives to this naive algorithm. The first alternative is a symbolic approach to finding the uncovered parts of the system. The second alternative is an algorithm that makes use of overlaps among the modified systems — since each modification involves a small change in the original system, there is a great deal of work that can be shared when we model check all the modified systems. Both algorithms work for full CTL, and the ideas in them can be adopted to various definitions of coverage. Once the set of covered states is found, we suggest a few helpful outputs to the user (more helpful than just the percentage of covered states).

Due to lack of space, many details are omitted from this version. A full version of the paper can be found in the authors' URLs.

2   Coverage Metrics

In this section we suggest several coverage metrics for temporal logic model checking. As describe in Section 1, we distinguish between a state-based and a logic-based approach to coverage, and we distinguish between a system and its environment. Our definitions are independent of the temporal logic being used. We assume the reader is familiar with temporal logic. In particular, the algorithms we are going to present are for the branching time logic CTL. Formulas of CTL are built from a set AP of atomic propositions using the boolean operators $\vee$ and $\neg$, the temporal operators X ("next") and U ("until"), and the path quantifiers E ("exists a path") and A ("for all paths"). Every temporal operator must be immediately preceded by a path quantifier. The semantics of temporal logic formulas is defined with respect to Kripke structures. For a full definition of Kripke structures, and the syntax and semantics of CTL, see [Eme90] and full version of this paper. For a formula φ (and an agreed Kripke structure K), we denote by $\|\varphi\|$ the set of states that satisfy φ in K, and use $cl(\varphi)$ to denote the set of φ's subformulas. A Kripke structure K satisfies a formula φ, denoted $K \models \varphi$ iff φ holds in the initial state of K. The problem of determining whether K satisfies φ is the *model-checking* problem.

We distinguish between two types of systems: *closed* and *open* [HP85]. A closed system is a system whose behavior is completely determined by the state of the system. An open system is a system that interacts with its environment and whose behavior depends on external nondeterministic choices made by the environment [Hoa85]. In a Kripke structure, all the atomic propositions describe internal signals, thus Kripke structures model closed systems. We study here open systems, and we model them by *sequential circuits*.

A sequential circuit (*circuit*, for short) is a tuple $\mathcal{S} = \langle I, O, C, \theta, \rho, \delta \rangle$, where I is a set of input signals, O is a set of output signals, and C is a set of control signals that induce the state space 2^C. Accordingly, $\theta \in 2^C$ is an initial state, $\rho : 2^C \times 2^I \to 2^C$ is a deterministic transition function, and $\delta : 2^C \to 2^O$ is an output function. Possibly $O \cap C \neq \emptyset$, in which case for all $x \in O \cap C$ and $s \in 2^C$, we have $x \in s$ iff $x \in \delta(s)$. Thus, $\delta(s)$ agrees with s on signals in C. We partition the signals in $O \cup C$ into three classes as follows. A signal $x \in O \setminus C$ is a *pure-output* signal. A signal $x \in C \setminus O$ is a *pure-control* signal. A signal $x \in C \cap O$ is a *visible-control* signal. While pure output signals have no control on the transitions of the system, a specification of the system can refer only to the values of the pure-output or the visible-control signals.

We define the semantics of CTL with respect to circuits by means of the Kripke structure they induce. A circuit $\mathcal{S} = \langle I, O, C, \theta, \rho, \delta \rangle$ can be converted to a Kripke structure $K_\mathcal{S} = \langle I \cup C \cup O, 2^C \times 2^I, R, \langle \theta, \emptyset \rangle, L \rangle$, where for all s and s' in 2^C, and i and i' in 2^I, we have $R(\langle s, i \rangle, \langle s', i' \rangle)$ iff $\rho(s, i) = s'$. Also, $L(\langle s, i \rangle) = \delta(s) \cup i \cup s$. Note that each state in $K_\mathcal{S}$ has $2^{|I|}$ successors, reflecting external nondeterminism induced by the environment of $\mathcal{S}$. We assume that the interaction between the circuit and its environment is initiated by the circuit, hence the single initial state. The other possibility, where the interaction between the circuit and its environment is initiated by the environment, corresponds to a Kripke structure with a set $\theta \times 2^I$ of initial states. Our definitions and algorithms assume a single initial state, yet they can be easily modified to handle multiple initial states.

We now define what it means for a specification to cover a circuit. Let $\mathcal{S}$ be a circuit that satisfies a specification φ. We want to check whether the specification describes $\mathcal{S}$ exhaustively. Intuitively, the uncovered part of $\mathcal{S}$ is the part that can be modified without falsifying φ in $\mathcal{S}$. Formally, we suggest several definitions of coverage, reflecting the various possible ways in which a part of $\mathcal{S}$ can be modified.

We start with the state-based definition. Here, we check whether the satisfaction of φ is sensitive to local changes in the values of output and control signals; i.e., changes in one state.

For a circuit $\mathcal{S} = \langle I, O, C, \theta, \rho, \delta \rangle$, a state $s \in 2^C$, and a signal $x \in C$, we define the x-twin of s, denoted $twin_x(s)$, as the state s' obtained from s by dualizing the value of x. Thus, $x \in s'$ iff $x \notin s$. Now, given $\mathcal{S}$, s, and a signal $x \in O \cup C$, we define the dual circuit $\tilde{\mathcal{S}}_{s,x} = \langle I, O, C, \tilde{\theta}, \tilde{\rho}, \tilde{\delta} \rangle$ as follows.

- If x is a pure-output signal, then $\tilde{\theta} = \theta$, $\tilde{\rho} = \rho$, and $\tilde{\delta}$ is obtained from δ by dualizing the value of x in s, thus $x \in \tilde{\delta}(s)$ if $x \notin \delta(s)$.
- If x is a pure-control signal, then $\tilde{\delta} = \delta$, and $\tilde{\theta}$ and $\tilde{\rho}$ are obtained by replacing all the occurrences of s in θ and in the range of ρ by $twin_x(s)$. Thus, if $\theta = s$, then $\tilde{\theta} = twin_x(s)$ (otherwise, $\tilde{\theta} = \theta$), and for all $s' \in 2^C$ and $i \in 2^I$, if $\rho(s', i) = s$, then $\tilde{\rho}(s', i) = twin_x(s)$ (otherwise, $\tilde{\rho}(s', i) = \rho(s', i)$).

- If x is a visible-control signal, then we do both changes. Thus, $\tilde{\delta}$ is obtained from δ by dualizing the value of x in s, and $\tilde{\theta}$ and $\tilde{\rho}$ are obtained by replacing all the occurrences of s in θ and in the range of ρ by $twin_x(s)$.

Intuitively, dualizing a control signal x in a state s in $\mathcal{S}$ means that all the transitions leading to s are now directed to its x-twin. In particular, the state s is no longer reachable in $\tilde{\mathcal{S}}_{s,x}$ (which is why we do not have to redefine $\tilde{\rho}(s,i)$). For a specification φ such that $\mathcal{S} \models \varphi$, a state s is x-covered by φ if $\tilde{\mathcal{S}}_{s,x}$ does not satisfy φ.

Note that it makes no sense to define coverage with respect to observable input signals. This is because an open system has no control on the values of the input signals, which just resolve the external nondeterminism of the system. In a closed system, the set of input signals is empty, and thus the system has the control on all its variables. Therefore in closed systems we can define coverage with respect to all signals.

Our second approach to coverage, which we call *logic-based* coverage, does not refer to a particular state of $\mathcal{S}$, and it examines the possibility of fixing some control signals to 0 or 1. For a circuit $\mathcal{S} = \langle I, O, C, \theta, \rho, \delta \rangle$ and a control signal $x \in C$, the x-*fixed-to*-1 *circuit* $\mathcal{S}_{x,1} = \langle I, O, C, \theta', \rho', \delta \rangle$ is obtained from $\mathcal{S}$ by replacing all the occurrences of x in θ and in the range of ρ by 1; i.e., $\theta' = \theta \cup \{x\}$, and for all $s \in 2^C$ and $i \in 2^I$, we have $\rho'(s,i) = \rho(s,i) \cup \{x\}$. Similarly, the x-*fixed-to*-0 *circuit* $\mathcal{S}_{x,0}$ is defined by replacing all the occurrences of x in θ and in the range of ρ by 0. A control signal x is 1-*covered* if $\mathcal{S}_{x,1}$ does not satisfy φ. Similarly, x is 0-*covered* if $\mathcal{S}_{x,0}$ does not satisfy φ. [3]

3 Algorithms for Computing Coverage

In this section we describe algorithms for solving the following problems. Let φ be a specification in CTL.

- Given a circuit $\mathcal{S}$ that satisfies φ and an observable output or control signal x, return the set of states not x-covered by φ in $\mathcal{S}$.
- Given a circuit $\mathcal{S}$ that satisfies φ, return the set of control signals that can be fixed to 0 or fixed to 1.

All these problems have a naive algorithm that model checks each of the corresponding dual circuits. For example, in order to find the set of states not x-covered by φ in a circuit $\mathcal{S} = \langle I, O, C, \theta, \rho, \delta \rangle$, with the observable signal x being a pure-output signal, the naive algorithm executes the model-checking procedure $|2^C|$ times, once for each dual circuit, where each dual circuit is obtained from $\mathcal{S}$ by dualizing the value of x in one state. A similar thing happens in the naive algorithm with the observable signal being a control signal, only that here the dual circuits also differ in some of

---

[3] The logic-based definition of coverage is closely related to the notion of *observability don't care conditions* as presented in [HS96]. There, there is a set $C' \subseteq C$ of control signals and an assignment for the signals in C', denoted by the set $\alpha \subseteq C'$ of signals that are assigned **true** in this assignment, such that the behavior of the output signals in all the states $\alpha \cup \beta$, for all $\beta \subseteq C \setminus C'$, is the same. Thus, whenever the system is in a state in which the control signals in C' has value α, the value of the other control signals is "don't care".

their transitions. Finally, the naive algorithm for the logic-based coverage executes the model-checking procedure $|C|$ times, once for each control signal.

We present two alternatives to the naive algorithm. The first is a symbolic algorithm that manipulates pairs of sets of states, and the second is an algorithm that makes use of overlaps among the various dual circuits. We are going to describe our coverage algorithms in terms of Kripke structures. For that, we first need to adjust the definitions in Section 2 to Kripke structures. For a Kripke structure K, an observable signal q, a set $Y \subseteq W$ of states, and sets Z^+ and Z^- of transitions in $W \times W$, the *dual Kripke structure* $\tilde{K}(q, Y, Z^+, Z^-)$ is obtained from K by dualizing the value of q in states in Y, adding to R transitions in Z^+, and removing from R transitions in Z^-. It is easy to see that all the dualizations of circuits mentioned in Section 2 can be described in terms of dualizations of the Kripke structures they induce.

For simplicity, we describe in detail the algorithms for computing the set of x-covered states for a pure-output signal x and the case $I = \emptyset$. The same ideas work for the more general cases. Some generalizations are very simple (e.g., releasing the requirement for I being empty) and some result in a significantly more complicated algorithm (e.g., when the modification involve control signals, where transitions are modified). For the detailed explanation of the required modifications in both algorithms presented below see the full version of this paper. For our special case, we define, for a specification φ, a Kripke structure K that satisfies φ, and an observable atom q, the set of states q-covered by φ in K as the set of states w such that the dual Kripke structure $\tilde{K}_{w,q} = \tilde{K}(q, \{w\}, \emptyset, \emptyset)$ does not satisfy φ. Thus, a state of K is not q-covered if we can flip the value of q in it and still satisfy φ. This definition, which is studied in [HKHZ99], corresponds to the special case of the observable signal being a pure-output signal and I being empty. So, in the algorithms below, we are given a Kripke structure $K = \langle AP, W, R, w_0, L \rangle$ that satisfies a CTL formula φ and an observable atom q, and we look for the set of states w such that $\tilde{K}_{w,q}$ does not satisfy φ.

The naive algorithm for computing the set of q-covered states performs model checking of φ in $\tilde{K}_{w,q}$ for each $w \in W$. Since CTL model-checking complexity is linear in the Kripke structure and the specification, the naive algorithm requires time $O(|K| \cdot |\varphi| \cdot |W|)$, which is quadratic in the size of structure[4]. Our symbolic algorithm returns an OBDD of the q-covered states. Our improved algorithm has an average running time of $O(|K| \cdot |\varphi| \cdot \log|W|)$.

3.1   Algorithm 1: A Symbolic Approach

Consider a Kripke structure $K = \langle AP, W, R, w_0, L \rangle$ and an atomic proposition $q \in AP$. For a CTL formula φ, we define

$$P(\varphi) = \{\langle w, v \rangle : \tilde{K}_{v,q}, w \models \varphi\}.$$

Thus, $P(\varphi) \subseteq W \times W$ contains exactly all pairs $\langle w, v \rangle$ such that w satisfies φ in the structure where we dualize the value of q in v. The definition of $P(\varphi)$ may not appear

---

[4] The algorithm for computing the set of q-covered states in [HKHZ99] runs in time $O(|K| \cdot |\varphi|)$. As we discuss in Section 1, however, the algorithm calculates the set of q-covered states according to a different definition of coverage, which we found less intuitive, and it handles only a restricted subset of ACTL.

helpful, as we are interested in the set of states in which dualizing the value of q falsifies φ. Nevertheless, the q-covered set in K for φ can be derived easily from $P(\varphi)$ as it is the set $\{w : \langle w_0, w \rangle \notin P(\varphi)\}$.

Our symbolic algorithm computes the OBDDs $P(\psi)$ for all $\psi \in cl(\varphi)$. The algorithm works bottom-up, and is based on the symbolic CTL model-checking algorithm. We assume that we have already performed symbolic model checking of φ in K; thus the sets $||\psi||$ have already been computed for all $\psi \in cl(\varphi)$. Let $S(\psi)$ denote the set of pairs $||\psi|| \times W$. In each step of the algorithm, it calculates $P(\psi)$ for some $\psi \in cl(\varphi)$, based on the sets $S(\psi')$ for $\psi' \in cl(\psi)$, and on the sets $P(\psi'')$ for $\psi'' \in cl(\psi) \setminus \{\psi\}$.

The algorithm uses the procedures $PairEX$ and $PairAX$ that take an OBDD $P(\psi)$ of pairs of states as an argument, and output an OBDD of pairs as follows: $PairEX(P(\psi)) = \{\langle w, v \rangle : \text{there exists a successor } u \text{ of } w \text{ such that } \langle u, v \rangle \in P(\psi)\}$. The procedure $PairAX(P(\psi))$ is defined dually. Thus, the procedures $PairEX$ and $PairAX$ work as in symbolic CTL model checking, only that here we compute sets of pairs instead of sets of singletons. The procedures apply the modalities to the first element of the pair, assuming the second is fixed.

We can now describe the algorithm. Given a CTL formula ψ, we define $P(\psi)$ according to the structure of ψ as follows (we describe here only the existential modalities. The universal ones are defined dually using $PairAX$, and are described in the full version).

- $\psi = p$ for an atomic proposition $p \neq q$. Obviously, changing the value of q in some state does not affect the value of p in any state. Therefore, $P(p) = \{\langle w, v \rangle : p \in L(w)\}$.
- $\psi = q$. Since the satisfaction of q in w depends only on the labeling of w, changing the value of q in some state v affects it iff $v = w$. Therefore, $P(q) = \{\langle w, v \rangle : w \neq v, q \in L(w)\} \cup \{\langle w, w \rangle : q \notin L(w)\}$.
- $\psi = \psi_1 \vee \psi_2$. A state w satisfies ψ in the dual structure $\tilde{K}_{v,q}$ iff it satisfies either ψ_1 or ψ_2 in $\tilde{K}_{v,q}$. Therefore, $P(\psi) = P(\psi_1) \cup P(\psi_2)$.
- $\psi = \neg\psi_1$. A state w satisfies ψ in the dual structure $\tilde{K}_{v,q}$ iff it does not satisfy $\neg\psi$ in $\tilde{K}_{v,q}$. Therefore, $P(\psi) = (W \times W) \setminus P(\psi_1)$.
- $\psi = EX\psi_1$. A state w satisfies ψ in the dual structure $\tilde{K}_{v,q}$ iff there exists a successor of w that satisfies ψ_1 in $\tilde{K}_{v,q}$. Therefore, $P(\psi) = PairEX(P(\psi_1))$.
- $\psi = E\psi_1U\psi_2$. A state w satisfies ψ in the dual structure $\tilde{K}_{v,q}$ iff w satisfies ψ_2 in $\tilde{K}_{v,q}$, or w satisfies ψ_1 in $\tilde{K}_{v,q}$ and there exists a successor of w that satisfies ψ in $\tilde{K}_{v,q}$. Therefore, $P(\psi)$ is computed using the least fixed-point expression $\mu y.P(\psi_2) \vee (P(\psi_1) \wedge PairEX(y))$.

The symbolic algorithm for CTL model-checking uses a linear number of OBDD variables. The algorithm we present here doubles the number of OBDD variables, as it works with sets of pairs of states instead of sets of states. By the nature of the algorithm, it performs model-checking for all $\tilde{K}_{w,q}$ globally, and thus the OBDDs it computes contain information about the satisfaction of the specification in all the states of all the dual Kripke structures, and not only in their initial states.

The algorithm is described for the case that the Kripke structure K has one initial state, and can be easily extended to handle a set W_0 of initial states. Indeed, given the set $P(\varphi)$ of the set computed by the algorithm, the q-covered set in K for φ is the set of all states w such that there is an initial state $w_0 \in W_0$ such that $\langle w_0, w \rangle \notin P(\varphi)$.

3.2 Algorithm 2: Improving Average Complexity

Consider a Kripke structure $K = \langle AP, W, R, w_0, L \rangle$, a formula φ, and an atomic proposition q. Recall that the naive CTL coverage algorithm, which performs model checking for all dual Kripke structures, has running time of $O(|K| \cdot |\varphi| \cdot |W|)$. While for some dual Kripke structures model-checking may require less than $O(|K| \cdot |\varphi|)$, the naive algorithm always performs $|W|$ iterations of model checking; thus, its average complexity cannot be substantially better than its worst-case complexity. This unfortunate situation arises even when model checking of two dual Kripke structures is practically the same, and even when some of the states of K obviously do not affect the satisfaction of φ in K. In this section we present an algorithm that makes use of such overlaps and redundancies. The expectant running time of our algorithm is $O(|K| \cdot |\varphi| \cdot \log |W|)$. Formally, we have the following:

Theorem 1. *The set q-cover(K, φ) can be computed in average running time of $O(|K| \cdot |\varphi| \cdot \log |W|)$, where the average is taken with respect to all possible assignments of q in K.*

All possible assignments of q in K are all possible labelings of the structure K with the observable signal q, where the value of q is chosen in each state of K to be **true** or **false** with equal probability.

Our algorithm is based on the fact that for each w, the dual Kripke structure $\tilde{K}_{w,q}$ differs from K only slightly. Therefore, there should be a large amount of work that we can share when we model check all the dual structures. In order to explain the algorithm, we introduce the notion of *incomplete model checking*. Informally, incomplete model checking of K is model checking of K with its labeling function L partially defined. The solution to the incomplete model checking problem can rely only on the truth values of the atomic propositions in states for which the corresponding L is defined. Obviously, in the general case we are not guaranteed to solve the model-checking problem without knowing the values of all atoms in all states. We can, however, perform some work in this direction, which is not needed to be performed again when missing parts of L are revealed.

Consider a partition of W into two equal sets, W_1 and W_2. Our algorithm essentially works as follows. For all the dual Kripke structures $\tilde{K}_{w,q}$ such that $w \in W_1$, the states in W_2 maintain their original labeling. Therefore, we start by performing incomplete model checking of φ in K with L that does not rely on the values of q in states in W_1. We end up in one of the following two situations. It may be that the values of q in states in W_2 (and the values of all the other atomic propositions in all the states) are sufficient to imply the satisfaction of φ in K. Then, we can infer that all the states in W_1 are not q-covered. It may also be that the values of q in states in W_2 are not sufficient to imply the satisfaction of φ in K. Then, we continue and partition the set W_1 into two equal sets, W_{11} and W_{12}, and perform incomplete model checking that does not rely on the values of q in states in W_{11}. The important observation is that incomplete model checking is now performed in a Kripke structure to which we have already applied incomplete model checking in the previous iteration. Thus, we only have to propagate information that involves the values of q in W_{12}. Thus, as we go deeper in the recursion described above, we perform less work. The depth of the recursion is bounded by $\log |W|$. As we shall analyze exactly below, the work in depth i amounts in average to model checking of φ in a Kripke structure of size $\frac{|K|}{2^i}$. Hence the $O(|K| \cdot |\varphi| \cdot \log |W|)$ complexity.

It is easier to understand and analyze incomplete model checking by means of the automata-theoretic approach to branching time model checking [KVW00]. In this approach, we transform the specification φ to an alternating automaton $\mathcal{A}_\varphi$ that accepts exactly all the models of φ. Model checking of K with respect to φ is then reduced to checking the nonemptiness of the product $\mathcal{A}_{K,\varphi}$ of K and $\mathcal{A}_\varphi$. When φ is in CTL, the automaton $\mathcal{A}_\varphi$ is linear in the length of φ, thus the product is of size $O(K \cdot |\varphi|)$.

The product $\mathcal{A}_{K,\varphi}$ can be viewed as a boolean circuit $G_{K,\varphi}$ (unlike boolean circuits, the product $\mathcal{A}_{K,\varphi}$ may contain cycles. In the full version we show how to handle these cycles) . The *root* of $G_{K,\varphi}$ is the vertex $\langle w_{in}, \varphi \rangle$. The leaves of $G_{K,\varphi}$ are pairs $\langle w, p \rangle$ or $\langle w, \neg p \rangle$. The formula φ is assumed to be in a positive normal form, thus negation applies only to the leaves of $G_{K,\varphi}$. The inner vertices of $G_{K,\varphi}$ are labeled with **true** or **false**, and the leaves are labeled with literals (variables or their negations). Initially, each leaf $\langle w, p \rangle$ or $\langle w, \neg p \rangle$ has a value, **true** or **false**, depending on the membership of p in $L(w)$. The graph has at most $2 \cdot |AP| \cdot |W|$ leaves. Intuitively, incomplete model checking corresponds to *shrinking* a boolean circuit part of whose inputs are known to an equivalent minimal circuit. The shrinking procedure (described in detail in the full version of this paper) replaces for example, an OR-gate one of whose successors is a leaf with value **true**, with a leaf with value **true**. In each iteration of the algorithm we assign values to half of the unassigned leaves of $G_{K,\varphi}$ and leave the other half unassigned. Recall that our average complexity is with respect to all assignments of q in K. Therefore, though we work with a specific Kripke structure, and the values assigned to half of the leaves are these induced by the Kripke structure, the average case corresponds to one in which we randomly assign to each unassigned leaf the value **true** with probability $\frac{1}{4}$, the value **false** with probability $\frac{1}{4}$, and leave it unassigned with probability $\frac{1}{2}$. The complexity described in Theorem 1 then follows from the following result from circuit complexity.

Theorem 2. *Boolean circuits shrink by at least the factor of ϵ under a random assignment that leaves the fraction of ϵ variables unassigned and assigns **true** or **false** to other variables with equal probability.*

Theorem 2 follows from the fact that boolean circuits for parity and co-parity, which are the most "shrink-resistant" circuits (shrinking a parity or co-parity circuit according to a random partial assignment to the variables results in a parity or a co-parity circuit for the remaining variables), are linear in the number of their variables (see [Weg87,Nig90]). Let m be the size of the graph $G_{K,\varphi}$. By Theorem 2, incomplete model checking in depth i of the algorithm handles graphs of size $\frac{m}{2^i}$, and there are 2^i such graphs. Hence, the overall average running time is

$$O(m) + 2 \cdot O(m/2) + 4 \cdot O(m/4) + \ldots + 2^{\log |W|} \cdot O(1),$$

which is equal to $O(m \cdot \log|W|)$. Since m is $O(|K| \cdot |\varphi|)$, the $O(|K| \cdot |\varphi| \cdot \log|W|)$ complexity follows.

Remark 1. In fact, the algorithm usually performs better. First, since the graph $G_{K,\varphi}$ is induced by a top-down reasoning, it may not contain leaves for all $\langle w, q \rangle \in W \times \{q\}$. States w such that $\langle w, q \rangle$ does not exist in $G_{K,\varphi}$ are obviously not q-covered, and the algorithm indeed ignores them. In addition, note that in the first iteration of the algorithm (that is, the first shrinking of $G_{K,\varphi}$), the unassigned leaves are exactly all the leaves of $G_{K,\varphi}$ of the form $\langle w, q \rangle$, and all the other leaves have values. While we cannot apply Theorem 2 directly and get shrinkage with $\epsilon = \frac{1}{|AP|}$ for this case (this is since we defined the average performance of the algorithm with respect to random assignments to q only, and since $G_{K,\varphi}$ typically contains less than $|W| \cdot |AP|$ leaves), we can still expect significant shrinkage in this call.

The algorithm can be easily adjusted to handle multiple initial states, where we check whether the modification falsifies the specification in some initial state. A naive adjustment repeats the algorithm for each of the initial states. A better adjustment handles all the initial states together, say by adding a new single initial state with transitions to all the initial states, and replacing the specification φ by the specification $AX\varphi$.

4   Presentation of the Output

Once we found the parts of the system that are not covered, there are several ways to make use of this information. For a circuit $\mathcal{S}$ and a signal x, let x-cover $(\mathcal{S}, \varphi)$ denote the set of states x-covered by φ in $\mathcal{S}$. One can compute x-cover$(\mathcal{S}, \varphi)$ for several output signals $x \in C \cup O$ (possibly, each of the properties that together compose the specification has a different set of signals that are of potential relevance to It). In [HKHZ99], coverage is defined as the ratio between the number of states that are members of x-cover $(\mathcal{S}, \varphi)$ for at least one signal x and the number of states in the design. This ratio indeed gives a good estimation to the part of the system that has been relevant for the verification process to succeed. In their implementation, Hoskote et al. also generate computations that lead to uncovered states.

We believe that once we worked hard and calculated x-cover$(\mathcal{S}, \varphi)$ for signals x, there are more helpful things that can be done with these sets. First, before merging x-covered sets for different signals, it is good to check whether x-cover $(\mathcal{S}, \varphi)$ is empty for some of the x's in isolation. An empty set may indicate vacuity in the specification (see also Section 5). In addition, we can use the sets x-cover$(\mathcal{S}, \varphi)$ in order to generate uncovered computations. Consider a state s of $\mathcal{S}$ that is not x-covered. The fact that s is not x-covered means that the specification fails to distinguish between $\mathcal{S}$ and the dual circuit $\tilde{\mathcal{S}}_{s,x}$. Therefore, possible errors caused by an erroneous value of x in s are not captured by the specification. So, a computation that contains the state s may be an interesting output. Even more interesting are computations that contain no covered states or many states that are not covered. Indeed, such computations correspond to behaviors of the circuit that are not referred to by the specification. Recall that the circuit models an open system. Thus, these computations are induced by input sequences that are ignored by the specification.

It is not hard to generate computations that consist of uncovered states only (if such computations exist) — we just have to restrict the transition function of S to uncovered states, which can also be done symbolically. In addition, computations that have many uncovered states can be found symbolically using the following greedy heuristic: we start from the initial state. Whenever we are in state s, we apply the *post* operator (given a set T of states, $post(T)$ returns the set of successors of states in T) until we encounter a set of states that contains an uncovered state, from which we continue. Alternatively, we can start with maximal computations consisting of uncovered states only, and connect them with transitions via covered states.

The above methodology can be applied also to the logic-based definition of coverage. Obviously, if we discover that a control signal x can be fixed to 1 or to 0 without violating the specification, this means that x is useless in the circuit according to the specification. This should not happen in a correct implementation of a complete specification. Therefore, a valuable output in this case is the list of uncovered control signals.

Recall that model-checking tools accompany a negative answer to the correctness query by a counterexample to the satisfaction of the specification. When model checking succeeds, we suggest to accompany the positive reply with two computations: one is the *interesting witness* of [BBER97], which describes a behavior of the system that cares about the satisfaction of all the subformulas of the specification. The second is a *non-interesting witness*: a computation that is not covered by the specification. We believe that both outputs are of great importance to the user. While the first describes some nontrivial correct behavior of the system, the second describes a possibly incorrect behavior of the system that escaped the verification efforts.

5   Discussion

In this section we briefly discuss some more aspects of coverage metrics for temporal logic model checking. An extended discussion can be found in the full version.

Definition of coverage metrics   There are several interesting possible relaxations of the definitions given in Section 2. One of them is allowing nondeterministic circuits. In nondeterministic circuits we can examine more coverage criteria: check the circuit obtained by merging s and $twin_x(s)$, check the circuit obtained by fixing a control signal to "don't care" (i.e., replace a transition to $\alpha \subseteq C$, with two transitions, to $\alpha \cup \{x\}$ and to $\alpha \setminus \{x\}$), etc. Another possibility is to allow different types of modifications in the system, for example flipping the value of q simultaneously in several states. Our definitions and algorithms can be easily modified to handle simultaneous modifications of the system. The corresponding algorithms, however, need to examine exponentially many modified systems and their complexity is much higher. Finally, we can think of δ as a function that maps the output signals to **true**, **false**, or *don't care*, thus allowing the designer to specify in advance that the values of certain signals are not important in some states. In this case we say that a system satisfies a specification φ if φ is satisfied no matter how q is assigned in states where its value is don't care. Our definitions of coverage apply also to designs with incomplete δ as above. Our algorithms can be easily adjusted to such designs.

Properties of coverage metrics The covered sets defined in Section 2 are *sensitive to abstraction*, in the sense that there is no correlation between the covered states in a system and its abstraction. From the other hand, the set of covered states is not sensitive to applying *cone of influence reduction*, where we abstract away parts of the systems that do not contain variables appearing in the specification or influence variables that appear in the specification [CGP99]. We also note that the notions of coverage and *vacuity* [BBER97,KV99] are closely related. Vacuity can be viewed as a coverage metric for the specification. Also, if there is a signal x that does not influence the satisfaction of φ in the system, then no state in the system is x-covered by φ. Our coverage metrics are *compositional*, in the sense that the intersection of the uncovered sets for the underlying conjuncts is equivalent to the uncovered set for their conjunction. Formally, if S_1 is the set of states not q-covered by φ_1 and S_2 is the set of states not q-covered by φ_2, then $S_1 \cap S_2$ is the set of states not q-covered by $\varphi_1 \wedge \varphi_2$. On the other hand, the coverage criteria defined in [KGG99], as well as the covered sets found by the algorithm in [HKHZ99] are not compositional.

There are still several open issues in the adoption of coverage metrics to temporal logic model checking. For example, it is not clear whether and how a coverage metric that aims at checking incompleteness of the specification should be different from a metric that aims at finding redundancies in the system. Another issue is the feasibility of coverage algorithms. While the algorithms that we presented have better complexity that the naive algorithm, their complexity is still larger than model checking. This may prevent a wide use of coverage metrics for temporal logic in formal verification. Clearly, there is room for improving the current algorithms, as well as searching for the new ones both for CTL and for other temporal logics, in particular LTL logic. Finally, while it is clear that outputs as these described in Section 4 are very helpful to the user, it is not clear whether high coverage is something one should seek for. Indeed, there is a trade-off between complete and abstract specifications, and neither completeness nor abstraction has clear priority.

Acknowledgment We thank Orna Grumberg, Yatin Hoskote, Amir Pnueli, and Uri Zwick for helpful discussions.

References

BB94.   D. Beaty and R. Bryant. Formally verifying a microprocessor using a simulation methodology. In *Proc. 31st DAC*, pp. 596–602. IEEE Computer Society, 1994.

BBER97. I. Beer, S. Ben-David, C. Eisner, and Y. Rodeh. Efficient detection of vacuity in ACTL formulas. In *Proc. 9th CAV, LNCS* 1254, pp. 279–290, 1997.

BCG88.   M.C. Browne, E.M. Clarke, and O. Grumberg. Characterizing finite Kripke structures in propositional temporal logic. *Theoretical Computer Science*, 59:115–131, 1988.

BH99.   J.P. Bergmann and M.A. Horowitz. Improving coverage analysis and test generation for large designs. In *IEEE Int. Conf. for CAD*, pp. 580–584, 1999.

CE81.   E.M. Clarke and E.A. Emerson. Design and synthesis of synchronization skeletons using branching time temporal logic. In *Proc. Workshop on Logic of Programs, LNCS* 131, pp. 52–71. Springer-Verlag, 1981.

CGMZ95. E.M. Clarke, O. Grumberg, K.L. McMillan, and X. Zhao. Efficient generation of counterexamples and witnesses in symbolic model checking. In *Proc. 32nd DAC*, pp. 427–432. IEEE Computer Society, 1995.

CGP99. E.M. Clarke, O. Grumberg, and D. Peled. *Model Checking*. MIT Press, 1999.

CK93. K.-T. Cheng and A. Krishnakumar. Automatic functional test generation using the extended finite state machine model. In *Proc. 30th DAC*, pp. 86–91, 1993.

DGK96. S. Devadas, A. Ghosh, and K. Keutzer. An observability-based code coverage metric for functional simulation. In *Proc. CAD*, pp. 418–425, 1996.

Eme90. E.A. Emerson. Temporal and modal logic. *Handbook of Theoretical Computer Science*, pp. 997–1072, 1990.

FAD99. F. Fallah, P. Ashar, and S. Devadas. Simulation vector generation from hdl descriptions for observability enhanced-statement coverage. In *Proc. 36th DAC*, pp. 666–671, 1999.

FDK98. F. Fallah, S. Devadas, and K. Keutzer. OCCOM: Efficient Computation of Observability-Based Code Coverage Metrics for Functional Simulation. In *Proc. 35th DAC*, pp. 152–157, 1998.

HH96. R.C. Ho and M.A. Horowitz. Validation coverage analysis for complex digital designs. In *Proc. CAD*, pp. 146–151, 1996.

HKHZ99. Y. Hoskote, T. Kam, P.-H Ho, and X. Zhao. Coverage estimation for symbolic model checking. In *Proc. 36th DAC*, pp. 300–305, 1999.

HMA95. Y. Hoskote, D. Moundanos, and J. Abraham. Automatic extraction of the control flow machine and application to evaluating coverage of verification vectors. In *Proc. ICDD*, pp. 532–537, 1995.

Hoa85. C.A.R. Hoare. *Communicating Sequential Processes*. Prentice-Hall, 1985.

HP85. D. Harel and A. Pnueli. On the development of reactive systems. *NATO Advanced Summer Institutes*, volume F-13, pp. 477–498. Springer-Verlag, 1985.

HS96. G.D. Hachtel and F. Somenzi. *Logic Synthesis and Verification Algorithms*. Kluwer Academic Publishers, MA, 1996.

HYHD95. R. Ho, C. Yang, M. Horowitz, and D. Dill. Architecture validation for processors. In *Proc. of the 22nd Annual Symp. on Comp. Arch.*, pp. 404–413, 1995.

KGG99. S. Katz, D. Geist, and O. Grumberg. "Have I written enough properties ?" a method of comparison between specification and implementation. In *10th CHARME, LNCS* 1703, pp. 280-297. Springer-Verlag, 1999.

KN96. M. Kantrowitz and L. Noack. I'm done simulating: Now what? verification coverage analysis and correctness checking of the dec chip 21164 alpha microprocessor. In *Proc. of DAC*, pp. 325–330, 1996.

Kur98. R.P. Kurshan. *FormalCheck User's Manual*. Cadence Design, Inc., 1998.

KV99. O. Kupferman and M.Y. Vardi. Vacuity detection in temporal model checking. In *10th CHARME, LNCS* 1703. pp. 82-96, Springer-Verlag, 1999.

KVW00. O. Kupferman, M.Y. Vardi, and P. Wolper. An automata-theoretic approach to branching-time model checking. *Journal of the ACM*, 47(2):312–360, 2000.

LP85. O. Lichtenstein and A. Pnueli. Checking that finite state concurrent programs satisfy their linear specification. In *Proc. 12th POPL*, pp. 97–107, 1985.

MAH98. D. Moumdanos, J.A. Abraham, and Y.V. Hoskote. Abstraction techniques for validation coverage analysis and test generation. *IEEE Trans. on Computers*, 1998.

MP92. Z. Manna and A. Pnueli. *The Temporal Logic of Reactive and Concurrent Systems: Specification*. Springer-Verlag, 1992.

Nig90. R. G. Nigmatulin. *The Complexity of Boolean Functions*. Nauka, Main Editorial Board for Phys. and Math. Lit., Moscow, 1990.

QS81. J.P. Queille and J. Sifakis. Specification and verification of concurrent systems in Cesar. In *Proc. 5th Int. Symp. on Progr., LNCS* 137, pp. 337–351. Springer-Verlag, 1981.

Weg87. I. Wegener. *The Complexity of Boolean Functions*. John Wiley & Sons, 1987.

Parallel Model Checking for the Alternation Free μ-Calculus

Benedikt Bollig, Martin Leucker, and Michael Weber

Lehrstuhl für Informatik II, RWTH Aachen, Germany
{bollig, leucker, michaelw}@i2.informatik.rwth-aachen.de

Abstract. In this paper, we describe the design and implementation of a parallel model checking algorithm for the alternation free fragment of the μ-calculus. It exploits a characterisation of the model checking problem for this fragment in terms of two–person games. Our algorithm determines the corresponding winner in parallel. It is designed to run on a network of workstations. An implementation within the verification tool TRUTH shows promising results.

1 Introduction

Model checking is becoming more and more popular for the verification of complex hardware and software systems. These systems are usually given by a formal description which can be transformed into a transition system. A desired property of the system, on the other hand, is usually specified as a formula of a temporal logic. A model checking algorithm answers the question whether the (transition) system satisfies this property. Numerous case studies have shown that this approach improves the early detection of errors [3].

Despite the developments in the last years, the so–called *state space explosion* still limits its application. While *partial order reduction* [20] or *symbolic model checking* [17] reduce the state space by orders of magnitude, typical verification tasks still last days on a single workstation or are even (practically) undecidable due to memory restrictions (see for example [7]).

On the other hand, cheap yet powerful parallel computers can be constructed of Networks Of Workstations (*NOW*s). From the outside, a NOW appears as one single parallel computer with high computing power and, even more important, huge amounts of memory. This enables parallel programs to utilise the accumulated resources of a NOW to solve large problems. Hence, it is a fundamental goal to find parallel model checking algorithms which then may be combined with well–known techniques to avoid the state space explosion gaining even more speedup and further reducing memory requirements.

A famous logic for expressing specifications is Kozen's μ–calculus [11], a temporal logic offering boolean combination of formulae and, especially, labelled *next*–state, minimal, and maximal fixpoint quantifiers. For practical applications, however, it suffices to restrict the μ-calculus in order to gain tractable model checking procedures. The alternation free fragment, denoted by L_μ^1, prohibits the nesting of minimal and maximal fixpoint operators. It allows the formulation of many *safety* as well as *liveness* properties. While this fragment is already

T. Margaria and W. Yi (Eds.): TACAS 2001, LNCS 2031, pp. 543–558, 2001.
© Springer-Verlag Berlin Heidelberg 2001

important on its own, it subsumes the logic CTL [6] which is employed in many practical verification tools. It can be shown that the model checking problem for this fragment is linear in the length of the formula as well as the size of the underlying transition system, and, starting with [4], several sequential model checking procedures are given in the literature (see [13] for a comparison). The algorithms can be classified into *global* and *local* algorithms. Global algorithms require the underlying transition system to be completely constructed while local algorithms compute the necessary part of a transition system *on-the-fly*. In plain words, global algorithms typically compute the fixpoints in an inductive manner while the local algorithms decide the problem by a depth–first–search. [13] compares the algorithms in detail.

Before starting to think about a concrete algorithm, we should consider its limitations, i.e. its complexity. In complexity theory it is a well–accepted view that problems within the class NC admit a promising parallel computing algorithm. NC is based on the Boolean circuit model for computation and describes the problems computable in polylogarithmic time with polynomially many processors. It can be shown that NC is contained in P. Problems outside of NC are consequently considered to be inherently sequential. However, it is not known whether NC=P. If not, then especially P–complete problems cannot be in NC. Hence, we call P–complete problems *inherently sequential* [8].

We show that model checking L^1_μ is inherently sequential, limiting our enthusiasm for finding a (theoretically) good parallel model checking algorithm. Even worse, depth–first-search is also P–complete, hence, promising parallel local algorithms are unlikely to exist [21]. Despite these theoretical limitations, we present a parallel global model checking algorithm. We implemented it within our verification tool TRUTH [14] and found out that it behaves very well for many practical problems.

Our algorithm is based on a characterisation of the model checking problem for this fragment in terms of two–person games due to Stirling [24]. Strictly speaking, we present a parallel algorithm for colouring so–called game graphs corresponding to the underlying model checking problem. This colouring answers the model checking problem and allows a derivation of a winning strategy. The latter may be employed by the user of a verification tool for debugging the underlying system interactively [24].

Another characterisation of this model checking problem can be given in terms of so–called 1–simple–weak–alternating–Büchi automata [12]. However, these correspond to game–based model checking [16]. Hence, our algorithm can also be used for checking the emptiness of these automata in parallel.

Until today, not much effort has been taken to consider parallel model checking algorithms. [25,1] present parallelised data structures which employ further computers within a network as a substitute for external storage. The algorithms described in [19,2] divide the underlying problem into several tasks. However, they are designed in the way that only a single computer can be employed to sequentially handle one task at a time. Stern and Dill [23] show how to carry out a parallel reachability analysis. The distribution of the underlying structure is similar to the one presented here. But their algorithm is not suitable for model checking temporal logic formulae. [9] presents a parallel reachability analysis algorithm for BDDs. They argue that many safety properties can be formulated as a reachability problem. In this way, their algorithm allows checking safety formulae. However, *liveness* properties which can be expressed within L_μ^1 are not supported. Furthermore, [10] argues that explicit state representation as well as BDDs have application domains in which they outperform the other one. Moreover, BDD–based algorithms generally do not provide counter examples, which are important in practice. Our main contribution is the first parallel model checking algorithm for L_μ^1 that supports interactive debugging.

The syntax and semantics of the μ–calculus are introduced in the next section. Furthermore, it is shown that L_μ^1 is inherently sequential. In Section 3, we describe model checking games for the μ–calculus and provide an important characterisation of the game graph which will be the basis for our parallel algorithm. Section 4 discusses our parallel model checking procedure and is followed by experimental results. We conclude by summing up our approach as well as giving directions for future work.

2 The μ-Calculus

In this section, we recall the syntax and semantics of the (modal) μ-calculus and its alternation free fragment. Furthermore, we show that model checking this fragment is inherently sequential.

2.1 Syntax and Semantics

Let *Var* be a set of variables and $\mathcal{A}$ a set of actions. Formulae of the modal μ–calculus over *Var* and $\mathcal{A}$ in positive form as introduced by [11] are defined as

$$\varphi ::= \texttt{false} \mid \texttt{true} \mid X \mid \varphi_1 \wedge \varphi_2 \mid \varphi_1 \vee \varphi_2 \mid [K]\varphi \mid \langle K \rangle \varphi \mid \nu X.\varphi \mid \mu X.\varphi$$

where $X \in Var$ and K ranges over subsets of actions $\mathcal{A}$. Like [24], we allow sets of actions instead of single actions appearing in modalities.[1] It is a simple exercise to extend our approach towards the propositional μ–calculus (cf. Section 4).

A formula φ is *normal* if every occurrence of a binder μX or νX in φ binds a distinct variable, and no free variable X in φ is also used in a binder μX or νX. Every formula can easily be converted into an equivalent normal formula. If a formula φ is normal, every bound variable X of φ *identifies* a unique subformula $\mu X.\psi$ or $\nu X.\psi$ of φ where X is a free variable of ψ.

Let $\mathcal{T} = (S, T, \mathcal{A}, s_0)$ be a *labelled transition system* where S is a finite set of states, $\mathcal{A}$ a set of actions, and $T \subseteq S \times \mathcal{A} \times S$ denotes the transitions. As usual, we write $s \xrightarrow{a} t$ instead of $(s, a, t) \in T$. Furthermore, let $s_0 \in S$ be the *initial state* of the transition system. We employ valuations V mapping a variable X to a set of states $V(X) \subseteq S$. Let $V[X/E]$, $E \subseteq S$, be the valuation which is the same as V except for X where $V(X) = E$. Given a labelled transition system

---

[1] $\langle - \rangle \varphi$ is an abbreviation for $\langle \mathcal{A} \rangle \varphi$.

$\mathcal{T} = (S, T, \mathcal{A}, s_0)$ and a formula φ over Var and $\mathcal{A}$, the satisfaction of φ wrt. $\mathcal{T}$ and a state $s \in S$ is defined for **true**, **false**, disjunction, and conjunction in the usual way, and for the temporal and fixpoint operators as follows:

$\mathcal{T}, s \models_V [K]\varphi$ iff $\forall a \in K$: if $s \overset{a}{\to} t$ then $\mathcal{T}, t \models_V \varphi$

$\mathcal{T}, s \models_V \langle K\rangle\varphi$ iff $\exists a \in K$: $s \overset{a}{\to} t$ and $\mathcal{T}, t \models_V \varphi$

$\mathcal{T}, s \models_V \mu X.\varphi$ iff $\forall E \subseteq S$: if $s \notin E$ then $\exists t \in S : t \notin E$ and $\mathcal{T}, t \models_{V[X/E]} \varphi$

$\mathcal{T}, s \models_V \nu X.\varphi$ iff $\exists E \subseteq S, s \in E$: and $\forall t \in E : \mathcal{T}, t \models_{V[X/E]} \varphi$

We shorten $\mathcal{T}, s \models_V \varphi$ by $\mathcal{T}, s \models \varphi$ for a formula φ without any free variables and $\mathcal{T}, s_0 \models_V \varphi$ by $\mathcal{T} \models_V \varphi$ and use identifiers like $\varphi, \psi, \ldots$ for formulae, $s, t, \ldots$ for states, and $a, b, \ldots$ for actions of the transition system under consideration. K denotes a set of actions. Whenever the sort of the fixpoint does not matter, we use σ for either μ or ν. For a formula of the μ–calculus, we introduce the notion of *subformulae* and *free* and *bound* variables as usual.

The *alternation free fragment* of the μ–calculus is that sublogic of the μ–calculus where no subformula ψ of a formula φ contains both a free variable X bound by a μX in φ as well as a free variable Y bound by a νY in φ.

Given a labelled transition system $\mathcal{T}$ and a formula φ, *model checking* is the problem whether $\mathcal{T}$ satisfies φ, i.e. whether $\mathcal{T} \models \varphi$. The *combined complexity* of the model checking problem is its complexity wrt. the product of the size of the transition system and the size of the formula. Its *program complexity* considers the complexity only wrt. the size of the transition system.

In [26], it was shown that the combined complexity for the alternation free μ–calculus is P–complete and, for a version of the alternation free μ–calculus employing two actions, that its program complexity is P–complete. [12] shows the latter result by using a formula with two propositions. We strengthen both results by employing neither propositions nor any action labelling.

Lemma 1. *The program complexity of the alternation free μ–calculus is P–hard.*

Proof. We reduce the P–complete *Game Problem* [8] to checking a formula of the alternation free μ–calculus wrt. a corresponding labelled transition system. A two player game is a tuple $G = (P_1, P_2, M, W_0, s)$. P_1 and P_2, $P_1 \cap P_2 = \emptyset$, are positions, in which it is the turn of Player 1 or Player 2, resp. $M \subseteq (P_1 \times P_2) \cup (P_2 \times P_1)$ is the set of moves the respective player can make. $W_0 \subseteq P_1 \cup P_2$ denotes the *succeeding positions*, $s \in P_1$ the *starting position*. The players move alternately beginning with Player 1. We call $x \in P_1 \cup P_2$ *winning* iff either x is succeeding ($x \in W_0$), or $x \in P_1$ and there is a winning $y \in P_2$ such that $(x, y) \in M$, or $x \in P_2$ and for all $(x, y) \in M$, y is winning. The Game Problem is the question whether s is winning.

Corresponding to this, we define a transition system $\mathcal{T}_G = (P_1 \cup P_2, T)$ by $T = (M - \{(p, q) \in M \mid p \in W_0\}) \cup \{(p, p) \in P_1 \times P_1 \mid p \notin W_0$ and there is no transition from p in $M\}$.

T is defined in the way that every deadlock state, i.e. state with no outgoing edges, is a state of W_0 or a state of P_2 in which Player 2 is not able to move. Hence, deadlocks are winning. They can be characterised in the μ-calculus by $\varphi_{W_0} = [-]\mathbf{false}$ where a formula $[-]\varphi$ indicates that φ is satisfied in all successor states, Further winning positions for Player 1 are states of P_1 such that there is a successor state (in P_2) whose direct successors (in P_1) are all winning. Hence, the formula $\varphi = \mu X.(\langle - \rangle [-] X \vee \varphi_{W_0})$ is satisfied in exactly those positions of P_1 which are winning where $\langle - \rangle \varphi$ guarantees the existence of a successor state in which φ holds. Note that φ may be satisfied in further positions of P_2 which does not bother us. We conclude that s is winning in the game $G = (P_1, P_2, M, W_0, s)$ iff $\mathcal{T}_G, s \models \varphi$. Observe that the construction of the transition system can be done in LOGSPACE. Note, we do not make use of propositions. Furthermore, we manage without actions at all by slightly adapting the modal fragment of our logic.

Together with a lineartime algorithm [12,13], we have the following theorem:

Theorem 1. *Model checking the alternation free μ-calculus is inherently sequential wrt. the combined complexity as well as the program complexity.*

3 Games for the μ–Calculus

Given a labelled transition system $\mathcal{T} = (S, T, \mathcal{A}, s_0)$ and a formula φ over *Var* and $\mathcal{A}$, we are able to define the *model checking game*. Its board is the Cartesian product $S \times Sub(\varphi)$ of the set of states and the set of subformulae. The game is played by two players, namely ∀belard (the pessimist), who wants to show that $\mathcal{T}, s_0 \models \varphi$ does *not* hold, whereas ∃loise (the optimist) wants to show the opposite.

The model checking game $G(s, \varphi)$ is given by all its *plays*, i.e. (possibly infinite) sequences $C_0 \rightarrow_{p_0} C_1 \rightarrow_{p_1} C_2 \rightarrow_{p_2} \ldots$ of *configurations*, where $C_0 = (s, \varphi)$ and for all i, $C_i \in S \times Sub(\varphi)$ and p_i is either ∃loise or ∀belard. We write $\rightarrow$ instead of $\rightarrow_{p_i}$ if we abstract from the player. The players do not have to move alternately, instead, the next turn is determined by the current subformula of φ. Hence, the second component of a configuration C_i determines the player p_i who is to choose the next move. ∀belard makes universal $\rightarrow_\forall$-moves, ∃loise makes existential $\rightarrow_\exists$-moves. More precisely, whenever

1. $C_i = (s, \mathtt{false})$, then the play is finished.
2. $C_i = (s, \psi_1 \wedge \psi_2)$, then ∀belard chooses $\varphi = \psi_1$ or $\varphi = \psi_2$, and $C_{i+1} = (s, \varphi)$.
3. $C_i = (s, [K]\psi)$, then ∀belard chooses $s \xrightarrow{a} t$ with $a \in K$ and $C_{i+1} = (t, \psi)$.
4. $C_i = (s, \nu X.\psi)$, then $C_{i+1} = (s, \psi)$.
5. $C_i = (s, \mathtt{true})$, then the play is finished.
6. $C_i = (s, \psi_1 \vee \psi_2)$, then ∃loise chooses $\varphi = \psi_1$ or $\varphi = \psi_2$, and $C_{i+1} = (s, \varphi)$.
7. $C_i = (s, \langle K \rangle \psi)$, then ∃loise chooses $s \xrightarrow{a} t$ with $a \in K$ and $C_{i+1} = (t, \psi)$.
8. $C_i = (s, \mu X.\psi)$, then $C_{i+1} = (s, \psi)$.
9. $C_i = (s, X)$ and X identifies φ, then $C_{i+1} = (s, \varphi)$.

As the moves 1,4,5,8 and 9 are deterministic, no player needs to be charged with them. With regard to the winning strategies and the algorithm, we will speak of ∀*belard-moves* in cases 1–4 and 9 if $\sigma = \mu$, and ∃*loise-moves* in all other cases. C_i is called ∀–configuration or ∃–configuration, respectively. ∀belard wins a play G, iff

- $G = C_0 \rightarrow \cdots \rightarrow C_n$ and $C_n = (s, \texttt{false})$ for any state s.
- $G = C_0 \rightarrow \cdots \rightarrow C_n$ and $C_n = (s, \langle K \rangle \varphi)$ and $\nexists t : s \xrightarrow{a} t$ for any $a \in K$.
- $G = C_0 \rightarrow \cdots$ has infinite length and the outermost fixpoint which is unwinded infinitely often is a μ-fixpoint.

Dually, $\exists$loise wins a play G, iff a configuration with the formula $\texttt{true}$ is reached, $\forall$belard gets "stuck", or the outermost fixpoint which is unwinded infinitely often is a ν-fixpoint [24].

Please note that, given a transition system and a formula, there are several plays and these not necessarily have the same winner.

To characterise plays, we introduce the notion of witnesses and judgements. Configurations C in which no move is possible are called *judgements*. A judgement is further called $\exists$–judgement ($\forall$–judgement) iff it is an $\exists$–configuration ($\forall$–configuration). For finite plays, it is obvious that $\exists$loise ($\forall$belard) wins the play iff it contains an $\exists$–judgement ($\forall$–judgement).

Configurations of the form (s, X) where s is any state of the transition system and X is a variable are called *witnesses* since in the following move, X is unwinded. If X is bound by a μ–quantifier, it is called an $\forall$–witness, otherwise $\exists$–witness. Witnesses have a natural partial order given by the nesting within the originating formula. A witness (s, X) is less than (s, Y) iff $\sigma X. \varphi(X, Y)$ is a subformula of $\sigma' Y. \psi(X, Y)$ where $\eta(X, Y)$ means that η may contain the free variables X, Y. For infinite plays, it is easy to see that it has a unique maximal witness and that the winning condition can be formulated as *$\forall$belard wins iff this witness is an $\forall$–witness, $\exists$loise wins iff it is an $\exists$–witness*. Please note that no configuration can be a judgement as well as a witness.

A *strategy* is a set of rules for a Player p telling her or him how to move in the current configuration. A *winning strategy* now guarantees that the play which p plays regarding the rules will be won by p. [24] shows that the model checking problem for the μ–calculus is equivalent to finding a winning strategy for one of the players: Let $\mathcal{T}$ be a transition system with starting state s, and let φ be a μ–calculus formula. $\mathcal{T}, s \models \varphi$ implies that $\exists$loise has a winning strategy starting at (s, φ), and $\mathcal{T}, s \not\models \varphi$ implies that $\forall$belard has a winning strategy starting at (s, φ). Since a formula either holds or is falsified, this result also implies that model checking games are *determined,* i.e., for every game, either $\forall$belard or $\exists$loise has a winning strategy.

All possible plays for a transition system $\mathcal{T}$ and a formula φ are captured in the *game graph* whose nodes are the elements of the game board (the possible configurations) and whose edges are the players' possible moves. The game graph can be understood as an *and-/or-graph* where the *or*–nodes (denoted by $\bigvee$) are $\exists$–configurations and *and*–nodes (denoted by $\bigwedge$) are $\forall$–configurations. Furthermore, the notion of witnesses and judgements carries over without any modification. A play corresponds to a path in the game graph and vice versa.

In the following, we concentrate on the alternation free μ–calculus. The following characterisation of the game graph for this fragment is useful for formulating a sequential algorithm and essential for our parallel algorithm.

Theorem 2. *Let $\mathcal{T}$ be a labelled transition system and φ a formula of the alternation free μ-calculus. Furthermore, let (Q, E) be their game graph. Then there exists a collection of $Q_1, \ldots, Q_m$ such that the following holds:*

1. *the collection of the Q_i is a partition of Q, i.e., $Q = \bigcup_{i \in \{1, \ldots, m\}} Q_i$ and for all $i, j \in \{1, \ldots, m\}$ with $i \neq j$, it holds $Q_i \cap Q_j = \emptyset$.*
2. *The subgraph induced by Q_i is exactly one of*
   (a) a non-trivial maximal strongly connected component (Type I).[2]
   (b) a singleton containing a judgement (Type II).
   (c) a maximal directed acyclic graph without any judgements (Type III).
3. *every Q_i of Type I either contains at least one $\exists$-witness and no $\forall$-witnesses or contains at least one $\forall$-witness and no $\exists$-witnesses.*
4. *there is a partial order $\leq$ on the Q_i's such that for every $q \in Q_i$ and $q' \in Q_j$ with an edge from q to q', we have $Q_j \leq Q_i$. Thus, moves from a configuration in Q_i lead to configurations in either the same Q_i or a lower Q_j.*

Proof. The proof is inspired by a characterisation of the game graph in terms of weak alternating automata [16]. First, consider the nodes of maximal non-trivial strongly connected components. These only occur because of unwinding fixpoint formulae. Hence, they contain witnesses. Alternation freeness now guarantees that these are all of the same kind, i.e. either $\exists$-witnesses or $\forall$-witnesses. Second, consider the leaves of the game graph, i.e. configurations without outgoing edges. These cannot be members of strongly connected components of Type I. By definition, every such Q_i is a judgement. Third, it is now easy to see that all remaining nodes belong to directed acyclic graphs which do not contain any leaves of the original game graph. Please note that maximality of the strongly connected components guarantees the order defined to be a partial order.

To prove our parallel algorithm to be free from deadlock, we need the following insight which holds since on every cycle, a fixpoint formula is unwinded.

Proposition 1. *Every strongly connected component of a game graph with more than one element contains at least one witness.*

Let us sketch a sequential algorithm deciding which player has a winning strategy [12]. It labels a configuration q by *green* or *red*, depending on whether $\exists$loise or $\forall$belard has a winning strategy for the game starting in this configuration q. It will be extended to a parallel version in the next section.

Let us consider a game graph. By Theorem 2, there exists a partition of its nodes Q into disjoint Q_i of Type I–III, and every Q_i of Type I either contains $\exists$-witnesses or $\forall$-witnesses. Also, there exists a partial order $\leq$ on the Q_i such that for $q \in Q_i$ and $q' \in Q_j$ for which there is a possible move from q to q', we have $Q_j \leq Q_i$. As seen before, every infinite play gets trapped within a single Q_i, and the winner depends on whether Q_i contains $\exists$-witnesses or $\forall$-witnesses. By Prop. 1, every infinite play visits such a witness infinitely often.

The game graph can be coloured by processing all Q_i upwards according to the partial order. To make the algorithm deterministic, enlarge the partial order

---

[2] A component is called non-trivial if it contains a least two nodes.

on the Q_i to a total order. Let Q_i be minimal wrt. $\leq$. Then it is of Type I or Type II. Furthermore, from any configuration of Q_i, every move leads to Q_i. If in Q_i there is an $\exists$–witness or Q_i consists of an $\exists$–judgement, all its nodes are labelled with *green*, otherwise *red*.

Once a configuration $q \in Q_i$ is labelled with *red* or *green*, its predecessors are labelled if possible. That means, an $\wedge$–node is labelled with *red* if q is *red*, but labelled *green*, if all successors are *green*. An $\vee$–node is treated dually. Furthermore, if a node could be labelled, its outgoing edges are erased. Such labelling is propagated further.

Let Q_j be the next set of configurations wrt. the total order. Then, all configurations in $Q_i \leq Q_j$ are already coloured by either *red* or *green*. If Q_j is of Type III, all of its configurations must be labelled due to the propagation described before. For a set of Type I, some unlabelled configurations might remain. These are labelled according to the type of witnesses in Q_j, i.e. with *red* if Q_j has $\forall$–witnesses, otherwise with *green*.

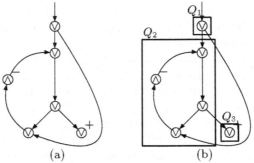

Fig. 1. State graph (a) and its partition (b)

Let us consider Figure 1. Part (b) is a partition of the game graph shown in (a). It contains components of types I, II, and III. Q_1 is a directed acyclic graph, Q_2 a non–trivial maximal strongly connected component, and Q_3 is a singleton containing a $\exists$–judgement (denoted by $^+$). The components can be ordered like $Q_3 < Q_2 < Q_1$. Since the minimal Q_3 contains an $\exists$–judgement, it will be labelled with *green*. The $\vee$–node from Q_2 to Q_3 and subsequently all nodes will therefore be labelled with *green* as well. Note how the $\forall$–witness (denoted by $^-$) has no influence here, since all nodes are coloured already.

4   Parallel Model Checking

Given a transition system and an L_μ^1–formula, our approach is both to construct the game graph as well as to determine the colour of its nodes in parallel.

4.1   Distributing the Game Graph

It is obvious that the construction of the game graph can be carried out in parallel by a typical breadth–first strategy. Given a node q, determine its successors $q_1, \ldots, q_n$. Now, the successors can be processed in the same manner in parallel.

However, to obtain a terminating procedure, only exactly the q_i *not* processed before must be expanded. All states generated have to be stored within the NOW, and load sharing m ust be guaranteed. On a shared memory arc hitecture, this does not involve big conceptual problems. For distributed memory mac hines, however, this is a little bit more difficult.

A first idea might be to distribute the first $q_1, \ldots, q_n$ to the first n processors, and these process the q_i as described before and distribute the successors to the next processors. However, deciding whether a q_i was processed before becomes an expensive operation. Every processor could have processed q_i and should therefore be consulted. In the worst case, for every node, such a broadcast is required. This yields no reasonable algorithm.

A different, often–employed way to store graphs on a distributed memory machine is to divide the graph's adjacency matrix $M \in \{0,1\}^{|V| \times |V|}$ into equal sized *blocks* and to store each block on a single processor [22]. This has several advantages. First, the blocks of the matrix can be generated in parallel. Second, given nodes $p, q \in V$, it is easy to check whether there is an edge from p to q, i.e. whether $M_{p,q} = 1$. Since there is a unique location for the block of the matrix containing the value for the pair (p, q), a single comm unication is needed. Third, every processor gets the same amoun t of data.

For our problem, this approach cannot be used. The num ber of nodes of our graph is unknown a priori but computed while constructing the graph.[3] Hence, the partition of the game graph in to blocks cannot be determined in advance.

W e propose the following way to construct and store the graph which is inspired by the work pool presentation of [15] and is similarly applied in [23]. Let f be a function mapping the states of the game graph to a processor of our net work. Usually, one takes a function in the spirit of a hash function assigning to every state an integer and subsequently its value modulo the number of processors. Then, f determines the location of every state within the network uniquely and without global knowledge. In a breadth–first manner, starting with the initial state q_0 of the game graph, the state space can be constructed in parallel with the help of f in the following way. Given a state q (and possibly some of its direct predecessors), send it to its processor $f(q)$. If q is already in the local store of $f(q)$, then q is reached a second time, hence the procedure stops. If predecessors of q were sent together with q, the list of predecessors is augmen ted accordingly. If q is not in the local memory of $f(q)$, it is stored there together with the given predecessors as well as all its successors $q_1, \ldots, q_k$, the states within the formula $\delta(q, a)$ which are computed. These are sent in the same manner to their (wrt. f) processors, together with the information that q is a direct predecessor. The corresponding processes update their local memory similarly .

4.2   Labelling the Game Graph

Given the game graph, a first possibility for labelling the nodes with *red* and *green* would be to apply a depth–first–search as done by sequential algorithms.

---

[3] In the context of model checking, the transition system is not given explicitly but expanded at run–time from a formal system description.

However, since this problem is P–complete [21], there is no hope to get a suitable parallel algorithm by adapting the ideas of depth–first–search, and there is no reason to do this.

Another possibility for labelling the nodes with *red* and *green* is applying typical algorithms for generating strongly connected components of our game graph in parallel which will be labelled in a second step [22]. However, labelling a connected component requires the knowledge whether the component can be "successfully abandoned" (cf. Section 3). It is neither clear how to obtain this information from the graph computed by these algorithms nor to modify these algorithms in the way that this information can be gathered easily.

We therefore propose the following method. The parallel colouring process is carried out *speculative*. For example, given an $\exists$–witness q, it determines an accepting component. This node is coloured *green* unless there is an $\bigwedge$–node with an edge to a lower component which is coloured *red*. The parallel algorithm, however, labels the witness q with *green*. Furthermore, a notification is sent to its direct predecessors $q_1, \ldots, q_k$. This notification tells each q_i that q changed its colour. Hence, they recompute their own colour according to the following obvious rule: If q_i is an $\bigvee$–node, then it is labelled with *green* if one of its successors is *green*. If all successors are *red*, it is labelled with *red*. Otherwise, some successors have no label yet and no colour is assigned to the current node. For an $\bigwedge$–node, the dual is carried out. If the colour of q_i has changed, it sends a notification to its predecessors where the same procedure starts again. Otherwise, the procedure is done. It is clear that the predecessors can be processed in parallel. The whole algorithm stops if all notifications are processed.

Theorem 3. *The algorithm described before labels a node* (s, ψ) *of the game graph with green if* $\mathcal{T}, s \models \psi$. *Otherwise, the node is labelled with red.*

Proof. We give a sketch of the proof. The *termination* of the algorithm can easily be seen by recalling that the game graph can be divided into components as aforementioned which are partially ordered. Labelling notifications are sent either within the current component or propagated to a higher one (wrt. the partial order). Since the colour operation is monotone (in the obvious sense), only a finite number of labelling notifications is generated.

When the algorithm terminates, the game graph is entirely labelled (*completeness*), because the components are either leaves (in which case they are labelled as described before), they contain a witness (cf. Proposition 1), in which case the speculative part of the algorithm jumps in and starts the labelling of this component, or completely depend on a lower component.

The sequential algorithm labels the nodes with a correct colour by processing the mentioned components according to the partial order. The labelling remains *correct* if the labelling of higher (wrt. the partial order) components is done speculative and corrected as soon as the correct colour of the lower component is determined. Note that the colour of *leaves* and *leaf components* (i.e. components which are minimal for the partial order) are correctly labelled from the beginning.

It should be mentioned that for an implementation, the two steps of constructing the game graph and labelling the nodes are carried out concurrently (cf. Section 4.3). The combined algorithm stops if no further labelling or state expansion steps have to be processed. For this task, we employ the DFG token termination algorithm, as presented in [5]. Due to space constraints, we will not go into the details of this algorithm.

4.3   The Algorithm

To describe our approach in more detail, we show an algorithm in *pseudo code* which combines the task of constructing and labelling the game graph in parallel. The termination check is omitted to simplify the presentation. This algorithm runs on every machine within the NOW. Note that initially one machine has to send the root of the game graph to its processor to start the procedure.

Let us consider Figure 2. Each processor's part of the graph is stored there in a relational structure consisting of one tuple for every node already processed of the form (**node, colour, preds, succs**) where **node** is the node together with its **colour**, its predecessors **preds**, and its successors together with their colours (**succs**, line 3). We introduce the colour *white* to denote unlabelled nodes. In line 7, a message is received. If the message requests to expand a given node, it is checked whether this node has already been processed before (line 10). If so, it might have a colour (not equal to *white*) which will be propagated to the new predecessors (lines 12–13). In any case, new predecessors are stored (line 11). If the delivered node has not been processed before (line 14), its successors are computed (with an initially *white* colour) and propagated to the corresponding processors (lines 15–18). Furthermore, it must be checked whether a labelling process must be initiated, i.e. whether the current node fulfils the requirements for being either an $\exists$– or an $\forall$–witness. If so, all predecessors are informed about the current node's colour (lines 19–25).

The second type of messages which are received are colouring messages (line 26) informing that a node's child has changed its colour. The current settings for *node* are extracted (line 27), and the new colour of the corresponding child is stored (line 28). If now the evaluation of the node's colour according to Section 4.2 yields a different colour than the old one, then all predecessors are informed in the previous way (lines 29–33).

It is easy to see that the space required by our algorithm is linear in the size of the game graph. The worst case run–time, however, is a factorial of its size. This case might turn up when the components of the game graph are of Type II, linearly ordered and alternating, i.e. Q_i contains an $\exists$–witness and Q_{i+1} contains an $\forall$–witness. Now, in every component a (speculative) recolouring up to the maximal (root) component may be initiated.

Since we already observed that the model checking problem for the considered fragment of the μ–calculus is unlikely to be in NC, we were warned that a parallel algorithm might not be optimal in every case. Despite these theoretical limitations, in practice the behaviour turns out to be feasible (cf. Section 5). An explanation for this fact is that the aforementioned kinds of game graphs require formulae with deeply nested fixpoints, which rarely occur as typical specifications.

```
 1    Process P
 2
 3    // graph : Node ⟶ (Colour × [Node] × [(Node,Colour)])
 4
 5    begin
 6      until hasTerminated do
 7          msg ← readMessage;
 8          case msg of
 9            Expand node pred:
10                if (node, colour, oldpreds, _) in graph then
11                    addPreds(node, preds)
12                    if colour ≠ White and pred ∉ oldpreds then
13                        sendMessageTo (Colour pred node colour) f(pred)
14                else
15                    succs ← computeSuccs(node)
16                    succss ← [ ( s, White) | s in succs ]
17                    for s ∈ succs do
18                        sendMessageTo (Expand s [node]) f(s)
19                    colour ← case
20                                   node is ∃−witness or ∃−judgement: Green
21                                   node is ∀−witness or ∀−judgement: Red
22                                   else: White
23                    addGraph (node, colour, preds, succss)
24                    if colour ≠ White
25                        sendMessageTo (Colour pred node colour) f(pred)
26            Colour node child colour:
27                (node, oldcolour, preds, succs) in graph
28                updateSucc(succs, child, colour)
29                newcolour ← computeColour(node, succs)
30                if newcolour ≠ oldcolour then
31                    updateGraph(node, newcolour)
32                    for p ∈ preds do
33                        sendMessageTo (Colour p node newcolour) f(p)
34    end
35
36    Function computeColour (node, succs)
37    begin
38      case
39          node is ⋁−node:
40            case
41                all (= Red) succs: Red
42                any (= Green) succs: Green
43                else: White
44          node is ⋀−node:
45            case
46                all (= Green) succs: Green
47                any (= Red) succs: Red
48                else: White
49    end
```

Fig. 2. A parallel construction and labelling algorithm

Let us consider the graph in Figure 3 as a simple example. It suggests that the distribution function f will map the given nodes onto two processors as shown. Starting with node 1, its successors
(2, 5) are computed and sent to processors p_1 and
p_2, resp. Now, 2 and 5 can be expanded in parallel
with the effect that nodes 3 and 6 are sent to p_2.
The successors of 3 are 5 and 4 which are delivered
to p_2. Since 6 is an $\forall$–witness (indicated by $^-$), it is
labelled with *red*, initiates a relabelling of 5, and issues an expand–2–message to p_1, which notices that

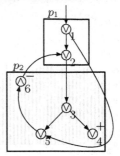

Fig. 3. A partition

2 is already expanded and registers 6 as one of 2's predecessors. p_2 carries on
with expanding 4, noticing that it is an $\exists$–judgement (indicated by $^+$), and sends
this information to 3. Next, the *red*–labelling of 5 is propagated to 3 and 1. However, 3 can now determine *green* as its colour and sends it to its predecessor. 2
propagates *green* to 1 and 6. Finally, the whole graph is labelled *green*.

5   Experim ental Results

We have tested our approach within our verification platform TRUTH [14]. W e
implem ented the distribution routine on its own as well as the com bined labelling
routine described in the previous section. As implem entation language we have
chosen the purely functional programmi ng language Haskell[4], which enabled us
to em bed this algorithm in the infrastructure of our verification tool TRUTH and
also to prototype a *concise* reference implem entation. The actual Haskell source
code of the algorithm has less than 300 lines of code. The comm unication layer
of our implemen tation is based upon MPICH[5], an implemen tation of the MPI
(Message P assing Interface) standard.

Now we will show some results we achieved when verifying properties of certain system specifications. Figures 4 and 5 show the measured results of state
distribution and the speedup when running our implem entation on a NOW consisting of up to 52 processors and a total of 13GB main memory . They are
connected with a conventional 100MBit F ast–Ethernet network.

The distribution routine shows that our approach is very well suited for
constructing large game graphs. We were able to construct graphs with several
hundred thousands of states within min utes. The game graph of the largest example we have constructed so far, a quad–parallel instance of the Alternating Bit
Protocol [18], consists of more than 1.6 milli on states, and we get a homogeneous
distribution of the state space on the workstations (Figure 4). The distribution
depends on our hash function f, and the results are quite good compared to
its simplicity. In fact, all our measuremen ts showed similar results, pro vided the
size of the graph is reasonably larger than the num ber of used workstations.

Our approach also scales very well with regard to the overall runtime (Figure 5). Unfortunately, because of the size of the game graphs we inspected, we

---

[4] http://haskell.org/
[5] http://www-unix.mcs.anl.gov/mpi/mpich/

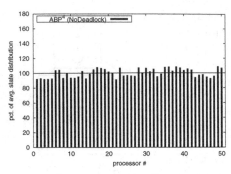
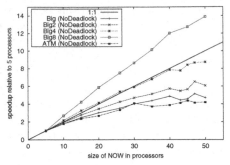

Fig. 4. state distribution   **Fig. 5.** runtime results

did not get results when running the algorithm on less than five workstations due to memory restrictions. Therefore the shown speedups are calculated relative to 5 processors instead of one. We found that we gain a linear speedup for reasonably large game graphs (in fact, for graphs with more than 500.000 states we even got *superlinear* speedups, which we will discuss later). The results are especially satisfying, if one considers that—for reasons of simplicity—we did not try to employ well-known optimisation means, for example reducing the communication overhead by packing several states into one message.

Due to our choice of Haskell as implementation language and its inherent inefficiency, we did not focus on optimising the internal data structures either. We use purely functional data structures like balanced trees and lists rather than destructively updateable arrays or hash tables. This is also the reason for the superlinear speedups we remarked before. We found that the overhead for insertions and lookups on our internal data structures dramatically increases with the number of stored states. We verified this by running all processes on a *single processor* in parallel and replacing the network message passing with inter–process communication. The expected result would have been to find similar runtimes as one process would achieve in this situation, or even slightly worse due to operating system context switches between the processes running in parallel. But we found that there is a significant speedup because the internal data structures are less crowded so that lookups and insertions are considerably cheaper.

Comparing our approach to the implemented sequential game–based depth–first–search model checking algorithm for L^1_μ, we have to learn that it is not possible for small examples to beat it. There are two reasons for that. In many cases, a formula can be proven or falsified by considering only a part of the game graph. Even parallel power does not outperform in these cases. Second, the communication between processors is dramatically slower within a NOW compared to accessing memory. Hence, as long as a problem fits into main memory it is difficult to beat a sequential algorithm by a parallel one running on a NOW.

The situation changes completely when most of a huge game graph has to be checked for proving a formula. This situation arises for example in the frequent case that a *NoDeadlock* formula is considered. To check whether a system description contains any deadlock requires the whole game graph to be analysed.

For large systems (several hundred thousand states), the parallel version beats the sequential one. More important, we were able to verify certain systems with the help of our parallel algorithm while the sequential failed due to memory restrictions.

6 Conclusion

In this paper, we presented a *parallel* game–based model checking algorithm for an important fragment of the μ-calculus. The demand for parallel algorithms becomes visible by considering the memory and run–time consumptions of sequential algorithms. Since the employed fragment of the μ-calculus subsumes the well–known logic CTL, it is of high practical interest. We have implemented our approach within the verification platform TRUTH. Systems with a million of states could be constructed within half an hour on a NOW consisting of up to 52 processors. We found out that the algorithm scales very well wrt. run–time and memory consumption when enlarging the NOW. Furthermore, the distribution of states on the processors is homogeneous.

Compared to the also implemented on–the–fly sequential model checking algorithm for L_μ^1, we learned that for simple examples a parallel *global* algorithm cannot outperform a local one. This is especially true for formulae like $\textbf{true} \vee \varphi$ being checked, where $\varphi = \nu X.\Phi$ yields a considerably big part of the resulting game graph. A local algorithm would be able to almost instantaneously present a solution, since the formula is dominated by an $\exists$–judgement ($\textbf{true}$).

To improve our algorithm for such cases, we head towards an "almost local" variant, which not only uses two colours but *colour weights*, with which e.g. the propagation of *safe* colours (resulting from minimal components Q_i) can be tracked better. So we eventually short-circuit the colouring process.

However, considering real world specifications yielding millions of states, even the here presented parallel algorithm gains the upperhand. Answers are computed more quickly, and, more important, there are numerous cases in which the sequential algorithm fails because of memory restrictions and the parallel version is able to prove a formula. From the practical point of view, it is a central feature of a verification tool to give an answer in as many cases as possible.

While our approach is already of practical interest since it allows to check larger systems, it should also be considered as a further attempt to develop parallel model checking algorithms. More research should be carried out in this direction. Especially, on–the–fly model checking and partial order reduction [20] should be analysed with respect to parallelisation. Furthermore, different (especially non–P–complete) specification logics might provide better parallel model checking algorithms.

References

1. S. Basonov. Parallel implementation of BDD on DSM systems. Master's thesis, Computer Science Department, Technion, 1998.

2. G. Cabodi, P. Camurati, and S. Que. Improved reachability analysis of large FSM. In *Proc. IEEE Int. Conf. on Computer Aided Design*, pages 354–360. IEEE Computer Society Press, June 1996.
3. E. M. Clarke and J. Wing. Formal methods: State of the art and future directions. Technical Report CMU-CS-96-178, Carnegie Mellon University (CMU), Sept. 1996.
4. R. Cleaveland and B. Steffen. A linear–time model–checking algorithm for the alternation–free modal mu–calculus. In *Proc. Computer Aided Verification (CAV '91)*, volume 575 of *LNCS*, Springer, 1992
5. E. W. Dijkstra, W. H. J. F eijen, and A. J. M. van Gasteren. Derivation of a termination detection algorithm for distributed computations. *Information Processing Letters*, 16(5):217–219, June 1983.
6. E. A. Emerson and E. M. Clarke. Using branching time temporal logic to synthesize synchronization skeletons. *Science of Computer Programming*, 2(3):241–266, 1982.
7. S. Gnesi et. al., A formal specification and validation of a critical system in presence of byzantine errors. In *Proc. 6th Int. Conf. on Tools and Algorithms for the Construction and Analysis of Systems*, number 1785 in LNCS. Springer, 2000.
8. R. Greenlaw, H. J. Hoover, and W. L. Ruzzo. *Limits to Parallel Computation: P-Completeness Theory*. Oxford University Press, 1995.
9. T. Heyman, D. Geist, O. Grumberg, and A. Schuster. Achieving scalability in parallel reachability analysis of very large circuits. In *Computer Aided Verification, 12th Int. Conf.*, volume 1855 of *LNCS*, pages 20–35. Springer-Verlag, June 2000.
10. A. J. Hu, G. York, and D. L. Dill. New techniques for efficient verification with implicitly conjoined BDDs. In *31st Design Automation Conference*, 1994.
11. D. Kozen. Results on the propositional mu-calculus. *Theoretical Computer Science*, 27:333–354, Dec. 1983.
12. O. Kupferman, M. Y. Vardi, and P. Wolper. An automata-theoretic approach to branching-time model checking. *Journal of the ACM*, 47(2):312–360, Mar. 2000.
13. M. Lange. Spielbasiertes Model-Checking für den alternierungsfreien mu-Kalkül. Master's thesis, Aachen, University of Technology, 1999. (German).
14. M. Lange, M. Leucker, T. Noll, and S. Tobies. Truth – a verification platform for concurrent systems. In *Tool Support for System Specification, Development, and Verification*, Advances in Computing Science. Springer-Verlag, 1999.
15. B. P. Lester. *The Art of Parallel Programming*. Prentice Hall, 1993.
16. M. Leucker. Model checking games for the alternation free mu-calculus and alternating automata. In *Proc. 6th Int. Conf. on Logic for Programming and Automated Reasoning*, volume 1705 of *LNAI*, pages 77–91. Springer, 1999.
17. K. L. McMillan. *Symbolic Model Checking*. Kluwer Academic Publishers, 1993.
18. R. Milner. *Communication and Concurrency*. Prentice Hall, 1989.
19. A. A. Narayan, J. J. J. Isles, R. K. Brayto, and A. L. Sangiovanni-Vincentelli. Reachability analysis using partitioned–roBBDs. In *Proc. IEEE Int. Conf. on Computer Aided Design*, pages 388–393. IEEE Computer Society Press, June 1997.
20. D. Peled. Ten years of partial order reduction. In *CAV, Computer Aided Verification*, number 1427 in LNCS, pages 17–28, Vancouver, BC, Canada, 1998. Springer.
21. J. H. Reif. Depth-first search is inherently sequential. *Information Processing Letters*, 20(5):229–234, June 1985.
22. S. H. Roosta. *Parallel Processing and Parallel Algorithms*. Springer, 1999.
23. U. Stern and D. L. Dill. Parallelizing the Murφ verifier. In *Proc. 9th Int. Conf. Computer Aided Verification*, volume 1254 of *LNCS*, Springer, 1997.
24. C. Stirling. Games for bisimulation and model checking, July 1996. Notes for Mathfit W orkshop on finite model theory, University of Wales, Swansea,.
25. A. L. Stornetta. Implementation of an efficient parallel BDD package. Master's thesis, University of California, Santa Barbara, 1995.
26. S. Zhang, O. Sokolsky, and S. A. Smolka. On the parallel complexity of model checking in the modal mu-calculus. In *Proc. 9th Annual IEEE Symposium on Logic in Computer Science*, pages 154–163, 1994. IEEE Computer Society Press.

Model Checking CTL*[DC]

Paritosh K. Pandya *

Tata Institute of Fundamental Research
Homi Bhabha Road, Colaba, Mumbai 400005, India
pandya@tcs.tifr.res.in

Abstract. We define a logic called CTL*[DC] which extends CTL* with ability to specify past-time and quantitative timing properties using the formulae of Quantified Discrete-time Duration Calculus (QDDC). Alternately, we can consider CTL*[DC] as extending logic QDDC with branching and liveness.

As our main result, we show a reduction of CTL*[DC] model checking problem to model checking of CTL* formulae. The reduction relies upon an automata-theoretic decision procedure for QDDC. Moreover, it preserves the subsets CTL and LTL of CTL*. The reduction is of practical relevance as model checking of CTL* as well as its subsets CTL and LTL are well studied and even implemented into a number of tools. We briefly discuss an implementation of a model checking tool for CTL[DC] called CTLDC, based on the above theory. CTLDC can model check SMV, Verilog and Esterel designs using tools SMV, VIS and Xeve, respectively.

1   Introduction

Logic CTL* is an expressive logic for the specification of properties of transition systems [8]. It has path quantifiers for specifying branching time properties as well as temporal operators for specifying how state of the system evolves along execution paths. For example, the following formula states that on all execution paths proposition P will hold infinitely often. (We only provide an intuitive explanation of what the properties states. A precise definition of the syntax and semantics of CTL* operators is given in Section 3.)

AGF P

Model checking algorithms for verifying CTL* properties of finite state transition systems are well studied [8]. Moreover, subsets CTL [4,5] and LTL [25] of CTL* have also been formulated and thoroughly investigated. Symbolic model checking algorithms for verifying formulae of these sub-logics have been implemented in tools such as SMV [18], VIS [2] and TLV [12].

In spite of its expressive abilities, there are situations where CTL* is restrictive. It has long been recognised [17] that availability of past modalities in

---

* Partially supported by the UNU/IIST offshore project *Semantics and verification of real-time programs using Duration Calculus: Theory and Practice*

temporal logics considerably facilitates formulation of complex properties. Secondly, specification of reactive systems must often deal with quantitative timing constraints [9]. In this paper, we will address these issues in an integrated fashion.

Discrete-time Duration Calculus (QDDC) [21,22] is a highly expressive logic for specifying quantitative timing properties of finite sequences of states (behaviours). It is closely related to the Interval Temporal Logic of Moszkowski [19] and Duration Calculus of Zhou et al [26]. It provides novel interval based modalities for describing behaviours. For example, the following formula holds for a behaviour σ provided for all fragments σ' of σ which have (a) P true in the beginning, (b) Q true at the end, and (c) no occurrences of Q in between, the number of occurrences of states in σ' where R is true is at most 3.

$$\square(\lceil P\rceil^0 \frown \lceil\lceil\neg Q\rceil \frown \lceil Q\rceil^0 \Rightarrow (\Sigma R \leq 3))$$

Here, $\square$ modality ranges over all fragments of a behaviour. Operator $\frown$ is like concatenation (fusion) of behaviour fragments and $\lceil\lceil\neg Q\rceil$ states invariance of $\neg Q$ over the behaviour fragment. Finally, ΣR counts number of occurrences of R within a behaviour fragment. A precise definition of the syntax and semantics of QDDC is given in Section 2. Formula $\eta = 3$ states that the behaviour fragment has length 3 (i.e. it spans a sequence of 4 states). QDDC is a convenient and highly expressive formalism for specifying quantitative timing properties. However, it cannot specify liveness or branching.

An automata-theoretic decision procedure allows checking of satisfiability (validity) of QDDC formulae [22]. This algorithm has been implemented into a tool called DCVALID [21]. The tool is built on top of MONA [11], which is an efficient and sophisticated BDD-based implementation of the Buchi-Elgot automata-theoretic decision procedure for Monadic Logic over Finite Words [3,7]. (See [13] for a recent paper on MONA.)

In this paper, we propose a straight-forward extension of CTL* where, in place of propositions, formulae of Quantified Discrete-time Duration Calculus $QDDC$ can be asserted within CTL* formulae. A $QDDC$ formula D holds for a node of a computation tree provided the unique path from the root of the tree to the node satisfies D. Thus, a QDDC formula D allows specification of the "past" of the node. Operators of CTL* allow specification of branching and liveness properties.

For example, the following formula states that on all execution paths QDDC formula D will become true infinitely often.

AGF D

The following formula states that once there is overload for 5 steps, there will be alarm until reset occurs.

AG $(true \frown (\lceil\lceil Overload\rceil \wedge \eta = 5) \Rightarrow \mathbf{A}(alarm \, \mathcal{U} \, reset))$

Logic QDDC provides a useful extension to the expressive power of CTL* by allowing past-time and quantitative timing properties to be expressed. It also significantly increases the expressive power of QDDC which is unable to specify liveness properties such as infinitely often D or branching. In a separate note [24], we list a number of real-life properties collected from model checking literature which are stated to be hard to formulate in CTL. W e show that these properties can be easily captured using CTL[DC].

As our main result, we show a reduction of CTL*[DC] model checking problem to the model checking of pure CTL* formulae by effectively transforming the transition system and the property. This transformation relies on the automata-theoretic decision procedure for QDDC. Thus, in effect, we show that by combining the model-checking procedures for CTL* and QDDC, we obtain a model-checking procedure for CTL*[DC].

Our reduction of CTL*[DC] model checking to CTL* model checking preserves the subsets CTL and LTL of CTL*. That is, a CTL[DC] formula reduces to a CTL formula and LTL[DC] formula reduces to an LTL formula. This reduction is of practical relevance as model checking of CTL* [8] as well as its subsets CTL [5] and LTL [16] are well studied and even implemented into a number of tools such as SMV [18,6], VIS [2] and TLV [12]. Based on this reduction, we have implemented a model checking tool for CTL[DC] called CTLDC [23]. It permits model checking of SMV, Verilog and Esterel designs using SMV [18], VIS [2] and Xeve [1] tools, respectively.

CTLDC permits well established CTL model checking tools to be used for analysing complex properties involving past and quantitative timing constraints. While there ha ve been several theoretical formulations extending LTL and CTL with past [14,15], CTLDC constitutes perhaps the first implemen tation of CTL with past. Moreo ver, the fact that we can integrate our approach with a wide variety of design notations such as SMV, Verilog, Esterel, and tools such as SMV, VIS, Xev e shows that the approach is rather generic and easy to build from componen ts.

The rest of the paper is organised as follows. W e provide a brief overview of the logic QDDC in Section 2. The syntax and seman tics of CTL*[DC] are given in Section 3. The reduction from model c hecking of CTL*[DC] to model checking of CTL* is given in Section 4. Finally, some examples of use of CTLDC, the model checker for CTL[DC], are described in Section 5. W e conclude the paper with a brief discussion.

2   Quan tified Discrete-Time Duration Calculus (QDDC)

Let $Pvar$ be a finite set of propositional variables representing some observable aspects of system state. Let

$$VAL(Pvar) \stackrel{\text{def}}{=} Pvar \to \{0,1\}$$

be the set of valuations assigning truth-value to each variable.

W e shall identify behaviours with finite, nonempty sequences of valuations, i.e. $VAL(Pvar)^{+}$.

Example 1. The following picture gives a behaviour over variables $\{p, q\}$. Each column vector gives a valuation, and the word is a sequence of such column vectors.

```
p    1   0   1   1   0
q    0   0   0   0   1
```

The above word satisfies the property that p holds initially and q holds at the end but nowhere before that. QDDC is a logic for formalising such properties. Each formula specifies a set of such words.

Given a non-empty finite sequence of valuations $\sigma \in VAL^+$, we denote the satisfaction of a QDDC formula D over σ by

$$\sigma \models D$$

We now give the syntax and semantics of QDDC and define the above satisfaction relation.

Syntax of QDDC Formulae Let *Pvar* be the set of propositional variables. Let p range over propositional variables, P, Q over propositions and D, D_1, D_2 over QDDC formulae.

The set of propositions *Prop* has the syntax

$$0 \mid 1 \mid p \mid P \wedge Q \mid \neg P$$

Operators such as $\vee, \Rightarrow, \Leftrightarrow$ can be defined as usual.
The syntax of QDDC is as follows.

$$\lceil P \rceil^0 \mid \lceil\lceil P \rceil\rceil \mid D_1 \,\widehat{}\, D_2 \mid D_1 \wedge D_2 \mid \neg D \mid \exists p.D$$
$$\eta \; op \; c \mid \Sigma P \; op \; c \qquad \text{where} \quad op \in \{>, =\}$$

Let $\sigma \in VAL(Pvar)^+$ be a behaviour. Let $\#\sigma$ denote the length of σ and $\sigma[i]$ the i'th element. For example, if $\sigma = \langle v_0, v_1, v_2 \rangle$ then $\#\sigma = 3$ and $\sigma[1] = v_1$. Let $dom(\sigma) = \{0, 1, \dots, \#\sigma - 1\}$ denote the set of positions within σ. The set of intervals in σ is given by $Intv(\sigma) = \{[b, e] \in dom(\sigma)^2 \mid b \leq e\}$ where each interval $[b, e]$ identifies a subsequence of σ between positions b and e.

Let $\sigma, i \models P$ denote that proposition P evaluates to true at position i in σ. We omit this obvious definition. We inductively define the satisfaction of QDDC formula D for behaviour σ and interval $[b, e] \in Intv(\sigma)$ as follows.

$$\sigma, [b, e] \models \lceil P \rceil^0 \quad \textbf{iff} \quad b = e \text{ and } \sigma, b \models P$$
$$\sigma, [b, e] \models \lceil\lceil P \rceil\rceil \quad \textbf{iff} \quad b < e \text{ and } \sigma, i \models P \text{ for all } i : b \leq i < e$$
$$\sigma, [b, e] \models \neg D \quad \textbf{iff} \quad \sigma, [b, e] \not\models D$$
$$\sigma, [b, e] \models D_1 \wedge D_2 \quad \textbf{iff} \quad \sigma, [b, e] \models D_1 \text{ and } \sigma, [b, e] \models D_2$$
$$\sigma, [b, e] \models D_1 \,\widehat{}\, D_2 \quad \textbf{iff} \quad \text{for some } m : b \leq m \leq e :$$
$$\sigma, [b, m] \models D_1 \text{ and } \sigma, [m, e] \models D_2$$

Entities η and ΣP are called *measurements*. Term η denotes the length of the interval whereas ΣP denotes the count of number of times P is true within the interval $[b, e]$ (we treat the interval as being left-closed right-open). Formally,

$$eval(\eta, \sigma, [b, e]) \overset{\text{def}}{=} e - b$$

$$eval(\Sigma P, \sigma, [b, e]) \overset{\text{def}}{=} \sum_{i=b}^{e-1} \left\{ \begin{matrix} 1 & if \ \sigma, i \models P \\ 0 & otherwise \end{matrix} \right\}$$

Let t range over measurements. Then,

$$\sigma, [b, e] \models t \ op \ c \quad \textbf{iff} \quad eval(t, \sigma, [b, e]) \ op \ c$$

Call a behaviour σ' to be p-variant of σ provided $\#\sigma = \#\sigma'$ and for all $i \in dom(\sigma)$ and for all $q \neq p$, we have $\sigma(i)(q) = \sigma'(i)(q)$. Then,

$$\sigma, [b, e] \models \exists p.D \quad \textbf{iff} \quad \sigma', [b, e] \models D \ \text{for some } p\text{-variant } \sigma' \text{ of } \sigma$$

Finally,

$$\sigma \models D \quad \textbf{iff} \quad \sigma, [0, \#\sigma - 1] \models D$$

We can also define some derived constructs. Boolean combinators $\vee, \Rightarrow, \Leftrightarrow$ can be defined using $\wedge, \neg$ as usual.

- $\lceil\lceil P \rceil\rceil \overset{\text{def}}{=} (\lceil\lceil P \rceil \frown \lceil P \rceil^0)$ states that proposition P holds invariantly over the closed interval $[b, e]$ including the endpoint.
- $\lceil \ \rceil \overset{\text{def}}{=} \lceil 1 \rceil^0$ holds for point intervals of the form $[b, b]$.
- $ext \overset{\text{def}}{=} \neg\lceil \ \rceil$ holds for extended intervals $[b, e]$ with $b < e$.
- $unit \overset{\text{def}}{=} ext \wedge \neg(ext \frown ext)$ holds for intervals of the form $[b, b+1]$.
- $\Diamond D \overset{\text{def}}{=} true \frown D \frown true$ holds provided D holds for some subinterval.
- $\Box D \overset{\text{def}}{=} \neg\Diamond\neg D$ holds provided D holds for all subintervals.
- $t \geq c \overset{\text{def}}{=} t = c \vee t > c$. Also, $t < c \overset{\text{def}}{=} \neg(t \geq c)$.
- $D^* \overset{\text{def}}{=} (\exists p. \ (\lceil p \rceil^0 \frown true \frown \lceil p \rceil^0) \wedge$
  $\qquad \Box((\lceil p \rceil^0 \frown unit \frown (\lceil\lceil \neg p \rceil \vee \lceil \ \rceil) \frown \lceil p \rceil^0) \ \Rightarrow \ D))$

Formula D^* represents Kleene-closure of D under the $\frown$ operator. It states that D^* holds for interval $[b, e]$ if there exists a partition of $[b, e]$ into a sequence of sub-intervals such that D holds for each sub-interval. Each sub-interval is characterised by p holding at both endpoints and nowhere in between, i.e. satisfying the formula $(\lceil p \rceil^0 \frown unit \frown (\lceil\lceil \neg p \rceil \vee \lceil \ \rceil) \frown \lceil p \rceil^0)$. It is not difficult to see that

$$\sigma, [b, e] \models D^* \quad \textbf{iff} \quad b = e \ \vee \ b < e \text{ and } \exists n, b_0, \ldots, b_n.$$
$$(b = b_0 \text{ and } \forall 0 \leq i < n. \ b_i < b_{i+1} \text{ and } b_n = e \text{ and } \sigma, [b_i, b_{i+1}] \models D)$$

Decidability of QDDC The following theorem characterises the sets of models of a QDDC formula. Let $pvar(D)$ be the finite set of propositional variables occurring within a QDDC formula D. Let $VAL(Pvar) = Pvar \to \{0,1\}$ be the set of valuations over $Pvar$.

Theorem 1. *For every QDDC formula D, we can effectively construct a finite state automaton $A(D)$ over the alphabet $VAL(pvar(D))$ such that for all $\sigma \in VAL(pvar(D))^*$,*

$$\sigma \models D \quad \textbf{iff} \quad \sigma \in L(A(D))$$

W e omit the proof of this theorem as it can be found elsewhere [22]. In outline, the proof relies on the following steps. Firstly, we can eliminate all measuremen t formulae of the form η *op* c and ΣP *op* c from a QDDC form ula D and find an equivalent form ula D' without these. Such form ulae are said to belong to subset QDDCR. Next we embed QDDCR into monadic logic over finite words. Thus for every form ula $D' \in QDDCR$ we construct a form ula ψ of monadic logic over finite words which has the same set of models as D'. This em bedding was first presented by Pandya [20]. Finally, the famous theorem due to Buc hi [3] and Elgot [7] states that for every form ula ψ of monadic logic over finite words, we can construct a finite state automaton which accepts exactly the word models of ψ. By com bining these steps, we can obtain the automaton $A(D)$ accepting word models of QDDC form ula D.   □

Corollary 1. *Satisfiability (validity) of QDDC formulae is decidable.*
Proof outline For checking satisfiability of $D \in QDDC$ we can construct the automaton $A(D)$. A word satisfying the form ula can be found by searching for an accepting path within $A(D)$. Such a search can be carried out in time linear in the size (num ber of nodes + edges) of $A(D)$ by depth-first search.   □

Example 2. The property of Example 1 can be stated in QDDC as form ula $\lceil P \rceil^0 \,\widehat{}\, \lceil \lceil \neg Q \rceil \,\widehat{}\, \lceil Q \rceil^0$. The automaton corresponding this form ula is given below. Each edge is labelled with a column vector giving truth values of variables P, Q as in Example 1. Also, letter X is used to denote either 0 or 1.

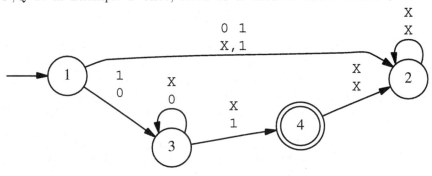

DCVALID The reduction from formulae of QDDC to finite state automata as outlined in Theorem 1 has been implemented into a tool called DCVALID [21], which also checks for the validity of formulae as in corollary 1. This tool is built on top of MONA [11,13]. MONA is a sophisticated and efficient BDD-based implementation of the automata-theoretic decision procedure for monadic logic over finite words [3,7]. DCVALID works by reducing QDDC formulae to this logic [22]. The automaton in Example 2 was automatically generated from the formula by this tool.

Complexity It must be noted that there is a non-elementary *lower bound* on the size of the automaton $A(D)$ accepting word models of a QDDC formula D. In the worst case, the complexity of the output automaton can increase by one exponent for each alternation of $\neg$ and $\frown$ operators. However, such blowup is rarely observed in practice and we have been able to check validity of many formulae which are 5-6 pages long with our tool DCVALID [21,22].

3 Logic CTL*[DC]

A transition system (also called Kripke structure) is a quadruple (S, R, L, S_0) where

S is the set of states,

$S_0 \subseteq S$ is the set of initial states.

$R \subseteq S \times S$ is the transition relation

$L : S \to VAL(Pvar)$ is the labelling function.

Recall that $VAL(Pvar) = Pvar \to \{0, 1\}$ is the set of valuations over $Pvar$. The labelling function $L(s)$ gives the truth-value of propositional variables at state s.

Syntax We have three sorts of formulae: $QDDC$ formulae, path formulae and state formulae. Let P range over propositions. Let D range over $QDDC$ formulae; α, β range over path formulae and ϕ, ψ range over state formulae.

Let $L(s) \models P$ denote that proposition P evaluates to true in state s with labelling function L. Also, for a given nonempty sequence of states $\langle s_0, \ldots, s_n \rangle$, let $L(\langle s_0, \ldots, s_n \rangle) \overset{\text{def}}{=} \langle L(s_0), \ldots, L(s_n) \rangle$ give the corresponding sequence of valuations in $VAL(Pvar)^+$. Hence for QDDC formula D over $Pvar$, we can define $L(\langle s_0, \ldots, s_n \rangle) \models D$ as in Section 2.

State Formulae of CTL*[DC]

$$P \mid D \mid \mathbf{A}\alpha \mid \mathbf{E}\alpha \mid \neg\phi \mid \phi \wedge \psi$$

Path Formulae of CTL*[DC]

$$\phi \mid \alpha \, \mathcal{U} \, \beta \mid \mathbf{X}\alpha \mid \alpha \wedge \beta \mid \neg\alpha$$

We can define some abbreviations for the path formulae. Let $\mathbf{F}\alpha \overset{\text{def}}{=} true \, \mathcal{U} \, \alpha$ and $\mathbf{G}\alpha \overset{\text{def}}{=} \neg\mathbf{F}\neg\alpha$.

Given $M = (S, R, L, S_0)$ and $s \in S$, let $Tr(M, s)$ denote the (unique) tree obtained by unfolding the state graph M starting with state s. In this tree, each node is labelled by a state from s. Moreover, a node n labelled s has as its immediate successors nodes labelled with s' for each distinct s' such that $R(s, s')$. We call such a tree a *computation tree*. Let $St(T, n)$ denote the state labelling the node n of tree T.

Given a computation tree T and an internal node n, let $hist(n)$ denote the finite sequence of states $s_0, \ldots, s_n$ labelling the nodes on the unique path from the root to n. A trajectory from n_0 is an infinite sequence of nodes $n_0, n_1, \ldots$ going into the future. Let $paths(n)$ be the set of all trajectories starting from n.

It should be noted that the label s of a node uniquely defines the subtree under it. However, distinct nodes n_1 and n_2 with same state label will have distinct $hist(n)$. The truth of formulae in our logic CTL*[DC] will depend upon both the subtree at n as well as $hist(n)$.

We now define the truth of state and path formulae. Let $T = Tr(M, s)$ be a computation tree. Let n be a node of T and let $\rho = n_0, n_1, \ldots$ be a trajectory in T. Then, the truth of state formula $T, n \models \phi$, and the truth of path formula $T, \rho \models \alpha$ are defined as follows.

State formulae:

$$T, n \models P \quad \textbf{iff} \quad L(St(T, n)) \models P$$
$$T, n \models D \quad \textbf{iff} \quad L(hist(n)) \models D$$
$$T, n \models \mathbf{E}\alpha \quad \textbf{iff} \quad T, \rho \models \alpha \text{ for some } \rho \in paths(n)$$
$$T, n \models \mathbf{A}\alpha \quad \textbf{iff} \quad T, \rho \models \alpha \text{ for all } \rho \in paths(n)$$

The boolean combinators have their usual meaning.

Path formulae: Let $\rho = n_0, n_1, \ldots$ denote a trajectory in T starting at a (not necessarily root) node n_0. For any $m \in Nat$, let ρ^m denote the suffix $n_m, n_{m+1}, \ldots$ of ρ starting with node n_m.

$$T, \rho \models \phi \quad \textbf{iff} \quad T, n_0 \models \phi$$
$$T, \rho \models \mathbf{X}\alpha \quad \textbf{iff} \quad T, \rho^1 \models \alpha$$
$$T, \rho \models \alpha\, \mathcal{U}\, \beta \quad \textbf{iff} \quad \text{for some } m \in Nat,$$
$$T, \rho^m \models \beta, \quad \text{and} \quad T, \rho^j \models \alpha, \text{ for } j : 0 \leq j < m$$

Finally,

$$T \models \phi \quad \textbf{iff} \quad T, n_r \models \phi \quad \text{where } n_r \text{ is the root of the tree } T$$
$$M, s \models \phi \quad \textbf{iff} \quad Tr(M, s) \models \phi$$
$$M \models \phi \quad \textbf{iff} \quad M, s \models \phi \text{ for all } s \in S_0$$

Subset CTL[DC] In this subset every temporal operator $\mathbf{X}$, $\mathcal{U}$, $\mathbf{G}$, $\mathbf{F}$ is preceded by a path quantifier $\mathbf{A}$, $\mathbf{E}$. If path formulae are restricted to the following syntax, we have the subset CTL[DC]

$$\phi\, \mathcal{U}\, \psi \mid \mathbf{X}\phi \mid \mathbf{F}\phi \mid \mathbf{G}\phi \quad \text{where } \phi, \psi \text{ are state formulae}$$

Subset LTL[DC] In this subset the formula is of the form **A**α where the path formula α is free of path quantifiers **A**, **E**. If path formulae are restricted to the following syntax, we have the subset LTL[DC]

$$P \mid D \mid \alpha \, \mathcal{U} \, \beta \mid \mathbf{X}\alpha \mid \alpha \wedge \beta \mid \neg\alpha$$

Subsets CTL*, CTL and LTL If a formula of CTL*[DC] does not contain any QDDC formula, then it is called CTL* formula. Similarly, we can define CTL and LTL formulae.

Example 3. The following CTL[DC] formula states that on all nodes of the computation tree which are at even distance from the root, proposition P must be true. Nothing is said about the truth of P on nodes which are at odd distance from the root.

$$\mathbf{A}\,\mathbf{G}((\eta = 2)^* \;\; \Rightarrow \;\; P)$$

This property cannot be expressed in logic CTL*. Thus our extension increases the expressive power of logic CTL*.

4   Decidabilit y of Model Chec king CTL*[DC]

Given a transition system M and CTL*[DC] formula ϕ, we construct a transformed transition system M' and CTL* formula ϕ' such that

$$M \models \phi \;\; \textbf{iff} \;\; M' \models \phi' \tag{1}$$

Thus, we reduce the model checking of CTL*[DC] to model checking of CTL*. In the rest of this section, we will define this transformation and prove its correctness.

Let the transition system $M = (S, R, L, S_0)$ and the CTL*[DC] formula be $\phi(D_1, \ldots, D_n)$, where $D_1, \ldots, D_n$ are the syntactically distinct $QDDC$ formulae occurring within ϕ. We construct the transformed transition system M' as follows.

Let $A(D_i)$ be the automaton recognising models of D_i as in Theorem 1. Such an automaton is called *synchronous observer* for D_i. We assume that $A(D_i)$ is in total and deterministic form. By this w e mean that from an y state q and for any valuation $v \in VAL(pvar(D))$ there is a unique transition leading to the state given by a total function $\delta_i(q, v)$.

W e define the synchronous product of M with the list of automata $A(D_i)$. Since each $A(D_i)$ is a finite-state acceptor and M is a Moore mac hine, we define the product such that we get a Moore mac hine. Let $A(D_i) = (Q_i, \delta_i, q_i^0, F_i)$. If M starts in state $s \in S_0$, the observers $A(D_i)$ observe this state and go to state $q_s^i = \delta_i(q_i^0, L(s))$ respectively. Also, if M moves from state $s \rightarrow s'$, each $A(D_i)$ moves from state $q_i \rightarrow \delta_i(q_i, L(s'))$. The observable propositions of the resulting system are valuations over $Pvar \cup \{End_i \mid 1 \le i \le n\}$. Proposition End_i holds when automaton $A(D_i)$ is in its final state. Thus, End_i holds precisely when the behaviour from start up to the current node satisfies the formula D_i. Formally, let

$$M' = (S', R', L', S_0')$$

where

$$S' \overset{\text{def}}{=} S \times Q_1 \times \ldots \times Q_n$$
$$S_0' \overset{\text{def}}{=} \{\langle s, q_1^s, q_2^s, \ldots, q_n^s \rangle \mid s \in S_0 \text{ and } q_i^s = \delta_i(q_i^0, L(s))\}$$
$$R' \overset{\text{def}}{=} \{(\langle s, q_1, q_2, \ldots, q_n \rangle, \langle s', q_1', q_2', \ldots, q_n' \rangle) \mid R(s, s') \wedge q_i' = \delta_i(q_i, L(s'))\}$$
$$L'(\langle s, q_1, \ldots, q_n \rangle) \overset{\text{def}}{=} L(s) \cup \{END_i \mapsto (q_i \in F_i)\}$$

The transformed formula $\phi(End_1, \ldots, End_n)$ is obtained by replacing each occurrence of QDDC sub-formula D_i by a proposition End_i which witnesses the truth of D_i.

Theorem 2. *Let* $\hat{s} = \langle s, q_1^s, \ldots, q_n^s \rangle$ *where* $q_i^s = \delta_i(q_i^0, L(s))$. *Then,*

$$M, s \models \phi(D_1, \ldots, D_n) \quad \textbf{iff} \quad M', \hat{s} \models \phi(End_1, \ldots, End_n)$$

Proof Outline Consider the computation tree $T = Tr(M, s)$ in M and corresponding computation tree $T' = Tr(M', \hat{s})$ in M'. There is a bijection $\pi : T \to T'$ between the nodes of T and T' as follows. For every node $k \in Tr(M, s)$ with state label $St(T, k) = s_k$, we have a node $\pi(k)$ with label
$$(s_k, \overline{\delta_1}(q_1^0, L(hist(k))), \ldots, \overline{\delta_n}(q_1^0, L(hist(k)))).$$
(Here, we have extended the transition function δ_i over VAL to $\overline{\delta_i}$ over VAL^+.)
From the above bijection, it is easy to prove that,
$$T, k \models P \quad \textbf{iff} \quad T', \pi(k) \models P.$$
The central property of T' is that
$$T, k \models D_i \quad \textbf{iff} \quad T', \pi(k) \models End_i.$$
From these, by structural induction on ϕ, we can prove that
$$T, k \models \phi(D_1, \ldots, D_n) \quad \textbf{iff} \quad T', \pi(k) \models \phi(End_1, \ldots, End_n). \qquad \square$$

Corollary 2. $M \models \phi(D_1, \ldots, D_n) \quad \textbf{iff} \quad M' \models \phi(End_1, \ldots, End_n)$ $\qquad \square$

Note that, if M is finite state then M' is also a finite state Kripke structure. Moreover, $\phi(End_1, \ldots, End_n)$ is a pure CTL* formula which can be model checked as follows.

Theorem 3 (Emerson and Lei [8]). *For a finite-state Kripke-structure M' and CTL* formula ϕ', there exists an algorithm to decide whether $M' \models \phi'$.*

Corollary 3. $M \models \phi(D_1, \ldots, D_n)$ *is decidable if M is finite-state.* $\qquad \square$

5   CTLDC: A Tool for Model Chec king CTL[DC]

We have implemen ted the reduction outlined in Corollary 2 into a tool called *CTLDC*. The tool is constructed on top of QDDC validity checker DCVALID [21,22]. The tool allows CTL[DC] specifications of SMV, Verilog and Esterel designs to be model checked in conjunction with verifiers SMV[18], VIS[2] and Xeve [1], respectively. A separate report gives the details of usage and working of this tool [23].

Given an SMV module M and a formula $\phi(D_1, \ldots, D_n) \in CTL[DC]$, our tool *CTLDC* gives the transformed SMV modules corresponding to M' of Theorem 2 and also the formula $\phi(End_1, \ldots, End_n)$. We can then use SMV [18] to model check whether $M' \models \phi(End_1, \ldots, End_n)$. The tool works in a similar fashion for Verilog and Esterel designs. The reader may refer to [23] for details of these transformations.

5.1   An Example: V ending Mac hine

A vending machine accepts $5p$ and $10p$ coins. A chocolate costs $15p$. We model the working of such a machine by the following SMV module.

```
MODULE vend
VAR
    bal:{0,5,10,15};
    event: {p5,p10,choc, null};
INIT
    bal = 0 & !(event=choc)
TRANS
    next(bal) = case
                    bal <= 10 & event=p5       : bal+5 ;
                    bal <=5   & event=p10      : bal+10 ;
                    bal = 15 & event=choc      : 0  ;
                    event=null : bal;
                esac
```

The following QDDC formula holds for all behaviour fragments satisfying the condition that 15p worth of coins have been deposited and no chocolate has been obtained.

$$fifteenp \stackrel{\text{def}}{=} (\llbracket event \neq choc \rrbracket \; \wedge$$
$$(\Sigma(event = 5p) = 3 \; \vee \; (\Sigma(event = 5p) = 1 \wedge \Sigma(event = 10p) = 1) \;))$$

Then, a possible extension of any behaviour ending with *fifteenp* is that a chocolate is obtained next.

$$\mathbf{A\,G}\,(true \,^\frown fifteenp \quad \Rightarrow \quad \mathbf{EX}(event = choc))$$

Moreo ver, the only possible extensions are that a null event can occur or a chocolate can be obtained.

$$\mathbf{A\,G}\,(true \,^\frown fifteenp \quad \Rightarrow \quad \mathbf{AX}(event = choc \vee event = null))$$

W e consider the vending machine behaviours under a fairness condition which states that infinitely often non-null events are performed, i.e. $\mathbf{GF}(event \neq null)$ holds. The following specification holds for all fair behaviours of vending machine. Here the path quantifier $\mathbf{A}^f$ ranges over all fair behaviours.

$$\mathbf{A}^f\,\mathbf{GA}^f\mathbf{F}\,((fifteenp \frown unit \frown \lceil event = choc\rceil^0)^*)$$

The above three properties were checked using the tool CTLDC. In checking the last property, we made use of the fair CTL model c hecking abilities of SMV.

Synchronous Bus Arbiter In a more substantial verification using CTLDC, we checked some properties of the historic synchronous bus arbiter as modelled in SMV by McMillan [18]. A synchronous bus arbiter with n cells has request lines req_i and acknowledgement lines ack_i for $1 \le i \le n$. At any clock cycle a subset of the request lines are high. It is the task of the arbiter to set at most one of the corresponding acknowledgement lines high. Preferably, the arbiter should be fair to all requests. W e refer the readers to McMillan's book [18] (Section 3.4.1) for a detailed description of a specific synchronous arbiter circuit. Here, we are mainly interested in its properties.

The following property states that if req_i is held high for any interval of m cycles then there must be an ack_i during such an interval.

$$\mathbf{A\,G}\,\square((\lceil\lceil req_i\rceil \wedge (\eta = m) \;\Rightarrow\; true \frown \lceil ack_i\rceil^0 \frown ext)$$

For an $n = 5$ cell arbiter, we found using CTLDC that the property holds for the first cell for $m = n$. But for all other cells it, does not hold if $m < 2n$. For these cells, the property does holds for $m = 2n$. Hence we concluded that the first cell is guaranteed access to bus if its request is held high for n cycles whereas for all other cells, the request must be held high for $2n$ cycles to guarantee access.

The following property asserts that the arbiter will not service a request req_j first if an earlier request req_i is still pending (the so called "first come first serve" policy (see [27])).

Let $fifo(i,j)$ be defined as

$$\mathbf{A\,G}\,\square\neg(\lceil\neg req_j\rceil^0 \frown \lceil\lceil req_i \wedge \neg ack_i\rceil\rceil \Rightarrow \neg\Diamond\lceil ack_j\rceil^0)$$

Surprisingly, McMillan's bus arbiter with 5-cells satisfies $fifo(i,j)$ for the following pairs and for no other pairs. This was determined experimen tally using CTLDC.

$$(1,2),(1,3),(1,4),(1,5),(2,3),(3,4),(4,5)$$

A much more comprehensiv e analysis of the performance of McMillan's arbiter circuit, and its variants, can be found on the DCVALID web page [21].

6   Conclusions

In this paper, we have proposed an extension of the logic CTL* to CTL*[DC]. This extension allows specification of past-time properties in CTL* using form u- lae of Quantified Discrete-time Duration Calculus (QDDC). In our opinion, this simple extension considerably facilitates formalisation of complex requiremen ts. CTL*[DC] is especially useful for expressing past-time requiremen ts and quantitative timing constraints. In a separate note, we give many such examples [24]. The properties in previous section are also illustrative. Formally, the expressive power of the logic CTL* is increased as shown by Example 3. CTL*[DC] can also be considered as a significant extension of QDDC which allows liveness and branching properties to be stated.

We have shown a reduction of CTL*[DC] model checking problem to CTL* model checking problem. The reduction relies upon the automata theoretic decision procedure for QDDC. W e believe that this approach is practically relevant as a number of tools exist for CTL* and its subsets, CTL and LTL. We have implementated this reduction into a tool called CTLDC which permits model checking CTL[DC] specifications of finite-state transition systems.

The tool CTLDC can model check SMV, Verilog and Esterel designs by reducing the model checking to a form which can be checked by SMV, VIS and Xeve tools respectively. *In this sense, CTLDC is not a new model checker. It enhances the functionality of SMV [18], VIS [2] and Xeve [1] by adding ability to model check a much more richer logic CTL[DC]. It enables complex properties involving past and quantitative timing to be checked using existing checkers.* A separate report gives details of implemen tation [23]. Currently, CTLDC is one of the very few available tool for model checking CTL with past and timing. In context of Duration Calculi, CTLDC is the only tool allowing model checking. (It should be noted that our original tool DCVALID [21] only checked for the validity of QDDC formulae.)

The symbolic model checking algorithm for CTL has been extended to fair CTL model checking [18]. It is easy to see that our reduction of CTL*[DC] model checking to CTL* model checking by transforming the transition system M to M' (Theorem 2) preserves fair paths. Hence, our reduction also gives a method for CTL[DC] model checking under fairness constraints by reduction to Fair CTL.

An important aspect of model checking is error trace generation. In our reduction, an error trace of the transformed model M', in fact, gives an error trace for the original model M if we disregard (project out) the extra variables which have been added by the transformation. Hence, existing facilities of counter example generation in reduced model can be used for CTL[DC].

Our approach of combining QDDC with CTL* can equally be used with any other logic, say X, which specifies properties of finite state sequences. Moreo ver, if the logic permits an automata theoretic decision procedure, this can be used to reduce the model checking problem for CTL*[X] to CTL* by using exactly the same transformation proposed here. One could consider a form of L TL over finite sequence, or monadic logic o ver finite words which both have automata theoretic decision procedures. Or one could use a form of regular expressions. Hence, the approach presented here is quite generic. However, the expressive power (in a pragmatic sense) and facilities for quan titative timing constraint specifications which are found in QDDC may not be so easily available in all such logics.

The issue of complexity of CTL*[DC] merits discussion and further investigation. As stated in Section 2, even the subset QDDC of CTL*[DC] has a non-elementary lower bound on the complexity of validity checking [22]. The same lower bound carries over to model checking of CTL*[DC] formulae. Such high complexity can potentially be a source of in-feasibility and may sound hopeless. However, this complexity is rarely seen in practice. In fact, we have been able to check many formulae which are 5-6 pages long with our tool (see Pandya [21,22] for substantial examples and performance measuremen ts). However, we have also encountered a few pathological formulae leading to state space explosion.

It has been long recognised [17] that availability of past time modalities in temporal logics can considerably facilitate formulation of complex properties. There have been several formulations extending LTL and CTL with past. Their model checking problem has also been investigated [14,15]. Extensions of CTL such as RTCTL [9] allow quantitative timing properties to be expressed and to be model checked using tools such as NuSMV [6]. A precise comparison of the formal expressive power of our logics CTL[DC] and CTL*[DC] with these logics is currently under investigation. We conjecture that CTL[DC] is strictly more expressive than the logic CTL_{lp} proposed by Kupferman and Pnueli [14].

References

1. A. Bouali, XEVE: An Esterel Verification Environment, *Proc. Computer Aided Verification, CAV'98*, Lecture Notes in Computer Science, Springer-Verlag, 1998.
2. R.K. Bryton, G.D. Hatchtel *et al*, VIS: A system for verification and synthesis, in *Proc. Computer Aided Verification, CAV'96*, Lecture Notes in Computer Science 1102, Springer-Verlag, 1996.
3. J.R. Buchi, Weak second-order arithmetic and finite automata, *Z. Math. Logik Grundl. Math.* **6**, 1960.
4. E.M. Clarke and E.A. Emerson, Synthesis of synchronisation skeletons for branching time temporal logic, *Proc. Logics of Programs*, Lecture Notes in Computer Science 131, Springer-Verlag, 1981.
5. E.M. Clarke, E.A. Emerson and A.P. Sistla, Automatic verification of finite-state concurrent systems using temporal logic specifications, *ACM Transactions on Programming Languages and Systems*, **8**(2), 1986.
6. A. Cimatti, E.M. Clarke, F. Giunchiglia and M. Roveri, NuSMV: A Reimplementation of SMV, *Proc. International Workshop on Software Tools for Technology Transfer (STTT-98)*, BRICS Notes Series, NS-98-4, 1998.
7. C.C. Elgot, Decision problems of finite automata design and related arithmetics, *Trans. Amer. Math. Soc.* **98**, 1961.
8. E.A. Emerson and C-L. Lei, Modalities for Model checking: Branching time strikes back, *12th Symposium on Principles of Programming Languages*, New Orleans, La., (January) 1985.
9. E.A. Emerson, A.K. Mok, A.P. Sistla and J. Srinivasan, Quantitative temporal reasoning, *Proc. Computer Aided Verification, CAV'90*, Lecture Notes in Computer Science 531, Springer-Verlag, 1991.
10. M.R. Hansen and Zhou Chaochen, Duration Calculus: Logical Foundations, *Journal of Formal Aspects of Computing* **9**, 1997.

11. J.G. Henriksen, J. Jensen, M. Jorgensen, N. Klarlund, B. Paige, T. Rauhe, and A. Sandholm, Mona: Monadic Second-Order Logic in Practice, *Proc. Tools and Algorithms for the Construction and Analysis of Systems, First International Workshop, TACAS '95*, Lecture Notes in Computer Science 1019, 1996.

12. Y. Kesten, A. Pnueli, and L. Raviv, Algorithmic Verification of Linear Temporal Logic Specifications, in *Proc. 25th International Colloquium on Automata, Languages, and Programming, ICALP'98*, Lecture Notes in Computer Science 1443, Springer-Verlag, 1998.

13. N. Klarlund, A. Møller and M.I. Schwartzbach, MONA Implementation Secrets, to appear in *Proc. Fifth Conference on Implementation and Application of Automata, CIAA 2000*, Springer-Verlag, 2000.

14. O. Kupferman and A. Pnueli, Once and for all, in *proc. 10th IEEE Symposium on Logics in Computer Science, LICS'95*, San Diago, June 1995.

15. F. Laroussinie and P. Schnoebelen, A Hierarchy of Temporal Logics with Past, *Theoretical Computer Science*, 140(1), 1995.

16. O. Lichtenstein and A. Pnueli, Checking that Finite State Concurrent Programs Satisfy Their Linear Specification. In *Prof. 12 ACM Symposium on Principles of Prog. Languages, POPL'85*, January 1985.

17. O. Lichtenstein, A. Pnueli and L. Zuck, The Glory of the Past, *Proc. Logics of Programs*, Lecture Notes in Computer Science 193, Springer-Verlag, 1985.

18. K. McMillan, *Symbolic Model Checking*, Kluwer Academic Publisher, 1993.

19. B. Moszkowski, A Temporal Logic for Multi-Level Reasoning about Hardware, *IEEE Computer*, 18(2), 1985.

20. P.K. Pandya, Some Extensions to Mean-Value Calculus: Expressiveness and Decidability, *Proc. Computer Science Logic, CSL'95*, Paderborn, Germany, Lecture Notes in Computer Science 1092, Springer-Verlag, 1996.

21. P.K. Pandya, DCVALID User Manual, Tata Institute of Fundamental Research, Bombay, 1997. (Available in revised version at http://www.tcs.tifr.res.in/~pandya/dcvalid.html)

22. P.K. Pandya, Specifying and Deciding Quantified Discrete-time Duration Calculus Formulae using DCVALID: An Automata Theoretic Approach, Technical Report TCS-00-PKP-1, Tata Institute of Fundamental Research, 2000.

23. P.K. Pandya, Model Checking CTL[DC] properties of SMV, Verilog and Esterel Designs using CTLDC, Technical Report TCS-00-PKP-3, Tata Institute of Fundamental Research, September 2000.

24. P.K. Pandya, Examples of complex properties from VIS literature, Technical Note PKP-TN-2000-02, Computer Science Group, Tata Institute of Fundamental Research, July 2000. Available on Web at http://www.tcs.tifr.res.in/~pandya/dccheck/demo/sample.html.

25. A. Pnueli, The Temporal Logic of Programs, *Proc. 18th IEEE Symposium on Foundations of Computer Science*, 1977.

26. Zhou Chaochen, C.A.R. Hoare and A.P. Ravn, A Calculus of Durations, *Info. Proc. Letters*, 40(5), 1991.

27. Zhou Chaochen, M.R. Hansen, A.P. Ravn and H. Rischel, Duration Specification for Shared Processors, *Proc. Formal Techniques in Real-Time and Fault-Tolerent Computing, FTRTFT'92*, Lecture Notes in Computer Science 571, Springer-Verlag, 1992.

CPN/Tools: A Tool for Editing and Simulating Coloured Petri Nets
ETAPS Tool Demonstration Related to TACAS

Michel Beaudouin-Lafon, Wendy E. Mackay, Mads Jensen, Peter Andersen,
Paul Janecek, Michael Lassen, Kasper Lund, Kjeld Mortensen,
Stephanie Munck, Anne Ratzer, Katrine Ravn,
Søren Christensen, and Kurt Jensen

Department of Computer Science University of Aarhus
IT-parken, Aabogade 34, DK-8200 Aarhus N, Denmark
cpn2000@daimi.au.dk

Abstract. CPN/Tools is a major redesign of the popular Design/CPN
tool for editing, simulation and state space analysis of Coloured Petri
Nets. The new interface is based on advanced interaction techniques,
including bi-manual interaction, toolglasses and marking menus and a
new metaphor for managing the workspace. It challenges traditional ideas
about user interfaces, getting rid of pull-down menus, scrollbars, and even
selection, while providing the same or greater functionality. CPN/Tools
requires an OpenGL graphics accelerator and will run on all major plat-
forms (Windows, Unix/Linux, MacOS).

1 The CPN/Tools Interface

Interaction techniques for desktop workstations have changed little since the
creation of the Xerox Star in the early eighties. The vast majority of today's
interfaces are still based on a single mouse and keyboard to manipulate windows,
icons, menus, dialog boxes, and to drag and drop objects on the screen. While
these interfaces are now ubiquitous they are also reaching their limits: as new
applications become more powerful, the corresponding interfaces become too
complex. CPN/Tools [1] addresses this trade-off between power and ease-of-use
by combining new interaction techniques into a consistent and simple interface
for editing and simulating Coloured Petri Nets [2,3].

Coloured Petri Nets frequently contain a large number of pages, which are
similar to modules in programming languages. In CPN/Tools we have designed a
window manager that makes it easy to manage these modules. The workspace occupies the whole screen and contains window-like objects called *binders*. Binders
contain *pages*, each equivalent to a window in a traditional environment. Each
page has a tab similar to those found in tabbed dialogs. Clicking the tab brings
that page to the front of the binder. A page can be dragged to a different binder
or to the background to create a new binder for it. Binders reduce the number
of windows on the screen and the time spent organizing them. Binders also help

T. Margaria and W. Yi (Eds.): TACAS 2001, LNCS 2031, pp. 574–577, 2001.
© Springer-Verlag Berlin Heidelberg 2001

users organize their work by grouping related pages together and reducing the time spent looking for hidden windows.

CPN/Tools supports multiple views, allowing several binders to contain a representation of the same page. For example one binder can contain a view on a page including simulation information while another binder can contain a view on the same page without simulation information and at a smaller scale (Fig.1).

The CPN/Tools interface requires a keyboard and two pointing devices. For a right-handed user we use a mouse for the right hand and a trackball for the left hand. The mouse is used for tasks that may require precision, while the trackball is used for tasks that do not require much precision e.g. moving tools. For simplicity we assume a right-handed user in our description of interaction techniques.

The interface has no menu bars, no pull-down menus, no scrollbars and no dialog boxes. Instead, it uses a unique combination of traditional, recent and novel interaction techniques:

Direct manipulati on(i.e. clicking or dragging objects) is used for frequent operations such as moving objects, panning the content of a view and editing text. When a tool is held in the right hand, e.g. after having selected it in a floating palette, direct manupulation actions are still available via a long click, i.e. pressing the mouse button, waiting for a short delay until the cursor changes, and then either dragging or releasing the mouse button.

Bi-man ual manipulati on is a variant of direct manipulation that involves using both hands for a single task. It is used to resize objects (binders, places, transitions, etc.) and to zoom the view of a page. The interaction is similar to holding an object with two hands and stretching or shrinking it. Unlike traditional window management techniques, using two hands makes it possible to simultaneously resize and move a binder, or pan and zoom the view of a page.

Marking Men u[5] are radial, contextual menus that appear when clicking the right button of the mouse. Marking men us offer faster selection than traditional linear menus for two reasons. First, it is easier for the human hand to move the cursor in a given direction than to reach for a target at a given distance. Second, the menu does not appear when the selection gesture is executed quickly, which supports a smooth transition between novice and expert use. Kurtenbach and Buxton [5] have shown that selection times can be more than three times faster than with traditional men us.

Keyboard input is used only to edit text. Some navigation commands are available at the keyboard to make it easier to edit several inscriptions in sequence without having to move the hands to the pointing devices. Keyboard modifiers and shortcuts are not necessary since most of the interaction is carried out with the two hands on the pointing devices.

Floating palettes contain tools represented by buttons. Clicking a tool with the mouse activates this tool, i.e. the user conceptually holds the tool in the hand. Clicking on an object with the tool in hand applies the tool to that object. Floating palettes are moved with the left hand, making it easy to bring the tools close to the objects being manipulated, and saving the time spent moving the

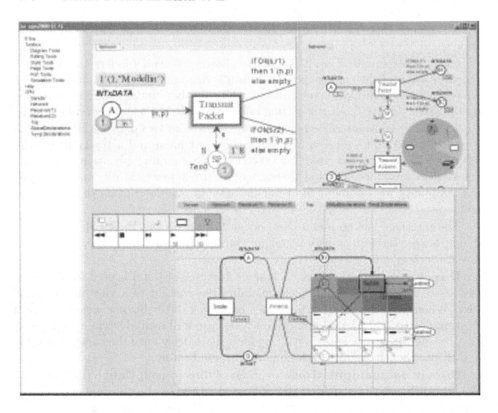

Fig. 1. The CPN/Tools interface. The left column is called the index. The top-left and top-right binders contain different views of the same page. The views are scaled differently and the view in the top-left binder contains simulation information. The bottom binder contains six pages represented by tabs: The page in front shows several magnetic guidelines (dashed lines). In the top right binder a circular marking menu has been popped up on a page. The palette with the VCR-like controls is a floating palette, while a toolglass is positioned over the page in the bottom binder. This toolglass can be used to edit colours, linetypes and linethicknesses.

cursor to a traditional menubar or toolbar. Floating palettes can be dropped in the workspace and become a standard toolpalette. In many current interfaces, after a tool is used (especially a creation tool), the system automatically activates a "select" tool. This supports a frequent pattern of use in which the user wants to move an object immediately after it has been created but causes problems when the user wants to create additional objects of the same type. CPN/Tools avoids this automatic changing of the current tool by ensuring that the user can always move an object, even when a tool is active, with a long click of the mouse. This mimics the situation in which one continues holding a physical pen while moving an object out of the way in order to write.

Toolglasses[4] like floating palettes, contain a set of tools represented by buttons, and are moved with the left hand, but unlike floating palettes, they are semi-transparent. A tool is applied to an object with a *click-through* action: The tool is positioned over the object of interest and the user clicks through the tool onto the object. The toolglass disappears when the tool requires a drag interaction, e.g. when creating an arc. This prevents the toolglass from getting in the way and makes it easier to pan the document with the left hand when the target position is not visible. This is a case where the two hands operate simultaneously but independently.

Magnetic guideli nesare used to align objects and keep them aligned. Moving an object near a guidelinet causes the object to snap to it. Objects can be removed from a guideline by dragging them away from it. Moving a guideline moves all the objects attached to it, maintaining their alignment.

Preliminary results from our user studies make it clear that none of the above techniques is always better or worse. Rather, each emphasizes a different, but common pattern of use. Marking men us work well when applying multiple commands to a single object. Floating palettes work well when applying the same command to different objects. Toolglasses work well when the work is driven by the structure of the diagram, such as working around a cycle in a Petri net.

2   Conclusion

CPN/Tools combine advanced interaction techniques into a consistent interface for editing and simulating Coloured Petri Nets. These interaction techniques have proved to be very efficient when working with Coloured Petri Nets, and we believe they will be suitable for graph editing and layout in general. Information about CPN/Tools including a more detailed tool-presentation can be found at http://www.daimi.au.dk/CPnets/CPN2000.

References

1. Beaudouin-Lafon, M., Lassen, M. The Architecture and Implementation of CPN2000, A Post-WIMP Graphical Application. *Proc. ACM Symposium on User Interface Software and Technology*, UIST 2000, November 2000, ACM Press, 2000.
2. Jensen, K. Coloured Petri Nets. Basic Concepts, Analysis Methods and Practical use, vol 1,2 and 3, *Monographs in Theoretical Computer Science*, Springer Verlag, 1992-97.
3. Kristensen, L. M., Christensen, S. and Jensen K. The Practitioner's Guide to Coloured Petri Nets *International Journal on Software Tools for Technology Transfer*, vol. 2, December 1998, pp. 98-132.
4. Bier, E., Stone, M., Pier, K., Buxton, W., De Rose, T. Toolglass and Magic Lenses: the See-Through Interface. In *Proc. ACM SIGGRAPH*, ACM Press, 1993, pp. 73-80.
5. Kurtenbach, G. & Buxton, W. User Learning and Performance with Marking Menus. In *Proc. Human Factors in Computing Systems*, CHI'94, ACM, 1994, pp. 258-264.

The ASM Workbench

A Tool Environment for Computer-Aided Analysis and Validation of Abstract State Machine Models

Tool Demonstration

Giuseppe Del Castillo*

Heinz Nixdorf Institut, Universität Paderborn, Fürstenallee 11,
33102 Paderborn, Germany (*giusp@uni-paderborn.de*)

Abstract. Gurevich's Abstract State Machines (ASMs) constitute a high-level state-based modelling language, which has been used in a wide range of applications. The ASM Workbench is a comprehensive tool environment supporting the development and computer-aided analysis and validation of ASM models. It is based on a typed version of the ASM language, called ASM-SL, and includes features for type-checking, simulation, debugging, and verification of ASM models.

1 Introduction

The ASM Workbench is a comprehensive tool environment supporting the development and computer-aided analysis and validation of Abstract State Machine models. Abstract State Machines (ASMs), defined by Yuri Gurevich in [4], are an effective approach for specifying and modelling state-based systems, which combines transition systems, used for modelling the dynamic aspects of a system, i.e., its behaviour, with first-order structures (algebras), used to model the static aspects, e.g., data types.

The ASM Workbench is based on a language called ASM-SL (ASM-based Specification Language), which extends the ASM language as defined in [4] by a type system and by constructs to define data types and functions (such extensions are very convenient in order to provide tool support for ASMs). The Workbench itself consists of a kernel, providing basic support for ASM tool development, and a set of tools built upon this kernel, which include a type-checker, a simulator, a debugger-like GUI, and a model-checker interface for formal verification support.

In this abstract, after recalling the basic ideas of Abstract State Machines (Sect. 2), we give an overview of the ASM-SL language (Sect. 3) and of the architecture of the ASM Workbench and of the tools it includes (Sect. 4). A complete account of ASM-SL and of the ASM Workbench, as well as of the underlying concepts and techniques, can be found in [1].

---

* Currently guest scientist at: Siemens AG, ZT SE 4, Otto-Hahn-Ring 6, 81739 München, Germany — E-Mail: *Giuseppe.DelCastillo@mchp.siemens.de*.

T. Margaria and W. Yi (Eds.): TACAS 2001, LNCS 2031, pp. 578–581, 2001.
© Springer-Verlag Berlin Heidelberg 2001

2 Gurevich's Abstract State Machines

Abstract State Machines (*ASMs*), introduced by Yuri Gurevich in [4], are a high-level state-based language for modelling discrete dynamic systems, which has been used in a wide range of applications, such as specifications of hardware and software architectures and operational semantics of programming languages (see [5] for a comprehensive overview of applications of ASMs).

The underlying computational model is essentially the well-known model of *transition systems*. Computations (*runs*) are finite or infinite sequences of states $\{s_i\}$, obtained from the *initial state* s_0 by repeatedly executing *transitions* δ_i:

$$s_0 \xrightarrow{\delta_1} s_1 \xrightarrow{\delta_2} s_2 \ldots \xrightarrow{\delta_n} s_n \ldots$$

In the simple case of deterministic ASMs without any communication with an external environment, there will be exactly one run. Otherwise, the set of possible runs can be represented, as usual, by means of a set $S_0 \subseteq S$ of initial states and a transition relation $R \subseteq S \times S$.

The peculiarity of ASMs is that *states* are first-order structures (algebras) over a given *vocabulary* Υ. In the traditional definition of transition systems, states are identified by the value of a finite number of state variables. In ASMs, instead, states are identified by the interpretation of function names from Υ, which are classified as *static*, *dynamic*, and *external*. Each transition may change the interpretation of dynamic function names in a finite number of places[1]. *External* function names are used to model the environment (their interpretation may change from state to state depending on the environment behaviour, like inputs of finite state machines), while *static* function names never change their interpretation (they typically correspond to operations on some data types).

A language of *transition rules* is defined in [4], which allows to specify ASM transitions. The most essential transition rule is the so-called *update rule*, of the form "$f(t_1, \ldots, t_n) := t$", where f is a n-ary dynamic function name, and t_i, t are terms over the vocabulary Υ. This rule has the effect of changing the interpretation of f such that $\mathbf{f}_{s_{i+1}}(s_i(t_1), \ldots, s_i(t_n)) = s_i(t)$. More complex transition rules can be built by means of additional rule constructors, such as conditionals, parallel composition, non-deterministic choice, etc.

3 The ASM-SL Notation

For the purpose of equipping the ASM method with tool support, it is necessary to extend the basic ASM language of [4]. In particular, the ASM definition does not indicate how to define universes and (static) functions, i.e., the data model underlying the transition system. Clearly, there are several options for specifying data, e.g., axiomatic descriptions in the style of algebraic specification. However, in order to obtain executable specifications, a model-based approach

---

[1] In this sense, ASMs constitute a generalization of transition systems (which can be considered as a special case of ASMs, where all dynamic function names are 0-ary).

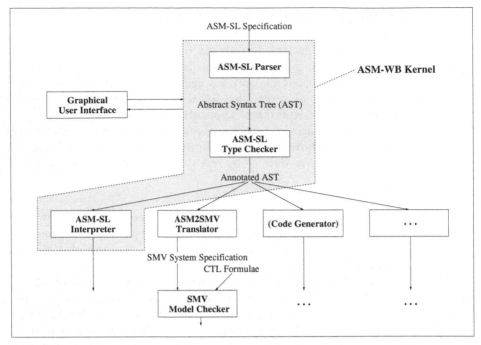

Fig. 1. The ASM W orkbench Tool Environment

was adopted, in the style of VDM [6]. A type system was also added (originally, ASMs are untyped). The result is ASM-SL[2], the source language of the ASM W orkbench, which extends the ASM language by some constructs borrowed from ML and VDM. The main features of ASM-SL can be summarized as follo ws:

- Specification of behaviour based on the ASM language of transition rules [4].
- Polymorphic type system based on the type system of Standard ML [8].
- Model-based approach to data specification, including: predefined elementary types (booleans, integers, strings) and type constructors (tuples, lists, finite sets, finite maps), user-definable free types, comprehension notation, pattern matching, recursive and mutually recursive function definitions.

4   The ASM Workbench Tools

The ASM W orkbench consists of a *kernel*, a set of modules implem ented in the functional language Standard ML [8], which provide basic functionalities (such as parser, type-checker, pretty-printer, and an interpreter-based evalua-tor), and a few additional components (Graphical User Interface, model-checker interface), built on the top of the kernel. Figure 1 shows the rough architecture of the W orkbench, which includes the mentioned tools and could be easily ex-tended by additional components (e.g., code generators), by reusing the kernel

---

[2] **ASM**-based **S**pecification **L**anguage.

functionalities. For reasons of space, it is not possible to go into details of the tool architecture. Instead, we give an overview of the existing tools.

The *type-checker* for ASM-SL is based on an efficient implementation of the well-known unification-based type inference algorithm [2]. In addition to type-checking, it performs other simple static checks. It can be used as a standalone tool or as a preprocessor for further elaborations.

The *interpreter* allows to simulate ASM runs, while keeping track of the computation history. In this way, computation steps can also be retracted (*backward step* feature). It also possible to simulate ASM models which interact with the environment by means of external functions. This can be done by means of an *oracle process*, which communicates with the interpreter in order to provide it with the values of the external functions, whenever needed.

A *Graphical User Interface (GUI)* allows to control the simulation and inspect its results, providing all the typical features of a debugger (browsing through the code, performing single steps forward or backward, setting breakpoints, observing the values of some terms, etc.).[3]

Finally, a *model-checker interface* provides support for formal verification of finite-state ASM models. Although ASM models have, in general, an infinite state space, the ASM-SL language provides a syntactic construct—so-called "finiteness constraints"—by which the finiteness of the model can be enforced by local modifications (restricting the ranges of dynamic and external functions to finite sets). Then, the ASM model is translated, by applying transformation techniques (unfolding and flattening of transition rules), into a model amenable to model-checking. The actual verification is performed by the SMV model-checker [7]. The ASM model is translated into the SMV language and then checked against a set of CTL formulae, to be provided separately (for details, see [3,1]).

References

1. G. Del Castillo. *The ASM Workbench: A Tool Environment for Computer-Aided Analysis and Validation of Abstract State Machine Models*. PhD thesis, Universität Paderborn (to appear in 2001).
2. L. Damas and R. Milner. Principal type schemes for functional programs. In *Proc. of the 9th ACM Symposium on Principles of Programming Languages*, 1982.
3. G. Del Castillo and K. Winter. Model checking support for the ASM high-level language. In *Tools and Algorithms for the Construction and Analysis of Systems, TACAS'2000*, LNCS 1785. Springer, 2000.
4. Y. Gurevich. Evolving Algebras 1993: Lipari Guide. In E. Börger, editor, *Specification and Validation Methods*. Oxford University Press, 1995.
5. J.K. Huggins. Abstract State Machines home page. EECS Department, University of Michigan. http://www.eecs.umich.edu/gasm/.
6. C.B. Jones. *Systematic Software Development using VDM*. Prentice Hall, 1990.
7. K. McMillan. *Symbolic Model Checking*. Kluwer Academic Publishers, 1993.
8. R. Milner, M. Tofte, and R. Harper. *The Definition of Standard ML*. MIT Press, 1990.

---

[3] A snapshot of the GUI can be found in the appendix.

The Erlang Verification Tool

Thomas Noll[1], Lars–åke Fredlund[2], and Dilian Gurov[2]

[1] Lehrstuhl für Informatik II***, Aachen University of Technology, Aachen,
Germany, noll@cs.rwth-aachen.de
[2] Swedish Institute of Computer Science (SICS), Kista, Sweden,
{fred,dilian}@sics.se

1 Introduction

The functional programming language Erlang w as developed by the Ericsson corporation to address the complexities of developing large–scale programs within
a concurrent and distributed setting. It is successfully used in the design and
implem entation of telecomm unication systems.

Software written for this application domain usually has to meet high quality demands such as correctness. Due to the high degree of concurrency and to
the dynamic behaviour of systems, testing is generally not sufficien t to guarantee these properties to a satisfactory degree. W e therefore follow a verification
approach, i.e., we employ formal methods to pro ve that a telecomm unication system implem ented in Erlang has certain properties specified in a suitable logic.

In view of the complexity of the verification problem in general it is mandatory to provide the user with powerful tool support. Therefore, in 1997 the
development of the EVT Erlang Verification Tool was started at the Swedish
Institute of Computer Science in collaboration with and with financial support
from the Ericsson Computer Science Lab and the Sw edish ASTEC (Advanced
Software TEChnology) competence centre.

To cope with the challenges of software verification in a highly dynamic setting, a semi–automati c theorem–proving approach was chosen as the underlying
framework. EVT is a proof assistant which offers powerful induction techniques
to handle dynamic process creation and unbounded data structures. Its graphical user interface provides comfortable access to proof resources. Several case
studies such as a billing agent [3] and a distributed database lookup manager [2]
have demonstrated the usefulness of the tool.

2 Foundations

2.1 The Erlang Programming Language

Erlang [1] is a concurrent functional programming language which allows to
implem ent dynamic networks of processes operating on data types such as integers, lists, tuples, or process identifiers (pids), using asynchronous, call–by–value
comm unication via unbounded ordered message queues called mailboxes.

The following code fragment specifies a simple concurrent server which repeatedly accepts an incoming query in form of a triple which is tagged by the

---

*** Most of the work was done during the author's employment at the Department of
Teleinformatics, Royal Institute of Technology (KTH), Stockholm, Sweden.

T. Margaria and W. Yi (Eds.): TACAS 2001, LNCS 2031, pp. 582–585, 2001.
© Springer-Verlag Berlin Heidelberg 2001

request constant, and which contains the request itself (matched by the variable **Request**) and the pid of the client process (**Client**). It then spawns off a process to serve the request (by using the **handle** function which is not considered here), and sends the result back to the client as a tuple tagged by the **response** constant.

```
server () ->
  receive
    {request, Request, Client} ->
      spawn (serve, [Request, Client]),
      server ()
  end.

serve (Request, Client) ->
  Client ! {response, handle (Request)}.
```

The starting point of any kind of rigorous verification is a formal semantics. Here we use an operational semantics (a variant of the semantics presented in [3]) by associating a transition system with an Erlang program, giving a precise account of its possible computations. The states are parallel products of processes, each of the form $\langle e, p, q \rangle$, where e is an Erlang expression to be evaluated in the context of a unique pid p and a mailbox q for incoming messages. A set of rules is provided to derive labelled transitions between such states.

This semantics is embedded in the proof system by allowing transition assertions to be used as atomic propositions, and by considering the modalities as derived formulae that are defined in terms of the transition relation (analogously to the treatment of CCS in [5,4]).

2.2 The Property Specification Logic

The logic that we use to capture the desired behaviour of Erlang programs and their components combines both temporal and functional features. It can be characterized as a many–sorted first–order predicate logic, extended with temporal modalities, least and greatest fixed–point operators, and some Erlang–specific atomic predicates. Due to its generality, it can be used to express a wide range of important system properties, ranging from more static, type–like assertions to complex safety and liveness features of the interaction between processes. An example for the latter is the following property of our concurrent server. It expresses that the process stabilizes on internal ('τ') and output ('!') actions, that is, only a finite number of these can occur consecutively:

$$\text{stabilizes} = \mu Z.[\tau, !]Z.$$

2.3 The Proof System

At the very heart of our approach is a tableau–based proof system [3,4] embodying the basic proof rules by which complex correctness assertions can be reduced to (hopefully) less complex ones. It operates on Gentzen–style sequents of the form $\Gamma \vdash \Delta$ where Γ and Δ are sets of assertions representing the premises and the conclusions, respectively, of the proof. For example, the following sequent expresses that the server process has the **stabilizes** property provided that the same holds, given any request r, for the **handle** function:

$$\forall q'.\forall r.\langle \mathtt{handle}(r), p, q' \rangle : \mathtt{stabilizes} \vdash \forall q.\langle \mathtt{server}(), p, q \rangle : \mathtt{stabilizes}$$

Summarizing, our proof system can be characterized by the following attributes:

- *laziness*: only those parts of the state space and of the formula are taken into account which are needed to establish the desired property, and so-called metavariables are used to postpone the choice of witnesses in a proof rule.
- *parametricity*: by representing parts of the system by placeholder variables (parameters), a relativised reasoning style for open systems is supported.
- *compositionality*: using a 'cut' rule, the end–system requirements can be decomposed in a modular and iterative way into properties to hold of the component processes.
- *induction*: to support reasoning about unbounded (or even non–well–founded) structures, inductive and co–inductive reasoning is provided based on the explicit approximation of fixed points and on well–founded ordinal induction. Inductive assertions are discovered during the proof rather than being enforced right from its beginning.
- *reuse*: by sharing subproofs and using lemmata, already established properties can be reused in different settings.

3   The EVT Tool

The verification task in our setting amounts to the goal–directed construction of a proof tree. Starting from the root with a goal sequent like the stabilization property of the server, the proof tree is built up by successively applying tactics until every leaf is labeled by an axiom. These tactics can attempt to construct complete proofs, or they can return partial proofs, stopping once in a while to prompt the user for guidance. The atomic tactics are given by the rules of the proof system, and more complex ones can be built up using special combinators called tacticals to obtain more powerful proof steps and, thus, to automate proofs, and to raise the abstraction level of reasoning.

Besides the actual construction of the proof tree, EVT provides support for proof reuse, navigation, and visualization. Due to the global character of the discharge rule which checks whether the current node of the proof tree is labeled by an instance of a previous proof sequent, the whole proof tree has to be maintained. EVT can thus be understood as a proof tree editor, extended with facilities for semi–automatic proof search.

A screen snapshot of EVT's graphical user interface is given in Fig. 1. It provides an easy and context–sensitive access to the proof resources like proof trees and their nodes, tactics, lemmata, and others. In the concrete situation, an example goal sequent is shown (with the premises and the conclusions above and below, respectively, the turnstile), and the user is just about to select a tactic which should be applied to the highlighted assertion.

A binary version of EVT can be downloaded from

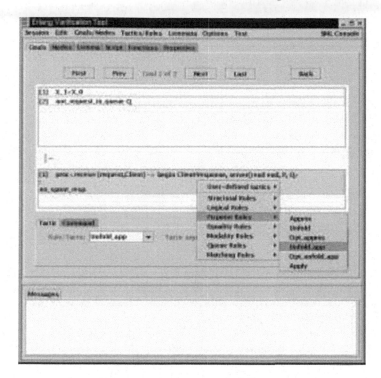

Fig. 1. The graphical user interface

```
ftp://ftp.sics.se/pub/fdt/evt/index.html
```

It is available for Intel x86 and Sparc architectures running under Linux and Solaris, respectively.

References

1. J.L. Armstrong, S.R. Virding, M.C. Williams, and C. Wikstr¨om. *Concurrent Programming in Erlang.* Prentice Hall International, 2nd edition, 1996.
2. T. Arts and M. Dam. Verifying a distributed database lookup manager written in Erlang. In *Proceedings of the World Congress on Formal Methods in the Development of Computing Systems (FM'99)*, volume 1708 of *Lecture Notes in Computer Science*, pages 682–700. Springer–Verlag, 1999.
3. M. Dam, L.-å. Fredlund, and D. Gurov. Toward parametric verification of open distributed systems. In *Compositionality: the Significant Difference*, volume 1536 of *Lecture Notes in Computer Science*, pages 150–185. Springer–Verlag, 1998.
4. M. Dam and D. Gurov. Compositional verification of CCS processes. In *Perspectives of System Informatics: Proceedings of PSI'99*, volume 1755 of *Lecture Notes in Computer Science*, pages 247–256. Springer–Verlag, 1999.
5. A. Simpson. Compositionality via cut–elimination: Hennessy–Milner logic for an arbitrary GSOS. In *Proc. LICS*, pages 420–430. IEEE Computer Society Press, 26–29 1995.

Author Index

Lecture Notes in Computer Science

For information about Vols. 1–1931
please contact your bookseller or Springer-Verlag

Vol. 1969: D.T. Lee, S.-H. Teng (Eds.), Algorithms and Computation. Proceedings, 2000. XIV, 578 pages. 2000.

Vol. 1970: M. Valero, V.K. Prasanna, S. Vajapeyam (Eds.), High Performance Computing – HiPC 2000. Proceedings, 2000. XVIII, 568 pages. 2000.

Vol. 1971: R. Buyya, M. Baker (Eds.), Grid Computing – GRID 2000. Proceedings, 2000. XIV, 229 pages. 2000.

Vol. 1972: A. Omicini, R. Tolksdorf, F. Zambonelli (Eds.), Engineering Societies in the Agents World. Proceedings, 2000. IX, 143 pages. 2000. (Subseries LNAI).

Vol. 1973: J. Van den Bussche, V. Vianu (Eds.), Database Theory – ICDT 2001. Proceedings, 2001. X, 451 pages. 2001.

Vol. 1974: S. Kapoor, S. Prasad (Eds.), FST TCS 2000: Foundations of Software Technology and Theoretical Computer Science. Proceedings, 2000. XIII, 532 pages. 2000.

Vol. 1975: J. Pieprzyk, E. Okamoto, J. Seberry (Eds.), Information Security. Proceedings, 2000. X, 323 pages. 2000.

Vol. 1976: T. Okamoto (Ed.), Advances in Cryptology – ASIACRYPT 2000. Proceedings, 2000. XII, 630 pages. 2000.

Vol. 1977: B. Roy, E. Okamoto (Eds.), Progress in Cryptology – INDOCRYPT 2000. Proceedings, 2000. X, 295 pages. 2000.

Vol. 1978: B. Schneier (Ed.), Fast Software Encryption. Proceedings, 2000. VIII, 315 pages. 2001.

Vol. 1979: S. Moss, P. Davidsson (Eds.), Multi-Agent-Based Simulation. Proceedings, 2000. VIII, 267 pages. 2001. (Subseries LNAI).

Vol. 1983: K.S. Leung, L.-W. Chan, H. Meng (Eds.), Intelligent Data Engineering and Automated Learning – IDEAL 2000. Proceedings, 2000. XVI, 573 pages. 2000.

Vol. 1984: J. Marks (Ed.), Graph Drawing. Proceedings, 2001. XII, 419 pages. 2001.

Vol. 1985: J. Davidson, S.L. Min (Eds.), Languages, Compilers, and Tools for Embedded Systems. Proceedings, 2000. VIII, 221 pages. 2001.

Vol. 1987: K.-L. Tan, M.J. Franklin, J. C.-S. Lui (Eds.), Mobile Data Management. Proceedings, 2001. XIII, 289 pages. 2001.

Vol. 1988: L. Vulkov, J. Waśniewski, P. Yalamov (Eds.), Numerical Analysis and Its Applications. Proceedings, 2000. XIII, 782 pages. 2001.

Vol. 1989: M. Ajmone Marsan, A. Bianco (Eds.), Quality of Service in Multiservice IP Networks. Proceedings, 2001. XII, 440 pages. 2001.

Vol. 1990: I.V. Ramakrishnan (Ed.), Practical Aspects of Declarative Languages. Proceedings, 2001. VIII, 353 pages. 2001.

Vol. 1991: F. Dignum, C. Sierra (Eds.), Agent Mediated Electronic Commerce. VIII, 241 pages. 2001. (Subseries LNAI).

Vol. 1992: K. Kim (Ed.), Public Key Cryptography. Proceedings, 2001. XI, 423 pages. 2001.

Vol. 1993: E. Zitzler, K. Deb, L. Thiele, C.A.Coello Coello, D. Corne (Eds.), Evolutionary Multi-Criterion Optimization. Proceedings, 2001. XIII, 712 pages. 2001.

Vol. 1995: M. Sloman, J. Lobo, E.C. Lupu (Eds.), Policies for Distributed Systems and Networks. Proceedings, 2001. X, 263 pages. 2001.

Vol. 1997: D. Suciu, G. Vossen (Eds.), The World Wide Web and Databases. Proceedings, 2000. XII, 275 pages. 2001.

Vol. 1998: R. Klette, S. Peleg, G. Sommer (Eds.), Robot Vision. Proceedings, 2001. IX, 285 pages. 2001.

Vol. 1999: W. Emmerich, S. Tai (Eds.), Engineering Distributed Objects. Proceedings, 2000. VIII, 271 pages. 2001.

Vol. 2000: R. Wilhelm (Ed.), Informatics: 10 Years Back, 10 Years Ahead. IX, 369 pages. 2001.

Vol. 2003: F. Dignum, U. Cortés (Eds.), Agent Mediated Electronic Commerce III. XII, 193 pages. 2001. (Subseries LNAI).

Vol. 2004: A. Gelbukh (Ed.), Computational Linguistics and Intelligent Text Processing. Proceedings, 2001. XII, 528 pages. 2001.

Vol. 2006: R. Dunke, A. Abran (Eds.), New Approaches in Software Measurement. Proceedings, 2000. VIII, 245 pages. 2001.

Vol. 2007: J.F. Roddick, K. Hornsby (Eds.), Temporal, Spatial, and Spatio-Temporal Data Mining. Proceedings, 2000. VII, 165 pages. 2001. (Subseries LNAI).

Vol. 2009: H. Federrath (Ed.), Designing Privacy Enhancing Technologies. Proceedings, 2000. X, 231 pages. 2001.

Vol. 2010: A. Ferreira, H. Reichel (Eds.), STACS 2001. Proceedings, 2001. XV, 576 pages. 2001.

Vol. 2013: S. Singh, N. Murshed, W. Kropatsch (Eds.), Advances in Pattern Recognition – ICAPR 2001. Proceedings, 2001. XIV, 476 pages. 2001.

Vol. 2015: D. Won (Ed.), Information Security and Cryptology – ICISC 2000. Proceedings, 2000. X, 261 pages. 2001.

Vol. 2018: M. Pollefeys, L. Van Gool, A. Zisserman, A. Fitzgibbon (Eds.), 3D Structure from Images – SMILE 2000. Proceedings, 2000. X, 243 pages. 2001.

Vol. 2021: J. N. Oliveira, P. Zave (Eds.), FME 2001: Formal Methods for Increasing Software Productivity. Proceedings, 2001. XIII, 629 pages. 2001.

Vol. 2024: H. Kuchen, K. Ueda (Eds.), Functional and Logic Programming. Proceedings, 2001. X, 391 pages. 2001.

Vol. 2027: R. Wilhelm (Ed.), Compiler Construction. Proceedings, 2001. XI, 371 pages. 2001.

Vol. 2028: D. Sands (Ed.), Programming Languages and Systems. Proceedings, 2001. XIII, 433 pages. 2001.

Vol. 2029: H. Hussmann (Ed.), Fundamental Approaches to Software Engineering. Proceedings, 2001. XIII, 349 pages. 2001.

Vol. 2030: F. Honsell, M. Miculan (Eds.), Foundations of Software Science and Computation Structures. Proceedings, 2001. XII, 413 pages. 2001.

Vol. 2031: T. Margaria, W. Yi (Eds.), Tools and Algorithms for the Construction and Analysis of Systems. Proceedings, 2001. XIV, 588 pages. 2001.

Vol. 2034: M.D. Di Benedetto, A. Sangiovanni-Vincentelli (Eds.), Hybrid Systems: Computation and Control. Proceedings, 2001. XIV, 516 pages. 2001.